National Summit on School Leadership

Crediting the Past, Challenging the Present, and Changing the Future

EDITED BY
CONNIE L. FULMER
FREDERICK L. DEMBOWSKI

ROWMAN & LITTLEFIELD EDUCATION

Lanham • New York • Toronto • Oxford

Published in the United States of America
by Rowman & Littlefield Education
A Division of Rowman & Littlefield Publishers, Inc.
A wholly owned subsidiary of The Rowman & Littlefield Publishing Group, Inc.
4501 Forbes Boulevard, Suite 200, Lanham, Maryland 20706
www.rowmaneducation.com

PO Box 317
Oxford
OX2 9RU, UK

British Library Cataloguing in Publication Information Available

Library of Congress Cataloging-in-Publication Data
National summit on school leadership : crediting the past, challenging the present, and changing the future / edited by Connie L. Fulmer, Frederick L. Dembowski.
    p. cm. — (NCPEA ; 13th)
 Includes bibliographical references and index.
 ISBN 1-57886-304-X (hardcover : alk. paper)
 1. School management and organization. 2. Educational leadership. I. Fulmer, Connie L., 1949– II. Dembowski, Frederick L. III. Series: Yearbook of the National Council of Professors of Educational Administration ; 13th.

LB2805.N455 2005
371.2'00973—dc22   2005013958

⊗™ The paper used in this publication meets the minimum requirements of American National Standard for Information Sciences—Permanence of Paper for Printed Library Materials, ANSI/NISO Z39.48-1992.
Manufactured in the United States of America.

NCPEA OFFICERS FOR 2005–2007

President
Duane Moore, *Oakland University*

Past President
Michael "Mick" Arnold, *Oakland University*

President-Elect
Gary Martin, *Northern Arizona University*

Executive Director
Theodore Creighton, *Sam Houston State University*

2004
Angus MacNeil, *University of Houston,* Jesse J. McNeil, *University of Texas, Arlington*

2005
Judith Aikan, *University of Vermont,* Frederick Dembowski, *Lynn University*

2006
Minnie Andrews, *Northern Arizona University,* Carolyn S. Carr, *Portland State University*

2007
Betty Alford, *Stephen F. Austin State University,* Alice Fisher, *Sam Houston State University,* Linda Morford, *Eastern Illinois University*

NCPEA HONOR ROLL OF PRESIDENTS, 1947–2005

1947 Julian E. Butterworth, *Cornell University*
1948 William E. Arnold, *University of Pennsylvania*
1949 Russell T. Gregg, *University of Wisconsin*
1950 Clyde M. Campbell, *Michigan State University*
1951 Dan H. Cooper, *Purdue University*
1952 Walter K. Beggs, *University of Nebraska*
1953 Robert S. Fisk, *University of Buffalo*
1954 Van Miller, *University of Illinois*
1955 Harold E. Moore, *University of Denver*
1956 Walter A. Anderson, *New York University*
1957 A. D. Albright, *University of Kentucky*
1958 Jack Childress, *Northwestern University*
1959 Richard C. Lonsdale, *Syracuse University*
1960 William H. Roe, *Michigan State University*
1961 Howard Eckel, *University of Kentucky*
1962 Daniel E. Griffiths, *New York University*
1963 Kenneth McIntyre, *University of Texas*
1964 Luvern Cunningham, *University of Chicago*
1965 William H. Roe, *Michigan State University*
1966 Willard Lane, *University of Iowa*
1967 Harold Hall, *California State University, Los Angeles*
1968 Kenneth Frasure, *SUNY, Albany*
1969 Samuel Goldman, *Syracuse University*

1970 Malcolm Rogers, *University of Connecticut*
1971 Paul C. Fawley, *University of Utah*
1972 Gale W. Rose, *New York University*
1973 Anthony N. Baratta, *Fordham University*
1974 John T. Greer, *Georgia State University*
1975 C. Cale Hudson, *University of Nebraska*
1976 John R. Hoyle, *Texas A&M University*
1977 J. Donald Herring, *SUNY, Oswego*
1978 Charles Manley, *California State University, Northridge*
1979 Jasper Valenti, *Loyola University of Chicago*
1980 Max E. Evans, *Ohio University*
1981 Lesley H. Browder Jr., *Hofstra University*
1982 John W. Kohl, *Montana State University*
1983 Bob Thompson, *SUNY, Oswego*
1984 Donald L. Piper, *University of North Dakota*
1985 Robert Stalcup, *Texas A&M University*
1986 Robert O'Reilly, *University of Nebraska, Omaha*
1987 Donald Coleman, *San Diego State University*
1988 Charles E. Kline, *Purdue University*
1989 Larry L. Smiley, *Central Michigan University*
1990 Frank Barham, *University of Virginia*
1991 Paul V. Bredeson, *Pennsylvania State University*
1992 Rosemary Papalewis, *California State University, Fresno*
1993 Donald Orlosky, *University of South Florida*
1994 Paula M. Short, *University of Missouri, Columbia*
1995 Maria Shelton, *NOVA Southeastern University*
1996 Clarence Fitch, *Chicago State University*
1997 Clarence M. Achilles, *Eastern Michigan University*
1998 Robert S. Estabrook, *Stephen F. Austin State University*
1999 Cheryl Fischer, *California State University, San Bernardino*
2000 Michael Martin, *University of Colorado, Denver*
2001 Judith Adkison, *University of North Texas*
2002 Paul M. Terry, *University of Memphis*
2003 Elaine L. Wilmore, *University of Texas, Arlington*
2004 Michael Arnold, *Southwest Baptist University*
2005 Duane Moore, *Oakland University*

Contents

Contributing Authors

Lola Aagaard, *Morehead State University*

Betty Alford, *Stephen F. Austin State University*

Judith Atkison, *University of North Texas*

David Barnett, *Morehead State University*

Robert Beach, *Alabama State University*

Genniver C. Bell, *Point Loma Nazarene University*

Lee Bolman, *University of Missouri–Kansas City*

Jim Bowman, *Central Missouri State University*

Naomi Boyer, *University of South Florida–Lakeland*

Bernard Brogan, *Widener University*

Sidney Brown, *Alabama State University*

Kermit Buckner, *East Carolina University*

Patti Chance, *University of Nevada–Las Vegas*

Julie Combs, *Texas A&M University–Commerce*

Pamela Eddy, *Central Michigan University*

Stacey Edmonson, *Sam Houston State University*

Robert Estabrook, *Central Michigan University*

Janis Fine, *Loyola University Chicago*

Thomas Fish, *University of St. Thomas*

Dorothy Garrison-Wade, University of Colorado at Denver and Health Sciences Center

Richard T. Geisel, *Grand Valley State University*

Michael Gilbert, *Central Michigan University*

Peggy Barnes Gill, *The University of Texas–Tyler*

Vivian Gordon, *Loyola University Chicago*

Marilyn Grady, *University of Nebraska–Lincoln*

Edward Graham, *California State University*

James Cengiz Gulek, *Pleasanton Unified School District*

Jean Haar, *Minnesota State University–Mankato*

Sandra Harris, *Lamar University*

Mitchel Holifield, *Arkansas State University*

Tim J. Ilg, *University of Dayton*

Marla Israel, *Loyola University Chicago*

Gary Ivory, *New Mexico State University*

Shirley Johnson, *Sam Houston State University*

Timothy Jones, *Texas A&M University–Commerce*

Beverly Kasper, *Loyola University Chicago*

Christine Kelly, *Dominican University*

Kaetlyn Lad, *Saint Mary's College of California*

Stephen Lawton, *Central Michigan University*

Ginny Lee, *Alameda County Office of Education*

James Machell, *Central Missouri State University*

Judy Jackson May, *Bowling Green State University*

Jane McDonald, *George Mason University*

James McDowelle, *East Carolina University*

Cheryl McFadden, *East Carolina University*

Rock McNulty, *Rio Vista Independent School District*

Nidelia M. Montoya, *Ysleta Independent School District*

Duane Moore, *Oakland University*

Fred Muskal, *University of the Pacific*

L. A. Napier, *University of Colorado at Denver and Health Sciences Center*

Steve Neill, *Emporia State University*

Joe Nichols, *Arkansas State University*

Sarah Noonan, *University of St. Thomas*

John Palladino, *Eastern Michigan University*

Kaye Peery, Maxwell Municipal Schools

Eleanor Perry, *Arizona State University (West Campus)*

A. William Place, *University of Dayton*

Terrence Quinn, *City University New York*

Ron Rebore, *Saint Louis University*

Rena Richtig, *Central Michigan University*

Carolyn S. Ridenour, *University of Dayton*

Shobana Rishi, *Modesto City Schools*

William Ruff, *Arizona State University (West Campus)*

Ross Sherman, *The University of Texas–Tyler*

A. Llewellyn Simmons, *University of Dayton*

David Stader, *University of Texas–Austin*

Barbara Storms, *California State University–Hayward*

Tina Sweeley, *Widener University*

Douglas Thomas, *Central Missouri State University*

Review Board

Preface

You are reading the 2005 NCPEA Yearbook titled *National Summit on School Leadership: Crediting the Past, Challenging the Present, and Changing the Future.* Inside this thirteenth volume in the series, you will find the published work of 36 chapters written by 67 authors from 47 different institutions of higher education. The review board, numbering 35 and representing 30 different organizations, did the heavy lifting by reviewing 59 manuscript submissions.

The submission process this year was conducted entirely online. The only postage involved was to send a hard copy of the manuscript to the publisher. Preparation for this volume started prior to the Branson conference last summer. Potential authors were recruited from those presenting. Email messages carried specifications for manuscript preparation to professors in the final stages of preparing their work for the Branson conference. The NCPEA website also was helpful with downloadable copies of preparation materials, deadlines, and a place for authors to upload finished manuscripts for publication.

The review process was also completed entirely online. Manuscript submission logs and reviewer logs were created and tracked electronically. Reviewer assignments were made and manuscript submissions were sent via email attachments to reviewers, along with an evaluation form. Each reviewer was asked to read six manuscripts. Reviewers were instructed to save the reviewer file with their initials and to return the review forms electronically with their recommendations to authors. As reviews came in the publication recommendations were recorded on a 2005 Yearbook manuscript log. Authors of manuscripts participated along the way to find missing references, dates, volumes, issues, and page numbers. I manned "computer central" and prayed that my hard drive would not crash until after the hard copy and CD were in the mail. Acceptance and rejection letters were also delivered electronically. The end result of

this human and technological infrastructure was an extremely smooth process that was timely, efficient, and productive.

This particular yearbook and the twelve that came before would not have been possible without the work of NCPEA members. First, it would not have happened if you were not teaching or doing research at your home institutions. Second, it would not have been possible if you and your colleagues had not attended NCPEA conferences. Without presenters and presentations there would be no need for a yearbook. Third, it was possible only because you submitted your work for publication in the yearbook. Thank you for, not only having confidence in your work, but also in the yearbook. Fourth, the editors and reviewers spent a considerable amount of time and effort on your work to get manuscripts ready for the next level in the process. I would like to thank my co-editor, Frederick Dembowski, and all reviewers who gave time during a busy part of the spring semester for service to NCPEA and this yearbook. The final editing of this tall stack of pages by Rowman & Littlefield editors, under the guidance of Cindy Tursman, transformed your work into the beautiful book you are holding today. As a result of this collective, our field is one book richer.

The 2005 Yearbook has four parts. Part I contains the invited lectures from the 2004 conference. One of these invited chapters was the Cocking Lecture given by Ronald Rebore, from Saint Louis University in St. Louis, Missouri. Another invitation went out to the Corwin Lecturer, Lee Bolman, from the University of Missouri at Kansas City. Next on the invitation list was the 2004 Living Legend Award recipient, Robert Beach, from Alabama State University in Montgomery. Of course, no yearbook would be complete without an opening message from the current NCPEA President, Duane Moore, from Oakland University in Rochester, Michigan.

The remaining 32 chapters were distributed into one of the three sections of the yearbook: Part II: *Crediting the Past*; Part III: *Challenging the Present*; Part IV: *Changing the Future.* One could argue about a particular chapter's placement in a particular section of the yearbook, but not with the contribution it made to the entire volume. It has been a pleasure working with all of the authors and reviewers on this 2005 NCPEA Yearbook project. Please enjoy the product of our collective efforts.

—Connie L. Fulmer

INVITED CHAPTERS

Crediting the Past, Challenging the Present, and Changing the Future

Duane Moore

THE THEME OF THE 2005 NCPEA YEARBOOK REMINDS me of an old Jewish proverb which goes something like, "May you live in exciting times." This wish has certainly come to pass for those of us engaged in educational administration and for NCPEA as an organization. For many of us who do not have the time or opportunity to step back and see the "big picture" or the larger whole of educational administration, this period is like a perceptual trick picture. From one angle we see exciting opportunities for change. Blink our eyes and we see the image as a frightening roadblock. Our 2005 national conference, I believe, will contribute to our understanding of the past, present, and future bigger picture in our common work as professors of educational administration.

During the fifty-plus years that NCPEA has been in existence the field of educational administration has experienced considerable turmoil—particularly the past 15 years. We are fortunate, nevertheless, as professors and as an organization to be in a dynamic field, as pointed out by our colleague, Louis Wildman, that contains at least 17 domains of knowledge in which to focus our attention on things that matter. Politicians, scholars, practitioners, and students have questioned the assumptions of education and educational administration, making countless suggestions for change. As professors of educational administration and leadership, we must continue to embrace the intellectual and moral responsibilities required to create more authentic preparation programs based upon solid knowledge, while acknowledging the changing dynamics of education and schools. Many of the demands and challenges of the past and present will be greatly different from those we will face in the future.

NCPEA is currently beginning a new and exciting major project to collect the knowledge base in educational administration and create small modules of information related to the major domains of leadership. The quality of the modules will be peer-reviewed and endorsed by NCPEA before being recommended to the profession. The first two modules we will work on are school law and improving student achievement in diverse populations. The knowledge base will be published online through Connexions, a collaborative venture with Rice University. Connexions is a professionally-driven approach to authoring that conveys the dynamic continuum of knowledge available and free of charge to anyone in the world, while maintaining original author license. This outstanding 2005 yearbook and annual conference is our first step in collecting and identifying the knowledge base for educational administration and leadership so school leadership can be strengthened at all levels. Thus, allowing us as an organization and as professionals to take "ownership" of what we are all about and to provide future leaders with the theoretical and practical base to be successful.

The Place of the Furies in Educational Leadership

RONALD W. REBORE

PART I: THE CONTEXT

DURING THE PAST EIGHT YEARS AS A PROFESSOR OF EDUcational leadership, I have come to the opinion that there is a cultural shift in the practice of educational leadership that is undermining certain basic humanistic principles. It appears to me that the accountability movement has placed an inordinate emphasis on using quantitative data in making decisions. This blind faith in quantitative data is evident not only in education but also in business and government. In fact, even religious organizations have begun to use quantitative market research techniques to determine the opinions of their congregations on a vast array of issues that include the effectiveness of preaching and the willingness of church members to increase their financial contributions.

I have formulated my opinion into the following hypothesis: The accountability movement seeks to control public educational policy through a radical rationalism. Of course, the accountability movement has many faces; thus, it is difficult to single out one person as its leader. Further, there is no formal organization of the movement. Rather, it is an attitude that many people have fostered which seeks to hold leaders responsible for the success of an organization. This is laudable in itself. The problem occurs when leaders believe that they should use only quantitative techniques to measure the success of an organization. Certainly, this is the prevailing perception of most leaders.

It is even more problematic to use only quantitative techniques to measure the success that individuals have attained in meeting the goals of an organization. While number of goods produced or sold is the vehicle for measuring success in many businesses and industries, test scores have become the vehicle for measuring success in education. Thus, if student test scores fall below the standard in a given state, the district in which the children are educated may be considered a failure in relation to the *No Child Left Behind*

Act. It is more troublesome when teachers are blamed for the failure of students to score at the pre-established testing standard.

Students are in school for a relatively short period each day, and the school year is approximately only nine months in duration. Thus, teachers and the school as an organization may not have a significant influence on a child's life outside the school. There are experiences at home and in the neighborhood with parents and others that most likely will affect how a child performs in school and on standardized testing. Yet test scores have become a rallying cry for many true believers in the accountability movement.

There are other indicators of this radical rationalism such as educational leadership courses being taught completely online, the overemphasis on data based decision making, zero tolerance policies, and the overemphasis on critical thinking. Certainly, *No Child Left Behind* is an example of legislation that knowingly or unknowingly supports radical rationalism. Good intentions do not mitigate the effects of ideology.

To avoid misunderstanding it is important to consider the concepts of *ideology* and *radicality*. Ideology in the context of this presentation means any belief or opinion that influences a person's actions. Further, in the context of this presentation, the definition of *radical* is unadulterated. Thus, a radical rationalism, as an ideology, allows no room for compromise. My experience with people who are committed advocates of rationalism is such that these people do not take into account the *furies* in their lives and in the lives of others.

The Furies

The title of this presentation, *The Place of the Furies in Educational Leadership*, is predicated on an ideology that is the complete opposite of rationalism. I have designated that ideology as *humanism*. Of course, humanism is an ideology with a long history, as is the case with rationalism. The present treatment, however, focuses on these two ideologies, as they are identifiable within the context of educational leadership.

The furies are better described than defined. Some people have a difficult time explaining why they love certain people. In spite of all failings, they just do. In like manner, it is difficult to explain why we *desire*; rather, it is more revealing to describe what humans desire. It is equally difficult to explain why we humans feel or think the way we do; however, in order to understand human existence, it is imperative to reflect on the content of human feelings and attitudes. Of course, the best expressions of the furies are exemplified in artistic endeavors: desires, attitudes, and feelings that motive human conduct and behavior are readily captured in literature and the fine and performing arts.

A Matter of Perspective

Of course, perspective is an all-encompassing human dynamic. The perspective that we have on life in general and on particular issues dictates our desires, attitudes, and feelings. Conversely, our desires, attitudes, and feelings influence our perspective. It is a reciprocal relationship. Thus a person's perspective may be constantly in flux or may be very stable depending on his or her desires, attitudes, and feelings.

As an example of the importance of perspective, consider the following two categories of people. Of course, the categories are mental constructs, and it is very difficult to find people who neatly fit into one or the other.

> **The Classic Worldview.** The person who holds this perspective views reality as static and immutable. Further, he or she sees the world as marked by objectivity and harmony. He or she utilizes deductive reasoning, and thus conclusions are always the same.[1]
>
> **The Evolutionary Worldview.** A person who has this perspective views reality as dynamic and evolving, historical and developing. Further, he or she sees the world as marked by progressive change and growth. He or she utilizes inductive reasoning, and thus conclusions change as the evidence changes.[2]

While arbitrary, the designations *Classical* and *Evolutionary* reflect the tension that exists in all organizations, including schools and school districts, between those who seek change and those who prefer the status quo. A case could probably be made that zero tolerance policies are predicated on a classic rather than an evolutionary worldview. Such policies negate the right of educational leaders to exercise their discretion.

Definitions

Before venturing into definitions of rationalism and humanism, it should be obvious from the above treatment that everything in life is ultimately filtered through an individual's personal perspective, the objectification of subjectivity. While there is an objective reality, each person's perspective of reality is tainted by his or her personal ideas, thought patterns, desires, attitudes, and feelings.

Rationalism is the tendency to use cognitive processes in conjunction with objective evidence as the primary basis for making decisions. Of course, scientific inquiry is an application of rationalism because it requires quantitative, objective evidence.

Humanism is the tendency to use both cognitive and affective processes in conjunction with both objective and subjective evidence in making decisions. Thus a person can enhance his or her decision-making evidence through using both qualitative and quantitative methods. Of course, the application of humanism is easily seen in the fine and performing arts because they use context to explore and describe phenomena.

Obviously the evolutionary worldview is supportive of a humanistic approach to decision making. Teacher evaluation and program assessment cannot be adequately viewed through only objective or subjective evidence. Both are required. That is the reason why test scores do not tell the entire story of how well a teacher teaches. The teacher who helps each student to achieve his or her greatest potential at a given period in his or her development is a good teacher, even if his or her students do not score at an adequate level on standardized tests. Most if not all teachers and educational administrators are aware of this.

It is because of these considerations that educators are often uneasy with alternative administrator certification. How can a former military leader or business leader acquire the appropriate humanistic *perspective* so necessary in the practice of educational leadership? He or she will probably not have the subjective qualities (desires, attitudes, and feelings) that a good teacher acquires through the instructional process. Teachers are engaged participants in the child growth and development process. That is also the reason why it is difficult to see how a principal can truly understand the learning-instructional process without first having been a teacher.

When the bottom line only focuses on financial or test score considerations, it is impossible to practice humanistic educational leadership.

The Phenomenon of Change

It has become somewhat a cliché to say that educational leaders are change agents. That is not true in the larger scheme of life. Rather, they are responsible for helping students, parents, teachers, other administrators, the board of education, and the public at large adapt to change. No educational leader is capable of maneuvering and manipulating major forces in society along any certain lines that eventuate in changing society itself. Rather, we are the recipients of forces and movements thrust upon us without our approval. The economy and the war in Iraq are examples of changes in our society that have had a profound effect on all Americans including teachers and administrators.

The great nineteenth-century novel *The Leopard*, written by Giuseppe di Lampedusa, is a literary work of art that speaks to the phenomenon of change in a timeless manner. It is about the political transformation that took place in Sicily in the mid-1800s. During that time, Sicily had been invaded by Garibaldi, which precipitated a change in its government from an aristocracy into a republic. The theme of the novel is summarized in a dialogue between the Prince of Salina and his nephew in which the nephew essentially says that if things are going to remain the same, then things will have to change.[3]

While the particulars of the story line may be foreign to contemporary readers, the underlying message is just as valid today as it was then because good literature helps us understand the deepest mysteries of life. If graduate programs in educational leadership are going to remain strong and vital, professors and deans must change their instructional and leadership styles. In like manner, if schools and school districts are going to remain strong and vital, teachers and administrators must change their instructional and leadership styles. For obvious reasons we, the professors and deans, should be the first to hypothesize and research how leadership practice should and can be adapted to meet the demands of change.

Signs of Our Times[4]

The canvas on which we paint our careers as professors of educational leadership is readily visible through the news media. We are bombarded not only with the events of our times but also with ongoing interpretations of those events through network television, cable television, the internet, and the print media. During the last two years, the following list of issues has emerged from the news media. It represents the majority of news-making events.

The Misconduct of Religious Leaders. An inordinate number of religious leaders had not notified civil authorities about the abuse of children by ordained men under their supervision. Compounding this neglect, they moved those pedophiles to other assignments, where they had further contact with children.

The Misconduct of Business Leaders. Thousands of people have lost their investments because some business executives lied about the solvency of their companies, which resulted in bankruptcy. However, before the financial condition of their companies became public, they further cheated investors and employees by selling stock in their companies at a price that was not reflective of its value, known as insider trading.

The Misconduct of Government and Military Leaders. Perhaps the most blatant misuse of authority occurred with the mistreatment of prisoners of war in Iraq by U.S. soldiers. The investigation of that mistreatment appears to indicate that it was not the deeds of only a few but at least had tacit approval of some people in the chain of command. The lack of cooperation between government agencies, especially in relation to intelligence information about terrorists, while not criminal, certainly carries the suspicion of misconduct. Finally, the untruthfulness and mean-spiritedness of politicians are reasons why many good people do not run for public office.

The Misconduct of Law Enforcement Officials. DNA testing has revealed that serious mistakes have been made in the arrest and prosecution of people wrongly accused of major crimes, resulting in their imprisonment for a significant number of years.

The Role of the U.S. in World Politics. The perception of other nations concerning the right of the U.S. to change and police the political structures in other countries has created tensions that, in essence, have somewhat isolated the U.S. in the world community. It is only our military strength and financial capability, rather than our moral strength that allows us to play a dominant role in world affairs.

The Financial Stability of Business and Industry. Certainly the stock market is the quintessential symbol of the financial health and stability of our nation, and the once bull market deceived us into believing that good times were everlasting. However, the most important economic fact is the increasing gap between the middle incomers and the wealthy. Tax breaks for the wealthy have not stimulated the economy to provide significantly better paying jobs for many Americans. Thus they do not have more money to spend.

Non-traditional Lifestyles. Perhaps, the most important lifestyle issue concerns the gay community. The ordination of a gay bishop in the American Episcopal Church and gay marriages occupied center stage for months. The gay marriage issue eventuated in major court decisions and legislation in some states.

Cloning Human Beings and Human Organs. The ethics of cloning and the research that produces the knowledge base for this phenomenon has serious consequences for everyone. It conjures both positive and negative images of the future.

Genetic Engineering. Transgenic manipulation is of particular concern because it is already widespread. Such genes have been introduced into crops for the sake of preventing disease and increasing output. The food chain issue makes us wonder about the long-range effects of such engineering. Certainly technology and research seem to have limitless horizons and possibilities; yet we, the humans creating the technology and designing the research, have definite limits.

Safeguarding Civil Rights in Dangerous Times. There is always the danger that civil rights will be abrogated when our country is threatened with enemies both within and without. When it is necessary to suspend certain civil rights, there must be checks and balances in place so that such measures do not become permanent.

Non-traditional Entertainment. Recreation and entertainment are reflections of a society in transition. Television shows that feature people eating worms and performing other disgusting or insensitive behaviors must give us pause as to the reasons why we enjoy such events. The same can be said about the news media as entertainment. Tragedies and court cases can occupy talk shows for weeks and months. What this phenomenon might suggest is the interest of Americans in second hand experiences. Instead of acting, people may prefer to just watch and listen.

Universal Access to Medical and Pharmaceutical Services and Products. These are of particular concern to senior citizens. Many Americans do not have medical insurance or cannot afford the premiums to purchase insurance. It is an ever-increasing problem because the cost of health care continues to rise.

Financial and Moral Support for Marginalized People. The number of people living at the poverty level appears to be increasing and some people who were in the middle-income bracket have now slipped into the ranks of the poor.

Terrorism. Of course, the most serious sign of our times is the threat of terrorism. Major issues concern not only the security of our borders but also the possibility that terrorists might use weapons of mass destruction within our borders. Thus, prevention of terrorism is of paramount importance. It goes without detailed commentary that the war in Iraq is an extension of the terrorism issue.

PART II: HUMANISTIC LEADERSHIP

In my opinion, educational leaders must explore the landscape of issues presented above in order to understand the perspective of their constituents. Professors of educational leadership should also consider these issues when preparing instructional strategies. Useful tools for such an exploration are the tenets of *humanistic leadership*. For this presentation, humanistic leadership refers to a way of life dedicated to leadership within and on behalf of the academic community and profession. Without this perspective, a superintendent or principal may concentrate on the performance of tasks and neglect reflecting on the overall reason why he or she became an educational leader. Humanistic leadership has a transcendental dimension, a notion that has been repressed in Western society since the enlightenment. Radical rationalism is a remnant of the enlightenment found in contemporary society.

The basic premise of humanistic leadership is that a person acts from the totality of who he or she is as a human being. Further, most administrators are generally aware of the fact that their decisions are influenced by more that just immediate circumstances, and the effects of their decisions can have an impact that goes beyond the present situation.[5]

There are seven dimensions of humanistic leadership: the reflection paradigm, the principle of subsidiarity, the evolutionary perspective, decision making based on qualitative and quantitative evidence, social justice, cultural pluralism, and public discourse.[6]

The first dimension, *the reflection paradigm*, takes into account the importance of practice as the phenomenon upon which theory and foundational values are based.[7] Everything begins with practice. Knowing and understanding what is occurring in schools and school districts is the only way to evaluate effective leadership. Leadership cannot be a top-down phenomenon but rather must begin with what is taking place in the classrooms, corridors, cafeteria, media center, parking lot, and playground. It also means knowing what is going on in relation to the school building. For example, is the HVAC system balanced and in good working order? Finally, it means knowing and understanding the desires, attitudes, and feelings of all stakeholders. Parents, students, teachers, staff members, administrators, and the public at large reflect in their daily lives the values, accomplishments, issues, and problems of public education.

It is from this base that school administrators can ascertain what they believe in terms of educational theory and determine if it really works. Does block scheduling work? How successful is teacher empowerment as a supervision strategy? What about the effectiveness of helping students develop critical thinking and critical feeling skills? The common mistake that many superintendents and principals are guilty of in relation to school reform is mandating change without sufficient evidence.

There is no question about the value and importance of educational theory. Practice without theory is chaos. Without a theoretical base, superintendents and principals move from one new approach to another in the hope that something new will work better than what is currently being tried. This is a regular occurrence in some schools and school districts, where good intentioned but ill-informed non-educational reformers with influence and an agenda capture the attention of school board members.

All theory is predicated on a system of values and beliefs, which will be referred to as *philosophy* in this section. Teacher empowerment is based on the belief that professional educators are skilled and dedicated professionals who are capable of making their own decisions not only about classroom management and student discipline but also about educational policy. At the school and school district level this means sharing the leadership responsibility with teachers and staff members. Thus theory without philosophy is also chaos. Not making the connection that theory is founded on philosophy is the same problem that arises when practice is not viewed as emanating from theory.

There is another important aspect to the decision-making paradigm. A reciprocal relationship exists between practice, theory, and philosophy. Not only does everything begin with practice but, in fact, practice can change theory, which in turn can change a superintendent's and principal's philosophy. Such a change in philosophy can further alter a person's theory, which will ultimately affect practice. The following figure presents schemata of this observation.

Third Level of Reflection → Philosophical Principles

↕ ↕

Second Level of Reflection → Leadership Theory Principles

↕ ↕

First Level of Reflection → Leadership Practice

Figure 1. Reflection Paradigm[8]

For purposes of discussion, practice can be considered the first level of reflection, theory the second level, and philosophy the third level. Reflection is the process and the paradigm is the method. This is a rather easy paradigm to understand, but it can be difficult to implement because reflection takes time and energy. Time and energy are commodities that most administrators do not have in abundance. Reflection requires a superintendent or principal to hesitate before making commitments and decisions. That is often very difficult to do when conflicts occur. However, the disposition of superintendents and principals to search for the relationship between practice, theory, and philosophy is more important than the mechanics of reflection.

Of course, this search takes self-knowledge and commitment. It also takes courage to ask the question: How does my practice, theory of leadership, and personal philosophy match up? It further requires a superintendent or principal to bring these three elements into synchronization, which in some instances could bring discontent on the part of faculty and staff.

The second dimension concerns *the principle of subsidiarity.*[9] This principle has a unique history that originated in social ethics and economics. The principle states that decisions should be made at the lowest possible level in an organization. There is no question as to the relevance of allowing teachers and staff members to do their jobs without interference from administrators. Also, there is no question about the firsthand knowledge and experience that teachers and staff members possess, which makes them eminently more qualified to handle many issues and problems.

The application of this principle empowers all other staff members as they carry out the responsibilities of their respective positions. In order to do this, decisions about budgeting, curriculum development, maintenance of facilities, public relations activities, technology implementation, and so forth, become shared responsibilities. As an example of empowerment, the superintendent becomes a consultant and mentor to assistant superintendents, directors, and principals; the principal becomes a consultant and mentor to teachers and other staff members.

Further, the mentor responsibility of the superintendent or principal is sometimes adaptive rather than technical. He or she must help others recognize how their values influence their behaviors in the face of new realities. Finally, this process of de-bureaucratization can lead to a better utilization of human, financial, and material resources.

In terms of decision making, the principle of subsidiarity requires superintendents and principals to develop a comprehensive monitoring system, whereby they will be able to know and understand the status of their school districts or schools. This will help them make informed decisions about which teacher, staff member, or administrator needs mentoring and/or consultation.

The third dimension of humanistic leadership is *the evolutionary perspective*. The discussion in the section *A Matter of Perspective* on the evolutionary worldview constitutes the explanation of this dimension.

The fourth dimension of humanistic leadership is *decision making based on qualitative and quantitative evidence*. In like manner, the discussion in the section *Definitions* that distinguishes between rationalism and humanism provides the background for this dimension.

The fifth dimension of humanistic leadership is *social justice*.[10] Justice is that human relations guide that regulates how people live out their lives as members of a given school or school district community. The substance of justice is entitlement that refers to those rights to which educators, parents, students, and other citizens have a claim. Distributive justice deals with the responsibilities that the school or school district has to individual educators, parents, students, and citizens. Legal justice deals with the responsibilities that educators, parents, students, and citizens have to the school or school district. Commutative justice involves those responsibilities that exist between educators, parents, students, and citizens. Justice also involves restitution, which is the right of a person to have an entitlement restored.

Contractarianism is a political philosophy, which sets forth the notion that people should design their own society. Thus government comes into existence through a contract or agreement among the people to be governed.

John Rawls is a contemporary contractarian. He describes his theory of justice in terms of fairness. His basic premise is that the best principles of justice for the basic structure of any society are those, which would be the object of an original agreement in the establishment of a society. Free, rational people as an initial position of equality would derive these principles. Rawls elucidated two principles, which he believed people would choose in the initial situation in order to implement the notion of fairness. The first principle asserts that each person is to have an equal right to a system of liberties that is compatible with a similar system of liberties available to all people. The second principle asserts that social and economic inequalities must benefit the least advantaged and that equal opportunity to secure offices and position must be open to all. Thus social justice requires these principles to be embedded within the curriculum and within the policies and procedures of the school and school district.

The sixth dimension of humanistic leadership is *cultural pluralism*. The United States is a nation of immigrants. Today most of them come from Asia and the Americas. Because of this phenomenon, the United States is now the most religiously diverse country on earth. It is a country of Christians, Jews, Muslims, Hindus, and Confucians. Thus, diversity precludes us from using religious norms as standards of human interaction.[11]

This has created a new challenge for superintendents and principals in terms of enculturation. The new immigrants must be able to interact with other people in the United States. Of course, such diversity requires dialogue between the new immigrants and educators. It is the only way that true understanding can take place. The purpose of such dialogue is not to compromise values, but rather it is an attempt to examine and explain the values of American education, the school, and the school district in relation to the values of the parents and students who come from new and different cultures.

The final dimension of humanistic leadership is *public discourse*.[12] Implementing the pluralistic point of view in educational leadership is not only a human-relations issue, but also a political issue because public school districts are state agencies. Jürgen Habermas is a contemporary philosopher who views public discourse as the pursuit of how conflicting interests can result in appropriate judgments. Embodied within his theoretical design is a procedure for human argumentation, which is reasoned agreement by those who will be affected by the norm. The central principle of public discourse is that the validity of a norm rests on the acceptability of the consequences of the norm by all participants in a practical discourse. This shifts reflection away from the solitary individual to the community of subjects in dialogue. Making a decision about the fairness of a norm cannot take place only in the minds of educational administrators; there must be actual discourse with school and school district stakeholders. Using Habermas's model, school board members, superintendents, principals, teachers, parents, students, and other citizens must be willing and able to appreciate the perspectives of one another.

Public discourse is difficult to implement. Habermas perceives the overarching problem to be the isolation that people experience in contemporary society. Therefore, his theory gives educational administrators encouragement to develop a framework within which stakeholders can communicate in a non-defensive manner. Consequently, communication can lead to decisions based on reason rather than on coercion. Further, the reasoned validity that people elucidate in discourse tends to transcend the present context and sets the stage for future discourse. Reasoning is the basis of all discourse and he asserts that participants must agree to this rationality if it is to be effective. Participants should be free from external and internal coercion other than the force of the best argument, which supports the cooperative search for truth. Because of the limitations of time and space, educational administrators must institutionalize discourse; the topics to be discussed and the contributions of participants must be organized in terms of opening, adjournment, and resumption of discussion. Parent-teacher meetings, school board meetings, school town hall meetings, faculty meetings, and administrator meetings are all venues for such discourse.

Discourse can be effective only if it is applied to questions that can be dealt with through impartial judgment. Thus the subject matter could deal with public educational policies such as student rights and responsibilities, parental involvement in the formal educational process, achievement testing, curricular programs, etc. This implies that the process will lead to an answer that is equally beneficial to all stakeholders. It does not mean that discourse seeks to reach consensus but rather to generate convictions in the participants. Further, Habermas sees the degree to which a society, its institutions, its political culture, its traditions, and its everyday practices permit a non-coercive and non-authoritarian form of ethical living as the hallmark of rational morality, which is derived from discourse.

CONCLUSION

My intention in preparing the Cocking Lecture was to incorporate into my presentation some elements from each of the three conference themes: Knowing the Way—Knowledge base for what we do; Showing the Way—Best practice in educational leadership programs; and Going the Way—Ethics, social justice, servant leadership, etc. I hope that the issues raised and perspectives set forth in Part I of this presentation helped to clarify *Knowing the Way*. The material and perspective on humanistic leadership was meant to address both *Showing the Way* and *Going the Way*.

As a final note, the question of ethics arises throughout this presentation. The ethics of educational leadership is predicated on two premises. First, most people do not seek bad things in their lives; rather, they badly seek things. Wanting good things very badly probably motivated the misconduct of religious, business, government, and law enforcement leaders. Some religious leaders wanted to protect their respective churches from scandal but refused to notify the civil authorities when allegations of child abuse surfaced. Some business leaders wanted to make more money and lavish on their families the best that money could buy, but they mislead investors into believing that their companies were in better financial shape than they were, and then sold their own stock at the inflated value. Some government leaders wanted to protect our country from terrorists but denied civil rights to some people. Some law enforcement leaders wanted to protect the public from criminals, but they manipulated the evidence.

The second premise involves the social covenant. All leaders, including educational leaders, are obligated to the organizations they serve through a contractual agreement. They are obliged to perform their responsibilities to the best of their abilities because of the agreement. Further, all members of the organizational community have an obligation to each other because they are bound together by the mission of the organization to which they belong. That obligation entails carrying out their roles and performing their responsibilities to the best of their abilities. The force behind the covenant is social justice.[13]

NOTES

1. Ronald W. Rebore, *The Ethics of Educational Leadership* (Upper Saddle River, New Jersey: Prentice-Hall, Inc., 2001), p. 21.
2. Ibid.

3. Giuseppe di Lampedusa, *The Leopard* (New York: Pantheon Books, 1960), p. 40.

4. The material in this section was gleaned during the 2003-2004 academic year through review of the New York Times and the St. Louis Post-Dispatch newspapers, and CNN Daily News.

5. Ronald W. Rebore, *A Human Relations Approach to the Practice of Educational Leadership* (Boston: Allyn & Bacon, 2003), p. 78.

6. Ibid., p. 79.

7. Ibid., pp. 79, 80.

8. Ibid., pp. 80, 81.

9. Ibid.

10. Ibid., p. 119.

11. Ibid., p. 105.

12. Ibid., pp. 125, 126.

13. Ronald W. Rebore, *Ethics*, p. 108.

SELECTED BIBLIOGRAPHY

deChardin, T. (1961). *The phenomenon of man.* New York: Harper & Row Publishers.

Eck, D. L. (1997). Challenged by a new georeligious reality. *In Trust, 8*(2), 10–12.

Frankl, V. E. (1984). *Man's search for meaning: An introduction to logotherapy.* New York: Simon & Schuster.

Habermas, J. (1993). *Justification and application: Remarks on discourse ethics.* Cambridge, Massachusetts: MIT Press.

Jung, C. G. (Ed.) (1968). *Man and his symbols.* New York: Dell Publishing.

Kekes, J. (1993). *The morality of pluralism.* Princeton, New Jersey: Princeton University Press.

Ong, W. J. (1982). *Orality and literacy: The Techologizing of the word.* New York: Methusen.

Rawls, J. A. (1999). *Theory of justice, revised.* Cambridge, Massachusetts: Belknap Press of Harvard University Press.

Rogers, C. R. (1961). *On becoming a person.* Boston: Houghton Mifflin Publishers.

Rousseau, J. J. (1974). *On the social contract, or principles of political right.* (C. M. Sherover, Ed. and Trans.). New York: New American Library.

What We Teach and How We Teach It: An Odd Couple's Odyssey

LEE BOLMAN

If you ask me what my poetry is, I have to tell you I don't know.

But if you ask my poetry, it will tell you who I am.

—Nerudo, Antología Esencial

WHAT WE DO TELLS MUCH OF WHO WE ARE, AND THE products of our action leave a series of traces, moving through time, that tell a story about where we have been. In this paper I focus on a collegial odyssey—my teaching and writing partnership with my colleague, Terry Deal. The focus will be on what we have learned and how we have evolved in our approach to teaching. That evolution is embodied in four books that we have written over a period of almost two decades. I hope to explore two basic questions all of us face every time we teach: (a) What should we teach? and (b) How should we teach it?

The four books vary significantly in their content and style, but all were written with a teaching purpose, and each reflected both the era in which it was written and who we were at the time. For each of the books, I will discuss four key attributes:

1. Sources of authority: On which basis did we claim authority to write and teach? On what sources of knowledge or wisdom did we rely?
2. Core assumptions: What central beliefs undergirded what we said and how we tried to say it?
3. Key ideas: What were the key ideas, and main content of what we hoped to offer?
4. Pedagogy: What were the teaching methods on which we relied.

A JOURNEY BEGINS

After finishing college, Terry had a brief career as a police officer in his home town of Laverne, California. He concluded that teaching might be safer than police work, and switched to education. After serving as a teacher, coach and principal of an alternative high school in San Francisco at the height of the 60s, he went back to school to earn a Ph.D. in education and sociology at Stanford. From there he came to Harvard in the Fall of 1976, where I had been teaching for about five years. As an undergraduate, I had planned on becoming a lawyer until I ran into Chris Argyris when I was a senior in college. That fateful encounter sent me in the direction of a doctoral program in organizational behavior and, ultimately, to the Harvard Graduate School of Education.

The first term that Terry came to Harvard, we were scheduled to teach together in a large course titled Organization Theory and Behavior. We began enthusiastically but soon realized we had a problem—we disagreed on almost everything. The readings that Terry wanted to assign fell mostly into two categories for me: (a) things I'd never read and (b) things I thought were boring or irrelevant. Terry had a similar take on the readings I wanted to assign. We compromised—he took half the classes with his readings; I took the other half. This was only partly successful. On occasion when Terry was lecturing, I found myself sitting in the back of the room shaking my head, worrying about the potential damage to students' careers if they took him too seriously. I sometimes felt it was my duty to open the next class by debunking his more outrageous claims. Terry was not reluctant to return the favor on his turn.

To us, this actually seemed interesting and exciting. Unfortunately, most of our students disagreed. Where we saw debate and intellectual ferment, they saw two instructors who couldn't get their act together. Many were particularly concerned about grading—how were they supposed to know what we wanted? That led to grumbling in the halls that began to spread over the school. Some of our colleagues began to drop hints that maybe we didn't know how to teach. Things came to a head when a delegation of students marched into the Dean's office to complain about the miseducation we were giving them. The Dean called to ask what was going on. "Academic freedom," we said. That incantation was sufficiently powerful to persuade the Dean to leave us alone, but it was getting clearer to us that we had a problem.

One of the older principles in social psychology is that a common enemy is a very powerful way to unify a group. We had a common enemy that included our students, our colleagues, and our boss. We bonded, and began a long, challenging series of conversations. We gradually abandoned our efforts to persuade the other—"I'm right and you're wrong." We realized we were both right, but we had different truths. It took us another year or so to clarify and delineate those truths, but that led to the concept of the four frames that have been central to our teaching and writing ever since. The key insight was that there were a number of competing ways to conceptualize or frame organizations, each with its own logic, each rooted in its own history and traditions. An overview of the model is shown in Table 1.

Each of us brought his own intellectual preferences and tensions. Terry was the primary contributor for both the structural and the symbolic frames. The structural frame, with its roots in Weber and a long tradition of sociological theory, emphasizes structure, order, and rationality. The symbolic frame, with roots in the arts as well as in anthropology and philosophy, centers on non-rational and meta-rational issues of belief, faith, meaning, and the importance of symbols in organizations. Meanwhile, I was the primary carrier for the human resource and political frames. Both focus on people but emphasize contrasting aspects of the social world. The human resource frame emphasizes a collaborative and self-actualizing view of humans, with a focus on integrating individual and organization. The political frame emphasizes scarcity, divergence, conflict and power.

MODERN APPROACHES (1984)

Once the four frames snapped into focus, we organized our teaching around them, which created a need for readings that supported our content. Material on structural and human resource issues was abundant, but political and symbolic readings were harder to find. We concluded that we needed a book that covered all four frames, and that the only way to get it was to write it ourselves. That eventually led to the 1984 publication of *Modern Approaches to Understanding and Managing Organizations* (see Table 2 for a summary of sources of authority, assumptions, content and pedagogy). It was, in the words of our colleague Bob Marx, of the University of Massachusetts-Amherst, "the pretty good book with the lousy title." (We hated the title as well, but lost that battle with our publisher.) Even though the theory movement in educational administration was waning by then, the idea that social science was the primary basis for professorial authority was still alive and influential in the book we produced. We tried to give it a readable, applied flavor, but it was still heavy on theory and research, and much lighter on case and example. Our basic assumption was that social science concepts could give professionals the more complex worldviews they needed. As we saw it, they typically oversimplified a complicated world because their personal theories, or conceptual maps, were too narrow and prevented them from seeing or knowing what to do about many of the challenges surrounding them. The solution we proposed was developing an appreciation for all four of the frames presented in the book.

Even in 1976, our teaching intent was to bridge the theory–practice gap. Most of our students planned to become educational practitioners, and we wanted them to be able to use the ideas that they learned. But we mostly taught theory through lectures and readings. Our primary method for linking theory to practice was group projects. Student teams conducted field

Table 1. Overview of Four Frames

Frame	Structural	Human Resource	Political	Symbolic
Metaphor for organization	Factory or Machine	Family	Jungle	Carnival, temple, theater
Central concepts	Rules, roles, goals, policies, technology, environment	Needs, skills, relationships	Power, conflict, competition, organizational politics	Culture, meaning, metaphor, ritual, ceremony, stories, heroes and heroines
Image of leadership	Social architecture	Empowerment	Advocacy	Inspiration
Basic leadership challenge	Align structure to task, technology, environment	Align organizational and human needs	Develop agenda and power base	Create faith, beauty, and power base

Table 2. Modern Approaches to Understanding and Managing Organizations

	Modern Approaches (1984)
Sources of authority	Social science
	Experience and example
Assumptions	You can't manage what you don't see
	Practitioners need more nuanced, flexible conceptual maps
Key ideas	Four frames: structural, human resource, political, symbolic
Pedagogy	Lecture
	Exercises, experiences

studies of organizational settings, trying to apply ideas from class to real world settings. We supplemented those with occasional in-class experiences and simulations. Some, like our power simulation (Bolman and Deal, 1979), worked very well. Others failed and were dropped.

REFRAMING ORGANIZATIONS (1991)

In the years after *Modern Approaches* came out, the four frames got a positive response from many of our students and from colleagues who began using the book in their own teaching. The primary complaints from both groups (other than the bad title) was that the book was too static and didn't go far enough in linking ideas to practice in useful ways that students could implement. When the time came to revise the book, we took that critique seriously. We greatly expanded the use of cases and examples, and sought to integrate them more tightly into the text. We expanded our discussion of leadership and organizational change, and put more emphasis on the art of leadership and management. Above all, we put the idea of *reframing*—an active process of looking at things from more than one direction—at the center of the book.

Meanwhile, our teaching was also evolving. After Terry moved to Vanderbilt in the early 1980s, we were mostly teaching separately, but there were many parallels in our individual evolutions. We spent less time

lecturing, and more time engaging students in the application of ideas in both experiential activities and case discussions. We made reframing a central idea in our classes and continually engaged students in reframing cases and experiences, both in and out of class. Our increased attention to artistry led to more focus on an action-reflection-feedback cycle.

TAPPING SPIRIT: LEADING WITH SOUL

From the time of *Modern Approaches*, we were often asked the question, "Is there a fifth frame?" Over the years, we received many proposed candidates. Among them, we often heard suggestions that the four-frame model could be enhanced by dealing more explicitly with ethics, values, and the spiritual dimension of leadership and organizations. That did not crystallize into a specific idea until a fateful lunch with some of our colleagues at our publisher, Jossey-Bass, in the Spring of 1993. We were at a restaurant in San Francisco, and the topic at hand was possible book projects. We discussed several different ideas that we had developed in advance, but none seemed to generate great enthusiasm. Finally, Lynn Luchow (Jossey-Bass's president at the time), interrupted the flow to ask a pointed question: "What would you guys *really* like to do?" That question produced a very long silence, during which Terry and I both realized that we didn't know what we *really* wanted to do. Somehow, out of that silence emerged a half-formed idea: a book about

Table 3. Reframing Organizations: Artistry, Choice, and Leadership

	Reframing Organizations (1991)
Sources of authority	Less social science
	More emphasis on cases and examples
Assumptions	Leadership and management are distinct, both are important
	Reframing is key skill
	Leadership as performing art
Key ideas	Four frames: structural, human resource, political, symbolic
Pedagogy	Less lecture
	More engagement
	Artistry: action-reflection-feedback cycle

Table 4. Leading with Soul: An Uncommon Journey of Spirit

	Leading With Soul (1995)
Sources of authority	Examples and stories
	Sacred texts
	Art and imagination
Assumptions	Faith & passion energize and sustain leaders
	Intuition, values and spiritual growth guide leadership
Key ideas	Spiritual journey (leaving home, questing, returning home)
	Leadership gifts (authorship, power, love, significance)
Pedagogy	Arts (poetry, music, story, theater, etc.)
	Reflection and dialogue

leadership and spirituality. By the time Lynn picked up the check, we had agreed to do it.

Once we were off on our own, I turned to Terry to ask, "Do you know anything about this?" He said, "No, I hoped you did." It didn't feel like a promising start, but it was the beginning of a challenging and powerful journey for us. We found ourselves reading very different literature, exploring new questions and issues, and making powerful intellectual and personal discoveries. We got a lot of help from the publisher and from many colleagues, and eventually produced *Leading With Soul* in 1995.

We had to go beyond our roots in the social science literature. We read sacred texts, poetry, fiction and philosophy in search of insights that we needed. We turned to parable as our primary instructional mode, and constructed a story of an embattled leader who had plunged into a spiritual crisis and was fortunate to encounter a wise sage who could help him move forward. Much in the story was autobiographical, constructed from bits and pieces of our individual spiritual journeys. The process of assembling a coherent narrative was a powerful experience for both of us.

We confronted questions of who we were and where we were going in our lives. We were fortunate that, for both of us, this led to strengthening our relationships with our wives and families, but it led to many other significant changes, including significant career and geographic shifts for both of us.

REFRAMING THE PATH TO SCHOOL LEADERSHIP

A recent milestone in our pedagogic odyssey was the 2002 publication of *Reframing the Path to School Leadership*. Our hope was to create a primer of what we had learned about leadership targeted particularly at aspiring principals and teachers. We wanted a short, highly readable book that would enable early-career professionals to understand basic insights about leadership and school organization, and to apply those insights to the challenges they encounter every day at work.

For this work our primary sources of authority were cases and experiences—our own and those of many teachers and principals we have known over the years. An underlying substratum of social science research still undergirds the ideas that we present, but it lurks quietly under the hood. As in *Leading with Soul*,

Table 5. Reframing the Path to School Leadership

	Reframing the Path to School Leadership (2002)
Sources of authority	Cases and experience
	Story and imagination
	Social science
Assumptions	Learn via vicarious immersion in a story moving through time
	Portable mentor is better than no mentor
	Administrative and teacher leadership are interconnected
Key ideas	Everyday life in schools (cast of characters, personal/professional concerns, how things work)
	Knowledge/know-how link
	Four frames
	Faith and values
Pedagogy	Diagnosis: what's going on here?
	Vicarious experiments (what would I do if…?; how could I apply this to my situation?)
	Reflection on personal cases
	Drama and role-play with feedback

we use story as a teaching vehicle. We interwove the stories of two rookies—a new principal and a new teacher—who found themselves working in the same school. Each faced leadership challenges. One of our key assumptions was that leadership lessons would be clearer and more helpful when they are rooted in the everyday life of schools—the challenges, the cast of characters, the personal and professional concerns that are always present. We hoped that our story would be an effective vehicle to bridge the gap between theory and practice, between knowing about and knowing how. Another core assumption was that teacher and administrative leadership are intertwined, and that both are critical elements in building schools that work.

The story is interrupted along the way by periodic conceptual interludes, where we try to explicate some of the key ideas that we hope the story illustrates. But we expected that the primary learning value would come through working with the story itself. It serves as an extended case that opens a range of pedagogical possibilities. Students can enhance their diagnostic skills by asking what is going on in the story and what it means, and by comparing their optic with that of their colleagues. They can enhance their ability to plan and strategize by answering the classic question, "What would you do if you were . . . ?", and by defending that answer in dialogue with others. They could engage in dialogue and reflection about their values and commitments by comparing their reactions to those of characters in the story.

Reframing the Path to School Leadership provides a compact overview of what we had learned to that point on our odyssey. The early chapters are key to our four frames. *Leading with Soul* is echoed in the use of story as the primary teaching vehicle, and in an emphasis on ethics and values, and on the spiritual dimension of teaching and school leadership.

TEACHING GIFTS

In *Leading with Soul*, we wrote, "Leading is giving. Leadership is an ethic, a gift of oneself" (Bolman and Deal, 2001, p. 106). We discussed four gifts that leaders might offer their constituents. All four are equally important and relevant in the relationship between teacher and student. The first gift, *authorship*, is what we offer whenever we enable students to do or create something that is uniquely theirs—that carries their signature. This gift is vital if we want to produce creative and self-reliant school leaders. If we rely on lectures and multiple-choice tests, we encourage our students to become passive and conformist, and to feel

that they are simply giving us what we want. This is hardly what we hope they will encourage as leaders. We need to invest effort and creativity to create challenging tasks that prod students to risk and learn and to express and develop their talents and interests.

We give the second gift, *power*, when we enable students to feel they can make a difference and have an impact on things that are important to them. It's easy to create a learning environment where students feel powerless, but what are we doing to future leaders if we put them in classrooms where they can't lead?

A third gift is *love*—manifested in the many ways that one individual can show caring for another. In our interactions with students, both in and out of class, we encounter a series of choice points where we can choose to invest more or less in our relationships. Pressures of time and task often lead us to avoid anything beyond quick and superficial encounters. But if we consistently choose distance over caring, what do we teach our students about priorities? We owe it to them and to ourselves to be mindful and intentional in manifesting our belief that all adults, as well as all children, can learn and are worthy of our caring and respect.

A fourth gift is *significance*. Significance can mean both importance and meaningfulness, and both are important. Working in schools is challenging and often exhausting. It brings moments of exhilaration and joy, but these are often tempered by periods of frustration and questions: Am I really making a difference? Do the payoffs really justify the energy I expend and the price I pay? Burnout is a problem across the profession. The alternative to burnout is faith, rooted in a deep sense of the importance and meaningfulness of the work. Rabbi Harold Kushner once wrote that we attend services not to find God, but to find a congregation. One of the most important things that we can do as teachers is to encourage our classes to become congregations of fellow seekers who share the questions and rigors of their respective journeys and, in the process, deepen one another's faith.

Burnout is a risk for professors as well as for teachers and school leaders. Tenured dinosaurs are one of the more notorious features of the academy. We have all known a few. If we hope to avoid joining that club, we need to keep traveling on our intellectual and spiritual journeys. The odd-couple odyssey on which Terry and I have been engaged is nearing the end of its third decade. We are proud of what we have been able to do and learn together but also clear that we need to keep on going—looking for new challenges and new ways to contribute. We are both sexagenarians, and we have begun to encounter some of the inevitable psychological and physical challenges of aging. We know there are more bumps on the road and that this journey cannot go on forever. But it's been a great ride, and we'll keep it going as long as we can.

REFERENCES

Bolman, L. G., and Deal, T. E. (1974). A simple but powerful power simulation. *Exchange: The Organizational Behavior Teaching Journal*, 4(3), 38-42.

Bolman, L. G., and Deal, T. E. (1984). *Modern Approaches to Understanding and Managing Organizations*. San Francisco: Jossey-Bass.

Bolman, L. G., and Deal, T. E. (1991). *Reframing Organizations: Artistry, Choice and Leadership*. San Francisco: Jossey-Bass.

Bolman, L. G., and Deal, T. E. (1995). *Leading with Soul: An Uncommon Journey of Spirit*. San Francisco: Jossey-Bass.

Bolman, L. G., and Deal, T. E. (1997). *Reframing Organizations: Artistry, Choice and Leadership* (2nd ed.). San Francisco: Jossey-Bass.

Bolman, L. G., and Deal, T. E. (2001). *Leading with Soul: An Uncommon Journey of Spirit* (2nd ed.). San Francisco: Jossey-Bass.

Bolman, L. G., and Deal, T. E. (2002). *Reframing the Path to School Leadership: A Guide for Teachers and Principals*. Thousand Oaks, CA: Corwin.

Bolman, L. G., and Deal, T. E. (2003). *Reframing Organizations: Artistry, Choice and Leadership* (3rd ed.). San Francisco: Jossey-Bass.

Neruda, P. (1971). *Antología Esencial*. Buenos Aires: Editorial Losada.

Educational Leadership: Knowing the Way, Showing the Way, Going the Way

ROBERT BEACH

WHAT NCPEA HAS ACCOMPLISHED

TWELVE YEARS AGO, IN 1993, JOHN HOYLE AND DWAIN Estes brought forward NCPEA's first yearbook *in a new voice*. It was wonderful. It was a volume that spoke to accomplishment, to the future, to optimism. Perhaps that is a path we might explore this afternoon, what NCPEA has achieved and reasons for optimism about our future—a future based on knowing, showing and going the way.

Optimism has roots in the past. Our organization has changed, has matured in twelve years. It can be hard to see the effects of this change inasmuch as most organizations, such as NCPEA, reach across a span of time that extends beyond our mortality, and for many of us, our memory. Consider our yearbook. From virtually unknown beginnings, it has taken twelve editors to bring this publication to the absolute respectability it enjoys today. Such change takes time, and time can bring forgetfulness. Although NCPEA's history is rich with accomplishments, today, let us examine where the past twelve productive years have brought us, and then consider how these gains have positioned NCPEA for going forward into the next several decades.

Since 1993, NCPEA has achieved the fiscal capacity—that is, the monetary power—to conduct operations across a broad spectrum of activities that allow us to engage in the professional dialog and activities that focus on and frame educational administration, at the national level. As I am sure Ted and the Board, who are moving this outfit forward, will confirm, this has taken the entire decade that began with Don Mc-Carty. This increased fiscal strength has not only generated the past years' developments, but also created a fiscally sound organization with the capability of achieving an optimistic future.

Along with the yearbook, we have seen two additional publications evolve that reflect NCPEA's development. The first of these is the journal *Educational Leadership Review*. This publication is becoming stronger and is providing an outlet for the scholarship being generated by NCPEA members. Publication of our own journal has been long in coming and has added to the visibility of the organization. Our ideas are also now reflected in the *AASA Professor*. At the same time, the assumption of Ken Lane's *Educational Administration Directory* has established a far-reaching touch of public professionalism that benefits our entire profession. With our developing web page and internet capability, we can communicate more effectively. This is development at a pace of one new dissemination effort every two years!

We have become increasingly attractive as an organization to many more professors than in the past. Membership is now over 800; this is two and a half times what it was ten years ago. The decade's explosion in membership reflects the reality, frequently overlooked, that our professors accept their responsibilities and struggle in virtual Sisyphus-like efforts as they work to improve, ultimately, the lives of children. We come to NCPEA to better undertake these increasingly difficult responsibilities. This conference has over 300 attendees! It was not so very far in the past when 150 was the benchmark for a successful conference. NCPEA has become the major professorial organization in educational administration.

A decade ago we were formally reaching out, as an organization, to only the National Policy Board for Educational Administration (NPBEA). Today, NCPEA holds a position on that Board and a voice in the national policy issues governing our field and profession. We now more fully understand the importance of linkages between organizations in achieving mutual goals and in building better organizations for the future. Enlarging on this perspective, the leadership of NCPEA and of the University Council of Educational Administration (UCEA) are engaged in a continuing dialogue that jointly strengthens the impact of our individual efforts to improve the profession. We now reach out to other organizations, organizations such as the National Association of Elementary and Middle Level Principals (NAESP), the National Association of Secondary School Principals (NASSP), and the American Association of School Administrators (AASA). We are building relationships that will provide support for creating mutually desired futures. In this area, we have begun cooperative responses to the challenges directed at the work we do in our preparation programs. The effort here has been hard but worthwhile; we are beginning to see that the separation between practitioners and professors has begun to narrow. This is largely due to the continuing efforts of our Board and of cooperating boards. Consider the impressive development of the Conference-within-a-Conference which has resulted from cooperation with the American Association of School Administrators (AASA). What a wonderful and mutually beneficial creation Ed Chance and Mike Martin have overseen!

During this decade, defacto national standards arrived, and, yes, NCPEA had a hand in this—especially our efforts in conjunction with the Interstate School Leadership Licensure Consortium (ISLLC), the Educational Leadership Constituency Council (ELCC), and through our participation in NPBEA. While neither, or any other, set of standards is much more than the beginnings of a foundation on which to build, most in the profession do look to the Policy Board and to the current standards as providing a focus for the profession, even if that focus serves as a lightning rod. Much progress has been made in this area. Five members are now serving in the program review area and a professor now serves on the ISLLC Board. This was not easily achieved.

There has developed a growing recognition that, indeed, we do have to revisit the knowledge base on which our work rests. Louis Wildman has made this clear. This has come about as a response to challenges by those who view our work as being without substance and without reference to a clear conceptual base of information, although it is difficult to find the knowledge base in use by most state departments of education, or most other education agencies. And it is correct that a periodic review of what we do as a profession is appropriate and is professionally helpful. All of us wish to be responsive to new knowledge and wisdom: this is absolutely critical in the environment that now surrounds us.

All the things that have been instituted are serving to define NCPEA as *the* organization for professors. All of these truly profound accomplishments create a platform for considering the future optimistically.

WHERE WE MIGHT CONSIDER GOING

Without question, our past efforts have been successful and must continue. The other day I came across a professor, the chair of a doctoral program, who was unaware of either UCEA or NCPEA. This individual worked with a good program and is bright and hard working. This week we have gathered 300 professors in professional development: that is great! However, in checking the *Directory* of faculty in educational leadership, one finds approximately 3,300 names listed. Allowing some reduction in numbers for deans and strictly higher education administration types, there are clearly over 2,300 faculty in our profession, in addition to ourselves, who could be here with us. Perhaps, by using the *Directory*, by contacting state departments of education, and by reaching out to state organizations of professors of educational administration, we can locate both individual professors and their programs and begin to familiarize each with our interests and goals, so that some may recognize the rewards of a mutual relationship. It is to everyone's benefit to find, show, and go with these individuals into a cooperative future.

We must continue to build linkages with other groups. NCPEA must continue to consider how to find ways to reach those with decision-making power. This is especially true with state-level educators. By this I mean state superintendents, state department personnel, and legislators on education committees. In many ways, these individuals are engaged in establishing and maintaining the environments in which not only our students work, but in which we work also. As these individuals engage in their daily activities, who provides them with the information necessary for making the decisions that impact our responsibilities? If we do not provide such information, others will—and do provide it. While some would be cool or even hostile to overtures from NCPEA, many more of these individuals would welcome information from a professional organization such as ours. Many might even find our conferences to be of interest.

Perhaps this can be achieved by considering a focused information dissemination effort with an ongoing newsletter, or brochure, being forwarded to important members of state legislative education committees, governors, state superintendents of schools, and others whom we define as important to our work. In this way, a few linkages may be created; as a minimum, we can provide a service by bringing our concerns and viewpoints before those who can be helped by our information. This July we will convene in Washington, D.C., and have opportunities to meet with several decision-making groups. This is a wonderful opportunity to begin an effort of this kind. We must begin to make our viewpoint heard—we are the legitimate voice of our profession and we must speak out. It is past time to voice our views. We have been silent too long.

NCPEA's involvement in the standards movement has never been clearly articulated. This involvement, this support, was never seen by the Board as an endorsement of a specific set of standards, for example, the ISLLC standards, but rather as support for the concept that national, trans-state guidelines might mitigate against hostile and/or professionally damaging deeds enacted by uninformed or pressure coerced states. Acceptance of the standards, per se, was not the issue. Establishing the capacity to reference national guidelines was. Something similar to the national standards aspect of this is now in being and we have had a central role in this. As anticipated, changes have been taking place relative to the standards themselves. The Policy Board is increasing its interest in this area. Modifying the current standards should become a serious interest for NCPEA. We should support the continual modification of these standards, helping to create greater flexibility, with the recognition that preparation programs and their missions and clients vary widely; assist in making them more professional and less touchy feely; and support efforts that help the standards to be embraced by our profession as a means of improving preparation programs and of informing the nation's educational leadership. We have been working in this area and should continue, and perhaps increase, our efforts. This might be done by establishing a joint standards oversight committee with other professional groups, where the charge is to monitor and impact those standards relating to preparation programs that are proposed or in use by accrediting agencies, standards groups and, if possible, by the states. A body having greater focus than the policy board and yet being less operationally oriented than the Educational Leadership Constituency Council (ELCC) is appropriate. Perhaps such a joint group should assume complete responsibility for program review. We have the wisdom and the capacity to establish something along these lines. John Hoyle and Chuck Achilles have been talking about this since the world discovered dirt! While this would involve a great deal of effort, certainly we can find ways to partially reward and recognize those members committed to an effort such as this.

As professionals we have a solid grasp of the essentials of our knowledge base. Work to improve ourselves in this area is ongoing. However, two things seem to be lacking. The first of these may be forthcoming but should be borne in mind so that it is not overlooked. This is the creation of some form of articulation relative to the knowledge base. We need to be able to point to some tangible codex and say, "Here is the knowledge base." Jim Berry has been working on this for some time. Our Connections project offers the opportunity to make this concept manifest. Yes, this codex will be a source of endless debate and challenge; so what? "Bring it on" and it will make us stronger! There exists a second concern. A problem exists with what most would consider an aspect of the knowledge base. There is no publication, manuscript, or book that adequately reflects craft wisdom. By this one can envision work along the lines of a principal's desk reference—really a how-to book: how to work with a secretary, how to sell tickets to a ball game, how to handle disruptive parents. For many of us, this is mundane "stuff." But it is part of the "stuff" of our knowledge base and hard-to-find "stuff" at that. Its absence echoes the continuing concerns that question the relevancy of our programs. Perhaps several things could happen here. While the practitioner organizations publish a considerable array of helpful information, some of which is related to this concern, their publications tend to focus on the instructional side. This is certainly a high priority concern that needs to be addressed, but it does not address the total role of the administrator in this area. Why not engage in a joint effort with our interested friends in the practitioner organizations and bring this desk reference forward. It could be useful in preparation programs and to professional practice, not to mention its usefulness as a royalty generator and advertisement for NCPEA.

Then there is the forgotten audience. By this I mean those that have the second heaviest involvement with the outcomes produced by our students, that is, the parents of the children in schools. The general public has only the vaguest notion as to what they should expect from a principal. Beyond discipline and on-time activities, parents have little understanding of school administration. Many misconceptions about public education exist in the public's mind. Little factual information is available to the general public in a form that is easily accessible and readily readable. We, as a profession, have done little to change fallacious beliefs or provide factual information on national education issues. As an example, when people learn that education spends $6,000 per child, there is an immediate tendency to multiply that number by the twenty or more children in the classroom. Well, $120,000 less the $60,000 for the teacher (including benefits), leaves a lot of dollars unaccounted for. Where are these dollars? The assumption is typically that the school must be wasting them! Well, we know where the dollars go. We can work toward correcting misimpressions such as this. We must show the way. Members might consider writing for popular publications, such as the *New Yorker*, the *Atlantic*, and even *Parenting*. Such writing might discuss what should be expected and what should be demanded of the principal if the school is to be effective. Certainly this type of publication may not be acceptable to some of our institutions for promotion and tenure purposes, but in many cases NCPEA members determine the appropriateness of what they and their colleagues write and can support dissemination efforts directed at providing public support. This issue is vitally important, for it is ultimately the public that drives those who drive us! We as a profession have failed to make that public aware of what we know

about effective schools and how such schools can be obtained. This we can do, and NCPEA might consider encouraging some of our members to undertake a public information effort through popular publications directed to parents and others in the general public.

It is time to be proactive, to build on the past, to continue and to improve our efforts at enhancing membership, to continue to build linkages, to adapt and support improved professional standards, to assume a significant role in national knowledge base efforts, and to consider engaging in efforts at improving public awareness.

Ted is exactly right when he encourages us to take back the profession. It is time that NCPEA go forward into a future of our making, not a future devised for some politically expedient but downward path. Our future is optimistic, for *we* know the way. But we are also challenged to show the way and to go the way. Let us accept these challenges and go the way.

In closing, let me thank you for the unexpected honor that has been shown by this award. It is a very humbling accolade.

CREDITING THE PAST

Superintendent Turnover and the Role of Successor Origin

RICHARD T. GEISEL

THE PROBLEM

ACCORDING TO A STUDY CONDUCTED BY METZGER (1997), "the superintendency is the least stable and secure position in education" (p. 44). McKay and Grady (1994) put it this way: "School systems change superintendents the way baseball teams change managers" (p. 37). Such observations can be a bit disconcerting for the person considering a career in educational leadership, not to mention the public school boards whose job it is to select good superintendents and enable them to develop and fulfill long term goals and plans for their school districts. A study of current superintendents in the year 2000 indicated that many superintendents are worried about where the next generation of superintendents will come from, citing "high turnover" as a major barrier to attracting new talent (Cooper, Fusarelli, and Carella, 2000). Of those surveyed, 92 percent expressed concern that "high turnover in the superintendency means a serious crisis in keeping strong leaders in the position" (Cooper, Fusarelli, and Carella, p. 4).

The consequences of having unstable leadership in a school district are numerous and varied. In a study of involuntary superintendent turnover, Metzger (1997) concluded that such turnover often leads to general turmoil in the district. Metzger cites a number of reasons for this, such as the perception by staff that superintendent turnover indicates a lack of direction and stability at the top of the school district, the financial costs of replacing a superintendent are high (which often includes legal involvement), and the staff begin to adopt a "circle the wagon" mentality that ultimately resists reform and risk-taking in favor of the status quo (p. 22).

THEORETICAL FRAMEWORK

Succession in leadership is an issue that all organizations must eventually cope with. According to Grusky (1960), succession research provides an important contribution to organizational theory for the simple reason that all organizations experience it, and the very nature of succession leads to some organizational instability. Finkelstein and Hambrick (1996) discuss the relation of executive turnover and succession to inside and outside candidates, but they do this strictly in the context of the business corporation. However, Finkelstein and Hambrick encourage further study in this area as applied to different fields (p. 183).

While there have been very few studies in the field of education that have analyzed the ramifications of successor origin on the educational leader and the school district, R. O. Carlson (1961) conducted a study forty years ago that led him to the conclusion that insider and outsider superintendents relate to their districts in different ways. Carlson found significant differences between insider and outsider superintendents regarding length of tenure (insiders had longer tenures than outsiders), salaries, attitudes toward mobility, succession patterns, ratios of insiders to outsiders, and their roles as either change agents or stabilizers. One of the objectives of this study was to refresh Carlson's work by testing his findings to see if they still held true in light of all the changes that the superintendency has undergone in the last forty years. Another objective of this study was to build upon Carlson's research by testing the relationship of successor origin to new areas, such as job satisfaction, communication, approval ratings, contract length, and others.

THE LITERATURE

According to Metzger (1997), the superintendency is the least stable job in education. The literature reveals two very solid factors for this phenomenon but falls short of thoroughly considering a host of other potential variables. According to Carter and Cunningham (1997), "the number one reason that most superintendents leave a school district concerns their relations with, and support from, the school board" (p. 96). Numerous studies bear this out (Anderson, 1989; Bradley, 1990; Carter and Cunningham, 1997; Eaton and Sharp, 1996; Giles and Giles, 1990; Grady and Bryant, 1988; Grady and Bryant, 1991; Hall and Difford, 1992; Lutz, 1976; Lutz and Iannaccone, 1986; McCurdy, 1992; McKay and Grady, 1994; Metzger, 1997; Moen, 1976; Palmaffy, 1998; Parker, 1996; Renchler, 1992; Schmuck, 1987; Sharp, 1994; Storey, 1987; Tallerico, 1993; Yee and Cuban, 1996).

The second most significant factor leading to frequent superintendent turnover involves the demographics of the district itself, particularly in terms of population. Studies show that both rural districts (Dlugosh, 1995; Eaton and Sharp, 1996; Grady and Bryant, 1988; Grady and Bryant, 1991) and urban districts (Cuban, 1976; Kowalski, 1995; National School Boards Association, 1992; Renchler, 1992) suffer from above-average superintendent turnover. The literature, however, gives scant attention to the relationship of these variables to the insider or outsider status of superintendents.

Past research has generally paid little attention to the possible effects, positive and negative, of hiring insider versus outsider superintendents, and whether insider or outsider status is a potential predictor of a superintendent's length of tenure, job satisfaction, effectiveness, or other important variables. Carlson (1961), for example, demonstrated that insider superintendents tend to have longer tenures than outsiders (p. 223). However, the variable of successor origin is almost always ignored in the national studies that have examined superintendent turnover and tenure.

There is a fair amount of literature in the fields of management and organizational leadership that addresses CEO succession. Some of the findings, generalizations and principles that have emerged from this research apply to, albeit indirectly, executive leadership succession in the education field. However, only a handful of succession studies deal directly with this subject in the education context. Fewer yet address the effects of succession on either the successor or the district (Smith, 1992). Instead, much of the literature focuses on the variables leading to succession and what factors lead a board of education to choose an insider versus an outsider when filling a superintendent position.

One thing that is conclusive in the literature is that succession tends to be a disruptive event (Grusky, 1960). How superintendents and school boards transition to a new superintendency can be critical in minimizing the disruption. Whether voluntary or involuntary, superintendent turnover is either a problem or opportunity for both the school district and prospective superintendent. Every school district in the country faces superintendent turnover, on average, every five to seven years (Glass, 1992). The succession event can either be the beginning or continuation of progress, a continuation of the status quo, or a disaster in the making.

PURPOSE OF THE STUDY

Although this study analyzed many factors, conditions, and effects that are associated with superintendent succession, the specific purpose of the study was to focus in detail on how the origin of the successor, as an insider or an outsider, impacts the organization and the perceptions of its leader. For the purposes of this study an "insider" was defined as a superintendent who was already an employee of the district in some other capacity immediately prior to being hired by the same district for the position of superintendent. An "outsider" was defined as a superintendent who was hired by a district to become the superintendent without being a prior employee of the district immediately before being hired.

As a result of his groundbreaking research some forty plus years ago, Carlson (1961) concluded that "the data demonstrate that school superintendents promoted from within and those brought in from outside relate to their organizations in different ways with different organizational consequences" (p. 210). This study builds on the research of Carlson and others by providing a more in-depth profile of insider and outsider superintendents. This study also explores the viability of Carlson's findings in light of the tremendous changes that have taken place in public education in the last 40 years.

METHODOLOGY

During the Winter of 2002 this study of the Michigan superintendency, with particular attention given to the issue of successor origin, was conducted. The purpose of the study was to learn more about the current makeup of Michigan superintendents as well as to compare the similarities and differences of those who were hired from within their current district versus those who were hired from outside their current district. Of the 524 superintendents anonymously surveyed online, 363 responded for a total response rate of 69 percent.

There were three phases of completion in this study, consisting of approximately four weeks. The first phase of responses (54 percent of the population) came within the first two weeks of the survey via email. The second phase of responses (15 percent of the population) came within the third and fourth weeks via email, and two responses (less than 1 percent of the population) came through the United States Postal Service and were the last questionnaires completed. The questionnaires returned were compared from phase to phase, and no discernable difference was observed between the questionnaires that were completed immediately when the survey began versus those that were the last to be completed.

SPSS software was used to analyze the data collected from the completed questionnaires. A descriptive analysis of all independent and dependent variables in the study was created, including an indication of the frequencies, means, standard deviations, and range of scores for these variables. Particular attention was given to documenting the number of outside superintendents and inside superintendents; typical succession patterns (insider to insider, insider to outsider, outsider to outsider, and outsider to insider); and comparing insiders and outsiders according to a number of attitudinal and performance variables detailed in the hypotheses listed in Chapter 1.

Depending upon the variables being analyzed, either a t test or a chi-square test was used to measure significance. A t test was used to compare the mean values of two different groups for significance where a continuous variable was involved. A chi-square test was used to compare two variables for significance where the data contained categorical information. Any comparison yielding a significance value less than 0.05 was considered to be statistically significant for purposes of this study.

RESULTS OF THE STUDY

Gender, Age, and Demographics

Seventeen percent of those responding to the survey were females, which is comparable, albeit slightly higher, to the national average. In *The 2000 Study of the American School Superintendency*, 14 percent of all superintendents were female (Glass, 1992, p. 16). Interestingly, the study of the Michigan superintendency revealed no difference between the number of female insiders and outsiders. Exactly 20 of the 40 female respondents indicated that they were insiders and 20 indicated that they were outsiders.

The vast majority of superintendents are in their fifties (64 percent) and are male (83 percent). Fifty-six

percent represent rural districts while only 5 percent represent urban districts. Most others identify their district as suburban or rural/suburban. Seventy-three percent of the superintendents responded that they were content with the size of their district, while most of the others indicated that they would like to be in a larger district.

Successor Origin

One-third of the superintendents surveyed were insiders at the time they were hired for their present superintendency and two-thirds were outsiders. Less than 10 percent of all superintendents have spent their entire career in just one district, indicating that even the majority of insiders have also worked in other districts throughout their career. Interestingly, 16 percent of outsiders were once insider superintendents before leaving their district for another superintendency.

Turnover

Another observation drawn from the data is that approximately one-third (32 percent) of all superintendents surveyed are in their first three years of being a superintendent, which indicates a fairly significant amount of superintendencies were turned over in the last three years. This is a trend that leaders in the state expect to continue due to a growing number of superintendents who are eligible to retire.

Superintendent/School Board Relations

The vast majority of Michigan superintendents reported that they have a positive relationship with their board of education. Surprisingly, only 3 percent indicated a negative relationship with their board. Of those reporting a negative relationship, all were outsiders. The vast majority of Michigan superintendents also characterized favorably the quality and frequency of communication with their board of education. Again, only 3 percent reported negatively regarding communication with their board. Generally, the superintendents view their own performance as either successful or very successful. Less than 4 percent were concerned about their success as a superintendent.

The majority of current superintendents (66 percent) have only held one superintendency. Of those who have held more than one superintendency during their career, 25 percent reported either conflict with the board of education or changes on the board of education as reasons for leaving their previous superintendency. Regardless of successor origin or other factors, most superintendents intend to remain in the profession as a superintendent until retirement.

Advantages and Disadvantages of One's Origin

Finally, perhaps the most enlightening feedback from the superintendents was their collective response to the last item on the questionnaire, which asked them to indicate the advantages and disadvantages of being an insider or outsider superintendent. While the answers varied, it was interesting to see the common threads that emerged from the 225 superintendents who responded to the question. Table 1 demonstrates the general themes that were repeatedly referred to as either advantages or disadvantages of being an *outsider*.

Many of the outsider superintendents responded that they felt that the opportunity for a fresh start with no baggage was a distinct advantage of being an outsider. For example, one superintendent stated that as an outsider, "history does not get in the way of problem solving." Another indicated that "as an outsider I can focus on the present instead of the past." The two most common responses regarding outsider advantage were with regard to bringing new ideas to the district and being able to operate with objectivity because no favors were owed to others in the district. For example, one superintendent stated that there were "no 'good old boy' issues to overcome." Another indicated that not having ties to friends made it easier to make the tough decisions.

Several disadvantages of being an outsider were also listed with the two most common responses being the time it takes to get caught up to speed and the time it takes to build trust. Some spoke about a loss of "institutional history," and others referred to the "inherent distrust of yet another outsider." A few superintendents saw the high expectations of change

Table 1. Advantages and Disadvantages of Being an Outsider

Outsider Advantages
    No personal baggage
    New ideas for the district
    No alliances/Can be objective
    Fresh start/Renewed motivation
    Ability to bring about change
Outsider Disadvantages
    It takes a while to get to know staff and community
    Do not know past history and culture of district
    Takes time to develop relationships and trust
    The Board has high expectations of change
    Unions do not like outsiders
    Moving/Relocating family

Table 2. Advantages and Disadvantages of Being an Insider

Insider Advantages
    Know staff and community (people and values)
    Credibility with staff already established
    Smooth transitions because of prior knowledge
    Trust is already established because the staff and community already know the superintendent
    Already know where the landmines are
    Do not have to move
Insider Disadvantages
    People already know your soft spots
    Some poor relationships already established
    Baggage comes along
    No honeymoon/Harder to change things
    Lack of new ideas/Too comfortable with status quo

as a disadvantage. For example, one superintendent stated that Boards call upon outsiders to get "their dirty work done."

Table 2 demonstrates the general themes that were repeatedly referred to as either advantages or disadvantages of being an *insider*.

The knowledge of the district and community, as well as the ability to hit the ground running were the most common advantages of being an insider that were listed by the respondents. For example, one superintendent stated, "I knew what areas needed to be addressed." Another indicated that "insiders know the unwritten rules and can navigate the culture with ease." Others referred to a "smooth transition" or an "easy transition." One superintendent commented that being an insider allowed a "consistency toward district goals" and an "ability to relate immediately to staff and the issues." Many saw the prior knowledge of the community as a distinct advantage. For example, one superintendent stated, "You know the people; many parents are former students."

There were also several disadvantages of being an insider that were listed. Several superintendents referred to the lack of new ideas, the baggage that comes along, and the difficulty of bringing about change. For example, one superintendent referred to the "baggage" he carried from his former position in the district. Another made reference to the fact that there was "no honeymoon," which made it difficult to initiate change. Others discussed the possibility of limited vision because of being in one place so long. Finally, one superintendent stated, "as an insider, you can get too comfortable."

Similarities and Differences

Most superintendents, irrespective of origin, reported similarly on items related to things such as superintendent/school board relations (overwhelmingly positive), communication (positive), job satisfaction (positive), years served (average tenure was 5 1/2 years regardless of origin), and board evaluations of their performance. However, this study did reveal that definite differences exist between the insiders and outsiders surveyed. Most notably, those differences include their perceptions of why they were hired to be a superintendent (insiders for stability and outsiders for change), the actual ratio of insiders to outsiders (1/3 insiders and 2/3 outsiders), the frequency and infrequency of various succession patterns (insider-to-insider is the least common pattern while outsider-to-outsider is the most common), their attitude toward mobility (outsiders being much more willing to think of their present assignment as temporary), and their level of contentment with the size of their district (outsiders demonstrated more dissatisfaction with the size of their current district than did insiders).

IMPLICATIONS FOR PRACTICE

The purpose of this study was to provide future superintendents and school boards with information pertaining to successor origin that would help them make informed decisions regarding what constitutes a good fit for the district. Insofar as this was the goal, the discovery that there is no relationship between successor origin and certain variables is as instructive and beneficial as the findings that indicate a relationship between successor origin and certain variables.

Based upon the findings in this study, there no longer appears to be a direct relationship between the number of years served in a superintendency and successor origin. The superintendency has changed dramatically over the past forty years. It would be inaccurate to assume that if a district hires an insider, the insider would be in the position for a longer time than an outsider would be. Carlson's (1961) research indicated that this was the case forty years ago, and it made intuitive sense based on the inherent differences between insiders and outsiders; however, much has changed in the last forty years in relation to the demands of the superintendency as well as the increased mobility of the population as a whole. Based upon this study, the difference between the length of tenure of insiders as compared to outsiders is negligible. Admittedly, however, this is the finding of just one study. Future research may indicate a different outcome.

One area that both superintendents and school boards should pay attention to in the hiring process is whether the district needs a stabilizing effect or needs a shake-up. There appears to be a significant relationship between change, stability, and successor origin. Carlson (1961) believed insiders were stabilizers while outsiders were called upon for creative performances when change was needed. Everything analyzed in this study reinforces this notion. For example, 23.2 percent of outsiders perceived that they were hired for their ability to create change while a mere 4.7 percent of insiders responded in the same way. Conversely, almost twice as many insiders (30 percent) as outsiders indicated that they were hired to provide stability.

In addition, many of the superintendents in the study made reference to the ability of outsiders to bring about change that insiders could not because of the honeymoon effect that outsiders have and the baggage that insiders carry from being in the district so long. On the other end of the spectrum, several superintendents responded that the advantages of being an insider included understanding the needs and resources of the district and being able to pursue the district goals without missing a beat. To the contrary, outsiders were viewed as having to take too much time to acclimate themselves to the needs and nuances of the district.

Perhaps the most significant reason successor origin really matters is that superintendents bring different skills to the table depending upon their origin, for very practical reasons such as familiarity or non-familiarity with the district, which can either be a hindrance or an asset depending upon the context. The key is knowing when it is important to match an insider with a district versus an outsider. In order to help determine what constitutes a "good fit," there are a series of questions that board members and superintendent candidates should reflect upon.

The findings of this study and the research reviewed as part of this study suggest that the following questions are important for school board members to address prior to the search for a new superintendent:

- Do we have consensus as a board on what our expectations are for this position?
- What tools do we have at our disposal to assess the needs of the district as perceived by various stakeholders such as staff, community and students?
- Does the feedback from various stakeholders reveal any consistent trends?
- How is our district currently making progress toward increasing student achievement for all students?
- Do we generally like the direction we are heading as a district?

- Is there inside talent that is qualified for the position?
- Do we already have someone in the district we can trust and be confident in?
- Is there a need for massive change that would be difficult for an insider to accomplish?
- What are the costs and benefits of maintaining stability versus initiating significant change?
- How will we clearly communicate the expectations of the position to prospective candidates?

There are also questions that prospective candidates for the superintendency should reflect upon. For the candidate who aspires to be a superintendent in the district he or she currently works in, the following questions should be addressed:

- Will a viable opportunity to become a superintendent in this district be available in the near future?
- Am I willing to wait for the position even though there are no guarantees that the board will hire an insider?
- Does waiting give me additional valuable experience or does waiting become a disadvantage in securing a superintendency?
- What will be the ramification be if I am not chosen for the position? How should I respond?
- Will I be an effective insider superintendent based upon my current relationships with staff and the board?
- Do I agree with the direction in which the district is currently going?
- Will others I currently work with expect favoritism? If so, how will I respond?
- How can I guarantee that the district does not stagnate for lack of new ideas and outside perspective?

Likewise, it is important for the outside candidate who is seeking a position as a superintendent to reflect upon the following questions:

- Am I willing to move my family?
- Am I willing to work at making new relationships and building trust?
- How will I overcome the stigma of being an "outsider," and am I mentally prepared for the resistance some staff will have to an "outsider"?
- How will I go about discerning who the movers and shakers are and utilizing their abilities?
- How can I affirm what is positive about the district and at the same time make the case for needed change?
- How much time will I spend communicating with the Board, staff and community?
- What will be my channels of communication?

- How can I build administrative loyalty?
- How can I build a positive culture?

One cannot overstate the need for the district to engage in an objective needs assessment prior to the search for a new superintendent. The needs assessment, at a minimum, must bring to light whether the district would, at this point in time, benefit from significant change or continued stability. Likewise, it is critical that individual candidates for the superintendency confront the issues that will inevitably be raised simply by nature of their origin as an insider or outsider. Ensuring a "good fit" requires the up-front work of addressing these critical questions by both the candidate and the board.

CONCLUSION

Carlson's (1961) research indicated that successor origin is a major variable in the study of superintendent succession because insiders and outsiders relate to their organizations in dissimilar ways. While several of the relationships tested in this study were not found to be statistically significant, this study did reveal that definite differences exist between insiders and outsiders. Most notably, those differences included superintendents' perceptions of themselves as stabilizers or agents of change, the actual ratio of insiders to outsiders, the frequency and infrequency of various succession patterns, attitudes toward mobility, perceptions of their relationship with the board, and level of contentment with the size of their district. This study was an attempt to refresh Carlson's research as well as explore new territory. There is, however, a lot more to learn about the effect successor origin has on the superintendent succession process and subsequent performance. It is hoped that future researchers will take up the mantle and expand upon this study in the ways suggested.

REFERENCES

Anderson, S. L. (1989). How to predict success in the superintendency. *School Administrator, 46*(7), 22, 24, 26.

Bradley, A. (1990, December 12). Rapid turnover in urban superintendents. *Education Week*, 3.

Carlson, R. O. (1961). Succession and performance among school superintendents. *Administration Science Quarterly, 6*, 210–227.

Carter, G. R., and Cunningham, W. G. (1997). *The American School Superintendent.* San Francisco: Jossey-Bass Publishers.

Cooper, B. S., Fusarelli, L. D., and Carella, V. A. (2000). *Career crisis in the school superintendency? The results of a na-*

tional survey. Arlington, VA: American Association of School Administrators.

Cuban, L. (1976). *Urban school chiefs under fire.* Chicago: The University of Chicago Press.

Dlugosh, L. L. (1994/95, Winter). The moving puzzle: School size, politics, and superintendent tenure. *Rural Educator, 16*(2), 16–20.

Eaton, W. E., and Sharp, W. L. (1996). Involuntary turnover among small-town superintendents. *Peabody Journal of Education, 71*(2), 78–85.

Finkelstein, S., and Hambrick, D. (1996). *Strategic leadership: Top executives and their effects on organizations.* Minneapolis, MN: West Publishing Company.

Giles, D. E., and Giles, S. (1990). *Where do all the superintendents go?* (ERIC Document Reproduction Service No. ED326938.)

Glass, T. E. (1992). *The study of the American school superintendency.* Arlington, VA: American Association of School Administrators.

Grady, M. L., and Bryant, M. T. (1988). *Superintendent turnover in rural school districts.* (ERIC Document Reproduction Service No. ED308032.)

Grady, M. L., and Bryant, M. T. (1991). School board turmoil and superintendent turnover: What pushes them to the brink? *School Administrator, 48*(2), 19–26.

Grusky, O. (1960). Administrative succession in formal organizations. *Social Forces, 39*, 105–115.

Hall, G. E., and Difford, G. A. (1992). *State administrators association director's perceptions of the exiting superintendent phenomenon.* (ERIC Document Reproduction Service No. ED351799.)

Kowalski, T. J. (1995). *Keepers of the flame. Contemporary urban superintendents.* Thousand Oaks, CA: Corwin Press, Inc.

Lutz, F. W. (1976). *Incumbent defeat and superintendent turnover: From assumptions to explanatory model and practical results.* (ERIC Document Reproduction Service No. ED123801.)

Lutz, F. W., and Iannaccone, L. (1986). *The dissatisfaction theory of American democracy: A guide for politics in local school districts.* (ERIC Document Reproduction Service No. ED274041.)

McCurdy, J. (1992). Building better board-administrator relations. Arlington, VA: American Association of School Administrators.

McKay, J., and Grady, M. (1994). Turnover at the top. *Executive Educator, 16*(8), 37–38.

Metzger, C. (1997). Involuntary turnover of superintendents. *Thrust for Educational Leadership, 26*, 20–22, 44.

Moen, A. W. (1976). *The effect of partisan elections on the incumbent defeat-superintendent turnover relationship.* (ERIC Document Reproduction Service No. ED122395.)

National School Boards Association (1992). Urban dynamics: Lessons learned from urban boards and superintendents. Alexandria, VA: National School Boards Association.

Palmaffy, T. (1998). Numero uno: El Paso superintendent Anthony Trujillo sets the standards for urban schools. *Policy Review, 91*, 12–39.

Parker, P. (1996). Superintendent Vulnerability and Mobility. *Peabody Journal of Education, 71*(2), 64–77.

Renchler, R. (1992). Urban superintendent turnover: The need for stability. Eugene, OR: ERIC Clearinghouse on Educational Management.

Schmuck, P. (1987). Women educators: Employees of schools in Western countries. Albany, NY: State University of New York Press.

Sharp, W. L. (1994). *Superintendent vulnerability and the bottom line.* (ERIC Document Reproduction Service No. ED384117.)

Smith, E. (1992). Careerbound and placebound superintendents: A study of leader succession in New Jersey Public Schools. Unpublished doctoral dissertation, Rutgers University.

Storey, V. J. (1987). *Leadership in uncertain times. Findings of a study of the British Columbia school superintendency, 1987.* (ERIC Document Reproduction Service No. ED293197.)

Tallerico, M. (1993). *Gender and politics at work: Why women exit the superintendency.* (ERIC Document Reproduction Service No. ED361911.)

Yee, G., and Cuban, L. (1996). When is tenure long enough? A historical analysis of superintendent turnover and tenure in urban school districts. *Educational Administration Quarterly, 32*, 615–641.

Transition Strategies and Networking: The Female Rural Superintendent

JEAN HAAR, JOHN PALLADINO, KAYE PEERY, AND MARILYN GRADY

RURAL SCHOOL DISTRICTS HAVE ALWAYS BEEN A PART OF the American educational system. In 2004, the United States finds rural schools educating a significant number of students. As noted in the Rural Trust report, *Why Rural Matters 2003: The Continuing Need for Every State to Take Action on Rural Education,* "Nearly one in three of America's school-age children attend public schools in rural areas or small towns of fewer than 25,000, and more than one in six go to a school in the very smallest communities, those with populations under 2,500" (http://www.ruraledu.org/newsroom/wrm_new.htm).

The role of the superintendent can affect the stability and the quality of a rural school. The position "has evolved from a position that included clerical as well as educational tasks, to one of business management, and finally to a position that integrates the tasks of chief executive officer and professional educational leader" (Chase, 1995, p. 34).

Although the role of superintendent has undergone changes during the twentieth century, the social characteristics of the superintendent have not. The position is dominated by white, middle-aged males (Blount, 1998; Garn, 2003). In 1990, only 3 percent of all superintendents were women; within the 3 percent, more women were superintendents in larger-sized districts than in smaller-sized districts (Blount, 1998). Chase (1995) noted the following:

> In 1991, 94.4 percent of superintendents were men; in 1990, 96.6 percent were white. . . . The male dominance of the occupation is striking because superintendents rise from the ranks of teachers, 70 percent of whom are women. While the presence of women in prestigious professions of medicine and law has increased slowly over the past twenty years, the superintendency has remained resistant to women's integration, despite the fact that half the graduate students in programs of educational administration are now women (p. 36).

Despite the increase of women graduating from educational administration programs, "almost half of all school districts have reported a shortage of qualified applicants [for administrative positions], with rural districts reporting slightly larger percentages" (Howley and Pendarvis, 2002).

Why have the number of women completing educational administration programs increased yet the number of women superintendents remained small? Why are there fewer women superintendents in rural districts than in suburban or urban districts? Studying women who have obtained an administrative position in a rural setting as well as studying women who have successfully remained in that position can provide answers.

PURPOSE AND METHODOLOGY

The purpose of the study was to examine the transitioning and networking strategies used by female rural superintendents. Rural was identified as communities with fewer than 2,500 people (*Why Rural Matters,* 2003). The study was a qualitative, multiple-case study. Structured interviews were conducted based on 22 open-ended questions. The main research question was "How do rural, female superintendents administer in rural school districts?" Subquestions were framed around four areas: leadership, relationships, change, and support. Participants were female superintendents employed with a rural school district in Michigan, Minnesota, Nebraska, and New Mexico. The names and locations of all possible participants were identified through the states' Departments of Education. The superintendents were invited to participate through telephone contacts that described the structure and purpose of the study. Fifteen were interviewed. The number interviewed was the result of the investigators' ability to contact the individuals and participants' willingness and availability to be interviewed during the timeframe of January through June 2004.

The interviews were approximately one hour in length. Three were conducted at the respective superintendent's school site; twelve were telephone interviews. IRB consent forms were signed and collected from each of the participants. The interviews were transcribed and Creswell's (2003) recommendations for data coding, analysis and interpretation were used. The collected data were separated into categories: career paths, circumstances, leadership, relationships, change, support, challenges and advice. Data were then analyzed for emerging patterns and themes. Conclusions were drawn from the categories.

FINDINGS

Career Paths

Although participants' experiences reaching the superintendency were unique, all began their profession in education. Thirteen followed the traditional path of teacher, building-level administrator, then superintendent; two moved into the superintendency from a teaching position, bypassing the building-level position. One went directly from the classroom into the superintendent office; another moved from the classroom to the state level agency position, to executive director of a nonprofit education cooperative before accepting a superintendent position. Five had leadership experiences and responsibilities along the way, such as dean of students, standards coordinator, or curriculum director.

The following provide examples of the different experiences that led participants to the superintendency:

> Although they've been quick and short, I've had a pretty varied experience from larger schools to smaller schools to almost all aspects of administration from supervising staff development to the truancy counseling-type of things with kids. I've seen a little bit of all of it.

> I was the high school principal for about two years. Then they were having trouble with the superintendent. They were going through firing him. So I ended up picking up some of his duties just because we had to have things done. We had to do it, and it fell on my desk. After he was fired, they had a consultant hired to help them decide what to do as a district. He suggested, "Just make this lady your superintendent." So they hired me as superintendent. This is my fourth year now here as superintendent.

> I have been with this district a long time. I was hired as an elementary teacher in the mid '80s. As consolidation happened, I applied to work at the middle school in a sixth grade position. I stayed in that for

about 7–8 years then became the K–8 principal . . . My superintendent was retiring and he said, "You need to apply for my position. You will do just fine. I'll help you." . . . And here I am.

> I taught ten years. I became certified as district superintendent, K–12 principal, and community director through a cohort program ("I did it only because of the fact that they brought it close to me. If I did it at this time, I already had overlapping classes, so it was a lot easier than to ever go back to do. I thought I wanted to be a principal.") and am now employed as all three. Technically, I am considered superintendent, principal K–8, and community director.

> The superintendent previous to me requested a sabbatical leave for a year . . . I thought to help the district out and to make an easy transition for everyone, instead of having somebody that doesn't know the system, I would at least check and see if it would work into my schedule [to obtain a superintendent license]. It was always kind of in the back of my mind that it would be neat to give that a shot but I don't think I would have taken the initiative to go back if this opportunity wouldn't have come up. I like the position. It is at the point where I hate to leave.

Circumstances

Professional and personal circumstances for entering the profession were shared. Most of the circumstances centered around four areas: (a) encouragement from others, (b) a sense of loyalty to the school and community, (c) the lack of quality candidates, and (d) individual situations and interests.

Colleagues, administrators, and family members spurred many of the participants toward administrative roles through encouragement. A participant commented, "When another administrator sees you have leadership abilities, qualities, and would do well in that position—it's a good feeling." One individual noted that the support was "initiated by former administrators but once I started doing the work, it was my own personal belief that if I am going to do something I need to be licensed."

A sense of loyalty and commitment to the school and community also affected a number of participants. One participant became superintendent after asking herself, "Who is going to hold this school together?" Another, "seeing the need and knowing that I could do it as well as anybody" stepped forward; while a third stated, "I offered stability to the school, to the community. I have been here 29 years; they know who I am; they know my family; I'm not going anywhere;

they know what you see is what you get. There's not going to be a whole lot of surprises."

A lack of quality from candidates in the position also influenced participants to actively pursue credentials in administration and apply for openings. One individual noted, "In small rural districts we don't frequently get a good pool of candidates to choose from." Not only a lack of candidates but also a lack of quality influenced decisions to pursue the position. Another participant commented, "When I was a teacher, I could see how things could be done better and was kind of critical of some of the decisions administration was making and I thought I could do a better job than that." One participant simply stated, "I didn't like my boss—I was working for someone I couldn't stand any more. It wasn't worth it."

Individual situations and interests also played a part in participants' decisions to move into the superintendency. Explanations included such statements as "My kids were through college so I could make that sacrifice [to obtain certification]"; "I am single and could move"; "I viewed it as another challenge"; "I've always been an overachiever"; "It was a location issue and job availability"; and "I had the desire to live in a rural community."

Leadership

With leadership style, most descriptions were process oriented. Participants described being collaborative in nature—often gathering consensus, developing ownership and buy-in, and leading by example. A participant summarized her process as "inclusive, collaborative when needed. I'm not afraid to make decisions and can make them when they are time sensitive. But for strategic or continuous improvement efforts, we have a district leadership team."

Participants described their leadership as "democratic," noting that "when people have ownership, you are more likely to get things accomplished." Other common descriptors were "situational," "team builder," "mediator," and "eclectic." Participants also described themselves as honest, supportive, and nurturing. As one participant stated,

[I am] relaxed, yet I have a subtle way of making myself forceful. I don't raise my voice. If there is a problem and I am upset, I take a deep breath and I always ask, "What can I do to help you?" I truly think that has made me more successful than the administrator who storms right out the door and puts everyone on the defensive.

And, finally, one participant described her style in the following manner: "I can tell you what I'm not. I do not like to micromanage. I operate on the premise, I want people in the right place and let them do their job and I'll support them."

Gender was also an area addressed with leadership. Participants were asked whether or not they felt gender played a role in how they led. The majority did not hesitate to make a connection between gender and their leadership style. For instance, one individual responded, "As a woman I am a little more tuned to people's feelings and respond to that—a little bit of a nurturing component." Another stated, "I think that females and males are different. . . . Our whole building is run by females. . . . We multitask. It has been said to us, 'We can't believe the amount of work you all can get done in one day.'" Other comments included "I think women, me included, are very hard workers. We probably put in way more time than we should"; "I think about it a lot actually when I'm with most of my colleagues who are male . . . just their attitude about how they proceed and make decisions. I think it is very much a gender factor"; and "I find it very difficult to do this job like a woman would do it. I find it hard to maintain a family. You approach it like you're the matriarch."

Two of the participants who did not make a connection between gender and their leadership style provided the following reasoning: "I don't think of it that way. . . . I coached volleyball and basketball and that wasn't always a female-dominated position either. I think you learn something through coaching. It's kind of a give and take and getting along." "I guess I've been one that really doesn't buy into the whole gender difference thing because my husband is also an administrator and we are very different in how we go about our days and 'stuff.' It's more a personality thing than a gender thing."

Two other participants noted the pros and cons of gender and leadership. They offered the following responses: "I don't know. I just know that there are many advantages and disadvantages . . . I try to use all the advantages to the maximum, and I really disregard the disadvantages." "I think [gender affects my leadership] sometimes negatively and sometimes positively. I know very often, when a decision is made, you just have to kind of 'bull' your way through it. If a female does it, she is a complete 'bitch' and if a male does it, he is just assertive. So that weighs a little bit on some things. Does it affect the end decision? For me, it doesn't."

Relationships

A large portion of the participants' leadership focused on establishing communications and building relationships. Participants discussed building relationships with (a) the school board, (b) the community, and (c) the staff, students, and parents.

With school boards, these female superintendents conscientiously developed processes for open communication and established close contact. On a regular basis, often weekly, they were in contact with board members through telephone conversations, email, personal visits, and weekly reports. One participant explained, "I do a cover letter with each Board packet. It explains what's in there. So they go into the board meeting knowing what to expect." Another commented, "If it's not confidential (e.g., 'you need to know that a swing broke and a kid got hurt'), I use email. If it's confidential (e.g., 'so and so is getting written up and you may get some flack'), I use the Friday packet . . . and I mark it confidential and send it." A third stated, "I think open, honest communication is real important . . . if I tell one board member, I tell all board members."

The participants, as a means of developing trust and respect, also commented on how careful they were to follow through with what they told the school board they would do. A participant explained, "I think a lot of it is building trust by making sure everything is taken care of. I give them information . . . so they can make an intelligent decision. . . . If I anticipate things, I will call the board chair. . . . I follow through on things." Yet another noted:

> Building relationships with them is key. I work with these people all the time. We are visiting at games; we are visiting at activities; we are on several committees outside of school—if it is the Foundation Board or the nursing home or the community clubs—we are working together in all capacities.

One final note, about building school board relationships, addresses a situation common in rural school districts: "If you work in a small town you usually know all the people anyway. There have been times when my cousin has been on the board and then good friends have been on the board. So, it's not difficult to build relationships; it's more the maintenance of the relationships."

With community relationships, participants focused on the importance of being visible and involved. Public relations were identified as a key responsibility of their position. Newsletters, presentations at community meetings, attendance at events, and use of various media venues were mentioned and used as a means to communicate with the community. Participants were members of various community groups

and organizations or were regular presenters at community meetings. Six were long-time residents of the community. Two grew up in the community in which they were now superintendents. One of those individuals commented:

> I know it helps that I am here. I graduated from here, and I try to be real active in the service organizations like the Lions Club. This community is phenomenal. We get more support than any school community I've ever seen. People are constantly giving donations or fundraising for different things for the school. Part of our bond project was for a fitness center for the whole community, an auditorium that the whole community can use. We really try to be the center of the community.

The other stated:

> I grew up in the community—left and came back, so I had a lot of relationships, knew some of the key players already without having to figure that out. But I'm not the little kid anymore. It is certainly a different role. I've been fortunate; people have accepted that. I think there is a little pride in the hometown girl coming back. But to maintain that, it is still a matter of respect—do I do what I say, do I follow through when I say things are going to happen—just to maintain that credibility with them.

Yet another superintendent who had been a long-time resident noted:

> I am just finishing my twentieth year in this district. Since I've been superintendent, we've passed two referendums. . . . I may have taught them or their children so there is a trust factor there. Those kids were in my class. Their parents respected me and thanked me for what I had done for their children, so I had a positive relationship there. When I had to pass a referendum, I called on those people and they came through.

Summing up how natural building relationships within the community can be for a long-time resident, one participant commented:

> I think those were established when I first started—it's been 29 years ago. My relationship, my stature in the community was developed when I came and stayed and worked with their children. I now have students' children and I'm getting close to having some of their grandkids here.

Participants also worked on relationships with staff, students, and parents. Having an open door policy, listening intently, and being available were mentioned. For instance, one individual described her process: "Talk to them about sensitive issues; let them know ahead of time things that are going to happen; be out and about; visit with parents, with staff whether it is certified, paraprofessionals, or the cooks, janitors—whoever; just be about and visible."

The participants also described ways in which they personalized their professional relationships. Personal contacts and visits, formal and informal conversations, and formal and informal notes were used to communicate appreciation to others. In general, many noted that building the relationships involved "listening to them, treating them with respect, giving them some feeling of ownership." One participant elaborated:

> I know what their family concerns are. . . . I think a female can move into that. You can move without suspicion into that kind of role. People are accepting of a woman asking, "How are the kids doing? Well, you know I have teenagers doing this . . . a woman is looked at as being more nurturing. So again, I try to build relationships based on that.

Participants also established processes for empowering others. Based on respect and trust of others, participants commented on the importance of empowerment, especially with implementing new initiatives and with gathering support for change. As one participant noted, "We have very talented staff with many good qualities. We just need to get those people 'sitting on the right seat on the bus.'"

Change

Change has become a constant in school systems. Participants were asked a series of questions centered on how they approached and handled the change process. One person commented, "A lot of times I'll start with a pilot and give them a lot of support, and let them share their success, then you will see other people wanting to get on board." In addition, she stated:

> You need to have people involved in the planning process and you need people to think about how things can be different. You need to look at visioning and where you want to be and have a large group of people involved in that initial process. Then you can identify ways in which you can get there.

Another said change, for their school district, occurred

through process and agreeing to stay the course—staying the course with our continuous improvement effort—it will be year four next year . . . we are finally starting to see some significant goals being identified in each building and then grade levels, departments, following where we are looking specifically at data, measuring results and asking the right questions.

Another articulated her role:

> I feel it is my job to get as much information on the change and share that. And share my opinion. I may say, "I don't agree with this. I'm here as a messenger. I don't agree with this, but it is what we have to do." I think once they see I am not trying to force it down their throats, it works.

Establishing buy-in, especially with stakeholders, and providing the necessary power and support needed were key points in the change process. One participant stated, "Having people part of the change, the decision making is important." Another participant approached requested changes from staff by stating, "It's an idea, but let's do some investigating before we do this and then it comes back to haunt us." She added, "I give them the power to do the changing." Yet another realized, "If it's an initiative I don't think anybody is going to grab hold of, I don't care how exciting I think it is, it's not going to go. I just know that by myself I cannot sustain it." Others noted, "There might be a step process. Gather some information, try to identify who are your key players, work with people and try to have ownership so the change can occur on a timeline." "Get your real good teachers and your supportive parents to back it"; then, "provide them with plenty of support." A participant shared the following example for obtaining buy-in:

> I started the first of July. By the end of July, we started with our audit and found out we were going to be in bad shape. . . . We needed to make drastic changes for 2003–2004. So I went to the communities. We scheduled two community forums; one in each town, so we gave everyone an opportunity to be there. . . . People had good questions. People also had misinformation. We could correct that. After [the forums], we set up committees. There were community people, teachers, administrators, school board members on each committee. We tried to run the full gamut of all categories of school spending. . . . Each committee met and came back with recommendations. I had a couple of board members who said, "We probably didn't learn anything we didn't already know." But we gave them the opportunity and they had ownership in it. We had to

make some tough calls on things. We cut some things that I know they didn't like but I think they understood. I had hardly any complaints about any of the decisions. They had their chance to speak; they had their chance to participate; and they had their chance to understand if they really wanted to. I think that helped us out. I liked that process. I was very comfortable doing that, because, again, I like to get the input of a lot of people. Then you can make an intelligent decision.

Many of the decisions to make changes were a result of mandates, such as No Child Left Behind. The participants accepted the mandates as a school reality. One individual noted, "We have to pick our battles, and there are mandated changes that we have no choice about." Another commented, "We might not agree but we have to do it. It's the law. It's our federal dollars. We keep plugging along and doing what they tell us we need to do to be in compliance." And, finally, a third individual contended, "It doesn't mean we like it all the time [but] it's all about attitude. Let's do it. It has to be handled and presented in the right way."

Although the participants stated they needed to be in compliance, not all the required procedures of the mandates were appreciated: "I think we need to follow the mandates. The problem is they keep changing it. I've learned to sit back a little bit and not be the first person to jump on board and believe it is actually going to stay." One participant commented:

We have a growing minority population. We have close to 20 percent Hispanic population at the elementary, and our special education population is pushing 10–15 percent, depending on the year, and our free and reduced lunch count is pushing 30 percent. The kids we are dealing with are needy kids. So when you have this ESL population, special education population and poverty population, you have to address the concerns but [with No Child Left Behind] to test them; to splatter it all over the paper that you're not doing well because you have this many kids and population; that's not doing anybody any favors.

Another individual concluded, "I'm concerned about losing with No Child Left Behind. I believe that public education is the foundation of democracy. But now public education is a place of burnout. We're trying desperately to protect our turf. Everything comes down with no resources, absolutely none."

Two participants had positive comments about mandates. One stated, "The state development reporting or the Title I funding reports, the expectations of

No Child Left Behind has really made us sit down and use actual data to evaluate." Another commented:

I think some things that have come out of it like the assessment part of it is really quite good. It makes people realize that maybe we need to look at different ways of doing things, maybe we need to look at a different curriculum in our math program, maybe we need more training for our staff in how to teach math, and look at what is being tested and make sure our students have that so they'll do well. We can't expect them to do well on the test if we've never taught it.

If the change was not due to a state or federal mandate, then it seemed to have to do with budgeting issues. As one participant stated, "Most of the changes have been state mandated. But we are looking at changing right now because of financial reasons." For another participant, changes due to budget constraints were about the only kind she had experienced as a superintendent:

The changes I have had to make, I've had support because we had the State Department on our back and we had all the red numbers to prove everything. To be quite honest with you, there was no questioning any changes we needed to make because the facts were so prevalent. That's not always true with change, especially when you are talking about curriculum and staffing, when you have money and resources. I haven't quite had that.

Demographic changes within the district also affected schools. Diversity, poverty, and declining enrollment were the most common reasons mentioned for changes, although technology and district-specific interests (e.g., agriculture, all day kindergarten) also impacted change. One participant noted, "Eight or nine years ago we added an ESL teacher because of our demographics, which is now 27 percent minority; and I've had to pay extra money to get interpreters in. Our special education population has grown from 10 to 14 percent, so I've added a second special education teacher." Another participant stated, "Our biggest challenge is our poverty. We have an extremely high free and reduced lunch count."

One participant explained how her district made adjustments to better meet the needs of a group of students:

We look at data. For example, to start an alternative school, we looked at the data; the number of students who were long-term suspended and the number who had dropped out. They were within graduation rate if they could accelerate the number of credits they could get a year. When we saw those numbers, we just said we're shooting ourselves in the foot. When you're long-term suspending 80 kids out of 500 kids from grades 8–12—something's not working. So we instituted an in-school suspension classroom and an alternative school. It does two things. It gives those kids a second chance that's not an environment where they shouldn't be, and it gets those kids out of the environment where they were disrupting. It helped the traditional high school teacher because they are not dealing with the kids who don't want to play the game, and it gets the kids in an environment where they still get an education.

Another addressed technology:

I think about what the future will bring and what our students will need in five or ten years, doing research on that, reading about different new approaches, being involved in discussion groups, attending conferences, looking at the future. Right now, I think technology is such an important piece and being able to give students the skills they need to be able to access the world is important.

Agriculture played a part in the following participant's school:

Because there are still viable agricultural areas . . . we started up an FFA after 35 years. It is a way for certain students to get involved with something they have close ties to, and I know there are a lot of jobs in this field. . . . We have students who have an aptitude for those areas—landscaping, forestry, wild rice research; it's just a natural for them. If we can encourage that and make them realize there are some good opportunities for them that will allow them to live wherever they want and maybe stay in [this area] or rural communities, we sustain our economy and keep things strong.

Open enrollment also entered the conversation:

There is a lot of open enrollment and people come and go. You make adaptations because you'll get some students with needs; maybe there are social services after them or the law. [So] you are just making some inroads, making some gains, have some programs and plans in place, and, poof, they are gone again.

Challenges

The superintendency poses many challenges. Participants were asked to describe how they balanced their personal lives with their professional lives. Responses indicated that maintaining a private life while administering in rural schools and communities is difficult and is not without sacrifices. One individual commented on how difficult it had been for her to "get comfortable being in the public eye and being scrutinized." Another noted, "that my outside circle of friends has diminished because of being in this role." Another stated:

Sometimes I can't go into this restaurant or I stay away from here. It is quite tough. But even if my husband and I are invited over, then it looks like favoritism or they will be talking about something and I kind of stifle the conversation. Since I have started here I probably don't do as much socially with people as I used to. It's really hard to be the superintendent and be in a social group. I've developed more of a private lifestyle.

One commented on her challenges, health-wise:

It is difficult to do. I am now at a point where I am taking more care of myself, personally. I had gained 40 pounds since I took this job. I have taken 20 off this last year. . . . I feel much better but it has been a real struggle to build in time for exercise and being more careful about my diet because I am a big stress eater.

Another contended:

It wears you out. I have become married to the job. I don't like that. I wish I could do a better job of balancing my personal and professional life, but my nature is to eat, sleep, and breathe my work. I consider myself a "people person" and am driven by that relationship end of things or approval.

Others seemed to accept the challenge of public scrutiny and responded in the following manner: "Being a part of this community means I am constantly a superintendent. I can't go out to eat. I can't go to the grocery store. I can't go anywhere without communicating about the school"; "I grew up in a rural community so it is familiar. I think my relationships become a part of my personal life"; and "I've pretty much perfected the line, 'I just don't know. I'll have to check on that.' Of course, by now they absolutely know I am lying because obviously I know."

The participants realized and accepted that the position called for an enormous commitment of time. As one person stated, "You could not leave your job behind because in a small setting, everyone knows you.

That's how you build relationships, too. I wouldn't last long if I said my office hours are 8:00–5:00." Another commented, "My children are grown and gone, so I do not have a young family that I need to be concerned about. My husband passed away so I am basically a single person. That assists me with my time commitment."

Three participants found they were able to remove themselves from the public eye because they lived outside the community: "Luckily (and I shouldn't say this too loud) I don't live in the community, which kind of helps. So at night when I am finished, I can go home"; "I live eight miles away, which still isn't far enough"; and "They have accepted that my family and personal life is somewhere else."

In summary, one individual offered the following view:

> I think as a person you need to have that self-confidence that you are doing what is best for you and still take into consideration how it might impact the district . . . like if you end up going to a local bar, and I feel strongly it's important for me to be in those places, too, because those people are the ones who are also voters and a lot of times might be the ones who have students who are more challenging so it's good for me to be there because a lot of them said, "I can't remember if a superintendent has ever been in our establishment." The school comes around and wants money but yet nobody wants to be in there.

Professional Support

Participants were not hesitant to contact others if they had a question or concern. They relied on the state level superintendents' association. Most attended regional meetings on a regular basis. They also called upon others for support and direction garnering professional support from mentors, predecessors, and area superintendents.

Other organizations mentioned included state level organizations of the school board association, the rural education association, and the department of education. However, the most supportive professional organization was the state level association for school administrators whose parent organization is the American Association of School Administrators (AASA). One participant explained how helpful the state level organization had been:

> Whenever I called and asked a question, I received a response. The first year was difficult. . . . I simply got to the point that I would say, "This is the rookie su-

perintendent with my question of the day." They were helpful in a good way. Never once did they make me feel like an idiot.

The national level was used "mainly as an informational tool." It was "mostly written materials and their daily news update, web-based hotline" that participants found helpful.

One individual found support from an organization not specifically tied to K–12 systems: "I am involved with the American Association of University Women on a national, state, and local level. . . . It's the networking with women and the ongoing support of women. . . . [T]hat organization has helped me more than any other in terms of encouraging me."

When seeking support or direction from specific individuals, participants often referenced other superintendents. For instance, one individual stated, "Those peer relationships with other superintendents are what pull a new superintendent through." Another noted:

> I will say that the area superintendents are wonderful. We meet every other month, informally. Any issues that come up, we talk about. I would have no hesitation to call any of these superintendents, and the majority of these are men. They do the same back. I am told that in the state our group is a little unique in that we do really get together and share ideas and don't really turf-protect so much.

One note of interest would be how quickly an individual moves from novice to expert. One participant shared, "When I started six years ago, there were probably three or four superintendents who I would call sometimes for advice on different issues. . . . Now I am one of the most experienced because of turnover, so I am probably more in the mentor role."

Graduate work and programs were cited minimally as helpful in preparing for the superintendency. Two participants specifically mentioned the finance course as irrelevant. One stated, "I can tell you the finance class really didn't help much." The other said, "I would say the financial piece was the piece missing . . . that is probably hard to do unless you are in a district." One individual did acknowledge a course as helpful: "One of the best courses I had was when an instructor who had been an administrator for 35 years—you know just an institution in himself—did a class on the superintendency. All he did was have experts come in from different areas (e.g., head cook, business manger)." Another appreciated the fact that she was in a situation where she could immediately apply what she learned, "The best experience is hands-on. I am glad I had a variance and was able to go to classes, learn something and go back and use it."

Guest speakers who were practitioners, adjunct professors who were in practitioner roles and fellow students who were practitioners were given the most credence for preparing the participants for their positions. For instance, one person acknowledged the contacts she had made in class as most beneficial: "I met some people through the program. Too much of it was theoretical. I think you need some theory but I do think you need more 'hands-on' experience." Another also cited fellow classmates as a powerful addition to her graduate program:

> The education courses were good because when I was going through, particularly for the superintendency, many of the students who were also in the group going through were superintendents from [a neighboring state] who wanted to come into [this state] and become licensed. So we had their expertise. Some of them had 15–20 years of being a superintendent.

One individual acknowledged coursework outside the graduate program as most helpful: "I would like to laud as wonderful preparation the LEAD programs. I found those, because they were practitioner-based, very valuable. Time management, leadership, problem-solving, personality, conflict resolution . . . "

Advice

Interviews concluded by asking participants what advice they would share with aspiring female superintendents. The responses ranged from broad, general advice to specific details; many held hints of individual experiences:

- "Enjoy the beauty of the rural community and the personalities in it."
- "You really have to make sure that you fit with the district philosophy."
- "You've got to step back. You've got to say to yourself, 'I can't do it all. I've got to let other people help.' Delegating is okay. In fact, it is more than okay, you have to do it. I think the whole stress level and work ethic for female superintendents gets to be a problem."
- "You have to be bold. You have to be able to say what you really think and don't let other people who are dominant around you dissuade you."
- "Don't underestimate your value and appreciate your differences. . . . Now that we are here, I think we need to be who we are and not try to do it like we're males. We're not."

- "Don't short change yourself. Have the confidence that you can do this. Use the advice and support you have from others to help you through the low spots."
- "Make connections with other colleagues. Find someone you can confide in. Don't be afraid to ask questions."
- "Don't take 'no' for an answer or that you can't do it."
- "Get those experiences. You have to try things; if they work, great; if they don't, you don't have to keep doing it."
- "The biggest thing I know and practice and am reminded all the time at home is to never promise anything you can't follow through on."
- "The key is to be honest."
- "Swallow your pride; be willing to ask questions."
- "Spend time shadowing someone for a couple of days."
- "Find a good mentor."
- "Be yourself. Don't put on someone else's clothes."
- "Communicate with the public and only show the community a role model."

DISCUSSION

Career Path and Circumstances

Garn (2003) noted, "48.5 percent of superintendents progress through a career path that includes classroom teacher, building-level administrator, and central office administrator. The second most common career path is from teacher to building-level administrator to superintendent with 31.2 percent of superintendents following this path" (p. 6). The majority of participants followed this career path, with only two bypassing the building-level position.

Seven of the participants only pursued the superintendency after they received encouragement from others or after they had an opportunity to experience what "being in charge" felt like. Only two specifically stated that it was their own personal interest that led them to pursue the superintendency.

Ten participants had fifteen or more years of experience in education before moving into the superintendency. They articulated that their years of experience provided them with a sense of confidence with handling the responsibilities of the superintendency.

Leadership and Relationships

A feminist leader works closely with personnel and develops personal relationships with co-workers that bond the members of the organization. Feminist organizations are characterized by practices such as participative decision making, systems of rotating leadership, promotion of community and cooperation, and power sharing. (Brown and Irby, 2003, p. 105)

Participants shared comments that display the characteristics of a feminist leader and a feminist organization. They described their collaborative leadership styles, how they worked with others, and the importance of open communications and of creating a caring atmosphere. They were not concerned about presenting themselves as "in control" but rather focused more on how much more could be accomplished by including others in the decision-making process.

They were also not concerned about displaying genuine interest and concern about people's feelings. They considered the fact that they were able to "tune into feelings" as an asset to their leadership style. These characteristics of caring provided them with a level of comfort and commitment found by other women who have served in the role of superintendent. Brunner (2000) observed, "This view of their work came about because they had one primary focus—caring relationships with adults and children. The development and support of caring relationships was the foundation of their work" (pp. 117–118).

The leadership styles of the participants also involved building strong relationships and open communications. They shared the strategies they used to establish and maintain relationships and for communicating with others. As noted by Wallin and Sackney (2003), "Because of this strong attachment between school and community, the administrator of a rural school must be, constantly aware of the community, its leaders, and its pressure points . . ." (p. 11). Because of the solid relationships these women had established, they had gained the trust and respect needed for them to succeed as leaders.

Change

Participants were attuned to the importance of the change process in order to garner support. Whether the changes were a result of mandates, budget constraints or local needs, participants emphasized how they obtained buy-in from the various individuals they considered as "key players." They worked hard to be inclusive and to empower those with whom they worked. They equated empowerment with professional respect.

Participants were also quick to note that the majority of the changes occurring within their districts were mandates or budgetary changes, thus making the issue of obtaining buy-in and developing ownership that much more challenging. Howley and Pendarvis (2002) summarized the situation:

Federal and state mandates have placed many new demands on administrators. Much of the pressure created by these mandates is caused by the lack of resources needed to address them. Superintendents say inadequate resources detract most from their effectiveness. . . . Shared governance requires school leaders to relinquish power as well as make use of highly developed skills in interpersonal communication, negotiation, and conflict resolution.

No matter how challenging the change was, participants were conscientious of being fiscally responsible and in compliance with mandates, identifying both as key responsibilities within their position.

Support

None of the participants hesitated to seek support for situations and issues that they felt warranted additional help or information. Professional organizations, especially the state level school administrator organization, and individuals were mentioned. Graduate programs did not receive the same accolades.

Participants realized the power of establishing strong networks of supporters. They did not view the need to seek out others for answers as a weakness. They identified the demands and stress of the position and the amount of continuous change within school settings, such as demographic changes and federal/state mandates, as legitimate reasons for anyone in the position to seek assistance. In fact, they viewed the lack of seeking out such assistance as irresponsible.

Quick to name individual colleagues and mentors, the participants also realized the value of those who were or had served in the role. They addressed the importance of networking and identifying a mentor in their advice to aspiring female superintendents. Wolverton and MacDonald (2004) agreed with their advice: "If states . . . want women superintendents they must embark on concerted efforts to identify and mentor female leaders. Mentors provide essential support and insights into the inner workings of the system" (p. 9).

A form of support not outwardly acknowledged by participants who had been long-time residents, but evident in their comments and examples, was the support they received within their buildings and communities. This support was the result of the reputations the participants had developed from the years they had committed and the loyalty they displayed to their schools and their communities.

Challenges and Advice

The participants were not without their challenges. They readily shared the trials and tribulations of being a rural female superintendent and their words of advice echoed of personal experiences. Most of the challenges seemed to reflect issues surrounding rural settings. Wallin and Sackney (2003) explained, "It has often been observed that rural schools are more tightly connected to their local communities than urban schools. In essence, the rural school becomes a symbol of community unity, community survival, and community values" (p. 11).

Participant challenges seemed to center around the personal issues of privacy in their lives and around the professional issues of demographic and budgetary concerns. Both areas can be daunting. Participants handled the issues of maintaining a private life while holding a public position by identifying escape avenues—either internal ones such as reminding themselves to be true to who they were or external ones such as scheduling time for their families or intentionally shopping in another town.

The professional issues were viewed in a broader, more visionary manner, and the participants' loyalty and commitment to the school and community became evident as they described strategies and solutions that they had been a part of that benefited both the school and the community. Their level of involvement within their communities, their representation on various local organizations, and their volunteerism were all a part meeting the needs of school and community alike.

RECOMMENDATIONS

"Current pools of administrative candidates come from practicing teachers and the majority of teachers are women. Yet few women are found in the superintendency" (Wolverton and MacDonald, 2004, p. 3). Therefore, the following recommendations are provided with the intent of increasing the pool of women willing to pursue the position:

- Provide more opportunities for females to broaden their experiences in the areas of leadership and governance;

- Provide situations for potential female leaders to establish networks with key leaders and organizations attuned to the knowledge and skills necessary to effectively lead schools;
- Encourage rural school districts to look to staff members who are committed to the school and the community and who have leadership ability as a means of obtaining and sustaining leadership;
- Develop mentorships and internships that expand potential candidates' experiences and skills;
- Encourage those recognized as having the knowledge, skills, and abilities to be successful in the superintendency to obtain the necessary licensure and degree; and
- Provide more hands-on, realistic experiences and establish more opportunities for networking in graduate programs.

Howley and Pendarvis (2002) acknowledged:

Always demanding of time and energy, the administrative roles of rural superintendents and principals are more complex and perhaps more stressful than ever before. In the past 25 years, administrators have had to address increasing demands for special programs, collaborative decision making and accountability. In addition, potential for conflict with school boards and various constituencies is greater in the face of heightened diversity of many rural communities.

The participants of this study are meeting the demands of being a female rural superintendent. They possess qualities that have served their districts and communities well. Hopefully, other females with leadership skills will join them.

REFERENCES

Blount, J. M. (1998). *Destined to rule the schools: Women and the superintendency, 1873–1995.* Albany, NY: State University of New York Press.

Brown, G., and Irby, B. (2003). The synergistic leadership theory: Contextualizing multiple realities of female leaders. *Journal of women in educational leadership, 1*(1), 101–116.

Brunner, C. C. (2000). *Principles of power: Women superintendents and the riddle of the heart.* Albany, NY: State University of New York Press.

Chase, S. (1995). *Ambiguous empowerment: The work narratives of women school superintendents.* Amherst, MA: University of Massachusetts Press.

Creswell, J. W. (2003). *Research design: Qualitative, quantitative, and mixed methods approaches* (2nd ed.). Thousand Oaks, CA: SAGE Publications, Inc.

Garn, G. (2003). A closer look at rural superintendents. *Rural educator, 25*(1), 3–9.

Howley, A., and Pendarvis, E. (2002). *Recruiting and retaining rural school administrators.* (Educational Resources Information Center Digest EDO-RC-02-7.)

Wallin, D., and Sackney, L. (2003). Career patterns of rural female educational administrators. *Rural educators, 25*(1), 11–25.

Why rural matters 2003: The continuing need for every state to take action on rural education. (n.d.). Retrieved April 14, 2003, from http://www.ruraledu.org.

Wolverton, M., and MacDonald, R. T. (2004). Women in the superintendency: Opting in or opting out? *Journal of women in educational leadership, 2*(1), 3–11.

Perceptions of School Culture toward Dimensions of Excellence: Do Stakeholders Agree?

TIMOTHY B. JONES, PEGGY BARNES GILL, AND ROSS SHERMAN

OVER THE PAST 20 YEARS, MOST EDUCATIONAL SYSTEMS have either participated in major change efforts, or tinkered with incremental changes in response to state and national mandates for academic excellence for all children (Myers and Goldstein, 1997). For many schools, the impetus for change has been a state accountability system coupled with the public's demand for accountability. Redesigning a school or school system to achieve excellence takes support from the entire constituency and time to stabilize or institutionalize the change. Only in an organizational culture that seeks and supports excellence can resulting efforts find the time and support needed. Elmore (2003) addressed the importance of culture explaining, "leaders understand that improving school performance requires transforming a fundamentally weak instructional core, and the culture that surrounds it, into a strong, explicit body of knowledge about powerful teaching and learning that is accessible to those who are willing to learn it" (p. 10). Given that the school administrators (leaders) have been identified empirically as having significant influence in school reform (Fullan, 1991; Leithwood, 1992), university efforts to provide meaningful preparation and ongoing staff development to school leaders should address both the existing culture and its transformation.

Despite a extensive research into learning organizations, empowered schools, brain-based learning, constructivism, and technology innovation, to name a few, schools and schooling generally have not successfully restructured in ways that provide meaningful and lasting results (Caine and Caine, 1997, 1999; Short and Greer, 2002). Organizational culture is a powerful predictor of whether a school will embrace and maintain the arduous work of successful restructuring (Collins and Porras, 1993). The purpose of this study was to identify the existing organizational culture of participants of a university-based, intensive, restructured schools institute, in order to design preparations pro-grams and ongoing professional development for school leaders that would enhance the likelihood of meaningful change. This institute will be further discussed later and hereafter referred to as "The Institute." Additionally, the study examined the degree to which stakeholders possessed the values that support organizational excellence (Peters and Waterman, 1982). The premise underlying the use of this population (members of The Institute) was that fee-paying participants in an optional restructuring schools institute would be highly motivated for school improvement and thus would provide insight to understanding what might represent the most favorable scenario of existing school culture for restructuring.

THEORETICAL FRAMEWORK

Organizational culture has been identified as significant in developing and maintaining excellence since the work of Weber (Schroeder, 1998) who argued that one cannot study organizations without understanding how organizations function, how organizations get the job done. Parsons (1960) further expanded these ideas to include the systemic nature of organizations. Parsons maintained that it is the continued and ongoing work of people and groups within the organization that provide organizational survival, and it is the shared beliefs and values that set the boundaries for what goals can and cannot be achieved by the organization. Bolman and Deal (2002), who place organizational culture in the symbolic frame of school leadership, suggest that it is organizational culture that provides the energy and zest to an organization and that a "weak culture calls out for change" (p. 105). Within this cultural frame, Short and Greer (2002) state that the reason for schools to restructure "revolves around providing opportunities for *individuals* to develop and mature as independent learners" (p. 11). It is this systemic learning of individuals that develops and supports an organizational culture of excellence.

The restructuring model utilized by The Institute that the study participants subscribed to integrates a body of literature that rejects the Cartesian and Newtonian thinking grounded in mechanistic theory and instead replaces it with systems thinking. The model centers on three areas: (a) re-organizational behavior of the restructured school; (b) organizational learning in the restructured school; and (c) organizational change in the restructured school. The following section outlines the body of literature that supports each component of the restructuring model. It is included specifically to provide a context of the professional development that the study participants had embarked and the comprehensive nature of the systemic restructuring that was ultimately desired.

Theoretical Underpinnings of the Restructuring Model

I. Organizational Behavior in the Restructured School
   A. New Sciences (Wheatley, 1999).
   B. Quantum Physics/Theory (Capra, 1997; Wheatley, 1999).
   C. Systems Thinking (Baskin, 1998; Banathy, 1991; Senge, 1994; Senge, 2000; Wheatley, 1999).
   D. Learning Organizations and Self-Organization (Capra, 1996; Caine and Caine, 1997; Wheatley, 1999; Senge, 2000).
   E. Organizational Culture (Bolman and Deal, 2002; Deal and Kennedy, 1982; Deal and Peterson, 1990; Sashkin, 1997; Peters and Waterman, 1982).
II. Organizational Learning in the Restructured School
   A. Constructivism (Brooks and Brooks, 1999; Lambert, 1995).
   B. Brain-Mind Principles/Brain Research (Caine and Caine, 1994, 1997, 2001; Jenson, 1998; Wiggins and McTighe, 1998; Tomlinson, 1999).
   C. Technology Integration (Picciano, 1998; Roblyer and Edwards, 2000).
III. Organizational Change in the Restructured School
   A. Complexity Theory (Capra, 1997; Baskin, 1998; Wheatley, 1999; Caine and Caine, 1997; Senge, 1994; Senge, 2000).
   B. The Journey of Inside Out Change (Senge, Kliener, Roberts, Roth, Ross, and Smith, 1999; Caine and Caine, 1997).
   C. The Edge of Possibility—Human Potential (Caine and Caine, 1997, 2001; Wheatley, 2002).

While it was the first area of the model, organizational behavior of the restructured school, which was of particular interest in this research, this study ultimately provided insights to all three of the model components.

The Institute set forth a path that empowered leaders and school stakeholders through changing the attitudes and beliefs of building principals and their leadership teams from a linear perspective to a systems thinking perspective. Thus, it is important to identify the existing attitudes and beliefs throughout the organization (Sashkin, 1997). These attitudes and beliefs form the boundary within which the school functions. By developing awareness of the patterns of shared beliefs, school leaders can cope more effectively with culture-based problems. Further, given a new awareness of these shared values and patterns of belief, the leadership team has the option of using that understanding to take actions to improve the culture in ways that have a positive and lasting effect in the school. Hence, The Institute attempted to motivate building principals and other school stakeholders to be proactive in facilitating the restructuring process.

METHODOLOGY

The study followed a single inventory (survey), descriptive research design. This research was guided by the following research questions:

1. What dimensions of organizational excellence are rated most favorably by educational leaders?
2. What dimensions of organizational excellence are rated least favorably by area educational leaders?
3. Is there a difference between the perceptions of administrators and teachers as to the presence or absence of the dimensions of excellence?

Instrumentation

The survey instrument used to collect data for this study was the *Organizational Behavior Questionnaire* (OBQ) (1997) developed by Marshall Sashkin, Ph.D. Specifically, the instrument measures "the overall excellence culture of an organization, as defined by ten values implicit and explicit in the beliefs identified by Peters and Waterman and expanded on by Collins and Porras" (Sashkin, 1997, p. 8). These values are referred to as the dimensions of organizational excellence.

The instrument consisted of a fifty item, double-sided optical scan form. The items were statements followed by a Likert-type alternative scale indicating Strongly Agree, Agree, Neither Agree Nor Disagree, Disagree, and Strongly Disagree. Strongly

Agree was scored as a 5 with Strongly Disagree being scored as a 1.

Content and construct validity is documented by Sashkin through validity assessment on more than 20 years of OBQ administration. Concurrent criterion validity and predictive criterion validity is also possible for measuring organizational behavior of one organization, but is not applicable for this study since the sample included participants from more than one organization. Internal consistency, based on a small sample provided by the survey author, sets reliability for nine of the ten scales according to Cronbach's Alpha at 0.60 or higher (Sashkin, 1997). A tenth scale, There Must Be Hands-On Management, was found to have low inter-item reliability in the small sample but along with the other nine scales yielded a higher inter-item reliability in the larger data sample.

Population and Sample

The population of this study consisted of school board members, superintendents, other central office administrators, principals, other building level administrators, teachers, and other certified non-administrative personnel. All members of The Institute who attended a formal institute meeting within a specified six-month period were selected as the sample representing each of the groups previously listed. There was one administration of the survey instrument for each type institute during the administration period including The Superintendent Institute, The Principal Institute and The Advanced Principal Institute. For the purpose of this study, The Institute refers to these three institute groups collectively. One hundred forty-two surveys were distributed to Institute members of which 133 (n=133) were completed by the participants representing a 93.66 percent response rate. The overall sample was proportionately representational among each demographic group (i.e., Board of Trustees, Superintendent, Teacher).

Institutional Context

The Institute was affiliated with the Department of Educational Leadership and Policy Studies at a comprehensive Texas regional university. The primary purpose of The Institute was to provide practicing school leaders opportunities for advanced professional development related to school restructuring and improvement utilizing the development of a center of excellence. Year-long Institute memberships included all levels of school leaders including school board members, superintendents, central office ad-

ministrators, building principals, other building level administrators, department chairpersons, teachers and other building level professionals. Services provided by the Institute were fee-based and paid by the membership's sponsoring school districts, limited external grant funds or individual participant's funds. Participation in this research project was strictly voluntary and responses collected were anonymous.

Analysis of the Data

Completed survey instruments were compiled and sent to the instrument publisher (HRD Press) for processing. Participants identified themselves by one of the following groups: (a) superintendent; (b) central office administrator; (c) principal; (d) other building administrator; (e) teacher or other professional; and (f) school board member. Data were processed for each of the groups in each of the ten scales and also as a single group (overall) in the ten scales. The ten scales or dimensions of excellence were as follows (Sashkin, 1997):

Dimension I:	Work Can Be as Much Fun as Play
Dimension II:	Seeks Constant Improvement
Dimension III:	Accept Specific and Difficult Goals
Dimension IV:	Accept Responsibility for Your Actions
Dimension V:	Care about One Another
Dimension VI:	Quality Is Crucially Important
Dimension VII:	Work Together to Get the Job Done
Dimension VIII:	Have Concern for Measures of Our Success
Dimension IX:	There Must Be Hands-on Management
Dimension X:	A Strong Set of Shared Values and Beliefs Guide Our Actions

The analysis includes identification of the beliefs that are strongest among the sample group, the beliefs that are weakest among the sample group, the statements of which most of the participants agree, and the statements of which most of the participants disagree. Demographic data included a breakdown of respondents according to ethnicity, time with the organization, gender and age. Finally, and most critically, percentage values of degree of agreement or disagreement for each response item were used in analysis. These values were then grouped or categorized by each identified scale to yield the overall organizational behavior analysis by characterizing the respondent as favorable, neutral or unfavorable to the applicable scale or dimension.

PRESENTATION AND DISCUSSION OF FINDINGS
Data in this section is presented in summary form as it was compiled and processed by the instrument publisher. Following the summary, each research question is addressed and discussed as it relates to the data.

Presentation of the Data
Tables 1 through 10 outline the analysis of the respondents of each participant group by the ten dimensions of excellence characterized by the OBQ. Whether the respondent was categorized as favorable, neutral or unfavorable was determined by the initial analysis provided by the instrument publisher.

Findings and Discussion
The following are the findings of the study coupled with some discussion that specifically addresses the three research questions previously posed.

Table 1.   Dimension I: Work Can Be as Much Fun as Play

Demographic Group	Favorable	Neutral	Unfavorable
School Board Member	71%	18%	11%
Central Office Administrator	45%	35%	20%
Other Building Administrator	68%	18%	14%
Principal	79%	13%	8%
Superintendent	80%	8%	12%
Teacher/Other Professionals	51%	19%	29%

Table 2.   Dimension II: Seeks Constant Improvement

Demographic Group	Favorable	Neutral	Unfavorable
School Board Member	82%	15%	3%
Central Office Administrator	67%	28%	6%
Other Building Administrator	77%	13%	10%
Principal	81%	12%	6%
Superintendent	92%	8%	
Teacher/ Other Professionals	56%	18%	26%

Table 3.   Dimension III: Accept Specific and Difficult Goals

Demographic Group	Favorable	Neutral	Unfavorable
School Board Member	85%	15%	
Central Office Administrator	41%	31%	28%
Other Building Administrator	65%	28%	7%
Principal	74%	18%	8%
Superintendent	80%	125	8%
Teacher/Other Professionals	36%	36%	28%

Table 4.   Dimension IV: Accept Responsibility for Your Actions

Demographic Group	Favorable	Neutral	Unfavorable
School Board Member	67%	20%	13%
Central Office Administrator	53%	20%	27%
Other Building Administrator	61%	16%	23%
Principal	67%	16%	17%
Superintendent	77%	0%	23%
Teacher/Other Professionals	55%	17%	22%

Table 5.   Dimension V: Care about One Another

Demographic Group	Favorable	Neutral	Unfavorable
School Board Member	72%	11%	17%
Central Office Administrator	49%	40%	11%
Other Building Administrator	73%	13%	14%
Principal	76%	12%	12%
Superintendent	80%	4%	16%
Teacher/Other Professionals	53%	15%	32%

Table 6. Dimension VI: Quality Is Crucially Important

Demographic Group	Favorable	Neutral	Unfavorable
School Board Member	55%	17%	28%
Central Office Administrator	40%	25%	35%
Other Building Administrator	59%	17%	23%
Principal	54%	16%	29%
Superintendent	64%	12%	24%
Teacher/Other Professionals	38%	23%	39%

Table 7. Dimension VII: Work Together to Get the Job Done

Demographic Group	Favorable	Neutral	Unfavorable
School Board Member	80%	18%	2%
Central Office Administrator	33%	40%	27%
Other Building Administrator	70%	21%	9%
Principal	82%	13%	5%
Superintendent	56%	28%	16%
Teacher/Other Professionals	53%	22%	25%

Table 8. Dimension VIII: Have Concern for Measures of Our Success

Demographic Group	Favorable	Neutral	Unfavorable
School Board Member	75%	8%	17%
Central Office Administrator	45%	38%	16%
Other Building Administrator	68%	17%	16%
Principal	62%	18%	20%
Superintendent	84%	8%	8%
Teacher/Other Professionals	49%	28%	23%

Table 9. Dimension IX: There Must Be Hands-on Management

Demographic Group	Favorable	Neutral	Unfavorable
School Board Member	74%	15%	11%
Central Office Administrator	56%	31%	13%
Other Building Administrator	68%	20%	12%
Principal	71%	18%	11%
Superintendent	64%	24%	12%
Teacher/Other Professionals	56%	26%	13%

Table 10. Dimension X: A Strong Set of Shared Values and Beliefs Guide Our Actions

Demographic Group	Favorable	Neutral	Unfavorable
School Board Member	64%	17%	19%
Central Office Administrator	32%	42%	26%
Other Building Administrator	62%	20%	18%
Principal	64%	17%	19%
Superintendent	80%		20%
Teacher/Other Professionals	48%	23%	29%

WHAT DIMENSIONS OF ORGANIZATIONAL EXCELLENCE ARE RATED MOST FAVORABLY BY EDUCATIONAL LEADERS? Overall, respondents generally indicated support for the ten dimensions of excellence. As a collective group, participants responded most favorably to Dimension II: Seeks Constant Improvement (74 percent favorable), Dimension I: Work Can Be as Much Fun as Play (67 percent favorable), and Dimension V: Care about One Another (67 percent favorable), as reported in Tables 1, 2 and 5. Generally, educators believe they work in a culture of continuous improvement where co-workers care about each other and enjoy work. These are strong cultural values upon which organizational leaders can build.

WHAT DIMENSIONS OF ORGANIZATIONAL EXCELLENCE ARE RATED LEAST FAVORABLY BY AREA EDUCATIONAL LEADERS?

Tables 4, 6 and 10 document the least favorably rated dimensions as Dimension VI: Quality Is Crucially Important (48 percent unfavorable or neutral), Dimension IV: Accept Responsibility for Your Actions (38 percent unfavorable or neutral), and Dimension X: A Strong Set of Shared Values and Beliefs Guide Our Actions (42 percent unfavorable or neutral). Given the national and state priority of accountability, the low rating of these dimensions is of some concern. Without a strong culture of shared values and commitment to quality, it is unlikely that a school or district will achieve and maintain organizational excellence.

IS THERE A DIFFERENCE BETWEEN THE PERCEPTIONS OF ADMINISTRATORS AND TEACHERS AS TO THE PRESENCE OR ABSENCE OF THE DIMENSIONS OF EXCELLENCE?

There is a consistent and persistent difference in the views expressed by the formal leadership (superintendents and principals) and the classroom teachers. The formal leadership (superintendents and principals) rated all dimensions more favorably than did teachers. The most striking difference was in Dimension III: Accept Specific and Difficult Goals (Table 3) where 74 percent of the principals and 80 percent of the superintendents saw their schools as accepting specific and difficult goals, but only 36 percent of teachers agreed with this assessment. Only 34 percent of teachers recognized a history in their schools of setting and attaining difficult goals, while only 24 percent of teachers agreed or strongly agreed that their schools set specific, difficult goals. Without specific and often difficult goals, organizations will seldom have the opportunity or capacity to improve and thus become a center of excellence.

In Dimension VIII: Have Concern for Measures of Our Success (Table 8), 84 percent of superintendents rated favorably, 62 percent of principals rated favorably, 68 percent of other building administrators rated favorably while only 49 percent of teachers rated favorably. Another 29 percent of teachers responded neutral to concerns for measures of success. This may be the most disturbing finding of this study as it suggests that despite years of high-stakes testing and the accountability movement, 51 percent of teachers respond that they have no concern or neutral concern for measures of success of their schools. It seems clear that administrators are feeling the pinch of accountability but that level of concern has not yet permeated the majority of the teaching and other professional ranks. This is further validated in the results of Dimension IV: Accept Responsibility for Your Actions (Table 4). In this dimension, 77 percent of superintendents and 67 percent of principals believe they are responsible for their actions while only 55 percent of teachers favorably share that responsibility.

Another notable difference is the teachers' low rating of the cultural value of caring measured in Dimension V: Care about One Another. In schools that are committed to excellence, people are told in many ways they are valued. People who believe they are treated fairly and equitably feel empowered. Celebrations of accomplishments, open communication, and a sense of ownership are examples of ways people feel valued and empowered. Table 5 illustrates that while 80 percent of superintendents and 76 percent of principals feel caring for one another is a cultural value in their schools, only 53 percent of teachers agree and thus feel the care. As reported in the first research question discussion, collectively this value was one of the strengths of the collective respondents. This is perhaps explained by the extremely high favorable response of four of the other five respondent groups. Only central office administrators (49 percent) responded lower than the teacher group. So while collectively it appears a strength that the schools have a feeling of caring, data documents serious discrepancies within the demographic groups thus suggesting a weakness. This phenomenon is also apparent in Dimension I: Work Can Be as Much Fun as Play. Table 1 shows that 80 percent of superintendents and 79 percent of principals responded favorably to this dimension while only 51 percent of teachers share that belief.

Working together to get things done, as measured in Dimension VII further delineates the beliefs of administrators versus teachers. While 56 percent of the superintendents and 82 percent of principals believe that working together results in the highest level of excellence, only 53 percent of teachers share that belief (Table 7). In other words, 47 percent of teachers do not believe that working together yields the highest level of excellence.

Dimension X: A Strong Set of Shared Values and Beliefs Guide Our Actions also yielded interesting results as indicated in Table 10. Superintendents responded favorably 80 percent of the time while principals responded favorably 64 percent of the time and teachers 48 percent of the time. This clearly indicates that decisions by superintendents are largely guided by a strong set of values and beliefs while far fewer decisions by principals, building administrators and teachers are so guided. In fact, more than one-half of the teachers responded that their decisions are not guided by a strong set of values and beliefs. While the reason is not clear in the data, this suggests that there is not a clear, shared set of values and beliefs in the schools of the respondents.

The implications of the Dimension X data are seemingly further confirmed in the results of Dimension VI: Quality Is Crucially Important. The elements of quality are normally a part of a shared set of values and beliefs. Only 38 percent of teachers responded favorably to quality being crucially important as opposed to 64 percent of superintendents and 54 percent of principals (Table 6). This clearly indicates that the importance of quality work is not being adequately communicated throughout the organization and not everyone at the school board level (55 percent) seemed to believe it was necessary to communicate such an expectation. Without commonly shared values and beliefs, quality being seen as crucially important by all members of the organization is highly unlikely.

It is also interesting to note the difference in how superintendents, principals and teachers responded to Dimension II: Seeks Constant Improvement versus Dimension VI: Quality Is Crucially Important. All three of these groups more favorably responded to Dimension II than Dimension VI. Seemingly, seeking improvement is a result of a stride toward quality. For example, 92 percent of superintendents seek constant improvement while only 64 percent of the same superintendents believe quality is crucially important. It certainly begs the questions why do we seek to improve? If only 38 percent of teachers believe that quality is crucially important, then why do 56 percent actually seek to improve?

In sum, individual respondent data paints a somewhat different picture of organizational culture than does the collective data. This clearly suggests that different stakeholders in the school organization have vastly different perceptions of the presence of the ten dimensions of excellence. While this section has focused primarily on the differences of superintendents, principals and teachers, data indicates many differences in perceptions among all of the six respondent groups. This difference will prevent an organization from becoming a center of excellence and true systemic restructuring hence becomes highly improbable.

CONCLUSION

This research project involving 133 educators was conducted in order to determine the presence of cultural values that are associated with organizational ex-cellence in hope of informing school leaders, administrator preparation programs and staff development providers about relevant issues concerning school restructuring, culture and improvement. Collectively, the majority of stakeholders surveyed agreed that the current culture seeks constant improvement, supports work as fun, and creates a climate of care for one another although the results of the subgroups suggest less agreement most notably with the teacher group. Participants indicated that commitment to quality, a shared sense of values, and acceptance of responsibility for ones' actions were less likely to be present in the current school culture. Teachers and Administrators frequently had strikingly different perceptions of the presence of a culture of excellence within the schools and were therefore less likely to see a strong culture.

Because there are differences in cultural perceptions among groups of stakeholders the core content of institutional preparation programs and the focus of professional development should be expanded to include more teacher leaders in order that a shared set of values and beliefs will guide the actions and beliefs of the organization. While there will always be differences of opinion about any school culture, there must be a closer alignment in the principal's and faculty's perception and commitment for excellence. Systemic reform, and thus organizational excellence, cannot occur unless all participants in the system are given the opportunity to participate in shared growth opportunities that build the capacity of the school to envision and enact meaningful and lasting change.

REFERENCES

Banathy, B. (1991). Systems design of education: A journey to create the future. Englewood Cliffs, NJ: Educational Technology Publications.

Baskin, K. (1998). *Corporate DNA: Learning from life*. St. Louis, MO: Butterworth-Heinemann.

Bolman, L., and Deal, T. (2002). *Reframing the path to school leadership*. Thousand Oaks, CA: Corwin Press.

Brooks, J .G., and Brooks, M.G. (1999). *In search for understanding the case for constructivist classrooms*. Alexandria, VA: Association for Supervision and Curriculum Development.

Caine, G., and Caine, R. (2001). *The brain, education, and the competitive edge*. New York, NY: Rowman and Littlefield.

Caine, G., and Caine, R. (1999). *Mindshifts: A brain-compatible process for professional growth*. Tucson, AZ: Zephyr Press.

Caine, R., and Caine, G. (1997). *Education on the edge of possibility*. Alexandria, VA: Association for Supervision and Curriculum Development.

Caine, R., and Caine, G. (1994). *Making connections: Teaching and the human brain*. Mento Park, CA: Addison-Wesley.

Capra, F. (1997). *The web of life: A new scientific understanding of living systems*. New York, NY: Anchor Books.

Capra, F., and Stendl-Rast, D. (1991). *Belonging to the universe: Explorations on the frontiers of science and spirituality*. San Francisco, CA: Harper Collins.

Deal, T., and Kennedy, A. (1982). *Corporate cultures*. Reading, MA: Addison-Wesley.

Deal, T., and Peterson, K. (1990). *The principal's role in shaping school culture*. Washington, DC: US Government Printing Office.

Elmore, R.F. (2003). A plea for strong practice. *Educational Leadership, 61*(3), 6–10.

Jenson, E. (1998). *Teaching with the brain in mind*. Alexandria, VA: Association for Supervision and Curriculum Development.

Lambert, L., Walker, D., Zimmerman, D.P., Cooper, J.E., Lambert, M.D. (1995). The constructivist leader. New York, NY: Teachers College Press.

Myers, K., and Goldstein, H. (1997). Failing schools, failing systems. In A. Hargraves (Ed.), *Rethinking educational change with heart and mind: 1997 ASCD yearbook* (pp. 111–127). Alexandria, VA: Association for Supervision and Curriculum Development.

Parsons, T. (1960). *Structure and process in modern societies*. New York, NY: Free Press.

Peters, T., and Waterman, R. (1982). *In search of excellence*. New York, NY: Harper and Row.

Picciano, A.G. (1998). *Educational leadership and planning for technology*. Upper Saddle River, NJ: Prentice Hall, Inc.

Roblyer, M.D., and Edwards, J. (2002). *Integrating educational technology into teaching*. Upper Saddle River, NJ: Prentice Hall, Inc.

Sashkin, M. (1997). *The organizational cultural assessment questionnaire*. Seabrook, MD: Ducochon Press.

Schroeder, R. (1998). *Max Weber, democracy and modernization*. New York, NY: Palgrave Macmillan.

Senge, P. (Ed.). (2000). *Schools that learn*. New York, NY: Doubleday.

Senge, P. (1994). *The fifth discipline: The art and practice of the learning organization*. New York, NY: Doubleday.

Senge, P., Kliener, A., Roberts, C., Roth, G., Ross, R., and Smith, B. (1999). *The dance of change: The challenges of sustaining momentum in learning organizations*. New York, NY: Doubleday.

Short, P., and Greer, J. (2002). *Leadership in empowered schools: Themes from innovative efforts*. Upper Saddle River, NJ: Merill Prentice Hall.

Tomlinson, C.A. (1999). *The differentiated classroom: Responding to the needs of all learners*. Alexandria, VA: Association for Supervision and Curriculum Development.

Wheatley, M.J. (2002) *Turing to one another: Simple conversation to restore hope to the future*. San Francisco, CA: Berrett-Koehler Publishers.

Wheatley, M.J. (1999). *Leadership in the new science: Learning about organization from an orderly universe*. San Francisco, CA: Berrett-Koehler Publishers.

Wiggins, G., and McTighe, J. (1998). *Understanding by design*. Alexandria, VA: Association for Supervision and Curriculum Development.

Understanding the Role of Metaphor in Leadership: Gaining Perspective, Seeing New Possibilities

SARAH NOONAN AND THOMAS FISH

Our creativity is proportional to our metaphorical diversity. The more metaphors we use, the more we enrich our view of life and the more unexamined aspects of life reveal themselves to us.

—Terry, *Authentic Leadership*

METAPHORS ARE HIGHLY INFLUENTIAL IN OUR THINKING, shaping our perspective regarding how situations are understood and what actions are expected or appropriate. Metaphors of leadership influence the way we think about such things as: the nature and purpose of leadership; the role and participation of leaders and followers (members, constituents); the actions associated with leadership activity; the skills or traits associated with effective leadership; and the representation of leadership found in various cultures.

Although we may not always be aware of the various metaphors that are operating in any situation (including our own and others), exploring various metaphors of leadership expand the capacity of leaders to frame and respond to many complex leadership challenges. To be effective, leaders must employ a variety of strategies to understand the situational and contextual challenges of leadership. This approach to thinking about leadership significantly broadens the ability of leaders to understand and function more effectively in their leadership environment.

The opportunity for creative thinking and the risk inherent in maintaining a limited perspective is explored through the lens of dominant (and sometimes "subliminal") metaphors that are "in use" in the popular and academic texts. Metaphorical thinking helps leaders *gain perspective, see new opportunities*, and *communicate their experience and ideas to others*. Well-prepared educational administrators should be highly aware of the importance and influence of metaphor in detecting, framing, and communicating about present and future realities.

THE IMPORTANCE OF METAPHOR

Metaphors, as *linguistic, image-generating devices*, help us think about what is not yet known or understood. Metaphorical thinking is an analytical and generative process where various characteristics or "referents" of two concepts are analyzed and compared for their similar and dissimilar elements. Metaphors associated with leadership help to explain the meaning of leadership as a phenomenon and human activity (Bass, 1990) including such things as: the nature and purpose of leadership; the role and participation of leaders and followers (members, constituents); the actions associated with leadership activity; the skills or traits associated with effective leadership; and the representation of leadership found in various cultures.

For example, Jason Szporn, a graduate student in Educational Leadership at the University of St. Thomas, explained his idea of leadership using a metaphor, comparing leadership to the game of chess. After describing the roles of the various chess pieces on the board, Jason described the importance of shared leadership, describing the potential opportunities available to a pawn for leadership:

The concept of emergent leadership is evidenced in the game. The pawn is perhaps the weakest piece on the chessboard, more canon fodder than anything else. Yet, should the pawn be able to make his/her way across the chessboard to the other side, the pawn gets the option of changing into any other kind of piece it would like (except the king). Usually, but not always, this means the pawn will choose to become a queen, the most powerful piece on the board. Under my definition of leadership . . . [the pawn is] . . . the most powerful piece on the board, the pawn (now queen) may be the individual the other pieces look to in order to improve their lives. (Szporn, 2004, p. 4)

Later on in his essay, Jason describes his reluctance to lead others because of his distrust and disappointment

53

with most leaders, "... most leaders are not leaders for the right reasons, and therefore one should be very careful about following anyone. Were I a bishop on a chessboard, I would most likely be a conscientious objector, and would likely be held in the king's dungeon at best, or beheaded at worst" (p. 5).

The insights made using the metaphor of "leadership is like a game," offer many of us the opportunity to gain new perspectives about leadership that were previously inaccessible to us. As Jason described his ideas to the class, nods of agreement and understanding appeared. We knew what he meant and began to consider more possibilities for thinking about leadership. How might the pawn be as powerful or more powerful than the king?

George Lakoff and Mark Johnson (1980) in their groundbreaking book, *Metaphors We Live By*, describe the influence of metaphor in our lives:

> Metaphor is pervasive in every day life, not just in language but also in thought and action. Our ordinary conceptual system, in terms of which we both think and act, is fundamentally metaphoric in nature. . . . Our concepts structure what we perceive, how we get around in the world, and how we relate to other people. Our conceptual system thus plays a central role in defining our everyday realities. If we are right in suggesting that our conceptual system is largely metaphorical, then the way we think, what we experience, and what we do every day is very much a matter of metaphor. (p. 3)

The use of metaphorical thinking about leadership can significantly broaden the ability of leaders to function more effectively in their environment due to their enlarged perspectives and expanded idea of the possibilities for strategic action. We need to examine our existing metaphors, identifying those that are "in use" and those lying undetected, exerting influence regarding the way we perceive events and our role in it. Morgan (1997) says, "Favored ways of thinking and acting become traps that confine individuals within socially constructed worlds and prevent the emergence of other worlds" (p. 219). Often, without even being aware of it, we create "mind traps" or "psychic prisons" that restrict our thinking. Leaders must avoid this.

If metaphors shape us, both consciously and unconsciously, then the limitations and possibilities of various metaphors for framing our experience and determining our future actions must be explored. The way we think metaphorically influences our actions.

Metaphors compress complicated issues into understandable images, influencing our attitudes, evaluations, and actions. A university head who views the institution as a factory establishes different policies than one who conceives of it as a craft guild or a shopping center. Consultants who see themselves as physicians are likely to differ from those who see themselves as salespeople or rain dancers. (Bolman and Deal, 2003, p. 268)

Metaphorical thinking influences our mental models. "Mental models are deeply ingrained assumptions, generalizations, or even pictures or images that influence how we understand the world and how we take action" (Senge, 1990, p. 8). Senge relates leader effectiveness to the continuous improvement of the leader's mental models. There is a danger of our mental models freezing, causing us to only see and remember that which reinforces what we already believe. Senge describes the trap of clinging to our existing mental models:

> We trap ourselves . . . in defensive routines that insulate our mental models from examination, and we consequently develop "skilled incompetence"—a marvelous oxymoron that Argyris uses to describe most adult learners, who are "highly skillful at protecting themselves from pain and threat posed by learning situations," but consequently fail to produce the results they really want. (p. 182)

To avoid these negative traps, we need more inventive and creative ways to expand our mental models and open up new avenues of thinking. We must avoid mindlessness. Ellen Langer (1989) in *Mindfulness* identifies the causes of "mindlessness" as (a) being trapped by categories [limiting how something is understood], (b) responding with " automatic behavior," and (c) acting from a single perspective (pp. 1–18). The effects of mindlessness can be seen when: a situation or problem is narrowly, poorly or inaccurately understood, responding inappropriately "without thinking" to various stimuli without noting differences in context or application, or limiting ideas or opportunities for understanding and taking action.

Charles Handy (1989) in *The Age of Unreason* encourages "upside down" or discontinuous thinking, recommending that we engage in processes that cause us to change our thinking by looking at everything in a new way. The value of ideas may be more important than the mark of individuals in the scheme of things. He believes that the power of thinking and new ideas may have a greater effect than a leader's influence at any particular time.

> In the long perspective of history it may seem that the really influential people were not Hitler or Churchill, Stalin or Gorbachev, but Freud, Marx, and Einstein, men who changed nothing except the way we think, but that changed everything. (p. 24)

Margaret Wheatley (1999) in *Leadership and the New Science* describes the uselessness of mechanistic or technical models for thinking about the future. Instead she encourages human interaction and collective knowing as a method for dealing with the future, describing the limitations of our current knowledge by drawing from the wisdom of Einstein: "As Einstein is often quoted as saying: No problem can be solved from the same consciousness that created it" (p. 7). Our future may depend on our ability to develop and share our individual and collective wisdom.

BECOMING WISE

Perhaps one of the most important aspects of leadership is wisdom. Sternberg (2003) relates certain aspects of thinking and "knowledge acquisition" to wisdom. Sternberg's "balance theory of wisdom" asserts that wisdom is largely a cognitive process where the "wise" individual engages in problem solving to define the problem, identify alternatives and assess their effects, weigh the potential impact of actions on self and others, and ultimately reach a balanced (wise) judgment. Sternberg imposes a limitation on what we think of as wisdom (and leadership). The leader's actions must result in a socially responsible end. This view of wisdom frames leadership from an ethical orientation. Leaders are those who are wise and motivated by the "greater good." Central to Sternberg's model is the importance of cognition in sensing, weighing, and determining a course of action based on contextual knowledge, analytical and creative thinking, and socially oriented values (p. 152). Wisdom is an important aspect of leadership. Wise leaders know how to skillfully examine issues from a variety of perspectives, engage in creative problem solving, and exercise effective judgment by selecting the "right" problem to solve, using a highly skillful strategy.

Harlan Cleveland (1985) offers a framework for understanding wisdom in *The Knowledge Executive*. He defines data as merely "undigested observations, unvarnished facts, until the data are organized [by others] into information" (p. 22). Organized data or information becomes knowledge when it is "internal-

ized by me, integrated with everything else I know from experience or study or intuition, and therefore useful in guiding my life and work" (p. 22). "Wisdom is integrated knowledge, information made super-useful by theory, which relates bits and fields of knowledge to each other, which in turn enables me to use the knowledge to do something" (p. 23).

Peter Vaill (1998) describes "process wisdom" as a strategy for leadership in *Spirited Leadership and Learning*. Process wisdom is the "feeling of moving through situations and problems and yet somehow, acting 'wisely,' in relation to them" (p. 25). Robert Terry (2001) in the *Seven Zones for Leadership* describes a similar phenomenon, calling it "adept wisdom" (p. 278). Reflective leaders are "smarter beginners"—those who open themselves up to the possibility of becoming wise through learning. An important aspect of wisdom is learning; wisdom is a learning process rather than a fixed state of being (Terry, 2001; Sternberg, 2003; Vaill, 1998).

Robert Terry (2001) relates skillful and creative metaphorical thinking to leadership:

> Moreover, I suggest that leadership will do well to make adept choices of metaphor in response to particular stirrings. If we think in terms of an inappropriate metaphor as we feel negative and positive stirrings in ourselves and in our organizations, we may miss the depth and scope of what these stirring signify, and our leadership may be less than adept. (p. 62)

Wise leaders "will do well" to make more visible the influence of metaphors "in use" and create new metaphors to open up possibilities for understanding and future action.

It may be valuable to view leadership as a learning process where wise, creative, and intelligent thinking is needed in response to *fluid, dynamic, and unknowable* circumstances. How then do we open ourselves up to the idea of becoming more skillful, adept and creative leaders? One way is to consider the use of metaphors and the development of metaphorical thinking as a useful tool to examine our mental models and increase our ability to respond to future challenges, creating more opportunities for wisdom.

THINKING METAPHORICALLY

Metaphors are linguistic, image-generating devices that help us think about what is not yet known or understood. Metaphorical thinking is an analytical and generative process where various characteristics or "referents" of two concepts are analyzed and compared for their similar and dissimilar elements. This process, described as "knowledge acquisition" (Sternberg, 2003), is an important aspect of problem solving. The characteristics of knowledge acquisition explain the cognitive processes involved in metaphorical thinking. During knowledge acquisition, we are engaged in: "(a) locating relevant information in context [selective encoding], (b) combining the information into a meaningful whole [selective combination], and (c) interrelating this information to what the reader [individual] already knows [selective comparison]" (p. 183).

Selective encoding requires us to select what is important and to eliminate distracting or irrelevant information. By reducing the information that is available, the most important aspects of a problem can be understood. This taking apart process then requires us to develop a new arrangement of information called *selective combination*. Using the metaphor of a detective searching for relevant information, Sternberg describes the process as a search for clues that, when successfully arranged, allow us to locate the suspect and solve the case. According to Sternberg, there is an optimal arrangement of the relevant facts. If the detective follows "false leads," then the case can't be solved (p. 184).

Finally, *selective comparison* requires us to compare the new information with what we already know, to give the new information meaning.

> New information can be related to old information, and vice versa, by the use of similes, metaphors, analogies, and models, but the goal is always the same: to give the new information meaning by connecting it to the old information that is already known. (Sternberg, 2003, p. 185)

Metaphorical thinking produces new learning. It is a meaning-making process that requires analytical and creative thinking, offering us the opportunity to understand something that was not previously known. Metaphorical thinking as described in the knowledge acquisition process, largely takes place during "selective comparison," *where we compare what is newly "organized" or noticed with other concepts, models or experiences to gain insight.* In the earlier example regarding how leadership is like a chess game, Jason notices certain aspects of leadership (not everything he knows about leadership, but *some* of its characteristics) and compares these aspects to some parts of his ideas related to chess (once again, not all of what he knows about chess is incorporated). He considers what he knows about "roles" in leadership and compares these roles to some of the players on the chessboard, producing the insight that the "pawn" is an emergent leader. This process of selective comparison (choosing certain aspects of two distinct concepts to compare) is the essence of metaphorical thinking. The exercise in metaphorical thinking helps Jason share his idea of leadership with us:

> There comes a time when a truly gifted person seeks to become a leader for truly altruistic purposes. This is a leader I can follow. Gandhi comes to mind. Mandela in South Africa. In short, a person who seeks to leverage power to improve people's lives in some meaningful way. Unfortunately there are very few of them. (Szporn, 2004, p. 6)

The metaphor helps us explore our thinking, pushing us toward expanded perspectives and sometimes, magically allowing us to generate moments of wisdom that, with a shock of awareness, we recognize as truth. The gift of the metaphor is that it allows our thinking to emerge and helps others understand just how we got there.

Metaphorical thinking is a useful tool for interpreting and communicating our knowledge and experience to others. It helps us describe and make sense of our experiences. For example, we might describe our work place as a "prison" or "factory" (Bolman and Deal, 2003; Morgan, 1997), evoking a cluster of images that tell us of the experience of work. Leaders may see themselves as kings, captains, commanders, or evangelists. Students may be talented players and teachers may be coaches, guiding students toward the finish line. The metaphor calls forth a mental schema that defines roles, relationships, norms, values, assumptions, activities, and so forth. Highly influential metaphors are embedded in our personal and cultural memories and widely shared.

Another one of our students described her work place as a "shark tank" and told us about how she avoided predator "fish." We knew immediately what she meant even though we had never experienced her work environment. Metaphors allow us to share the "unknowable" by linking what is known, enabling us to communicate our experience as a meaning-making activity to others. Because communication is a critical ingredient of leadership, expressing ourselves in metaphor allows others to access our ideas and builds a "collective" consciousness.

Metaphors are devices for creative thinking. We may ask, "How is a school like an extended family?"

This may generate new ideas about how schools can become more like a "home for the mind" or expand the idea of relationships between and among faculty, students and staff. A fellow student may be like a brother or sister or a beloved teacher may be like a wise aunt or uncle. Continuing with the metaphor, members of the school are encouraged to treat each other like members of an extended family. In this way, metaphors are generative devices for seeing new ways of thinking and acting. "A metaphor makes the strange familiar and the familiar strange. They help us capture subtle themes that normal language can overlook" (Bolman and Deal, 2003, p. 267). A leader can develop his or her wisdom through metaphorical thinking.

> Metaphors create new meanings of various types; without them, neither knowledge nor language can grow. Without cognitively based linguistic devices to juxtapose the old in unfamiliar ways, new ways of thinking and new expressions for those thoughts cannot emerge. (MacCormac, 1985, p. 207)

Metaphorical thinking helps us to *gain perspective, see new opportunities,* and *communicate our experience and ideas to others.* It is not surprising that metaphors are highly prevalent in the literature of leadership. We examined over 500 titles of the bestselling leadership books to locate the use of metaphors as a device for describing and explaining leadership. We identified dominant metaphors appearing in the works of the most influential authors (assuming that influence is related to highest number of sales). The methods and results of this study are described in the next section.

A REVIEW OF "BESTSELLING" LEADERSHIP BOOKS

A walk through any well-stocked bookstore reveals the intriguing (and growing) number of titles shelved in the section called "Leadership and Management." Titles such as *Leadership Secrets of Attila the Hun, Leading with Soul: An Uncommon Journey of Spirit,* and *Power Plays: Win or Lose—How History's Great Political Leaders Play the Game* evoke images of leadership through the use of metaphor, portraying leadership as a war, a pilgrimage or a game. A content analysis of 500 bestselling leadership book titles (250 titles each from an academic and a commercial catalog) was conducted to identify dominant metaphors in bestselling books. We selected WorldCat, a catalog and searchable database (the world's largest union catalog with over 500 million books), to locate the most popular

books in academic and public libraries in the world. The "bestsellers" were those books found in the greatest number of libraries.

We entered the keyword "leadership" and limited the book titles to those published in English between 1985–2005. This search yielded 776 titles ranked from the bestselling book (the top book was found in 3723 libraries) to the least popular (search conducted on 07-17-2004). We reviewed the top 250 books, analyzing whether a metaphor was contained in the title. In some cases, a synopsis was examined if the title was unclear. Next, we made a beginning list of metaphor categories and arranged the titles based on their popularity and dominant metaphor. We then expanded our search to the commercial market.

We conducted essentially the same search using the search engine provided by Barnes and Noble, a commercial bookseller (conducted 07-1-2004). We entered the keyword "leadership" using the Barnes and Noble search engine found on the website (http://www.bn.com) and rank ordered the 16,427 titles based on the criteria of "bestselling" titles. We examined the results of this second search, analyzed the first 250 bestselling titles, created a new list of metaphor categories, and arranged the titles based on their popularity and dominant metaphor.

Finally we refined our metaphor categories and developed a complete master list of book titles, organizing them by category and bestselling rank and merging the results of the two searches. The bestselling book titles that contain a dominant metaphor are organized in Tables 1–3. The metaphor categories are: leadership is like war; leadership is a spiritual journey; leadership is a game; leadership is a performing art; leadership is a natural process; and leadership is like operating a machine. Additional metaphors relate to vocational roles (captain, king, architect, explorer, detective, etc.) or experience metaphors (sailing in rough seas, navigating "permanent whitewater" (Vaill, 1996), escaping a fire, etc.). We describe the dominant metaphors in the next section.

EXPLORING METAPHORS

A dominant metaphor is that leadership is like a war: the leader is the general, workers are warriors, the competitive environment is a battleground, and the goal is to gain territory and defeat the enemy (see Table 1). Utilizing this metaphor, leaders emphasize strategy to gain ground or improve their position, workers are soldiers who follow commands from the highest authority, campaigns are planned and executed, and to the victor go the spoils! The most popular books utilizing the war metaphor are *The Prince, The Art of War, The Five Rings*, and *Leadership Secrets of Attila the Hun*. Three of the four books were written hundreds of years ago and are considered "classic" texts in battlefield strategy. The publisher's synopsis of *The Art of War* illustrates the war metaphor:

"A clever fighter is one who not only wins, but excels in winning with ease." So wrote Sun Tzu 2,500 years ago, and kings, soldiers, and statesmen have been turning to the Chinese master for his astute observations ever since. Sun Tzu's incisive blueprint for battlefield strategy is as relevant to today's combatants in business, politics, and everyday life as it once was to the warlords of ancient China. *The Art of War* is one of the most useful books ever written on leading with wisdom, an essential tool for modern corporate warriors battling to gain the advantage in the boardroom and for anyone struggling to gain the upper hand in confrontations and competitions. (Barnes and Noble Classics, 2004)

Another prominent metaphor is that leadership is like a spiritual journey. The leader is a spiritual guide or minister, followers are disciplines or believers, the competitive environment is represented as a struggle between good and evil, and the goal is to create meaning and seek fulfillment through service and the accomplishment of the greater good (see Table 2). Utilizing this metaphor, leaders seek their authentic selves as an expression of the "god" within us (for example, soul or "seed" work), identify and communicate ethical principles, define the mission and work based on shared values, emulate the actions of spiritual leaders and disciplines as living models for others, and seek salvation for humankind.

The most popular books are *Bearing the Cross: Martin Luther King and the Southern Christian Leadership Conference, Developing the Leader Within You, Principle-centered Leadership, The Servant: A Simple Story About the True Essence of Leadership, Stewardship: Choosing Service Over Self-interest*, and *Authentic Leadership: Rediscovering the Secrets to Creating Lasting Value*. The publisher's description of Hunter's (1998) *The Servant: A Simple Story About the True Essence of Leadership* illustrates the relationship between leadership and spirituality:

Table 1. War Metaphors

Sales Rank*	Bestselling Books
#12 BN	Machiavelli, N. (1999). *The prince (L. Ricci, Trans.)*. New York: Signet Classics.
#14 BN	Musashi, M. (1994). *The book of five rings (T. Cleary, Trans.)*. New York: Barnes & Noble Publishers.
#16 BN	Tzu, Sun (1994). *The art of war (R. D. Sawyer, Trans.)*. New York: Barnes & Noble Books.
#32 BN	Green, R., & Elffers, J. (2000). *48 laws of power*. New York: Penguin.
#48 WC	Roberts, W. (1989). *Leadership secrets of Attila the Hun*. New York: Warner Books.
#109 BN	Musashi, M. (2003). *The book of five rings (T. Clearly, Trans.)*. New York: Random House.
#129 WC	Kaplan, R. (2002). *Warrior politics: Why leadership demands a pagan ethos*. New York: Random House.
#130 BN	Barber, B. (2003). *No excuse leadership: Lessons from the U.S. Army's elite rangers*. New York: John Wiley & Sons.
#132 BN	Roberts, W. (1990). *Leadership secrets of Attila the Hun*. New York: Warner Books.
#142 BN	Ravina, M. (2003). *The last samurai: The life and battles of Saigo Takamori*. New York: John Wiley & Sons.
#145 BN	Pettet, G. (2004). *Lincoln's war: The untold story of American's greatest president as commander in chief*. New York: Random House.
#161 BN	Tzu, Sun (2003). *The art of war (D. Galvin, Ed., L Giles, Trans.)*. New York: Barnes & Noble Publishers.
#166 BN	Tzu, S. (2001). *The art of war for managers (G. Michaelson, Trans.)*. Holbrook, MA: Adams Media.
#173 BN	Cannon, J. & Cannon, J. (2003). *The leadership lessons of the U.S. Navy Seals: Battle-tested strategies for creating successful organizations and inspiring extraordinary results*. New York: McGraw-Hill.
#181 BN	Hanson, V. (2001). *Soul of battle: From ancient times to the present day, how three great liberators vanquished tyranny*. New York: Knopf Publishing Group.
#196 BN	Machiavelli, N. (1998). *The prince (P. Bondanella, M. Musa, Trans)*. New York: Bantam Books.
#201 BN	Machiavelli, N. (1981). *The prince (D. Donno, Ed.)*. New York: Bantam Books.
#207 BN	Machiavelli, N. (1981). *The prince (D. Baker-Smith, Ed., W. K. Marriott, Trans.)*. New York: David McKay.
#222 BN	Musashi, M. (2002). *The book of five rings (W. S. Wilson, Trans.)*. New York: Kodansha America.
#223 BN	Axelrod, A. (2001). *Patton on leadership: Strategic lessons for corporate warfare*. New York: Prentice-Hall Press.
#230 BN	Michael, E., Axelrod, B., & Handfield-Jones, H. (2001). *War for talent*. Cambridge, MA: Harvard Business School.
#241 WC	Roberts, W. (1993). *Victory secrets of Attila the Hun*. New York: Doubleday.

* Barnes & Noble Index (BN), WorldCat Index (WC)

Table 2. Spirituality Metaphors

Sales Rank*	Bestselling Books
#8 WC	Garrow, D. (1986). *Bearing the cross: Martin Luther King and the Southern Christian Leadership Conference.* New York: W. Morrow.
#19 BN	Maxwell, J. (2001). *Developing the leader within you.* Nashville, TN: Nelson Books.
#33 WC	Covey, S. (1991). *Principle-centered leadership.* New York: Summit Books.
#37 BN	Hunter, J. (1998). *The servant: A simple story about the true essence of leadership.* New York: Crown Publishing Group
#38 WC	Block. P. (1993). *Stewardship: Choosing service over self-interest.* San Francisco: Berret-Koehler Publishers.
#386 BN	George, B. (2003). *Authentic leadership: Rediscovering the secrets to creating lasting value.* San Francisco: Jossey-Bass.
#100 BN	Autry, J. (2001). *The servant leader: How to build a creative team, develop great morale, and improve bottom line performance.* Silver City, NM: Crown Publishing Group.
#108 BN	Jones, L. (1995). *Jesus, CEO: Using ancient wisdom for visionary leadership.* New York: Hyperion.
#131 BN	Blanchard, K., & Hodges, P. (2003). *Servant leader.* Woodstock, VT: J. Countryman Press.
#135 WC	Greenleaf, R., Frick, D., & Spears, L. (1996). *On becoming a servant leader.* San Francisco: Jossey-Bass.
#138 BN	Maxwell, J. (2002). *Running with the giants: What Old Testament heroes want you to know about life and leadership.* New York: Warner Books.
#139 BN	Greenleaf, R., & Spears, L. (Ed.). (2002). *Servant leadership: A journey into the nature of legitimate power and greatness.* Mahwah, NJ: Paulist Press.
#147 BN	Maxwell, J. (Ed.). (2003). *Maxwell leadership Bible.* Nashville, TN: Thomas Nelson.
#135 BN	Quinn, R. (1996). *Deep change: Discovering the leader within.* San Francisco: Jossey-Bass.
#179 BN	Bolman, L., & Deal, T. (1995). *Leading with soul: An uncommon journey of spirit.* San Francisco: Jossey-Bass.
#185 WC	Bolman, L., & Deal, T. (1995). *Leading with soul: An uncommon journey of spirit.* San Francisco: Jossey-Bass.
#190 BN	Badaracco, J. (2002). *Leading quietly: An unorthodox guide to doing the right thing.* Cambridge, MA: Harvard Business School Publishing.
#206 WC	Jones, L. (1995). *Jesus, CEO: Using ancient wisdom for visionary leadership.* New York: Hyperion.
#209 BN	Nouwen, H. (1993). *In the name of Jesus: Reflections on Christian leadership.* Silver City, NM: Crossroad Publishing Company.
#215 WC	Sergiovanni, T. (1992). *Moral leadership: Getting to the heart of school improvement.* San Francisco: Jossey-Bass.
#218 BN	Fullan, M. (2003). *The moral imperative of school leadership.* Thousand Oaks, CA: Sage Publications.
#225 BN	Jaworski, J. (1998). *Synchronicity: The inner path of leadership.* San Francisco: Berrett-Koehler.
#234 BN	Coles, R., & Goz, H. (2000). *Lives of moral leadership.* New York: Random House Publishing Group.
#237 BN	Blackaby, H., & Blackaby, R. (2001). *Spiritual leadership: Moving people on to God's agenda.* Nashville, TN: Broadman & Holman Publishers.
#241 BN	Covey, S. (1991). *Principle-centered leadership.* New York: Summit Books.
#277 BN	Hunter, J. (2004). *World's most powerful leadership principle: How to become a servant leader.* New York: Crown Publishing Group.

* Barnes & Noble Index (BN), WorldCat Index (WC)

In this absorbing tale, you watch the timeless principles of servant leadership unfold through the story of John Daily, a businessman whose outwardly successful life is spiraling out of control. He is failing miserably in each of his leadership roles as boss, husband, father, and coach. To get his life back on track, he reluctantly attends a weeklong leadership retreat at a remote Benedictine monastery. To John's surprise, the monk leading the seminar is a former business executive and Wall Street legend. Taking John under his wing, the monk guides him to a realization that is simple yet profound: The true foundation of leadership is not power, but authority, which is built upon relationships, love, service, and sacrifice. . . . If you are searching for ways to improve your leadership skills; if you want to understand the timeless virtues that lead to lasting and meaningful success, then this book is one you cannot afford to miss. (Crown Publishing Group, 1998)

Spirituality metaphors often describe individuals "who have lost their way." In *Leading with Soul: An Uncommon Journey of Spirit* (2001), a dispirited leader looks for meaning beyond the "bottom line":

At the heart of this groundbreaking book is a contemporary parable, which tells the story of Steve, a dispirited leader in search of something more meaningful in his life than an obsession with the bottom line. Through conversations with Maria—a mysterious sage whose wisdom was forged in her own hard-won business career—Steve unexpectedly discovers the true meaning of leadership. Having rediscovered his own soul, he is able to ignite the spirit of his organization. (John Wiley and Sons, 2001)

Another significant metaphor is that leadership is a game or sport, and teamwork is the key to success. The leader is the coach, followers are players or teammates, the competitive environment is the playing field or arena, and the goal is to win (see Table 3). Leaders as effective coaches, develop game plans, identify and support their most talented players, know the rules and "how" to play the game, devise a "winning" strategy, and inspire the team to achieve their best performance. Teamwork is emphasized and leadership is shared among team members. The most popular books are: *Now, Discover Your Strengths: How to Develop Your Talents and Those of the People You Manage,* *The Five Dysfunctions of a Team: A Leadership Fable, First Break All the Rules: What the Worlds Greatest Managers Do Differently, The 17 Indisputable Laws of Teamwork: Embrace Them and Empower Your Team,* and *Power Plays: Win or Lose—How History's Great Political Leaders Play the Game.* The coach-leader is talent scout and developer of people and teams:

Buckingham and Coffman explain how the best managers select an employee for talent rather than for skills or experience; how they set expectations for him

Table 3. Team Metaphors

Sales Rank*	Bestselling Books
#2 BN	Buckingham, M., & Clifton, D. (2001). *Now, discover your strengths: How to develop your talents and those of the people you manage.* New York: Simon & Schuster.
#7 BN	Lencioni, P. (2004). *The five dysfunctions of a team: A leadership fable.* New York: John Wiley & Sons.
#3 BN	Buckingham, M., & Coffman, C. (1999). *First break all the rules: What the world's greatest managers do differently.* New York: Simon & Schuster.
#6 BN	Maxwell, J., & Zettersten, R. (Ed.) (2001). *The 17 indisputable laws of teamwork: Embrace and empower your team.* Nashville, TN: Thomas Nelson.
#15 BN	Lencioni, P. (2002). *The five dysfunctions of a team: A leadership fable.* New York: John Wiley & Sons.
#18 BN	Morris, D., & Feldman, L. (2002). *Power plays: Win or lose—how history's great political leaders play the game.* New York: HarperCollins Publishers.
#46 BN	Smart, B. (1999). *How leading companies win by hiring, coaching and keeping the best people.* New York: Prentice-Hall Press.
#51 BN	Smith, D., Bell, G., & Kilgo, J. (2004). *The Carolina way: Leadership lessons from a life in coaching.* New York: The Penguin Group.
#51 WC	Wellins, R., Byham, W., & Wilson, J. (1991). *Empowered teams: Creating self-directed work groups that improve quality, productivity, and participation.* San Francisco: Jossey-Bass.
#65 WC	Schulman, J. (2001). *The game of life: College sports and educational values.* Princeton, NJ: Princeton University Press.
#87 BN	Kaplan, R., & Norton, D. (2000). *Strategy-focused organization: How balanced scorecard companies thrive in the new business environment.* Cambridge, MA: Harvard Business School.
#93 WC	Bradley, B. (1998). *Values of the game.* New York: Artisan.
#97 BN	Blanchard, K., Parisi-Carew, E., Bowles, S., & Carew, D. (2000). *High five.* New York: William Murrow.
#119 BN	Maxwell, J. (2003). *The 17 indisputable laws of teamwork workbook: Embrace them and empower your team.* Nashville, TN: Thomas Nelson.
#124 BN	Whitmore, J. (2003). *Coaching for performance: Growing people, performance and purpose.* Yarmouth, ME: Brealey, Nicholas Publishing.
#154 WC	Parker. G. (1990). *Team players and teamwork: The new competitive business strategy.* San Francisco: Jossey-Bass.
#170 WC	Schmidt, W., & Finnigan, J. (1992). *The race without a finish line: American's quest for total quality.* San Francisco: Jossey-Bass.
#171 WC	Cox. A. (1990). *Straight talk for Monday morning: Creating values, vision and vitality at work.* New York: John Wiley & Sons.
#189 BN	Blanchard, K., & Schul, D. (2001). *Little book of coaching: Motivating people to be winners.* New York: HarperCollins Publishers.
#191 WC	Larson, C., & LaFasto, F. (1989). *Teamwork: What must go right, what can go wrong.* Newbury Park, CA: Sage Publications.
#199 WC	Kotter, J. (1995). *The new rules: How to succeed in today's post–corporate world.* New York: Free Press.
#203 BN	Peterson, D. (1996). *Leader as coach: Strategies for coaching and developing others.* Minneapolis, MN: Personnel Decisions Inc.
#231 WC	Schrage, M. (2000). *Serious play: How the world's best companies simulate to innovate.* Boston: Harvard Business School Press.
#232 WC	Morris, D., & Feldman, L. (2002). *Power plays: Win or lose—how history's great political leaders play the game.* New York: HarperCollins Publishers.
#236 WC	Shula, D. (1995). *Everyone's a coach: You can inspire anyone to be a winner.* New York: Harper Business.

*Barnes & Noble Index (BN), WorldCat Index (WC)

or her—they define the right outcomes rather than the right steps; how they motivate people—they build on each person's unique strengths rather than trying to fix his weaknesses; and, finally, how great managers develop people—they find the right fit for each person, not the next rung on the ladder. (Simon and Schuster, 1999)

In *The Carolina Way: Leadership Lessons from a Life in Coaching*, many lessons can be learned from those with a winning record:

Coach Smith fully explains his entire coaching philosophy and shows readers how to apply it to the leadership and team-building challenges in their own lives. In his wry, sensible, wise way, Coach Smith takes us through every aspect of his program, illustrating his insights with vivid stories. Accompanying each major point is a "Player Perspective."

Each year Coach Smith gave his team the same three goals:

PLAY HARD: Insist on consistent effort. The final result is often outside your control. Create a system that demands effort, rewards it, and punishes its absence.

PLAY SMART: Execute properly. Understand and consistently execute the fundamentals. Reward their execution and punish their absence.

PLAY TOGETHER: Play unselfishly. Don't focus on individual statistics. Recruit unselfish players, reward unselfish play, and punish selfish play and showboating. (Penguin Group, 2004)

Other metaphors that appear in the review of bestselling titles are: leadership is like a performing art, leadership is a natural process (body, nature, universe), and leadership is like operating a machine. If leadership is like a performing art, then a traditional musical metaphor is used: the leader is the conductor, the followers are the musicians, the environment is the stage, the action is playing music, and the goal of the performance is applause and loyal fans. A more progressive metaphor is the shared and spontaneous leadership of a jazz ensemble. In this case, the leader is the musician who initiates the beat (drummer or base player), and then shares leadership with other musicians who improvise at various times during the performance. The metaphor allows us to consider emergent and shared leadership of the ensemble.

Some additional metaphors are derived from vocational or positional roles: captain, commander, president, king, explorer, architect, shepherd, detective, doctor, firefighter, and more. Often, these vocational metaphors offer the "secrets" of the profession, relating leadership experience in the field to more general lessons about the role of "leader." There are lessons to be learned from nearly all professions including Santa Claus in *The Leadership Secrets of Santa Claus* (Harvey, E., Cottrell, D., and Lucia, A., 2003)!

Our study of bestselling book titles reveals the dominance of metaphors as a construct for thinking about leadership. Metaphors can serve as a useful tool for understanding or they can serve as a trap, limiting our perspective due to habit-bound thinking and "automatic" responses. Metaphorical "exercises" can help us examine how leadership is "socially constructed" in various cultures. Through the use of metaphor as a thinking tool, leaders may learn how to uncover and discover the meaning of leadership in various organizational and community settings. It allows leaders to shape their leadership by consciously choosing appropriate metaphors to convey personal and institutional values—selecting those metaphors that fit our emerging view of leadership for the future.

IMPLICATIONS FOR EDUCATIONAL LEADERSHIP AND ADMINISTRATION PREPARATION PROGRAMS

Professors of Educational Leadership should engage students in the examination of metaphor. Metaphorical thinking exercises show us the possibilities of expanding our thinking, detecting the underlying theories of action in use, and explaining the complexities of our organizational life and experience. We might ask our students some of the following questions: What is useful about viewing leadership as a war, a spiritual journey, a game or a performance art? How can it explain our experience or help us to develop new understanding about leadership? What is limiting about the metaphor "in use" or those lying undetected just below our consciousness? What aspects of the situation are not explained by the metaphor? How much more can we understand when a new metaphor is employed? How can metaphors inspire, simplify, communicate, explain or distort?

Metaphors provide strategies for thinking about leadership. To be effective, leaders must employ a variety of strategies to understand the situational and contextual challenges of leadership. Terry (1993) connects perception to leadership:

Thus, metaphors are not only filters on reality, they also unite what is happening with implied suggestions for what is about to happen. They unite the true and the real in one vision of reality. In other words, metaphors mediate what is perceived to be authentic. Different metaphors yield different realities, resulting in different perceptions in what is really going on. (p. 161)

Metaphorical thinking may help leaders to:

- Gain insight regarding how the leader(s) and others view leadership
- Identify roles and relationships between leaders and participants in leadership (members, constituents, followers, etc.)
- Detect the expectations of leaders and members by locating the dominant and hidden metaphors, myths and stories for leadership operating in the environment
- Interpret the behaviors and interactions of others and analyze the alternatives to various situational challenges of leadership
- Assess the implications of various decision-making strategies
- Change or expand the metaphors for leadership to enhance the opportunities for productive change
- Reflect on the effects of various leader decisions in addressing the immediate challenges, and assess the impact of these decisions on the future.

The importance of metaphorical thinking is revealed when we consider the challenges ahead. Heifetz (1994) illustrates a change in the requirements of leadership by distinguishing between "technical" and "adaptive" challenges. Technical challenges require leaders to apply current know-how or expertise to address difficult but routine problems that can be mastered.

> These problems are technical because the necessary knowledge about them already has been digested and put in the form of a legitimized set of known organizational procedures guiding what to do and role authorizations guiding who should do it. (Heifetz, 1994, pp. 71–72)

However, adaptive challenges require leaders to learn new ways of thinking to uncover root problems, to examine underlying assumptions, to question existing ways of operating, and to discover new strategies to address challenges in highly unpredictable environments.

> Adaptive work consists of the learning required to address conflicts in the values people hold, or to diminish the gap between the values people stand for and the reality they face. Adaptive work requires a change in values, beliefs, or behavior. (Heifetz, 1994, pp. 71–72)

This change from technical to adaptive challenges requires that we shift our perspective from viewing leadership as the skillful application of technical knowledge to viewing leadership as a thinking and learning process where future problems and solutions are unknowable and routine ways of responding are not yet developed. Thus, we need to think differently, continuing to develop and expand our capacity to think analytically and creatively.

Metaphors shape the social construction of leadership in our culture. Because dominant metaphors are so pervasive, we may not thoughtfully examine the "subliminal" messages about leadership embedded in print and non-print media. Do we expect our leaders to be commanders, kings, coaches, captains, servants, artists, conductors, or spiritual guides? Are we disciples, warriors, actors, shipmates, travelers, or co-participants in leadership? These questions reflect the complexity of metaphor as a device to communicate our experience, construct its meaning, and gain perspective about the potential roles and responsibilities of leadership.

Because metaphors are so influential in framing our ideas about leadership, more exploration of their influence is needed. We believe that some popular metaphors represent the thinking of the past, rather than the thinking that is needed for the future. For example, thinking about leadership as a war may not be as constructive as thinking about leadership as a process or journey. Leaders with limited metaphors may act in mechanistic and sometimes, inappropriate ways to the adaptive challenges on the horizon. Adept leaders use metaphors to think creatively about current realities, gaining new perspectives and imagining more possibilities for strategic action.

We believe that metaphors are important devices to bring new ideas about leadership to the forefront; in fact, our future may depend upon it:

> Why must anyone seek for new ways of acting? The answer is that in the long run the continuity of life itself depends on the making of new experiments. . . . The continuous invention of new ways of observing is man's special secret of living. (Young as cited in Vaill, 1998, pp. 7–8)

REFERENCES

Barnes and Noble Classics (2003). *The art of war.* From the Publisher. [On-line], July 23, 2004. Available: http://search.barnesandnoble.com/booksearch/isbnInquiry.asp?userid=ye7M0kh92N&isbn=1593080166&itm=4.

Bass, B. M. (1990). *Bass and Stogdill's handbook of leadership: Theory, research, and managerial applications* (3rd ed.). New York: The Free Press.

Bolman, L., and Deal, T. (2001). *Leading with soul: An uncommon journey of spirit.* San Francisco: Jossey-Bass.

Bolman, L., and Deal, T. (2003). *Reframing organizations.* San Francisco: Jossey-Bass.

Buckingham, M., and Clifton, D. O. (1999). *First, break all the rules: What the world's greatest managers do differently.* New York: Simon & Schuster.

Cleveland, H. (1985). *The knowledge executive.* New York: E.P. Dutton.

Crown Publishing Group (1998). *The servant: A simple story about the true essence of leadership.* Retrieved July 23, 2004, from http://search.barnesandnoble.com/booksearch/isbnInquiry.asp?userid=ye7M0kh92N&bn=0761513698&itm=1.

Handy, C. (1989). *The age of unreason.* Boston: Harvard Business School Press.

Harvey, E., Cottrell, D., and Lucia, A. (2003). *The leadership secrets of Santa Claus.* Dallas, TX: The Walk the Talk Company.

Heifetz, R. (1994). *Leadership without easy answers.* Cambridge, MA: The Belknap Press of Harvard University Press.

Hunter, J. (1998). *The servant: A simple story about the true essence of leadership.* New York: Crown Publishing Group.

John Wiley and Sons. (2001). *Leading with soul: An uncommon journey of the spirit.* From the Publisher. [On-line], July 23, 2004. Available: http://search.barnesandnoble.com/booksearch/isbnInquiry.asp?userid=ye7M0kh92N&isbn=0787955477&itm=1.

Lakoff, G., and Johnson, M. (1980). *Metaphors we live by.* Chicago: University of Chicago Press.

Langer, E. (1989). *Mindfulness.* Reading, MA: Addison-Wesley Publishing Company.

MacCormac, E. (1985). *A cognitive theory of metaphor.* Cambridge, MA: MIT Press.

Morgan, G. (1997). *Images of organization.* Thousand Oaks, CA: Sage Publications.

Penguin Group (2004). *The Carolina way: Leadership lessons from a life in coaching.* From the Publisher. [On-line], July 23, 2004. Available: http://search.barnesandnoble.com/booksearch/isbnInquiry.asp?userid=ye7M0kh92N&isbn=159420005X&itm=1.

Senge, P. (1990). *The fifth discipline.* New York: Doubleday Currency.

Simon and Schuster (1999). *First, break all the rules: What the world's greatest managers do differently.* From the Publisher. [On-line], July 23, 2004. Available: http://search.barnesandnoble.com/booksearch/isbnInquiry.asp?userid=ye7M0kh92N&isbn=0684852861&itm=1.

Smith, D., Bell, G. D., and Kilgo, J. (2004). *The Carolina way: Leadership lessons from a life in coaching.* New York: Penguin Group.

Sternberg, R. (2003). *Wisdom, intelligence, and creativity synthesized.* New York: Cambridge University Press.

Szporn, J. (2004). *Leadership platform.* Unpublished manuscript, University of St. Thomas, Minnesota.

Terry, R. (1993). *Authentic leadership.* San Francisco, CA: Jossey-Bass.

Terry, R. (2001). *Seven zones for leadership.* Palo Alto, CA: Davies-Black Publishing.

Tzu, S. (2003). *The art of war.* New York: Barnes and Noble Classics.

Vaill, P. (1998). *Spirited leading and learning: Process wisdom for a new age.* San Francisco: Jossey-Bass.

Wheatley, M. (1999). *Leadership and the new science.* San Francisco: Berrett-Koehler Publishers.

Young, J. Z. as cited in Vaill, P. (1998). *Spirited leading and learning.* San Francisco: Jossey-Bass.

An Alternative Model on the Practice of Leadership: An Indigenous People's Perspective

L. A. NAPIER

ABSTRACT

IN THIS ARTICLE, THE AUTHOR REPORTS ON THE FINDINGS of The Indigenous Leadership Project. The purpose of the multiyear study was to examine a perspective on leadership that has been greatly ignored in the literature. A qualitative exploratory approach was utilized in reflecting upon and analyzing the influences on leadership development as determined by such cultural factors as ethnic teachings/values or community mores, motives/inspirations, spirituality and/or religion, and political schooling. The paradigm has been expanded to be more inclusive by providing more explanatory insights into the leadership phenomenon as viewed through a cultural lens. The findings reveal a unique relational model of collectivism and collaboration identified as Naturalistic Leadership.

INTRODUCTION

What is the nature of leadership? The rationale for acting on this query emerged from an individual lack of clarity surrounding the essence of leadership and our socialization to its purpose. For leadership scholars these are exciting times as there are numerous opportunities to get involved in the paradigm shift. The lessons to be learned seem endless. Leadership scholars now consider the industrial notions of leadership passé. Gone are the days of defining leadership for general consumption, studying characteristics and behaviors for purposes of duplication, and searching for the one exemplary leader who can deliver us from our own lack of initiative and purpose. The academic community welcomes new explorations into the realities of leadership—with alternative perspectives and processes for understanding encouraged.

Unfortunately, the industrial age leadership models are still often utilized in leadership development programs and continue to serve as guiding frameworks in the evaluation of those placed in leadership roles. Research need not be brought forward to recognize the ineffectiveness of these industrial models as applied to schools and other organizations.

Room must be made in the paradigm for alternative perspectives. Margaret Wheatly (1992) purports that "it is not important we agree on one expert interpretation or one sure-fire application. That is not the nature of the universe in which we live. We inhabit a world that is always subjective and shaped by our interactions with it" (p. 8).

Like Wheatly, Joseph Rost encourages the development of "theories that speak in a different voice, and that represent an alternative paradigm" (1991, p. 29). Alternative voices have not been part of the "club" (p. 29). According to Rost, what must be encouraged are new thoughts about the nature of leadership that use "postindustrial assumptions about human beings, organizations, societies, and the planet Earth" (p. 183).

Sometimes the past—insights about living and working in a collective society are the best lessons to inform us about leading organizations now and in the future.

PROJECT BACKGROUND

The Indigenous Leadership Project was a multi-year learning plan of growth, study, and reflection. The research was designed to address problematic issues of leadership theories as an area that could impact the common good.

A remarkable aspect of The Indigenous Leadership Project was that is was not a solo effort by one research

The author acknowledges the contributions of the doctoral students involved in the cultural leadership laboratory at The University of Colorado at Denver. Former laboratory participants who contributed in some aspect to this study include: Julee Brooke, Joseph C'de Baca, Maggie Lopez, Lilas Rajaee-Moore, Annie Rooney-French, Marcia Krett, Karen Myers, Yolanda Ortega-Ericksen, Maria Solano, Xeturah Woodley-Tillman, and my faculty colleague, Rodney Muth.

scholar. Also involved were future educational leaders who chose to accompany the researcher in this journey. They too sought answers and clarifications that would assist them in their own leadership education, personal understanding, and research. The process of research proved exciting and rewarding for all concerned. These educational leaders proved themselves invaluable in numerous aspects of the project including one intensive literature review, designing of the interview questions, and the pilot study data collection and analysis. In a limited capacity they also assisted in the actual project data collection and analysis.

The major contribution was by the actual project participants. These remarkable individuals were not viewed as "research subjects" but as "reflective practitioners" (Schon, 1984; as cited in Rost, 1991, p. 185). "Thinking women and men who understand that leadership is more complex than the mythology of leadership would have us believe" (Rost, 1991, p. 185). These reflective thinkers and practitioners know leadership must be viewed from their own perspectives if it is to meet "the wants and needs of the people, organizations, and societies of the twenty-first century" (p. 185). Equally important is that the alternative method for studying leadership allowed the project's participants to "see themselves as doing action research because they are at the center of where the action is, because they are involved in the paradigm shift, because they are agents of transformational change" (p. 186). These gracious participants understood "that there are quite literally no other people who have the perspective on leadership that they have because they are the ones who have been doing postindustrial leadership" (p. 186).

PURPOSE OF THE PROJECT

The purpose of the research was to explore the concept of leadership from the understanding of indigenous people who are knowledgeable and experienced in the leadership process based on traditional ways of knowing. Specifically, a view of leadership was obtained that is based on a more expansive cultural profile of the sources of leadership. The expanded profile provided the necessary contextual framework for exploring the impact of culture on those who lead.

The alternative perspective presented is a contribution to the expansion of the paradigm's boundaries making it more explanatory and inclusive "around more egalitarian themes" (English, 1994, p. 233). A contextual view of leadership developed from authentic stories representing "a variety of times and circumstances" and shaped by culture and its teachings (p. 232). The exploratory research was an attempt to move beyond discussion.

RATIONALE

Joseph Rost (1991), after an exhaustive review of 587 scholarly artifacts, concluded that leadership scholars have placed a great deal of time and effort into understanding the "peripheries of leadership" (p. 3). He identifies these peripheries as elements related to "traits, personality characteristics, 'born or made' issues, greatness, group facilitation, goal attainment, effectiveness, contingencies, situations, goodness, style, and, above all, the management of organizations—public and private" (p. 3). Primarily, Rost contends that the "peripheral elements are, for the most part, visible and countable, susceptible to statistical manipulation, accessible in terms of causality probabilities, and usable to train people in the habits of doing what those in the know may think is the right thing" (p. 3). He believes it is a "feel good" type of research for scholars because the process utilized in theory development conforms "to the best logical positivist framework for research" (p. 3). Rost makes the assumption that these peripheral type researchers failed to consider the significance of understanding more fully the nature of leadership. What seemed to be of most importance to these scholars "was that their research was based on empirical data and that it was done according to the traditional, quantitative methods" (p. 3). Rost believes what has been greatly ignored in leadership research is a focus on "the nature of leadership as a process" (p. 4) and "as a relationship" (p. 5).

The continual practice by scholars of contributing more proclamations than useful research is becoming increasingly perplexing to those practitioners searching for relevant and useful theories. Statements touting "no news may not be good but is still acceptable" are becoming habit forming in our writings. As scholars we rationalize that these kinds of statements are justifiable. It seems that if we are at least publishing about our lack of clarity, this will somehow academically legitimate our lack of action. Like Rost, I too was guilty of adding to the list of scholarly works that were introduced with such statements as "leadership is still a mystery after years of study." But no more—I took Rost seriously when he chided us. Scholars should no longer make "such introductory sentences" and then fail to act on the problem (p. 17). It is his contention that we can no longer "ignore the issue of what leadership is" (p. 17). Rost's suggestion—delve aggressively into the problem.

THEORETICAL FRAMEWORK

James MacGregor Burns, in 1978, approached leadership head-on like no one else before him. His identification of transforming and transactional notions of the leadership process began the redirection of how scholars and practitioners view leadership today. He dared to mention morality and leadership in the same sentence. He discussed socializing influences that contribute to leadership development. Burns described a relationship between leader and follower and differentiated between leaders and power wielders. His analysis of the leadership process was that "Leadership over human beings is exercised when persons with certain motives and purposes, mobilize, in competition or conflict with others, institutional, political, psychological, and other resources so as to arouse, engage, and satisfy the motives of followers" (1978, p. 18). He surmised that the purpose of leadership is to "induce followers to act for certain goals that represent the values and the motivations—the wants and needs, the aspirations and expectations—of both leaders and followers" (p. 19). Burns' critique of leadership research in 1978 was that they lacked a focus on the origins of leadership based on one's social environment. According to Burns, psychological queries have been important in understanding leadership but the psychological approach has also been hazardous based on conclusions "of control or rulership" as interpreted from "studies of animal behavior" (p. 49). Moreover, the psychological approach "has its own biases" (p. 50). One such bias is the commonly held perspective "that the critical influences on the shaping of leaders lie almost wholly in their early years. Another bias is a common reliance on psychoanalysis and psychobiography, "which are inescapably culture-bound. Psychoanalysis is a peculiarly Western invention and practice" (p. 50). Burns purports that the Western practice "follows certain assumptions, perceptions, and methods" that "may ignore or misperceive psychological motives or cultural attitudes—or even vagrant and idiosyncratic behaviors—that could be major sources of influence of leadership in other cultures" (p. 50). Burns attacked the nature of leadership head-on and surmised that the process can best be understood by examining those "basic forces that provide clues to the understanding of sources of leadership" (p. 63). For Burns, the "power lies deep in our origins" (p. 52).

Joseph Jaworski (1996) postulated that "the conventional view of leadership emphasizes positional power and conspicuous accomplishment" (p. 182). In Jaworski's opinion, "true leadership is about creating a domain in which we continually learn and become more capable of participating in our unfolding future" (17). He maintains that participation evolves more from "our being—our total orientation of character and consciousness—than with what we do" (p. 17). Jaworski surmises that "leadership is about creating, day by day, a domain in which we and those around us continually deepen our understanding of reality and are able to participate in shaping the future" (p. 17). Thus, this creation and understanding of our own realities "is the deeper territory of leadership—collectively 'listening' to what is wanting to emerge in the world, and then having the courage to do what is required" (p. 17).

METHODOLOGY

By design, the study was developed to formulate a general understanding of the nature of leadership as perceived by those who participate in some aspect of the leadership process. The findings provide a distinctive point of view from a methodology that by definition is more inclusive and sensitive to lessons of leadership learned from one's own culture.

The early beginnings of how best to proceed began with an investigation to determine what had been done in the past with respect to leadership research. The critique of leadership studies consisted of incremental steps of inquiry, discussion, and presentation of findings at national and international conferences.

How best to explore and gain insight into the nature of leadership was to develop a doctoral research laboratory comprised of students also concerned with expanding the leadership paradigm. A joint effort of faculty and students evolved into an excellent environment for examining and critiquing leadership research. Our focus was finding and discussing leadership studies that addressed the factors of ethnicity, gender, and/or culture even in a limited way. The purpose of the first two years of the laboratory effort was to critique the various research and methodological processes for examining leadership.

The doctoral laboratory's more extensive two-year review and examination of leadership research included: dissertations, ERIC, books, journals, and refereed papers. In our review we were also interested in locating and analyzing any cross-cultural methods utilized in leadership research. These two extensive literature reviews and assessments, coupled with laboratory discussions and the students developing knowledge base in leadership, leadership research, and cross-cultural methodologies proved fundamental in the research design.

THE RESEARCH DESIGN

Based on the review of the literature and laboratory discussions, we surmised that to change this research orientation would require "a critical reflective approach as recommend by Fenwick English (1994). This kind of approach would focus on the integrating of moral characteristics of leadership. However, we would explore moral leadership by using culture as the examination lens. According to English, "moral leadership is rooted in a context of values" that "is centered on people as centers of action, not merely as recipients of action" (p. 231).

Therefore, to obtain insight into these values a biographical approach was decided upon because it can "provide a rich source for understanding context and thereby establishing the meaning of leadership" (English, 1994, p. 232). English maintains that "as a source of data it is certainly not any more flawed than so-called 'scientific' studies of leadership [that] have been shown to be seriously compromised, including the contention that they are or were 'objective' or more rigorous" (p. 232). He further contents that "every study has a point of view. Science is no exception. Biography's point of view is perhaps a little more obvious and honest" (p. 232).

According to Rost, "studies grounded in biography could provide a rich contextual fabric to inform the field about the nature of leadership" (p. 232). Therefore, in our effort to explore "how" culture socializes individuals to perform leadership acts, a case study methodology was chosen as the research tool for obtaining the biographical data. "'How' and 'why' questions," according to Yin (1994), "are likely to favor the use of case studies, experiments, or histories" (p. 7).

A collective case study approach was chosen due to the absence of scholarly leadership theories of an indigenous people's perspective or any well-defined understandings of the leadership process from their interpretation. A researcher "may study a number of cases jointly in order to inquire into the phenomenon, population, or general condition" (Stake, 1994, p. 237). However, this study was not an examination of a collective rather it was an instrumental exploration extended to several cases. An instrumental study is used "to provide insight into an issue" (p. 237). It is important to note that the cases or the individuals interviewed for this project were not the primary interest of the research. They instead played "a supportive role" in "facilitating our understanding" of the nature of leadership (p. 237). The study was not designed to explore common characteristics. In fact, individuals were chosen because it was assumed "that understanding them" would contribute to a more refined understanding about the leadership process (p. 232). It is important to note that the case study approach utilized served as the qualitative explanatory method for obtaining their biographical data. These data were obtained via interviews from first person accounts for the purpose of providing insight into the social processes that might influence leadership for indigenous people. What makes this approach unique is that the project participants were allowed flexibility in the telling of their own stories, although, semi-structured questions were developed and used to guide their narratives so that a more complete cultural exploration of the nature of leadership could emerge.

The project is defined as exploratory in that no empirical research on the topic could be located. Furthermore, the researcher did not know from the conception stage, what the participants' perceptions would reveal. Therefore, the intent of the research was not to refine an existing theory. Rather the research was designed to provide an interpretative explanation of the "multiple realities" of the collective cases as guided by the interview questions developed from a well-researched theoretical framework.

The importance of formulating these guiding interview questions became the focus of the laboratory in the second year of its existence. The laboratory participants and two faculty members served as "experienced investigators" whose tasks included examining "previous research to develop sharper and more insightful questions about the topic" (Yin, 1994, p. 9). The laboratory also served as a tool to reduce any sloppiness of the pilot study investigators and lead researcher in allowing "equivocal evidence or biased views to influence the direction of the findings and conclusions" of the pilot study (p. 9). Another concern about case studies involves the generalizing of findings by qualitative researchers. "Case studies like experiments, are generalizable to theoretical prepositions and not to populations or universes. The finding of this study ". . . does not represent a 'sample,' and the lead investigator's goal was to expand and generalize theories (analytic generalization) and not to enumerate frequencies (statistical generalization)" (p. 10).

As mentioned earlier, a major source in the development of the interview questions was the Burns (1978) study of leadership. Burns suggested that scholars' examination of leadership should "move from the usual 'practical' questions to the most exacting theoretical and moral ones" (p. 4). His suggestion served to guide the laboratory in the development of the interview questions. Accepting his assumption "that leaders are neither 'born' nor 'made,' [we searched] for patterns in the origins and socializing of persons that account for leadership" (p. 4). Open-ended questions with follow-up probes were used as exploration guides for obtaining the perceptions of these indigenous leaders. The questions were designed from a profile developed from the lead researcher using the recommendation of Burns to move to a more "theoretical and moral" framework (p. 4) when examining the learning experiences of a people. The profile was also constructed to expand the socializing factors as identified by Burns to include other vital aspects of culture. The purpose was to include as many culturally socializing factors as possible: including traditional beliefs and practices associated with one's ethnicity and/or community mores and religion and/or spirituality.

The premise of developing questions from a cultural profile or framework is that Burns was correct in his belief that leadership is intertwined in relationships that are influenced by forces emanating from diverse realms of one's origins and socialization. In the quest to examine these cultural influences, questions were developed that would probe the concept of leadership from a distinctive perspective. Specifically, we wanted to explore the origins of leadership as influenced by "motivations" and "values" (p. 4) and identify the "forces that enable leaders to act on the basis of . . . [those] . . . values that, in turn, empower leaders to demonstrate genuine moral leadership" (p. 5). Also borrowed, was Burns' belief that leaders' cultural influences also evolve from lessons learned from their political schooling. The research design is significant in that we added to the scholarship of Burns through our development of questions that would investigate other cultural factors including traditional beliefs and teachings as it relates to one's ethnic community, spirituality and/or religion, or other influences as identified by the participants themselves.

THE SAMPLE PARTICIPANTS

The next step was to identify 20 indigenous individuals knowledgeable of the leadership process either through modeling or service to their communities (in any capacity and as they defined community). They were identified from the literature, an informal inquiry via the world wide web, word-of-mouth, and from leads resulting from a presentation of the project at The World Indigenous Peoples Conference: Education held in Albuquerque, New Mexico. Leads were also obtained from indigenous organizations.

The project sample included 10 women and 10 men who live in the world regions of North America, the Pacific Islands, Central America, New Zealand, and Australia. The project sample was not designed to be regionally representative, consequently, individuals selected were not drawn equally from each of the regions mentioned above. Only two criteria were used for the selection of participants. They were to be connected to their ethnic cultures through beliefs and practice of traditions and considered by others to be role models and/or change agents by those they serve or with the movements they participated in. Some of the participants selected are internationally and nationally known and some are known only in their communities, however, name recognition was not a criterion for selection. The participants worked in various capacities in the leadership process as they addressed social, political, and human rights issues; provided spiritual and religious guidance; influenced others through music and the arts; provided service in positions of leadership in federal and tribal governments; and in all levels of education. Another unique aspect of this leadership study is that the participants' identities were not held in confidence. All agreed to be identified because they believed strongly in the purpose of the study.

ANALYSIS

According to Huberman and Miles (1994), "the design of qualitative studies can in a real sense be seen as analytic" (p. 430). The selecting of a "conceptual framework, of research questions, of samples, of the 'case' definition itself, and of instrumentation all involve anticipatory data reduction—which . . . is an essential aspect of data analysis" (p. 430). The choices to be made "have a focusing and bounding function, ruling out certain variables, relationships, and associated data, and selecting others for attention. They also call for creative work" (pp. 430–431). The extensive preparation that goes into their design make them "not copyable, off-the-shelf patterns . . . [that most often must] . . . be custom-built, revised, and 'choreographed' (Preissle, 1991; as cited in Huberman and Miles, 1994, p. 431). The purpose of this study was "to describe and explain (at some level) a pattern of relationships, which can be done only with a set of conceptually specified analytic categories" (Mishler, 1990; as cited in Huberman and Miles, p. 431). It is quite "legitimate and useful" to get to these analytic categories gradually through inductive reasoning (Huberman and Miles, 1994, p. 431).

The specific method used to get at these analytic categories is referred to as "variable oriented strategies. It is an often used-approach [in] finding themes that cut across cases" (Huberman and Miles, 1994, p. 436). As is true for this study, "often a key variable comes clear only during cross-site analysis" (p. 436). The pattern is identified by Huberman and Miles as "pattern clarification" (p. 436).

FINDINGS

Presentation of the Data

It is important to remind the reader that the research participants were telling stories in most of their responses: stories about their beliefs and experiences. The findings of the study were extracted from these narratives. Throughout the presentation of these data, lengthy quotes by the participants are used to demonstrate a common way of thinking among several individuals. Great meaning can be grasped from these stories so these lengthy quotes were judged to be necessary.

Leadership

What is the nature of leadership? The search for the answer began by asking participants to describe good leadership. However, during the pilot study, it became evident that the pilot participants' responses might possibly be based on an assumption that there was a correct answer and that the goal of the research was to determine if they knew that answer. It was suspected that the descriptions they were providing might be originating from their formal mainstream schooling rather than from their own beliefs influenced by other sources but not excluding formal schooling. As a result, it was decided after the ninth pilot interview, to revise the interview schedule by adding an introductory question, "Do you have the word leadership or leader in your language?" This set the frame of reference for the interviews as it served to cue the participants that we were seeking a cultural perspective based on their own socializing influences and teachings.

Sixteen of the 20 participants answered no to having the term leader or leadership in their languages. However, most could think of a descriptive word or words or a generic term that could be used in reference. These translations were based on their view of the western definition of a leader. Some of these include spokesperson, boss, one out in front, a person in

front of all of us, and chief. Another participant, an Ojibwe from Michigan, also mentioned the term chief but clarified that it was a translation from a western perspective, and "has been influenced greatly from its original meaning." His goal is to get the tribe to eliminate the use of the western word chief because it is not in accordance to their original way. According to this participant, "the chief client system organization [was] created by another government [imposed] under a constitution" which reflects an organizational structure different from his people. An Australian Aborigine, made the point that "one out in front" is not the same concept as reflected in their traditional law. According to her beliefs, leadership is "a number of people taking responsibility." This was reiterated again by an Alaskan Athabaskan participant, she described how in her native village it was the people that recognized the person they looked up to or depended on, and this person was placed in a special role. She also emphasized that "the individual would never place themselves in a role of authority."

Most participants mentioned that historically and in many cases today the elders of the community appoint or place individuals in special leadership roles based on their wisdom and natural or acquired skills. In a couple of cases, where individuals were elected to a position, they still follow the traditional system of seeking guidance from elders before deciding to seek election.

The four that answered "yes" to the introductory question also indicated that the term in their language was not directly transferable to English but mentioned they had similar terms. However, it is important to note that the terms these individuals mentioned were translated based on their cultural perspective of leadership and not their perceived view of western leadership thought. The terms they mentioned are highlighted in bold and are followed by their interpretative meanings. They include **special advisor**: one that knows traditional laws; **concept of self-determination**: one who nurtures/this reference often given to a parent or teacher; **reverence**: this person suggests ways of going; and control over choices one makes on the journey of life: if one practices the intent behind the meaning of this interpretation one would be a good role model to others.

Once the introductory question was changed so was the follow-up question. "Based on your cultural understanding of leadership, describe a good leader." All of the descriptive responses are classified into three categories. The categories are numbered for reference only and are not utilized for ranking purposes. The descriptors follow each category as shown in Table 1.

All the participants' perceptions of good leadership evolved from seeing it, living it, and valuing the responsibilities. To put it simply, it is their culture (family, spirituality and/or religion, community mores, tribal laws/teachings and values) that has imprinted their perceptions of leadership. As one Australian Aboriginal elder explained, "simply because you were educated at a university does not make you a leader." This way of thinking was consistent in many of the responses. For example, an Athabaskan from Alaska, indicated you must go through a period of time of learning. It's not something you purchase—it is not a career. It's not something you planned. People have to see it as a fit for you. You just do it as long as it works and then you move on. There is no guarantee that it will always be yours.

Fifteen of those 20 interviewed for this project chose not to self-identify as a leader. Two participants

Table 1. Descriptive Responses Describing a Good Leader

Having a Commitment to the Common Good

Collective Leadership for the Good of the Community
Providing for the Community
A Servant to the People
Responsible for Social Functions and Has Responsibility for Maintaining Community
One That Has a Commitment to the Community

Knowing How to Communicate and Connect with Your People

Being an Idea Generator
One Who Knows How to Reach Consensus and Solidarity
Active Listener
Intuitive of Concerns and Needs
Walks the Talk
Exhibits Compassion

Knowing, Respecting, and Following Tribal Laws, Teachings, and Values

Caring
Sharing
Seeks Out Leaders Not Followers
Respect for Elders
Receives Counsel from Elders
Respects and Stays Connected to Nature and the Land
Respects and Follows the Teachings of the One's Ancestors
Exhibits Humility
No Self-Promotion
One Who Forgives, Teaches, and Learns from One's People
Acknowledges the Creator and Stay's Spiritually Connected
Exhibits Selflessness, Honesty, and Respects the Family/Clan Structure

from two different parts of the world provide responses that can best explain why these individuals chose not to self-identify. One participant remarked:

That's always a very hard question for me to answer because I feel it's a question coming from the western world, and my natural instinct would be to say no. However, I feel very blessed that a lot of people have turned to me for guidance.

Another believes

that communities or the people will let you know. You cannot advocate for yourself, even if you are well meaning. I don't know if I'll ever know that. I don't think a real Indian leader ever knows that.

Those five who did identify as a leader clarified their answers. For example, a Hawaiian native considers himself

to be a leader in the sense that I work with people in the way I have just described. But really in some sense everybody in our group is a leader because . . . [of their] . . . commitment to the work that we do. I think then that everybody has a contribution to make that allows us to reach our goals bit by bit.

In fact, all of the clarifications to those who answered yes were similar. A chief of a major tribe responded, "Yes, I consider myself to be a leader and not that I chose to be but in that the people chose me to be their leader." An Okanagon native from British Columbia, proudly answered "Sure I am. It's a natural part of my upbringing and a natural part of my commitment/responsibility to my community." Another participant replied "yes" and provided the following explanation. "I do, only because people have honored me with that description. . . . I recognize it as a function that I have in my community and I'll do it as long as it's what the people would like me to do."

When asked how they came to serve or what path they took to be recognized as a leader, all of the responses could be placed into one interpretation. Many spoke of their responsibility for developing their own gifts and when asked to serve by the elders or by others in their communities they did. An aboriginal native from Australia, explained how this is different from the western path. It was his perception that in the western world a person is ready to lead based more on "what you have been able to achieve in a career and what you've been able to produce to-date in terms of what quality you've been able to show and also implement."

For him, it was his role in community achievements that made people take notice and place him in his position of leadership.

Participants were asked to respond to the following quote, "Leaders are born not made." The question was not asked for the purpose of reputing or continuing the scholarly argument, rather it was asked for the purpose of delving more deeply into their perceptions surrounding leadership development. The majority of the participants believe it is both. An answer that exemplified many of their responses was made by a member of the Pueblo de Cochiti located in New Mexico. He believes "that while there are leaders who are already born, we also have leaders who have become leaders because of who they are—who are not appointed or designated at the time that they were born." A Quiche Indian from Guatemala and a Nobel Peace Prize recipient, responded that she did not know but thought it might be true. She explained, "Our grandparents always said, 'there are explicable things and there are inexplicable things.' Every one of our lives is accompanied by a mystery and that mystery is interpretation. Maybe that is a part of our lives." Another participant commented she thought there was "a lot of truth in that." In their traditional beliefs, "spiritual connections are inherited . . . goes through a family line."

When asked their likes about leading, most indicated it was the social responsibility that was fulfilling, the trust, and challenges involved with enacting change for one's people. The dislikes of leading centered on the politics that has emerged because of western influences. The influence "creates conflict in the community. It creates a complacency in people. A democratic system seems to say if you put an X on a piece of paper it absolves you of your responsibility." Another participant agrees that it is painful to have a divided community, but believes it is a leader's "responsibility to remind others in the way that we should conduct ourselves. Because that was a gift that was given to us by our grandfathers and grandmothers."

The next profile question exploring leadership as a concept dealt with the use of power. The participants were asked simply "how do you get what you want?" The majority of the participants mentioned they follow their traditional laws and values in bringing people together for the good of the community. A few responded that it was okay to ask for something only if guidance was received.

Another question was added to the last draft of the interview schedule for the purpose of obtaining more information about the sources of their cultural influences. Specifically, they were asked about their leadership teachers. Most mentioned their family, and many recognized the strength and the beauty of their matriarchal societies. Other responses included: nature, other indigenous leaders, elders, and good people.

TRADITIONAL BELIEFS/TRADITIONS

We wanted to know about the socializing influences resulting from the beliefs taught and practiced by ethnic communities and how significant the impact is in developing leadership among members of those communities. Therefore, inquiries were made about the most significant traditions they continue to celebrate in their family (as they defined family) and in their community (also as they defined community). Their interpretation of these concepts was essential, as we did not want to bias their responses with our own assumptions. It is important to note that the participants were informed in writing and verbally that the project would be respectful of secrecy obligations and that intent of the research was not to invade or extract information about these private teachings or practices.

Each described one or a few of their traditions as well as the importance each plays in their lives. However, in some cases, these traditions were not described in detail due to secrecy obligations. What emerged from their responses is that their cultural beliefs and ceremonies have as a primary purpose to teach, maintain, and show remembrance. These ceremonies deal with: the importance of community, respecting one's ancestors, spiritual and physical healings, the historical struggles, spiritual laws, the connection to and respect for nature, and rites of passage. It is evident from their responses that their cultural beliefs and traditions play a vital role in defining who they are today. One participant explained that his

community has a system or has many systems in place that basically tell us how we should conduct ourselves so that from the beginning of the year when new officers are appointed to positions, they understand very clearly that they have to continue certain traditions throughout the year—so our people have this calendar in place, an annual calendar, and it's the responsibility of our elders, our leaders, to insure that those traditions continue. And so the context in which we grew up says to us that we're going to be servant leaders. We're going to practice servant leadership and so leadership for me on an individual level means that I help to continue those traditions and the way in which I help to continue those traditions is to be there as a dancer, as a singer, and sometimes as a facilitator in the way that we may conduct our meetings. And it's always about recognizing the interconnectedness of all of life—and we're always taught that especially in the dialogue that whatever we have to say doesn't come from here but from one's heart.

Many of the societies represented by the participants have been influenced by assimilation policies and missionaries who introduced western beliefs and their accompanying ceremonies. However, only a few mentioned that these western ceremonies have become a part of their every day lives. The impact of assimilation has become a challenge for one Hawaiian participant. He has put his efforts in revitalizing the language and culture of his people.

We also inquired about possible conflicts between their cultural beliefs and how they choose to lead. If there were cultural conflicts, we wanted to learn how they dealt with these dilemmas. Fifteen of the 20 mentioned there were occasional conflicts in their communities and attributed the source of these conflicts to western influences that were either legislated or culturally brought in. Others reported that they only experienced conflicts when they were outside their communities working with western style organizations. Five participants have been lucky and report no conflicts to-date.

One additional question, in this section of the cultural profile, dealt with the environment. We knew from our pilot studies that nature was an important connection to indigenous people. Therefore, the question was designed to inquire into the lessons they have learned from nature and the world around them. The majority mentioned natural law throughout their responses and all remarked similarly with respect to every action having a consequence. This is why they believe so strongly in their interconnectedness with all living things. This way of viewing the world was explained through the Okanagan traditional teachings as told by a native.

> One of the real things that our people are clear on is our traditional laws and stories. . . . Our social order comes from how the natural world is understood by our people. . . . My growing up really depended on understanding how the world works from that view and then actually seeing it take place in terms of how the world actually does operate. So if I look around me all the things that surround me in my natural world are what gave us those laws or those teachings or those understandings in terms of interaction, as

well as our own interaction with them on a real world level. It's really clear to me that the environment is what dictates our social order and our laws and it's the natural world which creates for us a clear understanding of how we as Okanagans must operate on this land.

TRUTHS/VALUES—FAMILY/INDIVIDUAL

The questions emerging from this portion of the cultural profile were developed to determine the significant values these individuals continue to live by. In addition, we were curious how they confirmed these truths and values for themselves. Again, responses were directly related to following the traditional laws that personify the values they and their communities are obligated to follow. These values, if confirmed on a daily basis, bring cohesiveness to their way of life. It is their belief that values must be respected for the structure and guidance they provide. The value difference of a natural view and the western view was explained by a participant in this way:

> Somehow we need to recognize the humanness of all people and that we are all interrelated in life and that no group of people is better than another group. And that's probably very foreign to the western thought because I think that in western civilization, it's always been about conquest and I think that perhaps part of the reason is that they have really in many ways lost a sense of connection to our spiritual world and when I say the spiritual world, I mean the world of our grandfathers and our grandmothers. I don't know what else I could say, but it seems like leadership in the larger society is perceived as a situation where people either win or they lose and for our people it's not that, it's more about how you bring unity to the community.

SPIRITUALITY/RELIGION

Burns (1978) maintains that those who choose to function as leaders will do so because "of long and complex processes–psychological, social, and political" (p. 89). It was the researcher's predisposition that spirituality and/or religion were not processes that could fall easily into the processes mentioned by Burns. Therefore, it was deemed important to expand the cultural profile to include their interpretation of the influences spirituality and/or religion have had in their lives with respect to leadership.

The influence of religion (positive or negative) on these Indigenous participants was clear in most responses. Ten of the 20 chose to identify more from their spiritually part of their being. Spirituality in their view allowed them the freedom to be human and to individually interpret a way of living from their own sources of learning. A Maori native from New Zealand, emphatically stated that "spirituality allows you to express things in your way . . . religion is the controlled ethics of spirituality."

Nine of the 20 believe they are both religious and spiritual. They feel comfortable living life from a spiritual sense of who they are and in most of the cases participating actively in the organized religions introduced to their people by missionaries. According to an Alaskan native, he is influenced by both as both the spiritual aspects of traditional teachings and the Christian faith are connected closely to the values of his people. He indicated that approximately 90 percent of the tribal elders were strong in their Christian faith.

Only one participant defined "religion" as traditional ways of knowing. In her interpretation of the English word religion, it is a practice whereby "rituals" and "ceremonies" are conduced in a certain way to reflect the philosophies and beliefs of their traditional teachings. She is strongly connected to her traditional beliefs and their responsibilities and consequently her decision making is highly influenced. According to their traditions, "important decisions cannot be made without first taking it either to the sweat or to the long house, to our winter dance, or to have the pipe ceremony around it." Individuals facing personal dilemmas are instructed to go on a personal fast, the purpose of which is to seek clarification and guidance from a place inside of them where they know what they are doing is "right" in a spiritual sense. "Right" meaning that they have approached the issue from their four individual responsibilities (physically, mentally, emotionally, and spiritually). If clarity is not sought, one can easily take "the wrong fork in the road."

POLITICAL SCHOOLING/FORMAL AND INFORMAL

"The child's society is found in the home, the village road or the front stoop, the schoolroom or the city playground. But in recent decades, in most cultures, formal schooling has come to be seen as central in shaping political attitudes and behavior" (Burns, 1978, p. 85). Burns follows this point with an excellent clarifying statement that formal schooling can be greatly influential depending

> on the child, the school, and aspects of the school and the culture involved: the class and caste heterogeneity

of the student bodies, the curricula and school quality, and on the extent of the authority of these schools as agencies of national values, or of regional or community mores, and of religious doctrine. (1978, p. 85)

Therefore, to determine the shaping of political attitudes three questions were developed. "Are you politically involved?" was asked with a follow-up probe of "define politically involved." The researcher was aware of the general histories of most of the populations involved in the project and knew that many of the indigenous people worldwide have been exposed to western educational influences such as missionary, parochial, and federal boarding schools as well as colonizing legislation and military actions. It is also common knowledge that many indigenous people work or have worked for government agencies on behalf of their people. Therefore, it was important that we learn about the influences these institutions or organizations have had on their political agendas or beliefs. The closing request for completing this part of the profile was to ask them to describe other political influences other than institutional and what the nature of those influences were in developing or shaping their political views.

The majority (16 of 20) responded that they are politically involved and most believe they have to be. For many, being politically involved is a necessity for the survival of their people. For those individuals politically involvement means "serving through preserving" the interests of your own people from those who might seek to take advantage. Most mentioned that it was important to empower their people to move from the observer role to that of a more active participant. Politics can be a dirty process if one negotiates at the level of those without the best interest of the community at heart. Most believe there is a responsibility to inform and to speak one's mind on behalf of one's people. However, the responsibility must be accepted and demonstrated in "a good way" based on traditional teachings. This way of thinking is reflected in a participant's attitude toward empowerment. According to her, politics is a way

> to seek out as many people and empower them in terms of their thinking, their contribution, and their desire and need. I think that part for me is what my explanation of traditional leadership is and so of course I am involved in that and, of course, I think that is a political act. I don't think that you can sit back and just wait for everything to happen and let the chips fall where they may, if you are a responsible

person. . . . I think the word politics has taken on a dirty meaning because of the manipulative kind of dictatorial process which disempowers people. . . . We have to be totally involved in that negotiated process continuously or we have problems in our community. It's when people are not involved they abdicate that responsibility . . . that allows dictatorships to take over.

Only four participants answered "no" to being politically involved. One was disenchanted, after years of national and international political activity, primarily due to the unfair process of federal government negotiations. Two participants believed they were more political observers in their current leadership roles but believed they are professionally involved in many aspects that impact their people. The last respondent to answer with a no response believes she does not have the time to be politically involved due to her present work demands. It is important to note that she defined politically involved as serving in a political position.

ADDITIONAL COMMENTS

Finally, an opportunity was presented to the participants to speak about anything they wished to elaborate on or clarify. They were also requested to comment on issues that were perhaps on their minds but were not asked about. This proved to be most valuable in obtaining additional rich data and clarifying previous responses. It also provided a nice closure to a remarkable experience. Two such closing remarks dealt with the challenges of leadership education. One Australian Aborigine commented that

> this whole new age stuff to try to become indigenous is sad. Because if you want to find your way we will try to help you but it must be on our terms and our control. Not them trying to dominate and take what's left. That's the only thing that's left—our minds and our hearts. They've taken our land, they've taken our lives. We have to get our children to understand the things we have left. We can rebuild into our new life. You can become a modern indigenous person.

An Athabaskan native from Alaska, provided important insight while also sharing his hopes about leadership in the forth coming years. He remarked that many documents that you read today deal with leaders and leadership. He mentioned that it seems to be so "in vogue now to be a good leader." To him it seems like

> you've got to have a MBA at Harvard or some of the business schools. Maybe I am an old relic. I don't

know, but I am proud of the fact that I came out of a cultural environment. I came out of a family environment. I came out of a native environment that I still hold very dear. And some of the principles and some of the things that I have learned here I still apply today and I believe there are strengths in those beliefs and those practices—and in those demands that come from the native community and from the practices of our elders. . . . I am not saying that everything that comes out of management schools is bad. . . . I mean there is a place for that. But one of the difficulties with that type of education is it changes so often. . . . They have new theories coming out all the time. Many of the good strong beliefs that have evolved from the native perspective over a long period of time are going to be here for a long, long time. And I think we [must] recognize that it gives you more inner peace and the ability to deal with some pretty difficult issues in a way that brings compassion, understanding, and leadership through it. I really believe that. I am convinced of that. If there is one message it is that cultural learning, tradition, beliefs are very important in leading organizations.

SUMMARY OF THE PROJECT'S FINDINGS

Naturalistic Leadership

The concept of leadership from an indigenous people's perspective is identified as naturalistic leadership. It is identified as naturalistic because of the association made with the phenomenological form of inquiry identified as "naturalistic inquiry." Thomas Schwandt (1994) explains that Lincoln and Guba's work with "constructivism" was initially described as "naturalistic inquiry" (1985; as cited in Schwandt, p. 128). According to Schwandt, the "constructivist, interpretive, naturalistic, and hermeneutical [inquiries] are all similar notions" (p. 128). Primarily, "their particular meanings are shaped by the intent of their users. As general descriptors for . . . sensitizing concepts" (Blumer, 1954; as cited in Schwandt, 1994, p. 118). As a researcher, I am a proponent of this persuasion. In that I "share the goal of understanding the complex world of lived experience from the point of view of those who live it" (Schwandt, p. 118). I made it clear throughout this article that my desire for conducting the research was based on a "concern" to understand the "meaning" from the perspectives of those who live their own "reality" (p. 118). Clearly, the naturalistic researcher's goal embodies the nature of leadership as described in this study. Namely, these individuals observe and learn from their own "realities" which includes the world around them. For that reason, it seemed befitting to identify the leadership "realities" they described as naturalistic leadership.

The Process of Leadership

Leadership for indigenous people is not viewed as an option, therefore, it is not situational or conditional. It is a way of living that is demonstrated in the process of acknowledging and developing relationships—human and otherwise. If a definition can clarify descriptive explanations then the following definition is provided. Naturalistic leadership requires a clear understanding of the importance of traditional ways of knowing, established from the social order of the natural world. The servant role must be appreciated, respected, and accepted if the social responsibilities that are necessary for living in a collective society are to occur.

There are clear understandings that emerged from this research with respect to the nature of leadership as perceived by the research participants. There are few similarities between the perceptions of the western view of leadership and the indigenous people's ways of knowing. In their view it is not in good standing with traditional teachings to promote oneself as a leader. If one is to lead in a good way they must seek out and learn from those teachings that are available from the world around them. Learning is deemed essential in developing a clearer understanding of the obligations required for preserving a cultural way of life. Once an understanding is developed the learning process for how best to live in community cannot stop—it must be continuous. The personal commitment for contributing to the preserving of community is not optional but integral in the natural order for continuing human life.

Also important is the tenet that all community members must model the teachings of their culture. Communal leadership implies a collective responsibility in that all members of the community are expected to perform social leadership acts if they are to remain in good standing with traditional teachings. It is feared that if these teachings are forgotten or influenced too strongly from other cultures the unity among their community members will see increases in generational conflict and political strife. Moreover, the social responsibility of servant leadership could also be eroded and the coexistence between natural law and their own spiritual connectiveness might result in upsetting the equilibrium of both living structures.

IMPLICATIONS

The study was an attempt to move beyond mere discussion of the need to expand the leadership para-digm. Perhaps the alternative model presented will facilitate further research to refine the naturalistic leadership concept and analyze new ways of viewing leadership development and organizational structure to better serve all organizations and their members.

The major inference drawn from this study is that indigenous people's ways of viewing leadership evolves from knowing that nature is interconnected for a reason—survival. Naturalistic leadership, for them, is based on the importance of this interconnection. Leadership self-promotion is not necessary in a naturalistic leadership model. Conversely, placing community first is quite essential. The answers for how best to serve one's community can be found in the traditional teachings of our grandfathers and grandmothers, as drawn from the lessons learned from a well-designed system known as nature. A return to the strict adherence to traditional beliefs is not the implication or the recommendation of this study. Rather, what is called for is a deeper appreciation of the power generated by such teachings and a clearer understanding of these ways of knowing. Equally important is the necessary next step of exploring the boundaries of applicability for leadership development, leadership education, tribal governance, and organizational restructuring, specifically public, federal, and tribal schools. The answers we seek and the power to make a difference can be found among us if *we* begin the dialogue.

Taiaiake Alfred, author of *Peace, Power, Righteousness: An Indigenous Manifesto*, believes that "indigenous people have made significant strides towards reconstructing their identities as autonomous individual, collective, and social beings" (1999, p. 2). He emphatically maintains that "politics matters: the imposition of Western governance structures and the denial of indigenous ones continue to have profoundly harmful effects on indigenous people" (p. 2). What western societies need to grasp is that "land, culture, and government are inseparable in traditional philosophies; each depends on the others, and this means that denial of one aspect precludes recovery for the whole" (p. 2). The implication is that "without a value system that takes traditional teachings as the basis for government and politics, the recovery will never be complete" (p. 2).

What are the implications of the findings of this study on leadership education? Burns in 1978 asked the question "Can leadership be taught?" (p. 448). He surmised that leadership and education are vitally linked and should be viewed as a relationship. In his view, education should be viewed as a totality of experiences learned from the environment that surrounds us all. According to Burns, "education is not merely the shaping of values, the imparting of 'facts' or the teaching of skills, indispensable though these are; it is the total teaching and learning process operating in homes, schools, etc." (p. 448). All of these experiences are included in a reciprocal learning relationship between "both teachers and learners, engaging with the total environment, and involving influence over persons' selves and their opportunities and destinies, not simply their minds" (p. 448).

The "search for wholeness" should be the aim of leadership education. Burns purports that "leaders must be whole persons, persons with fully functioning capacities for thinking and feeling" (pp. 448–449). Finally, Burns describes the implication for education on the teaching of leadership. He believes it should be a joint venture in the seeking "of truth and mutual actualization" of both the teacher and learner. For indigenous people, the "search for wholeness" is part of the cycle of living human life. Indigenous people are taught to seek out the truth of their own realities for the betterment of their own communities and to increase good relations with all living things. The values and teachings of traditional beliefs prepare their members to care, share, think, feel, and act on behalf of the common good for those who are in relationships with them, human or not.

CONCLUSIONS

The nature of leadership as described by these indigenous leaders is significant and most powerful and must be examined more fully. The research was critically essential in answering the question: Where do these indigenous servants of leadership derive their ways of knowing?

The indigenous cultures, as described by the study participants, depict the development of leadership as a lifetime process through teachings and experiences that clarify the importance of traditional teachings. Again, the importance they place on building values over a lifetime confirms the ideal principles of learning about leadership being touted by others. Kunich and Lester (1997) are convinced "all leaders should study the great foundational works of their nation to learn of the struggles of prior generations, ponder them, make them a part of their being, determine how they apply to the situation at hand, and then transmit key principles to followers" (p. 13). It is their belief that "if values are thought to be only relative, if

there is no right or wrong, if one system of government is morally equivalent to all others, then there is nothing worth sacrificing for" (p. 13). And when values are only relative and not core to a community's existence, "the leader will be limited to appeals to local pride and self-interest in attempting to inspire excellence. The result will often be half-hearted effort—and failure" (p. 13).

As mentioned previously in the findings section, the leadership process for indigenous people is a relational concept. The structure of the natural order of the universe provides insight on how to act in a good way for the purpose of maintaining a relational balance. The findings indicate that the traditional values motivating the action is the most important aspect of their leadership—less important are the acts of leadership and those who perform them. These findings validate the contention made by Burns (1998) that scholars who use the key variables of the "'situation' or the 'context'" are coping out intellectually and analytically (p. 15). According to Burns, "the situation consists mainly of human beings with which our web interrelates—other leadership collectives . . . [and] . . . even in the event of sudden anticipated events . . . it is how people react to those events, not simply the events themselves, that affect the course of history" (p. 15). This might explain how many indigenous groups have survived countless attempts of assimilation policies and even termination efforts by their colonizers. It can also explain how the traditional view of following natural laws has sustained their existence in the very harsh environments in which most reside.

REFERENCES

Alfred, T. (1999). *Peace, power, righteousness: An indigenous manifesto.* Don Mills, Ontario: Oxford University Press.

Bolman, L. G., and Deal, T. E. (1995). Leading with Soul. San Francisco: Jossey-Bass Publishers.

Burns, J. M. (1978). *Leadership.* New York: Harper Colophon.

Burns, J. M. (1998). *Empowerment for change: Rethinking leadership.* College Park: Burns Academy of Leadership Press.

English, F. W. (1994). *Theory in educational administration.* New York: Harper Collins.

Gardner, H. (1995). *Leading Minds: An Anatomy of Leadership.* New York: BasicBooks.

Huberman, A. M., and Miles, M. B. (1994). Data management and analysis methods. In N. K. Denzin and Y. S. Lincoln, *Handbook of qualitative research* (pp. 428–444). Thousand Oaks, CA: Sage Publications, Inc.

Jaworski, J. (1996). *Synchronicity: The inner path of leadership*. San Francisco: Berrett-Koehler Publishers.

Kunich, J., and Lester, R. (1997). Profile of a leader: The Wallenberg effect. *The Journal of Leadership Studies, 4*(3), 6–19.

Rost, J. C. (1991). *Leadership for the Twenty-First Century*. Westport, CT: Praeger.

Schwandt, T. A. (1994). Constructivist, interpretivist approaches to human inquiry. In N. K. Denzin and Y. S. Lincoln, *Handbook of qualitative research* (pp. 118–137). Thousand Oaks, CA: Sage Publications, Inc.

Stake, R. E. (1994). Case studies. In N. K. Denzin and Y. S. Lincoln, *Handbook of qualitative research* (pp. 236–247). Thousand Oaks, CA: Sage Publications, Inc.

Wheatly, M. (1992). *Leadership and the new science: Learning about organization from an orderly universe*. San Francisco: Berrett-Koehler Publishers, Inc.

Yin, R. K. (1994). *Case study research: Design and methods*. Thousand Oaks, CA: SAGE Publications, Inc.

The Revival of Interpersonal Skills: Implications for School Leadership

JAMES MCDOWELLE

A RENEWED AND BURGEONING INTEREST IN INTERPERSONAL skills is evident in even a cursory review of current leadership literature (Fernandez-Araoz, 2001; Fleenor, 2003; Goleman, Boyatzis and McKee, 2002; Hernez-Broom and Hughes, 2004; McCauley, 2004; McDowelle and Buckner, 2002; Mumford, Zaccaro, Harding, Jacobs and Fleishman, 2000; Nahavandi, 2003; Northhouse, 2004; Sousa, 2003; Wong and Law, 2003; Zaccaro, Kemp, and Bader, 2004). A growing number of leadership theorists and researchers are asserting the importance of interpersonal skills such as communication, motivation, persuasion, conflict resolution and team-building in the exercise of leadership. Interpersonal skills are also called people skills, social skills, or in certain contexts, soft skills. Whatever the terminology, these skills are defined by the ability to interact effectively with followers or constituents and to influence followers and constituents toward the achievement of organizational goals and objectives.

The resurrection of interpersonal skills is particularly noteworthy because after a period of intense fascination with interpersonal skills in the 1960's and early 1970's interest waned and this aspect of leadership came to be referred to as "touch-feely." The term touchy-feely was meant to convey the belief that the use of interpersonal skills were based upon subjective feelings that could not be empirically verified and therefore lacked scientific authority (more on the issue of scientific authority and interpersonal skills later in this paper). The recent renascence of enthusiasm for interpersonal skills can be attributed to several factors:

1. Trends in leadership are cyclical but the emphasis always falls on either tasks or relationships. At some point in the cycle the emphasis will be on the skills required to accomplish the task, so called *hard skills*, e.g., budgeting, planning and organization. At some other point in the cycle, the emphasis will be on the skills necessary to nurture relationships, so called *soft skills*, e.g., the ability to empathize, develop trust, and listen actively. At the current time we are at a point in the cycle in which the emphasis is on soft or interpersonal skills. (Hernez-Broom and Hughes, 2004).

2. The current emphasis on soft skills can be explained because during periods of difficulty and change, followers and constituents of leaders become anxious and need the reassurance of effective interpersonal skills to help alleviate anxiety and maintain focus in the face of distractions (Fleenor, 2003). We are now in a period of change and difficulty in many areas of leadership.

3. Much of the focus on interpersonal and people skills has been generated by leadership literature that scrutinizes the causes for leadership failure. Many of those studies have cited a lack of interpersonal or people skills as the primary reason for ineffective leadership (Leslie and Van Elson, 1996; McCauley, 2004; Nahavandi, 2003; Nelton, 1997).

    "Lack of people skills and the inability to manage relationships are central issues [in leadership failure]. Leaders who are good with followers and other constituencies have a better chance of success" (Nahavandi, 2003, p. 79).

4. Emerging research in cognitive neuroscience and human behavior is allowing both practitioners and researchers to apply interpersonal skills with greater precision and effectiveness (Goleman, Boyatzis and McKee, 2002; Wong and Law, 2003). Some of this research involves the role of the emotions in decision making and leadership and can be subsumed under the heading of emotional intelligence. As mentioned earlier, previous literature on interpersonal skills was said to be subjective and lack scientific authority. Since much of the research on the emotions is based on brain imaging studies and other neurological inquiries it provides the area of interpersonal skills with a scientific aspect lacking when interpersonal skills were in vogue in the 1960's and 70's.

RESOLVING CONFLICTS WITH THE FUNDAMENTAL ATTRIBUTION ERROR

The area of conflict resolution provides an excellent illustration of how new research in human behavior is enhancing the application of interpersonal skills. Traditional leadership literature attributes conflicts to poor communication. This assertion is contradicted by emerging research in human behavior and conflict. Recent research cites structural relationships or personal differences as the cause of most conflicts. (Robbins, 2002). For example, almost every year in some school district a conflict arises between the director of finance and a principal. The conflict occurs when the director of finance declares that all school funds must be spent or encumbered in early spring. The principal then contends this directive is unreasonable because forcing the expenditure of funds so early in the school year is harmful to the instructional program. The director of finance contends that this action is necessary to ensure proper accounting practices. This conflict is not the result of poor communication but the structural relationships of the two protagonists.

Both structural relationship and personal difference conflicts are exacerbated by a behavioral phenomenon called the *fundamental attribution error* (Alred, 2000). The fundamental attribution error means that when we view our own behavior, we tend to attribute outside influences to what we do. On the other hand, when we view others' behavior we tend to attribute that behavior to character or character flaws. If we are late for a meeting with a significant other, we attribute that tardiness to traffic or pressing business (an external influence). The significant other will attribute our being late to a deficit in character that causes us to care more about what we are doing than keeping someone waiting. While resolving disputes, it is often helpful to discuss the fundamental attribution error and how it affects the way we view others' behavior. Although there are intellectual issues to be dealt with in every dispute, the emotions must be addressed before cognitive issues can be explored in any conflict. Both parties to the dispute need to fully express both the emotional and cognitive sides of their dispute while working toward a solution. Once the emotional issues have been analyzed and discussed then the conflict mediator can begin to structure solutions. Working with emotional issues lays a foundation in which both sides understand the others' position and take this position into account as they attempt to fashion a mutually acceptable solution.

IMPLICATIONS FOR SCHOOL LEADERSHIP

The need for interpersonal skills in the arena of school leadership has become prominent as the realization grows that school leadership takes place in an extremely people intensive environment (Goldring and Greenfield, 2002; McDowelle and Buckner, 2002). In fact Goldring and Greenfield (2002) contend that schools are one of the most intensive people environments in which leadership can be exercised. Aside from the field of Medicine, no other venue for leadership involves more interaction with fellow human beings. School leaders work with and through people (e.g., teachers, aides, counselors, and other administrators) with raw materials composed of people (students) and a final product consisting of people (graduating students). In addition, school leaders work closely with important constituents such as parents and government officials. This people intensive environment demands the application of highly effective people skills.

DEVELOPING INTERPERSONAL SKILLS

Business and industry have begun to stress the importance of interpersonal skills and are making a major investment in interpersonal skills development (Goleman, 1998; Nahavandi, 2003; Spenser, McClelland, and Kleiner, 1997; Sweeney, 1999). For example, General Electric Company spends approximately one billion dollars a year developing the social and emotional competencies that comprise interpersonal skills. L'Oreal has conducted research that indicates personnel with well-developed emotional competencies and interpersonal skills are more successful than those with less well-developed emotional and interpersonal skills. As a result of this research, L'Oreal has also devoted considerable resources to interpersonal competency development. American Express and the United States Air Force have also made a major investment in emotional competency and interpersonal skills training.

At least one state has recognized the necessity of interpersonal skills for school leaders. In Maine, the state's teacher and administrator associations, business leaders, and university systems collaborated to create an innovative leadership program for teacher leaders and principals. The program is called the Maine School Leadership Network (MSLN) and envisions three central dimensions of leadership knowledge as represented in the Leadership Development Plan Portfolio. The three dimensions are (a) cognitive aspects of leadership in schools, (b) interpersonal skills, and (c) intrapersonal skills. Early reports on the

MSLN have been positive (Donaldson, Bowe, MacKenzie and Marnik, 2004).

Although there has been little research conducted on the need for interpersonal skills training in Educational Leadership Preparation Programs (ELPP), research on other aspects of ELPP indicates that some interpersonal skills training is desired by experienced school leaders who are studying to enhance their skills. Pierce and Borden (2003) conducted research at the Principal's Center at Harvard University. Attending the Center were principals from rural, urban and suburban school districts across the country. Among the findings of the study were that 76 percent of the respondents believed conflict resolution to be highly relevant or relevant to the responsibilities of the principal but only 51 percent believed that information on conflict resolution had been well or adequately delivered in their ELPP. In contrast only 54 percent of the respondents in the study found the finance content they received in their preparation programs to be highly relevant or relevant.

Cherniss (2000) reports the most effective training models for developing interpersonal skills include the following components: (a) modeling, (b) role playing, (c) practice, (d) reinforcement, and (e) feedback. The implementation of this model, though proven to be effective, is time consuming and demanding for those conducting interpersonal skills training. Using this particular model could be particularly onerous in the context of current ELPP because of time constraints and the expertise required by those providing the training.

A KEY INTERPERSONAL SKILL: ACTIVE LISTENING SKILLS

Active listening provides a base for the use of other interpersonal skills. Communication between leaders and constituents is often delicate. Constituents sometimes find it difficult to be open about their concerns. They do not wish to be labeled complainers or malcontents. Communication is especially tentative early in a relationship. On this occasion, it is important for the leader to listen actively and watch for emotional cues in order to detect messages that are just below the surface of the verbal communication. Attentive listening also demonstrates concern and respect. Robbins and Hunsaker (1996) list eight behaviors that constitute active listening: (a) making eye contact; (b) making affirmative head nods and appropriate facial expressions; (c) avoiding distracting gestures; (d) asking questions; (e) paraphrasing; (f) avoiding interruptions; (g) avoiding over talking; and (h) making smooth transitions between the roles of speaker and listener. Listening is also key to the interpersonal skills of persuasion and motivation. Through listening we are able to find out what is important to our constituents. We can hear their needs and find out what drives them. Once we know this about the people with whom we work we are able to pinpoint what will persuade and motivate them. Although intellectual assertions are part of the act of persuasion, compelling persuasion is primarily based upon an emotional appeal (Conger, 1998; Gardner, 2004; Wills, 1994). Successful lawyers, politicians, and advertisers are well aware of this facet of human nature. The popular television commercial that urges you to use your credit card to purchase priceless moments is not appealing to your intellect. School leaders seldom have either the time or the resources to conduct market research and focus groups but active listening can serve the same purpose for the skillful practitioner. By asking open-ended questions and providing an empathetic audience the effective school leader can ascertain what persuades and motivates constituents. A real-life vignette highlights the importance of this key interpersonal skill.

A VIGNETTE

Brad Sneeden slowly sipped his second cup of coffee of his first working day as Superintendent of the Craven County, North Carolina School System. Brad still felt some of the elation that comes with your first appointment as superintendent but that elation was giving way to a bit of apprehension as he contemplated his first meeting of the morning. The meeting was with the associate superintendent of schools in Craven County. The associate superintendent had been Brad's most serious competitor for the job of superintendent and now the question was, what would be the nature of their relationship? Brad had received an abundance of advice on how to handle the situation. Some hardline administrators had advised him not to trust his former competitor, to freeze him out of the information loop and isolate him from important decisions. Others had counseled him to adopt a formal relationship with the associate superintendent and be on guard for any act of betrayal. Brad decided to reserve judgment until after a serious, one-on-one in-depth meeting with his fellow school district leader. After that meeting, Brad was convinced he could ignore the negative advice and build a trusting, mutually beneficial partnership with his erstwhile rival. Though no specific verbal assurances or commitments were stated in that meeting, both leaders used active listening skills, watched carefully for nonverbal, emotional cues, and then used emotional recognition to assess the other's emotional disposition. Their assessments proved correct. Working closely, the two school leaders helped make Craven County one of the most progressive school systems in North Carolina. Brad went on to be appointed Deputy State Superintendent of Schools and is now Associate Vice President for Leadership Development and Director of the Principal's Executive Program in the North Carolina Center for Leadership Development. His former associate superintendent is now Superintendent of the Craven County School System.

FUTURE DIRECTIONS

Given the impressive literature on the importance of interpersonal skills in leadership, there are many questions for professors of educational leadership. First and foremost, how many ELPP actually provide training in interpersonal skills development? Second, what type of training is provided? Does the training include the five components deemed necessary for effectiveness by Cherniss (2000) listed earlier in this paper? Once these questions have been addressed then the questions can be asked, "Does this training actually improve the exercise of school leadership?" The imposing research literature that asserts the necessity of interpersonal skills for effective leadership makes this inquiry an important concern for professors and practitioners of school leadership.

TAKE AWAY POINTS

1. A growing body of literature supports the importance of interpersonal skills for effective leadership.
2. Among interpersonal skills, active listening is a key ability.
3. Business, industry and government are making major investments in interpersonal skills training.
4. There is some indication that experienced school leaders desire interpersonal skills training.
5. The most effective model for interpersonal skills training requires a rigorous approach to skill development.
6. Because the school environment is people intensive, it demands highly developed people skills.

REFERENCES

Alred, K. G. (2000). Anger and retaliation in conflict: The role of attribution. In M. Deutsch and P. Coleman (Eds.), *The handbook of conflict resolution: Theory and practice.* San Francisco: Jossey-Bass Publishers.

Cherniss, C. (2000). Social and emotional competence in the workplace. In R. Bar-On and J. D. A. Parker (Eds.), *The handbook of emotional intelligence: Theory, development, assessment, and application at home, school, and in the workplace* (pp. 433–458). San Francisco: Jossey-Bass.

Conger, J. (1998, May–June). The necessary art of persuasion. *Harvard Business Review, 76*(3), 84–95.

Donaldson, G. A., Bowe, L. M., MacKenzie, S. V., and Marnik, G. F. (2004, March). Learning from leadership work: Maine pioneers a school leadership network. *Phi Delta Kappan, 85*(7) 539–544.

Fernanandez-Araoz, C. (2001). The challenge of hiring senior executives. In C. Cherniss and D. Goleman (Eds.), *The emotionally intelligent workplace: How to select for, measure, and improve emotional intelligence in individuals, groups, and organizations* (pp. 182–206). San Francisco: Jossey-Bass.

Fleenor, J. (2003, April). In tough times soft skills make the difference. *President and CEO,* pp. 37, 38.

Gardner, H. (2004). *Changing Minds: The art and science of changing our own and other people's minds.* Boston: Harvard Business School Press.

Goldring, E., and Greenfield, W. (2002). Understanding the evolving role of leadership in education: Roles expectations and dilemmas. In J. Murphy (Ed.), *The educational leadership challenge: Redefining leadership for the 21st century* (pp. 1–19). Chicago, IL: The University of Chicago Press.

Goleman, D. (1998). *Working with emotional intelligence.* New York: Bantam Books.

Goleman, D., Boyatzis, R., and McGee, A. (2002). *Primal leadership: Realizing the power of emotional intelligence.* Boston: Harvard Business School Press.

Hernez-Broom, G., and Hughes, R. L. (2004). Leadership, development: Past, present, and future. *Human Resource Planning 27*(4), 24–33.

Leslie, J. B., and Van Elson, E. (1996). *A look at derailment today.* Greensboro, NC: Center for Creative Leadership.

McCauley, C. D. (2004). Successful and unsuccessful leadership. In J. Antonakis, A. T. Cianciolo and R. J. Sternberg (Eds.), *The nature of leadership* (pp. 199–221). Thousand Oaks, CA: Sage Publications.

McDowelle, J. O., and Buckner K. G. (2002). *Leading with emotion.* Lanham, MD: Scarecrow Press.

Mumford, M. D., Zaccaro, S. J., Harding, F. D., Jacobs, T. O., and Fleishman, E. A. (2000). Leadership skills for a changing world: Solving complex social problems. *Leadership Quarterly, 11*(1), 11–35.

Nahavandi, A. (2003). *The art and science of leadership* (3rd ed.). Upper Saddle River, NJ: Prentice-Hall.

Nelton, S. (1997, May). Leadership for the new age. *Nations Business,* pp.18–37.

Northhouse, P. G. (2004). *Leadership: Theory and practice* (3rd ed.). Thousand Oaks, CA: Sage Publications.

Pierce, M. C., and Borden, A. M. (2003, Fall). Bridging the gap between theory and craft. *The AASA Professor,* *26*(2),10–14.

Robbins, S. P. (2002). *The truth about managing people.* New York: Prentice-Hall.

Robbins, S. P., and Hunsaker, P. L. (1996). *Training in interpersonal skills: Tips for managing people at work* (2nd ed.). Upper Saddle River, NJ: Prentice-Hall.

Sousa, D. A. (2003). *The leadership brain: How to lead schools more effectively.* Thousand Oaks, CA: Corwin Press Inc.

Spenser, L. M. J., McClelland, D. C., and Kleiner, S. (1997). *Competency assessment methods: History and the state of the art.* New York: John Willey and Sons.

Sweeney, P. (1999, February 14). Teaching new hires to feel at home. *New York Times,* p. 4.

Wills, G. (1998). *Certain trumpets: The nature of leadership.* New York: Simon & Schuster.

Wong, C., and Law, K. S. (2002). The effect of leader and follower emotional intelligence on performance and attitude: An exploratory study. *Leadership Quarterly, 13*(3), 243–274.

Zaccaro, S. J., Kemp, C., and Bader, P. (2004). In J. T. Antonakis, A. T. Cianciolo and R. J. Sternberg (Eds.), *Leader traits and attributes* (pp. 101–124). Thousand Oaks, CA: Sage Publications.

For the New Professor of Educational Leadership

MARILYN GRADY

THE PATH TO THE ROLE OF PROFESSOR OF EDUCATIONAL Leadership often includes a significant period of service as an administrator in a variety of administrative positions. These practitioner positions provide a rich array of information about "how to" administer in complex organizational settings. These experiences, however, do not prepare one for assuming the role of professor.

The university or college setting is a challenging environment of mystery and unwritten rules. Although there is no definitive handbook to guide the novice, there are several books that are valuable tools for the new initiate.

Cahn's (1993) *Saints and Scamps: Ethics in Academia* addresses the professorial life, scholarship and service, personnel decisions, and graduate education. This short text provides critical information about the concerns a new professor should have upon entering the academy.

Editors Cooper and Stevens (2002) in *Tenure in the Sacred Grove: Issues and Strategies for Women and Minority Faculty* provide a range of manuscripts concerning the work of professors. Sections of the text address the "landscape of the sacred grove," faculty as individual learners, and advice for professors. The multiple perspectives offered by the authors reflect years of experience in a variety of university settings.

Martinez Aleman and Renn (2002), editors of *Women in Higher Education: An Encyclopedia*, include selections on tenure and promotion in this comprehensive text. The accompanying references provide additional information that is important to the new professor.

Seldin's (2004) *Teaching Portfolio* is a slim text that suggests ways of documenting a professor's teaching excellence. In colleges of education, teaching excellence is a "given," it is "assumed" that all faculty are outstanding teachers. However, teaching graduate level classes and advising masters and doctoral students may be an entirely new experience for the school administrator new to the university setting! Seldin provides a framework that the junior professor can use to guide the path to teaching excellence at the graduate level.

McKeachie's *Teaching Tips: A Guidebook for the Beginning College Teacher* is an accessible text for those commencing a career as a professor. The information in the book suggests areas that the new professor should consider and plan for early in the career.

These books provide a solid foundation for the new professor. The references suggested by the authors are worthy of consideration as well.

In addition to these valuable texts, I offer the following findings of 20 years of observation, conversation, and study of the promotion and tenure challenges experienced by new or junior professors. These findings have been the focus of a session I have presented at the annual meeting of the National Council of Professors of Educational Administration.

INTRODUCTION

When you join a department or unit, you may be surprised to realize that the promotion and tenure experiences of the faculty members in that department or unit may not have been uniform. For instance, the oldest members of the department simply may have been informed that it was "time" for them to be tenured and promoted. These individuals may have never published in refereed journals. They may not have been required to prepare promotion and tenure materials for review. Their tenure decisions may not have been reviewed by peers or committees. These individuals were simply "tapped" for promotion. They may have been the beneficiaries of the "Old Boys Network."

Other faculty members may have been tenured at a "different time" in the institution's history. Changes in expectations for promotion and tenure are continuous. Changes in faculty membership, changes in department and college promotion and tenure committees, changes in deans or vice chancellors for academic affairs may precipitate changes in expectations. University regents or governance boards as well as legislative initiatives may influence changes in expectations.

Shifting emphases on number of publications, types of publications, research grants, amount of service, or focus on teaching may cause changes in expectations. In some institutions, excellence in teaching is sufficient for tenure and promotion. Faculty in a department may have very different and unequal publication records. Faculty may be appointed and given different assignments that do not involve significant research and writing expectations. Sometimes these "special assignments" are honored in the promotion and tenure process. In other instances, these individuals may be held to two different sets of standards. They may be held to their special assignment standards and then to the same expectations as other college faculty members.

These differences in the faculty may leave the new professor in a very lonely situation. The new professor may encounter faculty colleagues who have no publication records. There may be no faculty members with research skills. There may be no faculty members with experience as journal editors or members of editorial review boards. There may be no faculty members who make presentations at the annual national meetings of professional associations. Although the faculty in these departments may be supportive of the new faculty member's quest for promotion and tenure, these individuals may not be able to offer any "real" assistance to the new professor. New professors may feel isolated or extremely lonely while surrounded by professors of "good will" who possess "few tricks of the trade."

New professors may encounter these situations and many other unique conditions as they begin their careers in higher education. As new professors share their "new learnings" about the professoriate, they uniformly report encountering a workplace that has no peer in the professional world. Based on these conversations with new professors about their experiences as they sought promotion and tenure, the following "Tips" are offered to those who are new to the role of professor.

KNOW THE EXPECTATIONS

For individuals hired as professors, it is essential to "know the expectations." Each professor is hired with a unique set of expectations. As one assumes the professoriate, one recognizes that the expectations change from one generation of untenured professors to the next generation of untenured professors. This truth is revealed as the histories of a department's professors are examined. Even professors hired at the same time will have different performance expectations. Different individuals are hired to accomplish different institutional objectives. Tierney and Bensimon (1996) note that both women and men junior faculty are typically confused by the haphazard nature of the tenure and promotion process and do not understand the performance or procedural requirements or the time frame.

Different expectations exist at the department, college, and university levels. Since judgments are made about the tenure and promotion of professors at each of these levels, it is essential for the new professor to have as much understanding of these expectations as possible. This means that the new professor must review all written promotion and tenure materials available at the department, college and university levels. The new professor must discuss these documents with individuals who can offer clarification of the documents. Chairs of department promotion and tenure committees in the department or college may be helpful. The dean of the college may be helpful. Long-term faculty members who have served on promotion and tenure committees as well as faculty mentors can be helpful in clarifying expectations. Reviewing promotion and tenure portfolios of recently promoted and tenured individuals may be helpful. Permission to review these materials should be sought, particularly if the individual's work is in a similar area. The university's head of academic affairs may offer written materials or workshops related to promotion and tenure. Faculty groups on campus may offer workshops. These faculty groups are helpful in understanding the institution's "track record" concerning promotion and tenure.

Historically, there have been institutions of higher education that have encountered difficulties with promotion and tenure decisions. The *Chronicle of Higher Education* has been consistent in reporting these difficulties. Occasionally, at some institutions, new, junior faculty will be hired, will work for a number of years, and then not be granted tenure. It is important to understand the experiences of other junior faculty and other institutions so that a clear understanding of the expectations at your institution can be developed. The burden is on each individual faculty member to identify the expectations that will guide that individual's quest for promotion and tenure.

KNOW WHO CAN HELP—THE NETWORK

Perhaps each professor should have a Personal Guide through the promotion and tenure process. Some colleges and departments have created formal mentoring programs to assist new professors on the path to tenure and promotion. Thinking of the intricacies and complexities of the promotion and tenure process, a mentor or personal guide would be an asset.

Identifying "buddies" who are at similar career stages is essential. Buddies help in deciphering the unwritten rules of promotion and tenure. Sometimes individuals have colleagues in their own departments or colleges who can fill this colleague role. Often, however, the help must come from colleagues at other institutions.

New professors may find themselves in departments where they are the first new professors who have been hired in many years. The other professors were tenured during times when the expectations were different than the current conditions. In the absence of departmental colleagues who are up-to-date on contemporary promotion and tenure strategies, the new professor must seek colleagues who understand the current challenges of the promotion and tenure process.

Attendance at national meetings of professional organizations, such as the National Council of Professors of Educational Administration, provides an opportunity to meet other new professors in the same academic discipline. Because conference sessions are often grouped thematically, it is possible to meet others who share the same interests during these sessions. Being a presenter at national conferences provides the forum for meeting others interested in the same topics. Through these sessions, one has the opportunity to develop a network of national colleagues who can provide the support and guidance new professors need as they seek promotion and tenure.

The new acquaintances from the national meetings may lead to research and writing collaborations. Opportunities to contribute to journals, prepare book chapters, serve on editorial boards, serve on committees, or share in panels at national meetings may emerge from these associations. This national network also will be useful when it is time to seek external letters in support of promotion and tenure. The time, effort, and money invested in travel to national conferences are an excellent investment in a professorial career.

KNOW WHO CAN HURT

The academy is populated by a wide range of individuals who are variously talented and untalented. The higher education environment may foster some professorial behaviors that are dangerous to the new professor. *Saints and Scamps: Ethics in Academia* (1993), by Cahn, provides useful guidance in identifying the occupants of professorial roles.

The Vultures are particularly lethal to new professors. The Vultures recognize the talents, abilities, enthusiasm, and desperation of the new, untenured professor.

Consider the following scenario. On occasion, a tenured professor will approach a junior professor and invite the new person to collaborate on a research project. To the new professor, this may be very flattering. It may feel like a lifeline is being extended to the new person.

Beware the Vulture! The senior professor may be harvesting the junior professor's abilities and time. There have been instances when new professors have invested incredible effort in collaborations that have resulted in no publications and no recognition. Negotiating the intended outcomes of collaborations at the beginning of the experience is essential. Authorship and the order of authorship as well as a timeline for completion of activities are critical to the junior professor's future.

In a different scenario, a senior professor may block the publication of the results of a collaborative research project by insisting that the manuscript is not "ready" to be submitted. When a considerable investment of time and effort in a project does not lead to the submission of a manuscript for publication consideration, then the junior professor has lost time and momentum on the tenure and promotion clock. Junior professors are given a limited number of years before they must submit their promotion and tenure materials. Each person must carefully guard the use of time and ownership of work. It may be safer to work alone than to invest in collaborations that may not further the junior professor's career.

Jealous Peers also populate the academy. Not everyone who has been hired to a tenure line position or who has been tenured has the skills of a researcher or writer. Individuals who lack these skills may resent the new professor who has these skills. In universities where scholarly productivity is valued, those who do not have those skills may be jealous of those who do. Comments that disparage research, writing, and publication may be designed to undermine the work of the new professor. Jealous Peers may force the new professor into isolation. Work in the academy may require that one be comfortable working in isolation so that the expectations for promotion and tenure can be met.

Another group who may influence the new professor is the Effete Snobs. These individuals take pleasure in diminishing the work of the junior professor by finding the work to be inferior to the work of the senior professors. Given the opportunity to critique the junior professor's work, the Effete Snobs will make every effort to denigrate the new professor's contributions.

Given the existence of Vultures, Jealous Peers, and Effete Snobs, or as Cooper and Temple (2002) describe it: Dancing in a Snake Pit, the new professor would be well-advised to study departmental colleagues carefully and make alliances cautiously. A career in higher education is built through individual accomplishments. However, the academy is a political environment. The new professor needs to study the environment and be wary of traps embedded in the history of the department.

KNOW THE PEER REVIEW PROCESS

There are two types of review for promotion and tenure materials—internal and external. The internal review process includes the procedures that occur at the department, college, and university levels. At the department level, one expects the faculty to be most familiar with the junior professor's field—the journals, the professional organizations and the knowledge base or content areas. Department colleagues should recognize the individuals who hold the highest status in the field and the institutions that are considered to be most prestigious. Department colleagues review promotion and tenure materials with a specialized expertise. Because of their working proximity, they can reflect on the junior professor's contributions to the department, colleagueship, teaching, service as well as scholarly productivity. This is one level of internal review, but a very significant one. The department members or department promotion and tenure committee provides a letter that indicates the results of the review at the department level. The department chair may provide an independent review of the file as well. A letter is prepared by the chair that reflects the outcomes of the assessment.

At the college level, a promotion and tenure committee may exist that consists of representatives of the departments in the college. When materials are submitted to this group, the junior professor must remember that there will be a number of files presented for review. It is essential that the promotion and tenure materials be documented and arranged so that individuals from other departments understand: the contributions of the person applying for promotion and tenure, the contents of the file, and the impact of the person's work. Ambiguity must be eliminated. Providing a succinct statement of the work that aids in viewing the materials seems prudent. The college committee may present a letter that reflects the outcomes of the assessment of the file.

At the college level, the dean may conduct an independent review and judgment of the promotion and tenure file. How the file meets the college mission and goals should be represented in the materials prepared by the junior professor. The dean will provide a letter that reflects the results of the review.

A next level of internal review occurs in the university's office of academic affairs. The head of academic affairs may have a committee that reviews files at the university level or may review the files with other members of the office staff. The letters prepared at the department and college levels by faculty and administrators, specific materials prepared by the junior professor, and the external letters are examined. A decision on promotion and tenure is made and forwarded to the governing body of the university.

External letters are a second type of review. A formal procedure usually exists for soliciting the external letters. Sometimes the junior professor is permitted to suggest names of professors at other universities who will be asked to review the promotion and tenure materials. In other cases, the department decides who will be asked to review the materials.

At some universities, the candidate for promotion and tenure cannot be externally reviewed by individuals they have worked with, co-authored manuscripts with, or know. It is helpful to the new professor to understand these "rules" early in their professorial careers so that they can anticipate the procedures for soliciting external letters.

KNOW YOUR LINE OF INQUIRY

The time between being hired as an untenured faculty member and being considered for tenure and promotion passes rapidly. Establishing a line or lines of inquiry early is essential. Give consideration to your areas of expertise. The dissertation may provide several avenues of inquiry. The dissertation, itself, may provide several manuscripts.

Consider your passions. It is always easier to write about a topic for which you have passion. When the portfolio of materials is prepared for the promotion and tenure quest, the junior professor has to identify one or two areas of research expertise. This suggests that a steady stream of research and writing in those areas must be maintained throughout the professoriate.

Finding a niche is essential. All the research and writing matters little unless the manuscripts are publishable. One must select areas of inquiry that are valued by editors. Some areas are saturated, so writing in those areas may be futile. Writing in areas that are not sought by journal editors may be futile as well. Even though the topic may be important, if the journal editors do not have space in the journal or interest in the topic, the manuscript will not be published. Therefore, it would be wise to consider "what's publishable" and "what's hot and what's not."

As a research focus or foci are identified, keep in mind how deep one can dig in the areas. It is better to pursue areas that offer many aspects for exploration or veins of possibility. "One shot" explorations do not contribute to one's reputation as a "world's leading authority." Depth is good.

In the process of identifying the line or lines of inquiry, one should consider multiple thrusts in the beginning stages. By doing this, one has the opportunity to determine which areas of inquiry will be most productive and most marketable to the journals. Identifying the dry wells and dead ends early in a career is helpful as a research focus or line of inquiry is established.

KNOW THE OUTLETS

Journals have reputations. Some are considered extremely prestigious; others are not prestigious. Some journals have very low acceptance rates; others have high acceptance rates. Some journals have large circulations; others have miniscule circulations. Some journals are sponsored by professional associations; others are not. Some journals are national, some regional, some are state-based. Some journals are very specialized; others are general. Some journals only accept articles based on data-based research. Other journals will accept research articles as well as literature reviews. Some journals accept only quantitative research studies; others will accept both quantitative and qualitative research studies. Some journals are research journals; other journals are practitioner journals. Some journals are refereed; other journals are non-refereed. Some professors are required to publish only in refereed journals; other professors are permitted to publish in both refereed and non-refereed journals. Some journals are published monthly, some quarterly,

others semi-annually. Knowing the journals in your field and being aware of their status in relation to these issues will be helpful in identifying the outlets for your work.

Submitting your work to the "wrong" journal wastes your time and the time of the journal editor. Knowing the audience you are writing for is critical. An article prepared for the research community is written very differently than an article written for the practitioner community. Knowing the expectations of the university concerning appropriate outlets for your work is essential. Some professors are encouraged to publish only in the most prestigious, research-based, refereed journals.

KNOW THE PRODUCTION CYCLE

As you plan your research productivity, remember that it is essential to have several manuscripts in progress simultaneously. It can take as long as 18 months for an article to be published after it is submitted to a journal. Given this long time frame, the cautious junior professor must plan to have two or more different articles under publication consideration simultaneously. To achieve this objective, a constant cycle of writing, submitting, revising, and resubmitting must be maintained.

Remember—if a manuscript is rejected by a journal, review the editor's comments, make whatever revisions are appropriate, and submit the manuscript to the next appropriate journal on your list of outlets. A manuscript collecting dust on your desk is no help at all.

Establishing goals for the production cycle can be helpful. Multiple authors can lead to multiple products. If you find colleagues who are at similar career stages and share a similar work ethic, then it may be possible to collaborate and become more productive through the association. Working with similarly motivated individuals can be stimulating and rewarding, if the collaboration is based on equity and mutual benefit.

KNOW THE PITFALLS

Some departments are populated by senior faculty who are not helpful to the new professor. Sometimes this situation is described as a department that "eats its young." Hopefully, you will not find yourself in a dysfunctional environment. Clearly, not all higher education environments are negative places.

However, you may encounter senior professors "who could help, but don't" or "who would help, but can't." You also might encounter an attitude of "I've got mine, you get yours!"

You may encounter faculty who preach collaboration and teamwork in all areas, except research. Faculty members may be afraid to share as though "it" is an expendable resource that could be used up—only a finite amount is available—a scarce resource!

A WORD TO THE WISE

As you pursue your research and writing activities, consider whether you are simply describing "the disease" or whether you are searching for a "cure"? We probably know plenty about the "problems" and the "pathology." Rather than working on the negatives, try working on the positives, the promising, the "cure"!

REFERENCES

Cahn, S. M. (1993). *Saints and Scamps: Ethics in Academia.* Totowa, NJ: Rowman & Littlefield.

Cooper, J. E., and Stevens, D. D. (Eds.) (2002). *Tenure in the Sacred Grove: Issues and Strategies for Women and Minority Faculty.* Albany, NY: State University of New York Press.

Cooper, J. E., and Temple, J. B. (2000). Case studies: Learning from others. In J. E. Cooper and D. D. Stevens (Eds.), *Tenure in the sacred grove: Issues and strategies for women and minority faculty.* Albany, NY: State University of New York Press.

Martinez Aleman, A. M. M., and Renn, K. A. (2002). *Women in Higher Education: An Encyclopedia.* Santa Barbara, CA: ABC-CLIO, Inc.

McKeachie, W. J., and Hofer, B. K. (2002). *McKeachie's teaching tips: Strategies, research, and theory for college and university teachers* (11th ed.). Boston: Houghton Mifflin Company.

Seldin, P. (2004). *The teaching portfolio: A practical guide to improved performance and promotion/tenure decisions* (3rd. ed.). Bolton, MA: Anker Publishing Company.

Tierney, W. G., and Bensimon, E. M. (1996). *Promotion and Tenure: Community and Socialization in Academe.* Albany, NY: State University of New York Press.

Teachers' Perspectives on Danielson's Teacher Evaluation Model

TINA M. SWEELEY AND BERNARD R. BROGAN

THE PUBLIC AND THE FEDERAL GOVERNMENT'S FOCUS ON accountability for teachers' performance have grown in demand in recent years. The No Child Left Behind (NCLB) legislation enacted in 2002 has redefined accountability in public school education. The NCLB law affects nearly three million public school teachers in more than 89,599 public schools. The premise of the Act is based on four areas: accountability for results, flexibility and local control, options and choices for parents, and scientific-based teaching methods. Professors of educational administration are faced with the responsibility and challenge of preparing current and future administrators with the skills and competence to effectively respond to this movement toward accountability.

"Educators, researchers, and policymakers concur that the traditional view of learning, focused on knowledge and procedures of low cognitive challenge and the regurgitation of superficial understanding, does not meet the demands of the present and future" (Danielson, 1996, p. 23). "The two principle purposes of teacher evaluation, then, are (a) quality assurance and (b) professional development" (Danielson and McGreal, 2000, p. 8). Accomplishing these purposes will require carefully designed systems of evaluation that are developed and implemented through a partnership of teachers and administrators (Danielson and McGreal, 2000).

"Competitive industries in the twenty-first century will be those whose workers can solve complex problems and design more efficient techniques to accomplish work" (Danielson, 1996, p. 23). This goal is not only intended for students upon graduation, but also for teachers throughout their careers. In order to guide and nurture teachers into achieving this goal Danielson and McGreal (2000) recommend a framework for teaching model for evaluating teachers. This model has three instructor tiers: (a) the nontenured or probationary teacher, (b) the tenured or experienced teacher, (c) and the inadequate or needs assistance teacher. These three skill levels have varying abilities and needs. At each level, the administrators' role is different ranging from support and assistance to inquiry.

Danielson (1996) noted the teachers have been associated metaphorically with business managers, human relations directors, stage managers, actors, conductors, engineers, and coaches. "These metaphors remind us of the intellectual and emotional demands of teaching. . . ." (Danielson, 1996, p. 5). A teacher takes on many roles throughout a single day all the while bestowing knowledge on her students. "But even more demanding than its complexity is the level of stress that teaching generates" (Danielson, 1996, p. 5). With inclusion and increased needs among students in the same classrooms, teachers are mandated to plan for all children, meet federal and state guidelines, adhere to Individual Education Plans (IEPs), be collegial, communicate with parents, and uphold many other aspects of the job.

"For many years educators have agreed that the fundamental purposes of teacher evaluation are both quality assurance and professional development. Previous evaluation systems, however, have failed to achieve either goal" (Danielson, 2001, p. 15). Realizing this, school districts across the United States have begun to reshape teacher evaluations systems to more substantially reflect the quality of teaching (Danielson, 2001).

RESEARCH PROBLEM

Charlotte Danielson's approach of evaluating teaching is gaining popularity across the nation, and many school districts have decided to use this model, adapting it to meet their own needs (Danielson and McGreal, 2000). In Pennsylvania, for example, the Pennsylvania Department of Education (2003) adopted Danielson's recommendations and created a new system for evaluating all public school teachers beginning September 2004. The system considers all four of Danielson's domains as well as the subcategories and aspects of teaching.

According to the Pennsylvania Department of Education (2003),

> evaluators are encouraged to consider that teaching cannot be evaluated through classroom observations on any single day and that an accurate assessment of teaching requires that information be collected over a period of time. In order to completely assess actual practice, it is essential to use multiple measures of performance over time. (p. 1)

Therefore, this new approach to teacher evaluation is critical to the effects it will have on many new teachers as well as on teachers' eligibility for professional certification in the state of Pennsylvania.

Educational researchers and practitioners agree that teacher evaluation is an important component in providing quality education (Bolton, 1973; Gullatt and Ballard, 1998; Howard and McCloskey, 2001; Iwanicki, 2001; Manatt, Palmer, and Hidlebaugh, 1976). Many professors of education administration also believe the purpose of teacher evaluation is to improve teacher effectiveness, encourage professional growth, and remediate or terminate inadequate teachers (Wheeler, 1992; Wise, Darling-Hammond and McLauglin, 1984). These educators recognize that there are significant problems with current evaluation systems. These problems include misalignment with district goals, the use of one system that is too broad to fit a wide range of teachers along a continuum of content areas and experience, the role of the principal, and the lack of teacher input (Covey, 1991; Danielson, 1996; Danielson and McGreal, 2000; Howard and McCloskey, 2001; McGreal, Broderick, and Jones, 1984; Manatt, 2000; National Commission on Teaching and America's Future, 1996; National Governors Association Center for Best Practices, 2002; Painter, 2001). This lack of teacher input in the evaluation process is a very real barrier to effective evaluation and is a primary focus of this research.

PURPOSE OF THE STUDY

The purpose of this study was to determine the attitudes of teachers toward Danielson's *Framework for Effective Teaching*. Recognizing that successful implementation of any school reform initiative, especially teacher evaluation, requires upfront and continuous teacher involvement, this study sought to gage the degree to which teachers believe the various components of the evaluation system are important to quality teaching. To accomplish this purpose, the attitudes of teachers in one school district that is about to adopt the Danielson's model were surveyed.

Determining the degree to which teachers' believe specific domains are important to effective teaching is significant because school leaders can use this information to determine those areas that required more attention. The research also sought to identify differences in attitudes among school level, grade assignment, subject area taught, gender, and years of experience. With this information, school districts can determine which component areas are applicable for implementation within the district's evaluation instrument and plan a professional development program that addresses the specific needs of their teachers. According to Danielson (1996), "This process is critical to both enriching the professional lives of educators and to ensuring that the components used in a given setting actually do apply there. Only educators in that setting can make those determinations" (p. 5).

When teachers have the opportunity to share their opinions of what they believed are the elements of effective teaching, professional conversations regarding the development of the final evaluation instrument are meaningful. This process provides teachers with a sense of ownership and acknowledges that their professional opinions are considered important by the school district administration.

Today, there are continually increasing demands placed on administrators and teachers with accountability of school districts at an all time high. Professors of educational administration need to recognize these demands and provide their students with the knowledge and skills necessary to meet successfully these challenges. Teacher attitudes, such as those determined in this study, provide professors of educational administration a catalyst for professional development and training opportunities that promote quality teacher evaluation. Danielson's model is a promising alternative to the traditional system of evaluation and may provide administrators with a more comprehensive means of evaluating teaching (Danielson, 1996).

DANIELSON'S MODEL OF TEACHER EVALUATION

Charlotte Danielson is a seasoned educator. Her teaching experiences range from kindergarten to the collegiate level. She is the author and co-author of several books regarding teaching and enhancing the practice of teaching. Danielson has served as an educator and consultant across the United States and overseas in many areas such as curriculum planning, performance assessments, and professional development. Danielson's most noteworthy work is in the area of designing materials and training programs for Association for Supervision and Curriculum Development (ASCD), Educational Testing Service (ETS), and National Board of Professional Teaching Standards (NBPTS). "Her work has encouraged assessment in the service of learning by both teachers and students" (Danielson, 1996, p. iii).

Danielson (1996) developed a framework for teaching which represents all aspects of teaching and daily responsibilities. The components of the framework are comprehensive. They include planning and instruction, collegial interaction, parent communication, content knowledge, teacher reflection, and teacher interaction among the educational community (administrators, school board members, assistances, etc.). The 22 components are organized into four domain areas: planning and preparation, classroom environment, instruction, and professional responsibilities. The framework is divided into four domains of teaching responsibility. Each domain consists of three parts: rationale and explanation, documentation, and performance level. There are four performance levels: unsatisfactory, basic, proficient, and distinguished.

Domain One

This first domain has six components. The first component focuses on the teacher's demonstrating knowledge of content and pedagogy. The second component focuses on the teacher's knowledge of students. This area addresses knowledge of child development and age appropriate tasks, as well as students' skill levels, interests, and cultural heritage (Danielson, 1996). The third is selecting instructional goals. This involves setting purposeful goals, designed to achieve a clearly defined objective. The next component is demonstrating knowledge of resources. The two types of resources necessary are those for teachers and students. This area acknowledges the responsibility of teachers to use additional materials when necessary to go beyond what the school provides through curriculum. The student resources include items and services available to aid students in learning such as special services, and adapted materials. The next component is designing coherent instruction. This examines the type of instruction and determines whether it is suitable for the learning goal. Instructional strategies can be group work, independent activities, class lectures, and the materials used to achieve these goals. The final component in the first domain is assessing student learning. The assessment tools and methodology must correlate with the desired learning objectives. Documentation for the first domain can be demonstrated through lesson plans, course work, teaching materials, and student assessments (Danielson, 1996).

Domain Two

Domain two, the classroom environment, has five component areas. The first is creating an environment of respect and rapport. This examines the way teachers interact with their students and the manner in which the students are treated. The next component is establishing a culture for learning. This culture is viewed as a safe environment where students can take risks and are actively engaged in their own learning. The third component is managing classroom procedures. This area considers the management techniques used in the classroom such as transition strategies, procedures for gathering materials, supplies and clean up, student responsibilities within the classroom, and daily routines. Next is managing student behavior. This includes teacher expectations of students' conduct, monitoring, and responding to misbehavior. The final component is organizing physical space. In this component, safety and arrangement of furniture as well as accessibility for learning by all students is the primary focus. For this classroom environment domain, documentation is obtained through classroom observations (Danielson, 1996).

Domain Three

The third domain, instruction, has five components. The first is communicating clearly and accurately. This focuses on teaching oral and written language especially as it pertains to directions and procedures for students to follow. The next component is using questioning and discussion techniques. This area concentrates on the quality of questions, discussion techniques, and student participation during a lesson. The third area is engaging students in learning. The focus of this component is the activities and assignments students are engaged in to learn a concept. Other areas included are how students are grouped, what instructional materials are used, and how the lesson is structured and paced. The next component is providing feedback to students. The goal is to provide feedback to all students that is accurate, constructive, substantive, specific, and timely. Feedback is a valuable tool of communication that can be used to enhance students' learning. The final component in the third domain is demonstrating flexibility and responsiveness. Not all lessons are suitable for all students to learn a concept. When a lesson that is not suitable to all students occurs, a teacher must make appropriate changes to meet all the students' learning needs. Therefore, this component examines teachers' abilities to adjust lessons accordingly, to respond to students in need or for enrichment purposes, and to persist in seeking an effective approach for teaching the material. Documentation of these components is generally gathered through classroom observations and teaching portfolios (Danielson, 1996).

Domain Four

Domain four, professional responsibilities, contains six component areas. The first is reflecting on teaching. Reflection on teaching requires thinking about the instruction and details of the lesson. The reflections are assessed for accuracy and thoughtfulness pertaining to approaches to altering teaching methods and goals for future advances. The next component is maintaining accurate records. The areas of record keeping include student completion of assignments, student progress, and non-instructional records such as permission slips, etc. The third component is communicating with families. The focus is on the frequency of the information the teacher provides to parents concerning their students as well as the level of engagement expected for family participation in the students' learning. The next component addresses the teacher's contribution to the school and district. This area is divided between teachers' relationships with their colleagues, the service they provide to the school through volunteerism, and participation in district projects and leadership roles. The fifth component is growing and developing professionally. This includes enhancing knowledge and pedagogy through continuing education and professional journals. Another consideration is teachers' service to the profession. This involves research, supervising student teachers, partnerships with colleagues, study groups, writing articles, and making presentations. The final component is addressed in the way teachers demonstrate professionalism. This area includes a proactive role in serving students, advocating for children's needs, and making decisions committed to high professional standards. Documentation is gathered through teacher journaling, logs, reflection sheets, grade books, and daily interactions with families and colleagues (Danielson, 1996).

METHODOLOGY

The participants in this study included teachers from four elementary schools, one middle school, and one high school in a suburban school district in Pennsylvania. From this population 230 surveys were completed resulting in an 82 percent return rate. This sample consisted of 53 males and 177 females. On the elementary school level, five were males and 97 were females. From the middle school level, 13 were males and 41 were females. The high school level consisted of 35 males and 39 females.

The survey instrument was developed by Bernard R. Brogan and Tina Sweeley based on Danielson's 22 component areas. The instrument used a five-point Likert scale survey that included the choices strongly agree, agree, disagree, strongly disagree, and do not understand. The survey included 66 questions and asked eight background questions concerning years of teaching experience, years teaching in current position, teaching assignment, grade level taught, gender, subject(s) taught, level of education, and familiarity with Danielson's model.

DATA ANALYSIS

The data were analyzed using SPSS for Windows statistical software. Descriptive statistics were run in order to investigate the levels of significance and to determine whether or not the variables were normally distributed. An Analysis of Variance (ANOVA) was conducted to analyze the data collected. An examination of the variances between levels and within levels was analyzed to determine if differences existed in attitudes among groups investigated. If a difference among groups was significant, Levene's test for homogeneity of variances, a test to determine if the assumption of equal variances is valid, was conducted. If the results of the Levene's test revealed significant statistical values indicating differences among groups, then Scheffé's test was conducted. Scheffé's test determined where the differences occurred among the groups.

FINDINGS

Tables 1–4 provide selected demographic information pertaining to the participants in the study. Overall, the females responded more positively on the entire survey. The population consisted of 44 percent teachers from the elementary level, 23.5 percent from the middle school level, and 32.2 percent from the high school

Table 1. Gender

	Respondents' Gender	Frequency (Number of Occurrences)	Total Percentage of Occurrences
Valid	1 (Male)	53	23.0
	2 (Female)	177	77.0
	Total Respondents	230	100.0

Table 2. Teaching Assignment

	Teaching Assignment	Frequency (Number of Occurrences)	Total Percentage of Occurrences
Valid	1 (Elementary)	102	44.3
	2 (Middle School)	54	23.5
	3 (High School)	74	32.2
	Total Teaching Assignments	230	100.0

Table 3. Range in Years of Teaching Experience

	Range in Years of Teaching Experience	Frequency (Number of Occurrences)	Total Percentage of Occurrences
Valid	1 (0 through 10 years)	90	39.1
	2 (10.1 through 20 years)	71	30.9
	3 (20.1 through 30 years)	43	18.7
	4 (30.1 through 40 years)	24	10.4
	5 (40.1 through 50 years)	2	.9
	Total respondents	230	100.0

Table 4. Familiarity with Danielson

	Response	Frequency (Number of Occurrences)	Total Percentage of Occurrences
Valid	1 (yes)	79	34.3
	2 (no)	151	65.7
	Total Respondents	230	100.0

level. The largest percentage, 39.1 percent of respondents, had 0 through 10 years of experience. The percentage of teachers familiar with Danielson's work was 34.3 percent and those not familiar was 65.7 percent.

SUMMARY OF FINDINGS

Results of this study suggest that there is considerable agreement toward Danielson's domain areas of effecting teaching. Each domain area was analyzed using descriptive statistics.

Domain One: Planning and Preparation

The results indicated the teachers had a high level of agreement toward the planning and preparation section of the survey. Five of the twenty questions asked were scored in the extremely positive range. These five questions focused on demonstrating knowledge of content and pedagogy, selecting instructional goals, and designing coherent instruction. For planning and preparation, the largest difference was among elementary and high school teachers. These questions focused on demonstrating knowledge of students, selecting instructional goals, designing instruction, and assessing student learning. In each question resulting in a difference between elementary and high school teacher, the elementary teachers' attitudes were significantly more positive than the high school teachers' attitudes. Even though the results from this domain show an overall positive attitude toward planning and preparation, the elementary teachers felt planning and preparation was more important to effective teaching than did the high school teachers. The middle school level did not have a significant difference in attitudes compared to the elementary or high school levels with regard to Domain one.

Domain Two: Classroom Environment

The results indicated a high level of agreement among respondents with regard to the classroom environment items on the survey. Three questions revealed an extreme positive response concerning creating an environment of respect and rapport and organizing physical space. Domain two focused on creating an environment of respect and rapport, managing classroom procedures, managing student behavior, and organizing physical space. Of these questions, elementary teachers' attitudinal score were again significantly higher than those of high school teachers indicating that this area is thought to be more important to elementary teachers with regard to effective teaching. Middle school teachers did not have a significant difference in attitudes compared to elementary teachers. However, middle school teachers did differ significantly from high school teachers in this area. The differences focused on the areas of creating an environment of respect and rapport and organizing physical space. Middle school teachers' attitudes were more positive than high school teachers in these areas indicating middle school teachers' level of agreement is higher especially in the area of physical space. In fact, middle school teachers' mean scores were the highest with regard to physical space.

Domain Three: Instruction

The findings indicated a high level agreement amongst teachers in the area of instruction. Three questions were scored extremely positive. The three questions focused on using questioning and discussion techniques, engaging students in learning, and providing students with feedback. Domain three indicated elementary and high school teachers again had a difference in attitudes in the area of instruction. The differences occurred with questions concerned communicating clearly and accurately, engaging students in learning, and demonstrating flexibility and responsiveness. This indicated elementary school teachers view these areas more positively for effective teaching than high school teachers did. Middle school teachers had no significant difference compared to elementary and high school teachers.

Domain Four: Professional Responsibility

The findings indicated a moderate to high level of agreement in the area of professional responsibilities. However, five of the fifteen questions concerning domain three, instruction, were scored extremely positive. The questions focus on reflecting on teaching, maintaining accurate records, and showing professionalism. The fourth domain, professional responsibility, indicated once more that elementary and high school teachers differed in attitudes. The difference occurred among questions concerning communicating with families, contributing to the school and district, and showing professionalism. Among all of the questions where differences occurred, the middle school teachers' attitudes were the most positive, followed by elementary, then high school teachers, indicating that this area was considered most important for effective teaching among middle school teachers.

DISCUSSION

The findings of this study indicate that overall, the teachers agree with Danielson's framework for effective teaching. However, elementary teachers have the highest level of agreement, followed by middle school teachers, and then high school teachers. The research from this study shows that elementary, middle, and high school teachers have different levels of agreement regarding effective teaching.

Possible explanations for this occurrence could be the nature of the assignments in and of themselves. Perhaps middle school teachers have a combination of elementary and high school types of assignments such as teaching several subjects and grades, similar to elementary, versus teaching the same subject and one grade, similar to high school. The same combination can be applied to the students that are taught at the middle school level; sixth graders are more like elementary school children whereas eighth graders are more like high school students. Therefore, the teachers' attitudes were a combination of both elementary and high school teachers falling in the middle level of agreement.

A factor that may possibly influence teachers' attitudes toward effective teaching could be extraneous forces imposed on their students and the difficulties of handling them at each level. High school students may have greater and more pertinent problems interfering with learning than elementary students, thus causing a strain on the attitudes of their teachers toward effective teaching. With concerns about parental and family involvement, high school teachers have multiple families to contact, up to 150 students, versus the elementary level with up to 30 students. Perhaps elementary subject matter is taught with more breadth and high school is more in depth. Elementary school is more focused on the process of how to acquire information and retain it, whereas high school is more sophisticated and focused on the content of material and the substance of subjects. The nature of students' ability is also a factor. For example, tracking is more common on the high school level with students with disabilities or giftedness, whereas on the elementary level students are more likely to be included.

As indicated by the research, elementary teachers value planning and preparation the highest whereas high school teachers value it the lowest of the three groups. A possible reason for this high school phenomenon may be that these teachers, who often teach the same subject area, believe they have mastered their subject matter and planning instructional materials may not be considered as important for effective teaching. The breadth and depth of subject matter may also be a factor related to planning. Elementary teachers may be broader in their objectives whereas high school teachers may be more specific in learning objectives. For example, both fifth and eleventh-grade classes may study the American Revolution. The fifth-grade class objective may be to gain an awareness of independence and freedom, whereas the eleventh-grade class objective may be to gain an understanding of the underlying political and economic circumstances.

Middle school teachers indicated the highest level of agreement concerning physical space. Therefore, middle school teachers may have the greatest awareness of the need for physical space for their students and effective teaching. Middle school teachers also scored the highest in 50 percent of the questions concerning professional responsibility, particularly in the areas concerning communicating with families, contributing to the school and district, and showing professionalism. Elementary teachers also scored these areas with high levels of agreement and high school teachers had the lowest level of agreement. Middle school teachers indicated this area as the most important for effective teaching. Possible assumptions about the middle school level could be the students at this age have a greater rate of physical and emotional changes; therefore, conversations with parents that are more difficult in nature are necessary.

The category of professionalism includes questions about teachers working well within departmental teams. This middle school in this study is designed into teams, alpha and beta, and departmental groups. Perhaps team contributions are imperative to cohesiveness among staff and the success of students at the middle school level. Elementary and high school teachers may only have a few or no teachers who teach the same subjects or grades. For instance, there may be

only one physical education or speech teacher in an elementary building or one algebra or biology teacher at the high school level.

Overall, differences occurred among elementary, middle and high school teachers' attitudes toward effective teaching. This should clearly impact the approach that the school district takes in implementing the new evaluation model. Critical to the success of implementing a comprehensive evaluation system, such as Danielson's, is the need for the teachers' solid understanding of how and in what capacity the evaluation will be used. It is also important to identify the areas within each domain that will be included. Clear and identifiable benchmarks are necessary for teachers to judge themselves for areas of improvement and goal setting.

RECOMMENDATIONS

This study focused on one school district embarking on a new model of evaluation. Further study using the instrument developed for this study is needed to determine the extent to which these findings mirror the attitudes of teachers in other school communities. An analysis of the information gathered from the survey can also determine indicators of similarities and differences among teachers as well as identify the areas teachers feel are important to quality teaching. This information can assist educators in better preparing school teachers and administrators for promising new evaluation systems.

The following specific recommendations are based on the findings of this study.

1. Interview the teachers and provide time for professional discussions in an attempt to find data that are more objective. These data could provide answers and reasons to why the differences among the teachers' attitudes occurred throughout the domains about effective teaching.

2. The findings of this study showed that the teachers who were familiar with Danielson's work reported more positive attitudes and higher levels of agreement than those teachers who were not familiar. Therefore, provide in-service training and professional development opportunities for teachers to learn about Danielson's frameworks for effective teaching. Professional development could include workshops, speakers, presentations, distributing Danielson's book to teachers, handouts outlining the key components, and professional discussions.

3. Devise evaluation tools for the elementary, middle and high school levels using Danielson's four

domains with choices for demonstration of the indicators of effective teaching. Each domain has component areas listing indicators of effective teaching and some areas are more applicable to certain school levels as indicated by the findings. Danielson's level of performance scale, however, needs to remain consistent among school levels, the definition of an unsatisfactory, basic, proficient, and distinguished teacher must be the same for all teachers regardless of school level. Clearly, the findings showed a difference in attitudes and potentially the varying degree of needs and expectations expressed by the each level.

4. Include teachers in developing the evaluation system. As indicated in the literature this shared decision-making experience would promote ownership, cooperation, collaboration, and meaningfulness toward the evaluation device.

5. It will be important for school districts and educators involved in creating the evaluation system to give careful and critical analysis to how the term "effective" is defined when evaluating teachers using the new evaluation tool. Clear and identifiable benchmarks are also necessary for teachers to judge themselves for areas of improvement and goal setting. The literature demonstrates that what has been proven successful in one environment may not be successful in a different environment. Therefore, changes and adaptations to the evaluation tool to better suit districts' needs is a critical component to the success of the instrument.

6. Further investigations should be conducted to determine and identify the internal conditions and external factors that contribute to the teachers' responses. These variables may be related or mutually exclusive to teaching. However, they can still influence the teachers' attitudes.

7. Educate administrators responsible for using the evaluation instrument to ensure fair, consistent, and meaningful results, as well as provide time for administrators to communicate feedback concerning strengths and weaknesses with the teachers.

8. Danielson's framework focuses on effective teaching methods and pedagogy. Colleges and universities need to educate emerging teachers and administrators about Danielson's methods and philosophies. Moreover, they should initiate this process of evaluation with student teachers using a format adopted by their state and/or areas school districts.

CONCLUSIONS

The public and the federal government's focus on accountability for teachers' performance have grown in demand in recent years. The NCLB legislation enacted in 2002 has redefined accountability in today's public school system. The NCLB law affects nearly three million public school teachers and more than 89,599 public schools. The Act concentrates on four areas: accountability for results, flexibility and local control, options and choices for parents, and scientific-based teaching methods. The NCLB mandate requires that by the end of the 2005–2006 school year all public school teachers must be "highly qualified."

Federal guidelines, high stakes testing, and accountability are unavoidable challenges that are requirements for teachers and administrators. Danielson's method of evaluating teaching is designed to meet these increasing demands and better suit a wide range of teachers, content areas, years of experience, various principal roles, and include teacher input as a means of identifying the strengths and weaknesses of effective teaching (Danielson, 1996). This study found that teachers' attitudes toward the criteria of Danielson's evaluation method is generally positive and therefore opens the door for a more substantial dialogue on what effective teaching means and how it should be evaluated.

As stated in the research, educators across the nation agree that teacher evaluation is an important component in providing quality education. In addition, educators also believe the purpose of teacher evaluation is to improve teacher effectiveness, encourage professional growth, and remediate or terminate inadequate teachers. Clearly, the teachers in this research demonstrated that they are a very dedicated staff. Their high levels of agreement was evidenced by the findings showing a strong commitment to education and their students. These professionals hold themselves at high levels of accountability and are optimistic about providing their students with quality teaching. With that said, assuring that every teacher has a clear understanding of the criteria and expectations for being "highly qualified" is just the beginning.

REFERENCES

Bolton, D. L. (1973). *Selection and evaluation of teachers.* Berkeley, CA: McCutchan Publishing Corporation.

Carnegie Forum on Education and the Economy's Task Force on Teaching and Profession. *A nation prepared: Teachers for the 21st century.* New York. 1986.

Covey, S. (1991). *Principle-centered leadership.* New York: Fireside.

Cruickshank, D. R., and Haefele, D. (2001). Good teachers, plural. *Educational Leadership, 58*(5), 26–30.

Danielson, C. (1996). *Enhancing professional practice. A framework for teaching.* Association of Supervision and Curriculum Development.

Danielson, C., and McGreal, T .L. (2000). *Teacher evaluation to enhance professional practice.* Association of Supervision and Curriculum Development.

Gullatt, D. E., and Ballard, L. M. (1998). Choosing the right process for teacher evaluation. *American Secondary Education, 26*(3), 13–17.

Howard. B. B., and McCloskey, W. H. (2001). Evaluating experienced teachers. *Educational Leadership, 58*(5), 48–51.

Iwanicki, E. F. (2001). Focusing teacher evaluation of student learning. *Association of Supervision and Curriculum Development, 58*(5), 57–59.

Manatt, R. (2000). Feedback at 360 degrees. *The School Administrator, 57*(9), 10–11.

Manatt, R. P., Palmer, K. L., and Hidlebaugh, E. (1976). Evaluating teacher performance with improved rating scales. *NASSP Bulletin (60)*401, 21–24.

McGreal, T. L. (1980). Helping teachers set goals. *Educational Leadership, 37*(5), 414–419.

McGreal, T. L. (1982). Effective teacher evaluation systems. *Educational Leadership, 39*(4), 303–305.

McGreal, T. L., Broderick, E., and Jones, J. (1984). Artifact collection. *Educational Leadership, 41*(7), 20–21.

National Board of Professional Teaching Standards. Looking back at our roots: Early days, critical players. Retrieved September 27, 2003, from http://www.nbpts.org/about/lookingback.cfm.

National Commission on Excellence in Education, The. (1983). *A nation at risk: The imperative for educational reform.* Washington, DC: U.S. Department of Education.

National Commission on Teaching and America's Future. (1996). *What matters most: Teaching for America's future.* New York: Author.

National Governors Association Center for Best Practices. (2002, December). *Improving teacher evaluation to improve teaching quality (Issue Brief).* Carnegie Corporation, NY: Liam Goldrick.

Office of the Press Secretary. (2003, June 10). *President highlights progress in education reform.* Retrieved July 29, 2003, from http://www.whitehouse.gov/news/release/2003/06/print/20030610-4.html.

Painter, B. (2000). Using teaching portfolios. *Association for Supervision and Curriculum Development, 58*(5), 31–34.

Pennsylvania Department of Education. (2002). *No Child Left Behind in Pennsylvania.* Retrieved July 1, 2003, from http://www.pde.state.pa.us/nclb/site/default.asp?k12Nav=|1141|.

Pennsylvania Department of Education. (2003). *Level I to Level II evaluation forms.* Retrieved August 1, 2003, from http://www.teaching.state.pa.us/teaching/cwp/view.asp?a=3&q=84717&teachingNav=|93|94|.

Pennsylvania Department of Education. (2003). *Professional development assistance program (PDAP) executive summary.* Retrieved November 18, 2003, from https://www.tcs.ed.state.pa.us/PDAP/ExecSummary.asp.

State Board of Education. (2002). *Education regulations.* Retrieved July 2, 2003, from Pennsylvania Department of Education Regulations Online via Access: http://www.pde.state.pa.us/stateboard_ed/site/default.asp?g=0&pde_internetNa.

United States Department of Education (1998). *Goals 2000: Reforming education to improve student achievement.* Retrieved July 1, 2003, from http://www.ed.gov/pubs/G2KReforming/.

United States Department of Education. (2002). *No child left behind.* Retrieved July 1, 2003, from http://www.nclb.gov/.

Wheeler, P. (1992). Improving classroom observation skills: Guidelines for teacher evaluation. (EREAPA Publication Series No 92–5). Livermore, CA: (ERIC Document Reproduction Service No ED 364961).

Wise, A. E., Darling-Hammond, L., McLaughlin, M. W., and Bernstein, H. T. (1984). *Teacher evaluation: A study of effective practices.* Santa Monica, CA: The Rand Corporation.

An Examination of Individual and Collective Learning within a Cohort Model in Management Development

Jane McDonald

This phenomenological study examines management education within a cohort delivery model in higher education over a period of two years. The study explores how the group context influences individual cognition and group learning. Results of the study highlight specific tensions, or struggles, that characterize members' experiences of cohort life. These tensions revolve around group's purpose, membership, identity, and bonding. The study examines how the learning of individual members is related to the context of the group and has implications for understanding the group as a vehicle for cognitive change. By identifying key elements that facilitate individual and group progress and by highlighting critical tasks for cohort directors, this research offers valuable insight to university faculty, in a variety of disciplines, who want to design and implement cohort learning experiences in higher education.

Professional learning experiences in higher education are formative events for managerial development, and finding better ways to develop contexts that support executive learning is an on-going challenge for universities. Traditional attempts to improve management education programs have targeted three major areas: teaching methodologies, curriculum revision (Andre, 1985; Sullivan and Buttner, 1992), and student recruitment and selection practices (Devries, 1993; Hollenback, 1994). However, relying exclusively on these traditional approaches has failed to significantly alter managerial programs, increase the learning of participants (Barnett and Muse, 1993) or reduce the increased fragmentation experienced by students in large bureaucratic institutions. In response to the growing criticism of traditional management programs, universities are beginning to rethink their approaches to instruction.

One increasing approach to university preparation programs is the cohort model. Although the definition of cohort differs practically and theoretically among researchers, the most common understanding of a cohort is a "group of students who begin and complete a program of studies together, engaging in a common set of course activities and/or learning experiences" (Barnett and Muse, 1993, p. 140).

Many universities are attracted to a cohort model because it can be used both as a delivery format and a successful mode for learning. In addition, monitoring the academic progress of a cohort of students is an easier task for university faculty than following the records of students who self-select various courses and enrollment schedules. Many potential students are attracted to a cohort program because of the inferred promise of peer support and social connections (Chairs, McDonald, Shroyer, Urbanski, and Vertin, 2002; Zukas and Malcolm, 2000), its design to accommodate the schedules of working adults, and its predetermined sequence of course offerings. Regardless of why a cohort model is selected, the structure alone does not ensure that a cohort will succeed (Norris and Barnett, 1994). To the contrary, cohorts must be formed and maintained in a purposeful way if they are to foster student learning and development (Imel, 2002).

The formation and maintenance of successful cohorts requires student participants and faculty members alike to significantly alter familiar ways of teaching, learning and knowing. The traditional views of accepting the university instructor as the ultimate authority and of using independent learning styles to dominate the group environment are factors that can limit cohort effectiveness (Imel, 2002). In contrast, contemporary cohort programs are designed to create collaborative environments in which students are expected to shift from being dependent, passive receptacles of knowledge to being independent, autonomous, and self-directed learners who participate in interdependent activities (Griffith, 1987). University faculty members who instruct cohort students also are expected to adjust, from being the familiar "sage-on-the-stage lecturer" and ultimate knowledge authority to being learners themselves who facilitate the education process and serve as catalysts to help groups become cohesive learning communities.

The use of a cohort format in higher education has emerged slowly over a number of years, but cohort learning is relatively new as a focus of inquiry. Although there is increasing literature on cohorts and their potential as an alternative to traditional educational programs in universities, little is known about the cohort experience from the perspectives of student participants.

This paper reports the results of a phenomenological study that examines management education within a cohort delivery model over a period of two years. The research was conducted with members of a weekend, master's cohort program in human resource development. Informed by the fields of adult education, organizational learning and leadership development, this study uniquely describes a cohort from the perspective of its members and explores how participants manage both individual cognition and collective group learning. Specific tensions faced by cohort members during the two-year time frame are identified, and collective changes that occurred are highlighted and discussed. Suggestions offered to university faculty members who direct cohorts in higher education settings are inferred from the interview comments made by cohort participants.

SIGNIFICANCE OF THE STUDY

The study has direct implications for understanding the group as a vehicle for cognitive change. By examining the perspectives of cohort participants, this research contributes to the limited knowledge on cohort programs as a mechanism for instructional delivery and examines how the learning of individual members is related to the context of the group. By suggesting critical tasks for cohort directors, valuable insight is offered to university faculty members, in any discipline, who plan and implement cohort learning experiences in higher education.

METHODOLOGY

The study is designed to have student members of a management cohort reflect on and describe their cohort experience. The method of reflection that occurs throughout this study provides a logical, systematic and coherent resource for carrying out the analysis and synthesis needed to arrive at essential descriptions of experiences.

The qualitative research paradigm provides an excellent match to the phenomenon being studied. According to Van Mannen (1998), qualitative research emphasizes people's lived experiences and is well suited for locating the meaning people place on the events, processes, and structures of their lives. Within the qualitative research paradigm, a phenomenological approach was used because it seeks to describe what an experience really means for the persons who have had the experience.

Sampling Method

Unlike quantitative designs, phenomenological research is not conducted for the purpose of making generalizations, but rather to "detail the many specifics that give the context its unique flavor" (Lincoln and Guba, 1985, p. 201). Sampling in qualitative research is characterized as purposive or theoretical (Glaser and Strauss, 1967; Seidman, 1991; Strauss and Corbin, 1990; Taylor and Bogdan, 1984). The choice of participants is driven by the conceptual question, rather than by the concern for representation (Miles and Huberman, 1994). When studying the master's management cohort, we looked for data to provide the richest and broadest range of information about the learning perspectives of the cohort members, not to statistically represent the specific population.

Site and Participants

A two-year longitudinal study was conducted on members of a weekend cohort master's program in human resource development. The cohort consisted of fifteen students, all of whom voluntarily agreed to have researchers observe their class sessions. Nine students agreed to be interviewed three times during the length of the two-year program. Because two cohort members left the program during the first semester, the total number of students interviewed was seven. Our research goals were to secure a sample that had experienced the cohort phenomenon and produce trustworthy data on their experiences. Therefore, an adequate sample for qualitative research of this nature is small and appropriate for the context.

The seven participants, consisting of six females and one male, ranged in age from 29 to 45 years of age. Their average years in the workforce were ten. Six of the study participants were currently employed. Collectively, participants' work experiences were in both the private and public sectors and in diverse settings. None of the seven cohort members had participated previously in cohort experiences.

The program's curriculum was structured to present students with a clear understanding of the fundamental principles and theories of human resource development that underlie effective education and training in organizations. Principles were taught in the context of traditional lecture and discussion, along with relevant learn-by-doing tasks. Some of the course assignments were designed as team projects, as encountered in a typical job site. A course on group dynamics was taught during the first semester of study, in addition to the introductory course.

Data Collection

The primary means of data collection was in-depth interviews. Seidman's (1991) in-depth interview method was utilized because it brought the interviewer into the world of the person being interviewed (Patton, 1990). Seidman's method entails three interviews in which the interviewer examines an individual's (a) Past—the historical/biographical antecedents and context; (b) Present—the current experience; and (c) Future—the connections, reflections and meanings of experiences. Seidman suggests that interviews be conducted so that each of the three time periods is explored separately and all interviews are concluded within two weeks. We chose to modify the process so that we could capture and examine each participant's evolving experience of the cohort. Therefore, in each interview we explored the past, present, and future and also extended the period of time to complete the interviews from two weeks to two years.

Each of the participants was interviewed three times: once during the first semester of study, at the conclusion of the first year and at the conclusion of the second year. Primarily, open-ended questions were used in which participants were asked to reconstruct and reflect on their experiences with the cohort and express their views and feelings about their individual and collective learning within the cohort structure. To verify cohort members' recollection of their cohort experiences and to check their interview statements, we conducted class observations and spoke with faculty who taught the courses.

Data Analysis

Data were analyzed by using four primary steps suggested by Creswell (1994):

(a) *Bracketing.* A reflective process where researchers bracket their own preconceived ideas about the phenomenon; (b) *Horizonalizing.* A process of reviewing interview transcripts where all statements initially are given equal value. Later, repetitive statements and those irrelevant to the topic are eliminated, leaving only the horizons of the experiences; (c) *Clustering.* A process where the horizons of experiences are clustered into themes; and (d) *Organizing.* A process of arranging the horizons and themes into a coherent, textural description of what was experienced and a structural description of how it was experienced.

When analyzing the transcribed interview data, we first got a sense of the whole by carefully reading through all of the transcriptions and jotting down ideas as they emerged. We looked at the substance of the information and at its underlying meaning. Next, topics were identified and listed. Then, similar topics were grouped together, and relationships among the topics were sought and coded. In qualitative research, coding is grounded in data. The goal of coding is to "rearrange the data into categories that facilitate a comparison of data within and between these categories" (Maxwell, 1996, p. 78).

Trustworthiness

In qualitative research, issues of validity and reliability are recast into the broader concept of trustworthiness (Lincoln and Guba, 1985). Trustworthiness gives consideration to credibility, dependability, and confirmability. Confidence in the truth of the findings and the extent to which the findings of a particular inquiry have applicability in other contexts or with other respondents is considered credibility. The extent to which the findings of an inquiry can be replicated with the same or similar subjects and under the same conditions is considered dependability. Confirmability is the degree to which findings of an inquiry are determined by the subjects and conditions of the inquiry and not by the bias of the researcher.

RESULTS

In this section we review the results of the qualitative analysis. To set the context, we examined what the cohort meant to its participants and then reviewed the experiences of cohort life for its members.

Meaning and Experience of Cohort Life

PARTICIPANTS CONSIDERED THE COHORT A PSYCHOLOGICAL AND COGNITIVE SUPPORT GROUP. In the early stages of group formation, the psychological aspects were dominant. The following comments illustrate these sentiments:

"On the very first day I was blown away. I'd never been in a school situation where someone took me and my classmates to the library, to get [I.D.] cards, where to get lunch. So an expectation, indeed, was set and built. . . . Not only would we be a support to each other, which indeed happened, but the university would also continue with a lot of attention."

"It was really great to have someone comment on things that I had done in class and push me to keep doing those things. And, it wasn't a teacher. It was another student. I like being able to go through something with a lot of people. It's really nice not to feel like you're alone in a situation . . . there's nothing worse than that, because you get extremely stressed out."

As the second year of the program began, the emotional and psychological concerns of individuals that permeated the first-year adjustment period began giving way to a collective academic focus. One participant described the cohort's transition:

When we first got together it was getting together with a new group. Seeing that everybody succeeded, developed over time, and I think it became much more important as we went along. After the first year before the start of the second year, we started pushing for the quality of the work. Mainly in the second year of the program, everybody really was getting into the academic part of it and wanted the group to produce better results, better papers, better presentations, and so forth.

Comments by another cohort member accentuated the move to an academic focus. "The single most important thing that happened to me in this cohort was opening my mind to the HRD field in general, gaining new perspectives on individual learning and organizational learning, and team learning, and stuff that I never thought about before."

While the cohort was evolving into a strong cognitive support group, it continued to provide emotional support to cohort members. An example of how cohort members provided cognitive and psychological support was evidenced in the following participant reflection. "One of the cohort members wanted to drop out, and the group got together and literally prevented her and tried to help her along both in encouragement and also helping academically. In the second year, we had a couple of cohort members who had problems with completing course work and all of the cohort members wanted to get together and did get together to help those individuals."

PARTICIPANTS VIEWED SOME OF THEIR COHORT EXPERIENCES AS STRESSFUL AND FILLED WITH ANXIETY. The stress and anxiety experienced by individual cohort members

ranged on a continuum, from minor, temporary stress to stress caused by emotional situations and got in the way of learning. One participant explained stress as " . . . minor tensions that go on . . . anytime you're in a group of people." Others commented on the level of stress associated with performance anxiety. "I would get nervous that I hadn't said anything. You don't want to let your colleagues down." And, " . . . the first paper due in a graduate program. That's intensive by any stretch of the imagination, and you know stress was right off the scale." And, "In the afternoon, as group dynamics started to approach, my back would tense up. For me it would be like, oh, no. It's coming, it's coming." Still another cohort member described the effect of stress on learning. "You get uptight and you get stressed out, so you think more about what people are thinking than about what you are learning."

A particularly impactful tension-causing incident, witnessed by all cohort members, occurred early in the first semester of study, as the group was forming and learning how to communicate and work together. The experience involved a heated exchange among a few cohort members. Emotions were freely expressed, and assumptions about the beliefs of those involved in the exchange were angrily stated by one of the participants. The explosive communication was emotionally painful and stressful to some of the students who were involved in the incident and to others who witnessed the event. The opportunity to work through the hostility with a neutral party was not presented, and the incident was not discussed openly in the group again. In our later interviews with individual cohort members, some said this incident was a significant emotional force that determined the extent of group cohesiveness and defined the boundaries of openness when discussing controversial issues or ideas in future group conversations. Most individuals were reluctant to revisit the confrontation. A typical response was given by one of the cohort members. "In general, the class is very supportive, but there have been some individual instances where there's tension, and we need to be able to air that better." As time passed, the event itself and the internal emotions around the event became "undiscussible" in the cohort's culture (Argyris, 1990). A popular organizational consultant states that "individual differences and behaviors can either support or take away from team effectiveness" (Hartzler and Henry, 1994, p. 129). This incident, left unconfronted, is an illustration of how the group context can negatively influence individual cognition and group learning.

SOME PARTICIPANTS FELT CONSTRAINED BY THE COHORT DECISION-MAKING PROCESS AND STRUCTURE. Typically, the cohort used a consensus process to make decisions. When questioned about the process, several members claimed it encouraged "group think." The following statements are illustrative of their opinions.

"I learned to be careful of 'group think' and group mentality. There's power in groups that I am very weary of—the power to make fun of someone, to set somebody up as . . . the one to be ridiculed for the two years."

"People got swept along in a group. There's a lack of thinking sometimes. Don't make waves. Or, we all want to dress the same way because there's comfort [in sameness]."

Other cohort participants voiced their opinions on how the consensus decision-making process could conflict with personal wishes. A hypothetical situation was posed by one of the participant. "I might reach a point that I might want to take a specific elective that my cohort might not want, and . . . I have to compromise." This sentiment was confirmed in another comment. "The biggest problem in the cohort is that you're not on your own. Being on your own is very important because then you can go at your own pace. Then, you can take the courses you want to take, take electives you want to take. Here, you are in constraint of 14 other individuals who might have 14 different ideas on where they want to go."

In retrospect, the cohort participants spoke about the limitations associated with interacting with and hearing the perspectives of only 14 peers throughout the two-year program. They viewed the inclusion of outside participants in some of the courses as a positive cognitive experience for cohort members because it brought new perspectives on organizational theory and practice into the group. One cohort member expressed the positive influence of having " . . . non-cohort students attend classes. The [group] barriers were totally dropped." Several cohort members wanted to have the option of enrolling in electives outside the cohort structure, without first getting the cohort's consensus on the choice of courses. "I'd most like to [have taken] elective courses . . . it would have been much easier for me . . . or for anybody . . . so, definitely, [that was] the negative part of the cohort." Another cohort participant gave a compelling reason for favoring personal selections of elective courses over the consensus model: "I need freedom to choose electives that would truly benefit me from an educational standpoint."

IN GENERAL, COMMENTS BY PARTICIPANTS ABOUT THE MEANING AND EXPERIENCES OF COHORT LIFE WERE COMPLIMENTARY. However, when asked if participants would recommend the cohort experience to others, their answers were mixed, ranging from no benefit to high praise. The following responses exemplify the range of answers. "Would I do it again? No, I wouldn't go into a cohort. I haven't seen any benefit." Other comments gave credit to the support received from cohort colleagues. "The support, the whole atmosphere, the whole deal has been so good that I would have done it again. If I had to choose between the cohort and non-cohort (I had that choice when I started), I'm glad I chose this." Another participant claimed, "I never would have gone back to school if it weren't for the cohort."

CHANGES IN THE COLLECTIVE COHORT

Change is an unavoidable aspect of cohort learning, and group contexts influence individual and group learning. As the cohort experiences progressed over the two-year period, the system became more defined and both individual and collective changes became more evident. As expected, individual changes were more striking than the incremental movements that characterized the collective whole. The major areas of collective change are summarized in Table 1 below.

Table 1. Changes in the Collective Cohort

From	To
Concerned about fitting into the group	Concerned about academic outcomes and program completion
Emphasized psychological support	Provided psychological support but emphasized academic support
Focused on personal success	Became concerned about group success
Showed little trust	Developed trust in selected areas
Showed strong reluctance to freely express ideas and feeling	Expressed ideas more freely but in limited contexts
Used defensive behavior and lacked internal harmony	Used less defensive behavior and was more internally harmonious
Took events at face value without much processing	Was actively engaged in understanding the meaning of events
Wanted knowledge about management theory, content, problem solving	Became knowledgeable about management, theory, content, problem solving
Showed dependency—wanted to be taken care of	Became interdependent

TENSIONS EXPERIENCED BY COHORT MEMBERS

Four tensions and/or struggles characterized members' experiences in the cohort life. These tensions are comparable to the paradoxes of group life described by Smith and Berg (1987) in that the cohort members experienced contradictory and opposing emotions, thoughts, and actions that coexisted inside the group. These contradictions were related to (a) purpose, (b) membership, (c) identity, and (d) bonding. Table 2 illustrates these cohort tensions.

Purpose

The group members continually struggled with what they considered to be the purpose of the cohort. Some individuals saw the group as a support mechanism for personal learning. As an example, "[The cohort means] getting through graduate school with support. Especially when you're working." Another participant described the cohort's purpose as a mechanism for professional development. "One of the purposes why I came into the program was to learn more of the conceptual background, theories, and what's going on in research. I need more of a basis for that . . . at work, for my own professional growth." One member viewed the cohort purpose as a combination of both professional and personal growth. "In the beginning of the program I started to learn about the workplace. I ended up learning about the learning itself. And, that was a great learning experience." Another participant stated, "The [purpose] of the group was to stay together, nurture each other, learn, certainly to learn from each other."

The tension between personal and professional purposes for the cohort also was reflected in the symbolism that some participants used to describe the group. Several individuals overlapped their cohort experiences with earlier childhood memories and family members. Examples of these comments are: "I can close my eyes and see my mother asking me a question." And, " . . . [In the cohort] everybody stays in their family role: this is mother, this is father, this is, you know . . . Aunt Lily . . . I was like the child that wanted to run away."

Table 2. Tensions Experienced by Cohort Members

Tensions	Opposing Emotion	Opposing Emotion
Purpose	Personal	Professional
Membership	Inclusion	Exclusion
Identity	Individual	Collective
Bonding	Obligated	Cohesion

Membership

Some participants struggled with their own sense of belonging in the group. One cohort member stated, "When I first came to class I was extremely intimidated by everybody." Another said, "One of the biggest things I was accused of was that I was interrupting when other people were talking. So, I became real conscious of this . . . and later saw those who accused me were participating in the same behavior."

As individual members struggled with who should be physically and psychologically in the cohort, they looked at the connection of diversity and the tension of group membership. On one hand, participants agreed that diversity was welcomed in the program. Examples of comments that supported this claim are, "I wanted to do this program because of the stated attempt by the university to get a diverse combination of participants" and " . . . being around diverse people who think is . . . the best part [of the cohort experience]." Also, cohort members welcomed non-cohort students who attended cohort classes because they brought diverse academic ideas to the group. On the other hand, there were complaints about the diverse personalities and behaviors of cohort members. One example is, "It's a very diverse group of people, ages, experiences. Sometimes I don't see us really coming together." In addition, the early incident in which a heated, verbal exchange occurred between cohort members is another example of rejecting personalities and behaviors that proved divisive for the group. During the final interview at the end of the program, one participant came to terms with the diversity issue regarding group membership: "I developed an understanding of how and why people think the way they do. I developed more of an acceptance of people."

Identity

As with most groups, cohort participants vacillated between wanting to be treated and seen both as an individual and as a group member. One participant described this tension as "the battle between individuality and the group experience." Another participant identified the cohort as a team and stated, "The culture of the cohort is teamwork. More than anything else, you see yourself part of a larger team and not just you for your own sake. We wanted to succeed ourselves, personally, but also we really did want everybody else to succeed in the program and to finish the program. That was a very strong part of the culture."

Some participants, however, wanted to maintain an individual identity, without a sense of collectivism.

One cohort member explained, "While the group affiliation is important to me . . . I believe strongly that it is important to look beyond the identity of group boundaries. I would describe myself as an independent thinker." Another participant was asked how maintaining separateness affected the identity of the group. The response was, "Frankly, I don't care. I want to do this program, but I want to survive it intact."

Bonding

A feeling of group cohesion did not come easily for these cohort members. Throughout the program participants struggled with their sense of obligation to themselves and to the group as a whole. Several cohort members said they "felt obligated and didn't want to let others down." At the same time, others didn't want to sacrifice their own learning for the sake of group cohesiveness. Because group members were wary of losing their individual identities, participants occasionally mistook group harmony as "group think" and thwarted a chance to collectively bond.

At the beginning of the second year of study, the participants in the cohort searched for and found a common goal among all of the members that would unite the group with a common focus. The goal was to complete the program and graduate. Once this collective focus was verbalized and targeted, it served as a bonding force that began the development of some trust and cohesion within the group.

Ultimately, the level of bonding was different for everyone. One individual, who thought it was important to maintain some distance from the group, was pleased to comment, " . . . even out of the cohort experience, I came up with a concept of myself." For another participant, however, the sense of bonding was particularly strong. "I care about these people now. I care about what's going on in their daily lives, what they're worried about. What their concerns are, not just with school, but with other things. They've become my friends . . . like my family . . . I have to admit it is hard being separated for two weeks at a time."

The themes of group purpose, membership, identity, and bonding have a direct impact on the planning and administration of a diverse learning cohort. Next, we will explore the leadership responsibilities for university faculty who are interested in designing, refining, or maintaining educational learning experiences in a cohort format.

IMPLICATIONS FOR DIRECTING A COHORT

Learning within a cohort model in higher education is complex. Because of the complexity, we believe a co-hort director is key to providing successful learning experiences for students who participate in the cohort model. Most directors learn their responsibilities through trial and error, so the critical tasks that facilitate individual and group progress are important to identify. The director's tasks that we suggest in this section are inferred from our interviews of the cohort members and class observations. These critical tasks, or leadership responsibilities, are highlighted below.

Focus on the Selection Process

One critical task of a cohort director is the selection of applicants into the program. To the best of their judgment, directors need to select participants for a cohort model who do not have a background of family and/or personal experiences that will place the cohort member at high risk when under the pressures that naturally occur as groups are forming. In other words, do not select members for the cohort delivery model who require "extreme maintenance" to the extent that their emotional needs continually dominate the learning goals of the group. The behavior of individuals within groups "can have a positive or negative influence on teamwork and can impact overall team results" (Hartzler and Henry, 1994, p. 142). Although a stringent selection process does not guarantee a good fit for group learning, vigilance in the selection process of participants in cohort learning is important, particularly if applicants do not have substantial support from others outside the group.

Build a New History

Because cohort participants usually have little or no shared experiences prior to joining the group, a second key task of the director is to create a new history among the cohort members. To accomplish this task, the director needs to create and maintain a safe, respectful, and inclusive learning environment that includes specific structures and processes to help establish psychological and academic boundaries, group purpose and goal attainment, and professional and personal development. At the same time, expect and encourage the involvement by all cohort members in planning activities to meet their individual and collective needs.

Establish Group Purpose and Learning Goals

Explain the purpose of the cohort and what it is *not*. Have students set initial learning goals for themselves and for the collective, even though some of these goals will be revised once the program is underway.

Throughout the program, relate the learning activities to the purpose and goals of the cohort so participants understand the relevance of their experiences.

Establish Psychological and Academic Boundaries

At the initial meeting of the cohort, discuss the structures and processes available to support students and their learning environment. Discuss individual and group expectations for academic achievement, group participation, and university obligations. State and display the ground rules for communication within the group. Revisit these rules throughout the duration of the cohort, if needed. Cohort members can add to or revise the initial rules once a safe learning environment is established. Prior to beginning the cohort, give careful thought to the sequence of learning activities, especially during the group's formation period, and include both social and team building activities throughout.

Conduct On-going Assessments of Individual and Group Needs

Throughout the program, another critical task of cohort directors is to conduct assessments of the content taught and of the learning process. Then, adjustments can be made as needed. Soliciting a critical analysis from cohort participants is a vital piece of this assessment. Therefore, a regularly scheduled time for reflection can contribute to personal and organizational learning.

Avoid "Group Think"

Avoid "group think" by creating elasticity in the cohort's boundary. Creating elasticity can be accomplished by purposefully planning activities that intellectually permeate and extend the group's routine responses and thinking patterns. Examples are to allow cohort members to take an elective outside of the cohort schedule, invite other students to enroll in selected courses with the cohort members, and approach class discussions and problem solving from a variety of viewpoints.

Be Flexible to a Point

Be prepared to deal with whatever incident comes along by remembering to remain flexible, keep a sense of humor, and make decisions with participants that are based on the cohort's purpose and learning goals.

Establish and Integrate Dual Learning Tracks for Professional and Personal Development

Finally, to accelerate learning, the cohort director needs to establish two integrated learning tracks within the cohort. Design one track to include the professional content of the courses being taught. Design the other track to help cohort members learn about group behavior, conflict management, communication skills, and the process of change. The latter track can assist cohort participants to better understand cohort undercurrents and professional experiences rather than interpreting these events solely from the limitations of personal perceptions.

CONCLUSION

Closely planned and managed university cohorts are critical to optimizing individual and group learning. As university cohort directors strive to create effective leaning communities, it is important to be mindful of the structures that provide appropriate psychological and cognitive supportive for diverse participants. Additionally, to deal with the complexities of cohort-based learning, directors need to develop competencies that go beyond the skills used to lecture, teach a single course, or monitor administrative tasks. These expanded competencies include skills in asking challenging questions, being open to change, facilitating in-depth discussions and student reflection, strengthening cohort relationships and completing tasks, communicating clearly, dealing with conflict and defensiveness, and building teams. Also useful to cohort directors is a strong knowledge base in the theory and practice of adult education, organizational studies, group dynamics, leadership development, and change.

The cohort model for learning is not a one-size-fits-all phenomenon. Even with sensitive planning some students may become frustrated with a cohort's lack of flexibility in certain contexts, while other individuals may thrive in the familiarity of a cohort environment. As one cohort participant summed up the two-year cohort experience, "The cohort is more than a collection of individuals. It has a life of its own."

REFERENCES

Andre, R. (1985). Designing a course in international OB/HRM. *Organizational Behavior Teaching Review, 10*(2), 48–59.

Argyris, C. (1990). *Overcoming organizational defenses*. Englewood Cliffs: Prentice-Hall.

Barnett B. G., and Caffarella, R. S. (1992). *The use of cohorts: A powerful way for addressing issues of diversity in prepara-*

tion programs. Paper presented at the annual convention of the University Council for Education Administration, Minneapolis, MN.

Barnett, B., and Muse, I. (1993). Cohort groups in educational administration; promises and challenges. *Journal of School Leadership, 19*(3), 400–415.

Basom, M., Yerkes, D., Norris, C., and Barnett, B. (1995). *Exploring cohorts: Effects of principal preparation and leadership practice.* (ERIC Document Reproduction Service No. ED 387 857.)

Brooks, P. A. (1998). Cohort communities in higher education: The best example of adult education. In *39th Annual Adult Education Research Conference Proceedings, San Antonio, TX, May 15–16, 1998.* Retrieved from http://www.edst.educ.ubc.ca/aerc/1998/98brooks.htm.

Chairs, M. J., McDonald, B. J., Shroyer, P., Urbanski, B., and Vertin, D. (2002). Meeting the graduate education needs of Minnesota extension educators. *Journal of Extension, 40,* 4. Retrieved on December 31, 2004, from http://www.joe.org/joe/2002august/rb4.shtml.

Creswell, J. W. (1994). *Research design: Qualitative and quantitative approaches.* Thousand Oaks, CA: Sage Publications.

Creswell, J. W. (2003). *Research design: Qualitative, quantitative, and mixed methods approaches.* Thousand Oaks, CA: Sage Publications.

Devries, D. L. (1993). *Executive selection: A look at what we know and what we need to know.* Greensboro, NC: The Center for Creative Leadership.

Eisehardt, K. M. (1989). Building theory from case study research. *Academy of Management Review,* 14, 532–550.

Fenning, Kristine. (2004). Cohort based learning: Application to learning organizations and student academic success. *College Quarterly, Winter, 7,* 1. Retrieved from http://www.senecac.on.ca/quartrly/2004-vol07-num01-winter/index.html.

Forsyth, P. (2000). Uneasy collaborators must learn to redesign leadership preparation together. *Universities in the lead: Redesigning leadership preparation for student achievement.* Atlanta, GA: Southern Regional Education Board.

Geltner, B. B. (1993). *Collaborative action research: A critical component in the preparation of effective leaders and learners.* Paper presented at the Annual Meeting of the University Council of Education Administration, Houston, TX.

Glaser, B., and Strauss, A. (1967). *The discovery of grounded theory: Strategies for qualitative research.* Chicago, IL: Aldine.

Griffith, G. (1987). Images of interdependence: Authority and power in teaching/learning. In D. Boud and V. Griffin (Eds.), *Appreciating adults learning from the learner's perspective* (pp. 51–63). London: Kogan Page.

Haeger, J. D. (1999). *Defining graduate education.* Paper presented at the Fifty-fifth Annual Meeting of the Midwestern Association of Graduate Schools, St. Louis, MO. Retrieved from www.smsu.edu/mags/1999mags/Harger.htm.

Hartzler, M., and Henry, J. E. (1994). *Team fitness: A how-to-manual for building a winning team.* Milwaukee, WI: ASQC Quality Press.

Hollenbeck, K. (1994). *The workplace know-how skills needed to be productive (Technical Report).* Kalamazoo, MI: Upjohn Institute for Employment Research. (ERIC Document Reproduction Service No. ED 413 712.)

Imel, S. (2002). *Adult learning in cohort groups.* Practice Application Brief No. 24. Washington, DC: U. S. Department of Education. ERIC/ACVE.

Lawrence, R. I. (1996). *Co-learning communities: A hermeneutic account of adult learning in higher education through the lived world of cohorts.* Unpublished doctoral dissertation, Northern Illinois University.

Lawrence, R. I. (1997). The interconnecting web: Adult learning cohorts as sites for collaborative learning, feminist pedagogy and experiential ways of knowing. In *38th annual adult education research conference proceedings, Stillwater, OK.* Oklahoma State University. Retrieved from http://www.edst.educ.ube.ca/aerc/1997lawrence.html.

Lincoln, Y. S., and Guba, E. G. (1985). *Naturalistic inquiry.* Beverly Hills, CA: Sage Publications.

Maxwell, J. (1996). *Qualitative research design: An interactive approach.* Thousand Oaks, CA: Sage Publications.

Mezirow, J. (1995). Transformation theory of adult learning. In M. Welton (Ed.), *In defense of the lifeworld: Critical perspectives on adult learning* (pp. 39–70). Albany, NY: State University of New York Press.

Miles, M. B., and Huberman, A. M. (1994). *Qualitative data analysis (2nd ed.).* Thousand Oaks, CA: Sage Publications.

Murphy, J. (2001). The changing face of leadership preparation. *The School Administrator, 58*(10), 14–17.

Nesbit, T. (2001). Extending the boundaries: Graduate education for nontraditional learners. *Journal of Continuing Higher Education, 49*(1), 2–10.

Norris, C. J., and Barnett, B. (1994). *Cultivating a new leadership paradigm: From cohorts to communities.* Paper presented at the annual meeting of the University Council of Educational Administration, Philadelphia, PA, October. (ERIC Document Reproduction Service No. ED 387 877.)

Patton, M. Q. (1990). *Qualitative evaluation and research methods.* Thousand Oaks, CA: Sage Publications.

Reynolds, K., and Hebert, F. T. (1998). Learning achievements of students in cohort groups. *Journal of Continuing Higher Education, 46*(3), 34–42.

Reynolds, K., and Sitharaman, S. (2000). Business education in cohorts: Does familiarity breed learning? *Journal of Business and Training Education, 9,* 29–44. (ERIC Document Reproduction Service No. ED 461 738.)

Schutz, A. (1967). *The phenomenology of the social world* (Walsh, G. and Lehnert, F., Trans.). Chicago, IL: Northwestern University Press.

Schwandt, T. (2000). Three epistemological stances for qualitative inquiry: Interpretivism, hermeneutics, and social constructionism. In N. Denzin and Y. Lincoln (Eds.), *Handbook of qualitative research* (2nd ed., pp.189–214). Thousand Oaks, CA: Sage Publications.

Scribner, J., and Donaldson, J. (2001). The dynamics of group learning in a cohort: From nonlearning to transformative learning. *Educational Administration Quarterly, 37*(5), 605–636.

Seidman, I. E. (1991). *Interviewing as qualitative research: A guide for researchers in education and the social sciences.* New York: Teachers College Press.

Smith, K. K., and Berg, D. N. (1987). *Paradoxes of group life: Understanding conflict, paralysis and movement in group dynamics.* San Francisco, CA: Jossey-Bass.

Strauss, A. L., and Corbin, J. (1990). *Basics of qualitative research: Grounded theory procedures and techniques.* Newbury Park, CA: Sage Publications.

Sullivan, S. E., and Buttner, E. H. (1992). Changing more than the plumbing: Integrating work and gender differences into management and organizational behavior courses. *Journal of Educational Management, 16*(1), 76–89.

Taylor, S. J., and Bogdan, R. (1984). *Introduction to qualitative research methods: The search for meanings.* New York: John Wiley & Sons.

Tesch, R. (1990). *Qualitative research: Analysis types and software tools.* New York: Falmer.

Van Mannen, J. (1998). *Tales of the field: On writing ethnography.* Chicago, IL: University of Chicago Press.

Yin, R. (1981). The case study crisis: Some answers. *Administrative Science Quarterly, 26*(1), 58–65.

Zukas, M., and Malcolm, J. (2002). Pedagogies for lifelong learning: Building bridges or Building walls? In R. Harrison, F. Reeve, A. Hanson and J. Clarke (Eds.), *Supporting lifelong learning: Volume 1—Perspectives on learning.* New York: Open University: Routledge/Falmer.

The Great Juggling Act:
Administering Rowley in Our Time

VIVIAN GORDON, BEVERLY KASPER, MARLA ISRAEL, AND JANIS FINE

VIGNETTE

LEE, A NINE-YEAR-OLD THIRD GRADER, ATTENDS HAMIL-TON Public School. He has a learning disability in reading and written expression. When Lee first entered school as a kindergartner, his teacher observed his difficulties and provided some help, giving him extra support on letter recognition. In first grade, his teacher referred Lee for pre-referral services of reading recovery. In third grade, Lee made some progress with reading recovery. However, when he took the state assessment along with his peers, which was routinely administered statewide, his performance in reading and written expression did not meet state standards. In mathematics, Lee did meet state standards.

The pupil services team, upon recommendation of the teacher, with the consent of Lee's parents, conducted an initial case study evaluation. The result of the evaluation indicated that Lee had a learning disability in reading and written expression. The IEP team, along with the parents, seeks to provide a free, appropriate public education for Lee.

Certain conditions typically exist in public schools such as Hamilton Public School. Like school leaders at all public schools around the country, the principal at Hamilton must balance concerns regarding limited resources and competing demands from multiple stakeholders. Further, the principal must address issues related to legal mandates, ethical considerations regarding staff, and questions of distributive, social and commutative justice when considering the nature and level of special educations services to provide. School leaders, like the principal at Hamilton, must juggle all these considerations in light of U.S. Supreme Court cases like *Rowley* (*Rowley vs. Hendrick Hudson District*, 1982), the No Child Left Behind Act (No Child Left Behind, 2000), and the reauthorized Individuals with Disabilities Act (IDEA, 1997).

LEGAL HISTORY

The impact of U.S. Supreme Court decisions on public school administrative practice is evidenced not only in *Brown* (*Brown vs. Board of Education*, 1954) but also in relation to a more recent historic exclusion of children from schooling: exclusion of children with disabilities. After a series of cases prompting Congress to act to stop excluding these disabled children, such as the *Pennsylvania Association of Retarded Citizens vs. Pennsylvania* (PARC, 1972) and *Mills vs. Board of Education of the District of Columbia* (Mills, 1972), it responded with Public Law 94–142, the Education for All Handicapped Children Act (P.L. 94–142, 1975). This landmark legislation was designed to ensure not only the substantive right to a free, appropriate public education, but also to ensure extensive procedural protections. The legislation was further interpreted by U.S. Supreme Court in its decision in *Rowley* (*Rowley vs. Hendrick Hudson District*, 1982). In that decision, the Supreme Court determined that schools must give handicapped children an individualized IEP that is reasonably calculated to provide some educational benefit. The Court stated that

> the Act's Requirement of a free appropriate education is satisfied when the State provides personalized instruction with sufficient support services to permit the handicapped child to benefit educationally from that instruction. Such instruction and services must be provided at public expense, must meet the State's educational standards, must approximate grade levels used in the State's regular education, and must comport with the child's IEP, as formulated in accordance with the Act's requirements. . . . The IEP should be reasonably calculated to enable the child to benefit from his education. (*Rowley vs. Hendrick Hudson District*, 1982)

111

And

while Congress sought to provide assistance to the States in carrying out their constitutional responsibilities to provide equal protection of the laws, it did not intend to achieve strict equality of opportunity or services for handicapped and nonhandicapped children, but rather sought primarily to identify and evaluate handicapped children, and to provide them with access to a free public education. The Act does not require a State to maximize the potential of each handicapped child commensurate with the opportunity provided nonhandicapped children. (*Rowley vs. Hendrick Hudson*, 1982)

The Individuals with Disabilities Education Act (IDEA, 1997), a progeny of Public Law 94–142 (P.L. 94–142, 1975) and its reauthorization in 1997 (IDEA, 1997), has brought increased litigation and concomitant redefinition of what is required by our public schools in the arena of special education. The least restrictive environment requirement, or LRE, mandates that children be educated to the maximum extent appropriate in the least restrictive environment with his or her nondisabled peers (IDEA, 1997). One aspect of this LRE requirement is a presumption that children be educated outside the regular classroom "only when the nature or severity of the disability is such that education in regular classes with the use of supplementary aids and services cannot be achieved satisfactorily." The LRE requirement must be viewed in light of the individual needs of the child.

In *Rowley* (*Rowley vs. Hendrick Hudson District*, 1982), the Supreme Court identified two areas of inquiry in determining whether a state, through its public schools, has met its responsibilities to our disabled children under IDEA (IDEA, 1997):

> [A] court's inquiry in suits brought under Sec. 1415 (i)(B)(2) is twofold. First, has the State complied with the procedures set forth in the Act? And second, is the individualized educational program developed through the Act's procedures reasonably calculated to enable the child to receive educational benefits? If these requirements are met, the State has complied with the obligations imposed by Congress and the courts can require no more. (*Rowley vs. Hendrick Hudson District*, 1982).

Thus, in accordance with Rowley, a school administrator must be concerned with following IDEA procedures and providing an eligible disabled child with an individualized education plan, better known as an IEP, which is reasonably calculated to enable the child to receive educational benefits.

What constitutes educational benefit? Reviewing Rowley, the Court rejected an argument that IDEA required the provision of educational services that would "maximize each child's potential commensurate with the opportunity provided other children" (*Rowley vs. Hendrick Hudson District*, 1982). Reviewing the language of IDEA and legislative history, the Court concluded that the basic floor of opportunity provided by Public Law 94–142 consists of access to specialized instruction and related services that are individually designed to provide educational benefit to the handicapped child. While specifically disclaiming any attempt to define educational benefit, the Court did hold that the school system satisfies this requirement by "providing personalized instruction with sufficient support services to permit the child to benefit from that instruction" (*Rowley vs. Hendrick Hudson District*, 1982).

How does a school administrator measure educational benefit to disabled children eligible for special education? One factor that has been urged by school districts as evidence that a child's program has provided educational benefit to the child is the fact that a child has been promoted from grade to grade. In many cases, schools argue that passing from grade to grade is evidence of educational benefit. In other cases, progress is difficult to measure or quantify, leaving schools vulnerable to assertions by parents that the Rowley standard has not been met and their children have not received educational benefit.

Many schools now say that the Rowley standard of "some benefit" is not enough, calling Rowley ruling outdated. Scott Johnson asserts that the "some benefit" standard should be changed to a higher standard (Johnson, 2003). Others assert that as handicapped children gain access to the general curriculum, and they are tested on that material as well as being held accountable for the content, the "educational benefit" test should be strengthened as well. As a result, they argue the basic floor of opportunity is no longer all that may be required.

Courts are also asking questions like: Does a free, appropriate public education require a "Cadillac" of services or a "Chevrolet" of services? In the Tullahoma School District case (*Doe vs. Board of Education of Tullahoma*, 1993), the Court determined that a free, appropriate public education does not require a "Cadillac" but does require a "Chevrolet." Other cases have held that the IDEA calls for more than a trivial educational benefit and requires an individualized educational program to provide significant learning and confer meaningful benefit.

Measuring a free, appropriate public education can be a challenge for school administrators. An evaluation of the student's circumstances as a whole is still required. If a behaviorally disordered student is making gains in school but no progress at home, he is still considered to be receiving an educational benefit. Many states have recognized IDEA as a floor of educational opportunity and not a ceiling. These states have adopted a more demanding standard of appropriateness than IDEA.

In light of new statutory and judicial views, the advent of No Child Left Behind (No Child Left Behind, 2000), and increased demand for accountability by parents, school administrators find themselves doing a juggling act while trying to serve the needs of their disabled children. The resolution of this balancing dilemma may be found by examining varied lenses for use in decision making by school leaders: the lenses of social justice, ethics and best practice.

THE LENS OF JUSTICE
For this discussion, just will be defined as fidelity to the claims of a relationship. Specifically, the discussion will focus on three kinds of relationships found in schools: (a) Distributive justice: the claims that occur between groups of persons in the distribution of goods and resources; (b) Social justice: the claims that exist between groups of persons based on internal institutional patterns and structural conditions; and (c) Commutative justice: the claims that exist in relations between individuals. In other words, do the "cared for" feel cared for under just policies?

Today's school leaders must understand the histories and contours of our present legislative and judicial challenges and in consideration of them, explore new ways of fulfilling the promise of justice in our schools. Any coherent discourse on behalf of justice requires clear reasoning. Justice requires a capacity for critical examination—for living what Socrates called "the examined life." This entails not only being self-critical, but also critical of the way the world is organized and critical with respect to the "normal model" or prevailing paradigm. It requires courage to embrace those particularly difficult questions that often for reasons of "political correctness" go unaddressed. How, then, do we organize the examination of Rowley in today's climate for today's administrator? This requires an inclusive set of justice categories that will be of assistance in evaluating the relationships that prevail in our schools.

Distributive justice focuses upon the relationships and claims that occur between groups of persons in a given society. This mode of justice considers and specifies the obligations of a civil society to care for the basic welfare of its members (Rawls, 1971). Distributive justice specifies the right that all persons have to a just share in those goods that are fundamental for human existence. The problem or challenge of distributive justice usually hinges on how one defines exactly what it is that should be distributed, that is, what is required for human flourishing and excellence. Questions of distributive justice must be pursued in discussions of curricular content, processes and assessment.

- Has the IEP team assessed how the student's disability impacts his/her ability to participate in and progress in the general curriculum?
- Has the IEP Team developed the student's access skills needed to satisfy the content and proficiency standard?

Questions of distributive justice extend, too, to our hiring practices.

- To what extent are our hiring practices driven by a desire to achieve broad representation and social diversity, not simply out of moral imperative, but out of full recognition that a diversity of backgrounds, cultures, and views is essential to a vital public culture?
- To maintain the values of a just system, have we developed a means by which our hiring and promotional practices of the school district reflect our value system?
- Do the hiring and promotional practices reflect the priority of our vision while being just to potential candidates and protective of academic standards?

Social justice concerns the internal institutional patterns and relations of a society, the way in which the major social institutions distribute fundamental rights and duties and determine the division of advantages from social cooperation (Rawls, 1971). Social justice refers to those structural preconditions, many of which may be subtle and unspoken, that make it possible (or impossible) for there to be justice at all. And, it focuses critically on the underlying (and often invisible) power structure of class, race, gender, and—critical to the Rowley discussion—ability level. It provides tools for evaluating social models and systems in terms of their efficacy for addressing the human needs of a common citizenry. In our globalized world of today, social justice will involve more than ever before an examination of the expanded circle of relationships that stem from belonging to an ever-expanding common citizenry. Questions of social justice to be pursued:

- How do we ensure access in the general curriculum to the maximum extent possible?
- Have we designed the curriculum so that the educational standards apply to all children?
- Are students with disabilities receiving educational services based upon the high expectations for all children in state educational standards?
- Are we providing our students with educational services targeted towards the acquisition of sufficient skills to be successful in society?

Commutative justice concerns the claims that exist in relations between individuals. The obligation of commutative justice protects our ordinary everyday interactions and encourages us to handle these with mutuality and care, a demand that clearly requires constant vigilance, dialogue, and reflection (Calvez, 1991). Because a justice orientation must involve follow-up questions of care, questions of commutative justice must be pursued to examine the quality of the experience for those students who undergo the consequences of our decisions based in social and distributive justice:

- Once students with disabilities have access to the general curriculum to the maximum extent possible, and have performance goals and standards consistent with those set for all children: Do the children with disabilities, in fact, feel cared for? Has there been damage to their self-esteem? Have relationships between the disabled and non-disabled, in fact, been weakened?
- Does requiring the same curriculum of everyone create the condition for massive failure?
- Does the same curriculum cause boredom at one end of the spectrum and feelings of inadequacy at the other?

ETHICAL CONSIDERATIONS

When examining the Rowley standard of providing special needs children with an individualized educational program (IEP) that is reasonably calculated to provide "some educational benefit," the school administrator will note that the requirements detailing who may provide this education are not specified. Rowley has been silent about the specifics of teaching certification and has left the human resource manage-

ment of special education to the will of the individual states (*Henrick Hudson District Board of Education vs. Rowley*, 1982).

However a major shift occurred with the No Child Left Behind Act of 2000. NCLB mandated that all schools must provide "highly qualified staff in all aspects of the educational program," or be found out of compliance. While NCLB allows states to provide the definition and requirements of "highly qualified," the term itself suggests a stricter standard of personnel certification then ever before and is certainly stricter than the Rowley standard of "some educational benefit." The No Child Left Behind Act demands that school districts that do not have "highly qualified staff" provide written notification to parents of this deficiency and create an action plan to remedy this inadequacy or be put on a "watch" and subsequently a "warning" list (U.S. Department of Education, 2002).

As further motivation, federal funding is also tied to the requirement of providing "highly qualified staff in all aspects of the educational program." Specifically, federal funding of IDEA, Title I Reading and Title VII Bilingual Education, programs that either totally or partially serve special education children, are dependent upon meeting this new requirement. Therefore, school boards, due to these aforementioned fiscal deterrents, as well as concerned parents hold school administrators to this new standard of providing highly qualified faculty when evaluating the services and the personnel delivering special education programs. For example, within the State of Illinois, the following are the requirements for faculty working with special education students (Illinois State Board of Education, 2004).

Certified Staff
- All teachers must hold an appropriate special education degree and pass the state test for the grade level and/or subject matter.
- All certified staff, regardless of whether or not they work with special education students, must focus a percentage of their staff development hours on special needs populations.

Paraprofessional Staff
- All paraprofessionals working with Special Education or Title I students must now have 60 hours of college credit or obtained an associates degree, or met a formal State assessment plus college credit.

In an era of diminishing fiscal resources, these human resource requirements have ramifications concerning hiring, dismissal and remediation. Ethical considerations must be weighed in order for the administrator to make appropriate decisions that meet the Rowley standard of "some educational benefit," the NCLB standard of "highly qualified," and the desire to provide a quality education for all children within limited resources.

In reviewing these considerations, the administrator can first use a utilitarian perspective of providing the greatest good for the greatest number of people (Rachels, 2003). Using the utilitarian perspective the question becomes, how does one justify the costs of the new certification requirements for special education staff when these staff members educate a minority of the school population? The administrator could justify these costs solely on the point of the sanctions within the No Child Left Behind mandate. Not complying with the mandate of highly qualified personnel will result in the school district losing needed resources that directly or indirectly serve all students. But the utilitarian ethics of greatest good for the greatest number of students is only partially satisfied with this viewpoint. To fully meet the utilitarian ethical standard, the school administrator needs to purposefully recruit and hire dually certificated staff that can teach both special education children and regular education children. Additionally, once hired, great attention needs to be made guaranteeing that appropriate induction and mentoring are provided so that these dually certified personnel are not lost to competing districts. If such care is provided for these dually certified teachers, the utilitarian ethic would strongly encourage that all personnel are afforded with this type of mindful induction and mentoring so that all staff benefit and in turn so would all children.

Within the No Child Left Behind mandate, the rules promulgated within Illinois detail that at least one third of all future professional development for all teaching and paraprofessional staff be devoted to the issues of special education (Illinois State Board of Education, 2004). Again, using the utilitarian perspective, professional development will need to be developed that not only satisfy the requirements of No Child Left Behind but that also provide the greatest good to the greatest number of staff and children. To do this, the school administrator will need to offer common professional development that supports the school's mission of educating all children while providing strategies for special education instruction. Using a utilitarian perspective, the school administrator will need to be creative in providing this professional development focus on special education instruction without sacrificing the needs of gifted, bilingual or other populations within the school—such as differentiating the instruction. In the long term, the ethical perspective of utilitarianism can provide the focus for crystallizing the school mission and clarifying the goals and components of professional development. This focus on professional development aligned with school mission can result in the greatest good provided for the greatest number of faculty and students as well as satisfy the No Child Left Behind mandate (Ciulla, 2003; Kidder, 1995).

When looking at the issues of hiring, dismissal and remediation through a Kantian perspective, the school administrator must question whether these mandated certification requirements are universal (Beck, 1997; Rachels, 2003). In other words, do hiring, retaining, and training faculty with these special education requirements for highly qualified personnel serve the school community best? This question has two answers. If the certification and training requirements for becoming a special education teacher result in best teaching practice for all students then the answer to this question is yes. However, when school administrators, due to a limited hiring pool, hire and/or retain less than satisfactory teachers solely because they have the necessary certification to be designated "highly qualified," then the community is not best served. To best serve the community, it is the duty of universities and colleges to increase educational opportunities for prospective teachers to meet these certification requirements in "workforce shortage" disciplines. Additionally, it becomes the school administrator's responsibility to provide necessary remediation to less than satisfactory, yet highly qualified, personnel. Furthermore, it becomes the school administrator's responsibility to educate the local board of education and the parents as to the ethical responsibility of dismissing "highly qualified staff" in a workforce shortage discipline if remediation does not result in a standard of acceptable teaching from the employee.

Finally, using the ethics of care, focusing on relationships, the school administrator must ask, "Are the certification requirements for becoming and maintaining highly qualified status respectful of people and relationships?"(Kidder, 1995; Rachels, 2003). If the school administrator can ensure that recruitment, hiring and professional development focus on best practice for educating all students then these certification requirements are certainly respectful of students and parents. However, the ethics of care become most acute when the school administrator must either retrain or reclassify veteran faculty who do not currently maintain highly qualified certification. It becomes critical that school administrators keep current about these requirements, as state boards are often frequently reinterpreting and promulgating new rules. Most importantly, the school administrator must take all essential steps to provide veteran employees with the time, resources, training options and compassion necessary to complete this process of meeting highly qualified status. As veteran staff transition to highly qualified status, the ethics of care often collide with not only contract requirements but also with issues of justice.

IMPLICATIONS FOR LEADERSHIP PRACTICE

The pragmatic question that remains for educational leaders is this. How do effective principals juggle all of these considerations within the contextual pieces of schools and create a culture that meets individual student needs as well as those of all members of the school community? While Deal and Peterson (1999) assert that the principal's leadership is instrumental in shaping the school culture, they admonish that it cannot be a solo act; all members of the school community must be involved. How does this happen? It happens when the principal perceives of him or herself as a change agent who recognizes and respects the talents of all the stakeholders and becomes the facilitator of the reculturing efforts (Kouzes and Posner, 1995). This principal understands that an inclusive culture doesn't just happen, rather it is created. With purposeful leadership, i.e., considerations of the ethical and just implications of legal mandates, the principal facilitates the stakeholders in the development of a common set of shared beliefs and values—the vision—which forms the scaffold to support teaching and learning within their school community (DiPaola and Walther-Thomas, 2003). From this vision evolves the mission—the commitment providing direction to the practices of a school. Such a mission will clearly communicate what the school stands for—the success and achievement of all students; that every child is an individual and will be empowered as a learner with academic and social skills to make responsible choices.

When purposeful leaders set the tone and establish a culture of acceptance it becomes the norm. Therefore, the principal must first look to these lenses and come to terms with the critical questions raised by each lens. The purposeful leader will assess the current reality of his/her school and use the assessment as a tool to bring his/her constituencies together for conversations around the issues of the legal mandates, ethical considerations, and questions of justice. Understanding that no two schools have the exact same needs and realities, the responsive leader facilitates the conversations to establish a culture that is contextually responsive. Yet creating a shared vision and supporting the mission is just the beginning, for without constant nurturing and support through purposeful leadership, the culture will stagnate or revert to past practice (Deal and Peterson, 1999). A purposeful and responsive principal models the vision and communicates the mission by encouraging an instructional climate that provides the contexts which support learning for all students (Crockett, 2002). How does the responsive principal do this? DiPaola and Walther-Thomas (2003) believe that it is the principal's role to use staff development to educate his/her constituencies about the law and its day-to-day instructional implications in order to remove obstacles to learning.

> These obstacles are removed when the principal engages his/her faculty in conversations addressing the instructional issues raised by ethical and just considerations of the law. Appropriate, targeted, and continual staff development is fundamental to maintaining and supporting the vision to foster academic and social success for students of all abilities. If all teachers are to continue to expand their capacity to provide opportunities for all children they must have appropriate training—co-teaching models, collaboration, teaming, modifications, accommodations—coupled with classroom support—common planning time, role flexibility, human and material resources, etc. (p. 10)

Education and training should not be limited to teachers but should include everyone—paraprofessionals, bus drivers, lunch staff, office staff, custodial staff, etc. When all stakeholders embrace and model a shared voice of acceptance issues of student placement, participation in co-curricular activities, general education classrooms, etc., become opportunities for collaborative decision making rather than wedges between teachers and/or programs.

CONSTRUCTS

The following constructs describe the impact of incorporating the lenses of law, justice, ethics and practice on a student population. Through schematic diagrams, these constructs imply that when these lenses are adopted by the school leader, the students that are affected are not only the special education students but also the entire student body. The large circle of each of the figures represents the entire student body and the smaller circle contained within the larger represents the students who are eligible for special education. It should be noted that the size of the two circles were not contemplated to be representative of the actual size ratio between the groups in any one school. The sections indicated with arrows represent the lens used by the school principal at any given time.

Examination of Figure 1 indicates the infusion of the lens of the law on special education decision making. The diagram demonstrates that legal decision making by a school leader impacts special education students as well as regular education students. This is consistent, for example, with IDEA's mandated least restrictive environment concept.

Figure 2 indicates the infusion of the lens of justice. When a school leader employs the lens of justice in special education decision making, there is an impact on the special education students as well as the regular education students. There is also an impact on the way the principal implements the law.

Figure 3 indicates the infusion of the lens of ethics. When a school leader employs the lens of ethics in special education decision making, decision making through principles of justice and law are also impacted. The special education students and the entire student body are influenced.

Figure 4 indicates the infusion of the lens of practice. When a school leader employs sound supervision and leadership principles to those of law, justice and

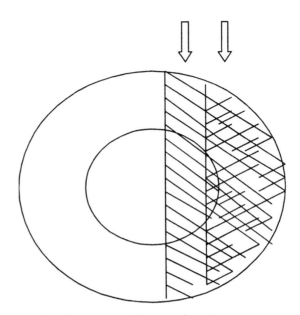

Figure 2. The Lenses of Law and Justice

ethics, special education students and the entire school population are appropriately served.

FINAL THOUGHTS

In conclusion, as the chief communicator for his/her school, the responsive principal uses critical thinking to examine the legal mandates through the lenses of ethical considerations and questions of justice tempered by the contextual framework. The principal then educates the greater school community regarding educational programs at his/her school and how they

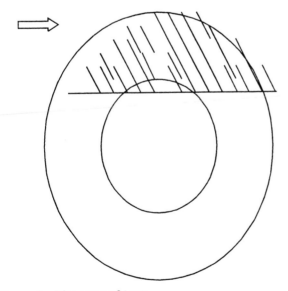

Figure 1. The Lens of Law

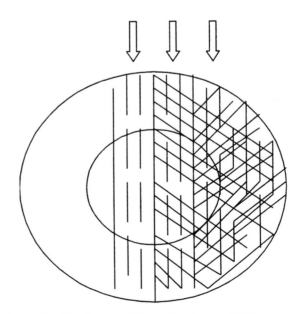

Figure 3. The Lenses of Law, Justice, and Ethics

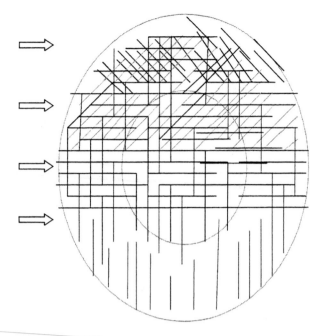

Figure 4. The Lenses of Law, Justice, Ethics and Practice

address the needs of all the students. As the ambassador of the school's vision and a communicator of the mission, the principal must use every opportunity to gather community support and understanding of what the school is about (DiPaola and Walther-Thomas, 2003). When it is announced that the school did not make AYP (Annual Yearly Progress) and students with IEP's are identified as the group that missed the goal, a community knowledgeable of the issues of law, ethics, and justice is likely to be more understanding. By the same token, when all stakeholders share a common voice of acceptance, a voice that is grounded in conversations of the ethical and just considerations within the legal mandates, AYP results can serve as a diagnostic tool to expand a community's compassion and commitment to educating all children.

REFERENCES

Beck, L. W. (1997). *Kant: Foundations of the metaphysics of morals* (2nd ed.). Translated by L. W. Beck. Upper Saddle River, NJ: Prentice-Hall.

Brown vs. Board of Education, 347 U.S. 382 (1954).

Calvez, J. S. J. (1991). *Faith and justice: The social dimension.* St. Louis: The Institute of Jesuit Sources.

Ciulla, J. (2003). *The ethics of leadership.* Belmont, CA: Wadsworth.

Crockett, J. (2002). Special Education's Role in Preparing Responsive Leaders for Inclusive Schools. *Remedial and Special Education 23*(3), 157–168.

Deal, T. E., and Peterson, K. D. (1999). *Shaping school culture: The heart of leadership.* San Francisco: Jossey-Bass.

DiPaola, M. F., and Walther-Thomas, C. (2003). *Principals and special education: The critical role of school leaders.* (COPPSE Document No. IB–7). Gainesville, FL: University of Florida, Center on Personnel Studies in Special Education.

Doe vs. Board of Education of Tullahoma City Schools, 20 I.D.E.L.R. 617 (6th Cir. 1993).

Illinois State Board of Education. (2004). *What districts should know about the new rules for certification and assignment of staff.* Springfield: Illinois State Board of Education.

Individuals with Disabilities Act, 20 U.S. C. A. Sections 1401–1491.

Individuals with Disabilities Act, Least Restrictive Environment, 20 U.S. C. Section 1412(a)(5).

Johnson, S. (2003). *Reexamining Rowley: A new focus in Special Education Law.* Retrieved August 29, 2003, from http://www.law2.byu.edu/jel/v2003_2/Johnson.pdf.

Kidder, R. (1995). *How good people make tough choices: Resolving the dilemmas of ethical living.* New York: Simon & Schuster.

Kouzes, J. M., and Posner, B. Z. (1995). *The leadership challenge.* San Francisco: Jossey-Bass.

Mills vs. Board of Education, 348 F> Supp. 866 (D.C. 1972).

No Child Left Behind Act of 2001, P.L. 107–110 (2002).

Pennsylvania Association of Retarded Citizens vs. Pennsylvania, 343 F. Supp. 279 (E.D. Pa 1972), modifying 334 F> Supp. 1257 (E.D. Pa. 1971).

Rachel, J. (2003). *The right thing to do: Basic readings in moral philosophy* (3rd ed.). Burr-Ridge, IL: McGraw-Hill.

Rawls, J. (1971). *A theory of justice.* Cambridge: Harvard University Press.

Rowley vs. Hendrick Hudson Board of Education, 458 U.S. 176, 102 S. Ct. 3034, 73 L. Ed. 690 (1982).

The Education for All Handicapped Children Act, P.L. 94–142 (1975).

U.S. Department of Education. (2002). No Child Left Behind. Washington, DC: U.S. ED. Retrieved October 26, 2004, from http://www.nochildleftbehind.gov/net/overview/index.html.

Part III

CHALLENGING THE PRESENT

Braving the New World of No Child Left Behind: What Really Counts in Overcoming the Challenge

Judy Jackson May

Facing the fiftieth anniversary of *Brown v. Board of Education*, America's schools remain in the midst of reform efforts addressing academic success for all students. The No Child Left Behind Act of 2001(NCLB) has inspired in-depth debate within public schools across the nation. This article examines an investigation of 64 public school superintendents regarding the challenges and impact of three NCLB components: (a) accountability measures associated with adequate yearly progress, such as school improvement, school choice, supplemental services, and subgroup accountability; (b) highly qualified teachers; and (c) issues relative to special education. The resulting data show that superintendents in more diverse, high poverty school districts were significantly more likely to report considerable challenges in meeting the guidelines established by the No Child Left Behind Legislation as compared to their peers in more affluent less diverse school districts. The author concludes that school district wealth and racial composition continue to be an inescapable factor in the success of America's school children, and legislative mandates cannot interrupt this cycle in the absence of honest acknowledgment and validation of the inequity of those challenges.

INTRODUCTION

Nearly 30 years after the landmark *Brown v. Board of Education of Topeka* equitable access case, the 1983 release of "A Nation at Risk," noted with sobering clarity that we were failing to adequately educate our youth. The release of this introspective interpretation of our system of public schools animated the failing and pervasive reform efforts launched to improve academic achievement through increased academic standards for all students. Continuing the quest of academic enlightenment through what has been deemed the most comprehensive reauthorization of the Elementary and Secondary Act of 1965, President George W. Bush's No Child Left Behind Act of 2001(Public Law 107–110) has earned the undivided attention of public educators and academics alike from all sectors of the educational community. As educational organizations continue to define and redefine the parameters of No Child Left Behind (NCLB), components of the Act continue to inspire spirited discourse and deliberation among educators regardless of district size, location, or demographics.

The fallout from the Nation report by the National Commission on Excellence in Education and others has provided the backdrop from which a preponderance of the Nation's school reform initiatives has originated. The NCLB educational agenda has been designed to provide a dramatic redirection for public schools in an attempt to address the failings originally cited in "A Nation at Risk," most notably poor and minority students who have failed to realize the academic success of their more affluent, white peers. This disparity in achievement between the poverty stricken and ethnic minorities, and more affluent white students, commonly referred to as the "achievement gap," has continued to serve as the focal point of reform efforts. Detrich (2000) asserted that the lowest performing students have suffered through a system that maintains low expectations; supplies minimal support for attainment of academic success; and, as Paul Houston (2003) pointed out, have been largely ignored as participants in the ladder of success. According to the United States Department of Education, the purpose of the NCLB Act is, "To close the achievement gap with accountability, flexibility, and choice, so that no child is left behind" (ESEA, 2002, ¶ 1). And in spite of the reported shortcomings of the legislation, the educational community must concede that the Act has forced a long overdue examination of the academic achievement of the students living in poverty that are disproportionately more likely to fail in the system (Rose, 2003). A major objective of the Act is to close the achievement gap by (a) holding state departments of education accountable for the success of all students, (b) raising the quality of education, (c) increasing parental participation and (d) ensuring significant accountability to guarantee that all students will show adequate yearly progress toward reading and math proficiency by the 2013–2014 school year.

Few educational leaders disagree with NCLB's imperative; vowing to leave no child behind is indeed laudable. Dissatisfaction with the legislation stems from disparaging reports from district leaders on the impact of NCLB's sanction-based accountability. Many of these leaders concur with Lewis (2002) who wrote that NCLB is "undermining many good policies, fostering some bad ones, and creating resentments that will not ease until better policies are developed and put in place" (p. 179). Enumerating the copious challenges encountered by school districts, Elmore (2003) branded NCLB as "the single largest nationalization of education policy in the history of United States, promoted paradoxically by a conservative administration with the docile cooperation of congressional liberals" (p. 6). Even some congressmen who assisted in crafting the legislation, as well as strongly endorsing the efficacy of the components, have joined the voices of educational leaders, expressing reservations in lieu of the implementation fallout of NCLB (Bacon, 2003; Richard and Robelen, 2004). Robelen (2004) further described the events of a January 2004 debate in which Senator John Edwards of North Carolina reflected on casting a positive vote for NCLB, and was quoted as saying, "We put too much faith in a Bush administration administering that policy, and it's clear that there are changes that need to be made, changes in the standards." (p. 1). Not a few superintendents, whose positions have placed them on the front lines of this nationwide reform effort, have echoed the sentiments of educational researchers who have noted that policymakers who constructed the NCLB legislation appear to have scant knowledge of the challenges for which they presume to make sweeping policy (Elmore, 2003; Houston, 2003; Rose, 2003).

The No Child Left Behind Legislation is comprehensive and encompasses substantial hurdles for some districts and opportunities for continued success for others. The stipulated mandates, procedural regulations, reliance on assessment, and subsequent sanctions may serve to increase organizational focus on student achievement; however, continued challenges lay in the unanticipated consequences of well intentioned legislation.

LITERATURE REVIEW

Many educators, and most notably superintendents, challenge the legislation, not on its merits, but instead on its premise that schools across the nation compete on a level playing field, with student populations who have equitable access to achievement opportunities, failing to legitimize challenges presented by issues that have historically contributed to the achievement gap. Hunter and Bartee (2003) examined these challenges in a compelling article that discussed research by Heubert and Hauser (1999), Irvine (1990), Jencks and Phillips (1998), McNeil (2000), Miller (1995), and Viadero (2000) that acknowledged and supported the fundamental link between equitable access and equality of opportunity in standardized test outcomes, noting that "neither African Americans nor Hispanics have faired well in these areas" (p. 151). Inattention and disregard for social circumstances that may place certain individuals at a higher risk of academic failure not only supports the ideologically dogmatic belief that social contexts are irrelevant (Bowman, 2001; Haycock, 2001; Hoover, 2000; Leroy and Symes, 2001; Pellino, 2002) in student academic achievement, but also fails to validate the inequitable and often immense efforts of administrators, staff, and teachers who serve those populations. Research continues to support the postulation that district demographics related to poverty and social circumstances, such as mobility rate, unemployment, parental age and education, homelessness, inadequate and inappropriate educational experiences, and parent involvement are variables that strongly influence achievement on standardized tests and need to be considered in the development of policies aimed at eliminating the achievement gap (Hunter and Bartee, 2003; Pellino, 2002).

Explored in this review is the impact of four NCLB components on school districts as reported by superintendents and the interaction and influence of district demographics on their success in meeting NCLB mandates. The components of the landmark NCLB legislation chosen for inclusion in this study were (a) accountability measures associated with adequate yearly progress, such as school improvement, school choice, supplemental services, and subgroup accountability, (b) highly qualified teachers, and (c) issues relative to special education. This investigation sought to explore how district leaders from rural, suburban, and urban school districts perceived the impact of these NCLB components on their schools. Superintendents were asked to assess how significantly their students and staff had been challenged by the specified legislative components. The study also examined the relationship of district demographics on the superintendent perceptions of successfully meeting these NCLB challenges. Presented in the following paragraphs is a brief historical perspective of reform initiatives in the United States and their social and cultural significance in the evolution of our system of public schools.

Ideological Context of School Reform

Discourse relative to reform efforts through the use of high stakes assessments is not a new concept and has been used throughout the twentieth-century America both in and out of the educational arena to make life altering decisions and maintain ideological social systems. According to Amrein and Berliner (2002), high stakes tests have been used to grant or deny entrance of immigrants to the United States, grant or deny participation in the military, grant or deny participation in accelerated and gifted programs, and to provide reinforcing data in support of student placements in special education and tracking programs.

Historically, political attention was drawn to the state of education in America with the Soviet launch of Sputnik in 1957. Perceptions that our cold war adversary was surpassing America in scientific gains, debunking steadfast beliefs of American superiority, caused politicians to seek educational reforms promoting achievement in science and math for certain segments of the school population, which was monitored through the increased use of testing (Amrein and Berliner, 2002). Fueled by continued fears that America's children were not achieving at levels comparable to their foreign counterparts, states moved toward improved educational measurements and established minimum competency testing during the decade of the 1970s. This period focused on teaching and testing basic skills that would ensure that each child would achieve at least minimum competency by graduation. By the early 1980s, concerns began to emerge that the minimum standards movement had become maximum expectations, especially in urban schools, as the public perceived the minimum competency standards as a "dumbing down" of academic content (Amrein and Berliner, 2002). The release of A Nation at Risk drew grave attention to our nation's failure to adequately educate our nation's youth and created a fury of school reform initiatives, whose unspoken rhetoric conveniently placed the blame for failure squarely on the bruised shoulders of the public school system.

Lending little credence to role of contributing societal issues, the nation's response to the Com-mission's "Risk" report calling for more effective school reform was a focus on the concept of performance-based accountability. Performance-based accountability emerged in the mid-eighties and became an attractive political tool, as state legislatures could be commended for efforts to reform schools without substantial financial commitment, and were able to conveniently leave the details of implementation to state and local educators and policymakers (Elmore, 2002). The appeal of standardized tests is not difficult to imagine; they are easily mandated, inexpensive to administer and implement, and provide unambiguous, observable results (Elmore, 2002), which also served to validate steadfast belief systems that some students were naturally more prone to academic achievement than others, thereby diminishing the influence of societal factors.

While the testing based reform movements of the seventies and eighties fell perilously short of the goal of increased academic achievement, the nation has continued to rely on standardized assessments to answer the call to raise academic standards and hold educational leaders accountable.

The No Child Left Behind Act of 2001

With the president's commitment to full funding, the Act passed with an 87-10 bi-partisan vote in a period of wide public concern for educational standards and accountability, expanding the breadth of the federal government's role in local education. In addition, the federal government is taking an active role in promoting consequences for schools that don't "measure up," mandating the qualifications of instructors, and comprehensively measuring district achievement based on the performance of students who have traditionally shown the least measure of success (Jennings, 2002). The legislation radically expanded the tentacles of the Federal Department of Education and propelled the challenges of public education to the national forefront, creating additional requirements for districts to meet the goal of having 100 percent of the nation's school children proficient in reading and math within 10 years, thereby leaving no child behind.

There is general agreement in the educational community that conceptually NCLB attempts to address the failings originally cited in A Nation at Risk; still, school leaders are confronted with momentous challenges as they move to comply with the accountability-based measures, making decisions that will likely impact the school and community for years to come.

NO CHILD LEFT BEHIND COMPONENTS EXPLORED IN THE STUDY

The specific NCLB components explored in this investigation include (a) accountability measures associated with adequate yearly progress such as subgroup accountability, school improvement, school choice, and supplemental services, (b) highly qualified teachers, and (c) issues relative to special education.

Under the Adequate Yearly Progress component of No Child Left Behind, each state is required to establish achievement benchmarks demonstrating yearly progress as well as leveling sanctions against schools not meeting the progress achievement mark. In addition schools must demonstrate that 95 percent of the mandated subgroups (African American, Native American, Asian/Pacific Islander, Hispanic, Multi-Racial, White, Economically Disadvantaged, Limited English Proficient, and Students with Disabilities) have participated in the state mandated assessment and meet or exceed the state established minimum. Schools not meeting AYP as indicated on state assessments are placed on school improvement status and are subject to state mandated sanctions determined by the number of years the school has failed to meet state mandated standards with increasing consequences each subsequent year.

The school choice requirement of NCLB stipulates that before the beginning of each school year, districts must identify schools failing to make AYP for three consecutive years. These schools must offer students the option of attending a higher performing district school of their choice. In addition, supplemental educational services must be made available to the student/parents. Supplemental educational services are additional academic instruction provided outside of the regular school day, such as tutoring, remediation and other educational interventions designed to increase the academic achievement of students in low-performing schools (Ohio Department of Education, 2004). The district is responsible for the financial costs incurred through mandatory transportation and the cost of supplemental services supplied by approved providers. Both the school choice and supplemental services options of AYP have proven to effect larger districts disproportionately and the funding is costing districts millions of dollars annually.

Irrespective to research on what constitutes a "qualified teacher" and what type of teaching produces the most academic achievement, No Child Left Behind deems a qualified teacher as one that holds at least a bachelor's degree and is fully licensed in subjects they teach. Additionally, the Act mandates that paraprofessionals must have completed two years of college, earned an associate's degree or complete formal assessments established by the district demonstrating their knowledge and ability to assist teachers. Fueling the debate are the concepts that teacher quality is relative to many intervening variables, such as parental support and socio-economic status, and that schools in depressed socio-economic areas are more likely to employ teachers who did not major or minor in the subject matter in which they teach (Wickham, 2002).

No Child Left Behind represents a major emphasis shift from legal accountability based Individual Education Program's (IEP) to academic accountability measured with the general population (McLaughlin and Thurlow, 2003). The Individuals with Disabilities Education Act (IDEA) requires that the IEP team decide which students receive alternative assessments; this is a fundamental conflict with NCLB, which mandates that "only students with the most significant cognitive disabilities are to be included in alternative assessments" (Allbritten, Mainzer, and Ziegler, 2004, p. 74).

By their very definition, Limited English Proficient (LEP) students are not proficient in English and it is improbable to believe their success on state assessments can mirror those of their native English-speaking peers. Schwartzbeck (2003) asserted that the expectation that students with disabilities and LEP will meet the same academic assessment standards as other students imposes an unrealistic one-size-fits-all approach ignoring the unique characteristics of individual students.

NO CHILD LEFT BEHIND AND THE ACHIEVEMENT GAP

Educators do not disagree that continued reforms are necessary, much of the NCLB criticism in the literature emanates from the impact of NCLB's test-based accountability on the adequate yearly progress component, and the mandates that are either unfunded or severely underfunded (Kluver and Rosenstock, 2003; Lewis, 2002; Linn, Baker, and Betebenner, 2002).

Schools are merely micro-reflections of the communities in which they serve, and NCLB further penalizes low-performing students with unattractive labels for test performance that is deemed unsuccessful (Mathews, 2003). Lowell Rose (2002) pointed out that "a failing label will be assigned frequently, based on the crushing impact of poverty" (Rose and Gallop,

p. 41). The same Rose and Gallop Poll noted as early as 2002 that schools with large diverse and disabled populations will experience extreme difficulty demonstrating progress. In addition, poverty stricken districts must deal with other challenges salient to the urban environment, such as the fact that students are more likely to enter kindergarten without benefit of enriching home and preschool experiences that research continues to report contributes significantly to life-long student success.

The legislative mandates of NCLB ensure that many schools will be persistently labeled as failing, not necessarily because superintendents, teachers, and staff have failed, but because of the great poverty and variability of community and school environments. This investigation focused on the interaction between the NCLB components that continue to spark widespread debate among educators, and the demographic variables that influence the districts' success in meeting the Act's mandates. The NCLB components explored in this study include those purported to improve the academic achievement of the disadvantaged, namely, (a) accountability measures associated with adequate yearly progress such as school improvement, school choice, supplemental services, and subgroup accountability, (b) highly qualified teachers, and (c) issues relative to special education.

STUDY DESIGN

This study utilized an analysis of variance design to evaluate the effects of several independent variables on a single dependent variable. The investigation, although quantitative in design, was exploratory in nature. The study was exploratory in that superintendent perceptions were initially used to gauge the impact of NCLB on their districts. Further explored was whether there was a significant relationship between the superintendent perceptions of the impact of NCLB and district demographic variables.

The study involved collecting data using a numeric survey instrument to ascertain how school district superintendents perceived the impact NCLB had on their districts in several areas. The research was guided by the following two questions:

1. How did superintendents perceive the impact of NCLB components dealing with (a) accountability measures associated with adequate yearly progress, school improvement, school choice, supplemental services, and subgroup accountability, (b) highly qualified teachers, and (c) issues relative to special education.

2. What was the interaction between the survey responses (dependent variable) and district demographic data (independent variables) such as (a) state academic ratings, (b) racial makeup, (c) percentage of students considered economically disadvantaged, (d) percentage of students with disabilities, and (e) student enrollment.

Instrumentation

The survey instrument was designed by the researcher using data gathered from a focus group comprised of seven selected superintendents who discussed the areas in which they felt they experienced the most challenges in meeting the guidelines established in the No Child Left Behind Legislation. Face validity of the instrument was established by the focus group of selected superintendents. The confidential survey was coded by district to allow the investigator to gather demographic data such as state academic ratings, racial composition, the percentage of disadvantaged and disabled students, and student enrollment. The instrument was a 21-item self-administered Likert-type survey which asked respondents to rate the impact of selected NCLB components on their school districts. Items 1–3 on the survey instrument requested the respondent's gender, age, and years as a superintendent. Items 4–20 on the survey instrument requested superintendents to respond to statements on a 6-point scale using very strongly agree, strongly agree, agree, disagree, strongly disagree and very strongly disagree. Question 21 on the instrument requested that respondents rate the degree of impact of discreet NCLB components on a scale of 1 to 4, with 1 indicating "No impact" on the district and 4 indicating "Significant impact" on the school district. A 45 percent return rate was realized with 64 responding superintendents.

Participants

The population for this study included all practicing superintendents (143) in a 20 county area in Midwest Ohio. A 45 percent return rate was realized in the sample of 64 superintendents, of which 58 were male and 6 were female. Six respondents were aged 30–40, 17 were aged 41–50, 38 were aged 51–60, and 3 were 60 and over. Thirteen percent of the districts had student populations of 500 or less students, 36 percent of the districts had student populations between 501 and 1000. Forty percent of the districts had populations between 1001 and 3000, 8 percent had populations of 3001 to 6000 and 3 percent of the districts had student of 6000 or more.

Data Analysis

A frequency distribution was configured using the raw data from the survey instrument responses and were reported as percentages. A series of analysis of variance were run at the .05 probability level to analyze mean differences between the dependent variable (survey instrument responses) and the independent variables (district demographic data). The district demographics that served as the independent variables used in the analysis are defined in the following paragraphs.

Independent Variables

The independent variables utilized in this study included District Ratings (DR), District Racial Makeup (RM), Percentage of Students that were Economically Disadvantaged (ED), Percentage of Students that were Disabled (SD), and Student Enrollment (SE).

For the 2003–2004 school year the state of Ohio established a total of 22 state indicators measuring the academic success or failure of each district and designating each district a District Rating (DR). Of the districts participating in this investigation, 10 were rated as Excellent, 24 were rated as Effective, 26 were rated as Continuous improvement, 2 were rated as Academic Watch, and 2 were rated as Academic Emergency.

For data analysis purposes in this investigation the independent variables were organized categorically in the following manner. Categories for District Ratings (DR) were Academic Emergency (6 or less indicators), Academic Watch (7–10 indicators), Continuous Improvement (11–16 indicators), Effective (17–20 indicators), and Excellent (21–22 indicators). Categories for Racial Makeup (RM) were 69 percent or less Caucasian, 70–89 percent Caucasian, 90–95 percent Caucasian, and 96–100 percent Caucasian. Categories for Economically Disadvantaged (ED) based on free and reduced lunch were 10 percent or less, 11–15 percent, 16–20 percent, 21–30 percent, and 31 or more. Categories for *Students with disabilities* (SD) were 10 percent or less, 11–15 percent, 16–20 percent, and 20 percent or more. Categories for Student enrollment (SE) were 500 or less, 501–1000, 1001–3000, 3001–6000, and 6001 or more.

FINDINGS

The analysis of variance revealed that four of the independent variables, District Ratings (DR), Racial Makeup (RM), percentage of Disabled Students (SD), and percentage of Economically Disadvantaged Students (ED) had a significant interaction with responses on the survey instrument. The significant findings are summarized in the following paragraphs.

Superintendents in districts with ratings of Academic Emergency, Academic Watch, Continuous Improvement, and Effective were significantly more likely ($F(4, 63) = 4.46$, $p = .0032$) to report facing achievement gap challenges between students of different socio-economic groups and levels than those superintendents in districts with Excellent Ratings.

Superintendents in districts with Excellent ratings were significantly more likely ($F(4, 59) = 2.63$, $p = .0044$) to indicate that NCLB will have a positive impact on high performing districts than were superintendents in districts with ratings of Academic Emergency.

Superintendents in districts with ratings of Academic Emergency, Academic Watch, and Continuous Improvement were significantly more likely ($F(4, 61) = 3.99$, $p = .0064$) to report significant challenges with hiring highly qualified paraprofessionals than superintendents in districts with Excellent ratings.

Superintendents in districts with student populations of 96 percent or more Caucasian were significantly less likely ($F(2, 62) = 5.58$, $p = .006$) to report achievement challenges relative to different socio-economic groups and levels than were superintendents in districts with 89 percent or less Caucasian student populations.

Superintendents in districts with 89 percent or less Caucasian student population were significantly more likely ($F(2, 60) = 6.50$, $p = .0028$) to report that hiring highly qualified paraprofessionals had a significant impact on their district than superintendents in districts with Caucasian populations of 96 percent or more.

Superintendents in districts with 89 percent or less Caucasian population were significantly more likely ($F(2, 60) = 2.48$, $p = .050$) to report school improvement issues as having a significant impact on their districts than superintendents in districts with 96 percent or more Caucasian population.

Superintendents in districts with 89 percent or less Caucasian populations were significantly more likely ($F(2, 60) = 4.63$, $p = .013$) to report the subgroup accountability component of NCLB as having as significant impact on their districts than were superintendents in districts with 96 percent or more Caucasian populations.

Superintendents in districts with 89 percent or less Caucasian populations were significantly more likely ($F(2, 60) = 5.31$, $p = .0076$) to report the assessment guidelines for students with disabilities component of NCLB as having as significant impact on their districts than were superintendents in districts with 96 percent or more Caucasian populations.

Superintendents in districts with 89 percent or less Caucasian populations were significantly more likely $(F(2,59) = 3.49, p = .0037)$ to report charter school issues as having a significant impact on their districts than were superintendents in districts with 96 percent or more Caucasian populations.

Superintendents in districts with 21 percent or more economically disadvantaged student population were significantly more likely $(F(4, 63) = 6.27, p = .0003)$ to report facing achievement gap challenges between students of different socio-economic groups and socio-economic levels than were superintendents in districts with economically disadvantaged populations of 15 percent or less.

Superintendents in districts with 16 percent or higher disabled student populations were significantly more likely $(F(2, 62) = 4.32, p = .017)$ to report that they believed NCLB would increase academic success of the majority of students in their district than were superintendents with 10 percent or less disabled student populations.

Superintendents in districts with 11–15 percent disabled student populations were significantly more likely $(F(2, 62) = 5.22, p = .0081)$ to report that NCLB has necessitated district policy changes than were superintendents in districts with 10 percent or less disabled student populations.

Superintendents in districts with 16 percent or higher disabled student populations were significantly more likely $(F(2, 63) = 3.90, p = .025)$ to report that meeting the requirements of NCLB have invigorated and encouraged district staff members to work more closely to improve academic achievement than were superintendents in districts with disabled populations of 11–15 percent.

Superintendents in districts with 16 percent or more disabled student populations were significantly more likely $(F(2, 59) = 6.08, p = .004)$ to report that NCLB will have a positive impact on high performing districts than were superintendents in districts with disabled populations of 15 percent or less.

Superintendents in districts with 16 percent or higher disabled student populations were significantly more likely $(F(2, 61) = 5.20, p = .0083)$ to report that hiring highly qualified teachers had a significant impact on their district than were superintendents of districts with 10 percent or less disabled student population.

Additionally, near significant $(F(2, 60) = 5.58, p = .08)$ interaction was revealed when superintendents in districts with 89 percent or less Caucasian student population were more likely to report achievement challenges relative to different socio-economic groups and levels than superintendents in districts with 90 percent or more Caucasian student population.

RESULTS

The resulting data from the analysis of variance revealed that there were significant relationships between how superintendents perceive the impact of No Child Left Behind and the following district demographic variables: (a) district ratings, (b) the racial composition of the student body, (c) the percentage of students who are economically disadvantaged, and (d) the percentage of disabled students. These independent variables appear to have a significant effect on how superintendents perceive the likelihood of successfully meeting the most challenging components of NCLB. The resulting data showed that superintendents of districts with the lowest academic ratings of Academic Emergency and Academic Watch, leading districts whose racial makeup were 89 percent or less Caucasian with 21 percent or more economically disadvantaged and 15 percent or higher disabled, were significantly more likely to report substantial challenges with regard to socio-economic issues, hiring highly qualified paraprofessionals, subgroup accountability, assessment of students with disabilities, school improvement challenges and charter schools. These district characteristics such as increased minority student enrollment, higher percentages of students who are disadvantaged and disabled are statistically more likely to be representative of larger, more urban school districts.

Accordingly, superintendents of districts with the academic rating of Excellent who led districts with 15 percent or less disabled and economically disadvantaged populations and 96 percent or more Caucasian populations, were significantly less likely to note challenges relative to socio-economic issues, hiring highly qualified paraprofessionals, subgroup accountability, assessment of students with disabilities, school improvement and charter schools, and were more likely to report NCLB as having a positive impact on high performing districts. A composite analysis of the results reveal that the most significant NCLB compliance challenges in this study were reported by superintendents in districts that (a) had higher percentages of students who were economically disadvantaged, (b) had higher percentages of students with disabilities, and (c) had lower percentages of Caucasian students. These characteristics are more likely to be representative of districts with the rating of Academic Watch or Academic Emergency.

An optimistic finding of this study related to the change in behavior and attitudes superintendents reported relative to students with disabilities. Results of this investigation indicated that NCLB's AYP subgroup accountability components may have invigorated districts with higher disabled populations to devote more time and attention to the educational programs and progress of atypical students. Superintendents in districts with 16 percent or higher disabled student populations were significantly more likely to report that NCLB had invigorated and encouraged more collaboration among staff and were also more likely to believe that NCLB would improve the achievement of students in their districts. Accordingly, leaders in districts with 11–15 percent disabled populations were significantly more likely to report the initiation of district policy changes to comply with NCLB, which, relative to the achievement of students with disabilities, may be rather encouraging. Components of NCLB prompting districts to construct policy changes and institute initiatives to meet the academic achievement demands of disabled students are undoubtedly positive ones.

DISCUSSION

The enactment of the No Child Left Behind Act of 2001 sparked a firestorm of debate and a breadth of opinions across the United States. The assessment and accountability mandates tied to Title I funds, which most schools cannot financially operate without, have compelled districts to meet the compliance demands of NCLB. Touted by the Bush administration as a bipartisan success story, NCLB was reportedly designed to impact the way children learn in school and how schools and states are held accountable to students, parents, and educational communities (Castro, 2003). Supporters claim the legislation "shines a bright light on the students who are not making the grade," (Chaddock, 2004, ¶ 3) and will close the achievement gap between high and low performing students as well as minority and non-minority children by providing a "fair, equal, and significant opportunity" to obtain a high quality education (McLoughlin, 2003, p. 1). The results of this study found support for NCLB advocate claims only with respect to the achievement of students with disabilities, as a significant number of responding superintendents noted increased attention to their disabled student population. Opponents read-

ily assent that the Act's rhetoric of supporting the achievement of all students is noble (Mathis, 2003, p. 679), but on the practicality of implementation also lament that NCLB is "the cruelest illusion to promise far more than will ever deliver" (Mathis, 2003, p. 679), asserting that it was created by bureaucrats who do not posses a realistic concept of how schools operate and "rely on coercion rather than collaboration, and equate achievement with test scores and accountability with punishment" (Houston, 2003, ¶ 5).

The voices of this sample of superintendents appear to be quite representative of the current literature on No Child Left Behind as well as the dialogue and commentary among a myriad of educational leaders. While respondents believe accountability measures are necessary for effective school reform, the findings of the study indicated that superintendents question the overall effectiveness of NCLB in meeting the goals established in the legislation, as most reported, to varying degrees, that the components of No Child Left Behind present clear obstacles and few solutions, asserting that NCLB appears to disregard the influence of district demographic variables in student achievement, educational research relative to best practices and the necessity of adequate instructional and financial support.

EFFECT OF DISTRICT DEMOGRAPHIC VARIABLES ON STANDARDIZED ACHIEVEMENT RESULTS

As noted by superintendent responses in this investigation, the intent of NCLB to close the achievement gap is unarguably a noble one. But the burden of compliance appears to fall disproportionately on larger, more diverse and smaller rural districts, as the legislation fails to acknowledge and validate the unlevel playing field that exists between middle class students and those who hail from socio-economically depressed environments. Practitioners and researchers alike continually assert that the standardized achievement tests on which the success of NCLB is gauged, are more a reflection of the child's socio-economic status; a measure of what a child brings to school, not what they learn there (Beekley, 2003; Carlson, 2004; Krashen, 2002; Popham, 2000). Noticeably lacking in this test-based assumption is the inescapable effect of poverty and the influence of environmental variables on the academic performance of children (Pellino, 2002). Often children from low socio-economic environments are academically at-risk and cannot compete on a level playing field due to factors such as abuse and/or neglect, family dysfunction, homelessness, high mobility, low education level of young parents, substance abuse, unemployment, and most importantly, lack of exposure to educational experiences (Carlson, 2004; Kindle and Pelullo-Willis, 2002; Krashen, 2002; Pellino, 2002; Rothstein, 2002).

Race and the Achievement Gap

Results of this study strongly support recent literature and commentary pointing to AYP subgroup accountability as presenting the most significant challenges for superintendents in districts that are more diverse with higher populations of disabled and economically disadvantaged students. Although it presents the most significant challenges, the focus on closing the achievement gap between minority and white students is a component of NCLB that even the Act's critics applaud. However, disaggregating test score data by race and ethnicity as mandated by NCLB's AYP may actually reinforce strongly held beliefs by some that some groups are "naturally" inferior in ability to other students, resulting in the stance that there is no need to invest money or effort to try to improve their achievement (Carlson, 2004). Carlson (2004) further asserted that breaking out test scores by this misleading and easily collected data is a matter of convenience rather than intent to aid failing students. In addition, some experts purport that NCLB promotes reproduction of the current social order where European Americans are the standard that all "others" must live up to, further perpetuating and reinforcing stereotypes relative to the perceived lack of ability on the part of non-white students (McMillian, 2004).

Moreover, the conceptual framework on which NCLB is predicated is a superficial model (Dede, 2002), which focuses on "outputs of racial achievement gaps instead of inputs of resources, accessibility, and quality of instruction" (McMillian, 2004, p. 25).

Researched-Based Practices and Teacher Quality

As outlined in the NCLB legislation, schools are to use research-based practices and materials, and only those backed by evidence will be funded. Disregarding the spirit of the act's own mandate, NCLB developers reduced the probability that programs will be based on educational research by using fixed standards to measure AYP, that not only ignore the group variability at the starting gate, but also ignore the improvements made by students (Elmore, 2003; Rose, 2003). Calling AYP a "completely arbitrary mathematical function grounded in no defensible knowledge or theory of school improvement," Elmore (2003) cited research asserting that students do not necessarily improve

their achievement in equal annual increments (p. 7). Therefore, many schools that are truly succeeding in raising student achievement could be classified as failing, forcing states with formerly high standards to lower their standards in order to avoid penalties and sanctions (Allen, 2004; Dillon, 2003; Elmore, 2003).

Perhaps in the quest to enact effective reform initiatives legislators should be focusing on how to mitigate the harmful effects on any students whose low socio-economic environments put them at risk (Carlson, 2004), and create and promote effective ways of preparing students to live beyond the walls of the school. Instead of preparing students for the future, NCLB regresses to the outdated customs of the industrial age by narrowing the curriculum and sorting students through the use of standardized testing (Marshak, 2003). The industrial approach to schooling of the early twentieth century disregarded developmental psychology research which described the variability of childhood growth and development, and promoted the efficient model of production with cattle type movement of children from one grade to another with their peers (Marshak, 2003).

CONCLUSION

The sample of voices in this investigation appear to strongly support current pedagogy relative to the No Child Left Behind Act of 2001. Superintendents in districts of varying sizes are keenly aware of the continued urgency to address effective school reform, and in fact respondents in this study appear to believe the writings of Rose (2003) who surmised that "In fact for all its flaws, NCLB forces us to recognize that too many students, disproportionately minorities and those living in poverty, fail to find success in school" (p. 2). It is however, the implementation and lack of research-based and realistic expectations of NCLB that school leaders find objectionable. Elmore (2003) blames the enactment of this poor legislation, in part, on the lack of knowledge, lack of practice and lack of mobilization by public school educators. He charged all educators to work collaboratively, both professionally and politically, to solve the problems of education. Neill (2003b) suggested that educators and advocates need to lobby Congress to overhaul NCLB by creating strong grassroots coalitions at the local, state, and national level with a strong and united voice. Educators should move to develop "genuine accountability" that truly buttresses student learning through socially supportive and academically challenging standards without the destructive inflexibility of the current No

Child Left Behind legislation (Neill, 2003a, p. 227; Neill, 2003b).

REFERENCES

Allbritten, D., Mainzer, R., and Ziegler, D. (2004, Jan/Feb). Will students with disabilities be scapegoats for school failures? *Teaching Exceptional Children, 36*(3), 74–75.

Allen, T. (2004, January). No school left unscathed. *Phi Delta Kappan, 85*(5), 396–397.

Amrein, A. L., and Berliner, D. C. (2002, March 28). High-stakes testing, uncertainty, and student learning. *Education Policy Analysis Archives, 10*(18). Retrieved April 28, 2003, from http://epaa.asu.edu/epaa/v10n18/.

Bacon, P. (2003, September). Struggle of the classes. *Time, 162*(12), 42–44.

Beekley, C. X. (2003, September 20). New law is burdensome for public schools. *The Toledo Blade*, p. 9.

Bowman, B. (2001). The challenge of diversity. *Phi Delta Kappan, 76*(3), 234–238.

Carlson, K. (2004). Test scores by race and ethnicity. *Phi Delta Kappan, 85*(5), 379–380.

Castro, O. (2003). *Uncle Sam wants . . . your child's name, phone number, and address.* Retrieved on February 9, 2003, from www.afsc.org/youthmil/news/nochild.htm.

Chaddock, G. R. (2004, January). Bush education law transforming schools. *The Christian Science Monitor.* Retrieved on February 1, 2004, from www.csmonitor.com/2004/0108/p03s01-lgn.html.

Detrich, D. (2000, Fall). *High stakes testing: Do tests with bite help or hinder our efforts to improve teaching and learning?* North Central Regional Educational Library. Retrieved March 10, 2003, from http://www.ncrel.org/policy/pubs/html/linc_f00/high.htm.

Dillon, S. (2003, May 22). States are relaxing education standards to avoid sanctions from federal law. *New York Times*, p. 29. Retrieved on July 10, 2004, from http://www.nytimes.com.

Elementary and Secondary Education Act (2002). Retrieved on April 23, 2003, from http://www.ed.gov/legislation/ESEA02/beginning.html.

Elmore, R. F. (2002, September–October). Testing trap. *Harvard Magazine, 105*(1), 35–41. Retrieved on March 29, 2003, from http://www.harvard-magazine.com/online/0902140.html.

Elmore, R. F. (2003, November). A plea for strong practice. *Educational Leadership, 61*(3), 6–10.

Haycock, K. (2001). Closing the achievement gap. *Educational Leadership, 58*(6), 6–11.

Heubert, J. P., and Hauser, R. M. (1999) (Eds.). *High stakes testing for tracking, promotion and graduation.* Committee on Appropriate Test Use, National Research Council, Washington, DC: National Academy Press.

Hoover, R. (2000). Forces and factors affecting Ohio Proficiency Test performance: A study of 593 Ohio school districts. Retrieved May 10, 2002, from www.cc.ysu.edu/~RLHoover/Optimism.html.

Houston, P. (2003, March). The bigotry of expectations. *No Child Left.com, 1*(3). Retrieved on February, 2, 2004, from www.nochildleft.com/2003/mar03bigotry1.html.

Hunter, R. C., and Bartee, R. (2003, February). The achievement gap: Issues of competition, class and race. *Education and Urban Society, 35*(2), 151–160.

Irvine, J. (1990). *Black students and school failure: Policies, practices, and prescriptions.* Westport, CT: Greenwood.

Jencks, C., and Phillips, M. (1998) (Eds.). *The black-white test score gap.* Washington, DC: Brookings Institution.

Jennings, J. (2002). Knocking on your door. *American School Board Journal, 189*(9), 25–27.

Kindle Hodson, V., and Pelullo-Willis, M. (2002, June/July). Substandard housing: A barrier to learning. *Habitat World.* Retrieved on September 10, 2002, from www.habitat.org/hw/june-july-02/feature6.html.

Kluver, J., and Rosenstock, L. (2003, April). Choice and diversity. *Principal Leadership Middleschool Education, 3*(8), 12–18.

Krashen, S. (2002, February). Poverty has a powerful impact on educational attainment, or, don't trust Ed. Trust. *Substance.* Retrieved November 12, 2003, from www.fairtest.org/k12/krashen%20report.html.

Leroy, C., and Symes, B. (2001, Winter). Teachers' perspectives on family background of children at risk. *McGill Journal of Education, 36*(1), 45–60. WilsonWeb, January 20, 2002.

Lewis, A. C. (2002, November). A horse called NCLB. *Phi Delta Kappan, 84*(3), 179–180.

Linn, R. L., Baker, E. L., and Betebenner, D. W. (2002, Aug/Sept). Accountability systems and implications of requirements of the No Child Left Behind Act of 2001. *Educational Researcher, 31*(6), 3–16.

Marshak, D. (2003, November). A foolish race into the past. *Phi Delta Kappan, 85*(3), 229–231.

Mathews, J. (2003, February). *The ups and downs of No Child Left Behind.* Washingtonpost.com. Retrieved on February 9, 2004, from www.washingtonpost.com/ac2/wpdyn?pagename=article&node=&contentId=A56818.

Mathis, W. J. (2003, May). No Child Left Behind: Cost and benefits. *Phi Delta Kappan, 84*(9), 679–686.

McLaughlin, M. J., and Thurlow, M. (2003, September). Educational accountability and students with disabilities: Issues and challenges. *Educational Policy, 17*(4), 431–451.

McLoughlin, C. (2003, September). NCLB primer for parents and educators: The federal No Child Left Behind Act of 2001. *National Association of School Psychologists,* 1–4.

McMillian, M. (2003/2004, Dec/Jan). Is No Child Left Behind 'Wise schooling' for African American male students? *The High School Journal,* 25–33. Retrieved on March 13, 2004, from www.muse.jhi.edu.

McNeil, L. M. (2000). *Contradictions of school reform: Educational costs of standardized testing.* New York: Routledge.

Miller, L. S. (1995). *An American imperative: Accelerating minority educational advancement.* New Haven, CT: Yale University Press.

Neill, M. (2003a, November). Leaving children behind: How no child left behind will fail our children. *Phi Delta Kappan, 85*(3), 225–228.

Neill, M. (2003b, Fall). Don't mourn, organize. *Rethinking Schools Online.* Retrieved on February 3, 2004, from www.rethinkingschools.org/special_reports/bushplan/nclb181.shtml.

No Child Left Behind Act of 2001, Pub. L. No. 107–110, 115 Stat. 1425. Ohio Department of Education (ODE). (2004). Retrieved February 1, 2004, from http://www.ode.state.oh.us/esea.

Pellino, K. (2002). *The effects of poverty on teaching and learning.* Retrieved August 20, 2002, from www.teachnology.com/tutorials/teaching/poverty.

Popham, J. W. (2000, December). The mismeasurement of educational equality. *The School Administrator, 56*(11), 12–15.

Richard, A., and Robelen, E. W. (2004, March). Federal law is questioned by governors. *Education Week, 23*(25), 1, 17.

Robelen, E. W. (2004, January). "No Child" Law faulted in democratic race. *Education Week, 23*(18), 1, 23.

Rose, L. C. (2003, September). Public education's Trojan Horse? *Phi Delta Kappan, 85*(1), 2.

Rose, L. C., and Gallup, A. M. (2002). *The 34th annual Phi Delta Kappan/Gallup poll of the public's attitudes toward public schools.* Retrieved April 29, 2002, from www.pdkintl.org/kappan/kpol0009.htm.

Rothstein, R. (2002). *Out of balance: Our understanding of how schools affect society and how society affects school.* Chicago: Spencer Foundation.

Schwartzbeck, T. D. (2003). Targeting subgroups. *School Administrator, 60*(11), 16–20.

United States Department of Education (1983). *A nation at risk.* Washington, DC.

Viadero, D. (2000, March 22). Lags in minority achievement defy traditional explanations. *Education Week 19*(28), 1, 18–19, 21–2. Available from www.nochildleftbehind.gov/next/overview/index.html.

Mentoring Needs of New Superintendents

ROCK MCNULTY AND JUDITH ADKISON

IN 1999 THE TEXAS LEGISLATURE PASSED A LAW REQUIRING all first-time superintendents in Texas to participate in a year-long mentoring program. The research reported here was designed in response to this legislation to determine whether new superintendents thought they needed mentoring, and, if so, what they thought the critical elements of a mentoring program should include. While there is considerable literature on mentoring of students and new teachers and some literature on mentoring principals, little attention has been given to the mentoring needs of superintendents or of chief executive officers in private sector organizations. This article reviews definitions of mentoring, discusses mentor characteristics identified in the literature, and examines literature on superintendent mentoring. It describes the research design and reports the findings about first-year superintendent's perceptions of the need for mentoring, benefits of a mentoring relationship, critical characteristics of an effective mentor, and knowledge areas where support is needed. It concludes with recommendations for superintendent mentoring programs.

WHAT IS MENTORING?

In the classical view of mentoring, an older, experienced person advises a younger, less experienced person. Beyond this, there are different views of the purpose of mentoring and of the mentor role. While mentoring occurs in educational settings between teacher and student, and mentoring can occur outside a work setting to develop an individual, most of the interest in mentoring has focused on its socialization function in organizations and professions. The purposes of mentoring relationships or programs include acquiring or improving job skills, personal development, and career advancement. Since the concept has been operationalized in many ways, it has been difficult to conduct research on the extent of mentoring

and how it affects mentors, the mentored, and the organization (Merriam, 1983).

Kram (1985) identified two functions of mentoring in corporations. The career function emphasizes learning the ropes of the profession and preparation for a career move, while the psychosocial function involves the development of the individual in his/her social environment. The career function brings about professional promotion, while the psychosocial function affects the individual on a personal level by clarifying role identity and acclimating the fledgling employee to the work environment. Similarly, the Crow and Matthews (1998) mentoring model for school administrators includes three functions. The professional development function concentrates on the development of knowledge, skills, behaviors, and values for dynamic school leadership. The career development function helps the mentored develop career satisfaction, awareness, and advancement. The psychosocial development function promotes the mentored person's personal and emotional well-being, clarifies role expectations, and reduces organizational conflict.

To clarify the many types of relationship seen as mentoring, Shapiro, Haseltine, and Rowe (1978) developed a continuum of advisory/support relationships that facilitate career development in management and business. The roles on the continuum range from supportive colleague or coworker to the intense and paternalistic relationship of the mentor. Figure 1 shows five roles that have been labeled "mentoring."

Mertz (2004) developed a more elaborate model that incorporates levels of intensity and different purposes in the arrangement. The model arranges the roles in a pyramid to reflect both increasing involvement and intensity in the relationship and the change in intent from the lowest level (psychosocial development) to the highest level (career advancement). The

Peer Pal	Someone at the same level with whom one can share information, strategy, and mutual support for mutual benefit.
Guide	A person who can explain the system but is not usually in a position to champion a protégé.
Sponsor	Someone who is less powerful than a patron in promoting and shaping the career of a protégé.
Patron	An influential person who uses his/her power to help the protégé's career advancement.
Mentor	An individual who assumes the role of both teacher an advocate in an intense paternalistic relationship.

Figure 1.   Continuum of Mentor Roles

six levels are: (a) Role model, peer pal, or supporter; (b) teacher or coach; (c) counselor, advisor, or guide; (d) sponsor or benefactor; (e) patron or protector; and (f) mentor. She explained that the intent of patrons and mentors is career advancement and thus, the focus of the relationship is on the future rather than on improving current job skills.

One-on-one mentoring programs have long been a part of management development in major corporations, but the emerging concept of the "learning organization" has sparked renewed interest in mentoring (Fritts, 1998, p. 3). Fritts defined the learning organization as a company committed to the continual development of individuals and groups to meet changing business needs. The futuristic learning organization sees mentoring as a key human resource strategy and uses mentoring to ensure that it will have the leadership talent to move the company into the future. Similarly, in education, continuing development and support of leaders has been seen as important for assuring effective schools, and mentoring or peer-coaching programs are frequently proposed to meet that need (Daresh, 2004).

Daresh (2004) argued that, in teacher education and administrator development, mentoring has become so popular that mentoring relationships have "generally been viewed as a kind of panacea for dealing with many of the limitations often felt to exist in education as well as in many other fields" (p. 498). However, formal mentoring programs have been shown to benefit the mentor, the mentee, and the organization. The relationships also can be problematic when lack of time, personal or professional differences, and unclear expectations about the relationship occur (Daresh, 2004; Ehrich, Hansford, and Tennent, 2004).

CHARACTERISTICS OF EFFECTIVE MENTORS

Most discussions of mentoring or mentors include two dimensions of mentor behavior. The effective mentor addresses both. The first dimension includes efforts to help the mentee acquire skills and knowledge related to a job. The second includes behaviors that promote the mentee's personal growth (e.g., Crow and Matthews, 1998). Fraser (1998) emphasized the importance of the rapport between the mentor and mentee, arguing that the relationship will grow stronger if the partners feel a kinship, openness, and trust as they work toward a common goal.

Several sources identified mentor behaviors that establish a personal relationship with the mentee. Cohen (1995) described a developmental mentor model designed to help mentors motivate mentees to take the necessary risks to make decisions without certainty of successful results and to overcome difficulties in their own journeys toward education. Mentors offer personal thoughts and genuine feelings to emphasize value of learning from unsuccessful or difficult experiences rather than treating them as failures; show a realistic belief in the mentees' abilities to pursue goals; encourage them to take action; and project a confident view of the necessary and appropriate risk taking needed to develop personally, professionally and educationally. Cohen and Galbraith (1995) believed that the importance of the relationship for the mentee becomes stronger through the collaborative learning experience. Daresh and Playko (1994) found that one of the attributes of mentoring is a relationship that is both developmental and supportive in its nature. Luna (1994) similarly describes mentoring as a "functional" supportive relationship in which both the mentor and the one mentored receive professional and personal benefits. The significance of the personal relationship suggests the importance of a good match between the mentor and mentee. Both mentors and mentees have reported that incompatible personalities, ideologies, or levels of expertise lead to a problematic relationship (Ehrich et al., 2004).

MENTORING THE SUPERINTENDENT

Mentoring has been suggested to help non-traditional candidates move into the superintendency and to help superintendents hired from outside education to succeed. Glass (2000) recommended state-funded year-long superintendency internships for women administrators to give them a close view of the position. He reported that one of the reasons there are fewer women in the superintendency is that they seem to have a less developed mentoring system than men. This is important since mentors many times "act as go-betweens among superintendent candidates and school boards" (p. 31).

Mathews (1999) argued that mentoring might be especially beneficial to first-time superintendents hired from outside the field of education. He reported that a growing number of school boards purposely target non-traditional sources of superintendents because of their impatience with low student achievement and high educational costs. On-the-job learning is necessary when new superintendents come from the military, business, public service such as city managers, and legal professions. He reported that many non-traditional superintendents independently seek out mentors among fellow superintendents. They find that they benefit from other superintendents' advice in handling a variety of situations and basic day-to-day tasks, as well as the idiosyncrasies of teacher-people skills. Their mentors provided "crash courses" in "edu-speak" and "edu-accounting" and protocol for school boards (Matthews, 1999, p. 28). However, there are few formal programs for the new superintendent to enter into an apprenticeship, coaching, cohort, or mentoring relationship.

Formal mentoring programs for preservice administrators have been developed. For example, the Danforth Foundation supported an experimental program to stimulate structured mentoring relationships between students in university-based preparation programs and school district administrators (Barnett, 1990). Milstein (1993, p. 30–31) believes that if university programs can select a cadre of successful practitioners who willingly bond with, model for, and demonstrate to talented novices the best of administrative practice, the mentoring experience can be successful. Administrator preparation programs, including those for the superintendency, include formal internships, where a mentoring relationship may or may not develop. Hoyle, English, and Steffy (1998) recommended a Professional Studies Model (PSM) designed for full-time administrators seeking the doctorate. This model includes a cohort design that makes possible the "peer pal" relationship among graduate students and provides other levels of mentoring from faculty and school administrators.

However, mentoring programs for practicing superintendents are rare. The Texas Association for School Administrators (TASA) has initiated a mentoring program in response to the legislative mentoring requirement described in the following section. Little is known about how superintendents actually are mentored. There is no specific research on the mentoring needs of administrators who are entering the chief executive level in public education.

Mentoring the superintendent would appear to be different from the more conventional or traditional model of a senior, experienced person taking a novice under his or her wing to teach and help within the same organization. In the traditional sense, mentoring allows for mediated career entry in which novices move gradually from simple to more demanding tasks, and from modest to substantial responsibility, all under the supervision of acknowledged masters whose skill and longevity have earned them status with an occupation (Peper, 1994). This view of mentoring seems inappropriate to the mature individual who already has moved through a variety of teaching and administrative positions and received specialized graduate training. The new superintendent cannot be eased into the role but must handle all responsibilities associated with the job whether prepared or not. As chief executive officer the superintendent has no senior person in the organization to serve as a mentor.

TEXAS MENTORING REQUIREMENTS

To address the challenge of large numbers of new superintendents with little or no experience in the superintendency, the 1999 Texas Legislature passed a law requiring that all new superintendents participate in a mentoring relationship. At the time of the study Texas had the only state-required mentoring program for school superintendents in the United States. The law required that, beginning September 1, 2000, first time public school superintendents must adhere to Chapter 19 of the Texas Administrative Code (TAC) Section 242.25 which states that specific guidelines must be followed if a school district has as its chief executive officer a first-time superintendent. The state guidelines require that first-time superintendents (including the first-time in the state) must participate in a one-year mentorship to include at least 36 hours of professional development directly related to the state standards for a superintendent. The law requires that the superintendent has contact with his or her mentor at least twelve times during the one-year mentorship. The new superintendent must complete the mentorship program for first-time superintendents within the first 18 months of employment in the superintendency in order to maintain the standard certificate.

Table 1. New Superintendents in Texas 1999–2000

District Enrollment	Total Positions Statewide	New Sup'ts.	Male	Female	Anglo	African American	Hispanic
<500	345	34	28	6	33	0	1
500–999	211	15	12	3	15	0	0
1,000–2,999	253	18	14	4	15	03	
3,000–9,999	152	5	5	0	3	11	
>10,000	81	5	4	1	1	0	4
Totals	1,042	77	63	14	67	1	9

The intended relationship appears closest to the "guide" level of the Shapiro, Hazeltine, and Rowe (1978) continuum or the teacher, counselor, guide, advisor roles in the Mertz (2004) model. This level of mentoring emphasizes knowledge and skill development in job-related areas rather than individual growth or career advancement.

METHODOLOGY

The method of inquiry was a structured interview of 20 superintendents who completed their first year as a superintendent in the state of Texas in the school year of 1999–2000, the year before the law went into effect. The interviewees were selected to get the maximum variation in range of people to be representative of the larger population (Tagg, 1985; Seidman, 1998).

Table 1 shows demographic information about new superintendents in Texas in 1999–2000.

Table 2 shows the demographic information for the sample.

The first-year superintendents interviewed for this study reflected the population of the state's new superintendents. The range of district sizes, gender, and ethnicity in the population was represented in the study.

Data were collected in personal face-to-face or telephone interviews that were taped and transcribed after the interview. Four interviews were conducted by telephone because of geographical distance and the inability to match schedules. The interviews, approximately 90 minutes in length, followed a common structured protocol.

The questions requested demographic information including district size, career path, formal training, and experience with a mentor during the first year of the superintendency. Those who did not have a mentor were asked what they would have wanted from a mentoring relationship.

Field notes of the researcher's impressions, ideas, and observations were maintained in a notebook. These notes were written immediately following an interview as a reflective exercise and to add meaning to each interview. Follow-up phone calls were conducted if, after reviewing the written transcripts, clarification or additional information was needed. Field notes and informal self-evaluation were reviewed and evaluated after each interview to determine if the interview instrument was yielding the desired data. Additionally after each interview, the audiotape was reviewed for clarity and to ensure all answers from each participant were clear and answered fully. The taped interviews were transcribed soon after the interview. The scripted interview was then reviewed and compared with the questions to ensure full understanding of the participant's answer. Interview questions did not have to be modified to elicit the data.

The first-year superintendents were asked to discuss what formal and informal mentoring they had experienced. Reflecting on their first year of the superintendency, they identified the areas of the job where they would have benefited most from a mentor and how that mentor might have assisted them in meeting the responsibilities and expectations of their role in the position of superintendent.

Table 2. Superintendents in the Sample

District Enrollment	N	Male	Female	Anglo	African American	Hispanic
<500	7	4	3	7	0	0
500–999	3	3	0	3	0	0
1,000–2,999	5	4	1	5	0	0
3,000–9,999	3	3	0	2	1	0
>10,000	2	2	0	0	0	2
Totals	20	16	4	17	1	2

DEVELOPMENT OF THE INTERVIEW QUESTIONS

The interview questions were developed from the review of the literature and Texas statutory requirements. The professional standards of the superintendency as outlined by Texas statute and the Texas Association of School Administrators served as sources to structure the interview questions about specific knowledge and competencies. An interview instrument based on the research questions, statutory requirements, and literature review was developed. Broad, open-ended questions determined the areas a first-year superintendent identified as areas where a mentor can assist him or her in meeting the expectations, functions, role, and responsibilities of the job. The sources for the questions were the Texas Professional Standards for the Superintendency, Texas Education Code Provisions 11.201—Superintendent Duties, State Board of Education Rules Texas Administrative Code Title 19 Part 7 Chapter 242 Rule 242.15 Standards Required for the Superintendent Certificate, and Commissioner's Rules Concerning Superintend Appraisal 150.1021. These sources, which outline superintendent responsibilities, were also compare to the responses of interviewed first-year superintendents. Also used as a source for questions was *Skills for Successful 21st Century School Leaders* (Hoyle, English, and Steffy, 1998). The instrument served as a guide during the interview process. However, there was some variation in interviews because there was an occasional need for follow-up questions to responses.

The interview instrument was submitted to an advisory panel to obtain face and content validity for the completed survey. The panel consisted of one university professor in the field of educational administration, three superintendents with over twenty years of experience, and one past superintendent who is currently a state educational service center director. One of the members served on the committee that assisted the Texas legislators in writing the law requiring the mentoring of first-year superintendents. The panel members were asked to assess the instrument for content validity, question relevance, clarity, and appropriateness. Panel members were asked to complete an evaluation instrument, which allowed them to respond to the validity of each question on the interview for.

PERCEIVED NEED FOR MENTORING

The interview protocol used three approaches to determine if the new superintendents thought they needed mentoring. The first was to ask whether they were prepared for the new position. The second asked them about their current and previous experiences in a mentoring relationship. Finally, a direct question asked if they felt they and other new superintendents needed a mentor.

When asked to recall a circumstance or incident during their initial year where they felt unprepared by their professional or formal training, all of the first-year superintendents stated they felt unprepared for some aspect of the job. However, only one felt totally unprepared for the role, stating: "I didn't feel prepared for anything."

New superintendents without respect to district size, gender, or ethnicity identified situations related to school finance that they were unprepared to handle easily. Seven related difficult situations that centered on developing and meeting a budget. For example, one faced the challenge of suddenly having the district classified as a "Chapter 41 district." Texas school districts in this category are considered "wealthy" when the property value is over 300,000 district property value per student and must send any locally collected funds over the $300,000 per student ceiling to the state agency to be distributed among the less wealthy districts. She explained that this law affects few small school districts in the state and, consequently, it was hard to find another superintendent to help her understand the challenges of administering the budget and explaining the situation to the board of community.

Four superintendents reported the difficulties of trying to develop a budget and making budget-cutting decisions to balance the budget after revenue shortfalls. Another described the emotional drain and difficulty in explaining a reduction in force to the board and staff. Neither he nor the board had been aware of the severity of the finances when he took the job. Three others expressed the difficulty in getting their board of trustees to understand the problems in the budget. Two superintendents related the more subtle but heavy feeling of realizing the responsibility they had to the entire community and school district through the proper development of the budget for the coming year. They described the experience as "frightening," when realizing "the buck stops here," or "I'm it." One participant described a conflict over property values with the appraisal district and coming to the realization of the importance of the situation when he had to return to his office and individually sign every employee's paycheck. There were nearly 200 paychecks to be signed. He realized the "awesomeness of the responsibility" as he signed each individual's paycheck. It "hit" him that property values meant revenue, which meant salaries of people in the community. He felt strongly that he was an advocate not only for children but also for his community. He also noted that through this experience he realized just how "political the position is," referring to the experience of dealing with other government agencies.

Another common realization was that the role requires facing multiple, significant problems at the same time. Four superintendents described immediately having to handle controversial situations such as conflict on the board of trustees, continual negative press from the local printed media looking for scandals, and handling formal complaints that required investigation and reporting to the state agency. Each of these situations required quick study, organization of ideas, and problem solving in order to learn and carry out their responsibilities. Each of the superintendents reported that, while trying to concentrate on one main issue, they also had the pressures of having to meet other needs that were unfamiliar to them within the school district. One participant described that on his first day of work there was a bomb threat in which he had to act. He stated, "You find out quickly who everyone comes to for the answers." Another reported feeling unprepared for "the reality of the superintendent experience . . . and the constant demand for immediate answers to a wide variety of questions from many different areas."

Other first-year superintendents described more general and subtle unease. One administrator of a district of under 500 students recalled that on the second day on the job after walking into his office he thought, "Where do we go from here?" He elaborated, "There are no guidelines of what you do day-to-day as a superintendent." Another new superintendent in a district under 500 students described a similar feeling:

I'm it. When I was a principal I could always tell people that I needed to ask the superintendent. Now I couldn't pass the work on or know that someone would check me.

A participant in a district of 1,000 to 2,999 students described the "butterflies" of the first board meeting and realizing, "there is no one else to take the heat." A superintendent of a district over 10,000 students simply identified the feeling as, "the reality of the superintendent experience."

Two first-year superintendents in districts of 1,000 to 2,999 students recalled the constant work required to build and maintain relationships and understand the political powers that seek to influence the decisions of the superintendent. One described being approached by an individual board member who expected her to honor and work on a special request immediately. She described the feeling of not being prepared on how to respond to the individual board member, "one of her bosses." Another described feeling the great responsibility of having to broker between the board of trustees, administration, and teachers in order for them to cooperate, understand each other, and develop common goals together. He stated:

Trying to speak and understand the same language is a challenge. Everyone is different. Sometimes we have some lively exchanges of ideas and discussions. You can't educate children the same way you run a farm or business.

A common theme was that most of the new superintendents felt unprepared for the "day-to-day" activities and responsibilities of the superintendency. The constant input, questions, decision, and problem solving that take place in a day with little time to study, think, or reflect on decisions was a challenge. The connection between theory and basic knowledge of the job and actual practice was not a part of the majority of the participants' formal education. Time management was another area in which all superintendents appeared to struggle when first in the position of superintendent. They expressed there was not enough time to get everything done that needed to be accomplished.

Experience in Mentoring Relationships

Nineteen of the new superintendents had firsthand experience with mentoring at some point in their careers. The majority (14) reported having one mentor. All of the men had mentors at the time of the interview. In some cases, the relationship with the mentor had lasted throughout the career, and in three cases it began when the superintendent was a high school student and the mentor was a teacher or coach.

Three of the four women did not have mentors at the time of the interview, and one never had a mentor. They served in rural, isolated districts. Two had been promoted from within the district, and the third had been hired from a neighboring district. Two had been mentored as assistant principals or principals in larger districts and had served as interim superintendents before being named superintendent. They both remained in contact with their former mentors but did not have a close relationship. While they discussed aspects of the job, they noted that they did not ask the former mentors for "much assistance," and that the mentors did not refer them to other resources when they did ask for advice. One did state that the mentor gave her verbal encouragement and was available. Likely the former mentors, who were not superintendents, lacked the expertise and experienced to continue the mentoring relationship.

Four first-year superintendents in districts smaller than 3,000 students had established recent mentor relationships through business or professional association rather than through working in the same school district. The relationships developed in different ways: One superintendent participated in a formal mentoring program developed by the state administrators' organization; others had a helpful superintendent in a neighboring district, a business relationship with another superintendent, or met the mentor at a professional meeting. While these relationships began as advisory relationships focused on the job, they all developed into friendships. One superintendent found that as he gained experience and expertise, the relationship with the mentor became a peer relationship in which both parties shared knowledge and helped each other. The mentors were good role models as well as teachers. They displayed a "willingness to do whatever it took as far as answering questions," and coached in a way that "didn't make me feel like I should know the answers already." These mentors could provide "just in time" information or assistance so that the novice did not have "to spend a long time looking for information in books." They were not condescending: "He doesn't have an attitude that I should already know this." They also took an interest in the personal and emotional well being of the mentored superintendent. One first-year superintendent explained that his mentor is

> interested and knows the stress of the job. He understands and allows me to blow off steam. He encourages me to take care of myself, my health, my family, my children, and take time for myself. [He] helps with problems.

Even though the relationship was relatively new, a basis of trust had been established. Mentor and mentored discussed "personal challenges" and the mentor provided emotional support. For example, a new superintendent reported feeling as if, "I'm in the well and can't see out of it and he can help me. I trust him."

In summary the four superintendents with recently acquired mentors reported that "the relationship is more important than the knowledge . . . and the experience [was] more important in connection with the relationship." It was important that the mentor had had similar experiences, being able to say, "I've been there too, and it's tough right now but tomorrow the sun will still come up and you'll still have your job." The value of this relationship included support, giving the mentored "the confidence I needed to at least act like I knew what I was doing."

All other mentoring relationships fell into the patron/mentor categories on the Shapiro, Haseltine, and Rowe (1978) and Mertz (2004) models. Their mentors established close, personal relationships, helped them learn, and helped them advance. At least 10 of the 13 in this group had worked for their mentor in the past. All enjoyed a long-term relationship sometimes beginning when the mentored person was a high school student working with a teacher or coach who moved into administration. All mentors and protégés were connected by being part of the same school district at some point in their careers. The mentor helped the protégé move up the ranks, often taking him or her along as he moved up the career path. The relationship continued until the mentor and the new superintendent/protégé became colleagues and friends. Two men were mentored by women superintendents, and the one woman was mentored by a male superintendent. Figure 2 summarizes the 20 mentoring relationships.

Those who had participated in a patron/mentor relationship reported a positive experience in which the mentor was concerned not only with the protégé's career and professional knowledge but also with the mentee's physical and emotional well-being. The superintendents reported that family concerns were part

No current mentor	Two had mentors earlier in their career as principals or assistant principals. One had never been
3 women	mentored. All sought substitutes for mentoring to gain needed information and advice.
Peer Pal/Guide	Acquired mentors as superintendents. Only one found the mentor through a formal mentoring
4 men in districts <3,000	program. Relationship moved from technical assistance to friendship.
Patron/Mentor	Long-term relationships that helped the mentee advance throughout the career. In some cases
13 sup'ts	a paternalistic relationship developed when the mentee was a teenager. The mentor may
12 men	have brought the mentee along to new districts as his own career advanced. Relationships are
All 3 minorities	close and personal as well as professional.

Figure 2. Mentoring Experiences as Superintendent

of the conversations with the mentors, and in three cases the relationship broadened to include interaction as couples with their spouses and spending leisure time with each other. However they did continue to discuss how to successfully fulfill the superintendent roles and handle specific responsibilities. In some cases the relationship moved from a subordinate to a peer relationship. In two cases the relationship had become less intense as the mentee's career moves created geographic separation.

When asked how the mentor had helped them most in carrying out their roles and responsibilities as a superintendent, the responses emphasized the mentor's support and encouragement using words like "confirmation," "reinforcement," "positive support," and "believing in me." A second theme was the help mentors gave in guiding them in how to develop appropriate relationships with various groups. In districts smaller than 3,000 students, new superintendents received valued assistance in finance issues such as planning and procedures in passing a bond. Those in the larger districts felt that their mentors helped the most with encouragement and acting as a sounding board, sharing and discussing their experiences in the superintendency, and providing honest feedback. One noted: "I think probably the most effective help has been the fact that he gave me somebody to bounce ideas off of and caused me to think sometimes in ways that I would not have thought otherwise." In the districts over 3,000 students superintendents were more likely to mention exchanging ideas than learning about specific knowledge areas.

In summary, all 17 superintendents with mentors felt the relationship was positive and benefited them personally and professionally. All but one relationship began voluntarily and informally when a mentor identified a promising protégé or the mentee sought advice and support from a peer.

Perceived Need for Mentoring

All 20 felt that they had benefited from the mentoring relationship or would have benefited had they had a mentor in their first year. The superintendents who did not have a mentor sought substitutes for the relationship by developing networks of other superintendents. The one who had never been mentored actively sought information and assistance from other superintendents in her region, from the education service center, by attending professional meetings, and by reading the professional literature. These first-year superintendents felt that new superintendents needed a mentor. One summarized:

> Everyone needs one [a mentor]. Everyone needs someone they can call. I don't care who you are, where you come from, what your training has been, if you are a first time superintendent, whether it be in Texas or wherever, you have to have that person or people.

WHAT DO SUPERINTENDENTS NEED FROM A MENTORING RELATIONSHIP?

Given that new superintendents feel they need mentoring, what do they want and need from the relationship? The interview was designed to elicit information about needs for specific knowledge related to the role and responsibilities as well as information about the critical mentor characteristics needed for the helping relationship. These superintendents had clear ideas about how to be a successful mentor. When asked what advice they would give to someone about to mentor a first-year superintendent, they focused on personal characteristics, the nature of the relationship, and availability and approachability. The recommendations did not differ by district size, the nature of previous mentoring relationships, gender, or ethnicity.

Skills and Knowledge

As one function of mentoring is the development of knowledge, skills, and behavior needed for success in the job, the interviews sought to identify the most important knowledge and skill areas in which new superintendents needed help. Near the end of each interview, participants were given a checklist in which the interviewer read a list of superintendent skills, responsibilities, and roles while the participant read through the same list. They were asked to check the areas in which they felt they could have benefited from or would have wanted assistance from a more experienced mentor superintendent. All identified specific knowledge areas. Table 3 shows a rank ordered list of skills and knowledge where new superintendents felt a mentor's assistance was needed.

All but one superintendent wanted or had assistance from a mentor in the area of school finance. The exception, a superintendent in a district of 3,000–9,000 students, had been an assistant superintendent of business in a similar district. Fourteen identified working with the school board as a need. A majority saw needs in facility planning and capital projects, budget creation and management, preparing for board meetings, and curriculum development and

Table 3. Areas Where New Superintendents Need Mentoring

Skill, Responsibility, or Role	N	Percentage
School Finance	19	95%
Board Relationships & Development	14	70%
Community Relations	13	65%
Facility Planning/Capital Projects	12	60%
Budget Creation/Management	11	55%
Board Meeting Management, Agenda, & Preps	11	55%
Curriculum Development & Alignment	11	55%
Employee Relations	9	45%
Team Building (Staff & Board)	9	45%
Transportation	9	45%
Investment of School Funds	8	40%
Employee Health Insurance	8	40%
Strategic & District Improvement Plans	8	40%
Food Services	8	40%
Fed. Programs & Management	6	30%
Communication Skills	6	30%
Maintenance & Custodial Service	6	30%
Calendar Creation & Process	6	30%
Insurance—General Risk Management	5	25%
Development of Policy	5	25%
Leadership Skills & Techniques	5	25%
Planning Functions	5	25%
Staff Development	5	25%
Grants	4	20%
Athletics & Extracurricular Activities	4	20%
Vision Articulation	3	15%
Total	20	100%

alignment. Some needs varied by district size. Superintendents in the smallest districts did not report needing a mentor in community relations, while almost all superintendents in districts larger than 1,000 students identified this as an area of need. Superintendents in districts under 3,000 students sought or received mentoring assistance in board relationships. All three superintendents who needed a mentor in the area of vision articulation were in the smallest districts. Superintendents in the largest districts were most likely to need mentor assistance in communication skills. Areas where few new superintendents in any size district felt a need for assistance were athletics and extracurricular activities, writing and acquiring grants, and staff development.

Critical Mentor Characteristics

When asked what advice they would give to someone about to mentor a first-year superintendent, the participants focused on personal characteristics, the nature of the relationship, and availability and approachability. The recommendations did not differ by district size, the nature of previous mentoring relationships, gender, or ethnicity.

The most frequently identified critical mentor characteristics were honesty and the ability to establish a relationship based on trust in which a free exchange of thoughts and ideas are shared without fear of belittlement, embarrassment, or damage to the relationship. Mentored superintendents must be able to trust their mentors to maintain confidentiality and tell them the truth. One explained:

> Be very honest, have a relationship . . . that goes beyond just the professional [level]. It has to go beyond the professional because, many times, you're talking about focus, re-focusing; many times he'll use that technique to bring me back around as a reality check. Sometimes this job gets to you. It's so overwhelming and so much to be done and you need someone to give you that reality check every now and then.

Another advised that the

> relationship needs to be first. Take some time, go spend some time with that person, take them to lunch. Get to know a little bit about them and their family. Get to know what makes them tick and what doesn't make them tick. Because if you have that relationship and you build that trust, then I think you have a lot better chance of being effective and helping.

Another advised:

> Know your limitations. If someone is calling needing help, don't play around with him or her. If you don't know something, tell them. Be honest with your own limitations, and be honest with that person.

Across school district size, gender, and ethnicity, new superintendents mentioned patience as a critical quality in a mentor. In explaining patience, one noted: "Don't try to accomplish it all on the first day."

The new superintendents recommended that the mentor be non-directive, offer options rather than solutions, listen, and help the mentored superintendent reflect. They advised mentors not to be critical and to remember that the mentored person cannot be exactly the person that the mentor is. Mentors should offer constructive criticism while also demonstrating care in a way that does not leave the mentored person feeling inadequate, "dumb," or "as if they already should know" how to do something.

The importance of "walking through a problem" and "acting as a sounding board" while listening were mentioned. A participant recommended: "The first thing is that you actually need to listen to the person you are mentoring. It's not just information going from you to them. [It's] helping to work through [issues]." Another said: "See the whole picture. Consider all the angles instead of just trying to solve the problem by looking at one part of it. Take every issue or concern serious. It may be silly, but take it serious [sic]."

Another characteristic is demonstrating care for the novice by making time without giving the impression that the contact is an imposition or interruption. They even advise the mentor to be proactive in developing and maintaining the relationship:

> Be available. Be compassionate and verbally supportive. . . . I'd tell them to pick up the phone and call the person they were mentoring occasionally because that person is probably going to be so bogged down, their head spinning and going in so many different directions. Time is just so confined that sometimes you don't even have time to pick up the phone and ask the question; you just try to get through it.

New superintendents recommended that the mentor maintain regular contact and establish a relationship where the mentee feels comfortable calling and asking questions, no matter how trivial. Most interviews mentioned the importance of the mentor's availability and maintaining regular contact even if it is by phone or e-mail.

They felt that good mentors encourage their protégés by listening, verbally affirming, and showing interest in both personal and professional growth. They motivate by "cheering on" the new superintendent when he or she is frustrated, confused, or discouraged. They let the protégés know that they are not alone and others have traveled the same path.

Participants recommended that a mentoring program match new superintendents with mentors who were in similar districts and in districts in close proximity. One felt that a program should match people who are compatible in personality, prior experiences, and interests. Another noted that the press of time makes it difficult for superintendents to serve as mentors. He suggested finding mentors who have recently retired from the superintendency. They would have the needed experience and knowledge as well as time to develop a relationship.

SUMMARY AND CONCLUSIONS

New superintendents clearly felt that they needed a mentor and that mentoring programs for new superintendents are needed. Most of them had mentors as first-year superintendents, and over half had participated in intensive mentoring relationships in which the mentor not only helped them learn but sponsored their career advancement. All of these voluntary relationships were positive, providing both technical assistance and, more importantly to this group, support. While all first-year superintendents identified specific areas of the superintendent's role and responsibilities in which assistance from a mentor was needed, when asked to identify important mentor characteristics, content expertise was not a priority. Instead, the ability to develop and maintain a trusting, supportive relationship with the mentored person, the ability to guide in reflection and problem solving, showing care and concern for the individual as a person not just as a superintendent, and offering encouragement and support were critical for them without regard to district size, ethnicity, or gender. While content knowledge was not as critical, it was important that the mentor was experienced as a superintendent so that he or she understood the mentee's concerns and emotions.

Mentoring programs for new superintendents clearly can perform a valuable service in helping the novice acquire specific information. However, new superintendents have other avenues for acquiring information about their roles and responsibilities and having their questions answered. Professional organizations offer programs for new superintendents. For example, the Texas Association of School Administrators (TASA) offers a first-time superintendent academy that provides training in most of the superintendent responsibilities in which this group felt unprepared. Participation in such a program also gives new superintendents a cohort group where peer pal relationships can form as well as access to experienced superintendents and experts in the knowledge areas. State and national conferences also include sessions on the content areas where these administrators felt unprepared.

What cannot be obtained as easily is the supportive relationship with an individual who understands the many emotions associated with the role. While new superintendents felt unprepared in some areas of their role and were able to prioritize knowledge and skills where mentor assistance was desirable, they seemed to want more than content knowledge from the mentor relationship. Superintendents who had been in long-term mentoring relationships and those whose relationships were recent valued the same mentor characteristics and behaviors. The mentor's support, empathy, listening, and help in problem solving and reflection were more valued than the task-related information provided. The high value new superintendents give to the quality of the relationship argues for careful matching of mentor and mentee in any formal program and suggests that both parties have some choice in entering the mentor-mentee relationship.

The interviews provided information that can be used to improve university-based preparation programs. First-year superintendents lacked confidence in their ability to apply the knowledge they learned in their graduate programs. Preparation programs could help ease the transition and help them gain confidence by including more assignments and activities that require graduate students to apply their knowledge in school district settings rather than in classroom simulations. Similarly, internships could be designed to provide realistic experiences for interns likely to become superintendents.

Superintendent preparation programs that formally plan for mentoring can give the preservice superintendent a head start. This can be done through forming cohort groups of students with realistic possibilities of becoming superintendents as well as by helping the preservice superintendent develop mentoring relationships with superintendents. Internships that include extended time in which the intern "shadows" the superintendent and has an opportunity to reflect with this mentor on what he/she has observed could help the preservice administrator gain a better understanding of some of the realities of the job that can affect them personally and emotionally. Because of the time demands on superintendents, availability of this kind of internship should be based on the realistic chances of the intern becoming a superintendent in the near future. Paid full-time internships for promising future superintendents also could help ease the transition into the new role. This is especially important for administrators in small districts where most superintendents come straight from building-level positions.

While a mandated program for all new superintendents may be overkill, there is a need for formal superintendent mentoring programs. Most new superintendents in the study were able to find satisfactory mentors without benefit of a formal program. The three superintendents in this study who did not have mentors as superintendents sought other sources of information from meetings and from peers, but they did not have the supportive relationship that the others found most valuable. Most mentoring relationships are informal and voluntary. In this study some superintendents had outgrown their former mentors. Others had mentors of convenience from neighboring districts identified by chance at professional meetings. Individuals whose neighbors are not able to serve as mentors or who do not encounter a good mentor elsewhere will not have the opportunity for a supportive relationship that can contribute to their effectiveness.

An effective mentoring program requires planning. Ehrich, Hansford, and Tennent (2004) found that some formal programs in school districts resulted from a "hasty decision that mentoring had much to offer," but the resulting programs often "lacked intellectual rigor, were poorly planned, and were inadequately resourced" with untrained mentors and participants who did not understand the program objectives (p. 534). Goal clarity is important. For example, the Texas legislative intent likely was for a program to give new superintendents specific skills and knowledge, as the only specific learning requirement is that superintendents spend a minimum of 36 hours of professional development directly related to the state standards required for the superintendent certificate. As the new superintendents appear to find the supportive relationship more valuable than specific knowledge, there is a basis for misunderstanding about the purposes of the program and dissatisfaction with the quality of the experience. A formal program should develop clear expectations that are communicated to all parties. As noted above, mentor selection, training, and matching with the mentee are critical for a successful mentoring experience. Finally, a voluntary program in which new superintendents who did not have mentors could be linked to an experienced administrator could reduce the size, complexity, and costs of the program.

REFERENCES

Barnett, B. (1990). The mentor-intern relationship: Making the most of learning from experience. *NASSP Bulletin, 74*(526), 17–24.

Cohen, N. H. (1995). *Mentoring adult learners: A guide for educators and trainers*. Malabar, FL: Krieger Publishing Company.

Cohen, N. H., and Galbraith, M. W. (1995). Mentoring in the learning society. In N. H. Cohen and M. W. Galbraith (Eds.), *Mentoring: New strategies and challenges* (pp. 5–14). San Francisco, CA: Josey-Bass.

Crow, G. M., and Matthews, L. J. (1998). *Finding one's way: How mentoring can lead to dynamic leadership*. Thousand Oaks, CA: Corwin Press, Inc.

Daresh, J. (2004). Mentoring school leaders: Professional promise or predictable problems? *Educational Administration Quarterly, 40*(4), 495–517.

Daresh, J. C., and Playko, M. A. (1994). *Mentoring for school leaders*. American Educational Research Association Convention Paper. American Educational Research Association Annual Meeting, April 1994.

Ehrich, L. C., Hansford, B., and Tennent, L. (2004). Formal mentoring programs in education and other professions: A review of the literature. *Educational Administration Quarterly, 40*(4), 518–540.

Fraser, J. (1998). *Teacher to teacher: A guidebook for effective mentoring*. Portsmouth, NH: Heinemann.

Fritts, P. J. (1998). *The new managerial mentor: Becoming a learning leader to build communities of purpose*. Palo Alto, CA: Davies-Black Publishing.

Glass, T. E. (2000). *Where are all the women superintendents? The School Administrator, 6*(57), 28–32.

Hoyle, J. R., English, F. W., and Steffy, B. E. (1998). *Skills for successful 21st century school leaders*. Arlington, VA: The American Association of School Administrators.

Kram, K. E. (1985). *Mentoring at work: Developmental relationships in organizational life*. Glenview, IL: Scott, Foresman.

Luna, G. (1994). The development of female leadership: Women executives as mentors. American Educational Research Association Convention Paper. American Educational Research Association Annual Meeting, April 1994.

Luna, G., and Cullen, D. L. (1995) *Empowering the faculty: Mentoring redirected and renewed*. Washington, DC: The George Washington University Press.

Mathews, J. (1999). On-the-job learning of nontraditional superintendents. *The School Administrator, 56*(1), 28–33.

Merriam, S. (1983). Mentors and protégés: A critical review of the literature. *Adult Education Quarterly, 33*(3), 161–173.

Mertz, N. T. (2004). What's a mentor, anyway? *Educational Administration Quarterly, 40*(4), 541–560.

Milstein, M. M. (Ed.) (1993). *Changing the way we prepare educational leaders: The Danforth experience*. Newbury Park, CA: Corwin Press. Inc.

Peper, J. B. (1994). *Mentoring, mentors, and protégés*. Discussion of the papers presented on mentoring at the American Educational Research Association Annual Meeting, April 4–10, 1994. (ERIC Document Reproduction Service No. SPO35511.)

Seidman, I. (1998). *Interviewing as qualitative research: A guide for researchers in education and the social sciences* (2nd ed.). Teachers College, NY: Teachers College Press, Columbia University.

Shapiro, E. C., Haseltine, F., and Rowe, M. (1978). Moving up: Role models, mentors, and the patron system. *Sloan Management Review, 19*, 51–58.

Tagg, S. K. (1985). Life story interviews and their interpretations. In M. Brenner, J. Brown and D. Canter (Eds.), *The research interview: Uses and approaches* (pp. 163–199). London: Academic Press.

Thody, A., and Crystal, L. (1994). Mentoring: Cultural reenforcement or destabilization? *American Educational Research Association Convention Paper*. American Education Research Association Annual Meeting, April 1994.

A Rubric to Improve Educational Leadership Candidates' Ability to Systematically Analyze a Written Problem

David L. Stader

A TRADITIONAL UNIVERSITY EDUCATIONAL LEADERSHIP course may include a variety of assessments of leadership candidates' knowledge including mid-term and final exams or a large literature-driven research project (Montgomery, 2002). These assessments certainly have a place in the preparation of tomorrow's educational leaders. One of the weaknesses however, is the assumption that candidates who acquire knowledge about leadership will know when to apply that knowledge and how to use it appropriately (Bridges and Hallinger, 1997). As Leithwood and Steinbach (1992) point out, in the absence of knowledge one has nothing to think about. In the absence of connections with the real world of campus leadership, one does not know what to do with the knowledge one has.

Making the connection between knowledge acquisition and the real world is particularly important in the development of the requisite skills to solve the types of problems educational leadership candidates will likely face as future principals. However, research into the development of problem-solving skills in educational leadership candidates is not well developed (Bridges and Hallinger, 1997; Copland, 2000; Leithwood and Steinbach, 1992). Consequently, the purpose of this research is to determine the efficacy of a self-scoring rubric on the problem-solving skills of prospective school leaders. Specifically, this research tests the hypothesis that the use of a self-scoring rubric based on the various subcomponents of problem-solving is associated with greater skill in analyzing and responding to a written problem scenario among educational leadership licensure candidates.

THEORETICAL PERSPECTIVES

Rubrics

"Rubric" has evolved into the term used to describe scoring guides for assessing the quality of student learning. Rubrics are usually used with a relatively complex assignment, such as a culminating project, an essay, or the analysis of a written problem. Regardless of the purpose, all rubrics share three commonalities: (a) evaluative criteria, (b) quality definitions, and (c) a scoring strategy (Andrade, 2000; Goodrich, 1997; Popham, 1997). Rubrics can either be holistic or analytic. In the holistic strategy, the evaluative criteria are considered and a single, overall quality judgment is derived. An analytic strategy requires a criterion-by-criterion approach that may or may not be aggregated into an overall score (Popham, 1997). Regardless of the rubric strategy, good rubrics should make instructor expectations very clear and improve performance by showing students how to meet these expectations (Andrade, 2000; Goodrich, 1997). The point of rubrics is to guide students toward the production of better final products, not disaggregate students. The criterion must be known in advance by students so they can apply them as they work through the assignment. Students and instructors can make formative judgments along the way and modify responses as well as instruction as the products emerge (Montgomery, 2002). Candidates should always have ample time to reflect on and revise their work after peer or instructor pre-assessment (Goodrich, 1997).

Rubrics however, are notoriously difficult to develop (Andrade, 2000; Popham, 1997). James Popham (1997) lists four common rubric flaws: (a) Many rubrics display task-specific evaluative criteria. In other words, the rubric is specific for a task; (b) Another common flaw is excessively general evaluative criteria. Effective rubrics must provide guidance for instructors and candidates about what is genuinely significant; (c) Another shortcoming is dysfunctional detail. Lengthy rubrics are not useful. In contrast, short but useful rubrics are far more valuable to instructors and candidates; and (d) The final flaw is equating the test of the skill with the skill itself. For example, scoring candidate responses to a written problem only in ways that are consistent with instructor beliefs and attitudes would defeat the purpose of a rubric designed to improve candidates' overall ability to respond to a problem.

In contrast, effective rubrics

- Contain three to seven teachable evaluative criteria (Popham, 1997)
- Capture the key attributes of the skill being assessed (Popham, 1997)
- Avoid unclear and unnecessarily negative language (Goodrich, 1997)
- List criteria and articulate levels of quality (Andrade, 2000)

*Making connections: Leadership
and Problem-solving*

Common sense (and scholarship in the field) suggests that future principals will be required to understand, frame and solve problems they will encounter on the job (Copland, 2000). For example, Walker (1990) used the key skills identified by the NASSP Assessment Center project as a framework for an in-depth study of three exemplary principals serving elementary, middle, and secondary schools. This study found that these exemplary principals were skilled problem-solvers with the ability to (a) analyze problems within the context of their particular school, (b) seek out facts before making decisions, (c) confront issues with both sensitivity and decisiveness, and (d) develop a plan of action in response to the problem.

The types of problems school leaders face can be defined in a variety of ways. Most useful to this research is the classification of problems into routine, well-structured problems and non-routine, ill-structured problems (Leithwood and Stager, 1989; Leithwood and Steinbach, 1992). Well-structured problems present familiar issues that experienced principals have solved many times before. Conversely, ill-structured problems are more complex and are often characterized by a lack of clarity, present a number of issues, and pose numerous potential obstacles. In short, ill-structured problems are "messy" in that a clear resolution is not apparent.

In a study of problem-solving skills, Leithwood and Stager (1989) found that principals typically encounter both structured and ill-structured problems. However, while expert and non-expert principals respond similarly to structured problems, expert principals are much more adapt at solving complex, ill-structured problems. Expert principals attempt to understand ill-structured problems by relying on past experience, collecting new information, and making explicit, relevant, and reasonable assumptions. Non-experts tend to rely more on assumptions that may or may not be explicit and relevant, rather that collect information. Expert principals more readily accept personal responsibility for effectively solving ill-structured problems. Non-experts either ignored the issue of personal responsibility or in some cases rejected responsibility by referring the problem to someone else. Expert principals spent considerable effort in planning for the solution process. Non-experts paid little attention to planning. Finally, expert principals did not become involved in irrelevant issues.

One of the real life challenges of problem-solving is the social context inherent in many ill-structured problems (Leithwood and Steinbach, 1991, 1992). In fact, it is the social context more than the problem itself that makes for an ill-structured problem (Leithwood and Steinbach, 1992). A significant part of the social context of problem-solving is the fact that the way problems are presented to school leaders frequently reflects the particular preconceived notion of the individual or group presenting the problem (Copland, 2000). This bias creates a preconceived solution generated from the frame of reference of the problem presenter. For example, a parent may call a principal with a request for their child to drop a challenging class or a teacher may request moving a problem student to another teacher. In both cases, the problem is presented from a frame of reference with a predefined solution already built into the problem. Effective principals do not dismiss the solution as presented. As Copland (2000) points out, the problem framing of the parent and teacher in the preceding example may be absolutely correct. However, the fatal mistake occurs when the principal embraces a preconceived solution before the problem has been clearly defined.

Consequently, effective principals recognize that a problem has been presented with a preconceived solution and reframe the problem in solution free terms. This reframing allows for the anticipation of obstacles that are likely to arise from various solutions and figure out how the obstacles may be addressed when and if they do arise (Copland, 2000). This is the process of "thinking like a school leader" that is addressed in this research.

EXPERIMENTAL RUBRIC DESIGN

Goor and Thorp (2003) reported excellent results in the use of a rubric in improving the problem-solving skills of pre-service teachers. However, research on the use of rubrics (or frameworks) to improve the problem-solving process of educational leadership candidates is thin at best. Therefore, the problem-solving research of Copland (2000), Leithwood and Stager (1989), Leithwood and Steinbach (1992), and Walker (1990), served as a theoretical framework for the development of the rubric used in this research. Most problem-solving strategies are not question driven (Richetti and Sheerin, 1999). Consequently, one of the objectives of this rubric design was to create the flexibility to guide participants in asking the right questions when faced with a written problem.

Consistent with the research in effective rubric development, the experimental rubric has the following characteristics: (a) seven evaluative criteria based on the research concerning the problem-solving skills of expert principals, (b) descriptors for each of the evaluative criteria, and (c) a scoring strategy. Each criterion has three skill levels: developing (0 points), proficient (1 point), and accomplished (2 points). The evaluative criteria based on the common themes from the research in problem-solving skills of expert principals include:

1. Number of key issues: Expert principals do not become involved or distracted by irrelevant issues. In other words, effective problem-solving begins with the ability to identify the relevant issues.
2. Context or clarification: Seeking further information and clarification was a common theme found in the research regarding effective problem-solving skills of expert principals.
3. Professional language: It makes little difference whether or not the resolution is made verbally or in writing (Copland, 2000). What is important is the ability to clearly and succinctly articulate a resolution to the problem. The nature of this research required a written response.
4. Standards based knowledge: One rationale for the very existence of educational leadership programs is that there is a relevant body of knowledge fundamental to effective school leadership.
5. Assignment of responsibility: Effective principals accept responsibility for addressing ill-structured problems and pursue a resolution that is in the best interests of the school community rather than assign blame or refer the problem to someone else.
6. Perspectives: Expert principals understand the need to clarify the perspectives of the problem presenters, anticipate obstacles to successful resolution, and seek the perspectives of others involved in the problem.
7. Analysis: Expert principals consistently develop more detailed plans to resolve ill-structured problems than their less effective counterparts.

Leithwood and Stager (1989) found that expert principal responses to an ill-structured problem showed greater coherence (or inter-relatedness) across problem-solving components than non-experts. Consequently, the rubric was designed as an analytical model with the individual criterion aggregated into a total score. Total scores were divided into three ranges: (a) 11–14 points = accomplished, (b) 7–10 = proficient and (c) 0–6 = developing. The experimental rubric is illustrated in Figure 1.

METHODOLOGY

Participants

The participants in this study were 15 educational leadership licensure candidates enrolled in a state university master's degree program located in Louisiana. Most (11) of the participants are female, range in teaching experience from 3 to 15 plus years, and represent elementary, middle school and high schools throughout Southeastern Louisiana.

Study Design

Assessment of the participants' problem-framing ability was accomplished though a pre- and post-test design. The purpose of the design was to determine whether the use of the self-scoring rubric and subsequent practice using the rubric as a problem-framing guide would improve the participants' ability to conceptualize and respond to an ill-structured problem scenario. All 15 participants completed the pre- and post-test scenarios under similar conditions. Participants were given little guidance for the pre- and post-test other than instructions to respond in writing to the problem. Candidates self-scored their responses using the rubric and submitted their responses and self-score to the instructor for validation. The instructor used the same scoring guide as the participants. Responses were collected in such a manner as to ensure a blind validation process.

Pre-Test

In the pre-test, participants were asked to react to and write a response for a problem scenario obtained from the ETS (2001) testing booklet (Scenario One: The Holiday Concert). Participants responded in one sitting under typical classroom conditions. Participants were not allowed to discuss or comment on the scenario until everyone had finished. Participants were then presented with the scoring rubric. Participants were led through a discussion of the rubric and asked to apply the rubric to self-score their responses.

Criteria	Developing (0 pts)	Proficient (1 pt)	Accomplished (2 pts)
Number of **key issues** cited by the candidate	Vague or omits reference to any of the key elements of the case	Cites one key issue from the case	Cites at least two key issues from the case
Context of the response (seeks clarification or further information)	Cites personal experience or opinion. Does not seek further information or clarification.	Case evidence used to make a point. Seeks some clarification or information.	Demonstrates clear understanding of the case, cites multiple sources of needed information or clarification.
Professional **language**	Incorrect use of language	Some professional language, minor	Professional language evident
Standards based knowledge evident in response	Lack of knowledge or incorrect use evident.	Some germane **knowledge** evident.	Clear demonstration of professional knowledge
Assignment of **responsibility**	Externalizing, blaming others, does not accept responsibility	Assumes some responsibility. Some externalization evident	Clear understanding and acceptance of responsibility for the fair resolution to the case
Perspectives on the case	Personal perspectives and biases evident. Little thought to the perspectives of others involved in the case	Demonstrates some thought to the perspectives of the individuals/groups involved in the case	Clearly demonstrates an understanding and appreciation of the multiple perspectives of individuals impacted by the case
Analysis of the case (Plan of action)	Cites opinion, no supporting information, and plan of action not evident. Personal perspective and biases evident.	Analysis reflects some supporting information. Plan of action incomplete, clarification from single source. Single perspective.	Clear analysis of the case. Clear plan of action that seeks clarification/information from a variety of sources and perspectives.

Case Study Cumulative Scoring Guide (0-12 pts)   11-14 points: Accomplished   7-10 points: Proficient   0-6 points: Developing

Figure 1. Case Study Rubric

SCENARIO ONE: THE HOLIDAY CONCERT

It is early December and the students in an elementary school are practicing for the annual holiday concert. A parent phones the school to insist that her child not be required to sing any of the Christmas songs. The principal excuses the child from participation in the music practice. Do you agree with the principal's action? Give a rationale, citing factors that are relevant to a principal's decision in such situations. * Available: www.ets.org/sls/slstestprep.html.

Post-Test

Participants were provided with several scenarios of increasing complexity over the course of the semester. The scenarios were presented in a format similar to the pre- and post-test in that participants were asked to write their responses to the problem under classroom conditions and not allowed to discuss the problem until everyone was finished. Participants were encouraged to share their responses and scoring with peers and then with the instructor. From this interaction the participants had the opportunity to reflect on their responses and the instructor had the opportunity to adjust instruction according to the needs of the participants. This point is particularly important. The instructor needs to play an active coaching role as participants' struggle with the reframing of ill-structured problems in solution free terms (Goodrich, 1997; Leithwood and Steinbach, 1992; Montgomery, 2002).

Participants were presented with a final problem scenario (Scenario Two: A Memorial Weight Room for Riverboat). This scenario, written by the researcher, was designed to reflect several characteristics of an ill-structured problem, including: (a) the social context of a preconceived solution on the part of the problem presenters, (b) multiple key issues, (c) multiple perspectives, and (d) successful resolution will require detailed planning.

SCENARIO TWO: A MEMORIAL WEIGHT ROOM FOR RIVERBOAT

The start of Sharon Grey's second year as principal of Riverboat High School was not any easier than her first. Two very popular members of the football team had been tragically killed in a one-car auto accident the previous spring. Both fathers were active in the booster club and had asked family and friends to donate money for a school weight room rather than send flowers. A tidy sum had been collected, and with Sharon's enthusiastic support the board of education had approved the club's request to begin construction. All had gone well and as the facility neared completion one last fundraising effort by the club had generated $22,000 for equipment. At the last booster club meeting the parents of the two boys presented the Club President with a check for equipment and a plaque for the weight room. Sharon unsuspectingly took the plaque, which read "This weight room is dedicated to Timothy and Michael who accepted Jesus as their Savior. We pray that others will use this equipment in the name of Our Lord and Savior and follow Mike and Tim by opening their hearts to Jesus Christ." Sensing Sharon's hesitation, the parents made their position very clear. If Sharon refused to hang the plaque, the weight equipment would not be purchased. This position was solidified the next day in an emotional letter to Sharon from the parents. The superintendent failed to see any reason to reject the plaque, and remarked, "Almost everybody in the school is the same religion. I don't see how a plaque can hurt."

Participants were asked to write their responses to the problem. Participants responded to the final scenario in one sitting under typical classroom conditions. Participants were not allowed to discuss or comment on the scenario until everyone finished. Participants were led through a discussion of the rubric and self-scored their responses. Again, self-scores were submitted to the instructor for validation. The researcher as well as independent assessment by two additional educational leadership colleagues with K–12 campus leadership experience judged self-scores to be accurate.

RESULTS

Pre-Test Results

Written responses to the pre-test scenario (The Holiday Concert) revealed the majority of the participants scored at the developmental stage as defined by the rubric. Total scores ranged from 3–7 points. Of the 15 participants who participated in the project, 13 scored in the Developing range (0–6) and two scored in the Proficient range (7–10 points). See Pre-Test Sample Responses.

Pre-Test Sample Responses

Sample One: "I agree with the principal's decision. The child could be from a religious background that restricts her from singing the Christmas songs. It was a simple request from the mother which she has her reasons for. This is not a situation where a principal should do battle."

Sample Two: "Yes, I agree with the principal's action. Christmas is a Christian holiday. Parents and students have the right not to participate in events with religious context."

Post-Test Results

Post-test scores revealed an aggregate improvement in candidate responses. The total scores ranged from 7–12 aggregate points with 13 of the scores in the Accomplished range (11–14 points) and two scores in the Proficient range (7–10 points) as measured by the rubric. In addition to better scores the quality of responses for all participants markedly improved (see Post-Test Sample Response).

Post-Test Sample Response

There are several conflicting key issues addressed. First, the principal is reluctant to hang the plaque because of the religious content. The parents of the deceased athletes have made it clear that if the plaque is not hung, the weight equipment will not be purchased with the donations. The Superintendent has also failed to see Ms. Grey's point in rejecting the plaque.

Ms. Grey must first dialogue with the key people involved to try to reach an understanding upon which to base her decision. She needs to meet with the parents and hear their perspective. She also needs to speak to the Superintendent to hear his concerns. Ms. Grey can also get some good feedback from members of the booster club to get their perspectives.

Once she gathers all the information, she should discuss the different perspectives with the Superintendent and make a decision. Once the decision is made she needs to notify the parents and booster club members to explain the decision.

The results of the pre- and post-test are summarized in Table 1.

Table 1. Pre- and Post-Test Scores

N = 15	Developing (0–6 pts)	Proficient (7–10 pts)	Accomplished (11–14 pts)
Pre-Test	13	2	0
Post-Test	0	2	13

VALIDITY

Of particular concern for this research is the content validity of both the scenarios and the criteria selected for the rubric. Content validity concerns how well the problem scenarios mirror the real life problems experienced by principals and how accurately the rubric reflects the problem-solving process of expert principals (Copland, 2000; Kurtz and Mayo, 1979). In a study of problem-based learning and participants' problem-framing ability, Copland (2000) suggests that the content validity of problem scenarios can be assessed along two axes: abstractness and fidelity of the measure.

Abstractness is an assessment of the likelihood that a campus leader may actually confront a problem similar to the one outlined in a scenario. The relative abstractness of the scenarios is inversely proportional to the likelihood that a similar problem will arise in practice. In other words, the less likely that a similar problem will arise in practice the higher the abstractness of the measure. The more likely that a similar problem will arise in practice the lower the abstractness of the measure.

Similar to Copland's (2000) approach in determining the relative abstractness of problem scenarios in his research, the scenarios used in this research were taken from the ETS study guide (ETS, 2001) and from the professional experience of the instructor. The scenarios were selected to represent a concrete area commonly encountered by elementary, middle, and high school principals. As suggested by Copland (2000), the scenarios were also read by two university instructors with K–12 school leadership experience. These individuals found the scenarios to represent common problems. Therefore, the abstractness of the scenarios can be assessed as relatively low.

Fidelity is defined by Copland (2000) as an assessment of the extent to which the problem scenario replicates the manner in which a principal would encounter a problem in practice. Again, the fidelity of the scenarios is inversely proportional to the extent to which it mirrors real life. The scenarios were purposely designed to be ill-structured enough for participants to construct their own response from their particular frame of reference. It is clear that the open-ended nature of this type of problem more closely represents on-the-job dilemmas rather than selecting the "best" answer from a multiple choice test. However, it is exceedingly difficult to replicate the context, nuances and emotion surrounding many parent, teacher, and student problems. Therefore the fidelity of the scenarios can be considered to be moderate.

The validity of the rubric can be assessed along the same two axes of abstractness and fidelity. Rubric abstractness is a measure of the likelihood that a principal may actually need to use the rubric criterion when faced with an ill-structured problem. The theoretical framework developed by Copland (2000), Leithwood and Stager (1989), and Walker (1990) would indicate that expert principals would use these skills. Thus the abstractness of the rubric would be low.

The fidelity of the rubric assesses how closely the rubric criterion mirrors the real life problem-solving process of expert principals. This is a more difficult assessment. The thinking process of a number of expert principals facing a similar problem may be quite different and each may reach a different conclusion based on the interactions of the particular circumstances and context of the problem situation. However, there would seem to be at least some consistency in the manner in which expert principals approach an ill-structured problem. At the very least, the rubric criterions provide a starting point for thinking about effective problem-solving. Therefore, the fidelity of the rubric can be judged as medium.

DISCUSSION

This research tested the hypothesis that a self-scoring rubric based on the various subcomponents of problem–solving would be associated with greater skill in analyzing and responding to a problem scenario among educational leadership licensure candidates. Results demonstrated a consistent and appreciable improvement in the ability of the participants to frame and respond to ill-structured scenarios of ever increasing complexity. For example, an examination of the typical responses to the pre-test scenario (The Holiday Concert) reveals answers from the single frame of reference of the problem presenter. The problem framing of the parent may be the correct one. But, the typical responses to the problem reveal the common mistake of embracing the preconceived solution of the problem presenter before the problem has been clearly defined (Copland, 2000). Typical responses also demonstrate little planning, are based on assumptions, do not demonstrate an appreciation for the perspectives of the music teacher, and demonstrate little seeking of further information necessary to make an informed decision.

In contrast, the typical response to the post-test scenario (A Memorial Weight Room) demonstrates an emerging awareness that problems are often presented with an embedded preconceived solution by the problem presenter, the importance of reframing problems in solution free terms, the importance of seeking further information and clarification, the importance of a plan of action, and the acceptance of the responsibility to make a decision that is in the best interest of the school community.

This research did not compare methods or approaches to problem-solving instruction. Rather, it assesses the impact of a self-scoring rubric based on the various subcomponents of problem solving in analyzing and responding to a problem scenario among educational leadership licensure candidates. Evidence supports two claims: (a) the problem-solving skills of educational leadership candidates can be improved, and (b) there is tentative support for the use of a rubric to guide the general problem framing of educational leadership candidates. To the knowledge of the researcher, this is the first study to address the efficacy of a rubric developed and applied in this manner. Consequently, the need for validation and further research is necessary before any definitive conclusions, either positive or negative, can be made.

LIMITATIONS

This research has several limitations including: (a) the relatively small sample size makes sweeping conclusions difficult to defend; (b) there is always the possibility that participants viewed the problem-solving scenarios as a test and naturally attempted to determine what answer the professor thinks is important; (c) the lack of a control group makes comparisons impossible; and (d) the carry-over value of the rubric and problem-solving exercises on participants' responses to future problems they will encounter as a school administrator is impossible to determine.

FOR FURTHER RESEARCH

Several areas of further research may evolve from this preliminary study, including:

1. The impact of the rubric on pre- and post-program problem-solving skills of school leader candidates.
2. Will a significant difference in constructed response state test scores such as the SLLA result from the use of the rubric?

3. Will the rubric apply to data-based scenarios?
4. Would peer scoring aid in candidate understanding of the rubric application?
5. What is the carry-over value of the rubric as candidates assume leadership positions?

REFERENCES

Anderson, R., and Puckett, J. (2003). Assessing students' problem-solving assignments. *New Directions for Teaching and Learning, 95,* 81–89.

Andrade, H. (2000). Using rubrics to promote thinking and learning. *Educational Leadership, 57*(5), 13–18.

Bridges, E., and Hallinger, P. (1997). Using problem-based learning to prepare educational leaders. *Peabody Journal of Education, 72*(2), 131–146.

Copland, M. (2000). Problem-based learning and prospective principals' problem-framing ability. *Educational Administration Quarterly, 36*(4), 585–607.

Goodrich, H. (1997). Understanding rubrics. *Educational Leadership, 54*(4), 14–17.

Goor, M., and Thorp, E. (2003). *Authentic assessments of teacher candidates: Rubric compares students' responses to cases.* Paper presented at the Annual AACTE Conference, New Orleans, LA.

Kurtz, A., and Mayo, S. (1979). *Statistical methods in education and psychology.* New York: Springer-Verlong.

Leithwood, K., and Stager, M. (1989). Expertise in principals' problem solving. *Educational Administration Quarterly, 25*(2), 126–161.

Leithwood, K., and Steinbach, R. (1991). Indicators of transformational leadership in the everyday problem solving of school principals. *Journal of Personnel Evaluation in Education, 4*(2), 221–244.

Leithwood, K., and Steinbach, R. (1992). Improving the problem-solving expertise of school administrators: Theory and practice. *Education and Urban Society, 24*(3), 317–345.

Montgomery, K. (2002). Authentic task and rubrics: Going beyond traditional assessments in college teaching. *College Teaching, 50*(1), 34–40.

Popham, W. J. (1997). What's wrong—and what's right—with rubrics. *Educational Leadership, 55*(2), 72–75.

Richette, C., and Sheerin, J. (1999). Helping students ask the right questions. *Educational Leadership, 57*(3), 58–62.

School Leader Licensure Assessment (2001). Princeton, NJ: Educational Testing Service. Retrieved on December 31, 2004, from www.ETS.org/sls/.

Walker, J. (1990). Shadowing the skills of exemplary principals. *Education Digest, 56*(1), 45–50.

Reinvesting in Mid-level Leadership through Professional Development Courses

CHRISTINE KELLY

CLINICAL SUPERVISION OF TEACHING STAFF OR PERSONNEL can take on various forms and serve various purposes. The most common of these is that of staff evaluation and retention. Yet a more useful purpose, but seldom considered, is that of altering the culture of the school. Peterson and Deal (1998) define culture as "the underground stream of norms, values, beliefs, traditions and rituals that has built up over time as people work together, solve problems, and confront challenges" (p. 28).

When the culture of a school becomes entrenched, drastic measures might need to be taken to provide staff development to turn that culture around to become more productive. "Probably the most important—and the most difficult—job of an instructional leader is to change the prevailing culture of a school" (Barth, 2002, p. 6). Calling mid-level, designated faculty leaders to reevaluate their leadership role is at the heart of significant cultural change.

CASE IN POINT

When mid-level leaders have longevity in a school, and their positions are viewed by them as strictly administrative rather than providing leadership, the culture of the school becomes less and less responsive to the needs of the classroom teacher and therefore those of the student body. An attempt at fostering a professional development program can fall far short of its intended mark of reinvesting in and calling for the instructional leadership so needed for the growth and "health" of a school. Often even monetary incentives fall short of rekindling the desire to lead.

Clearly, the professional growth of the teaching staff must be encouraged by the mid-level administrators (department chairpersons, team leaders, etc.) but when they themselves have reached a point in their own professional development where they could utilize various techniques to facilitate professional growth in their peers, interventions need to be put into place. To develop what Lambert (1998) refers to as "a culture of inquiry that includes a continuous cycle of reflecting, questioning, gathering evidence, and planning for improvement" (p. 19) among teachers, mid-level leaders must be called to be reflective, questioning, researching and future planning individuals.

A plan for such a bold move of creating a culture of inquiry among mid-level leaders must be well thought out and orchestrated to make it obligatory yet practical for this group of highly-influential individuals who often are allowed to form a complacent culture. Smith (1999) refers to such actions on the part of an effective administrator to redefine leadership in his or her school as recognizing "that they must stand firm with regard to the organization's commitment to the shared mission" (p. 603).

Such a plan must utilize several paths toward ensuring the success of the program as well as the satisfaction of the participants. For ensuring the success and satisfaction of this highly influential peer group, there is the distinct possibility and hope that it could result in the professional development of their department members or faculty. One is seldom able to encourage the revitalization of one's department, team or school without being convinced of the value of the time devoted to such an endeavor. This professional development of department members, if configured well, would ensure ongoing professional growth of each department centered around peer and supervisory observation and feedback. To create a climate where staff development is a welcome experience, the lead teachers must be treated as professionals in this experience (DuFour, 1991). This climate can be best provided by a collaborative juncture between university administrative leadership programs and schools.

MODEL COURSE DESIGN

A course developed for such a cohort should be one of Clinical Supervision and Evaluation of Personnel.

When the course meets on the regular university calendar and is conducted by university personnel from the administrative leadership program, the participants discuss required readings from *Techniques in the Clinical Supervision of Teachers* (Acheson and Gall, 1997) as a text. Each participant is required to search out articles from professional journals or magazines that relate to supervision or evaluation of teachers. These readings are reported in a written form one-third of which is the participants' reflection on how this might or might not be useful to them in their present or some future position as an instructional leader. These course participants should be given time to share, with their peers, the articles and reflections and carry on a discussion of the contents with the group. Additional reading on staff development, teacher leadership, and peer coaching through clinical supervision are assigned and guided discussions in small groups become a regular part of the weekly class meeting.

The research and inquiry into most common and best practices available and recommended to encourage instructional leadership becomes the theoretical framework for developing a positive, supportive structure for the leadership as well as the faculty. Still another component of such a course is to discuss education-related current events which serve to heighten the participants' awareness of what is happening in the larger local and national education communities. This can become a platform for not only further inquiry into models available for revitalizing current practice but also well thought out and well founded future planning.

As a requirement of such a course, each participant should conduct three clinical observation cycles—one with a member of the study group and two with department members. The observation cycle should follow the guidelines presented by Acheson and Gall (1997) as a recommended technique for supervising teachers. These observations should be a substitute for the annual evaluation observation that each of the department chairpersons or assistant principal is required to conduct with each department member or faculty member. Paralleling already established responsibilities of providing an annual observation/ evaluation of all their department or faculty members with the new strategies being presented in the class, it is expected that the new observation techniques would be used not only for those cases that fulfilled the requirement for the course, but also for other teachers on the faculty.

This practical application with peer feedback and support of both course participants and university professors of educational leadership creates a sort of "education laboratory" for practice, reflection and questioning in a supported environment. Ideally, two university professors can be instructors of record— one university instructor to conduct class, direct discussion, create and present scenarios for consideration, the other university instructor to meet with the participants to discuss pre-conference questioning, techniques to be used in the observation, and, if requested, attend the feedback conference along with the participant—a sort of field experience supervisor. A meeting after the teacher observation, between the university instructor and the participant in the program, should also be built into the program. This is done so that the techniques being learned in the course and employed in the ordinary supervisory responsibilities of the participants, can be collegially critiqued building in the cyclic process of improvement.

Keeping the course on a pragmatic level and sustaining interest, involves participants being required to create a tailor-made observation or evaluation tool for their department or school as their final assignment. This can be accomplished by examining the existing tool the participants use and, with knowledge gained by participating in the course, and course related research, change or adjust it to suit the unique needs of the particular department or school. Participants should be encouraged to search web sites for existing evaluation instruments and also use these to help them fashion their new instrument. This can be accomplished by creating an assignment for each participant to search out a given number of web sites for evaluation tools and/or observation techniques. In critiquing the web sites, participants reflect on their own professional needs to provide leadership, both instructional and collegial, to their faculty and school. This kind of investigation provides the opportunity again to reflection on present practice, question the need for change or fine tuning, and open the door to future planning for more effective feedback and growth potential of faculty members.

Participants should be encouraged to work in co-operative groups especially for their midterm and final assessment experiences. All participants receive graduate credits from the participating university in a course that will apply toward the requirements for state administrative certification or recertification.

In conducting a course such as the one described herein, instructors need to make it very clear that this is not another layer of responsibility imparted on a group of individuals who perceive themselves as already responsible for too much. Rather, it should be emphasized at every opportunity, that clinical supervision, not evaluation, will lead to collegial relationships that in turn will foster staff development and thereby create a richer environment for both faculty and students. The constant reminder that the supervisor is asking the teacher to allow them to be "another set of eyes" (Acheson and Gall, 1997) is in fact asking the teacher to enter into a collegial relationship with the supervisor for the purpose of being more aware of what is going on in their classroom. This premise also asks the supervisor to reserve the judgment of evaluation for another time and emphasizes the support of the teacher in answering the questions which the teachers pose to help them record, observe and collect data on the personnel and student actions which occur in their classrooms each day.

Because the participating mid-level leaders are required to practice the observation techniques learned in class in observing one another first, there is a greater appreciation of each other's discipline and skills generated. This in itself can create a cultural shift by opening doors to what really happens at other grade levels and other departments as opposed to the assumptions that usually prevail as to what is not done in other disciplines or at other grade levels. This collegial observation puts the emphasis on what is really happening and, possibly, where colleagues can support and interface with one another. A culture of inactivity and desire to keep the status quo can be changed into a different culture, one that expresses the excitement that department members, after clinical observation, show toward continuing the dialogue in the hopes of perfecting the craft of teaching.

A culture in which the supervisor (department chairperson, team leader, etc.) might have gone through the motions of a checklist evaluation, sometimes peppered with oft-duplicated narrative, can evolve into a culture that wants to invest in the members of their respective departments because they know that students will be the ultimate beneficiaries of better teaching. The shift from a complacent culture to one of enthusiasm is about mentoring and investing in teachers. DuFour (1991) refers to this cultural shift as one to "satisfaction and productivity" (p. 29).

Requiring outside reading of professional journal articles of the leaders' choice, provides the participants an opportunity to search out topics of interest to them as well as those that might support their stance on su-

pervision and evaluation or open them up to considering that this "collegial relationship" building just might be the glue that will create a cohesive department for them as well as cohesiveness of the entire faculty. Professional reading and discussion should continue to be part of the new culture well after the course concludes.

Still another area of emphasis by university instructors is that of coaches for change or content area coaches among supervisors and department or faculty members (Guiney, 2001). It should be emphasized that these roles could be undertaken by any department or faculty member and that classroom teachers doing peer clinical observation is just as useful, or possibly more so, than the hierarchical form of supervision most faculty are accustomed to. Mid-level leaders being willing to relinquish some of this activity can readily identify some department members who are more skilled at content coaching and anxious to share that expertise with other teachers. This would take us another step closer to a culture shift and reflective practice.

The final component of such a course is to emphasize the responsibility the mid-level leaders have to leadership in staff development. While this may, at first glance, seem to be a given, attitudes in such a culture may have arrived at leadership as just another layer of tasks thrust upon an already overextended pseudo-administrator. Again, through supplemental readings that emphasize the influence leadership has on school culture, and good teaching, the mid-level leaders will begin to see themselves in a different kind of leadership role (Peterson Deal, 1998), again a cultural shift toward the positive.

PROPOSED COURSE OUTCOMES

Ownership in School Mission

Where prior to such a supervision course, the targeted group of individuals may see every call to leadership in their position as another "job" or "chore," they now become assertive leaders willing and desirous of sharing the *responsibility* of leadership with the administration rather than just the exertion of the *power* of leadership. This new view of leadership should be observed in monthly group meetings with the administration where there is an increase in ownership in the mission of the school. This shift to co-ownership should be observed in the desire to share in the responsibility of more significant aspects of leadership with the administration.

Observation/Evaluation Reports

Planned observations and follow-up sessions with faculty members are more productive and plan for professional improvement initiated by the teacher after exposure in such a course. This behavior indicates more investment in the process and the personnel than might have been previously displayed. Written observation reports should indicate a greater commitment to successfully mentoring teachers beyond their first year of teaching. This too is a cultural shift from the obligation to mentor only first year teachers to having a long term investment in already established teachers. If this shift takes place, Senge (1990) would note that the new culture could support, among other things, team learning. Sangor (2000) in his book *Guiding School Improvement with Action Research* would go one step further and note that since this activity of supervision by collegial observation has become meaningful as well as attractive to the mid-level leaders, they will "find time to sustain the effort" it takes to plan such observation cycles (p. 181).

The emphasis on collaboration of members of the group during the university course should result in a less territorial and more collaborative atmosphere in the education arena as a result of their work together in the university course. Modeling this kind of attitude and behavior will, most probably, filter down to the department or team level where many teachers are eager to try some interdisciplinary approaches but might have previously met with resistance or no encouragement from the department chairpersons or team leaders who believe that is another layer of responsibility and work for them.

Self-evaluation Tool

Lastly, the group can collaboratively create a tool of self-evaluation for their position. The process of creating a reflective tool that can be used as an indicator of effectiveness in their position can now be undertaken as a sincere desire to evaluate the results of the process derived from the university course. This new tool can also be used to evaluate the depth of the cultural shift that has taken place as a result of calling these individuals to recognize their responsibilities in the arena of collegial supervision and the level of investment on the part of the mid-level administrators, rather than resistance to the true role of leadership and being in conflict with the administration. The newly configured culture should be one of investment in the future of the teachers who are part of each departments or

school. In the trickle down affect, it should also prove to be a renewed investment in their school and the mission of the school and therefore new investments in teaching and learning at the school.

CONCLUSIONS AND RECOMMENDATIONS

Recommendations are made to sustain professional reading through "Professional Sharing Circles" including the mid-level administrators or team leaders and interested teachers. The process of identifying teacher leaders can take place within the context of such sharing sessions. The call to leadership in this way is a natural evolution and investment as well as an authentic nurturing of potential leaders from within the teaching faculty resulting in a more aggressive plan for improving staff development.

As a result of these actions with a case study group, the university can use this impetus to create new courses to fulfill the state's professional development requirement for recertification. Courses such as those emphasizing creating self-evaluation and development plans and mentoring for department chairpersons and other supervisory personnel will not only be the result of such university/school collaboratives for the resurfacing and reinvesting in instructional leadership at the mid-level and teacher positions. The collegial, university based approach described herein addresses continuing recertification efforts but, more importantly, continuing school improvement efforts.

REFERENCES

Acheson, K. A., and Gall, M. D. (1997). *Techniques in the clinical supervision of teachers: Preservice and inservice applications.* New York: Longman.

Barth, R. (2002). The culture builder. *Educational Leadership, 59*(8), 6–11.

DuFour, R. (1991). *The principal as staff developer.* Bloomington, IN: National Educational Service.

Guiney, E. (2001). Coaching isn't just for athletes: The role of teacher leaders. *Phi Delta Kappa, 82*(10), 740–743.

Lambert, L. (1998). How to build leadership capacity. *Educational Leadership, 55*(7), 17–19.

Peterson, K. D., and Deal, T. E. (1998). How leaders influence the culture of schools. *Educational Leadership, 56*(1), 28–30.

Sagor, R. (2000). *Guiding school improvement with action research.* Alexandria, VA: Association for Supervision and Curriculum Development.

Senge, P. M. (1990). *The fifth discipline: The art and science of the learning organization.* New York: Doubleday.

Smith, W. F. (1999). Leadership for educational renewal. *Phi Delta Kappan, 80*(8), 602–605.

"Divertual" Learning in Education Leadership: Implications of Teaching Cultural Diversity Online vs. Face-to-Face

CAROLYN S. RIDENOUR, A. LLEWELLYN SIMMONS, TIMOTHY J. ILG, AND A. WILLIAM PLACE

Wisdom on the page correlates with wisdom in the writer about as frequently as a high batting average correlates with a high IQ: they just seem to have very little to do with one another. Witty and charming people can produce prose of sneering sententiousness, and fretful neurotics can, to their readers, seem as though they must be delightful to live with. Personal drabness, through some obscure neural kink, can deliver verbal blooms. . . . Speech is somatic, a bodily function, and it is accompanied by physical inflections—tone of voice, winks, smiles, raised eyebrows, hand gestures—that are not reproducible in writing. Spoken language is repetitive, fragmentary, contradictory, limited in vocabulary, loaded down with space holders ("like," "um," "you know")—all the things writing teachers tell students not to do. And yet people can generally make themselves understood right away. As a medium, writing is a million times weaker than speech. It's a hieroglyph competing with a symphony.

—Menand, Bad comma; Lynne Truss's strange grammar

INTRODUCTION

MENAND (2004), IN THE QUOTATION ABOVE, CAPTURES one of the dilemmas of online courses offered by colleges and universities. Writing, when competing with speech, he claims, is a "hieroglyph competing with a symphony." If restricted only to writing (a medium that is "a million times weaker than speech," in his words) students are seriously limited both in being understood and in understanding others. Being enrolled in an online course restricts students to Menand's "hieroglyphics." Interactions among students, their teacher, and their peers are carried out only through words typed on the computer monitor.

What are the consequences of this teaching-learning situation when graduate students in a Department of Educational Leadership are enrolled in a course on cultural diversity? Might the words on the computer screen be completely unrelated to the humanity, personality, style, interpersonal behaviors, and dispositions of the student writing them, as Menand suggests? Or, might the detachment provide a security in which the most honest and unadulterated discourse can be shared between teacher and students, as some proponents hope? In this chapter we explore responses to this dilemma. We attempt to capture this situation in our label: "divertual learning," a neologism coupling "diversity" with the "virtual" reality of the learning situation.

The two questions included in the call for proposals for the UCEA 2004 annual meeting, The Changing Face of Educational Leadership: UCEA at the Crossroads, were *"What is/should be the role of educational leadership in addressing issues of equity and social justice?"* and *"How do we define 'effective' leadership preparation programs in light of the rapidly changing demographics of the United States?"* This chapter falls into the nexus of these two questions that were drivers of the most recent conference of academics in education leadership. These questions also capture a place in space and time for us. We are in the midst of research into the transition of some components of our educational leadership preparation program to an online mode of delivery. Simultaneously, we are probing into whether or not a course focusing on cultural diversity and social justice can legitimately and effectively be delivered in an online environment.

Specifically, in this chapter we attempt to discuss the efficacy of delivering online a graduate course in issues of diversity (what we call "divertual" learning) versus teaching that course in a traditional face-to-face graduate classroom. Many colleges and departments of educational leadership face parallel issues: first, a need to strengthen the social justice mission as increasingly diverse constituents are being served by the graduates of these programs and second, the influx of distance education into graduate schools of education by university administrators seeking financial gain in a competitive marketplace.

PURPOSE

The purpose of this chapter is to raise questions and perhaps begin to shed light on delivering online a course in cultural diversity to future school administrators as opposed to delivering the course within a traditional face-to-face classroom setting. Questions are naturally raised by a shift from face-to-face traditional instruction, in general, to an online delivery system. The shift to an online environment for a cultural diversity course, in particular, may raise an even more important question: how can education for social justice be effective when divertual arrangements impede authentic and holistic human interaction in shared physical time and space? How can educational objectives that require graduate students to wrestle with dimensions of human difference and their own identities be accomplished within a milieu that masks most of those human differences?

Addressed in four sections of this chapter are selected dynamics that need attention when comparing the two learning venues. In the first section, we discuss the challenge of teaching cultural diversity and social justice *at all*, let alone comparing the two settings in which "they" are "taught." Next, in the second section, we explore several benefits and drawbacks of each instructional setting; and, thirdly, we raise the question of interpersonal dynamics: How does student-student interaction and teacher-student interaction differ in face-to-face classrooms from those same human interactions in an online situation? And how do these differences inform the teaching of issues of cultural diversity? Importantly, how do students relate with one another and the instructor in ways that can effectively dismantle individual and institutional sexism and racism?

Finally, in the fourth section, we attempt to examine both learning environments as to their potential to foster personal transformation, an important goal of change when learning surrounds issues of cultural diversity, such as race, gender, ethnicity, religion, social class, sexual orientation and physical and mental abilities and disabilities.

We admit that this chapter is only a work in progress. We are only at the beginning of a long process of examining these important academic, social, economic, and ethical issues about online education, particularly as they impact future school administrators.

"TEACHING" ISSUES OF CULTURAL DIVERSITY

Can We Teach Cultural Diversity?

In the mid-1990s our Department of Educational Leadership designed two courses addressing issues of cultural diversity for aspiring school administrators. One course, entitled, *Issues of Diversity in Schools*, was designed to consider race, gender, social class, ethnicity, religion, special needs, and sexual orientation as dimensions of society that influence school culture, which can privilege or marginalize both students and educators. A second course, *Leadership in Diverse Communities*, was designed to move students forward from the basic course into applying new understandings about cultural diversity to school organizations. We were not alone in filling this void that we called "cultural diversity." The decade saw numerous educational administration preparation programs redoubling their energies toward issues of race, gender, social class and children who had been historically underserved (Murphy, 1999).

Can one actually teach leadership in diverse communities? Can one teach acceptance, tolerance, social justice and antiracist attitudes? Our stance is that no, we cannot teach this as subject matter, but we can create a learning situation that allows graduate students to experience new awareness, learn about cultural difference, and reflect on their own cultural identities, transform their thinking and dispositions, develop cultural proficiency (Lindsey, Robins, and Terrell, 2003), and perhaps reconstruct their values and beliefs to become advocates for the success of children and families in diverse cultures. In short, we cannot "teach cultural diversity" but students can "learn cultural diversity."

We recognized that these issues were routinely addressed in our existing educational administration courses that address curriculum, law, personnel, supervision, and leadership. The departmental consensus, however, was that we needed to bring cultural diversity from the background to the foreground. An increasing multicultural society was clearly playing a growing role in the academic success of children, the instructional role of teachers, and the communities with whom administrators interact. No longer wanting to leave these issues to chance in other courses and because they were growing in importance to school leadership, we devoted ourselves to these two

3-semester hour courses. Within about a year, however, two changes outside the department were catalysts for cutting back on the progress we had made.

First, changes in Ohio licensure requirements and second, our move from an academic calendar structured into quarters to a calendar of semesters forced us to make difficult decisions toward streamlining the required credit hours. We needed to eliminate some courses. One of the diversity courses was discontinued. As a result, we no longer offer two courses but combined the two into one course. This course which continues to be offered today is entitled *Leadership in Diverse Communities*. And, since 2001, the course has been offered both online and in face-to-face traditional classrooms.

The Face-to-Face and Online Courses in Cultural Diversity

In the face-to-face course, students engage in multiple activities: they assess their own attitudes and values; maintain weekly written journals; interact face-to-face with those who might not share their beliefs, values, and cultural backgrounds; deliberate on marginalized social groups; consider issues of equity and social justice; identify racism and sexism and other marginalizing forces in schools, curriculum, policies and practices; question the role of schools in the context of wider societal cultures; discuss the possible roots of the majority-minority gaps in student achievement; and, locate themselves as agents of change and advocates of social justice (ISLLC, 1996). In the face-to-face course instructors use dialogue, simulations, small group deliberations and problem solving, case studies, journaling, self reflection and self assessment, invited guests who share diverse experiences and beliefs with enrolled students, and various media (videos, films, novels, and websites). Students demonstrate growth through journaling, group dialogue, personal reflections, presentations (group and individual), a scholarly paper and written exams. Required books have included those by Delpit (1995), Gollnick and Chinn (2004), Gruwell and The Freedom Writers (1999), Jelloun (1999), Lindsey, Robins, and Terrell (2003), McIntyre (1997), and Payne (2003), as well as other readings.

"Online education" needs to be contextualized and defined for each specific situation. In our situation, online education consists of three masters' level courses[1] and five postmasters level courses for Ohio principal licensure. Each online course, including the *Leadership in Diverse Communities* course, is uni-

formly structured into ten modules and enrollment is limited to 18 students in each course. The course is delivered asynchronously, although required timelines for completed assignments are included. Students are assigned to small groups; they respond to readings by writing to probes of the instructor. Students respond to the writings of peers in their group, using threaded discussions. Students do not interact with the instructor or their colleagues in any planned face-to-face meetings. This course is delivered by both full-time and adjunct faculty. Those teaching online have had no special training in this delivery medium.

To further illuminate the context, our university is a Catholic and Marianist school whose central mission is "community." This value should be evidenced in all that we do, particularly in teaching and learning, the center of our efforts. The goal of the course is not merely the effective management of issues of diversity. Studying cultural differences is only one of several steps toward the wider cause of social justice. Building a community committed to social justice requires vigilance so that we can reflect on and reject any of our behaviors that perpetuate inequity (hooks, 2003). Diversity merely outlines the dimensions of difference, but our behaviors, attitudes, and dispositions are our responses to diversity (Simmer-Brown, 2003). Whether or not the *facts* of diversity can be learned similarly in traditional and face-to-face environments is less our concern than is the question of whether or not our *responses* to diversity can be experienced and perhaps transformed in these two settings.

GENERAL BENEFITS AND DRAWBACKS OF FACE-TO-FACE AND ONLINE SETTINGS AS EDUCATIONALLY EFFECTIVE AND POWERFUL

Origins of Online Learning

Some authors report that little research into the benefits of online coursework has been conducted (Speck, 2000) and, of the research that has been completed, most is flawed by weak theoretical foundations (Merisotis and Phipps, 1999). While strong evidence is not yet firmly established, Moore and Anderson (2003) have recently edited a *Handbook of Distance Education* that includes online learning situations within a wider spectrum of distance learning options.

Not all distance education is labeled "online." In his introduction to that volume, Michael Moore characterizes distance education as the educational experience in which the teacher and students are in different locations. Not all of these arrangements are "online."

He admonishes those who *start* with the technology when they study any form of distance education. Technology and distance education are not synonymous. It is the technology, the computers, and the internet, that are new and not empirically supported. According to Moore, researchers have confused the technology with the education and many have discounted what actually is a rich body of knowledge and established understanding about distance education (2003).

Only recently has distance education entered the mainstream of acceptable educational venues (Moore, 2003) after having been an option as far back as the establishment of the U.S. postal service. Two dynamics: globalization and expanded communications technology generated this exponential growth in the last few years. The explosion of online courses in higher education seems to have been driven not by evidence of its advantages to teaching and learning but because of its financial benefits to universities and other sponsoring organizations. No groundswell of faculty seeking to teach online courses has driven this avalanche. Generally, it has been driven by top-down decisions of university administrators (Speck, 2000). That online learning continues to proliferate absent much research into its impact demonstrates continued disinterest in its pedagogical warrants and blind acceptance of its presumed profitability. Given this context, however, we are not absolved of responsibility to ask questions about these courses and to assess their current and potential impact.

Instructors

Moving from traditional face-to-face classroom settings to online settings changes the role of the instructor. But, the extent of the changes depends on the instructor, the content, and the goals of the course. According to McLoughlin and Oliver (1999), within the traditional setting, the teacher's role is "manager, expert, disciplinarian, controller, dispenser of information, goal setter, timekeeper," while in the online environment, the teacher's role changes into a supportive role as "coparticipant, scaffolder, colearner, moderator, facilitator, coach, monitor, adviser." These distinctions may be dichotomous and extreme. Each circumstance has unique contextual variables. These distinctions make stereotypical assumptions about instructors in traditional classrooms that are not always valid. Many face-to-face instructors conduct learner-centered classrooms; they coach their students and moderate lots of collaborative participation of students. Simplistic reductions that stereotype

all online courses and *all* face-to-face courses hinder what might be more productive dialogue. However, they are sometimes difficult to avoid.

Educational leadership is an applied field, a professional realm of study. Application of what preservice principals learn to their professional roles in schools is the goal of what we do in the classroom. School, according to bell hooks (2003) must always be made a definite part of the "real world" (p. 41). Educational administration is a profession largely engaged in face-to-face human interaction, communication, negotiation, deliberation, and conflict resolution.

From which venue, face-to-face or online, are students better prepared to transfer their learning to their professional lives as school administrators? An important concern, this has been voiced by many. Indeed, in his 1999 book on preparation programs for educational administrators (co-edited with Forsythe), Murphy, in the concluding essay, questions why the knowledge base in educational administration has been unrelated to the real-world practice in schools. Would online learning exacerbate or lessen that putative disconnect? Conflicting points of view have been expressed about the connection between courses and the world outside the "classroom."

Transfer of Learning to Practice

Students can very easily be oblivious to any links between a classroom and the rest of their lives. Students in educational administration programs may perceive that learning statistics or finance or law is not immediately connected to "what they will do tomorrow" in their K–12 classrooms. However, it is fair to say that the face-to-face classroom is never set totally apart from the external world in terms of cultural diversity. In these classes, graduate students are constantly interacting with others in shared physical time and space. Some of their peers and instructors come from similar cultural heritages and some come from different backgrounds. Thrown together, they discuss the problems of schools.

However, graduate students, who are teachers and administrators, can routinely disconnect their university experiences from their professional work. If successfully decoupled, the potential transfer of learning from any college courses to the practice of teaching and administration is minimized.

Given the likelihood of this alienation in traditional classrooms, does an online learning isolate students even more from "real world" contexts and peers who are struggling with them? Does it reinforce the false assumption that what students do in class is not relevant to their lives outside graduate school? Are the online learning communities in which students share ideas in writing to their classmates sufficient to strengthen transfer to professional practice? Learning needs to be holistic, integrated, and relevant rather than narrow and isolated if it is to make a substantive difference in students' lives (Nussbaum, 1997; Palmer, 1998).

Some might even claim that transfer to practice is enhanced online; they would reject the isolationism of online learning. They promote online learning as *liberated* from traditional classroom constraints. Online learning can connect the students to rich and multiple sources of information, expert opinion, virtual realities, web-based expertise, and, according to Dabbagh and Bannon-Ritland (2005), linking students to a universe of multiple realities. Here, the authors assume a particular category of online learning that consists of multimedia, options from which enrolled students select to meet their needs, and a variety of socially constructed learning communities. They might say that relevance to the "real world" is perhaps more immediate when one is linked to a streaming video of a building principal in action. However, in terms of personal connection and interaction in a course on cultural diversity, this is not the same experience as visiting that principal's school or conversing with her in a graduate seminar.

Moreover, those instructors in traditional classrooms who exclusively lecture may subject their students to linear, time-bound, narrow subject matter sources, and rigid teacher control, according to Chambers (cited in Dabbagh and Bannan-Ritland, 2005, p. 4), and in so doing, reinforce the disconnection between learning and practice.

INTERPERSONAL DYNAMICS: FACE-TO-FACE VS. ONLINE INSTRUCTION

Given what we have claimed about this course in educational leadership, both "divertual learning" and "classroom-situated learning" necessarily involves very different types of interpersonal behaviors and relationships. These warrant some discussion. What are the dynamics of interpersonal relationships in divertual and face-to-face situations? Is it fair to ask: To what extent is one or the other superior in a course addressing cultural diversity? Or, are they equally effective?

Major Emphasis of Face-to-Face and Online Courses: Content or People

University learning settings are focused on academic content knowledge. However, in a leadership preparation program, the focus must be on the people as well as the subject matter. And, even more importantly, in a cultural diversity course the emphasis on the people must be even stronger.

Much of the research into online education has been conducted in the context of distance education, and the emphasis is on *distance*. These studies have investigated the dynamics of teaching and learning that span oceans and continents. Whether or not the value of online education can be similarly argued when students are within the same city, county, or region, for example, as most of our students are, is a separate question. Students who are thousands of miles away from their instructors and peers are almost always in different cultures. These groups of students are unlikely to encounter their instructor or fellow students in shared physical space. These cultural diversities are manifest primarily in writing, requiring expressive language skills of students. "Technology-mediated interaction" seems to be an accurate term for online learning, one used by Vrasidas and Zembylas (2003) to capture the essence on online communication.

On the other hand, students who are in relatively close proximity to one another and to their instructor might easily engage in at least some face-to-face interaction. Not all of their interactions need to be "technology-mediated," of course. And, some online programs include at least some face-to-face encounters between students and instructors (Dabbagh and Bannan-Ritland, 2005). Distance learning markets, however, encompass increasingly large geographic areas, reducing the possibility of these personal face-to-face encounters.

Examining face-to-face learning and comparing it to the interpersonal dynamics of online learning was the focus of a British researcher, Nigel Blake (2000). He turns the argument about face-to-face instruction and online instruction upside down. The burden of proof, he hints, is on face-to-face. Cutting off all human contact *benefits* learning, he claims, lending the experience a dimension of scientific disinterestedness. In what might have been a condescending tone (if he were face-to-face and not writing text), he describes the almost "primitive" need for physical proximity that humans crave to satisfy. However, he argues that teaching is better considered synonymous with *study*, an activity that is traditionally more solitary. Blake attempts to make parallel the notions of "teaching/learning" and "study":

> Instead of the text actually teaching, the student has to actively study the text, just as she might also study

primary sources . . . behind the text is a writer who is plausibly described as 'teaching at a distance.' . . . The solitude of the student is as compatible with teaching as with study. (p. 185)

Intellectual discourse values disinterestedness, according to Blake (2000); academic "decorum" is strengthened by "bracketing off" the personal, such as facial expressions, body language, and voice intonations. These are intrusions on both sides of the teaching-learning duo, according to Blake, intrusions that must be "tamed" (p. 188). It is the academic voice to which the interaction should be directed, not the raced or gendered voice. To quote Blake further:

> And much of what is screened out or clouded in online education is precisely the kind of personal characteristic that can interfere irrationally in human interaction, and in education can distort, disrupt and at the extreme pervert the interaction of tutor [teacher] and student. And students are no less vulnerable to the same possible irrationalities, either taking against a tutor [teacher] as a kind of person they just 'don't get on with' or 'falling for them' as seductively attractive—and treating them with unjustified skepticism or perhaps undue deference. (p. 190)

On the other hand, perhaps Blake protests too much about the disadvantages of personal human contact. The personal dimension might be totally irrelevant in Carstens and Worsfold's (2000) conceptualization of online courses, insofar as the focus is solely on *content*. They suggest that online courses focus only on "knowledge" objectives (as opposed to, say, performance, dispositions, or transformation).

From three separate authors come three examples of similar language used to convey the meaning of online education, i.e., its primary focus on subject matter content. For instance, Berge (2000) writes:

> When it comes to learning, there are essentially two kinds of interaction. One occurs when a student individually interacts with content. The other is more social: a student interacts with others about the content. (p. 25)

In either case, according to Berge, the focus is the *subject matter content*, not the students themselves. A second example comes from Simonson (2000) when he writes that

> learning outcomes are the observable, measurable behaviors that are a consequence of online instruction.

When learning activities are designed it is important that some expectations for students be identified to guide the selection of appropriate technologies. (p. 31)

Similar "subject matter-focused" language comes from Canada (2000), when he writes in "product" language about both environments. The difference in Canada's characterization is that he disparages *both* learning settings. If his argument holds up, *neither* the traditional face-to-face classroom *nor* the online environment is suitable to achieve personal transformation, our goal in the *Leadership in Diverse Communities* course. We aim for cultural proficiency, personal transformation, in our students (Lindsey, Robins, and Terrell, 2003). Canada depicts both environments as oriented toward some *product*, rather than oriented toward personal transformation.

> An online course resembles a traditional course in many ways. In both environments, for example, a teacher guides students through a body of knowledge and skills. Students, in turn, show the teacher—and themselves—how much they have learned by producing something, perhaps a paper or a test. Finally, the teacher evaluates the product, often suggesting ways the student can improve. (p. 35)

Divertual Interpersonal Relationships

Weiss (2000) claims that the online environment might not only be "antiseptic" but also might lead to potentially unethical behaviors and responses. She suggests that

> the removal of the human element creates an environment that is not conducive to maintaining ethical behavior among students. If the student does not see the pain of a hurtful remark, then it must not exist. (p. 48)

With the absence of the "human element," how *do* students sense the impact of a hurtful remark? How do they grow in their interpersonal relationships? How do they experience growing forgiveness for hurting and being hurt? Discussions of race, gender, religion, and social class situate people in vulnerable positions; faculty members who facilitate these discussions establish their classrooms as safe havens for such discussions. When communicating face-to-face, meaning depends on whether words are said in respect, anger, frustration, humor, or love (Weiss, 2000). Such cues are unavailable online.

In an online environment, how can students look another human being in the eye, a human being who is different than they are? How do they experience personal transformation? How well do they get to merely know one another, the foundation of productive human relationships? Aspiring school administrators face a role in which human interaction is crucial to their effectiveness. Can human beings relate to one another in personally transforming ways when they experience one another as only moving words on a screen?

There may not be one answer to that query. Personal relationships develop in online communication quite frequently. And, the question itself, to some, might be moot. Entrepreneurs have latched on to the profit potential for linking individuals with one another online. From contacting old high school classmates to dating services, sharing hobbies and social concerns, political and social bloggers, the personal connections online have proliferated (Correll, 2002; Imel, 2003).

Evidence for meaningful interpersonal relationships in online courses, however, is inconclusive, at best. For example, one student that Canada (2000) quotes made these remarks:

> The only adverse part of this course is that you don't know me and I don't know you. Voices only. When teaching any class, I think the passion and professor's actions communicate a lot about what he or she is attempting to teach. With an online class you miss that. (p. 39)

The feeling of Canada's student is the opposite of a student of one of the authors of this chapter. The student visited her recently, lauding the success of her online course —she loved it! Her first comment was, "I got to know the other students so well!" In this course, the students would ultimately meet face-to-face at a concluding session of presentations. She was eagerly anticipating that session. "I can't wait to meet them!" Notwithstanding that the sequence of the two feelings seemed to be reversed (i.e., one usually meets others *before* they get to know them), her remarks showed passion about others she knew only through technology mediated communication, in the absence of interaction with them in shared physical time and space.

An online message from a student in a masters program was written at the end of a two-year online program in response to a probe to reflect on the experience. Her words capture the mixed blessings of this teaching-learning medium insofar as divertual learning is concerned, here recapitulated by Vrasidas and Zembylas (2003):

In my opinion, technology influences our cross-cultural online interaction by making us simply reflect on each other's opinions posted in words, and not based on biases, stereotypes, misconceived perceptions, or misinterpretations due to someone's skin color, physical appearance, gestures, or facial expression. . . . Part of the problem of this medium is that it forces our relationships to remain on a very "textual" level by relying on just the typewritten characters that make up our words, sentences, and meaning. This is not exactly a negative aspect. . . . Perhaps another way technology has influenced our cross-cultural online interaction is that it "muffled" some of the insensitivity that we sometimes experience in face-to-face environments. Since most of us are now living on or are originally from the islands where people share a lot and are very close with each other, this technology has at least assisted us and facilitated our "islander" longing to communicate, socialize, and make lasting relationships. (p. 271–272)

The price we pay for "muffling" the insensitivity may be actual learning that is lost. Personal transformation, for some individuals, involves the uncomfortability of facing racism and stereotypes that perhaps one has not previously been aware of or acknowledged.

Cyber relationships, however, grow from very different purposes than do online graduate courses. To what extent are personal relationships important for success in graduate courses? Are gains in knowledge sufficient? For the course we are discussing in this chapter, personal relationships are indispensable as learning grounds for students aspiring to cultural proficiency.

Learners Bring Cultural Differences

Teachers have been continually encouraged to attempt to tailor their teaching to the styles and cultures of the learners in their classrooms (Brown, 2003; Ingram, Conley, McDonald, Parker, and Rivers, 2003). The cultural backgrounds and related learning preferences of students enrolled in online courses are worthy of discussion, perhaps even more relevant to an online course in cultural diversity. For instance, individualism tends to be more valued in Western cultures and collectivism, an emphasis on the group, tends to be valued in Nonwestern cultures (Matsumoto, 1996). And, it is also the case that some individuals in both cultures behave differently when they are interacting with family members in intimate relationships (mostly in a collective spirit) than they do with others outside their families (mostly individualistically), according to a synthesis of research by Gunawardena,

Wilson, and Nolla (2003). The isolation in an online learning setting might reinforce individualism and privilege those from Western cultures; the independent learning setting might be inconsistent with those from cultures that place a higher value on relationships and the collective.

Unfortunately, the picture is not that clear. One might argue just the opposite. Individualistic cultures, such as ours in the United States, tend to have more groups to which people can align themselves, but individuals do tend to abandon groups that are too demanding and "their relationships within their groups are marked by a high level of independence or detachment. In collectivist cultures, depending on the effective functioning of the group, a member's commitment to an ingroup is greater" (Gunawardena, Wilson, and Nolla, 2003, p. 755). This seems to imply that it is possible that members of individualistic cultures maintain more detachment from online learning groups than do those from collective cultures. In either case, success as an independent learner bodes well for students in an online learning setting (Dillon and Greene, 2003).

Online learning creates potential challenges for those from what Hall (1998) refers to as "high-context cultures," cultures in which indirect nonverbal contextual cues are important to successful personal interaction and communication. (Low-context cultures depend on the explicit verbal message and less on the contextual cues.) Online text-based education can privilege those from low-context cultures, such as the United States, while those from some Hispanic, Native American, and Japanese cultures might be disadvantaged (Gunawardena, Wilson, and Nolla, 2003). When those from high-context and low-context cultures communicate, those predisposed to the former might participate less and learn less.

Similarly, silence is perceived very differently in different cultures. Some Asian cultures consider silence as powerful and useful; it is nurtured along with a posture of reserve and formality. On the other hand, the United States and other Western cultures are more apt to value assertion and aggressive verbal behavior (Ishii and Bruneau, as cited in Gunawardena, Wilson, and Nolla, 2003). In an online learning situation, silence renders a student invisible. In face-to-face learning settings, silence and reserve might not be barriers to the extent they are in online courses. The instructor is much more able to navigate the teaching-learning dynamics to maximize the participation of all learners in both nonverbal as well as verbal ways. A nod, a gesture, a questioning look can signal understanding.

Students for whom English is not their first language may also experience more flexibility in communicating face-to-face than they do online. As people engage in the give and take of speaking and listening, clarification of meaning can be immediate and effective. Perhaps communication is easier and more effective with less struggle for new users of English when it is carried out face-to-face than it is online.

Calculating the quality of students' work online and the quality of instructors' feedback online differs from the face-to-face classroom (Dillon and Greene, 2003). Online educators are encouraged to provide timely feedback to students who submit their assignments, just as face-to-face educators are. In the online environment, that immediacy is calculated differently and so is the quality. The cultural dynamics, however, come in to play in both venues. For example, absent personal human contact, a lengthy response by an online instructor can be perceived negatively, depending on the predispositions of the student (Dillon and Greene, 2003). It may well be that, because instructors and students do not become acquainted in a rapport building phase and get to know one another more holistically as persons as they do in face-to-face classes, an intervening step is needed whereby online instructors learn how their students respond to feedback. Students, too, may need to learn to be independent learners, if they are not personally or culturally predisposed to learn that way. This shift could eventually produce unintended consequences if all students' learning dispositions and behaviors become more standardized in all environments.

Cultural dispositions are brought to all learning environments; learning styles and preferences play a role in students' capacity to maximize learning. The restrictions of a divertual setting may render it unsuitable for some learning goals. But, on the horizon are other more dramatic shifts that may diminish the impact of this mismatch. The goals of the courses themselves may be modified to fit an online environment. Revolutionizing the way educators consider learning styles and learning preferences might be an outcome in the explosion of distance education, moving away from learning styles to emphasizing metacognition (Dillon and Greene, 2003). Students need to learn how to learn in a variety of settings, regardless of any traits they display. Because the technology favors students who learn independently and in isolation, more and more educators will likely train students to learn independently, over and above whatever cultural values they bring to the "classroom."

ONLINE VS. TRADITIONAL: HOW CAN WE PROMOTE PERSONAL TRANSFORMATION THAT STRENGTHENS THE VALUES OF CULTURAL DIVERSITY AND SOCIAL JUSTICE?

Personal transformation implies change from within. Rather than solely emphasizing cognitive goals, the goals for learners are dispositional. Students are taught to examine their own values, beliefs, and attitudes about their professional role in the wider world. They are confronted with the need to change or expand the repertoire of their personal behaviors and attitudes. Educational processes are intended to be holistic, encompassing the entire person, mind, body, and spirit. Grounded in ISLLC standards, we are obligated to define our work this deeply: preparing students to manage schools in ways that guarantee that students are treated fairly, ethically, and with understanding of the larger cultural context (ISLLC, 1996). Teaching that encourages personal transformation is teaching holistically. Building awareness and new understandings about culturally diverse communities and the attitudes and behaviors of those who lead them is our goal in the *Leadership in Diverse Communities* course. Our goal is personal transformation. That we must teach holistically is required not only by ISLLC, but also by our local institutional mission, the Marianist characteristics that are our legacy.

If it is offered online, teaching a course on cultural diversity, i.e., divertual learning, must be carried out through this framework with no less purposefulness than in delivering the class face-to-face. Online it cannot be the same course as it is face-to-face. Colleagues in K–12 education join us in this commitment. Concerns are no different in their K–12 schools than they are for us in departments of educational leadership. For example, the Executive Director of AASA, Paul Houston, expressed concern that time spent sitting before a computer screen rather than interacting with those unlike oneself may limit children's social education. In his own words, he expressed the fact that

> as children are growing up in an increasingly diverse world, they need to have exposure to people different than themselves. I'm not saying it can't happen outside the public system, but it happens easily in the public system in many cases (Cox, 2004).

What stance must we take in our own graduate classrooms that might parallel a similar concern?

We must ponder the real possibility that the online classroom may be appropriate for "knowledge transfer" but "not to personal transformation and the development of human values," according to Carstens and Worsfold (2000). And it is personal transformation that should be at the heart of a course focused on social justice and equity. For example, cultural proficiency theory (Lindsey, Robins, and Terrell, 2003, a book sometimes used in this course we are studying) maintains that some educators move along a 6-point continuum as they develop cultural proficiency, the

> point at which educators and the school environment optimally facilitate effective cross-cultural interaction. . . . [Culturally proficient] educators recognize that culture involves far more than ethnic or racial differences. They demonstrate an understanding of the cacophony of diverse cultures each person experiences in the school setting . . . a conscious awareness of the culture of their communities, districts, or schools. (p. 30–31)

Lindsey et al. began to chart the course of one's personal development toward cultural proficiency as a journey through "contact" with others unlike oneself, through "disintegration" of long held personal values and attitudes, on through more steps toward the goal of cultural proficiency. Authentic transformation of values, attitudes, and beliefs within students almost always requires personal discomfort. In other words, this graduate course is not solely focused on knowledge gained. The course aims at personal transformation. Other theories, such as Janet Helms' (1992) theory of white racial identity, pose similar developmental schema that include the disintegration of one's previously held beliefs, values, and behaviors and their subsequent rebuilding.

In both theories, these are not just *any* beliefs and values. These are beliefs and values about one's identity, about how one ascribes value to other human beings, about one's sense of power and self-worth, about one's family heritage, about one's appearance in an appearance-obsessed culture, about one's religious beliefs, social class, and economic status, about one's physical abilities and disabilities, about one's sexuality, and about one's often unrecognized but lifelong fears of those unlike oneself.

Delineating these many beliefs and values brings to mind the notion that *education* is about finding one's place in the world, according to Parker Palmer (1998) about empowerment, transcendence, healing and wholeness. In the educational leadership milieu, this means that *education* is about our students' finding their place in the world of schools where they assume much responsibility for children and teachers and accountability to the community. Their own personal identities, their personal beliefs and value for strong relationships with others influence the heart of their leadership style and its eventual effectiveness.

Personal transformation carries them toward their place in the world. And we must admit that the globalization discourse, the discourse that dominates online learning, creates a reality about the world that substantially reduces cultural pluralism. The communication technology, in fact, constructs one networked culture. Not unexpectedly, some doubt that a "mediated technology communication" environment can encourage true human interaction that is transformational (Mason, 2003). Thus, online learning may not be suitable for a course in cultural diversity which aspires to such transformation.

Some proponents of online learning ground its effectiveness in the very social processes that doubters might claim are missing. For example, Dabbagh and Bannan-Ritland (2005) characterize asynchronous learning networks as potentially strong social groups

> where groups of learners or professionals with a common goal congregate to share information and resources, ask questions, solve problems, and achieve goals, and in doing so, collectively build new knowledge and evolve the practices of their community. These distributed forms of interaction are made possible by telecommunications technologies, which . . . are fundamentally responsible for increasing the interconnectedness and scope of interactions and activities and providing a global perspective on a particular area of study. (p. 10)

This perspective strongly suggests that personal transformation might be logically consistent with an online learning environment. In whatever ways they construct the learning environment, however, it is absent the physicality of actual culturally diverse human beings sitting together in shared physical space with their flesh and blood counterparts who embody the human encounters potential school leaders will soon have, if they hope to successfully manage future schools.

CONCLUSIONS

Our conclusions at this point in time surround five ideas. First, globalization has changed how we think about education. Second, the competition that has generated the proliferation of online learning may outweigh attention paid to the learning values, if not closely monitored. Third, there is real difficulty in

concluding that online and face-to-face can support exactly the same goals; this is even truer for a cultural diversity course. Fourth, we admit that there are limitations of each venue; but, finally, the cultural dimensions that activate all learning situations are even more consequential for online teaching.

Globalization: A Way of Thinking About Oneself and Others

"Globalization" has begun to structure the discourse on distance education, including online venues and, we believe, divertual learning. At first glance, "globalization" would not seem a relevant construct to the interpersonal relationships in an online course in an educational leadership program in Ohio. However, we concluded that this construct does inform our questions about divertual learning because it addresses a dimension fundamental to theories of all distance learning—how one thinks about oneself in relation to the rest of the world. At first glance, the term "globalization" is automatically connected to discussions of competitive markets, global trade, and international relations. We believe that the dramatic influence of globalization over the past couple of decades does play a role in how individuals consider online education. In essence, people have begun to think about themselves and their "distance" from others in new ways. The notion of "I" and "others" has begun to change. These new ways of thinking have begun to influence educational delivery systems, even when the system is within the borders of one country or state.

In arriving at this conclusion, we considered at least three ways of thinking about globalization—three perspectives that are quite different from one another. Evans (1997), a prolific researcher in the field of distance education, defines "globalization" as the notion that "most people, if not all, are connected more or less contemporaneously with distant events, sometimes whether they like it or not" (p. 18). His meaning, here, implies an embodied connectedness. Staying with definitions, we considered Mason's (2003) definition. To her, the construct is simpler: in educational circles the term is used synonymously with borderless education, virtual education, and online education. Vrasidas and Zembylas (2003) conceptualize "globalization" in less neutral ways than do Evans and Mason, structuring the phenomenon through a lens of power, a second perspective. They state:

> Although there is no agreement among scholars on what globalization means, there are some identifiable

characteristics that focus mainly on its impact. Such characteristics include the dominance of a world capitalist economic system, the increased use and reliance on new information and communications technology, the strengthening of transnational corporations and organizations, the erosion of local cultures, values, and traditions, and the emergence of what some call a "global culture" (Giddens, 1990) within a "network society" (Castells, 1996, p. 272).

In this quotation we're most interested in Vrasidas and Zembylas's allusion to cross-cultural reliance on "new information and communications technology" and the "network society," the latter to which they cite Castells (1996). All of these authors integrate two areas of progress: communications technology and the forces that have promoted increased globalization. In the history of distance learning these are inseparable phenomena (e.g., see Moore, 2003).

We considered yet a third perspective, that of Dabbagh and Bannan-Ritland (2005) who, in fact, based their perspective on Evans' ideas as expressed in a 1995 article. These authors add another dimension to the meaning of globalization—the ways in which people think. Ultimately, this construct brought the issue back to the forefront of divertual learning. They state:

> Globalization can be described as a psychological phenomenon that can be applied to many contexts to imply that most people are connected simultaneously with distant events, directly or indirectly, intentionally or unintentionally, which promotes a perception or an awareness of the globe as a single environment. (Evans, 1995, p. 8)

In this context, globalization becomes psychological, a way of thinking about oneself in relation to the world. More importantly, this way of thinking promotes the world as a single environment, a single culture. Combined with Vrasidas and Zembylas's claim, this discourse privileges a single culture paradigm at the expense of local cultures. Because of the dominance of the United States on the internet and in technology, globalization may well be interpreted as Americanization (Evans and Nation, 2003).

The phenomenon of globalization, then, when accepted as a psychological construct, as a way of thinking about oneself in relationship to the world, has implications for divertual learning. This course we teach is heavily laced with issues of identity, both personal and professional. Identities constructed through race, ethnicity, gender, religion, geography, sexual orientation, social class—are all issues of sociocultural importance to

those who aspire to be school leaders. Constructing one's identity as a learner, a scholar, a teacher, or a school administrator within a globalization discourse may be carried out in ways that reinforce certain power structures and diminish others. In cultivating cultural proficiency within our classrooms (or online) we are simultaneously teaching in a world where the very notion of culture itself has been dramatically altered.

The Bottom Line

A second conclusion is related to finances. Comparing face-to-face education and online education cannot be considered without considering market share, and ultimate revenue for the university and resulting viability of our program in educational administration. Online education promises to bring in more students and potentially more revenue for universities. Our online course, *Leadership in Diverse Communities*, may sustain or increase the university's revenues if we can attract students to our program with the online option who may have otherwise gone elsewhere. Regardless of the responses to the four questions we have considered about divertual learning in this chapter, market forces may dominate any decisions about the relative appropriateness of online vs. face-to-face learning environments.

Appropriate and Inappropriate Online Course Goals

Third, we have concluded that online and face-to-face educational settings are sufficiently different. Establishing the same goals for students in the same course in both settings is problematic. Some may argue that no courses in educational leadership should be delivered online. Others may make finer distinctions, pointing out meaningful differences between courses such as law or finance or research (where, they say, knowledge trumps personal transformation as a course goal) and a cultural diversity course (where enlightened human interaction and personal transformation are course goals). The former courses, to these decision makers, might be more easily relegated to an online environment with the same goals and objectives as those in the face-to-face venue. If a course in cultural diversity is to be put online, however, the nature of the desired outcomes would necessarily have to differ due to the absence of human interaction in shared physical time and space.

Cultural Dispositions of Students and Instructors

Fourth, we concluded that the cultural dispositions that students and instructors bring to their learning experiences matter. Students' sense of self, their communication styles and preferences, and their dispositions as learners play a role in their success. In the traditional face-to-face classroom, the instructor's role has a longer history and is better understood. The flexibility of the face-to-face instructor maximizes his/her potential to adapt to changing learner's needs. Instruction online is not well understood and is less familiar to those responsible for students' academic and personal growth. Less flexibility in the online environment can minimize instructors' ability to adapt to learners' needs. Technology mediated communication, in itself, supports certain learning preferences and limits others. Those assigned to deliver online courses need to reflect on their own instructional preferences and be given time to prepare for this new way of interacting with their students. They need to acknowledge the cultural preferences that both they and their students bring to the learning situation.

Next Steps

We have merely scratched the surface of our ideas in this chapter. The conversations will continue and much more knowledge, understanding, research, and organizational collaboration must go into new learning technologies before they can be effectively implemented. Accomplishing the mission of our educational leadership department must always be held up as the criterion for whether or not we are effectively carrying out the legacy of our academic ancestors in a contemporary world of schools, rather than whether or not we are incorporating the newest technology.

We began this chapter arguing that there were two reasons that compelled us to examine these four questions. First, our students in educational administration will face increasing diversity among the students and families they will serve in the future, making it imperative that we include cultural diversity in our preparation programs. That future school leaders be culturally proficient and embody the dispositions and behaviors that serve diverse families equitably is one way to regain excellence in all schools, especially those schools that we have historically served less well. Second, graduate students who want to study educational administration have multiple options from which to choose; we want to remain viable within that market by considering when online learning might be appropriately considered and when it might not be.

Of these two issues, both must be addressed, but the obligation for meeting the needs of all children and families is most important. This comes first; designing the best ways to prepare culturally proficient school leaders must be our first obligation. Whether those strategies are best delivered face-to-face or online is secondary and should be decided based on the results of those established criteria.

NOTE

1. We will develop all ten masters level courses for online delivery over the next couple of years; currently only three courses in the masters program are delivered online.

REFERENCES

Berge, Z. L. (2000). Components of the online classroom. In R. E. Weiss, D. S. Knowlton, and B. W. Speck (Eds.), *New Directions for Teaching and Learning, 84*, 23–28.

Blake, N. (2000). Tutors and students without faces or places. *The Journal of the Philosophy of Education Society of Great Britain, 34*(1), 183–198.

Canada, M. (2000). Students as seekers in online courses. In R. E. Weiss, D. S. Knowlton and B. W. Speck (Eds.), *New Directions for Teaching and Learning, 84*, 35–40.

Carstens, R. W., and Worsfold, V. L. (2000). Epilogue: A cautionary note about online classrooms. In R. E. Weiss, D. S. Knowlton, and B. W. Speck (Eds.), *New Directions for Teaching and Learning, 84*, 83–88.

Chang, M. J. (1999). Does racial diversity matter? The educational impact of a racially diverse undergraduate population. *Journal of College Student Development, 40*(4), 377–395.

Correll, S. J. (2002). The ethnography of an electronic bar: The lesbian café. In S. B. Merriam and Associates (Eds.), *Qualitative research in practice: Examples for discussion and analysis* (pp. 239–258). San Francisco: Jossey-Bass.

Dabbagh, N., and Bannan-Ritland, B. (2005). *Online learning: Concepts, strategies, and application.* Upper Saddle River, NJ: Pearson.

Delpit, L. (1995). *Other people's children.* New York: The New Press.

Dillon, C., and Greene, B. (2003). Learner differences in distance learning: Finding differences that matter. In M. G. Moore and W. G. Anderson (Eds.), *Handbook of distance education* (pp. 235–244). Mahwah, NJ: Lawrence Erlbaum.

Evans, T. D. (1997). Encountering globalization: Issues for open and distance educators. In L. Rowan, L. Bartlett and T. D. Evas (Eds.), *Shifting borders: Globalisation, localisation, and open and distance education* (pp. 11–22). Geelong: Deakin University Press.

Gollnick, D. M., and Chinn, P. C. (2004). *Multicultural education in a pluralistic society* (6th ed.) Upper Saddle River, NJ: Pearson.

Gruwell, E., and The Freedom Writers. (1999). *The freedom writers diary.* New York: Doubleday.

Gunawardena, C. N., Wilson, P. L., and Nolla, A. C. (2003). Culture and online education. In M. G. Moore and W. G. Anderson (Eds.), *Handbook of distance education* (pp. 753–776). Mahwah, NJ: Lawrence Erlbaum.

Helms, J. E. (1992). *A race is a nice thing to have: A guide to being a white person or understanding the white persons in your life*. Topeka, KS: Content Communications.

hooks, b. (2003). *Teaching community: A pedagogy of hope*. New York: Routledge.

Imel, S. (2003). *Informal adult learning and the internet: Trends and issues alert no, 50*. (ERIC Clearinghouse on Adult, Career, and Vocational Education, ED481327.)

Ingram, K. W., Conley, C., McDonald, S., Parker, V., and Rivers, J. (2003). *What factors affect the way teams interact in an on-line graduate course?* (ERIC Document Reproduction Services No. ED482681.)

Jelloun, T. B. (1999). *Racism explained to my daughter*. New York: The New Press.

Kleinfeld, J. S., and Yerian, S. (1995). *Gender tales*. New York: St. Martin's Press.

Lindsey, R. B., Robins, K. N., and Terrell, R. D. (2003). *Cultural proficiency: A manual for school leaders* (2nd ed.). Thousand Oaks, CA: Corwin.

Mason, R. (2003). Global education: Out of the ivory tower. In M. G. Moore and W. G. Anderson (Eds.), *Handbook of distance education* (pp. 743–752). Mahwah, NJ: Lawrence Erlbaum.

McIntyre, A. (1997). *Making meaning of whiteness*. Albany, NY: SUNY Press.

McLoughlin, C., and Oliver, R. (1999). Pedagogic roles and dynamics in telematics environments. In M. Selinger and J. Peaarson (Eds.), *Telematics in education: Trends and issues* (p. 39). Kidlington, Oxford, UK: Pergamon Press.

Menand, L. (2004, June 28). Bad comma; Lynne Truss's strange grammar. *New Yorker*, 102–104.

Merisotis, J. P., and Phipps, R. A. (1999). What's the difference: Outcomes of distance vs. traditional classroom-based learning. *Change, 31*(3), 12–17.

Moore, M. G. (2003). This book in brief: Overview. In M. G. Moore and W. G. Anderson (Eds.), *Handbook of distance education* (pp. xiii–xxiii). Mahwah, NJ: Lawrence Erlbaum.

Moore, M. G., and Anderson, W. G. (Eds.) (2003). *Handbook of distance education*. Mahwah, NJ: Lawrence Erlbaum.

Murphy, J. (1999). The reform of the profession: A self-portrait. In J. Murphy and P. B. Forsyth (Eds.), *Educational administration: A decade of reform*, (pp. 39–68). Thousand Oaks, CA: Corwin.

Nussbaum, M. C. (1997). *Cultivating humanity: A classical defense of reform in liberal education*. Cambridge, MA: Harvard University Press.

Palmer, P. (1997). *The courage to teach: Exploring the inner landscape of a teacher's life*. San Francisco: Jossey-Bass.

Payne, R. (2003). *A framework for understanding poverty*. Highland, TX: Aha Process.

Simmer-Brown, J. (2003). In b. hooks, *Teaching community: A pedagogy of hope* (p. 47). New York: Routledge.

Simonson, M. (2000). Making decisions: The use of electronic technology in online classrooms. In R. E. Weiss, D. S. Knowlton and B. W. Speck (Eds.), *New Directions for Teaching and Learning, 84*, 29–34.

Speck, B. (2000). The academy, online classes, and the breach in ethics. In R. E. Weiss, D. S. Knowlton and B. W. Speck (Eds.), *New Directions for Teaching and Learning, 84*, 73–82.

Vrasidas, C., and Zembylas, M. (2003). The nature of technology-mediated interaction in globalized distance education. *International Journal of Training and Development, 7*(4), 271–286.

Weiss, R. E. (2000). Humanizing the online classroom. In R. E. Weiss, D. S. Knowlton and B. W. Speck (Eds.), *New Directions for Teaching and Learning, 84*, 47–52.

Internship: Ensuring Practitioner Success

SHIRLEY JOHNSON AND STACEY EDMONSON

DEVELOPING EFFECTIVE ENTRY LEVEL SCHOOL LEADERS IS perhaps the greatest challenge any educational leadership program faces. A well-developed internship program offers multiple opportunities often not available in the traditional classroom setting used by most preparations programs. While coursework on topics such as law, curriculum, leadership, special programs, and others are addressed in the coursework, campus level projects that integrate the content into applicable, authentic experiences (Capasso and Daresh, 2001). This movement from comprehension into application is critical for the development of effective leadership skills (Peel, Wallace, Buckner, Wrenn and Evans, 1998). Effective leaders must have the opportunity to develop critical leadership skills at the campus level in order to create an effective transfer of skills and cognition (Dosdall and Diemert, 2001).

Principal preparation programs are one of the few areas where internship experiences are not utilized effectively. For example, teachers are required to spend at least a full semester in a classroom with students; doctors are required to complete an extensive residency where they practice knowledge application and are monitored closely for development; counselors are also required to complete an extensive practicum. Unlike most professional internship experiences, such as student teachers who are typically expected to be full practitioners in a classroom of students during their internship experience, administrative interns often receive minimal amounts of true responsibility and less monitoring and development. These interns are usually full time employees of the district or campus in which they are completing their internship and are expected to somehow incorporate the "part time" responsibilities of a school principal into a full time classroom teaching job (Creighton, 2002). Consequently, principal interns often have to "squeeze in" internship activities during non-instructional time, such as before or after school hours or during their conference period. These scenarios do little to provide interns with substantial opportunities to engage in activities just as a school principal would experience.

Complicating this issue is the lack of appropriate supervision by administrators who either are not trained in mentoring experience or do not have a genuine interest in developing the intern's leadership potential for a variety of reasons. However, interns are expected to be competent administrators upon completion of internships with supervisors who have little or no time to devote to "training" an intern. Because of time constraints on the part of both supervising administrators and the interns themselves, internship activities sometimes consist of menial tasks such as bus duty, taking attendance, or monitoring the cafeteria during lunch. These types of activities often enable the students to develop a narrowly focused set of operational leadership skills, but do not effectively encourage the development of instructional leadership skills that are required in today's era of accountability.

In light of this problem, the faculty at Sam Houston State University (SHSU) has begun the careful examination of improving the activities and requirements experienced by principal interns. The faculty has considered the number of obstacles that will be encountered by both interns and the supervisors and are willing to confront each problem.

Through the years, SHSU has served the students of its region well in successfully preparing aspiring principals and assistant principals for administrative positions in surrounding school districts. Standardized testing requirements, student demographics, and the rapidly retiring baby boomers have emerged a need for educators to become certified with more attention directed to the "real world" connections associated with schools. SHSU has chosen to respond to these demands by redesigning the master's program internship with the input of superintendents, alumni, and research.

Prodded by Hale and Moorman's (2003) research for the Institute for Educational Leadership, the SHSU's department of Educational Leadership reviewed its current offerings as it considered the following: "In a survey of educational leaders conducted by Public Agenda, 68 percent of the principals responding indicated that traditional leadership preparation programs were 'out of touch with the realities of what it takes to run today's schools'" (p. 5). Even though hard to examine what the department thinks is well done, the following also reinforced the need for reexamination.

Because they are rewarded for empirical research, these faculty members have few incentives to engage in meaningful dialogue and partnerships with K–12 educators. Thus, they seldom spend time in public schools—*and practitioners rarely read their publications.* The United States has a history where the K–12 and university levels remain distinctly separate. But greater linkages between K–12 schools and institutions of higher education will be necessary to better prepare future school leaders (Combs, Miser, and Whitaker, 1999, www.ASCD.org).

Professors in educational leadership understand change cycles and related theory, but they are susceptible to missing the variables in the environment that signal the need for reviewing and revamping programming just as any other business or educational entity. Moving beyond the traditional thinking is not easy and is subject to question; however, there is no longer a choice. The crisis in educational leadership is to the point that strategic tactics are required to shape future progress. The variables sounding the alarm are as follows:

- Current leadership at the campus and superintendent levels is retiring rapidly.
- Replacements for the retirees are younger and lack the maturity to immediately support effective leadership.
- Leadership demand is requiring problem solving that moves beyond the traditional university course sequence and degree requirements as noted in the state or national certification requirements (State Board for Educator Certification [SBEC], n.d.).
- Demand mandates that leadership development move to the field where theory and application are immediately evident and on-site practice required (Gooden and Spencer, 2003).

Finally, Bottoms and O'Neill (2003) with the Southern Regional Education Board (SREB) echoed many of the same concepts, but went on to specifically address areas of the principal's job that were not being appropriately addressed by higher education. In a passionate plea they wrote, "It is time for local districts to think about how they will attract high-performers. It is time for universities to create school leadership preparation programs that will make a difference in improving schools and student achievement" (p. 2). In the light of Bottoms and O'Neill's work, SHSU's Educational Leadership Department used research and the experience of its seasoned staff to reshape the internship program and consider other innovative ways to meet the demands of practicing principals and superintendents.

The revisions in both the curriculum and in program implementation of the internship program are predicated on very strong beliefs shared by other professionals (Bottoms and O'Neill, 2001; Hale and Moorman, 2003; Hipp, 1997) and those of the SHSU faculty. The following summarizes the tenets upon which the revisions are justified. The principal

- is an instructional leader possessing the capabilities to positively impact student performance through quality instructional analysis, design, and strategic implementation of curriculum, instruction, professional development, and related resources.
- is a collaborative leader who effectively distributes leadership to improve student achievement, build trust, and positively impact school culture and climate.
- is able to articulate visionary beliefs and motivate faculty, staff, students, and the community to generate results.
- is able to craft effective collaboration among parents, business partners, and community members to create a seamless support for student success.

From these tenets evolved a more authentic approach to preparing aspiring school leaders. This approach demanded the redesign of the current internship and modifications to the existing curriculum.

REDESIGNED INTERNSHIP
The redesigned internship consists of two parts: (a) an on-site internship to be served with a mentor who meets regularly with the student and provides specific on-site duties for the intern to complete, and (b) completion of a leadership behavior assessment accompanied by a seminar where results are explained and a development plan created to assist the student in behavior awareness. Students entering the internship must understand that this is an important part of the

degree and/or certification. It is rigorous but designed to prepare the student for an administrative position.

ON-SITE INTERNSHIP

The on-site internship is designed to provide the intern with a high quality experience that provides the student with information and experience from the field that enables him or her to readily assume an administrative position. This experience is to be completed during the student's final semester in the leadership program. The student seeking internship is responsible for obtaining permission to serve in an internship on his/her campus of choice. Before the internship can begin, the supervising professor, the building principal, and the intern must meet to discuss, agree to, and sign a contract that enables the intern to complete the activities mentioned below. It is

important to note that this internship is different from those in the past, and the principal must make arrangements for the intern to have an additional period each day or designated time other than their conference period to complete the internship activities.

If the student is unable to arrange the internship on the campus, then it will be necessary for the student to make other arrangements for a campus assignment. Because of these substantial changes, it will be important for the students to be informed in the beginning level courses of this requirement and to communicate with the administration of their school to accept and support this internship. In addition to the Leadership Profile assessment described below, the following five areas of focus are utilized in the internship: (a) Instructional Delivery and Curriculum Analysis, (b) Personnel and Student Management, (c) Special

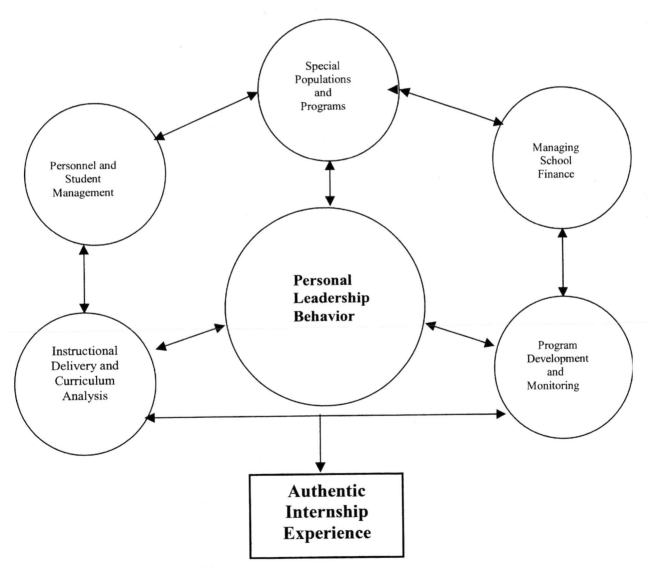

Figure 1. Revised Internship Model

Populations and Programs, (d) Managing School Finance, and (e) Program Development and Monitoring. Each area includes an intense interactive seminar as well as leadership behaviors and activities to be completed after the seminar.

Instructional Delivery and Curriculum Analysis

In this seminar, participants will receive intensive assistance in instructional supervision in order to highly develop observation, analysis, and feedback skills to support the continued improvement of instructional supervision. The objective of this area is to coach teachers to deliver quality instruction that creates quality student performance. Interns must (a) implement basic components of instructional leadership to support improve student performance, and (b) design instructional units to include lesson plans with appropriate instructional strategies to enhance the instructional program. The culminating project in this area requires interns to observe 20 percent of the instructional faculty and create an instructional profile. They match teachers' student performance with instructional abilities and make recommendations for possible professional development that specifically targets student improvement.

Personnel and Student Management

In this seminar, participants learn the basic components of school culture and how to motivate and manage personnel at the campus level. This seminar will include the legal processes associated with personnel management as well as cultural issues that enhance the instructional environment. The objective of this seminar is to enable participants to lead the school climate and culture through the implementation of effective human resource management. The interns must (a) implement strategies to improve the school culture and climate that consider personnel development and enhance the learning environment, (b) provide quality personnel management strategies and discipline management techniques to support a positive school culture, and (c) conduct quality conflict resolution strategies to solve parent, student, and faculty problems. The final project for this area requires interns to conduct a climate survey of the entire faculty and generate conclusions from the data. They must design a series of activities/strategies to address areas of concern and/or strengthen areas of concern. In addition, they must conduct at least two conflict resolution sessions to resolve a conflict between teachers and/or students.

Special Populations and Programs

The objective of this seminar is for interns to implement effective programming for students of special populations. Students will receive training from highly trained specialists who understand and have implemented programs for students of special populations. The seminar will be divided into three distinct sessions: (a) describe special education programming, manage the IEP process, and oversee appropriate paper work; (b) provide quality Bilingual/English as a Second Language (ESL) programming that meets the specific needs of the second language learners as well as improves student achievement; and (c) lead the implementation of funding provided by No Child Left Behind to enhance instructional programming to successfully improve student achievement. For the final project in this area, interns must conduct a complete analysis of the current ESL/Bilingual and Special Education programs on the campus. They should determine the strengths and concerns of both programs and recommend changes to one or both programs in the form of an action plan that is prepared for implementation.

Managing School Finance

The objective of this seminar it to design a campus budget that reflects the use of district funds, federal/state funds, and any other allotted monies. Participants will explore the school finance policies and procedure in order to design and implement a campus budget, interact with the district budget, and understand the impact of the state or federal law on the management of district monies. Interns must complete the following activities: (a) describe the funding formulas necessary to support public schools and then relate the formula to the participant's district, and (b) create a school budget that reflects equity and support of the instructional and co-curricular programs. The final project requires interns to create a budgetary process that creates maximum participation by the faculty and administration in the design of the budget. Additionally, students must assemble the budget and explain the results to the faculty.

Program Development and Monitoring

This seminar extends a significant opportunity to examine data describing the health of the curricular and instructional program. Participants learn how to analyze the existing programming in their building and provide suggestions in the form of an action plan to improve student performance. The objective of this seminar is for aspiring leaders to create curricular programs that improve and sustain quality student performance. In addition, the interns must (a) analyze current trends and performance indicated by the district accountability indicators, and (b) design programming to alleviate current student performance issues and strengthen current instruction. The final project for this objective requires the intern to lead a data inquiry of at least math and English Language Arts teachers to determine strengths of current student performance and areas of concern. Once the areas of concern have been determined then recommendations will be generated for action plans to improve student and/or teacher performance.

Other Relevant Internship Components

ROLE OF THE UNIVERSITY SUPERVISOR. When a student meets the requirements for the internship, the coordinator will assign the interns to a professor who will guide the student throughout the semester in a much different manner than before. The internship professor will

- meet with each intern to assist in the selection of a mentor.
- meet with the mentor and the intern to discuss the objectives of the program and obtain a signature that ensures the mentor is willing to provide the opportunities for the intern.
- work with the mentor to provide feedback and assistance throughout the program.
- guide the interns through the simulations required for completion of the course.
- tutor interns who do not have success with the simulations and need remediation of any kind.

MENTOR SELECTION AND PROCESS. To secure the mentorship process, the department chair of Educational Leadership or his/her designee will obtain a written agreement from the superintendent of each district of the aspiring interns. The superintendent will be made aware that the internship is intended to meet the demands of superintendents regarding the preparation of aspiring assistant principals and requires that the intern be assigned an additional period during which the intern will complete the assigned duties. The superintendent or principal may provide additional time if the district so chooses, but only an additional period is requested.

PERSONAL LEADERSHIP BEHAVIOR

In addition to the above seminars and activities, each intern will complete the Leadership Profile to deter-

mine their personal Profile regarding personal behaviors that underlie all leadership skills. The Leadership Profile provides a principal with important information relative to a person's usual behavior, their underlying needs, and the points of stress that seriously affect their most productive usual behavior. All of the data summarizes into a Lifestyle Grid that describes how the principal prefers to work and interact with other people. They also are provided information as to when their stress behavior begins to materialize as a result of their basic needs not being met. The Lifestyle Grid is further defined by eleven components categorized into behaviors underlying leadership that produce responses to the usual behavior, underlying needs, and stress points of each principal (Birkman, 1995).

The results provide each administrator with a comprehensive view of self and how they prefer to behave. These results also enable participants to consider the profiles of others who are different and gain understanding as to how different people will respond in various situations. The results for teams are often overwhelming, but the understanding always creates improved working relations and productivity simply because people better understand one another.

Following the administration of the Profile, students will participate in a feedback seminar and interact with peers to understand the different behavior profiles and how to effectively interact with each. When the seminar is completed, each student will develop a personal growth plan that will enhance personal strengths and highlight areas of growth from both the Leadership Profile and the on-site internship. Feedback and assistance will be provided to students by the faculty.

CURRICULUM IMPLICATIONS

To provide students with the necessary on-site experiences of both engaging faculty and staff in significant projects and in bringing the project to closure, changes must be made in the curricular offerings of the program to support the internship experiences. Each of the core courses in the curriculum offerings must be modified so that the student understands the theory and/or practice associated with the internship experience. In addition to the curriculum revisions, each course requires students to complete a comprehensive project that will contribute to the successful completion of simulations during the internship program.

Administration and Organization of Public Schools

Administration and Organization of Public Schools is designed to provide a foundation of content and theory important to understanding past and current public schools. To reshape the course to reflect the current needs of the field, the following must be added to this curriculum:

- Current information and theories regarding school reform and networks
- Major concepts that affect leadership and schools
- Comparative work of current issues schooling needs with those of the past
- Complete a current project understanding the important concepts necessary for change whether school or district.

Instructional Leadership

Instructional Leadership provides the foundation for developing quality instructional leadership skills. In addition to the theory related to supervision styles and cycles, Instructional Leadership I must include the following:

- Focusing aspiring principals on the primary job of positively affecting instruction
- Finding effective strategies that apply leadership and research-based knowledge to solve field-based problems
- Developing leadership skills to create and implement comprehensive school-improvement designs

Curriculum Planning

The function of Curriculum Planning is to acquaint the aspiring principal with the principles of curriculum and its usage in the school. The program must ground the theory and principles in the school with a relationship to the district curriculum and with methodology for using research-based resources and programs to address appropriately identified problems and implement professional development for new programs and sustain training for effective programming. Curriculum Planning project should include:

- Collaborative inquiry to analyze all AEIS and other school data to determine program strengths and concerns
- Data must include: Attendance data, Drop out (if appropriate), subject area scores, AYP, Discipline infractions, etc.
- Analysis of instruction from each core content area
- Recommendations for professional development

- Campus Improvement Plan developed from process that includes
  - CIP goals and objective
  - One set of action plans/strategies for one goal and objective

Special Programs and Special Populations

This course provides the basics of special populations programs that are essential to each public school and to certain private schools. Students will be expected to tie the essentials of special populations programs to curriculum and to the campus improvement plan. The project for this course should include:

- Program designs for Bilingual/ESL
- Program designs for Special Education
- Design of the Bilingual/ESL and Special Education program for the particular needs of the school.
- No Child Left Behind requirements
- Addition of a project that requires identification of projects, programs, or curriculum additions that are supported by special populations funding.

School Support Services

Since this course is designed to acquaint students with support services that enable schools to function, the course project should include:

- Facilities planning to support school improvement or reorganization
- Bus utilization that supports school improvement
- Technology that supports both instruction and administration
- Complete a facilities project that details the integration of all support services as they support a campus.

Federal, State, and Local School Law

This course provides the legal underpinnings for managing schools. The course project should include action research into:

- Personnel Management and Due Process
- Discipline Management
- FERPA implementation
- Special Education
- Bilingual Education and other special programs
- Student and teacher rights
- Addition of a project that is scenario based that requires the use of at least all three of the above points and demands a solution to be examined by the superintendent, the board, and interested parties.

Role of the Principal

The Role of the Principal is one of the most important courses in the program because it integrates many of the concepts of each of the core courses. The course project must include:

- Leadership skills and behaviors that support the creation or maintenance of a positive culture and climate
- Creation of a community of learners
- Organizational systems and principles that create effective school management
- Creation of effective team development and maintenance

Instructional Leadership Development

Instructional Leadership Development will require the following:

- Full analysis of an instructional unit
- Observation of three lessons of an instructional unit
- Cognition and knowledge of the state adopted standards
- Conference planning and implementation
- Completion of a classroom observation to include:
  - Analysis of lesson plans related to the observation
  - Analysis of the observation
  - Conference planning
  - Conduct the conference

The projects required in each of the above mentioned courses will provide the basis for authentic assessment of skills required in the school setting. The required activities and seminars for the internship are relevant to the completed coursework.

CONCLUSIONS

The requirements of this internship are aggressive and demanding of the student. These requirements can also be demanding of a mentor who already has a very demanding and busy schedule. However, the student has the opportunity to practice these very important skills in a "safe" environment where immediate feedback can be provided by a practicing administrator and where corrections can be made without serious implications. The difficulty with this internship can occur with an administrator who does not deem the student as a worthy candidate and does not completely support the work completed by the student or who does not give the student an opportunity to accomplish any of the activities in an authentic setting. Consequently, it is vital that the university liaison complete an appropriate screening of the attitudes of both the mentor and the intern. This internship can be the most important experience aspiring principals can experience, but it can also be a defeating experience if the liaison fails to detect difficulties and resolve the conflict.

Overall, this approach to internship can be difficult for intern supervisors because they must understand the importance of their regular visitations and management of the student's work. Intern supervisors in the past have had little to do with the actual process taking place in the internship experience, and consequently many students were not afforded the opportunity to learn or apply what they know in the actual school setting. This process can also be difficult for the student in that they risk influencing their mentor with skills that are less mature and that need nurturing before the intern actually begins practicing as a school leader. The burden on the university to protect the quality of the internship and the performance of it students dramatically increases with this program. However, the awards far outweigh the possible negatives.

REFERENCES

Birkman, R. (1995). *True colors*. Houston, TX: Birkman International.

Bottoms, G., and O'Neill. (2001). *Preparing a new breed of school principals: It's time for action*. Atlanta, GA: Southern Regional Education Board.

Capasso, R. L., and Daresh, J. C. (2001). *The school administrator internship handbook: Leading, mentoring, and participating in the internship program*. Thousand Oaks, CA: Corwin Press.

Combs, A., Miser, A., and Whitaker, K. (1999). On becoming a school leader: A person-centered challenge. [Electronic Book Version]. Retrieved September 4, 2004 from, www.ASCD.org.

Creighton, T. B. (2002). Toward a leadership practice field: An antidote to an ailing internship experience. *AASA Professor, 25*(3), 3–9.

Dosdall, E., and Diemert, N. (2001). Working from a higher rung. *Journal of Staff Development, 22*(1), 26–29.

Gooden, J., and Spencer, L. (2003). Reforming educational leadership programs: Identifying the ideal principal mentor. *Connections*. Online Publication retrieved February 27, 2003, from www.principals.org/publications/connections/index.cfm.

Hale, E., and Moorman, H. (2003). *Preparing school principals: A national perspective on policy and program innovations*. Edwardsville, IL: Institute for Educational Leadership, Illinois Education Research Council.

Hipp, K. (1997). Documenting the effects of transformational leadership behavior on teacher efficacy. Paper presented at the annual meeting of the American Educational Research Association. March 1997.

Peel, H. A., Wallace, C., Buckner, K. G., Wrenn, S. L., and Evans, R. (1998). Improving leadership preparation programs through a school, university, and professional organization partnership. *NASSP Bulletin, 82*(602), 26–34.

State Board for Educator Certification. (n.d.). Approved programs. Retrieved July 30, 2004, from http://www.sbec.state.tx.us/SBECOnline?approvedprograms.asp?=1.

Non-Degree (Add-On) "A" Certification: Meeting the Needs of the New Principal

SIDNEY BROWN

INTRODUCTION

THE IDEA FOR THIS STUDY AROSE FROM A CONVERSATION with an inner city elementary school principal in Mobile, Alabama. She was expressing frustration over the increased responsibilities of the principalship that have expanded over the last decade. She stated, "Since 1990, my duties have expanded to include some of the following: to prepare staff, community, and students for standardized achievement tests, realigning curriculum standards, remediation, test analysis, and intervention planning. I have to write school improvement, technology and safe school plans, and must monitor and evaluate all three of those plans annually. Also, I work with emotionally disturbed students and provide inclusion for all students, while maintaining an acceptable dropout rate." She felt that her formal administrative certification training did not adequately prepare her to anticipate and address all of these issues.

RATIONALE

There are currently two models used to qualify candidates for administrative certification for the principalship in the state of Alabama. One model requires the candidates to obtain at least a master's degree in Educational Administration and earn certification through course work and a structured 300-clock hour administrative internship. The second model is for the candidate who holds at least a master's degree in any field of education. Through this model, the candidate must apply for admission to a 300-clock hour Non-Degree (Add-On) "A" administrative certificate program. This program consists of six core courses with the last two courses consisting of an intensive internship. However, these experiences are disjointed because placement should be based on need rather than on the availability of space, which is the common practice. The intern is placed in a year-long internship in four different administrative settings (elementary school, middle school, high school, and central office).

An example of the administrative internship concept conducted through the College of Education at a four-year institution in Alabama, and is based upon the high school as the candidate's desired level of certification. The candidate must complete 300 clocks hours of meaningful internship experience during one academic year (22 objectives, with performance documented through a student portfolio). Of those 300 hours, the candidate must complete 150 hours at the high school (home school) level. The candidate must then complete 50 hours of internship at the elementary level, 50 hours at the middle school level, and 50 hours at the central office level. During this internship the candidate must satisfy 22 objectives mandated by the Alabama State Department of Education. These 22 objectives encompass the knowledge areas of curriculum, professional development, school and community, student services, fiscal management, and communication. A minimum of three of the objectives must be satisfied at each internship site. The candidate must be assigned to and complete the internship with a state certified principal mentor in the public schools; this mentor must have served in the principalship for at least three years (Brown, 2003). Upon completing all coursework and internship requirements, the candidate must receive a passing grade on the institution's graduate comprehensive final examination. This examination is facilitated through the institution's Graduate School though no degree is involved. The final phase requires the candidate to submit an application for state certification for the principal ship through the Director of Certification in this institution's College of Education.

As a result of the conversation with Principal X, the following question is posed: *Is the Non-Degree (Add-On) "A" administrative certificate awarded by the state of Alabama meeting the professional and personal needs of new principals?* The question serves as the central premise for this study, and is relevant as it is today for two distinct reasons asserted by Klemper and Richett (2002): (a) 40 percent of all principals are currently eligible for retirement with the next decade; and (b) the number of qualified candidates for the principalship is dangerously low. Based on these assertions, the shortage of skilled leaders can reach serious proportions. In Alabama, the recruitment of principal candidates has been further exacerbated by variables such as long hours, low salaries, less prestige and poor working conditions. These variables have contributed to notable shortages of qualified principals in the workforce. Dramatic changes have occurred in education reform legislation of 1995, and as a result, the responsibilities of school administrators and those who prepare school administrators have changed dramatically. The significance of the question is further enhanced by school reform efforts, accountability standards, and high stakes testing in which all are at a pinnacle for the 2001 No Child Left Behind (NCLB) legislation.

According to recent research, filling principals' shoes is a difficult task (Keller, 1998). In Alabama new accountability standards were designed to increase the quality of teachers and administrators; however this strategy has had an adverse effect and become an added stressor to the already overburdened task of being a principal.

Alabama reflects the national trend with respect to principal retirement. During the 2001–2002 academic years, over 60 public schools were noted as having at least 50 percent of principals eligible for retirement in the next 5 to 10 years. Also, many experienced principals retire from the state of Alabama and then obtain employment in neighboring states. This is done to receive full retirement benefits from the state of Alabama, while obtaining and maintaining full-time employment as a principal or assistant principal in a neighboring state.

Paradoxically, it has also been noted that at least 20 percent of the remaining principals in the Alabama workforce are under the age of 32. This is relevant to the preparation of future principals during their internship programs because the lack of experienced principal mentors available for candidates seeking administrative certification is limited. Some school districts provide opportunities for teachers to enhance their knowledge and skills through a prospective principals' academy. However, Alabama does not provide release time for candidates to participate in these academies thereby reducing the state's capacity to ensure a developmental pipeline for producing effective, highly qualified novice principals. Members of Alabama's

administrative professional organization can participate in an existing leadership academy to receive training in the Professional Educators Personnel Evaluation (PEPE) skills/knowledge areas: seven habits of highly effective people, faculty meetings as tools for capacity building, special education legal issues, and building successful school teams. All of these areas are important for PEPE performance evaluation, but they do not address the immediate knowledge/skills base needed by the novice principal.

As noted by Keller (1998), in addition to there being a shortage of highly qualified principals, there are few qualified people applying to the principalship (cited in Fusarelli and Smith, 1999). Principals must be carefully recruited, mentored, and educated in the latest skills and knowledge domains if this problem is to be corrected.

Lashway (2003) stated:

> If experienced principals feel their jobs to be exhausting and stressful—most surveys indicate so—then what is it like for the novice principal? Not surprisingly words such as "lost," "overwhelmed," and "shell shocked" pervade the literature on first-year principals. (p. 1)

With such demonstrative words by novice principals, there is little wonder why there are growing shortages in this level of educational administration.

REVIEW OF RELATED LITERATURE

Webster's Dictionary defines leadership as a direction-setting task. Effective leaders (principals) direct schools in a manner that puts student success at the forefront in the learning community. For example, Kouzes and Posner (1997) stated that people who lead engage in "visioning" (p. 91). Furthermore, the leader as a facilitator is a good model and point of reference for all programs designed to train principals. Effective leaders demonstrate high moral and ethical traits. They have high expectations for their students and staff, and communicate on a daily basis the three Cs to success: be clear, concise, and have consistent goals. Candidates seeking school administration certification who demonstrate appropriate leadership dispositions are the qualities most Colleges of Education are struggling to develop in their graduates. The knowledge and skills learned while completing the administrative and supervision certification programs must be reinforced with consistently high quality for professional development. Such professional development must focus on current issues, and should address such topics as new accountability standards, new curriculum standards, related stressors, leaving no child behind, and community troubles permeating the school that used to be handled in the home.

The demands of today's principalship are excessive. Because the day-to-day operations of a school have become so strenuous and time consuming, one could not expect to have a good quality of life and be an effective school leader (Boris-Schacter and Langer, 2002). Principals would like to terminate ineffective teachers, and reduce excessive paperwork (Archer, 2002). As a result of these practices and hindrances, concern over bureaucracy and the politics of the job have led many principals to leave the profession (Archer, 2002).

Developing quality leadership for student success is of utmost importance. Without leadership, schools cannot expect to develop and/or maintain standards of quality and character. In its full breadth, the maturation of school leadership requires understanding the principal's role and becoming an expert in the knowledge and skills of all 11 leadership domains identified by Smith (1996) as essential for finding capable leaders. Those leadership domains are: (a) past leadership, (b) capacity to catch or create a vision, (c) the person needs to feel the thrill of a challenge, (d) a constructive spirit of content, (e) the person has practical ideas, (f) a willingness to take chances, (g) a completion factor, (h) mental toughness, (i) peer respect, (j) family respect, and (k) possess a quality that makes people want to listen to you.

These aforementioned knowledge and skills areas must be developed in new principal candidates through structure training paradigms if they are expected to become successful principals. Lashway (2003) stated that the skills needed today vary greatly from the skills needed by the principal of yesteryear, when it was believed that effective leadership meant that principals managed vending machines, retained an effective bookkeeper, and were good disciplinarians. Today's principal is responsible for keeping sound financial records, writing federal and state grants, managing school personnel, and providing instructional leadership. Today's principal must develop the knowledge and skills of an Instructional Leader/Manager (ILM). In essence, the principal of the past was reactive to the changes of education, where the future principal must take a proactive stance based on theory and practice.

The College of Education at one four-year public institution in Alabama has recently completed its seven-year National Council for the Accreditation of Teacher Education (NCATE) review process. The purpose of this peer review is partly to assess the effectiveness of all educational program offerings of the college. These reviews are important for accountability purposes. This becomes especially important in the light of assertions by Lashway (2003) that "by reputation principal-preparations programs are not highly effective" (p. 1). The College of Education at this particular institution has implemented the theme *The Educator as Decision Maker*. This theme is important in part because principals must be able to make research-based decision quickly. These decisions are evident early in the process of an administrative candidate's choice of program offerings.

This particular Non-Degree (Add-On) "A" program has historically provided a constant flow of qualified administrative graduates. The question is how the quality of this program can be improved to meet the ever-changing demands of the new principal. In order to define some of the program's weaknesses, the following issues have been identified based on the author's experiences as a university supervisor interacting with administrative internship candidates:

1. The candidates are certified for every level of school administration. *Each administrative graduate is certified to serve in any administrative position in the school system.*

2. The four internships are disjointed. *The interns are usually placed by the local school system based on availability of space rather than on home school level, which can lead to the experience exceeding the university expectation of a 1-year experience.*

3. There are no level-specific internships. *The interns are certified at all levels of administration (elementary school, middle school, high school, central office, and superintendent).*

4. Internships are not a continuous yearlong process. *Interns often engage before and after school activities, which do not give a true picture of the demands, knowledge, skills and depositions, which need to be developed.*

5. Candidates do not have the opportunity to develop a sense for the ebb and flow of a school year. *Interns are normally placed at a site when there is space available. Their intern experience can exceed the expected yearlong expectation.*

6. There is no capstone licensing for Alabama. *Currently the State Department of Education allows its institutions' Colleges of Education to interpret what activities should be completed within their respective certification programs.*

These weaknesses are problematic because research has shown that accountability standards are crucial to the overall development of quality schools and leadership. In order to change, schools reformers have realized that steps must be taken to standardize the process by which school administrators are prepared (Bolman, Johnson, Murphy, and Weiss, 1990; Griffiths, Stout, and Forsyth, 1998; Jacobson, 1996). A report by the National Commission on Excellence in Educational Administration recommends that principal preparation programs mirror the criteria of "professional schools which emphasize both theoretical and clinical knowledge, applied research and supervised practice" (Griffiths, Stout, and Forsyth, 1988, p. 17). The candidate for the principalship must be afforded the necessary knowledge and skills to navigate a school leadership position.

Any one of the two previously mentioned degree/non-degree options (minimum master's degree in Educational Administration or in other fields of education) must be taken at the university level if a candidate pursues certification in a leadership position in the Alabama public school system. However, local boards of education can also petition the State Department of Education for a waiver of the rules in order to obtain emergency certificate for an administrator. These waivers can be renewed for three consecutive years without penalty. At the end of the third year cycle, the waived certificates must be replaced by an administrative degree certificate from one of the degree-granting Colleges of Education at an institution in the state. If the administrator does not receive state certification he or she must be removed from that administrative position.

Flanary (2002) stated that to ensure that prospective school leaders are prepared today and well into the future, it will take a total team of prospective stakeholders. State Boards of Education, colleges, universities and community groups play a key role in that effort by ensuring that aspiring school administrators have the targeted training that they need to obtain employment and to retain employment.

University leadership preparation programs must look inward and outward to ensure progress in building and maintaining quality school administration programs. Schools cannot expect to improve the teaching and learning process without strong competent leaders who must possess the ability and dispositions to be collegial in the decision-making process.

The Alabama Department of Education further enhances its administrator quality and professional development by requiring that every administrator be certified in the implementation of Alabama's PEPE program. Without this certification, administrators cannot supervise and evaluate personnel. PEPE certification involves an intensive, weeklong odyssey that was adopted with new accountability standards set by the Alabama State Board of Education in 1995 and approved by the state Legislature. The main thrust of the program was to ensure the public trust that all teachers and principals would be evaluated annually through an objective performance-based system. This would, in effect, ensure the perceptions of quality teaching and learning annually in Alabama public schools. Further evidence of the success of the principal preparation program is that students consistently meet state goals in the PEPE program.

FOCUSING ON THE GROUP

The Department of Instructional Support Programs in the College of Education at a particular four-year public institution houses the administrative preparation program. As this department began collecting data for NCATE documentation and visiting with the administrative interns throughout this state, faculty members in the administrative preparation program observed that the teachers seeking the Non-Degree (Add-On) "A" certificate were more focused and better prepared than candidates who enter graduate degrees programs in Educational Administration. This was a surprising conclusion. The author informally reviewed 37 annual performance (PEPE) evaluations of principals and assistant principals (AP) that had gone through both programs. This was accomplished by asking all 37 recently placed administrators for copies of their individual PEPE evaluations. The results of this assessment were that the average scores of the 20 administrators who received the Non-Degree certificate was a 3.00 average score on a 4.00-point maximum scale. Of the 17 Educational Administration program certification completers placed, 10 received an average score of 2.8. While one may surmise that the Non-Degree candidate would not be better prepared for the PEPE evaluation, the Non-Degree program certification completers may have earned higher PEPE evaluations because they were given more opportunities to take on leadership roles earlier in their careers. Their experiences mirror the 11 traits identified by Smith (1996) earlier in this paper.

The author has found that the aforementioned traits of leadership identified by Smith (1996) correlate well with the expectations that administrative candidates will face with their performance evaluations, as outlined in the State Board of Education PEPE Evaluation Manual for Principals. What follows are the 11 knowledge and skills each principal will be evaluated (PEPE) on, and the knowledge and skills that the Non-Degree program certification completers are already demonstrating:

1. *collaboration*—geopolitics—most were chosen by management, and given opportunities to lead colleagues;
2. *communication*—they have obtained a master degree or higher;
3. *organizing for results*—some have been appointed to roles requiring outcome-based organizational skills such as SACS/title 1/budget committee chair;
4. *assessment/evaluation*—some have been promoted to roles requiring performance assessment such as department chair;
5. *planning*—they have demonstrated the ability to set goals, deadlines, and timelines for instructional improvement;
6. *laws and policies*—promotion to policymaking roles such as (AAI) administrative assistant of instruction;
7. *problem solvers*—promotion to problem-solving roles such as (API) assistant principal of instruction;
8. *leadership of human resources*—they are PEPE certified by the Alabama State Department of Education;
9. *innovation*—they have demonstrated effective use of educational technology;
10. *school operations and management*—they have gained experience in fiscal management and paper trial knowledge while chairing committees; and
11. *fiscal leadership and management*—they have been promoted to successful principalships.

Through this grooming and mentoring process, the state Non-Degree (Add-On) "A" certification program can possibly serve as a viable method for addressing the need to produce a pool of qualified new principals. These new principals can feel confident in the quality of their preparation at their respective university preparation program.

Finn (2002) states, "most administrators believe that the University Administrative preparation programs are not adequate. Sixty-nine percent of the principals and 80 percent of the superintendents surveyed stated that "these programs are out of touch with the day-to-day realities of the job" (p. 23). This study was designed to address part of this issue by surveying current Non-Degree candidate' perceptions of their program and by assessing current administrators' success on the job through conversation and PEPE evaluation results.

DATA COLLECTION

A questionnaire was developed by the author to gather data for this study. This questionnaire was designed to ascertain the perceptions of administrative Non-Degree (Add-On) "A" intern (ANDIC) candidates regarding the internship experience. ANDIC participants were given questionnaires in both of Administrative Internship Fall 2003 classes. Questionnaires were completed and returned anonymously.

RESULTS

Candidates Comments

Comments received were grouped according to administrative candidate responses to questions. The responses were recorded in the highest frequency mode for reliability purposes. The first question was: "Do you perceive the Non-Degree (Add-On) 'A' certificate a quality program? Please explain."

- One hundred percent of the candidates responded, "Yes, I perceive the Non-Degree certificate is a quality program because of direct instruction from the college professor."
- One hundred percent of the candidates responded, "Yes, I believe it will afford adequate experiences in supervision and administration."
- One hundred percent of the candidates responded, "Yes, this program is of quality"; however, one answer varied slightly.

The second question was: "Do you believe this program will help further your career goals? Please explain."

- One hundred percent of the candidates responded, "Yes, this program will further my career goals."

The third question was: "Do you believe the program needs improvement? If yes, please explain."

- Sixty-six percent of the candidates responded, "No, does this program need improvement."
- Thirty-three percent of the candidates responded, "Yes, the program should be improved."
- Some of their additional comments were: "Give no comprehensive exam," "placements should be ready at the beginning of the semester," and "the

internship needs to be improved to allow one complete calendar year to complete."

The fourth question was: "Do you believe that you will be prepared to assume the position of principal, central office employee, or superintendent? Please explain."

- One hundred percent of the candidates responded, "Yes, they were prepared to assume the principalship."

An additional comment revealed that "The program is very in-depth and requires a lot of work." Interestingly none of the candidates assumed that they were ready for a position higher than the principalship.

The fifth question was: "Do you believe that your internship experience has prepared you to become a successful principal?"

- Seventy-eight percent of the candidates responded, "Yes, they were prepared to become successful principals."
- Twenty-two percent of the candidates responded that they had not completed the internship.
- Ten percent of the candidates responded that they were out on maternity leave.

The sixth question was: "Do you believe the internship should be level specific or should the program continue as it is?"

- Eighty-nine percent of the candidates responded, "No, the internship should stay as it is."
- Ten percent of the candidates responded that "the internship should be optional and based on the needs of the student."

An excellent summary comment came from an administrative internship candidate who had completed half of her internship hours. This student wrote that she feels that this is a rigorous training program that will allow her to be successful in any administrative position.

CONCLUSION

The novice principal needs leadership skills that are relevant to current issues in education, i.e., No Child Left Behind, IEP days, knowledge of curriculum, time management, school law, money management, and stress management. Their predecessors' primary focus was reactive day-to-day management activities. Today's proactive research-based leadership is developed not only on the job, but also during the process of their administrative experience training to become effective instructional leaders and managers (ILM). These new hires in the principalship will continue to feel isolated, confused, and overwhelmed, and the demand on their time can cause desperation without responsive reform of the training process that reflects skills, knowledge, and dispositions needed for today's principals. Without the appropriate training, novice principals cannot totally focus on teaching, learning, and leadership, nor do they have the time to develop a networking support system which is so important to their overall success. If the Non-Degree certificate is implemented effectively as described above, it may become a model for reform and eventual adoption by other states. Several states in the U.S. are experiencing principal shortages (Keller, 1998). While Alabama has not yet demonstrably reached a critical shortage of principal candidates to date, this may be due, in part, to the aforementioned Non-Degree certificate program/process. This process is one of apprenticeship (internships) mentoring, grooming, and creating a climate for success for new principals and their students and school community.

RECOMMENDATIONS

The following suggestions should be considered for improving the Non-Degree (Add-On) "A" certificate at degree-granting colleges and universities.

1. Currently, in some institutions the Graduate School admits candidates to the program. The program faculty should be involved in the admissions process.
2. Once graduate students complete coursework, they can apply for state certification. However, a formal recommendation process facilitated through program faculty should be implemented within the certification application process.
3. Currently, administrative interns complete their internship at four different site levels (elementary, middle school, high school and central office). Interns should select one site in which to gain expertise.
4. At present, administrative interns are required to complete 300 clock hours for laboratory experience; however, there is no specialization for the internship. If this process continues it will be necessary to enhance this standard. The candidate must at least complete a school improvement to enhance his/her level of expertise at the particular level.

5. Administrative preparation programs offer general knowledge and skills training for administrative interns; thereafter, professional development activities, once on the job, must be relevant to current issues in education.

6. Principal mentors should complete a formal, structured, mentor training program prior to receiving administrative interns.

7. Each principal mentor should hold state administrative certification and should have been in present position at least three consecutive years in a public school to demonstrate stability.

8. The instructional support program which facilitates this program should engage in longitudinal tracking of program completers into the principalship. Results of the questionnaire showed that interns perceive the preparatory qualities of the internship program. Performance-based tracking of these interns after entry into the principalship will further evaluate the effectiveness of the training experience for their preparation and administrative development.

REFERENCES

Alabama State Board of Education (1999, February). *Professional education personnel evaluation program of Alabama (PEPE)*. Alabama Department of Education Website.

Archer, J. (2002, April 7). Principals: So much to do so little time. *Education Week, 21*(31), 1, 20.

Bjork, G., and Ginsberg, R. (1995). Principles of reform and reforming principal training: A theoretical perspective. *Educational Administration Quarterly, 31*(1), 11–37.

Bolman, L. G., Johnson, S., Murphy, J. T., and Weiss, C. H. (1990). *Re-thinking school leadership: An agenda for research and reform*. Cambridge: National Center for Educational Leadership.

Boris-Schacter, S., and Langer, S. (2002, February 6). The plight of the modern principal. *Education Week, 21*(24), 34.

Brown, S. (2002, August). Administrative Internship Handbook.

English, F. (2002, Winter). Cutting the Gordian Knot of educational administration: The theory-practice gap. *The Review, XLIV*(1), 1.

Finn, E. C., Jr. (March 15, 2002). Strong leadership critical to improving education. *Montgomery Advertiser*, Opinion, p 14.

Fusarelli, L. D., and Smith, L. (1999). Improving urban schools via leadership: Preparing administrators for the new millennium. *Journal of School Leadership, 9*(6), 534–551.

Griffiths, D. E., Stout, R. T., and Forsyth, P. B. (Eds.) (1998). *Leaders for American schools: The report and the papers of the National Commission on Excellence in Educational Administration*. Berkley, CA: McCutchan Publishing Corporation.

Jacobson, S. L. (1996). School leadership in age of reform: New direction in principal preparation. *International Journal of Educational Reform, 5*(3), 271–277.

Keller, B. (1998). Principals' shoes are hard to fill, study finds. *Education Week, 17*(27), 3.

Klemper, R. A., and Richett, C. T. (2001, December 12). Greening the next generation of principals. *Education Week Journal, XXI*(15), 34.

Kouzes, J., and Posner, B. (1997). The leadership challenge (pp. 91–120). San Francisco: Jossey-Bass Publishing.

Lashway, L. (2003, February). Transforming principal preparation. *ERIC Digest, 165, 1–7*.

Lashway, L. (2003, August). Inducting School Leadership. ERIC *Digest, 166, 1–8*.

Murphy, J. (1990). *Preparing school administrators for the twenty-first century: The reform agenda*. Cambridge, MA: National Center for Educational Leadership.

National Policy Board for Educational Administration (1993). *Principals for our changing schools: manual*. Balmar Printing & Graphics.

Principal shortage, funding concerns drive NASSP Board to take a stand. (2002, September). *Newsleader, 50*(1), 3.

Smith, F. (1996, Fall). Leadership qualities. *Leadership Journal, XVII*(4), 30.

Stricherz, M. (2001). School leaders feel overworked. *Education Week, 21*(12), 5, 4/5.

Ubben, C. G., Hughes, W. L., and Norris, L. C. (2001). *The principal: Creative leadership for effective schools* (4th ed.). Boston: Allyn & Bacon.

The Contribution of Inquiry to Developing Collaborative Leaders

BARBARA A. STORMS AND GINNY LEE

WHETHER AND HOW PREPARATION PROGRAMS FOR SCHOOL administrators can meet the challenges of preparing effective leaders for twenty-first century schools remains an open question. Amidst increasing public scrutiny of schools, preparation programs are implementing new strategies for leadership development including innovations such as problem-based pedagogy (Barrows, 1996; Bridges, 1992), cohort formats (Barnett, Basom, Yerkes and Norris, 2000), and ethical/caring/moral program perspectives (Beck, Murphy and Associates, 1997; Shapiro and Stefkovich, 2001). As departments of educational leadership enact these and other reforms, their efforts come to represent hypotheses or theories of action (Argyris and Schön, 1974; Malen, Croninger, Muncey, and Redmond-Jones, 2002; Schön, 1983) about what kind of leader is likely to affect needed educational change and what kind of preparation is likely to produce such a leader.

This paper examines the impact of one component of a preparation program in which school leaders were coached to use inquiry as a tool for school improvement. This master's degree requirement for leading an inquiry was intended to accomplish multiple goals underlying one department's theory of action. Assuming that the most challenging problems faced by schools are complex ones that cannot be successfully addressed by applying existing knowledge, this theory emphasized the need for practitioners to engage in continuous learning organized around the specific needs of their sites. Collaborative inquiry was considered a powerful tool for supporting continuous learning and addressing complex issues. This model for leadership preparation also assumed that mastering inquiry tools was best accomplished through a constructivist model of learning, coupled with ongoing opportunities for reflection.

For school leaders to achieve the potential benefits of applying inquiry to site issues, they need to incorporate into their practice the understanding, skills, and dispositions required to mobilize, engage, guide, and sustain collaborative groups in authentic examination and analysis of issues. The idea that teachers' joint engagement around questions of practice supports teaching and learning is viewed as a condition for individual and organizational development (Bray, Lee, Smith and Yorks, 2000; Lambert, 2002). While studies of collaboration have cautioned against the idea of contrived collegiality (Hargreaves, 1994; Sagor, 1995), studies of school reform support authentic professional collaboration as a necessary condition for meaningful change (Darling-Hammond, 1993; Little, 1982; Morris, Chrispeels and Burke, 2003).

Initiating and guiding collaborative work without falling prey to contrived collegiality requires that leaders attend to both the substantive and process-related elements of joint work. The study reported in this paper examines situations in which early career school administrators used site-based inquiry as a tool for school improvement. Specifically, the authors wished to examine leaders' constructed understandings of professional collaboration as they emerged in the inquiry process and how these understandings, in turn, influenced early career administrators' ideas about the role of leaders and effective leadership practices for guiding school improvement.

CONCEPTUAL FRAMEWORK

The concepts of inquiry, action research, and practitioner research are seen as important strategies for school improvement (Anderson, Herr and Nihlen, 1994; Burnaford, Fisher and Hobson, 1996; Calhoun, 1994; Langer and Colton, 1994). While individual teachers may use inquiry to improve instruction, moving to a process by which a larger portion of a school community (e.g., grade level or entire faculty) identifies and explores issues together is viewed as a powerful school reform strategy (Calhoun, 1994;

Sagor, 1997; Szabo, 1996). The literature on collaborative inquiry identifies a common set of activities for the inquiry process: identification of a focal question; gathering of data; analysis of information; and action decisions based on the analysis (Calhoun, 1994; Gay and Airasian, 2003; Sagor, 1992, Stringer, 1996).

Calhoun's work emphasizes the cyclical and recursive nature of the inquiry process (Calhoun, 1994). Thus initial gathering and examination of data may result in an inquiry group realizing that its original questions require reframing, or data analysis may suggest needing to "go back" and gather more information. Uncertainty and ambiguity are inherent in the process as participants attempt to "make sense of" experience and information. Such ambiguity demands leaders who support participants in grappling with and addressing differences in perception, perspective, and understanding (Garmston and Wellman, 1999; Sergiovanni, 1992; Weick, 1995). Without support for shared meaning-making, inquiry can become a *pro forma* exercise resulting in superficial "agreements" that have little impact on practice.

Much recent literature about school improvement efforts focus on the importance of educational leaders facilitating shared understandings. In *The Constructivist Leader*, Lambert and her colleagues stress processes such as surfacing assumptions, questioning for understanding and regular professional dialogue as essential for engaging colleagues in authentic efforts to create common understandings (Lambert, 2003; Lambert, L. L., Walker, Zimmerman, Cooper, Lambert, M. D., et al., 2002, 1995). Other authors talk about constructivist leadership as important in community building which is, in turn, important for individual and organizational development and improvement (Barth, 1992, 2001; Sergiovanni, 1992, 1996). School change processes are complex yet rely on a shared sense of purpose, goal, or direction (Bray, Lee, Smith and Yorks, 2000; Sergiovanni, 1992) and an understanding of the complexity of change process itself (Schön, 1983; Fullan, 1991; Sergiovanni, 1996; Lee, 1991). To lead effective school improvement efforts, leaders facilitate dialogue that helps school communities understand the meaning of change and the process by which it takes place (Fullan, 1991).

Sergiovanni (1992) articulates that how one carries out work is based on the mental models that one holds about "how the world works." According to Schön (1983) and Argyris and Schön (1974), reflective practice is important to a leader's development as it allows a leader to examine and test his/her theories of action.

Developing a consciousness of the ways in which they make meaning, including the values, beliefs, and preferences that inform this process are also fundamental dispositions of effective leaders (Sergiovanni, 1992, 1996; Barth, 1992, 2001). Thus, successful educational leaders facilitate shared meaning making within their school communities, but also engage in reflective practice for their own professional growth.

In this study, school leaders facilitated site-based inquiry to examine policy and practice. These inquiries required site leaders to engage groups of colleagues in identifying a significant issue at the site and carrying out one or more cycles of inquiry during a single school year that would result in action or recommendations for next steps. Because leadership in collaborative inquiry was a new endeavor for these early career leaders, guiding and implementing the inquiry process were opportunities for learning not simply about the substantive topic of the inquiry but also the process of facilitating the collaborative inquiry process.

While both research and applied literature tend to regard professional collaboration as a powerful lever for improvement (Sergiovanni, 1996; Barth, 1992; Fullan, 1991), researchers have identified differences between cordiality, collegiality, and authentic collaboration around the real work of schools (Little, 1982; Hargreaves, 1994). Hargreaves (1994) points out that, under the guise of facilitating collaboration, school leaders may conceive of and create teacher groups that are charged with undertaking cooperative tasks not of their own choosing or priority. Under these conditions, their effort is "administratively regulated, compulsory, implementation-oriented, and predictable" (Hargreaves, 1994, pp. 195–196), resulting in work that is ultimately contrived and a distraction from engaging in more authentic activities. In contrast, Hargreaves points to collaborative cultures in which teachers' joint work is "voluntary, development-oriented, and unpredictable" (Hargreaves, 1994, pp. 192–193). For study participants, the inquiry experience provided numerous occasions to implement, guide, facilitate, experience, and reflect on the nature of collaborative work and to construct meaning about the concept of professional collaboration.

METHODOLOGY

Setting of the Study

For the Department of Educational Leadership at California State University, Hayward, "leadership is

Table 1. Participants by Role and Year in the Study (n = 47)

	Total	01–02	02–03	03–04
Principals	9	6	2	1
Assistant Principals	32	15	8	9
Other Site Administrators	4	1	2	1
District Administrators	2	1	1	0
Totals	47	23	13	11

about learning together, and constructing meaning and knowledge collectively and collaboratively" (Lambert, 1998, p. 5). In the 1990's this department replaced the traditional master's degree thesis with a yearlong research cohort organized around the enactment of collaborative inquiry to bring about school improvement. The outcome of the students' inquiry is a product for other educators about the findings from the site-based research. (See Lee and Storms, 1999, for prior research on this program.)

This current study encompasses data from cohorts in three different academic years, from 2001 to 2004. The research cohort for the 2001–2002 academic year served as a "living laboratory" to examine the experiences of practicing administrators in conceptualizing, organizing, and implementing collaborative inquiry and to establish research methods that were used throughout study (Lee, Storms, Camp and Bronzini, 2002).

Sample

PARTICIPANTS. Over the three years of this study, 107 candidates enrolled as master's degree candidates in educational leadership. The final three-course requirement for the degree placed them in a research cohort where each candidate would carry out a collaborative inquiry at his/her site. Of those 107 candidates, 57 (53 percent) were school administrators. A subset of 47 school leaders was the focus of this research (see Table 1). This subset was selected on two criteria: 1) each held an administrative position, and 2) each was enrolled in either an on-line research seminar or practicum, both of which served as major sources of data for the study.

The research cohort is the culminating master's degree experience for candidates in educational leadership. When candidates were admitted to the administrative credential program (the initial sequence of courses before candidates enter the research cohort) nearly all of them were classroom teachers. However, as noted in Table 1, by the time educators enter the research cohort (typically one year later), many had taken on their first administrative role. Study participants were largely school site administrators at all levels of the K–12 system who represented diverse ethnicities and both genders (see Table 2).

Research Methods

This research study largely employed qualitative research methods (Bogdan and Biklen, 1998; Patton, 2002) in the collection and analysis of data. Given that the purpose of the study was to examine the administrators' perceptions regarding the inquiry process, collaboration, and their work as leaders, the choice of qualitative methodology was necessary and appropriate. The initial research team in 2001–2002 was comprised of the two authors and two graduate assistants, both of whom were practicing school administrators and graduates of the program. This team conceptualized the research and collected and analyzed data from administrators in the 2001–2002 research cohort (Lee, Storms, Camp and Bronzini, 2002). Data collection and analysis procedures developed in the first year of the study were used for all three years of the study.

Table 2. Description of Study School Administrators (n = 47)

Role	Level				Ethnicity				Gender	
	High School 9–12	Middle School 6–8	Elem. K–5	Other (preK–12, 6–12, adult)	White	African-American	Latino	Asian	Male	Female
Principal	1	0	6	2	7	1	1	0	3	6
Assistant Principal	13	11	7	1	18	8	3	3	19	13
Other Site Admin.	0	0	2	2	1	1	2	0	1	3
District Admin.	0	0	0	2	2	0	0	0	0	2
Totals	14	11	15	7	28	10	6	3	23	24

DATA SOURCES. Multiple forms of data were collected including responses in on-line threaded discussions and written assignments submitted over the course of the year and, during 2001–2002, observations of research cohort class discussions (Lee, Storms, Camp and Bronzini, 2002). Across data sources, the administrators described and reflected on the processes of initiating and leading collaborative inquiry efforts from their positions as leaders.

DATA ANALYSIS. The responses in the on-line discussions were stored in a database, organized according to responses by question, and responses of each individual administrator across all of the questions. Responses were then evaluated for common themes using coding systems developed in the initial year of the study. In 2001–2002, classroom observations provided information that helped refine the coding systems for this study. The written assignments (site context portrait, inquiry summaries and reflections on leadership) were important data sources about the way in which administrators viewed their roles and collaborations.

FINDINGS

Inquiry Topics

In the process of selecting inquiry topics, the administrators enrolled in the research cohort were asked to collaborate with others at their site to identify "significant" topics related to equitable learning outcomes for all students. Inquiry topics addressed several major categories of school improvement including student achievement, curriculum, instruction, school climate and school design. Student achievement topics looked primarily at the academic success of students (e.g., reducing the achievement gap for English Language Learners). Topics in the curriculum category generally looked at the implementation or effectiveness of a particular curricular program (e.g., reading series implementation) while topics about instruction looked at how teachers were delivering content or using particular strategies (e.g., use of differentiated instruction). School climate topics looked at school policies such as discipline policies as well as efforts to engage a variety of stakeholders (e.g., parents), whereas topics in school design looked at organizational structures such as class schedules.

In this study, principals were largely engaged in inquiries related to student achievement and instruction while assistant principals inquired across topic categories, though most heavily in the area of school climate. Other administrators focused mostly on in-struction, climate and curriculum (See Storms, 2004, for a more extended study on inquiry topics.)

Collaboration

The requirement that participants in the research cohort engage in collaborative inquiry meant that the administrators needed to identify an issue that was, at the minimum, of interest to a group at the site. An underlying assumption of this study was that the more authentic collaboration is, as Hargreaves (1994) presented, the more likely that collaboration will yield useful outcomes for the school. In analyzing data, one of the variables the authors looked at was the level of authenticity in the collaboration. Three levels of authenticity emerged from the data based on the type of collaborative group (on-going, interest-based, created for this inquiry), and the administrator's access to/role in the collaborative group (an active member, organizer, controller). The three categories of collaboration that emerged included:

> *Most Authentic*—the administrator was welcomed into and became an active member of an on-going group that was already working on a significant topic at the school.
> *Somewhat Authentic*—the administrator brought together an interest-based group that had not previously organized themselves to work together on the topic. The administrator served as the organizer, usually calling the meetings.
> *Inauthentic*—the administrator identified others who should be interested in a topic, then controlled most of the group activities including meetings, data collection and analysis.

In the "most authentic" collaborations, administrators worked with others who were, prior to this inquiry, engaged in a naturally occurring, interest or responsibility-based group. These types of collaborations included such groups as teachers designing or implementing a new program or curriculum, or established committees. For example, in one inquiry, a group had been working with parents and community members to explore if and how a charter school might better meet the needs of students who were not succeeding in the regular program. Over the course of the academic year, the administrator who had previously only been involved peripherally in the discussions, joined the group and was immersed in data collection and analysis and school design discussions that led to an application for a new small school.

In "somewhat authentic" collaborations, administrators developed interest-based groups to work with them. These collaborations were initiated, generally, by soliciting volunteers who were interested in a particular topic. In most of these collaborations, the interest in the topic had existed at the site for some time, but had not been acted upon in any organized way. For example, English teachers at a particular grade level who were trying to implement district-mandated differentiated instruction were brought together by a school administrator in on-going discussions to develop lessons, try them out, and review student work. The administrator organized many of the group meetings and supported the group with release time. At the end of the year, the group presented the lessons and student work to other faculty at the school.

In "inauthentic" collaborations the administrator identified colleagues based on a nominal or perceived link to a topic. In these efforts, the topic was principally of interest to the administrator. The leader most often controlled the group interactions including data collection and analysis. For example, teachers at a high school who were generally recognized as strong teachers were interviewed and asked to document how they taught reading. The effort resulted in a report that could be shared with other teachers if the occasion arose. Inauthentic collaborations were contrived for the purpose of the administrator meeting the requirements of the degree. Table 3 provides information about the level of authenticity for the collaborations in this study.

DISCUSSION

The Influence of Role

Many factors influenced the ways in which the collaborative inquiries evolved including the leaders' range of experience, interests and expectations. Because the inquiry was part of a degree program, it likely influenced the perceptions that participants brought to their role as leader and participant in the inquiry process. Many began with the idea that a collaborative inquiry meant that they needed to lead a group of followers. Some learned, however, that this approach would not necessarily lead to authentic or meaningful engagement on the part of others.

The role of the administrator influenced the collaboration. Principals were able to more easily join ongoing groups or convene interest-based groups than were assistant principals. Most often assistant principals had to identify staff members who had a nominal link to the topic and convince them to participate. Other site and district level administrators were able to engage in more or less authentic collaborations by using their role (e.g., coordinate a particular program) as leverage to enter or develop a collaborative team (Brynjulson and Storms, 2005).

How administrators viewed their leadership responsibilities influenced the choice of topics. Principals tended to see all issues at their schools as topics that deserved their attention. For principals, the deciding factor about a topic had to do with gauging priorities for reform with the readiness of the school community. However, assistant principals often viewed their responsibilities as specific. "I do discipline" was a chorus often heard from assistant principals. This view of the role may have greatly limited assistant principals' perceived sphere of influence and narrowed both the topics they felt they could address and the pool of possible collaborators.

Emerging Themes

As the school administrators worked with colleagues, their thinking about collaboration, leadership, and inquiry itself shifted and expanded. As they experienced the process of working within a group, they were confronted on a regular basis with having to negotiate meaning. Five themes emerged in their observations and reflections about their experiences:

- Recognizing the Need for and Developing Specific Leadership Skills
- Modeling Appropriate Dispositions
- Laying Aside Preconceived Notions
- Supporting Authentic Engagement in Collaboration
- Constructing New Understandings of Leadership

Table 3. Type of Collaboration Group and Collaborators by Administrator Roles Across Years (n = 47)

	Total	More Authentic	Less Authentic	Inauthentic
Principal	9	7	1	1
Assistant Principal	32	13	4	15
Other Site Administrator	4	2	2	0
District Administrator	2	1	1	0
Totals	47	23	8	16

Each of these is described in turn in the remainder of this section.

RECOGNIZING THE NEED FOR AND DEVELOPING SPECIFIC LEADERSHIP SKILLS. All of the school leaders in the study reported broadening and refining their sense of the kinds of skills required of a leader in a collaborative inquiry endeavor. As they recognized that their role was not to direct the inquiry but to engage as part of a collaborative group, they realized that this required them to develop facilitation skills, with a special attention to careful listening. Comments such as the following were typical:

- *Listening has been one of the ways I've been able to establish trust within the inquiry group—to erase the line that divides the administrator and the teacher.* Middle School Assistant Principal
- *Understanding is attained through attentive listening. The inquiry process has truly emphasized to me the value of listening to others. Listening leads to improved communication, stronger collaborative relationships, mutual understanding, and the establishment of trust. When there is trust in a relationship, powerful and positive things can happen. I think that relationships with my colleagues have improved because I am learning to become a better listener.* Middle School Assistant Principal
- *I have improved in truly being open to what is being said, recognizing who is saying it, and prompting them to elaborate. Even more important in the listening process is to analyze who is not speaking.* District Office Administrator

As demonstrated by these statements, leaders viewed listening skills as serving both a functional and symbolic capacity. Careful listening signaled the importance of hearing all voices, of considering all comments, and of treating each person as a worthwhile contributor. Listening contributed to group trust and shared understanding.

MODELING APPROPRIATE DISPOSITIONS. Leaders realized that the quality of relationships within the collaborative groups depended on individuals feeling valued and respected by all. They spoke of the importance of demonstrating empathy, respect, and integrity in their interactions with individuals and with the group. These dispositions were important not only for the inquiry, but also for their broader leadership effectiveness at the site.

- *I believe that teachers need to feel understood and appreciated. They must sense that the school leader sympathizes and empathizes with their struggles, issues,*

and concerns. I don't think you can lead something you don't understand. Middle School Assistant Principal
- *Collaborating with others, truly listening, and respecting diverse opinions are also very important skills I am working to develop as a leader.* District Office Administrator
- *One of my learned lessons this year is that I can't be the one who delivers all information. I have to give my staff/collaborators the time to develop the questions and thinking . . . I am really sitting in the passenger seat as the navigator not the driver. The group has to have ownership and feel connected to the inquiry. Shared leadership allows the teachers to truly feel like they . . . can be trusted to make decisions in the best interest of the school.* Elementary Assistant Principal

Leaders saw these dispositions as necessary conditions for members of the collaborative group to participate openly and honestly. As one high school assistant principal put it, "When dealing with a topic that is sensitive and requires individuals to evaluate themselves, the tact used can make or break the collaboration." Another leader spoke of the importance of validating the thoughts of the less forthcoming members of the group:

For the silent ones in the crowd, I try to engage with them individually. . . . My hope is they will feel safe to speak up. If they have a divergent opinion, I feel it is my role to "protect" their right to voice their position, at the very least. Elementary Principal

Leaders supported inquiry groups in developing and demonstrating the kinds of dispositions that would support open and equitable participation. For one elementary principal, this took the form of agreed-upon group norms: "Some of the norms that we truly value are honoring perspectives, validating ideas, and asking questions of each other."

LAYING ASIDE PRECONCEIVED NOTIONS. In working collaboratively, leaders regularly found themselves in situations in which prior experience with a person or issue had shaped a set of expectations that were not useful in the current inquiry endeavor. They realized that they needed to set aside or step outside these ideas or expectations for the inquiry and the collaboration to be open and a potentially productive process.

- *What I am learning about myself as a leader is that I can't let my previous experiences, observations, or expectations about someone influence what I see.* Middle School Assistant Principal

- *The collaborative process affords us the opportunity to learn more about each other and break down barriers and preconceived notions.* Middle School Assistant Principal

In some instances, the preconceived notions that needed to be set aside were related to the very concept of leadership. Most of the study participants voiced the importance of shared leadership and engaging as an equal participant. One elementary principal observed what happened when this didn't occur in his group: "Because I don't sit at the table as a peer, there is often a culture of submission and acquiescence that bothers me." Another spoke of giving others the "opportunity to guide the way." Letting go of preconceived ideas helped leaders support the engagement and authenticity of the collaborative group.

SUPPORTING AUTHENTIC ENGAGEMENT IN COLLABORATION. For some of the leaders, an outcome of inquiry was an understanding of the potential power of authentic collaboration. As an elementary school principal described it, "I have key players in the school who can effect change, utilize research, are open to communication, and are team players." She observed that when the work and participation are authentic, staff "find the time to plan and take action." Another elementary principal commented that authentic collaboration occurred when a group shared "the same vision." She noted that authentic collaboration could lead "to systemic change and not just slapping a band-aid on a recurring problem." A principal at an elementary school invoked the notion of democracy in collaboration, emphasizing her belief in teachers' "inherent right to actively participate in decisions [that] affect [them]."

Many leaders talked about overcoming their own need to control outcomes as a way to ensure authentic collaboration. One elementary assistant principal commented, "one of most difficult things to do is to let go of the work and let others do the work." A high school assistant principal echoed what many of the administrators struggled with when he stated, "When I need something done, I used to trust only me." Through the process of engaging in inquiry, many of the school leaders confronted their need to control and worked to involve others more fully.

- *I usually like to do things myself, because I know what kind of outcome I would like to see. However, I have found that when I give others the opportunity to take charge of something, they not only develop self-confidence and leadership skills but they usually come*

up with the same idea(s) I came up with or something better. Other Site Administrator
- *You just keep thinking "it's easier to do it myself" which is a terrible thing to do. Collaboration helps me realize that some people are as eager as I am to get the job done—and are willing to help out. A project feels like an insurmountable task when you look at it alone—but when you start talking to people . . . you realize what a yahoo you were to think you had to do it all yourself.* High School Assistant Principal
- *Being a leader doesn't mean controlling people or assuming you know what they need. People need to ask their own questions and construct their own knowledge.* Elementary Principal

Several of the leaders saw authentic collaboration is necessarily unpredictable. An assistant principal at an elementary school said that she realized " . . . solutions and answers may not be the ultimate goal." The curriculum coordinator for an elementary school spoke of developing a culture "in which true introspection, constructive critique, and lifelong professional learning continue happening." Yet another leader associated professional community with "a journey of discovery."

CONSTRUCTING NEW UNDERSTANDINGS OF LEADERSHIP. A common theme in the comments of leaders engaged in inquiry was an increased appreciation for the power of collaboration and of collaborative cultures. Many of them saw such cultures as contributing to more affirming and congenial workplace environments for teachers and leaders. They also considered the potential power of actively engaging the professional community in cycles of inquiry and recognized "shared leadership" that equalizing of power among the members of the professional community, a flattening of hierarchical relationships between administration and faculty. As one assistant principal at an elementary site observed, "Leadership does not mean that one is an expert or should [act like] the expert." They emphasized concepts of capacity building and of working to undo "dysfunctional" feature of schools, such as "factions [and] favoritism." For some, this appreciation of more collaborative, facilitative, and constructivist concepts of leadership represented a significant shift from the ideas they had held as they began the process of collaborative inquiry:

- *It seems that now I have internalized a very different vision of what school leadership means to me. Whereas before in my experience as a teacher I would have perceived the job of a school administrator as one that manages, sets and enforces policies for both students and teachers, I now see my role as that of the facilitator that is able to define a clear vision of a learning community, build capacity among teachers to collaborate and help develop a voice that matters among all participants in this endeavor.* Elementary Curriculum Coordinator

- *I'm learning to be an observer of systems to see how sometimes the system is the cause of the lack of progress on an issue.* Principal, 6–12 School

Taken together, this set of themes represent evolving conceptions of inquiry, collaboration, leadership, and approaches to school reform. For many of the administrators enrolled in this master's program, these evolving conceptions moved them away from comfortable and predictable practices and patterns of interaction. As leaders began to trust the power of the collaborative groups to grapple with complex issues, many came to recognize, appreciate, and develop new skills and capacities to facilitate and support their colleagues.[1]

STRENGTHENING CONCEPTIONS OF LEADERSHIP

The experience of leading site-based collaborative inquiry not only deepened early career administrators' knowledge concerning particular issues, but also provided a hands-on opportunity to extend their understanding of leadership and collaboration. For many, this applied work experience was one of finally "getting" the meaning of concepts such as collaboration, facilitative leadership, and group process. As individuals engaged in inquiry they were implementing and testing aspects of their own theories of leadership. Across the set of individual experiences, the authors consider the following four "common insights" to be important for the development of school leaders:

1. *Appreciation of authentic engagement.* Leaders came to recognize the power of collaborative groups in which all of the members were genuinely invested with an issue. They saw that ownership and caring about an issue generated meaningful engagement on the part of teachers. They recognized that teachers were very willing to "take on" issues that were genuinely important to them and that such authentic engagement was pivotal to open and honest work around difficult or challenging questions.

2. *Shift from product to process.* Many leaders came to recognize that the success of the inquiry effort required significant attention to the process itself. Leaders' experiences in collaboration focused attention on matters of communication, democratic process, conditions of trust, valuing ideas, encouraging honesty, withholding judgment, and other similar elements of effective group work.

3. *Collaborative inquiry as an example of professional community.* Leaders came to recognize that the inquiry process they were facilitating could be considered a prototype for the kind of professional community needed for school reform and improvement to take hold. They realized that asking questions, using data, and working together to identify and make choices were all part of the meaning-making process.

4. *New conceptions of leadership.* The experience of working collaboratively with colleagues served as an opportunity for individuals to test and refine their personal theories of leadership. With varied levels of conscious awareness, the leaders engaged as much in inquiring about their own leadership as the topic that was the focus of the collaborative work. Leaders reflected on working with individuals and groups and arrived at conclusions about what was required of them for the collaborative inquiry to be successful. Out of this came new conceptions of leadership that focused on more facilitative approaches that would support shared dialogue and meaning-making.

As the participants themselves came to recognize, this set of ideas is relevant not only for collaborative inquiry, but also for the work of professional communities and of leaders in those communities. While the authors recognized the power of this experience to support such insights, we are also aware of its fragility.

Changes in pedagogy and coaching of the master's degree students were intended to make this department of educational leadership's theory of action more explicit. A primary intent, of course, was to strengthen the learning process and support candidates in achieving proficiency in guiding reform efforts and in using inquiry skills in a meaningful way at their sites. Most administrators in this study reported significant shifts in their thinking about collaboration and leadership. Such fundamental changes in perspective, we believe, are essential for leadership development.

NOTES

An earlier version of this paper (Lee, Storms, Camp, and Bronzini, 2002) was presented at the Annual Meeting of the American Educational Research Association in New Orleans. The authors would like to thank Penny Bronzini and Marianne Camp for their assistance with this research, including their contributions to the AERA paper. The authors want to thank Gloria Rodriguez, Ph.D. (UC Davis) for her help in collecting data for this study.

1. Not all participants exhibited such growth, of course. Preliminary data analysis suggests that leaders with inauthentic collegial groups tended to address topics less related to teaching and learning.

REFERENCES

Anderson, G., Herr, K., and Nihlen, A. (1994). *Studying your own school: An educator's guide to qualitative practitioner research.* Thousand Oaks, CA: Corwin.

Argyris, C., and Schön, D. A. (1974). *Theory in practice: Increasing professional effectiveness.* San Francisco: Jossey-Bass.

Barnett, B. G., Basom, M. R., Yerkes, D. M., and Norris, C. J. (2000). Cohorts in educational leadership programs: Benefits, difficulties, and the potential for developing school leaders. *Educational Administration Quarterly, 36*(2), 255–282.

Barrows, H. S. (1996). Problem-based learning in medicine and beyond: A brief overview. *New Directions for Teaching and Learning, 68,* 3–12.

Barth, R. S. (2001). *Learning by heart.* San Francisco: Jossey-Bass.

Barth, R. S. (1992). *Improving schools from within.* San Francisco: Jossey-Bass.

Beck, L. G., Murphy, J., and Associates (Eds.) (1997). *Ethics in educational administration: emerging models.* Colombia, MO: University Council of Educational Administration.

Bogdan, R. C., and Biklen, S. K. (1998). *Qualitative research for education: An introduction to theory and methods* (2nd ed.). Boston: Allyn and Bacon.

Bray, J. N., Lee, J., Smith, L. L., and Yorks, L. (2000). *Collaborative inquiry in practice.* Thousand Oaks, CA: Sage.

Bridges, E. M. (1992). *Problem-based learning for administrators.* Eugene, OR: ERIC Clearinghouse on Educational Management, University of Oregon.

Brynjulson, M., and Storms, B. A. (2005). Working together: One district's inquiry. *Leadership, 34* (3), 16–19.

Burnaford, G., Fischer, J., and Hobson, D. (Eds) (1996). *Teachers doing research: Practical possibilities.* Mahwah, NJ: Earlbaum.

Calhoun, E. (1994). *How to use action research in the self-renewing school.* Alexandria, VA: Association for Supervision and Curriculum Development.

Darling-Hammond, L. (1993). Reframing the school reform agenda: Developing capacity for school transformation. *Phi Delta Kappan, 74*(10), 752–761.

Fullan, M. G. (1991). *The new meaning of educational change* (2nd ed.). New York: Teachers College Press.

Garmston, R. J., and Wellman, B. M. (1999). *The adaptive school: A sourcebook for developing collaborative groups.* Norwood, MA: Christopher-Gordon Publishers.

Gay, L. R., and Airasian, P. (2003). *Educational research. Competencies for analysis and application* (7th ed.). Upper Saddle River, NJ: Pearson.

Hargreaves, A. (1994). *Changing teachers, changing times: Teachers' work and culture in the postmodern age.* New York: Teachers College Press.

Lambert, L. (2003). *Leadership capacity for lasting school improvement.* Alexandria, VA: Association for Supervision and Curriculum Development.

Lambert L. (2002). A framework for shared leadership. *Educational Leadership, 59*(8), 37–42.

Lambert, L. (1998). *Building leadership capacity in schools.* Alexandria, VA: Association for Supervision and Curriculum Development.

Lambert, L. L., Walker, D., Zimmerman, D. P., Cooper, J. E., Lambert, M. D., Gardner, M. D., and Ford Slack, P. J. (1995). *The constructivist leader.* New York: Teachers College Press.

Lambert, L. L., Walker, D., Zimmerman, D. P., Cooper, J. E., Lambert, M. D., Gardner, M. D., and Szabo, M. (2002). *The constructivist leader* (2nd ed.). New York: Teachers College Press.

Langer, G. M., and Colton, A. B. (1994). Reflective decision making: The cornerstone of school reform. *Journal of Staff Development, 15*(1), 2–7.

Lee, G. V. (1991). Instructional leadership as collaborative sense-making. *Theory Into Practice, 30*(2), 83–90.

Lee, G., and Storms, B. A. (1999). Evolving conceptions of school leadership: Preparing administrators for cultures of inquiry. *Educational Leadership and Administration: Teaching and Program Development, 11,* 71–82.

Lee, G., Storms, B. A., Camp, M., and Bronzini, P. (2002). *When school leaders use inquiry as a reform tool: Developing leadership for collaboration.* Paper presented at the Annual Meeting of the American Educational Research Association, New Orleans, LA.

Little, J. W. (1982). Norms of collegiality and experimentation: Workplace conditions of school success. *American Educational Research Journal, 19*(3), 325–340.

Malen, B., Croninger, R., Muncey, D., and Redmond-Jones, D. (2002). Reconstituting schools: "Testing" the "theory of action." *Educational Evaluation and Policy Analysis, 24*(2), 113–132.

Morris, M., Chrispeels, J., and Burke, P. (2003). The power of two: Linking external and internal teachers' professional development. *Phi Delta Kappan, 84*(10), 764–767.

Patton, M. C. (2002). *Qualitative evaluation and research methods* (3rd ed.). Thousand Oaks, CA: Sage.

Sagor, R. (1997). *Collaborative action research for educational change.* In Hargreaves, A. (Ed.). Rethinking educational change with heart and mind, 1997 ASCD Yearbook. Alexandria, VA: Association for Supervision and Curriculum Development.

Sagor, R. (1995). Overcoming the one-solution syndrome. *Educational Leadership, 52*(7), 24–27.

Sagor, R. (1992). *How to conduct collaborative action research.* Alexandria, VA: Association for Supervision and Curriculum Development.

Schön, D. A. (1983). *The reflective practitioner.* New York: Basic Books.

Sergiovanni, T. J. (1996). *Leadership for the schoolhouse: How is it different? Why is it important?* San Francisco: Jossey-Bass.

Sergiovanni, T. J. (1992). *Moral leadership: Getting to the heart of school improvement.* San Francisco: Jossey-Bass.

Shapiro, J. P., and Stefkovich, J. A. (2001). *Ethical leadership and decision making in education: Applying theoretical perspectives to complex dilemmas.* Mahwah, NJ: Lawrence Erlbaum Associates.

Storms. B. A. (2004). The Impact of High Stakes Accountability on the Attentions of School Leaders. Manuscript submitted for publication.

Stringer, E. T. (1996). *Action research: A handbook for practitioners.* Thousand Oaks, CA: Sage.

Szabo, M. (1996). *Rethinking restructuring: Building habits of effective inquiry.* In McLaughlin, M. W., and Oberman, I. (Eds), *Teacher learning: New policies, new practices.* New York: Teachers College Press.

Weick, K. E. (1995). *Sensemaking in organizations.* Thousand Oaks, CA: Sage.

Principal Preparation Programs: Problems, Prospects, and Promising Practices

TERRENCE QUINN

IT IS A WELL-ESTABLISHED PRINCIPLE OF SCHOOL LEADERSHIP that administrators occupy crucial roles in promoting successful schools. Much of the success of school leaders depends on the quality of training they receive through professional preparation programs administered by universities. Adequate professional development for school administrators is a challenge to the present system of preparation that, if addressed intelligently and with foresight, can change the future of our schools. For the past forty years numerous studies of the history of principal professional preparation programs have revealed continuing irrelevance and poor quality. Numerous impediments and conflicting priorities that are outlined in this article have combined to dilute effective preparation for school leaders. In recent years, however, there have appeared glimmers of progress towards the development of more reality-based programs adequate to the task of effective principal preparation. This article traces the history of these problems and identifies promising initiatives that may significantly alter the study of school leadership.

The demands placed on schools of today are greater than ever before. No Child Left Behind legislation, new accountability measures, teacher quality, the introduction of parent choice through charter schools and vouchers, the application of quickly-changing technology to school management practices, high stakes testing, a perplexing achievement gap, funding issues, curriculum standardization, and new approaches to school governance all combine to pose powerful challenges to school leaders.

To what extent are educational administrators prepared to address these thorny issues? While the research is clear that successful schools are the product of successful leadership (Hallinger and Heck, 1996; Leithwood and Riehl, 2003; National Association of Secondary School Principals, 2004; Ruebling, Stow, Kayona, and Clarke, 2004; Waters and Grubb, 2004;

Waters, Marzano, and McNulty, 2003), it is less clear that leadership development programs administered by institutions of higher education are satisfactorily preparing principals to become more successful in leading schools of today into the world of tomorrow (Hess, 2003; McCarthy, 2001; Shakeshaft, 1999).

The literature on leadership is often a paean to the indispensable role that principals play in school improvement yet the training for school leaders is problematic for colleges and universities. The quality of leadership training for school administrators is the 800-pound gorilla in the living room that everyone sees but few are willing to address. President Bush's first Secretary of Education Rod Paige has suggested that leadership development is the "stealth issue" in the battle for school reform. The stakes are high in this battle because the federal government and state governments have placed increased responsibilities on the schools as never before. Competent leadership on the ground is an essential strategy to winning that battle.

Numerous indictments, however, have been directed against leadership development programs that threaten to scuttle the battle for reform of our nation's schools. The indictments are not a recent occurrence. As early as 1960, the American Association of School Administrators (1960), regarded as a pre-eminent professional organization for school superintendents and principals, described leadership preparation as dismal. Even prior to that attack, other critics argued that such programs relied too much on "naïve empiricism" (Halpin, 1957, p. 156).

Since those early days, the criticism has continued unabated. The National Commission on Excellence in Educational Administration (1987, pp. xvi, xvii) identified numerous deficiencies in leadership preparation programs. The commission's report, titled Leaders for America's Schools, laid many of the shortcomings of principal preparation programs at the doorstep of the nation's colleges and universities. The following are among the shortcomings of leadership development programs:

- Lack of a definition of good educational leadership
- Lack of leader recruitment programs in the schools
- Lack of collaboration between school districts and universities
- Lack of quality candidates for preparation programs
- Lack of program relevance to the job demands of school administrators
- Lack of sequence, modern content, and proper field-based experiences.

Since the commission's early attack on preparation programs, criticism has not subsided. Joseph Murphy (1992), a veteran scholar and analyst of preparation programs, issued his own list of deficiencies of such programs:

- Uninspiring instructional methods
- Fragmented curriculum
- Lack of connection to real world practice
- Minimal academic rigor
- Part-time student body that is tired, distracted, and pressed for time
- An ill-defined knowledge base with few standards.

Several years later, Murphy (1999a) lamented that "educationally uninformed administrators provide a poor foundation for school success" (p. 5).

Gerald Tirozzi (2001), executive director of the National Association of Secondary School Principals, observed, "The training candidates receive from administrator preparation programs is often inadequate, and ongoing professional development is episodic at best" (p. 437). Lashway and Anderson (1997) issued their own caustic comment: "If administrator training programs were movies, the reviews would be unanimous: two thumbs down" (p. 77). Martha McCarthy (2001), Chancellor professor of education at the University of Indiana, stated, "The bad news is that we do not have data linking reforms in administrator preparation to our asserted purpose of producing capable leaders. . . . Virtually no studies track changes in leadership preparation to success as a school leader, much less to student performance in the schools they lead" (p. 1). In their survey of leadership preparation programs, Grogan and Andrews (2002) concluded that many essential skills and much important knowledge cannot be delivered by a traditional, university-based program.

Even professors of educational administration whose task it is to prepare graduates to assume positions of leadership question whether they can effectively handle their new assignments (Hallinger, 2003). It is equally unclear that leadership students receive appropriate instruction in the burgeoning demand for knowledge of instructional practices. For example, a national survey of 1400 middle school principals commissioned by the National Association of Secondary School Principals reported that more than one-third had not taken any coursework or study in middle school educational practices, and that over 70 percent had taken two courses or less (Petzko, Clark, Valentine, Hackmann, Nori, and Lucas, 2002). Graduates of leadership preparation programs are equally dismayed at the quality of their training. For example, a survey (Farkas, Johnson and Duffet, 2003) found that 67 percent of principals believe that educational leadership programs are out of touch with what it takes to run a school district. In this same study only 4 percent praise their graduate studies, and a majority of respondents reported that they derived the best training from professional mentors and guidance from colleagues.

The national media has also weighed in on the subject of leadership development programs. As Guthrie and Sanders (2001, p. A 46) have written,

> University preparation of educational administrators has fallen into a downward spiral dominated by low-prestige institutions, diploma mills, outmoded instruction and low expectations. Many of these sub-par programs have virtually no entrance requirements, save an applicant's ability to pay tuition.

How did leadership development programs come into such disrepute? What obstacles to change exist? What are the prospects for improvement? What are some promising practices that universities are adopting? This paper addresses these issues.

Any overhaul of preparation programs faces several significant challenges that have the potential to dilute the effectiveness of educational leadership programs. These include (a) little support from university administrations; (b) curriculum controversies; (c) the self-selection nature of the applicant pool for such programs; (d) the narrow focus of program content; and (e) a chasm between the theory and the reality of school administration.

LITTLE UNIVERSITY SUPPORT

University officials are generally unaware of the particular needs of leadership development programs.

Over the years this lack of familiarity and lack of knowledge has produced a low level of university support (Young and Petersen, 2002). Vartan Gregorian (2004, p. 36), President of the Carnegie Corporation of New York and a keen observer of the American educational scene, noted that since so few schools of education have endowments to rely on, "they frequently find themselves doing what's expedient rather than what's right for themselves and their students, meaning they resort to increasing enrollments and lowering standards in order to raise income."

The study of education in general and educational leadership in particular is at a crossroads as numerous studies and reports confirm the need for significant improvement in the form of higher standards for students and for educational leadership programs. The impetus for these reforms may emanate from national accreditation agencies like the National Council for the Accreditation of Teacher Education which was established to help increase the quality of departments and schools of education. NCATE accreditation is a voluntary, peer review system based on national leadership standards designed by practitioners and professors. Of an estimated 500 colleges and universities that offer programs in educational leadership, approximately 300 have chosen accreditation through NCATE. These programs seek the designation of "National Recognition" by the Educational Leadership Constituent Council (ELCC). The ELCC, an affiliation of the National Association of Secondary School Principals, the National Association of Elementary School Principals, the Association for Supervision and Curriculum Development, and the American Association of School Administrators, is authorized by NCATE to engage in rigorous peer assessments of educational leadership programs using standards determined by the National Policy Board for Educational Administration. ELCC has reviewed 166 of these programs since 1996 and has awarded "National Recognition" to 111 institutions.

Still, many universities may unwittingly continue to stifle reform efforts. One example is the entire concept of university promotion and tenure for faculty. That policy has long emphasized the importance of research and publication in scholarly journals. Under this system college teaching and service are consigned to minor status, and junior faculty who immerse themselves in teaching, community outreach, or even applied research—at the expense of pure research—jeopardize their own careers. McCarthy and Kuh (1997, p. 253) cautioned that universities "have not given high status to applied research and have relegated field-based and other outreach activities to a distant third tier in the reward system." University reluctance to recognize service and teaching as elements of effective scholarship was reported over a decade ago by Clark (1989) who noted that universities have become increasingly firm that tenure and promotion should be rewarded on the basis of research and publication in scholarly journals. Such unwillingness remains common thinking to this day.

CURRICULUM CONTROVERSIES

In recent years, universities, public institutions in particular, have begun to face increasing budget pressures. This constraint expresses itself in dwindling resources for faculty seeking professional growth to study curriculum changes in principal preparation programs. This precarious financial outlook for colleges has compelled many professors to subsidize their own professional development—a not altogether pleasant prospect for college faculty in general and untenured faculty in particular. The result then becomes one of failure to remain current in the important areas of research, best practices, new models of leadership and change, and new theories of adult learning. Murphy (1999b, p. 176) found that "nearly all of the professional development opportunities were individualistic in nature.... Very little of it seemed to be organizationally anchored."

The proper curriculum to prepare school administrators is itself the subject of some controversy because there is no consensus with respect to the ideal curriculum that university faculty can plan and organize. Field administrators argue for a set of learning modules that emphasize the management and administration of schools. University faculty, on the other hand, emphasizes a curriculum rooted in instruction and a positive teaching-learning process.

It is significant to note that the emphasis on management and administration topics does not necessarily lead to pupil achievement. If the mission of schools is to promote student success, then principals must be trained in ideas, philosophies, and techniques to attain that goal. A quiet, orderly and efficiently managed school does not always translate into an achieving school and may, in fact, impede the goal of student success by ignoring or failing to support curriculum innovation simply because new initiatives are not priority.

One illustration of this controversy revealed itself in a study conducted by the Charlotte Advocates for Education (2004) of the Charlotte-Mecklenburg schools in North Carolina. When a focus group of principals was asked what they would like to have learned prior to becoming school leaders, they responded with a variety of recommendations:

- Time management in schools
- Team building techniques
- Working effectively with parents, volunteers, and the larger community
- Building relationships with staff while still completing needed tasks
- Understanding the nuts and bolts issues such as building a budget, a master schedule, navigating the school system, organizing classrooms, hiring quality staff
- Providing highly effective professional development to staff in an efficient manner.

Another study (Portin, Schneider, DeArmond, and Gundlach, 2003) sought to address the learning needs of school leaders by examining their day-to-day work situations. Given all the demands imposed on principals, this team questioned whether it is realistic to expect that they would spend the bulk of their time in classrooms? Should school administrators focus on instruction when the school may face other serious issues like student safety, parent-teacher conflict, declining enrollment, or an influx of newcomers to a stable community? In an effort to determine exactly what school administrators do every day, this team of researchers conducted in-depth interviews with educators (principals, vice principals, and teachers) in 21 schools in four cities across four states. They found that there is no one single formula for success as a principal. Instructional leadership was but one of several critical functions that all combined to produce an achieving school. Other critical leadership functions include cultural, managerial, strategic, external development, micro-political, and human resource leadership. Their interviews with principals revealed several areas of study the administrators wished had been taught in their own preparation programs: conflict resolution, cultural sensitivity, problem diagnosis and solving, organizational theory, and, most of all, business and financial administration.

What kinds of leadership training do the professional associations and academicians recommend for school administrators that will ensure student success? They suggest a curriculum that includes the following: vision and values, instructional leadership, data-based decision making, building a positive school culture, management and leadership, and school improvement and the change process (Kelly and Peterson, 2000; National Staff Development Council, 2000).

The recommendations put forth by the principals and those suggested by professional associations continue to pose a dilemma for universities. As much as principal preparation programs may seek to reshape curriculum in order to accentuate the importance of the teaching and learning to the entire educational enterprise, school leaders in the field continue to focus on management and administration as their priorities. The dichotomy of views between research-oriented university academicians and the practical needs of field administrators exposes this tension. The task for both groups is to come to a common understanding of the core requirements that will lead to school improvement. The task may be a Herculean one.

Nonetheless, a report issued by the Southern Regional Education Board (2004) recommends that educational leadership departments place a higher priority on (a) curriculum study and instruction-related content, (b) assignments based on real life instructional problems, (c) assessments that measure whether administrators fully understand best practices research, and (d) well-defined school-based experiences that extend the learning process beyond classroom walls of the university campus.

THE SELF-SELECTION NATURE OF THE APPLICANT POOL

Among the many criticisms leveled at preparation programs is the inadequate applicant pool. This deficiency reveals itself in acceptance rates of as high as 90 percent to leadership development programs. According to Creighton (2002), any effort to strengthen educational administration preparation programs will have little positive impact on education until the policy makers give more serious attention to improving selection criteria. Any pool overhaul would obviously require a more carefully selected array of candidates and a more rigorous screening process for leadership positions. Jacobson (1990, p. 35) has complained, "for too many administrator preparation programs, any body is better than no body."

Griffiths (1988) noted that graduate school students who were planning to specialize in school administration and educational leadership scored poorly on the Graduate Record Examination in relation to students who were specializing in other areas. Griffiths pointed out that those students planning to specialize in educational leadership scored fourth from the bottom (among 94 majors) in GRE scores. A decade later, this lamentable state had not ameliorated. According to McCarthy (1999), educational leadership students again scored near the bottom as noted in the *Graduate Record Examinations: 1996–1997 Guide to the Use of Scores*. Murphy and Forsyth (1999) underscored McCarthy's description of leadership programs with their observation that students seeking certification in the field of educational administration often were not quite willing to devote the necessary time or effort to their leadership studies. Such students scored poorly on tests designed to measure academic achievement. They were also found to score poorly in risk-taking.

An even more recent review of data published in the Graduate Record Examination Guide (2001) noted the continuing deterioration in the quality of applicants seeking to study school leadership. Students entering educational administration programs from 1996 to 1999 earned GRE scores that ranked them near the bottom when viewed in comparison with seven areas of academic specialization. Educational administration ranked second from the bottom in verbal reasoning (above physical education majors), third from the bottom in quantitative reasoning and second from the bottom in analytical reasoning (Creighton, 2002). If these measures are accurate indicators of the achievement levels of prospective administrators, then educational reform and the change process that are the essence of school improvement may be destined to proceed at a glacial pace.

It may be too simplistic to blame universities for the dearth of quality applicants. Young (2004) identified numerous other factors that impact the recruitment and selection process by which candidates are admitted into educational leadership programs. These include program location, the number of hours required for program completion, cost of tuition to complete the program, program recruitment plans, encouragement from mentors, size and quality of the applicant pool, and internship requirements.

NARROW FOCUS OF PROGRAM CONTENT

The position of school leader is undergoing radical change. Whereas in the past school administrators may have emphasized competence in management issues of programming, budgeting, and a generally orderly and quiet work environment, priority today for future success emphasizes leadership in areas of curriculum, instruction, professional development, assessment, data-based decision making, and creating an environment that enhances the learning process. It is questionable how comfortable university prepara-

tion programs are with respect to transforming their courses of study to meet the changing nature of school leadership today. The split becomes more evident when despite the plethora of research attesting to the importance of instructional leadership for their job success, school administrators today continue to express a preference for a curriculum that emphasizes traditional management issues.

Just as the practice of educational leadership is producing new priorities that call for greater pupil achievement throughout the nation's schools, preparation programs can best respond by submitting to their own program change. This is a difficult proposition for universities as well because many programs continue to offer courses focusing on traditional aspects of school leadership tasks. School finance, administrative theory, school law, computer scheduling, and personnel administration are but a few of the traditional courses in the principal preparation program curriculum.

What are the prospects for improving program content? To be fair, efforts to modernize the curriculum may prove difficult for several reasons. First, McCarthy (1999) bemoans the complacency and congeniality that characterize too many programs, and a concern that faculty members themselves do not perceive a need for change in preparation of school leaders. A second reason that impedes program improvement is the absence of data that might validate the effort. In commenting on Hofstra University's plans to strengthen its program of educational leadership, Shakeshaft (1999) concluded that "after a decade packed with meetings, curriculum discussions, shared ideas, strategies, and program tinkering . . . (we) have no way to gauge whether or not all of our extra work is worth the effort we expend" (pp. 237, 245). Young, Petersen, and Short (2001) reinforced Shakeshaft's concern with their observation that "until we have a process for determining whether or not educational leadership preparation has any of the impacts that we hope for them, it is not likely that we will have adequate information to engage in effective program development" (p. 10).

An uncertain quest with an equally ambiguous payoff may also deter faculty involvement. Another reason exists to complicate any desire for curriculum reform, and this reason is related to the previous reasons described above. This refers to the fact that few incentives exist to transform programs. Curriculum reform is tedious and time-consuming. The work of faculty in this area may not be recognized or rewarded because research and scholarly publication, as noted earlier, remain more assured routes to the attainment of promotion and tenure than the uncertain change effort that surrounds course revision.

One force for change may be state education departments that are responsible for program accreditation and student licensure as school leaders. Through their power to license and to accredit, or deny accreditation, to university-sponsored programs, state departments and agencies command powerful roles in ensuring that qualified and meritorious candidates are licensed and certified. The downside here is that major decisions and policy formulations become the jurisdiction of state agencies. University licensure becomes subject to state guidelines, and the role of educational leadership faculty is that of sideline observers.

CHASM BETWEEN THEORY AND REALITY

The effectiveness of preparation programs for school leaders can be gauged in the application of knowledge, skills, and attitudes to the world of practice. This is not always the case due to the haphazard and irrelevant nature of these programs. The gap between the theory of educational leadership and real practice in the frenetic, day-to-day world of school administration has been well documented (Cambron-McCabe, 1999; Young, Petersen, and Short, 2001). This gap expresses itself in the conflict of priorities between the university and the school. As noted earlier, the university emphasizes research and scholarship, and does not reward active involvement or collaborations with schools. The following excerpt offers insight into the dichotomy: "Universities and school districts are 'uneasy collaborators,'" states Patrick Forsyth, Williams Professor of Educational Leadership at Oklahoma State University. They are institutions "that are quite different in how they operate and how they think" (Young, 2004). The result here is a Berlin Wall mentality that fails to capitalize on the resources the university and the school district can offer each other.

The chasm also expresses itself in an outdated curriculum that must be patched together again, or completely re-sewn, to accommodate the additional duties of school leaders. Programs that emphasize school management to the detriment of leadership opportunities become agents of the status quo, and are oblivious to the ubiquitous demands for school change. The goal of revamped leadership preparation programs must be to serve as a catalyst for change and stronger instructional achievement.

The National Policy Board for Educational Administration (NPBEA, 1989) was among the first to call for program reform as a means to resolve the difference in priorities that exist between the needs of schools and the needs of the university. Its early recommendations for improved curriculum included the following:

- Societal and cultural influences on schooling
- Teaching and learning processes and school improvement
- Organizational theory
- Methodologies of organizational studies and policy analysis
- Leadership and management processes and functions
- Policy studies and politics of education
- Moral and ethical dimensions of schooling.

Failure to resolve the differences in priorities will only have deleterious consequences for all parties. Candidates for licensure become victims of inadequate preparation because they do not develop the necessary skills, competencies, and knowledge required to address educational challenges. The result is substandard performance on their part, greater job frustration, and in all too many cases, increased leader turnover, and ultimately, shortages of school administrators. The shortfall in qualified administrators has become a national concern (Quinn, 2002). Teachers and students become casualties of poor preparation programs because they are denied the dividends of improved learning environments that are fostered only by good leadership.

Perhaps the greatest damage that stems from the school-university gap is inflicted on the universities themselves. They run the risk of continued irrelevancy and may find their preparation programs in competition with newly created programs organized by professional associations and private industry. In 1980 leadership academies to train school administrators were non-existent. Leadership development was virtually the sole province of universities (Cooper and Boyd, 1988). A decade later, the number of organizations in the United States that identified themselves as leadership academies and principal centers exceeded 150 (Hallinger, 2002). In recent years numerous professional leadership associations, including superintendent, elementary and secondary principal associations, all have begun training programs to certify school administrators. The private sector has seen the birth and development of leadership initiatives through New Leaders for New Schools, the DeWitt Wallace Foundation, the New York City Principals Leadership Academy, the Broad Foundation, Danforth Foundation, and the Kellogg Foundation. The latter foundation has developed a collaborative program with former Michigan Governor Engler to create an urban Superintendents Academy without any input or relationship to a university.

Some states and local jurisdictions have begun to approve alternative principal and superintendent certification programs bypassing university participation. In California, for example, aspiring school leaders can now pass a test with no university course work or internship and receive administrative certification (Young and Creighton, 2002). Florida and Michigan have rolled back their certification rules to allow leaders from fields other than teaching to serve as principals. Georgia established an Office of School Improvement to train school leaders in the critical issues that impact on their job success and student achievement. The office developed its own leadership training modules. Sample modules include using data to lead change, creating a high performance learning culture, literacy and numeracy leadership, providing sustained professional development, and leading instruction.

Several cities, including Boston and New York, have initiated their own principal preparation programs that have little real affiliation with local universities. These two cities offer an intensive, one-year leadership experience consisting of a four-day-a-week school residency for future principals and teaching provided by incumbent school leaders. Each of these groups stresses the reality-based leadership experience of their programs because their trainers and governing boards are, for the most part, former school administrators. In another instance of independence from university-based leadership training programs, the Springfield, Massachusetts school district successfully petitioned the Massachusetts State Education Department to run its own preparation programs. The district may now certify administrators who graduate from its leadership academy. Los Angeles has a similar district-led principal development program.

It is ironic that at a time when "the press is clearly toward external control mechanisms (e.g., competition) as the stimulus to drive educational improvement" (Clark, 1999, p. 233), knowledgeable observers like Michelle Young and George Petersen, Executive Director and Associate Executive Director of University Council of Educational Administration, report "we are not convinced that educational leadership faculty are disinterested in improving their programs. Rather, we have observed a great deal of support and

effort dedicated to program improvement" (2002, p. 14). Among recent initiatives are case studies, course realignment, problem-based learning, action research with a field base, introduction of cohort groups, student portfolios, ongoing fieldwork, and more meaningful university-school partnership programs (Jackson and Kelley, 2002).

PROSPECTS FOR IMPROVEMENT

Are critiques of educational leadership programs destined to remain a staple of negative conversation in school lunchrooms and central offices? What are the prospects for reform in leadership preparation? In recent years there has been some evidence that universities are abandoning the apathy and irrelevance that are woven into too many educational leadership programs. Since the release of the National Policy Board for Educational Administration's report (NPBEA, 2002), *Standards for Advanced Programs in Educational Leadership for Principals, Superintendents, Curriculum Directors and Supervisors*, university programs are working to align curriculum with standards that more accurately reflect the nature of school leadership today with strong value placed on positive school culture, vision, professional development, and instruction.

The work of NPBEA has been augmented by the issuance of the Interstate School Leadership Licensure Consortium standards (CCSSO, 1996). These standards are driving efforts in areas of licensing, preparation programs, accreditation, program assessment, and course improvement. Today nearly 40 states have adopted the ISLLC standards in their entirety or some adapted form of the standards. Through its work in the licensure and accreditation of preparation programs, the National Council for the Accreditation of Teacher Education has also stimulated further reform in leadership development.

UNIVERSITY INITIATIVES

How have universities reconstructed their leadership programs to accommodate new research and heightened demands for program improvement? What promising practices are universities implementing in the quest for more course relevance and rigor? Several examples come to mind. Oklahoma State University rebuilt its leadership program to include 12 credits of course work in instructional leadership. This is at least twice the number of credits typically given to study of this issue. And administrators from neighboring school districts work with OSU faculty to integrate problem-based learning activities into course work.

East Tennessee State University has contracted with an outside curriculum expert whose task it is to design leadership courses that focus on issues related to instruction. Faculty at the University of North Texas are integrating leadership standards with course content and student assignments. UNT is also working with the Dallas Independent School District to create a program that recruits future school leaders. The district requested principals' input to nominate talented teachers for possible admission into UNT's school leadership program.

New Mexico State University is working to bring together practitioners, university faculty, and legislators to design an innovative program to prepare border and binational school superintendents. The City University of New York has drafted plans that invoke the use of a cohort structure, the integration of ISLLC standards into all course work and the internship, as well as partnership initiatives with local school district superintendents.

The University of Washington has redesigned its preparation program to emphasize the moral and ethical leadership components of school decision making. The program also requires a 10-day summer institute as part of the bonding experience inherent in a cohort model.

California State University at Fresno has created a two-tier leadership program that focuses on instruction in the first tier with candidates required to complete 120 hours as master teachers. The second tier addresses transformational leadership issues in which adjunct faculty, many of whom are school administrators, teach content areas of school practice.

POLICY RECOMMENDATIONS

What policy recommendations emerging from this review of the state of leadership preparation should universities consider in their efforts to strengthen their programs? A number of recommendations are offered below:

1. review principal licensure programs to determine that the curriculum addresses the research attesting to the relationship between principal leadership and student achievement.
2. ensure that licensure programs are taught by faculty that possesses the knowledge and the skills needed to teach leadership practices.
3. undertake a more proactive approach to recruiting prospective candidates for leadership study. The self-selection approach does not always provide the universities and school districts with motivated and talented individuals.

4. revise program content around issues pertaining to instructional leadership, curriculum, data-based decision making, and student achievement.
5. revamp field-based internship experiences to focus on problem solving and action research.
6. identify research-based criteria to select worthy applicants for leadership. Criteria should certainly include expertise in curriculum and instruction, a statement of educational values, and strong interpersonal skills.
7. form more dynamic partnerships with school districts that would jointly identify outstanding candidates for study of administration, review course syllabi for relevance, and create meaningful field work opportunities.
8. rethink the incentive system for faculty in ways that recognize and support involvement in school improvement and program formulation. Here faculty must be rewarded with promotion and tenure for their work in schools.
9. encourage efforts to hire faculty who understand, and know how to implement, the change process in schools.
10. support the appointment of faculty members as non-tenured professors of practice and who possess field leadership experience.
11. conduct research to determine the relationship between educational leadership programs and (a) leader effectiveness on the job, and (b) student achievement.
12. give faculty time and resources to conduct school-based research.
13. provide the required funding to maintain high-quality, research-based professional development programs for prospective administrators.
14. sensitize field administrators that their preference for a curriculum based on management and administration issues does not lead to instructional improvement.

CONCLUSION

The challenges that schools face today are growing at an unprecedented pace. The challenges are exacerbated, of course, by the dearth of effective leaders to address the host of problems that cross their desks every day. Shipman (2001) cautions that "if universities do not accept standards-based reform, and quite soon, they will be out of business within a decade" (p. 13).

The numerous urgent calls for school reform that emanate from government pronouncements, commission reports, and research findings require that schools and universities join together to embark on a more comprehensive dialogue that will identify, recruit, and train the next generation of leaders. Strengthening the selection and training process for prospective administrators must assume a higher level of importance in university leadership preparation programs. University departments of educational leadership cannot wait any longer to make the needed changes in what is taught, how it is taught, and how faculty interact with K–12 principals and school leaders. To ignore the many mandates to improve may well stall or derail the cause of educational improvement.

REFERENCES

American Association of School Administrators (1960). *Professional administrators for America's schools* (Thirty-eighth AASA Yearbook). Washington, DC: National Education Association.

Cambron-McCabe, N. H. (1999). Confronting fundamental transformation of leadership preparation. In J. Murphy and P. B. Forsyth (Eds.), *Educational administration: A decade of reform* (pp. 217–227). Thousand Oaks, CA: Corwin Press.

Charlotte Advocates for Education (2004). *Role of principal leadership in increasing teacher retention: Creating a supportive environment.* Charlotte, NC: Author.

Clark, D. L. (1999). Searching for authentic educational leadership in university graduate programs and with public school colleagues. In J. Murphy and P. B. Forsyth (Eds.), *Educational administration: A decade of reform* (pp. 228–236). Thousand Oaks, CA: Corwin Press.

Clark, R. R. (1989). The academic life: Small worlds, different worlds. *Educational Researcher, 18*(5), 4–8.

Cooper, B., and Boyd, W. (1988). The evolution of training for school administrators. In D. Griffiths, R. Stout and P. B. Forsyth (Eds.), *Leaders for America's schools* (pp. 251–272). Berkeley, CA: McCutchan Publishing Co.

Council of Chief State School Officers (1996). *Interstate school leaders licensure consortium: Standards for school leaders.* Washington, DC: Author.

Creighton, T. (2002). Standards for education administration preparation programs: Okay, but don't we have the cart before the horse? *Journal of School Leadership, 12*(5), 526–551.

Farkas, S., Johnson, J., and Duffett A. (with Syat, B., and Vine, J.). (2003). *Rolling up their sleeves: Superintendents and principals talk about what's needed to fix public schools.* New York: Public Agenda.

Graduate Record Examination Guide to the Use of Scores (2001). Princeton, NJ: Educational Testing Service.

Gregorian, V. (2004, November 10). No more silver bullets. *Education Week, 24*(11), 48–50.

Griffiths, D. E. (1988). *Educational administration: Reform PDQ or RIP* (UCEA Occasional Paper No. 8312). Tempe, AZ: University Council for Educational Administration.

Grogan, M., and Andrews, R. (2002). Defining preparation and professional development for the future. *Educational Administration Quarterly, 38*(2), 233–256.

Guthrie, J. W., and Sanders, T. (2001, January 7). Who will lead the public schools? *The New York Times,* A 46.

Hallinger, P. (2003). The emergence of school leadership development in an era of globalization: 1980–2002. In P. Hallinger (ed.), *Reshaping the landscape of school leadership development: A global perspective* (pp. 3–22). Lisse, The Netherlands: Swets & Zeitlinger Publishers.

Hallinger, P., and Heck, R. (1996). Reassessing the principal's role in school effectiveness: A review of empirical research, 1980–1995. *Educational Administration Quarterly, 32*(1), 5–44.

Halpin, A. W. (1957). A paradigm for research on administrator training. In R. F. Campbell and R. T. Gregg (Eds.), *Administrative behavior in education.* New York: Harper & Row.

Hess, F. M. (2003). *A license to lead? A new leadership agenda for America's schools.* Washington, DC: Progressive Policy Institute.

Jackson, B., and Kelley, C. (2002). Exceptional and innovative programs in educational leadership. *Educational Administration Quarterly, 38*(2), 192–212.

Jacobson, S. L. (1990). Reflections on the third wave of reform: Rethinking administrator preparation. In S. L. Jacobson and J. A. Conway (Eds.), *Educational leadership in an age of reform* (pp. 30–44). New York: Longman Publishing Co.

Kelly, C., and Peterson, K. (2000). *Principal inservice programs: A portrait of diversity and promise.* Paper written for the National Center on Education and the Economy and the Carnegie Foundation. Washington, DC.

Lashway, L., and Anderson, M. (1997). Developing school leaders. In S. C. Smith and P. K. Piele (Eds.), *School leadership: Handbook for excellence* (3rd ed., pp. 72–100). Portland, OR: ERIC Clearinghouse on Educational Management.

Leithwood, K., and Riehl, C. (2003). *What we know about successful school leadership.* Philadelphia, PA: Laboratory for Student Success, Temple University.

McCarthy, M. M. (1999). The evolution of educational leadership preparation programs. In J. Murphy and K. S. Louis (Eds.), *Handbook of research on educational administration* (2nd ed., pp. 119–139). San Francisco: Jossey-Bass.

McCarthy, M. M. (2001). Challenges facing educational leadership programs: Our future is now. *Newsletter of the Teaching in Educational Administration Special Interest Group of the American Educational Research Association, 8*(1).

McCarthy, M. M., and Kuh, G. (1997). *Continuity and change: The educational leadership professoriate.* Columbia, MO: University Council for Educational Administration.

Murphy, J. (1992). *The landscape of leadership preparation: Reframing the education of school administrators.* Thousand Oaks, CA: Corwin Press.

Murphy, J. (1999a). *Reconnecting teaching and school administration: A call for a unified profession.* Paper presented at the annual meeting of the American Educational Research Association, Montreal, April 1999.

Murphy, J. (1999b). Changes in preparation programs: Perceptions of department chairs. In J. Murphy and P. B. Forsyth (Eds.), *Educational administration: A decade of reform* (pp. 170–191). Thousand Oaks, CA: Corwin Press.

National Association of Secondary School Principals (NASSP) (2004). *Breaking ranks II: Strategies for leading high school reform.* Reston, VA: Author.

National Commission on Excellence in Educational Administration (1987). *Leaders for America's schools.* Tempe, AZ: University Council for Educational Administration.

National Policy Board for Educational Administration (NPBEA) (1989). *Improving the preparation of school administration: An agenda for reform.* Charlottesville, VA: Author.

National Policy Board for Educational Administration (NPBEA) (2002). *Standards for advanced programs in educational leadership for principals, superintendents, curriculum directors, and supervisors.* Arlington, VA: Author.

National Staff Development Council (2000). Learning to lead, leading to learn. Improving school quality through principal professional development. Oxford, OH: Author.

Petzko, V., Clark, D., Valentine, J., Hackmann, D., Nori, J., and Lucas, S. (2002). Leaders and leadership in middle level schools. *NASSP Bulletin, 86*(631), 3–15.

Portin, B., Schneider, P., DeArmond, M., and Gundlach, L. (2003). Making sense of leading schools: A study of the school principalship. Seattle, WA: Center on Reinventing Public Education, University of Washington.

Quinn, T. (2002). Succession planning: Start today. *Principal Leadership, 3*(2), 24–28.

Ruebling, C., Stow, S., Kayona, F., and Clarke, N. (2004). Instructional leadership: An essential ingredient for improving student learning. *The Educational Forum, 68*(3), 243–253.

Shakeshaft, C. (1999). A decade full or a decade half empty: thoughts from a tired reformer. In J. Murphy and P. B. Forsyth (Eds.), *Educational administration: A decade of reform* (pp. 237–251). Thousand Oaks, CA: Corwin Press.

Shipman, N. (2001). Repairing the bumps in the road. *Education Leadership Review, 2*(2), 10–13.

Southern Regional Education Board (2004). *Progress being made in getting a quality leader in every school.* Atlanta, GA: Author.

Tirozzi, G. (2001). The artistry of leadership: The evolving door of the secondary school principal. *Phi Delta Kappan, 82*(6), 434–439.

Waters, J. T., and Grubb, S. (2004). *The leadership we need: Using research to strengthen the use of standards for administrator preparation and licensure programs.* Aurora, CO: Mid-continent Research for Education and Learning.

Waters, J. T., Marzano, R. J., and McNulty, B. A. (2003). *Balanced leadership: What 30 years of research tells us about the effect of leadership on student achievement.* Aurora, CO: Mid-continent Research for Education and Learning.

Young, M. D. (2004). *Preparing school and school system leaders: A call for collaboration.* Paper presented at the 2004 AACTE Annual Conference, Chicago, IL.

Young, M., and Creighton, T. (2002). Who is framing the national understanding of educational leadership preparation and practice? *Leadership and Policy in Schools, 1*(3), 222–241.

Young, M. D., and Petersen, G. J. (Winter, 2002). Enabling substantive reform in the preparation of school leaders. *Educational Leadership Review, 3*(1), 1–15.

Young, M. D., Petersen, G. J., and Short, P. M. (2001). *The complexity of substantive reform: A call for interdependence among key stakeholders.* Paper commissioned for the National Commission for the Advancement of Educational Leadership Preparation. Columbia, MO: University Council for Educational Administration.

Assessing Outcomes from Educational Leadership Programs[1]

STEPHEN LAWTON, MICHAEL GILBERT,
ROBERT ESTABROOK, RENA RICHTIG, AND PAMELA EDDY

BOTH INTERNAL AND EXTERNAL AGENCIES ARE PRESSING administrators of college and university programs to demonstrate their success by providing hard evidence in the form of output measures. The Department of Educational Administration and Community Leadership (EACL) at Central Michigan University (CMU) has been challenged to respond to such demands by the National Council for Accreditation of Teacher Education (NCATE), the Higher Learning Commission (HLC) of the North Central Association of Colleges and Universities (NCA), the State of Michigan, and CMU's Assessment Council, Graduate College, Provost's Office, and Colleges of Education and Human Services (CEHS), all of which call for rational processes linking program goals, content, and processes with student outputs. Its experience illustrates a general problem in higher education as outcomes-oriented accountability systems are developed or imposed by a variety of authorities (Serban and Friedlander, 2004). The purpose of this essay is to describe one department's initiatives to respond and to illustrate the need for a more comprehensive solution.

ONE DEPARTMENT'S RESPONSE

Developing the Department's response to these calls for accountability is difficult due to the variety of frameworks selected by the various authoritative bodies, although this problem was not at first evident. Beginning in 1995, EACL adopted an assessment plan in accord with the CMU Senate's *Policy on Student Learning Outcomes Assessment*, which was subsequently approved by the Assessment Council. Then, based on *NCATE Program Standards: Advanced Programs in Educational Leadership for Principals, Superintendents, Curriculum Directors, and Supervisors*, which was prepared for the National Policy Board of Educational Administration (NPBEA) for the Educational Leadership Constituent Council (ELCC), EACL sought NCATE approval for its M.A. in Principalship

and Specialist in General Administration. Preparation of the submission entailed, among other steps, linking all course syllabi to ELCC's five program domains (*strategic leadership, instructional leadership, organizational leadership, political and community leadership, and internship*) and 63 program standards listed within the five program domains. In 2000, the department was granted "National Recognition" by ELCC for these programs.

Subsequently, the regulatory regime has changed while growing in diversity and complexity. First, the College of Education and Human Services (or, technically, the Professional Education Council) adopted its own model for accountability, CLEAR, which stands for *Concept and knowledge driven, LEArner centered,* and *Reflective practice*. Within each domain are three goals, each with three to six objectives, totaling 45 in all. For renewed NCATE re-accreditation, in 2003 EACL was required to realign its assessment activities, including course syllabi, to conform to the CLEAR model, thus jettisoning their alignment with the 1995 era ELCC standards.[2]

NCATE and ELCC also jettisoned the original ELCC standards, replacing them with a modified version devised by the Interstate School Leaders Licensure Consortium (ISLLC) in 1996. These *Standards for School Leaders*, developed under the auspices of the Council of Chief State School Officers, identify six domains: *school vision, school culture and instruction, operations and resources, communication and collaboration with community, ethical behavior,* and *political, economic, social and cultural context*.[3] Within each domain are lists of requisite *knowledge, dispositions,* and *performances*—149 in all. The widespread adoption of ISLLC standards by states and the development prompted a revision of the ELCC guidelines, with the National Policy Board on Educational Administration appointing a group to integrate the ELCC Guidelines within the ISLCC standards framework in a manner that could include doctoral program reviews and which would reflect NCATE's position that programs be assessed "on how well graduates are prepared to perform in the workplace rather than on the number of courses offered or on objectives listed in syllabi" (NPBEA, 2002b, p. 7).

The new NCATE standards for educational leadership programs includes an *internship*; drops the distinction between *knowledge*, *dispositions*, and *performances*; phrases criteria in paragraphs rather than ISLLC's point form, thereby reducing them from 149 to 71; and notes that preparation programs should include the three dimensions of *awareness*, *understanding*, and *capability*. Overall, in comparison to the original ELCC standards, the revised approach is less content- or course-oriented and more problem-centered, a difference reflected in the sample items provided by the Educational Testing Service (ETS, 2003) on the *School Leaders Licensure Assessment* (SLLA), an instrument used to assess achievement relative to the original ISLLC standards.

CHALLENGES AHEAD

Three challenges lie ahead for EACL's advanced professional education programs if the department responds to current expectations. First, it must update its assessment plan and the individual program assessment plans to focus on students.

Second, the CMU Provost's Office, in preparation for University re-accreditation by the Higher Learning Commission of NCA, is developing its own model for program assessment with five stages: *academic audit, self-study, external review, SWOT analysis,* and *ratings, dean review and provost review and recommendation* (CMU, 2004). Within the self-study phase are program-level outcomes in six domains: *student learning and effective teaching, assessment for learning, learning assessment planning and reporting, advising, learning environments,* and *preparing for the future.* A total of 27 program criteria are listed within the six domains.

Third, the State of Michigan has initiated voluntary approval process for principal preparation program based on a set of standard based on the framework developed by ISLLC in the mid-1990s. Two domains are added to those of the original six ISLLC standards: *technology leadership* and *internship.* As well, specific criteria, which are to be demonstrated at an *awareness, basic,* or *comprehensive* level, number 210. EACL is being encouraged by its College administration to apply for this voluntary recognition.

POSSIBLE SOLUTIONS

The puzzle, then, is how to align EACL's course and program assessment practices with college, university, and state standards without maintaining three or more parallel but overlapping systems. One approach is to begin with the transition point model for acquiring assessment data that was required as part of NCATE re-accreditation in 2003 and reflected in the model in Figure 1.

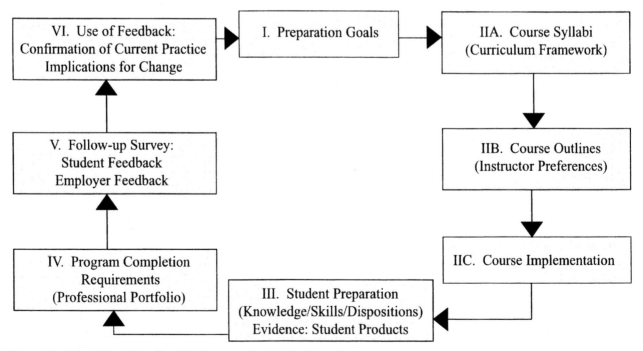

Figure 1. Educational Leadership Program Facsimile Flow Chart

In this flow model, data are collected at admissions, completion of course work, and completion of program. At each stage there must be one or more sources of data (portfolio, internship, activity, exam, essay, etc.), a measurement rubric for assessing the data, a scoring system for the rubric, and a score (see Figure 2). To complete the assessment, one or more follow-ups would be conducted (surveys, interviews, focus groups, etc.) and scored.

M.A. Principalship	M.A. Educational Leadership	M.A. Community Leadership	Specialist in General Educational Administration	Doctor of Education in Educational Leadership
Admissions Portfolio Rubric Scoring Score	**Admissions** Portfolio Rubric Scoring Score	**Admissions** Portfolio Rubric Scoring Score	**Admissions** Portfolio Rubric Scoring Score	**Admissions** Portfolio and Interview Rubrics Scoring Scores
Course Activities Rubrics Scoring Scores Grades	**Course Activities** Rubrics Scoring Scores Grades	**Course Activities** Rubrics Scoring Scores Grades	**Course Activities** Rubrics Scoring Scores Grades	**Course Activities** Rubrics Scoring Scores Grades
Internship Log and Activity Write-ups Rubrics Scoring Score	**Internship (optional)** Log and Activity Write-ups Rubrics Scoring Score	**Internship** Log and Activity Write-ups Rubrics Scoring Score	**Internship** Log and Activity Write-ups Rubrics Scoring Score	**Internship** Log and Activity Write-ups Rubrics Scoring Score

M.A. Principalship	M.A. Educational Leadership	M.A. Community Leadership	Specialist in General Educational Administration	Doctor of Education in Educational Leadership
Exit Portfolio Prof. Platform Rubric Score	**Exit Portfolio** Prof. Platform Rubric Score	**Exit Portfolio** Prof. Platform Rubric Score	**Field Study** Proposal Rubric Score Report Rubric Score	**Comprehensives** Exam Questions Rubrics Scores High Pass/Pass/ Marginal/Fail
Follow-up Survey Instrument Scoring Score	**Follow-up Survey** Instrument Scoring Score	**Follow-up Survey** Instrument Scoring Score	**Follow-up Survey** Instrument Scoring Score	**Dissertation** Proposal, Dissertation, and Abstract Rubrics Scores
				Follow-up Survey Instrument Scoring Score

Figure 2. Assessment at Transition Points in EACL Graduate Programs

CENTRAL MICHIGAN UNIVERSITY
College of Education and Human Services
Department of Educational and Community Leadership

Scoring Rubric for Theses/Dissertations

Name_____

In relation to the quality of work exhibited in the majority of accepted theses/dissertations, this criterion is:
   5 = exceptionally well done
   3 = marginally acceptable, not of high quality
   1 = substandard for advanced graduate level work

1.   The thesis/dissertation contains the elements of the format for theses/dissertations as appropriate for this particular study and the expectations of the student's committee.

2.   The thesis/dissertation reflects the quality of written expression commensurate with advanced graduate work; i.e., the discussion is logically sequenced, free of errors of grammar, punctuation and usage; sentences convey complete thoughts, paragraphs focus on a single topic; and the rhetoric easily advances the reader's understanding of the study.

3.   The statement of the problem is a logical argument that establishes the context in which the problem resides, critically, but briefly, examines that context for its virtues and limitations, identifies a particular limitation that requires focused investigation, and justifies the pursuit of that focus.

4.   The project has a clearly stated purpose in the form of either a direct statement or central research question(s), or both as appropriate to the study

5.   The review of related research further establishes the existence of the problem, reviews and critiques the existing research directly pertaining to the focus of the study, underscores the theoretical or logical premise of the study, and discusses explicitly the major variables or categories that are the subject of the investigation.

6.   The design of the study reflects an understanding of the principles of research design to an extent appropriate for the scope and purpose of the project.

7.   The design of the study (e.g., any relational propositions) is premised on sound theoretical assumptions (or commonsensical rationale), is realistic, and contributes worthwhile new knowledge.

8.   The methodology is internally consistent with the purpose(s) of the study and appropriate to the design.

9.   The description of the procedures or methodology creates for the reader a clear and thorough understanding of steps the researcher followed when carrying out the project.

10.   The procedural section of the thesis/dissertation specifies the method(s) to be used for collecting data, sources of data (subjects, sample, documents), instruments (if any) and their development; addresses issues of validity and reliability; and addresses legal, ethical and human relations requirements for the protection of human subjects in research.

11.   The analysis section of the thesis/dissertation contains an adequate discussion of data management and any statistical analysis that was used to test relational hypotheses or to describe how the results answered a central question or purpose.

12.   The discussion of the results was pertinent to the design of the study, to the questions posed, and to overarching issues in the field.

Total Points   _____

Unacceptable: Less than 36 points
Acceptable: 36 to 48 points
Target: Greater than 48 points

Figure 3.   Scoring Rubric

Each key activity or product would be of such a nature as to reveal levels of student proficiency relative to multiple criteria included in state, college, and university standards. In the process, adequate rubrics for scoring are important since they carry the weight of assigning proficiency levels to specific responses. A sample of a current rubric in use in EACL (Figure 3) provides an indication of progress to date. Scores from rubrics, currently available only in student files or faculty notes, would also need to be systematically collected and entered into a database with a record for each student. Otherwise, collating summary statistics of student outcomes would be impracticable.

Would such a system be adequate to address the challenges presented by the Provost's HLC Program Review, Michigan's principal program approval process, and the College's CLEAR model? Can all of these objectives be met without revising all course syllabi and maintaining several assessment systems? Or should there be recognized hierarchy of assessment and accountability systems so that if the most stringent requirements are met, other authorities would waive their standards? Certainly, from a department's viewpoint, this possibility is most attractive since in would reduce the overall effort while allowing it to focus its energy on meeting high standards rather than have it dissipated in the process of meeting multiple standards. Achieving this goal would require widespread recognition of the difficulties and, indeed, self-defeating nature that multiple frameworks for accountability create. Then, a consensus might develop to either agree upon a single approach or on an accepted hierarchy of standards that would allow units to obtain waivers from competing models of the highest standards were met. Hopefully, this essay represents a measured step towards this goal.

NOTES

1. Paper prepared for the Annual Conference of the National Council of Professors of Educational Administration (NCPEA), August 3–6, 2004, Branson, MO.
2. In addition to the formal institutional assessment systems, EACL was also required to comply with two short-time standards initiatives.

   In September 2003, the University's Office of Student Disabilities Services, in implementing the University policy to provide "individuals with disabilities reasonable accommodations to participate in university activities, programs and services" required submission of departmental guidelines for *Essential Functions and Technical Standards for Degree Programs*. EACL drafted polices linked to modified ISLLC standards and classified under four headings: *observational skills*, *psychomotor skills*, *cognitive skills*, and *affective/behavioral/interpersonal skills*. All criteria were to be performance based. For example, one observation skill listed is to "view various forms of prepared information, including written, projected, and artistic."

   In practice, such guidelines are used to determine if a new student requires accommodation, in which case the Office of Student Disabilities Services is contacted to determine if the disabilities exist within the meaning of the American's with Disabilities Act (ADA) and, if so, whether the student can meet the program's technical standards with "reasonable accommodations." As well, the Office assists departments and program coordinators in designing and providing accommodations when called for.

   In a sense, the *Essential Functions and Technical Standards* form what in the past have been implicit prerequisites or standards for admission. Some departments at CMU now require that all students accepting admission sign a statement indicating that they have read departmental *Essential Functions and Technical Standards* and that they do not require accommodation. Those who do not sign are required to contact the Office of Student Disabilities Services. EACL has not, at this time, taken this step. Also, although the EACL has indicated that its *Essential Functions and Technical Standards* are linked to ISLCC standards, no systematic demonstration of these linkages has been developed or validated. In fact, extensive research would be necessary to ensure the rigor of these functions and standards, as well as ISLCC standards. At present, both might be vulnerable to a court challenge by an individual who is denied admission to a program because reasonable accommodations were not, in the University's view, feasible.

   EACL prepared draft standards in less than three weeks to meet the deadline for submission for legal review by the University. Nine months later, no feedback has been received.

   The second short term demand was to a May 2004 memorandum from the Provost which included a chart titled *CMU Graduate Programs that Meet One or More Initial Screening Criteria*. It included a list of 40 programs that were to be reviewed within six weeks as to enrollment (demand), quality, and cost. Three of EACL's five programs were on the list. The only data provided to support the identification of the programs were one term's on-campus enrollment data. In addition, there was a list of ten questions, including one asking if the data provided were accurate. EACL responded with (a) correct data on actual on- and off-campus enrollments; (b) an reanalysis of cost data from the Institutional Research Office, which had omitted off-campus students revenue and enrollment while including relevant expenditures; and (c) a list of quality initiatives undertaken by EACL.

The College Dean was most helpful by reporting that there was strong demand and high regard for the programs evident throughout the state.

These short term assessment demands were disruptive at the department level since they superceded systematic efforts to address university, state, and national assessment programs. Their lack of integration with other assessment and standards initiatives resulted in redundant and disconnected activities which minimized their contribution to fulfilling long term improvement objectives.

3. This abbreviated version is taken from Cox (2002) who notes two additional standards, *instructional programs* and *policy implementation*, for district superintendents. ISLCC defined standards in short paragraphs that are difficult to summarize in a succinct manner. See the original sources for full statements.

REFERENCES

Central Michigan University. (March 2003). *Institutional self-study report for Central Michigan University*. Submitted to National Council for Accreditation of Teacher Education. Mt. Pleasant, MI: Author.

Central Michigan University. (2004). *Proposal for a revised program review process*. Retrieved August 1, 2004, from http://www.provost.cmich.edu/viceprovost/APC/ProgramReviewProposalFeb17.pdf.

Council of Chief State School Officers. (November 2, 1996). *Interstate School Leaders Licensure Consortium: Standards for school leaders*. Washington, DC: The Author. Retrieved August 1, 2004, from http://www.ccsso.org/content/pdfs/isllcstd.pdf.

Cox, E. (2002). Leadership programs and ISLLC. *The AASA Professor*, 24(4), 4–8.

Creighton, T., and Young, M. (2003). Conversation with Fenwick English: Standards without standardization. *NCPEA Education Leadership Review*, 4(1), 33–36.

Department of Educational Administration and Community Leadership, Central Michigan University. (October 21, 2003). *Essential Functions and Technical Standards for Degree Programs* (Draft). Mt. Pleasant, MI: The Author. Photocopy.

Department of Educational Administration and Community Leadership, Central Michigan University. (March 4, 2003). *Report on student and program assessment. Prepared for NCATE accreditation review*. Photocopy.

Department of Educational Administration and Community Leadership, Central Michigan University. (May 5, 2004). *Master of Arts Degree—School Principalship—Student Outcomes.* (Draft). Mt. Pleasant, MI: The Author. Photocopy.

Education Testing Service. (2003). Tests at a glance. School leadership series. Princeton, NJ: ETS. Retrieved August 1, 2004, from ftp://ftp.ets.org/pub/tandl/SLSTAAG.pdf.

Glasman, N., Cibulka, J., and Ashby, D. (2003). Program self-evaluation for continuous improvement. Paper prepared for the National Commission for the Advancement of Educational Leadership Preparation, Feb. 7–9, 2002. Retrieved July 27, 2004, from http://www.ncaelp.org/index.htm.

Jackson, B. L., and Kelly, C. (2002). Exceptional programs in educational leadership. Paper prepared for the National Commission for the Advancement of Educational Leadership Preparation, Feb. 7–9, 2002. Retrieved July 27, 2004, from http://www.ncaelp.org/index.htm.

Michigan State Board of Education. (February 10, 2004). Standards for the Preparation of School Principals. Program Standards for the Preparation of School Principals. Retrieved August 1, 2004, from http://www.michigan.gov/documents/SBE_Item_Stds_for_Prep_of_School_Principals_Feb_04_86551_7.doc.

National Council for Accreditation of Teacher Education. (September 1995). *NCATE Program Standards: Advanced Programs in Educational Leadership for Principals, Superintendents, Curriculum Directors, and Supervisors*. Retrieved August 1, 2004, from http://www.ncate.org/standard/new%20program%20standards/elcc.pdf.

National Council for Accreditation of Teacher Education. (n.d.). *A Listing of Approved and Denied University-Based Administrator Training Programs*. Retrieved on August 1, 2004, from http://www.npbea.org/ELCC/ELCC_approved_and_denied_list_1-13-04.pdf.

National Policy Board for Educational Administration. (January, 2002a). *Standards for Advanced Programs in Educational Leadership for Principals, Superintendents, Curriculum Directors, and Supervisors*. Retrieved August 1, 2004, from http://www.npbea.org/ELCC/ELCCStandards%20_5-02.pdf.

National Policy Board for Educational Administration. (January, 2002b). *Instructions to Implement Standards for Advanced Programs in Educational Leadership for Principals, Superintendents, Curriculum Directors, and Supervisors*. Retrieved August 1, 2004, from http://www.npbea.org/ELCC/Instructions%20to%20ELCC%20Standards.102.pdf.

Serban, A., and Friedlander, J. (Eds.) (2004). Developing and implementing assessment of learning outcomes. New Directions for Community Colleges, No. 126. San Francisco: Jossey-Bass.

There Oughta Be a Law!

MITCHELL HOLIFIELD

"THERE OUGHTA BE A LAW," A COMMON VERBAL REACTION to situations/happenings that perturb people, served as the impetus for a performance-based class project in the Ed.D. program in Educational Leadership at Arkansas State University. This project was a response to Arkansas's governor's complaint that higher education had not been involved in the state's efforts to devise a more equitable plan to fund education and to consolidate small school districts. So the idea emerged that the doctoral cohort could identify and choose educational issues to research and perhaps ultimately address with legislative bills to be submitted to a panel of state legislators. This paper describes the project: the accreditation standards addressed, the project's stages, the results of the 2004 doctoral cohort's efforts, concomitant issues, and the students' and professor's evaluation of the project.

STANDARDS ADDRESSED

The "Oughta-Be-a-Law" project primarily addresses Standard 6 of *Interstate School Leaders Licensure Consortium: Standards for School Leaders (ISLLC)*:

A school administrator is an educational leader who promotes the success of all students by understanding, responding to, and influencing the larger political, social, economic, legal, and cultural context. (1996, p. 20)

This same standard appears in *Standards for Advanced Programs in Educational Leadership* (2002, p. 14).

STAGES OF THE PROJECT

The Issue

Each of the twelve cohort members brought at least one educational issue to the class's attention; the class chose six issues to further investigate.

The Research

Utilizing multiple sources (professional literature, media, experts, and policy interest groups), pairs of students then did the initial research regarding the issue's facts/critical attributes. Subsequently, three issues were abandoned due to the fact that similar legislation was already in the "pipeline." (The members of these teams dispersed into the other three teams.)

Resolution

Each team wrote a bill.

The Ethical Test

Each student within the subgroup analyzed the group's bill utilizing the ethical reasoning model (see Table 1); then the group drew conclusions on whether or not there were ethical problems with the bill. When needed, the group made revisions to the bill and finally decided if the bill should indeed be presented to the entire cohort who then collectively determined if the bill should be included in the cohort's presentation to the panel of Arkansas legislators.

Presentations

Each group whose bill was approved by the cohort orally presented their bill and its rationale to a panel of Arkansas legislators.

PROJECT RESULTS/THE BILLS

Reserve Funds

One bill placed a 10 percent cap on fund balances of Arkansas's public schools. The cohort's research indicated that numerous Arkansas school districts had reserve fund balances well beyond the 10 percent recommended in the professional literature. In fact, some districts had the equivalent of 100 percent of

Table 1. Steps in Ethical Reasoning

1. What are the facts?
2. What is the ethical issue/problem?
3. Who are the claimants and in what way are you obligated to each one?
4. What do you think each of these claimants would prefer that you do regarding this issue?
5. Focus on each action with the following lenses:
    a. Utility: Is the greatest good for the greatest number achieved and do benefits outweigh costs?
    b. Individual Rights—Are fundamental, basic human rights and dignity respected and protected?
    c. Equal Treatment—Is the action fair in that burdens and benefits are evenly distributed?
    d. Categorical Imperative: Are you willing to make your decision a rule or policy that you and others in your situation can follow in similar situations in the future?
    e. Ethic of care: Are you fulfilling your duties as a "caregiver"?
    f. Can you live with this decision?

their operating budget in reserve. Furthermore, in the 2001–2002 fiscal year, fund balances totaled $519 million, a figure representing just over 20 percent of statewide operating budgets.

Athletic Deficits

Another bill addressed deficit spending in university athletics. The cohort's research revealed that of the five universities in the state that had a comprehensive athletic program (football in particular) only one university had an athletic surplus annually. The others had losses in 2003–2004 ranging from $342,222 to $1.5 million. The cohort constructed a bill that eliminated the use of profits from auxiliary services to address deficit spending in athletics at Arkansas's universities. Presently, state law allows $450,000 from general and unrestricted educational funds as well as profits from auxiliary services to be used to offset the deficit spending in athletics. The cohort reasoned that $450,000 should be sufficient and that tapping auxiliary services' profits to any degree desired takes funding away from programs such as housing and student services.

Instructional Time

A third bill was directed at the erosion of instructional time in Arkansas's 9–12 schools by extracurricular and interscholastic activities (i.e., sporting teams leaving school early to travel to athletic events, bands going to competitions, students leaving classes to decorate for the prom, etc.). The cohort found that 30–54 percent of instructional time was lost per month at the schools studied for this project. The rather lengthy bill limited these activities' intrusions into instructional time and established penalties for exceeding those limits.

CONCOMITANT ISSUES

An interesting caveat concerned the bill regarding deficit spending for inter-collegiate athletics, mainly football. A group decided to propose an amendment to a law allowing profits from auxiliary enterprises to be used to offset athletic deficit spending. The proposed amendment disallowed the use of these profits. Several cohort members were employed by the university in auxiliary enterprises and were concerned that addressing this very controversial issue might have impact on their careers at the university. There was considerable discussion on whether or not to advance this bill to the panel of legislators. The decision was to present the amendment.

In addition, the professor of the course initiated a discussion on whether or not it was ethical to be using a university class to perhaps stop the university's practice of using profits from auxiliary enterprises to address increasing deficit spending in the athletic department. Football had recently become a Division I program, a move considered to be an important stage in the university's efforts to become a research institution. If the cohort's bill were to be championed by a legislator and were to eventually become law, the university would almost assuredly have to abandon Division I status. The cohort decided that to create and present this bill was not unethical and was within the guidelines of academic freedom as noted in the AAUP's Code of Ethics. Since producing leaders who would be responsible risk-takers was one of the Ed.D. program's goals, the professor agreed with the cohort's decision's to present the bill to the panel of legislators.

THE PANEL'S RESPONSE

The panel consisted of a state representative, a state senator, as well as the staff attorney in the Legislative Counsel's Office within the Bureau of Legislative Research. They listened intently to the cohort's presentations, asked numerous questions, judged the bills to be well-written, concluded that they addressed serious issues that deserved attention, and "hoped the bills would find sponsors." In other words, all the bills were too controversial for the two legislators to champion.

EVALUATION OF THE PROJECT

Among student reactions to the project were the following:

- "Too realistic!"
- "One of the best assignments I've ever experienced."
- "This was the most intense work that I've had to do in any graduate course."
- "Very real world. I was not comfortable with being bound to decisions made by a group that I often disagreed with. I guess that's politics."

The professor of the course judged the project to have several positive characteristics:

1. Makes real the politics of resolving important educational issues,
2. Achieves authenticity to escape the typical "Ivory Tower" allegations,
3. Applies use of quantitative and qualitative research methods,
4. Seeks solutions for several crucial educational issues,
5. Utilizes all levels of Bloom's Taxonomy,
6. Sharpens students' oral and written communication skills,
7. Requires interactions between students and "main-team" stakeholders, and
8. Breathes life into making ethical decisions in a real situation, not just in a case study, and adds—at least from the perspectives of some of the students—an element of risk.

Therefore, the 2005 cohort will undertake the same project.

REFERENCES

Council of Chief State School Officers. (1996). *Interstate school leaders licensure consortium: Standards for school leaders.* Washington, DC: Author.

National Policy Board for Educational Administration. (2002). *Standards for advanced programs in educational leadership.* Arlington, VA: Author.

Supervising Novice Administrators: Purposeful Trust Building through Mentoring

PATTI CHANCE

RECRUITING QUALITY LEADERS TO FILL A GROWING NUMBER of administrative vacancies in America's schools is becoming a heightened concern as schools continue to be placed under increased scrutiny in the form of legislation and policies which demand more measures of accountability for student performance. Even though the importance of instructional leadership as an essential ingredient for increasing student achievement has been well documented over three decades of research (Blase and Blase, 1998; Edmonds, 1982; Harris, 1998; Lezotte, 1994; Purkey and Smith, 1983), continued professional development for school leaders has been largely ignored in educational reform initiatives. In a recent study of the concerns and perceptions of principals about their jobs, DiPaola and Tschannen-Moran (2003) found that principals were most concerned about their role as an instructional leader and almost all principals stated they needed more professional development in this area.

Furthermore, university principal preparation programs have been criticized for their apparent disconnect between theory and practice. Recommendations for principal preparation reforms call for increased use of field experiences and mentoring programs that match novice administrators with experienced principals (Griffiths, Stout, and Forsyth, 1988; Milstein, 1993; Playko and Daresh, 1993). Thus, a paradox is faced in the preparation of principals as instructional leaders. On one hand, aspiring and novice principals need experiences in the realities of the practicing principal's job. On the other hand, those already in the job believe they need additional professional development in the area of instructional leadership. Therefore, in order to provide quality field experiences for aspiring and novice administrators that will likely increase their capacity for instructional leadership, principal preparation programs must also address the profes-

sional development of supervising principals who serve as mentors to new leaders.

Mentoring refers to a relationship between an experienced role model and a novice, where the mentor guides the professional development of a lesser-experienced individual. Hersey and Hersey (1990) compared mentoring to coaching and stated that a mentor observes, provides feedback, probes, listens, analyzes, and gives suggestions to a protégé in a non-threatening environment. The term mentor comes from Homer's Odyssey, where Odysseus entrusted the care of his family to Mentor, who served as a teacher and guide to Odysseus' son, Telemachus. A mentor is commonly thought of as a trusted adviser, friend, and teacher, who offers wisdom, encouragement, and support for another less experienced person. Thus, mentoring encompasses two interrelated processes: (a) trust building and (b) reflection. This article explores the connections between trust and reflection based upon a two-part study of mentoring in a university-school district partnership for principal preparation.

MENTORING NEW PRINCIPALS

Playko (1995) identified four benefits that aspiring school leaders gain from the mentoring process. First, by working with a mentor, preservice administrators gain practical insights and understandings about the job of the school administrator. Second, protégés gain self-confidence about their competence to effectively perform in an administrative position. Third, mentoring assists people in becoming socialized to a new professional role. The socialization process involves an understanding of the formal and informal systems within the organization, such as learning the key people in the organization and community and the unwritten expectations about professional conduct or duties. Finally, the mentoring relationship leads to continued networking and help in future administrative placements.

Muse, Thomas, and Wasden (1992) warned of several potential problems with mentoring in administrator preparation programs. Among these were:

1. good principals may not be good mentors;
2. mentors may be too protective and controlling;
3. interns may receive only a limited perspective from a mentor; and
4. interns may become carbon copies of mentors.

These researchers further suggested that careful selection of mentors and ongoing professional development for mentors can mediate these potential pitfalls.

Professional development for mentors requires that mentors receive initial training as well as continued support through ongoing meetings to reinforce important concepts and practices of mentoring. In describing an initial mentor training program, Daresh and Playko (1991) identified five domains that provide a foundation for effective mentoring. The first is an orientation to mentoring which includes an operational definition of mentoring and outlines the benefits and concerns associated with the process. The second domain deals with instructional leadership, specifically emphasizing reflection as a tool for guiding the aspiring leader. Human relation skills related to adult learning and mentor process skills are the third and fourth domains. Mentor process skills include problem-solving strategies, interviewing techniques, and observation techniques. The final domain involves a review of specific goals of the mentoring program which are unique to the local context.

Effective mentors consciously move their protégés from dependence to autonomy and actively engage protégés in reflection (Barnett, 1995). Reflection between a mentor and protégé involves guiding and coaching through questioning that allow the protégé to examine and reconsider problems of practice (Schon, 1983). The reflective process of questioning and discussion also involves the examination and application of concepts and theories as frames of reference for effective practice. Barnett (1995) noted that experts use principles, concepts, and theories when solving problems whereas novices tend not to identify deep structures or underlying principles which may be applicable to a situation or problem of practice.

CONTEXT OF THE STUDY

The University of Nevada Las Vegas is situated in one of the fastest growing cities in America. Located in the most southern part of Nevada, Las Vegas is the metropolitan center of the Clark County School District, which encompasses approximately 8,000 square miles. Over the last ten years, the school district has experienced steady growth of approximately 8 percent each year, adding 12,000 to 15,000 students to its rolls each year and building an average of one new school each month. As student rolls continued to climb and new schools were erected, the district also expected that approximately half of their current administrative personnel would retire. This is the backdrop in which the University of Nevada Las Vegas (UNLV), in 1996, began a collaborative effort with the Clark County School District (CCSD) to prepare administrators ready to fill some of the 500 anticipated administrative openings.

The collaborative program has been in place for nine years, accepting one cohort class each academic year. Students participate in a two-year curriculum that integrates field experiences and course work. A key component of wedding theory and practice is the assignment of each student to a practicing principal who serves as his/her mentor throughout the program. Mentors supervise students' field experiences and internships. Mentors are considered to be master principals and are nominated by their supervisors or university faculty. Final selection of mentor principals is made by the district's regional superintendents. Once selected, mentors attend an initial training session that provides an overview of the program and introduces the concepts of mentoring and coaching. Expectations for mentors' supervision of field experiences are outlined. In addition, the training presents an explanation and rationale for the sequencing of field experiences and how these relate to concepts and theories presented in university course work. Ongoing communication is maintained through meetings with university faculty and mentors held throughout the year. Meetings consist of program updates, discussion of students' course work, expectations for mentors' supervision of field experiences, as well as special topics for professional development of mentor principals.

As a part of ongoing evaluation of the program, a study was undertaken in the fourth year of the program to determine the strengths and weaknesses of the mentoring process as perceived by mentors and protégés. Based on findings from this initial study, interventions and adjustments were made in the program and a follow-up evaluation was conducted after implementation of these changes.

INITIAL STUDY

Graduating students and their mentors were surveyed regarding their perceptions of mentor-protégé relationships, benefits and challenges of the mentoring process, and the impact of mentoring on the students' preparedness for administrative practice. In addition, in-depth exit interviews were conducted with program graduates and with randomly selected principals. The average length of time that the twenty principals surveyed had served as mentors was three years. Thus, these principals' perceptions and feedback were based on a solid, working knowledge of the program and the mentoring process.

The survey of mentors and protégés consisted of open-ended questions regarding the mentoring process. Respondents were asked to comment about the mentor-protégé relationship in terms of benefits and challenges to themselves and to the other party. Mentors were asked to reflect upon changes they noticed in their protégés over the course of two years and whether they felt the protégé was ready to assume an administrative position. Protégés were asked to describe how they had changed as a result of their involvement in the program and to identify factors they believed influenced those changes. Protégés were also asked to assess their own readiness for an administrative position. Interviews provided additional data and allowed for expanded responses and deeper reflection regarding perceptions of the mentoring process.

Specifically, a primary purpose of the study was to determine the extent to which mentors and students overtly considered the mentoring and learning processes, such as coaching, questioning, and reflecting. A content analysis of data was conducted in which responses were categorized into themes related to the benefits of mentoring to students as identified by Playko (1995) and references to metacognitive processes involved with mentoring. Data were classified into six categories reflecting respondents' references to

1. protégés gaining insight into the job of the administrator;
2. increasing self confidence of protégés;
3. protégés' socialization into the administrative role;
4. networking and help from mentors' for protégés' future placements;
5. overt and conscious attention to reflection in the mentoring process; and
6. overt and conscious attention to the application of theory and concepts to problems of practice.

Responses from students and mentors strongly confirmed two of the four benefits described by Playko. Eighty-six percent of the students surveyed and 100 percent of the mentors surveyed indicated that the mentoring process gave aspiring principals insight into the job of an administrator. This was further confirmed through student interviews, in which 63 percent mentioned this benefit in some way during the exit interview. Students' increase in self-confidence was the strongest benefit noted, with 100 percent of both mentors and students indicating such in the survey and 95 percent of students relating this in the exit interviews. Protégés' socialization into the administrative role was commented on to a lesser degree. Fifty percent of mentor and student survey responses alluded to the concept of socialization in terms of understanding the formal and informal workings of the district. However, in student exit interviews, 84 percent discussed socialization more overtly especially in terms of gaining a better understanding of the "bigger picture" of the school from the principal's viewpoint. A little over half of the protégés, in both surveys and interviews, discussed the idea of networking and continued help from their mentors. This was mentioned by only two (17 percent) of the mentor principals.

The reflective process and the application of theory to problems of practice were weakly reflected in the data. Fifty-eight percent of student survey responses alluded to the process of reflection, although only 11

Table 1. Percent of Respondents Referencing Themes Related to Benefits to Protégés and Metacognitive Processes

	Student Survey	Student Interviews	Mentor Survey
Benefits to Protégés			
Insight Into Job	86%	63%	100%
Increasing Self Confidence	100%	95%	100%
Socialization Into Administrative Role	50%	84%	50%
Networking for Future Placements	50%	50%	17%
Metacognitive Processes			
Reflection	58%	11%	9%
Application of Theory to Practice	14%	47%	17%

percent discussed this during their interviews. Only one mentor principal overtly referred to the reflective process. The application of theory to problems of practice was mentioned by 14 percent of the students in the survey but was discussed by 47 percent during their interviews. Two (17 percent) of the mentors surveyed touched upon merging theory and practice.

PRELIMINARY FINDINGS

Findings from this study strongly support the body of research literature that suggests that field-based experiences with mentor practitioners positively contributes to the preparation of preservice administrators. From both students' and mentors' perspectives, the mentor-protégé relationship clearly resulted in preservice administrators gaining insight into and deeper understanding of the principal's job and unquestionably had a positive influence on protégés' self-confidence to fulfill an administrative role. Protégés and mentors also recognized that the mentoring process assisted preservice administrators in becoming socialized to the formal and informal systems and expectations of the organization, although this factor was not consistently identified by either students or mentors. Similarly, the benefit of the mentor-protégé relationship in regard to helping the preservice administrator develop a network that could influence a future administrative appointment was not uniformly addressed. Students tended to be more cognizant of this aspect of the relationship than did mentors. Perhaps this can be attributed to the protégés' focus on their purposeful preparation for career advancement.

Most revealing was the analysis of data regarding the metacognitive processes of reflection and application of theory to practice. While the initial study indicated that for the most part protégés and mentors had developed strong relationships, the data suggested that there was little recognition of reflective dialogue as part of the supervision process. Typical comments from protégés who indicated strong relationships with their mentors were:

> I trust him.
> It will be everlasting—very trustworthy.
> [My mentor] tells you the truth.
> She believes in me.

Mentors' responses indicated almost no conscious awareness or intent to engage protégés in deliberate reflection about field experiences or to make connections between the university's teaching of fundamental concepts and theory to the problems of practice.

Moreover, while student responses suggested that some protégés were consciously reflecting and conceptually linking theory to problems of practice, these processes were not apparently purposeful or intentional.

That neither mentors nor students were generally participating in reflection as a part of the mentoring, or teaching, process suggested a significant gap in this principal preparation program. The purposes for utilizing mentors in the preparation of school leaders go beyond the notion of on-the-job training. Mentoring should help engage the learner not only in the ways things are done but, more importantly, in understanding how and why leaders' behaviors influence organizational outcomes and consequently impact student achievement. Reflection is a critical component in the process of supervision as a way to help novice administrators apply concepts and theory to problem solving and leading organizations through effective change. Results from this study affirmed Leithwood and Steinbach's (1992) findings that "on-the-job experience is a slow and unreliable way to improve problem-solving expertise" (p. 341).

PROGRAM MODIFICATIONS

It was evident that program modifications were needed to increase the reflective dialogue between mentor and protégé. While the reflective process was emphasized to mentors through their professional development and to students through coursework assignments, it seemed that more formal procedures for reflection needed to be developed. This was done by shifting more responsibility for reflection to the protégés through specific reflective requirements in their field experiences, internship, and portfolio development. In addition, findings from the program evaluation study were shared with mentor principals in an effort to heighten their awareness of the reflective process.

FORMALIZING REFLECTION: THE INTERNSHIP

The collaborative principal preparation program requires a culminating internship of approximately 150 contact hours under the supervision of the mentor principal. Utilizing a needs assessment for leadership development (Buckner, Flanary, Hersey, and Hersey, 1997), students evaluate their strengths and weaknesses before embarking on their internship experience. This reflective process is used to guide students in developing an individualized plan for their internship. Through dialogue with their mentor principals and the faculty internship director, students design an Individual Administrator Development Plan (IADP). The IADP outlines specific field-based activities and learning opportunities in which the intern will engage. In planning their internships, students organize proposed field-based experiences by categorizing activities according to the six broad Interstate School Leaders Licensure Consortium (ISLLC) standards (Council of Chief State School Officers, 1996). Thus, students must design their internship in such a way that they are involved in problems of practice related to (a) vision development, (b) student learning and staff professional growth, (c) management and operations, (d) family and community relations, (e) integrity and ethics of leadership, and (f) influencing the larger political, social, economic, legal, and cultural context. In addition, students are encouraged to include a variety of activities related to various leadership roles, skills, and processes. In this regard, students are asked to consider the 21 domains of principal leadership developed by the National Commission for the Principalship (1990) when planning their internship. This planning process encourages students to actively reflect upon the relationships, standards, leadership constructs taught through university coursework, and applications to practice.

During their internships, students are required to keep a log of their field-based experiences. In order to promote reflective practice, the on-line form requires students to indicate (a) the dates and number of hours involved in the activity; (b) the ISLLC standard(s) addressed; (c) the domains of leadership involved; (d) the intern's level of involvement (i.e., active, interactive, inactive); and (e) answers to six specific reflective questions. The six questions designed to engage students in reflection are

1. What was done?
2. Why was the task necessary?
3. What did you do (in sequence)?
4. What problems did you encounter?
5. How were they resolved?
6. What did you learn?

REFLECTION THROUGH PORTFOLIO DEVELOPMENT

A culminating project of the internship is the compilation of a portfolio that parallels the student's IADP. Like the IADP, portfolios are organized by the six ISLLC standards. Students select at least two artifacts for each standard that demonstrate their understanding and application of the standard in a leadership situation. Artifacts are defined as concrete examples of leadership accomplishments or experiences that demonstrate expertise or ability.

Each artifact is prefaced with a reflective summary which presents a rationale for the selection of the artifacts, describes the activity(ies), and analyzes the processes of leadership in light of how the selected activity(ies) relates to the standard and what the intern gained in terms of professional growth. Students are instructed in a reflective process suggested by Brown and Irby (1997) which integrates reflective practice into the portfolio development process through a five-step cycle.

At the end of the internship, each student presents his/her portfolio in a meeting with the mentor principal and educational leadership faculty. While each student plans a formal presentation of his/her portfolio, an important component of the presentation is the informal discussion that ensues. A reflective dialogue invariably emerges in which the mentor principal engages the intern in conversation that helps the intern place the experience into a larger context of leadership. The faculty member's role becomes that of teacher in which the faculty member (a) affirms the student's analysis of the experience by elaborating on theory-practice connections and (b) encourages the intern to make critical analyses through probing questions.

FOLLOW-UP STUDY

A year after implementation of the formalized reflection pieces, follow-up evaluation was conducted through the use of focus group interviews with mentors. One purpose of the focus group inquiry was to explore mentors' perceptions of the supervision process, especially in terms of the relationship between trust building and reflection. Thus, mentor principals were asked to discuss instructional supervision, trust development, reflective processes, and their own growth and development as a mentor. Principals who participated in the focus groups act as mentors, not only for this collaborative program, but also for new principals in the district and for teachers in their schools who are aspiring leaders.

Participants' responses regarding their behaviors as mentors fell largely into three domains: (a) modeling desirable behaviors; (b) guiding reflection through questioning; and (c) providing time to develop an effective mentor-protégé relationship. These themes emerged in all areas of discussion, whether principals were talking about instructional leadership, developing trust, or their own professional growth.

Deliberating on instructional leadership, one mentor commented:

> Model it. You have to show them what it truly means to be an instructional supervisor. You have to show them it means being in the classrooms on a regular basis. It is talking to teachers on a regular basis. It is that whole process, not just going in and writing up an observation.

Another stated that the relationship was not hierarchical. It's "not that I'm supervisor and you're here. It's that we really are a team. We have to work on it as a team."

In the conversations with mentor principals, the issue of trust was directly explored in relation to instructional leadership and supervision. Bryk and Schneider's (2002) study of Chicago schools found that in schools that were improving student achievement or that had demonstrated effectiveness, there were high levels of trust. Bryk and Schneider proposed a three-level theory of trust, which they termed relational trust. They explained that social exchanges in schools are organized around a distinct set of role relationships, such as teacher-student, teacher-parent, and teacher-principal. They found that there must be synchrony in the mutual expectations and role obligations in order for trust to grow and be maintained. Furthermore, they noted that in most cases role relationships are unequal, where one role is inherently more powerful than the other, and it is up to the person in the more powerful role to act in a way that reduces the other's vulnerability. Mentors' responses regarding trust building confirmed this notion. One mentor noted:

> I think you need to open up to people and show your human side to people. When you walk down the hallway, you're not just Mr. So and So or Mrs. So and So. You're [Tom] or [Mary] and you talk about your children and they start to get the humanization of it all. And then you open up to each other. And I think that sharing goes on, and that sharing builds a trust between one another—that you're not sitting on a pedestal by yourself.

Another mentor's comment supports the idea of multiple relationships that work toward building trust:

> Our leadership style is going to come through in your everyday interactions as you walk through classrooms and how children respond to you, how support staff respond to you, how the custodian responds to you. I think all of those things are key elements of trust. Are

they apprehensive? Are they comfortable? Will they share?

In discussing risk-taking, one mentor described how she works to reduce others' vulnerability:

> Part of taking a risk is urging them to do something that is different, knowing that you'll always be there to support that. So there's a safety net. . . . If you fail or it doesn't go right, we're still going to be there to support you and say it's okay.

Mentors noted that trust building is also developed over time. As one principal said, "Trust is not issued."

Certainly, coaching models of supervision (e.g., Costa and Garmston, 2002) emphasize that trust is essential to improving performance through reflective practice. Furthermore, current thinking on school reform emphasizes community building as a critical component for school improvement (Reeves, 2002; Schmoker, 1999; Sergiovanni and Starratt, 1998). Most of this literature stresses the importance of empowering others, but trust building is a reciprocal relationship. It involves building dense relational ties (Coleman, 1990) and communication networks (Rogers and Argarwala-Rogers, 1976), where communication is defined as a continuous loop between the source and the receiver. One participant described the role communication plays in trust when he said:

> Communication and dialogue back and forth is the key, whatever stage you're at. You can't be the type of person who says, "Here's a job; go down the hall and do it." . . . You become co's—you're co-principals, you're co-leaders. And you do things together. You communicate before, during, and after. The communication is the important process. . . . Communication has to keep flowing back and forth for both parties to grow. We grow as mentors by talking to protégés because the best learners are the people who teach others. We as principals learn more by teaching others.

Thus, the protégé is not the exclusive recipient of the effects of mentoring. The mentor also changes as a result of a trusting relationship with open communication focused on reflection about practice. One mentor noted, "For me, self-reflection has been huge. The longer I have been doing it, the more comfortable I am giving it away." Another described how she transferred reflective practice to a wider audience:

> The reflective piece is the greatest change for me. When you started emphasizing that in our gatherings,

I started using it. Not just with administrators and potential administrators, but with teachers. I found it to be a very powerful tool . . . probably one of the most significant changes in my mentoring style.

SUMMARY AND IMPLICATIONS

The results of the initial part of this study suggested that mentors and protégés understood the importance of trust building as fundamental to the learning process. However, without the conscious and overt focus upon reflection as a tool for professional growth, dialogue between mentor and protégé could be characterized as on-the-job training rather than professional growth and improvement. Formal procedures for reflection and emphasis on questioning and communication strategies provided tools for both mentors and protégés to focus upon professional growth in a safe and trustworthy relationship. Thus, trust building centered upon dialogue about connecting classroom learning to administrative practice. Through this process, both mentor and protégé experienced professional growth, each projecting their own perspective and considering the other's perspective. Mentoring

involved purposeful trust building, and reflection became a tool for teaching and learning.

The reciprocity of trust building and reflection, however, goes beyond the mentor-protégé relationship. In this case, the role of the university faculty might also be considered. The supervision of novice administrators is not the sole purview of the mentor. Relationships of trust must also be developed between university faculty and students and between faculty and mentors. These relationships, coupled with reflective processes focused on professional growth, may result in long-term institutional effects, i.e., schools led by instructional leaders who practice reflective processes with their faculty for school improvement.

The following diagram illustrates the outcomes of purposeful trust building and reflection through relationships among mentor principals, novice administrators, and university faculty.

Mentors and novices make connections between classroom learning and practice. Dialogue between mentors and university faculty results in professional development for mentors and sharing of best practices from the field. Exchanges between university faculty

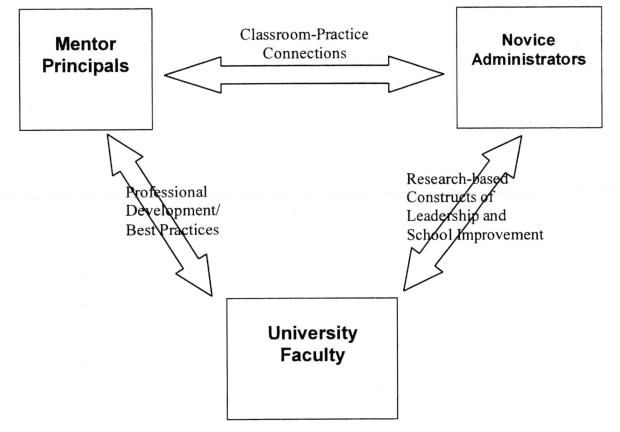

Figure 1. Outcomes of Reflective Practice and Trust Building

and novice administrators revolve around research-based constructs of education leadership and school improvement. All parties are affected when there is purposeful trust building focused on professional growth through reflective practice. As dense relational ties and communication networks become established, it would be expected that trust will be maintained and leadership performance will increase.

REFERENCES

Barnett, B. G. (1995). Developing reflection and expertise: Can mentors make the difference? *Journal of Educational Administration, 33*(5), 45–59.

Blase, J., and Blase, J. (1998). *Handbook of instructional leadership: How really good principals promote teaching and learning.* Thousand Oaks, CA: Corwin.

Brown, G., and Irby, B. J. (1997). *The principal portfolio.* Thousand Oaks, CA: Corwin.

Bryk, A. S., and Schneider, B. (2002). *Trust in schools: A core resource for improvement.* New York: Russell Sage Foundation.

Buckner, K. G., Flanary, R. A., Hersey, L. G., and Hersey, P. W. (1997). *Mentoring and coaching: Developing educational leaders.* Reston, VA: National Association of Secondary School Principals.

Coleman, J. S. (1990). *Foundations of social theory.* Cambridge, MA: The Belknap Press of Harvard University Press.

Costa, A. L., and Garmston, R. J. (2002). *Cognitive coaching: A foundation for renaissance schools.* Norwood, MA: Christopher Gordon Publishers.

Council of Chief State School Officers. (1996). *Interstate school leaders licensure consortium: Standards for school leaders.* Washington, DC: Author.

Daresh, J. C., and Playko, M. A. (1991). Preparing mentors for school leaders. *Journal of Staff Development, 12*(4), 24–27.

DiPaola, M., and Tschannen-Moran, M. (2003). The principalship at a crossroads: A study of the conditions and concerns of principals. *NASSP Bulletin, 87*(634), 43–65.

Edmonds, R. (1982). Programs for school improvement: An overview. *Educational Leadership, 40*(1), 4–11.

Griffiths, D. E., Stout, R. T., and Forsyth, P. B. (1988). *Leaders for America's schools: The report and papers of the National Commission on Excellence in Educational Administration.* Berkeley, CA: McCutcheon.

Harris, B. (1998). Paradigms and parameters of supervision in education. In G. R. Firth and E. F. Pajak (Eds.), *Handbook of research on school supervision* (pp. 1–37). New York: Simon & Schuster Macmillian.

Hersey, L. G., and Hersey, P. W. (1990). *Mentoring and coaching: Developing educational leaders.* Reston, VA: National Association of Secondary School Principals.

Leithwood, K., and Steinbach, R. (1992). Improving the problem-solving of school administrators: Theory and practice. *Education and Urban Society, 24*(3), 317–345.

Lezotte, L. W. (1994). The nexus of instructional leadership and effective schools. *The School Administrator, 51*(6), 20–23.

Milstein, M. M. (1993). *Changing the way we prepare educational leaders: The Danforth experience.* Newbury Park, CA: Corwin Press.

Muse, I. D., Thomas, G. J., and Wasden, F. D. (1992). Potential problems (and solutions) of mentoring in the preparation of school administrators. *Journal of School Leadership, 2*(3), 310–319.

National Commission for the Principalship. (1990). *Principals for our changing schools.* Fairfax, VA: Author.

Playko, M. A. (1995). Mentoring for educational leaders: A practitioner's perspective. *Journal of Educational Administration, 33*(5), 84–92.

Playko, M. A., and Daresh, J. C. (1993). Mentoring programs for aspiring administrators: An analysis of benefits to mentors. *ERS Spectrum, 11*(3), 12–16.

Purkey, S., and Smith, M. (1983). Effective schools: A review. *Elementary Journal, 83*, 427–452.

Reeves, D. B. (2002). *Holistic accountability: Serving students, schools, and community.* Thousand Oaks, CA: Corwin.

Rogers, E. M., and Argarwala-Rogers, R. (1976). *Communication in organizations.* New York: Free Press.

Schmoker, M. J. (1999). *Results: The key to continuous school improvement.* Alexandria, VA: Association for Supervision and Curriculum Development.

Schon, D. A. (1983). *The reflective practitioner: How professionals think in action.* New York: Basic Books.

Sergiovanni, T. J., and Starratt, R. J. (1998). *Supervision: A redefinition* (6th ed.). Boston: McGraw Hill.

Connecting the Dots: Online Instructional Design that Links to Leadership Abilities

Naomi Boyer

ONLINE INSTRUCTIONAL DESIGN LINKED TO LEADERSHIP ABILITIES

INSTRUCTIONAL DELIVERY (MEDIUM AND DESIGN) HAS BE-come a topic of debate within the field of educational leadership, which has online learning tagged as either bane or benefit to the development of leaders. Many argue that aspiring school administrators need to establish relationships and develop leadership traits that enforce humanistic principles, which is often negated by technology and distance. However, the current trend of many universities to venture into web-based, blended, and web-enhanced instruction has led to the creation of new online instructional frameworks that not only address content knowledge but also leadership competence. Technological skill can be merged with student-centered instruction to increase self-direction, time management, personal responsibility, reflection, communication skills, strategic planning, and organizational change.

CONNECTING THE DOTS

Design of online materials can provide the basic layout for leadership students to find personal pathways through a body of content, much like a large game of connect the dots. This does not refer to the game that has children moving from spot A to spot B and then on to spot C (this would relate much more to traditional professor-led models), but rather to a large square of dots in a 10x10 pattern that has one play against an opponent creating squares in a random fashion. Instead of playing *against the instructor* in this game, metaphorically the instructor provides the parameters and guidance via content, instructional design and interaction. This encourages students to follow their own prescribed learning path through the matrix creating *boxes* of learning as they travel around the grid. The owned self-designed knowledge then becomes much more valuable, meaningful and transforming than a simple task completion exercise that also lends itself to

problem solving, teaming, strategic planning, initiative, perseverance, and lifelong learning.

Therefore, the driving question for this paper explores the convergence between technological instruction (both delivery and content) and leadership capacity. In what ways does an online instructional design incorporating social, self-direction enhance leadership potential? The course content for this investigation was based on technology integration skills; leadership outcomes were integral components of this design rather than the primary focus. Therefore, this study examined both the content learning gains and the secondary leadership outcomes.

LEARNING CONTRACTS AND ASPIRING LEADERS

Adult learning theories of self-direction and andragogy establish the boundaries of socio-cultural and constructivist teaching methods in the described online instructional delivery. Self-directed learning has been defined as, " a process in which individuals take the initiative, with or without the help of others, in diagnosing their learning needs, formulating learning goals, identifying human and material resources for learning, choosing and implementing appropriate learning strategies, and evaluating learning outcomes" (Knowles, 1975, p. 18). The adult learning concept of andragogy includes key components of: (a) interaction, (b) task centeredness, (c) individualization, and (d) self-directedness (Knowles, 1986). These components are applicable to transformational adult learning regardless of the learning setting or instructional delivery method (Lane, 1997).

Knowles (1986) has suggested that adults have a deep psychological need to be self-directional and designing educational programs toward this end increases ownership of the learning experience. Evidence suggests that when "adults learn on their own initiative they learn more deeply and permanently than what they learn by being taught" (Knowles, 1986,

225

p. 27). Students who become empowered to control their own learning experience become transformed as individuals and therefore more engaged in their own learning process (Lane, 1997; Moore and Kearsley, 1996; Palloff and Pratt, 1999).

While self-direction has been considered a function of independent learning, the blending of self-direction with instructor guidance and social learning theory merges the concept of the individual with the collective, providing certain strategies and techniques that can be used in instructional practice. Traveling from an individual self-direction toward a concept of social, self-direction provides all of the value of active, constructed cognition as well as shared vision, language, and objectives. White and Weight (2000) argue that "working adults may be self-directed, but they also value the exchange of ideas and meaningful relations" (p. 43). These same meaningful relationships may also lead to deep knowledge construction with outcomes that far outweigh traditional instructional methods.

Frameworks for self-directed learning can be used as scaffolding that adapts and changes as learners ma-ture. This scaffolding can provide an academic structure to support a learner's plan as responsibility shifts from *teacher* to *learner*. These components, originally developed from Knowles (1975) work on self-direction, include: (a) self-diagnosis of needs, (b) learning contracts, and (c) continual reflection. Scaffold use begins with a *diagnostic instrument* to assess individual learner needs within a given body of knowledge (e.g., a professional development workshop, a formal course or an entire program). The students rate their current level of knowledge on objective statements that direct them to information that would enhance their learning. The second step in this process is the development of a *learning contract* with self-specified objectives, learning strategies, target dates (timeline), evidential products and external authentication. In the final phase of scaffold use signaled by completion of the learning contract, *reflective instruments* are introduced to assist in the process of assessing overall gained knowledge and personal reflection.

The learning contract example was designed by a group who chose to work on three group objectives

Learning Objective	Learning Strategies/Resources	Dates	Evidence of Learning	Authentication
1. Ability to identify, describe, and use data management systems.	1A: Attend Microsoft Access mini-workshop. 1B: Complete Microsoft Office Access Tutorial at the following web address: http://www .microsoft.com/office/using/tips /archives/wordtips.asp. 1C: Utilize Resource Pack A as a guide. Review all websites & provide feedback to group by May 28th.	1A: June 3, 2004 1B: June 3, 2004	1: Produce FCAT scores database report.	1: Mail and/or email CD of database and report samples to Professor.
2. Ability to identify, describe, and use publishing software.	2: Complete Print Shop (Multimedia) wizard.	2: June 11, 2004	2: Information brochure for TSSA technology standards (incorporating objective 2 and 3)	2A: Send copy of brochure as electronic file to all members of class for feedback (form to be attached). 2B: Send copy of brochure (with class feedback results) as electronic file to Professor. Note: The brochure will authenticate objective 3.
3. Ability to identify and respond to the basic technology standards as presented by TSSA (Technology Standards for School Administrators)	3A: Utilize Resource Pack D as a guide to include guiding questions for discussion in group discussion room. 3B: Review the following website: http://cnets.iste .org/tssal. **All Objectives:** Brainstorming	3A: Questions from Resource Pack D completed by June 11, 2004 3B: Brochure completed June 30, 2004	3A: Group discussion transcripts 3B: Each group member will submit a personal reflection paper.	3: Personal and group analysis of TSSA reflections

Figure 1. Sample learning contract showing format and level of detail

and two individual objectives (see Figure 1). A detailed listing of each category is included in the learning contract example that was submitted at the beginning of the course (two weeks into the semester). The students engaged in a negotiated process with the instructor regarding the appropriateness, completeness, and content of the designed learning contract, and used this scaffold as a pathway through the learning experience.

MODEL OF SOCIAL SELF-DIRECTED LEARNING

Many researchers interested in self-directed learning have utilized learning contract schematics to enhance adult, independent learning experiences (Aspin, Champman, Hatton, Sawano, 2001; Beitler, 2000; Doncaster, 2000; Greenwood, 2002–2003; Knowles, Holton and Swanson, 1998; Rossman, 2000; Vaughn, 2000; Waddell and Stephens, 2000; Wickett, 2000). Previous, research has also been done on the success of these tools with groups and learning communities. A model (see Figure 2) has been presented that addresses learning as a complex, dynamic system with individual input characteristics that mediate the process (cultural learning environment) and directly result in product (learning) outputs (Boyer, 2001; Boyer, 2003a; Boyer, 2003b; Boyer and Maher, 2003). The

model in Figure 2 emerged from online delivery of various content areas with adult, mature learners. As an instructional tool, this model appears to be quite successful in enhancing engagement, reducing isolation, minimizing/eliminating student attrition, and increasing work quality, particularly with educational leadership preparation populations.

Given the systems design of the model and the extensive data collection techniques, the instruments and protocols are best described in the following equation: *Input + Process + Output = Outcomes (I+P+O = Oc)*. This model is not intended to minimize the interdependence of the components that must be accounted for during data analysis. Each portion of the model *(I+P+O = Oc)* symbolizes mediating characteristics or events that must be considered myopically before looking at holistic relationships. This model has been used to design an online learning system that incorporates solid adult learning best practices (choice, variety of activity, learning style accommodation, engagement, etc.) with self-directed learning frameworks. The online instructional design does not homogenize learning; rather a process is provided personal and social growth inclusive of individuality and collective action. The input and output elements

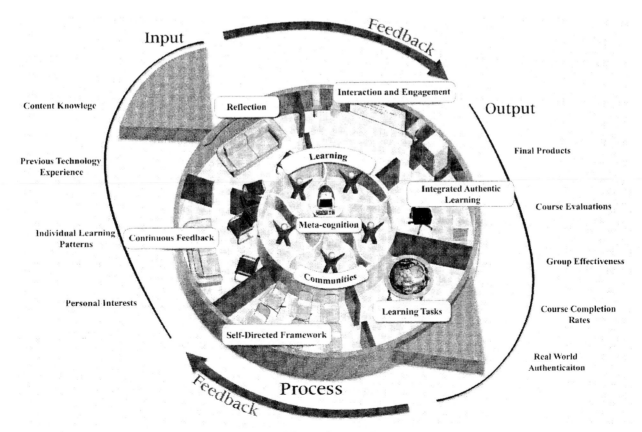

Figure 2. Model of Social Self-Direction Designed for Online Environments

merely support the assessment of mediating factors that contribute to the environmental constraints of the process dimension.

The outcomes of the model (not shown in figure above) represent an area of learning that is often ignored and yet quite important to the development of educational leadership competency. The outcomes of the system feedback (social, self-directed learning) are not comprised of an intentional cognition or learning enterprise. Instead, the outcomes of this model are defined as the resulting transformation and/or impact of the designed learning experience (including $I+P+O$ components) on both the individual and the contextual environment. In other words, the outcomes relate to the second order, collateral learning consequences beyond those objectives clearly stated in a syllabi or course description.

Instructional Design

The *connect the dot grid* symbolizes the instructional design used in this study. This curricular framework included many options, but still provided clearly established pathways. The described course had one full-day session at the beginning and one half-day sharing session at the end, integrated into the web-based design. The remainder of the instructional time (10 or 15 weeks) was spent online with continuous engagement and extensive interaction. Engagement was clearly defined as logging on to the course site at least three times a week, reading all discussion board messages in the appropriate forums, and responding to questions and/or requests. Students were encouraged to discuss topics and weekly resources with one another (included the instructor) and to check email at least three times a week.

The content within the course was available yet not mandated and centered on technology concepts and skills for aspiring school leaders. What did this look like in cyberspace? Students have multiple types of content available to them including readings, resources (electronic), websites, suggested activities, and practice assessments. Within these offerings, students found assessment rubrics, skills/concept lists that were necessary for knowledge demonstration, and suggested products. Despite the comprehensive availability of content, students utilized the frameworks of self-direction to chart their course through the content.

During an initial face-to-face orientation, students completed a diagnostic instrument that provided them with the accepted university content boundaries. Learning contracts were introduced and students practiced developing these within groups. Students selected their own objectives (within the course parameters), designed their own learning strategies and resources (pulling from the available online content described above), set their own timelines (within the timeframe of the course), established final products to demonstrate selected objectives, and selected individuals in their external environments (schools, communities, families, etc.) to provide documented feedback on their work (see Figure 3). Course requirements established the number of acceptable individual and group objectives.

Each of the steps described above provided an extension beyond the task itself and were completed individually and as group actions. For instance, the selection of objectives encouraged individuals to think about what is meaningful in their own lives within a content area. Students "owned" the material and content for that semester and met their individual learning needs. Through the self-design of a learning strategy and resource list, students considered individual/group learning preferences and anticipated the personal steps that were necessary to learn the identified skill. Target completion dates were determined that anticipate life events and set a timeline for successful time management. Designing evidential products provided the opportunity for students to demonstrate knowledge and connect learning to real, authentic products that have an impact not only on their learning but also on the world around them. By authenticating work products in the external community, students made their skills and knowledge a shared activity which provided recognition, personal confidence, and the possibility of implementation on a larger scale.

The tools for completing the process described above were available in the online course and received considerable attention during a full-day, face-to-face orientation session. During this day students were introduced and trained on how to use the University adopted courseware tool, Blackboard 6.0 (WebCT was used for the first four semesters), which included the course content, interaction tools (discussion, chat, whiteboard, and email), student homepages (developed by the students as part of course requirements), and other online course components. Students were also given a learning patterns profile and an activity to become familiar with the content during this initial session.

The learning contract activities that were completed during the first session initiated the learners to the group collaboration process. Student copies of

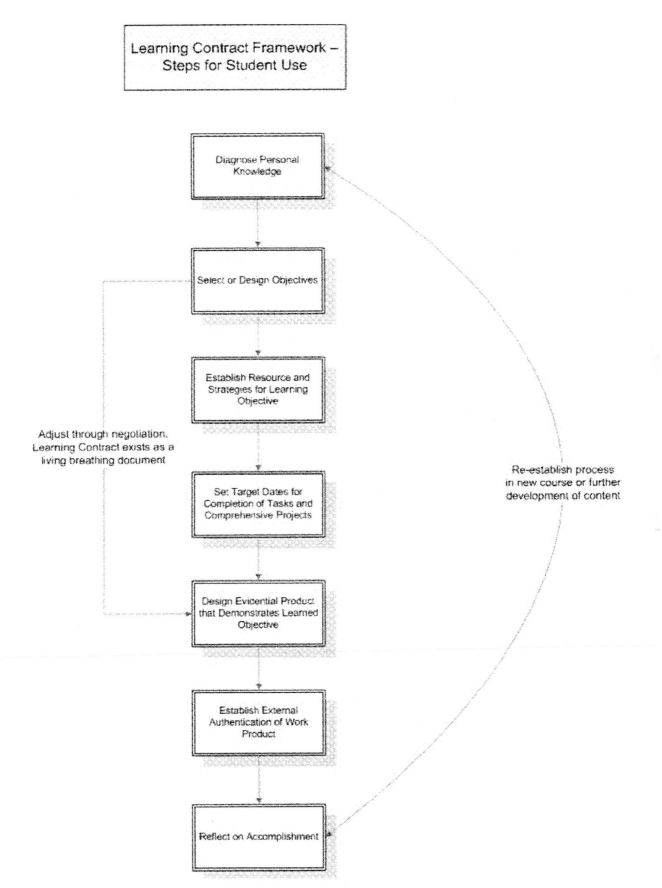

Figure 3.   Learning contract process used in instructional designs

these learning contracts were submitted after the first week of class to gain feedback and instructor guidance. Final copies based upon feedback and any additional changes were submitted two weeks into the class, providing students with a "map" of the learning that continued throughout the semester. The instructional design and course format provides a dimensional "playing board" and environment for student opportunity.

METHOD

The model described above has undergone extensive revision and consideration using design-based research guidelines. The model previously described in Figure 2 is a complex and dynamic system of individual and group learning. Such a model is appropriate to explore within the design-based research method (Sloane and Gorard, 2003). The three main stages of model design identified by Sloane and Gorard are: (a) model formulation, (b) estimation or fit and (c) model validation. Design-based research is particularly appropriate during the initial stages of this model formulation since it serves to identify the aspects of social, self-directed learning model outcomes that are linked to the leadership potential and environmental impact that are identified in the research question for this study. The question previously noted is as follows: In what ways does the instructional design incorporating social, self-direction enhance leadership potential?

The design-based research methodology addresses metaprocesses that can account for the complex environmental issues associated with learning. Cobb, Confrey, diSessa, Lehrer, and Schauble (2003) explain that "design experiments therefore constitute a means of addressing the complexity that is a hallmark of educational settings" (p. 9). Given the complexity of the model, this phase of the research has focused on the outcome knowledge gained from this approach and used mixed methods to analyze the output content knowledge and the collateral leadership potential gained from model implementation.

This phase of study utilized a mixed methods design that incorporated both statistical analyses with qualitative document analysis. The measure of course content knowledge acquisition (output) was based on the degree of growth noted by the difference in pretest and posttest scores (self-rated diagnostic instruments described below). The qualitative portion of the study included review of transcripts (pulled from email and discussion board postings) for emergent themes from which a coding matrix was designed. This coding matrix was then used by two raters to identify instances of these themes throughout the transcripts.

Sample

In the eight semesters of implementation of this online instructional design, there were 10 different course sections with a total of 203 students involved in the process. Each of the subjects were enrolled in the online Master's course, *Microcomputers for School Administrators*, a requirement of the Educational Leadership program. Participant ages ranged from 25–60 with a majority female representation as is the norm in the educational arena (see Table 1). Participants were involved in the study for a timeframe of 10–15 weeks depending upon the semester of enrollment.

Instrumentation and Reflective Feedback

They measured gathered information on the conceptual and skill based knowledge of the students at the beginning and end of the semester. The *Diagnostic Self-Rating Scale Needs Assessment (Pretest)* was designed by the researcher. This instrument was modeled on the learning objectives of the course in a format conceptually relevant to Knowles' (1986) learning contracts. While it has not undergone valid-

Table 1. Sample Designation, Activity Identification, and Gender Distribution for Global Study and Model Development

Semester	Additional Activity	Female	Male	Total
1	Content Pilot	23	6	29
2	Learning Contract Pilot	16	5	21
3	Content/LC Alignment—**Reflective Documents Begin**	22	5	27
4	Outcomes Assessment	20	2	22
5	Courseware to Blackboard	16	8	24
6	2 Simultaneous Sections—**Data available on both Pre/Post Assessment**	26	14	40
7	Weekly resources	12	5	17
8	2 Simultaneous Sections	18	5	23
	Total	153	50	203

Note that bolded text represents beginning point of data for this study which then extends to the final semester.

ity or reliability testing, the *Diagnostic Self-Rating Scale Needs Assessment (Pretest)* has been piloted and utilized in a variety of research settings. Students used this instrument to rate their level of knowledge on objectives and level of professional appropriateness of such an objective. The *Diagnostic Self-Rating Scale Outcomes (Posttest)* mirrors the initial diagnostic instrument, but was used by students to evaluate their knowledge after having gone through the formal/informal learning experience (outcomes).

The *Diagnostic Self-Rating Scale Needs Assessment (Pretest)* and the *Diagnostic Self-Rating Scale Outcomes (Posttest)* data were converted to numerical representations of student knowledge ratings (0 no knowledge—3 high knowledge). A t-test between pre and post values was used to indicate content knowledge gained via this instructional design. The results provided a snapshot of student perception of learning acquired as a result of this learning system.

Reflective tools and open-ended questions were used as a means for collecting information about the extended learning that might have occurred as a result of the system of social, self-directed learning as an instructional design. Students were asked reflective questions throughout the course (orientation reflection, update 1, update 2, and final update) and provided with tools to critically examine course performance and contribution (grading contracts and discussion analysis forms). This reflective component intentionally identifies student metacognition at the center of learning schematic and provides valuable information about student perception. These reflections were completed via email, the discussion board, submitted forms, and personal assessments. The open-ended reflection questions that were extrapolated from the overall data, for purposes of this study are listed below.

1. Reflection A: Provide a rundown on what you are working on, what you need further support on, and how you gauge your learning thus far.
2. Reflection B: Please provide some information about your individual progress, how you have been adapting to the format.
3. Reflection C: What did you learn in this class?

4. Reflection D: Did your work in this class have an impact in your surrounding settings (other classes, teaching assignments, school in general, household activities)? Please specify where and how you find yourself using your knowledge and skills.

These reflective instruments were reviewed for student stated examples of leadership traits that are noted as part of this semester-long learning process. Rather than identifying statements indicative of the learning of technological skills, specific leadership actions and behaviors were identified. Leadership programs often abstractly include leadership competencies/standards, but often have a difficult time extending the conceptual analysis to actual student behaviors. The emergent themes from this transcript analysis were used to demonstrate what, if any, leadership indicators resulted from the instructional design used in this study.

Findings

The described instructional design was not focused on a leadership curriculum. Therefore, it was important to determine if the intended learning did occur in the course. The measures (*Diagnostic Self-Rating Scale Needs Assessment* and *Diagnostic Self-Rating Scale Outcomes*) were completed by six course sections, over four semesters with complete data available from 79 subjects. Any student who completed and submitted one instrument (pre or post) but not the other was removed from the data set. The mean of the differences between the pre and post scores was 1.07. See Table 2 for additional descriptive information on both the pretest, posttest, and difference values. Given the results of the statistical analysis [t(78) = 18.44, p<.0001], learning did indeed occur. It is important to remember that these results were based on self-assessments of technology content knowledge, an area of study that often lacks initial knowledge, thus the highly significant difference between the pre/post measures.

An extensive list of personal learning was noted throughout the reflections which were available from the third semester to the eighth semester. See Table 3 for a list of the 23 themes that emerged from the reflections and the mean number (Rater 1 and Rater 2) of instance identification of these themes throughout

Table 2. Combined Descriptive Statistics on Pretest, Posttest, and the Difference Scores

	Mean	Standard Deviation	Median	Mode	Minimum	Maximum
Pretest	2.28	0.56	2.24	1.92	1.29	3.84
Posttest	3.36	0.42	3.42	4	2	4
Difference	1.07	0.52	1.08	0.92	−0.33	2.32

the text. An initially identified theme that was found to have less than two instances was removed from the coding schematic and listed as not generalizable across the sample. The theme with the least instance was the development of problem solving abilities, whereas co-operative work (group dynamics and teaming) had the most noted instances.

There were 13 categories that had more than 15 instances in the coded transcripts. It came as no surprise that the areas of confidence with technology, communication, research skills (library and web), and resource collection were noted as important learning obtained in the class. Given the content of the course and the online delivery, having learned about the use of electronic communication tools to enhance the faculty, student, and administration interaction was an obvious extended consequence. One student reflected:

> I personally learned a lot about the importance of keeping a schedule and an open line of communication. I also learned that flexibility is the name of the game in ANY educational setting.

However, a particularly intriguing theme was the enhanced ability to work collaboratively (included learning about group dynamics and teaming), which was identified an average of 39.5 times in the reflection documents. An example of an item that was coded within this category can be noted in the following statement:

> As much as I enjoy working and learning independently, the members of Mostly Sequential [group name] were supportive and real such that I am more apt to engage in future group experiences.

Other themes that were noted in excess of 15 instances include, the acquisition of self-knowledge, self-reflection abilities, personal responsibility for learning, time management skills, and the ability to take risks or step outside of traditional comfort zones (research skills using the library and web, confidence with technology, and cooperative also included but previously mentioned). An example of a statement that relates to both technology confidence and risk taking is as follows:

> The biggest impact for me was my attitude toward technology. Whereas before technology was a foe, it is now a formidable beast to be conquered and I'm sharpening my sword!

The other identified themes embedded in the text (<15 instances) also included other important leadership behaviors. For instance, the ability to multi-task, develop organizational skills, empower self and others, plan strategically and adapt were found throughout the reflective documents. Each of these themes

Table 3. Coding Themes and Number of Instances Identified in the Reflection Analysis

Identified Leadership Themes	Mean Number of Instance Identification
Problem Solving	5
Multi-Tasking	5.5
Developing a Vision—Awareness of the Bigger Picture	6
Organization Skills	6
Flexibility	6.5
Strategy Design for Successful Work Completion	6.5
Ability to Develop Others	7
Adaptability	7
Strategic Planning	7
Empowerment of Self	7.5
Ability to Empower Others	9
Resource Management	10
Communication	11
Resource Collection	12.5
Life-Long Learning	14
Perseverance	14
Risk-Taking	15
Research Skills—Library and Web	16
Confidence with Technology	16.5
Time Management	17.5
Personal Responsibility for Learning	18.5
Self-Knowledge/Self-Reflection	20
Cooperative Work/Group Dynamics/Teaming	39.5

relate directly to the learning that extends beyond course objectives and into the area of leadership potential.

CONCLUSIONS

The findings above indicate that instructional design incorporating social self-direction did indeed enhance leadership behaviors and potential skill, while still attending to the course content. These findings in no way suggest that this learning process was an easy one for students. Rather, many students report extreme discomfort in the course structure at the beginning of the course. However, the majority of students indicate an appreciation of the format, content, and learning experience by the end of the semester. For instance, one student wrote:

> I had never taken an internet based class before but thought it would be cool. After our first meeting in May I was ready to run for cover and never take a web based class again! Well I stuck it out . . . and I'm glad I did. I learned how to deal with my learning discomfort as well as my learning style.

Another student writes a similar reflection:

> I felt very uncomfortable at the beginning of this course with the apparent unstructured learning style; however, looking back, I think I've become more adaptable—this course forced me to do that. I enjoyed being able to go to a site and follow my desires instead of having a prescribed path.

The online instructional design was one of great initial challenge for students who have been successful in the "traditional" design of learning. Even at the end of the course, some students report that they would prefer to sit in class for 3–4 hours an evening and write a few papers for credit because it is too "hard" to plan ones own learning.

One must consider whether leaders should be prepared to follow orders and do what is requested or whether leaders should be competent to think and plan and problem solve on both specific and global issues. Does school leadership as a field need individuals who possess an ability to expand and learn or who express themselves as passive learners? In the first statement below the aspiring leader reflected the former; whereas in the second statement the latter was expressed.

> This course forced me to work outside of my comfort zone. By working through some basic fears and hesi-

tations, my comfort zone was expanded. I am excited about the potential for using my learning in this class.

> Because I was unfamiliar with Blackboard and the learning contract, the whole process seemed tedious. I would have been happy with a few research papers followed by several exams.

Self-knowledge and learning from reflection, along with the ability to adapt in various roles and ambiguous situations, are critical components of the administrative reality that will face many of these learners. Creating learning situations that support these skills provides the behavioral reinforcement that supports the transition from university learning to on the job experience.

The field of Educational Leadership has noted with alarming frequency the need to multi-task, manage time, be flexible and adaptive, and build relationships (Heifetz and Linsky, 2004; Portin, 2004). Yet, our traditional instructional design in university settings does not encourage leaders to build these types of skills. Similar to the outcry in industry for graduates who can think, problem solve, and critically analyze, school leadership demands those who can extend beyond rote learning to demonstrate not only content knowledge, but also leadership behaviors through strategic planning and meaningful action.

Other statements in the reflective documents suggest that students not only developed personal skills that encourage personal responsibility for learning but also managed to increase awareness, appreciation, and opportunities in the school context that surrounds their learning experience. There are comments that suggest many students utilized new knowledge to provide staff development in their school or put class products to use in the school settings. The authentication portion, of learning contract process, extended the learning, bringing school technology specialists, school administrators, and other colleagues in touch with the learning experience and therefore making them more knowledgeable about the individual's learning and potential role in the school.

The act of reflecting, as is expressed by many researchers, itself appeared to encourage some students and propel them to know about themselves as well as think about how to learn from this knowing (Barth, 2001; Thompson, 2004).

> It's a challenge for me to NOT be in control, and (even though it is not a comfortable thing usually) I like that challenge and enjoy seeing how each group member tackles our objectives. I'm also not one for

reflection (but you knew that), so once again, I enjoy the challenge and embrace the opportunity to think "outside of the box."

Another student also indicates the importance of reflection even in the face of discomfort and challenge.

> I had a difficult time with this class. I will be honest and say that I thought it would be a piece of cake. . . . I will need a different plan to attempt this again. . . . It has been a fantastic learning experience.

It is important to note that the quotes above indicate that the process can sometimes be painful and frustrating in the moment. Nevertheless, the overall learning system appears to transform individuals and provide secondary knowledge/behaviors that will be useful to aspiring leaders.

The online instructional design that has been described is not linear, but rather extensively complex in role, responsibility, and design. It requires extensive time and commitment on the part of both instructors and students. Satisfaction, of all of those involved, will be in considerable flux throughout each experience. Returning to the initial connect the dot metaphor, incorporating online instructional design that support social, self-directed learning into leadership programs transforms the initial white space of dots into a pattern that not only makes sense, but empowers learners to design the *learning game* themselves.

REFERENCES

Aspin, D., Chapman, J., Hatton, M., and Sawano, Y. (Eds.) (2001). *International handbook of lifelong learning, Part I–Part II.* Netherlands: Kluwer International Handbooks of Education.

Barth, R. S. (2001). Stepping back. *Journal of Staff Development, 22*(3), 38–41.

Beitler, M. A. (2000). *Self-directed learning readiness at General Motors Japan.* North Carolina. (ERIC Dcoment Reproduction Service No. ED447266.)

Boyer, N. R. (2001). *Building online learning: System insights into group learning in an online environment.* Unpublished doctoral dissertation, University of South Florida, Florida.

Boyer, N. R. (2003a). The learning contract process: Scaffolds for building social, self-directed learning. *The Quarterly Review of Distance Education, 4*(4), 369–383.

Boyer, N. R. (2003b, October). *Using social, self-directed learning frameworks to engage and transform aspiring school leaders.* Paper presented at the meeting of the Association for Education Communications and Technology Conference, Anaheim, CA.

Boyer, N. R., and Maher, P. A. (2003). Constructing scaffolds for social online learning: Using self-directed frame-

works with virtual groups. *International Journal of Self-Directed Learning, 1*(1), 26–38.

Cobb, P., Confrey, J., diSessa, A., Lehrer, R., and Schauble, L. (2003). Design experiments in educational research. *Educational Researcher, 32*(1), 9–13.

Doncaster, K. (2000). Learning agreements: Their function in work-based programmes at Middlesex University. *Education + training, 42*(6), 349–359.

Greenwood, S. C. (2002–2003). Contracting revisited: Lessons learned in literacy differentiation. *Journal of Adolescent and Adult Literacy, 46*(4), 338–350.

Heifetz, R. A., and Linsky, M. (2004). When leadership spells danger: Leading meaningful change in education takes courage, commitment, and political savvy. *Educational Leadership, 61*(7), 33–37.

Knowles, M. S. (1975). *Self-directed learning.* New York: Association Press.

Knowles, M. S. (1986). *Using learning contracts.* San Francisco, CA: Jossey-Bass Publishers.

Knowles, M. S., Holton, E. F., III, and Swanson, R. A. (1998). *The adult learning. The definitive classic in adult education and human resource developmen*t (5th ed.). Texas: Gulf Publishing Company.

Lane, C. (1997). Technology and systemic educational reform. In P. S. Portway and C. Lane (Eds.), *Guide to teleconferencing and distance learning* (pp. 179–226). Livermore, CA: Applied Business teleCommunications.

Moore, M. G., and Kearsley, G. (1996). *Distance education: A systems view.* Belmont, CA: Wadsworth Publishing Company.

Palloff, R. M., and Pratt, K. (1999). *Building learning communities in cyberspace: Effective strategies for the online classroom.* San Francisco, CA: Jossey-Bass, Inc.

Portin, B. (2004). The roles that principals play. *Educational Leadership, 61*(7), 15–18.

Rossman, M. H. (2000). Andragogy and distance education: Together in the new millennium. *New Horizons in Adult Education, 14*(1). Retrieved January 4, 2004, from http://www.nova.edu/~aed/horizons/vol14n1.htm.

Sloane, F. C., and Gorard, S. (2003). Exploring modeling aspects of design experiments. *Educational Researcher, 32*(1), 29–31.

Thompson, S. (2004). Learning from the eye of the storm. *Educational Leadership, 61*(7), 60–63.

Vaughn, C. (2000). *Reading out: A starter kit for adult education distance learning programs.* Richmond, VA: Virginia Adult Learning Resource Center.

Waddell, D. L., and Stephens, S. (2000). Use of learning contracts in a RN-to-BSN leadership course. *Journal of continuing Education in Nursing, 31*(4), 179–184.

White, K. W., and Weight, B. H. (2000). *The online teaching guide: A handbook of attitudes, strategies, and techniques for the virtual classroom.* Boston, MA: Allyn and Bacon.

Wicket, R. E. Y. (2000). The learning covenant. *New Directions for Adult and Continuing Education,* Spring *85*(35), 39–47.

Principals' Training or Lack of Training in Special Education: A Literature Review

DOROTHY GARRISON-WADE

NUMEROUS RESEARCH STUDIES HAVE EXAMINED THE ROLES of the school principal, but little is known about how a principal's training and experience affect the level of services received by students with disabilities. Some studies explore the nature of leadership roles, but none examine the administrators' role regarding the context of inclusive schooling (Chien, 2000). Various leadership and training programs prepare principals to tackle issues involving school law, safety issues, instruction, curriculum, policy, facilities, budget, etc. Nevertheless, in light of the growing number of students with a diverse range of disabilities, it is reasonable to review principals' training or lack of training in special education and its effects on students.

Lack of special education preparation for school principals is challenging their ability to serve all students (Goor, Schween, and Boyer, 1997). Special education is the factor reported as having the most consistent effect on principals' time, enthusiasm, ability to lead schools, and frustration level (Smith and Colon, 1998; Balt, 2000). Administrators report being ill prepared for the job and cite difficulties with role clarification and job specialization (Ashby and Maki, 1996).

Implementation of special education is the major component lacking in the training process for principals (Morton, 2000). It presents an enormous problem for school principals. School principals have a responsibility to all their students, including students with disabilities (Katsiyannis, 1994). Not only do principals have a responsibility to students with disabilities, but federal mandates require it.

Through literature review, this article reviews special education policies and implications for principals, principals' training, knowledge, skills, attitudes, and their impact on the services for students with disabilities. First, let us look at federal policies, mandates, and court cases influencing special education and the ramifications of these policies and mandates for school principals.

FEDERAL POLICIES/COURT CASES

As late as 1972, half of the eight million children with disabilities in the United States eligible for educational services received no services (Douvanis and Husley, 2002). The enactment of the Education of All Handicapped Children Act of 1975 (P.L. 94-142), predecessor to the Individuals with Disabilities Act (IDEA), drastically changed services for children with disabilities. IDEA requires that a continuum of placement options and services be available to students with disabilities. The legislation includes the following provisions:

- A mandate to provide free, appropriate public education for children with disabilities
- A requirement that an Individualized Education Program (IEP) be developed for each student identified as disabled
- A requirement that schools actively involve parents in planning their child's education
- A requirement that students with disabilities be placed in the least restrictive environment (Gaddy, McNulty, Waters, 2002).

Enactment of this law forced school systems to provide services to millions of children with disabilities who previously did not attend school or receive limited educational services. According to the U.S. Department of Education, approximately six million students ages 6 through 21 receive services under IDEA. (U.S. Department of Education, 2002). With increasing enrollment of students in special education, the role of the principal has drastically changed, particularly in light of identifying and providing required special education services. Many administrators are placed in an administrative role with minimum knowledge of laws relating to students with disabilities. Without knowledge of IDEA and Section 504, principals are often challenged to ensure equal and appropriate accessibility for qualified individuals (Katsivannis, 1994).

235

The reauthorization of IDEA 1997 extends significant implications for school administrators. The revised regulations mandate that school administrators possess knowledge of IDEA requirements (e.g., eligibility, placement, performance goals, and assessment of student outcomes); demonstrate awareness of instructional strategies that are conducive to the needs of diverse learners; possess the capacity to provide opportunities for necessary training of school personnel; and provide on-going support and assistance to teachers (Anderson, 1999). The most recent 2003 reauthorization of IDEA includes new provisions to streamline discipline policies, reduces paperwork requirements, and improves professional development (NAASP, 2001).

Federal regulations are comprehensive on the responsibility of the school principal to provide the least restrictive learning environment for all children. The responsibilities for assuring that IDEA regulation is implemented are clearly spelled out to school administrators. Ignorance or lack of knowledge of the law is not an acceptable defense for a principal not to enforce federal mandates and regulations.

Since the enactment of IDEA regulations, many lawsuits have been filed against school districts that challenged enforcement of special education regulations. Four examples of special education landmark cases include: *Roncker v. Walter*, 700F.2d 1058 (Sixth Cir. 1983), developed a two-part test to determine placement for students with disabilities; In *Greer v. Rome City School District*, 950F.2d 688 (Eleventh Cir. 1991), the court decided in favor of parents who objected to the placement of their daughter in a self-contained special education classroom; *Oberti v. Clementon School District*, 995 F.2D 1204 (Third Cir. 1993), changed from the IDEA's "mainstreaming" approach to the concept of "inclusion"; and *Sacramento City Unified School District v. Holland* 14F.3d 1398 (Ninth Cir. 1994), challenged the district on placement of a student and ruled that when determining placement, mainstreaming a student with disabilities in regular education classes with supplemental aids and services must first be considered prior to placement in a special education classroom.

IMPLICATIONS AND LIABILITIES FOR PRINCIPALS

The implications of principals not following the letter of the law could be costly for school districts. Case in point, Tucker (November, 2002) in *The Washington Post* reported that a federal judge ordered a district school system to pay one million dollars to two con-

tract schools, Educational Transition Services and Rock Creek Academy, for providing services to students. As a result of this order, the school district threatened to close their schools, because the amount was more than half of the $1.7 million the city owed for past services (Tucker, 2002).

Gaps in training regarding special education laws as reported by Rhys (1996) and Nardone (1999) confirm a lack of preparation; they state that school principals lack knowledge of special education legal issues, specifically in compliance and procedural requirements as legally mandated by Individuals with Disabilities Education Act (IDEA). The 1990 version of IDEA requires school administrators to participate in Individualized Education (IEP) meetings to determine appropriate services for students with disabilities (Goor, Schwenn, and Boyer, 1997). Yet, it is the tendency of many principals to delegate their responsibilities to others which increases liabilities (Goor, Schwenn, and Boyer, 1997). Decisions are sometimes made that do not protect the students' and parents' rights. Students' placements are sometimes inappropriate and consideration is not always given to placement in a less restrictive setting. In addition, principals are responsible for helping facilitate a transition plan for students with disabilities as they progress through the educational system (Alper, Schloss, and Schloss, 1996). Knowledge of special education legal issues needs to be an important component of a principal's educational background. Parents of students with disabilities are becoming more knowledgeable of complexities and ambiguities of legal mandates of special education. If principals are not knowledgeable of special education laws and regulations, they risk lawsuits and perhaps loss of their jobs. By not educating themselves in special education law, principals may place their district in jeopardy of not meeting compliance guidelines, and ultimately in unwanted litigation (Nardone, 1999). Most importantly, principals' lack of knowledge of these regulations may affect the outcome of services for students with disabilities.

TRAINING IN SPECIAL EDUCATION

According to Anderson (1999), despite the implication for school administrators to be trained in special education laws and policies, most school administrators have received little, if any training related to special education in their leadership preparation training. She further states that most principals continue to rely on central office staff (i.e., directors of special education and consultants) as primary sources of information and guidance in providing leadership to students, staff, and programs within their schools.

The significance of training for principals in special education is addressed by the NASBE Special Education Group (1992) in a report entitled, *Winners All: A Call for Inclusive Schools.* In this report, NASBE (1992) challenges principals to be accountable for the outcome of all students, including students with disabilities, by getting training in inclusive education. Balt (2000) indicates that many principals do not feel well prepared for those roles as administrators of special education programs. Most principals are unfamiliar with effective strategies to educate students with disabilities outside of special education classrooms (Morton, 2000). By acquiring knowledge of special education policies and procedures and learning instructional strategies that are supportive of inclusive education, principals are more capable of participating in and implementing inclusion of all students with disabilities in their schools.

Although there is a prerequisite for school administrators to have knowledge of strategies to address the needs of all students, the lack of training and knowledge in the area is largely attributed to the absence of a strong special education foundation within principal certification programs. Nardone (1999) states that only twelve states currently require special education course work for general administrative certification, and 45 percent of all states do not require general knowledge of special education in order to receive an administrative endorsement. The situation appears to be even worse in professional schools preparing school administrators; for there is usually only one program, and special education is largely missing from the curriculum (Sirotnik and Kimball, 1994).

Praisner (2003) found that preparation programs provided principals with a minimum amount of knowledge base deemed by special education experts as relevant in the implementation of inclusion. She also discovered that characteristics of disabilities, special education law, and behavior management may be adequately covered in preparation programs, but specific topics that present appropriate strategies and processes to support inclusion appear to be lacking. Patterson, Bowling, and Marshall (2000) further support these findings and conclude that principals are not adequately trained for leadership in special education.

KNOWLEDGE NEEDED

Typically, principals have the appropriate training and experience to facilitate instruction in regular educa-

tion but few have the background and experience in special education. Their backgrounds do not include the comprehensive knowledge necessary for ensuring that students with disabilities' needs are met and their rights protected (Goor, Schwenn, and Boyer, 1997). Sirotnik and Kimball (1994) state that principals should at minimum have knowledge of Public Law 94-142; state regulations governing special education practices; the Regular Education Initiative (REI); definitions and characteristics of handicapping condition; service delivery models; appropriate teaching strategies; financial, legal, and ethical implications of special education program; and know enough about background history on special education to understand current issues and debates. Without knowledge of IDEA and Section 504, principals are often challenged to ensure equal and appropriate accessibility for qualified individuals (Katsivannis, 1994). Knowledge of special education law and regulations is essential to ensure that all students' needs are met. Without the appropriate background in special education policies, principals are unable to provide leadership and make sound decisions to ensure that students with disabilities are getting quality services.

Another area in which principals feel they need additional knowledge is in dealing with technology for special education students (Rhys, 1996). Assistive technology allows many students with disabilities to function more effectively (Goor, Schwenn, and Boyer, 1997). Principals need to be aware of available assistive technology, whether it is simple or elaborate, as well as it's attendant costs. If the Individual Educational Program (IEP) team determines that additional equipment would enhance special education services, the principal needs to support the decision.

Principals should become knowledgeable of the referral-to-placement process and support and closely monitor the process (Salisbury and Smith, 1991). By actively participating in the placement process, principals can ensure compliance with the law and due process for students. In addition, knowledgeable principals are able to challenge excessive testing of students with disabilities, ask pertinent questions, and offer alternative programs and interventions for students not eligible for special education placement (Goor and Schwenn, 1995). Principals must also become aware of effective strategies used by other administrators that have proven effective in overcoming barriers in special education (Cardinal, 1991). For example, a special education teacher designs a transition plan for a student with disabilities to transition from middle school to high school; the teacher may seek advice from the principal on placement, and/or effective strategies that will help the student's transition.

Special education teachers often solicit principals' advice on discipline. All behavior management strategies may not be effective intervention for all students. When developing behavior management strategies for students with disabilities, the principal should take into consideration the student's disability and how the disability influences the student's behavior. Lack of awareness of the various types of disabilities and successful intervention strategies will limit the principal's effectiveness. The principal needs to know what to do if a student with disabilities has to be suspended from school for a severe problem and how the suspension will change the student's placement and services. A principal has to be careful when suspending students with disabilities, because the courts place the burden of proof on the school in determining if the behavior was a result of the student's disability (Bartlett, 1989). If principals are not aware of special education policies, strategies, or technique, they may be ineffective in developing an intervention plan to help correct students' behavior.

ATTITUDES TOWARD INCLUSION

Principals' overall attitude is important in creating a positive school climate and in influencing instructional practices (Kirner, Vautour, and Vautour, 1993). This is especially true for special education programs. The principal's attitude and genuine concern expressed for children with special needs influence the success of special programs (Burrello, Schrup, and Barnett, 1992). In contrast, principals' negative attitudes, based upon the belief that students with disabilities require a disproportionate amount of time and resources or that these students should be educated in more segregated environments, hamper the administration of special education in school buildings (Goor and Schwenn, 1995). Principals' attitudes toward inclusion could result in an increase or decrease of opportunities for students to be served in a general education class; therefore, the principal must display a positive attitude and commitment to inclusion (Evan, Bird, Ford, Green and Bichoff, 1992). Effective principals model positive attitudes towards acceptance of all children, visit special education classrooms, spend time with students with disabilities, tour the building daily, and become involved with the concerns of all students and programs (Van Horn, Burrello, and De-Cue, 1992).

Little research has been conducted to determine the influence of the principal's attitude toward inclusion and the impact principals' attitudes have on students' placement. Praisner (2000) conducted a research study to look at principals' attitudes toward students with severe/profound disabilities; relationship among personal characteristics, training, experience and attitudes toward inclusion; and relationship between principals' perception of appropriate placement for students with different types of disabilities and their attitudes and experience. A survey consisting of 408 elementary school principals was conducted. Some of the findings of the research study include: (a) most of the principals agreed with inclusion when it is phrased in a generic and unregulated manner; (b) the more hours and credits in special education taken by principals, the more positive their attitudes were toward inclusion; (c) the more positive the attitudes of the principals toward inclusion, the more inclusive the placements' selection; and (d) the more positive principals' experiences were with students with disabilities, the more positive their attitudes were toward inclusion (Praisner, 2003). The study also shows that most principals in the study had general knowledge of special education laws, characteristics of disabilities, and behavior management, but specific topics that address actual strategies were lacking. The research findings emphasized the importance of principals' positive experiences and attitudes on promoting "inclusionary" practices for students with all types of disabilities.

ATTITUDES CORRELATED TO TRAINING

How do principals' training and/or experience in special education correlate to their attitudes toward inclusion? Praisner's (2003) research revealed that principals exposed to special education credits through college courses generally had more positive attitudes toward inclusion. Her study also discovered principals with formal training in special education through courses, workshops, and/or a portion of courses (10 percent of content or more) developed positive attitudes toward inclusion. Yet, no previous research was found to relate the number of special education credits to positive attitudes. However, Hegler (1995) and Stoler (1992) did find a relationship between the numbers of in-service hours taken in special education toward creating a positive attitude. Many principals support the importance of in-service opportunities for teachers and administrators to promote positive attitudes and skills for working more efficiently in context areas (Murray, 1993). Other literature emphasizes the importance of special education coursework in developing positive attitudes toward inclusion (Greyerbiehl, 1993; Hyatt, 1987).

Since there is limited research to support the relationship between training content and attitudes to determine what specific topics influence principal preparation in special education, more research is needed in this area (Praisner, 2003). This type of research could be beneficial to principals' preparation programs in training principals to become effective instructional leaders for all students.

CONCLUSION

From the literature review, several assumptions could be made in regards to principals' training or lack of training in special education. The literature clearly supports the idea that most principals' preparation programs do not adequately train them for leadership in special education. Without appropriate training and/or experience in working with student with disabilities, principals do not have the necessary background to make sound decisions. The literature also revealed that principals' attitudes toward inclusion were influenced by their experience and training. Van Horn, Burrello and DeClue (1992) state, "the beliefs and attitudes of the principals toward special education are the key factors influencing their behavior toward students with disabilities and the most important role the principal plays in the inclusion of special education students into the school is that of symbolic leader" (p. 50). In addition, there were numerous examples in the literature review that showed that many principals are not knowledgeable of special education laws, terminology, strategies, and behavior interventions. Without the appropriate knowledge and training, principals are not able to offer professional assistance in placement meetings and transition planning.

More research is needed to determine the effect of principals' training on the impact of students' services. In spite of lack of research, it may be safe to say that principals need more training in special education to provide effective leadership for all students. From the literature review, it is obvious that special education training for school administrators is lacking and insufficient. There is a great need for more course offerings in principal licensure programs and for staff development to give school administrators essential tools needed to enforce special education laws. In order for school administrators to provide quality services for all students, there need to be more opportunities for them to receive appropriate training to deal with critical issues regarding special education services. What principals "most desperately need" is a firm foundation in special education policy and legal issues (Balt, 2000). Professional development for principals needs to be a "seamless garment" that extends through pre-service, induction, career changes, and retirement (National Association of Secondary School Principals, 2001). Today's principals need relevant and practical training giving them knowledge and skills they need to deal with managerial operations of schools, legal issues, problem analysis and various interpersonal skills (Balt, 2000).

Principals need adequate preparation for their most important role of providing educational leadership for all children. Preparation programs for principal leadership must improve their programs in preparing principals for leadership in special education by ensuring principals have requisite knowledge in assessing the impact of disabilities on student performance, monitoring referral-to-placement procedures, managing records and confidentiality issues, employing assistive technology, and facilitating parent involvement (Goor, Schwenn, and Boyer, 1997). The challenge is not easy, but those preparing for leadership need particular training in skills necessary to deal with critical issues around growing special education needs. In order for all children to obtain quality educational services, it is imperative that principals receive necessary training to acquire a knowledge base in special education and competence to ensure compliance of the law.

REFERENCES

Alper, S., Schloss, P. J., and Schloss, C. N. (1996). Families of children with disabilities in elementary and middle school: Advocacy models and strategies. *Exceptional Children, 62*, 261–270.

Anderson, K. M. (1999). Examining principals' special education knowledge and the inclusiveness of their schools. (Doctoral dissertation, University of North Carolina at Greensboro, 1999). Dissertation Abstracts International, 61, 02A.

Ashby, D., and Maki, D. M. (1996, February). What first year principals don't know: How you may be able to help new colleagues succeed. Paper presented at National Association of Secondary School Principals Annual Convention, San Francisco.

Balt, S. D. (2000). Preparing principals for leadership in special education. (Doctoral dissertation, University of California Riverside, 2000). Dissertation Abstracts International, 61, 06A.

Bartlett, L. (1989). Disciplining handicapped students: Legal issues in light of *Honig v. Doe. Exceptional Children, 55,* 357–366.

Burrello, L. C. (1991). The principal's blue book on special education: Part II: Principal instructional leadership and supervisory practices in special education programs. Council for Administrators of Special Education (CASE), Indiana University, IN.

Burello, L. C., Schrup, M. G., and Barnett, B. G. (1992). The principal as the special education leader. Bloomington: University of Indiana, Department of Educational Leadership and Policy Studies.

Cardinal, D. N. (1991). How to stay current with special education issues. *NASSPBulletin, 75*(535), 71–77.

Chien, Y. (2000). The principals' and pupil services director's role and relationship in the context of inclusive practices in two elementary schools. The University of Wisconsin-Madison.

Douvanis, G., and Hulsey, D. (2002, August). The least restrictive environment mandate: How has it been defined by the courts? Arlington: Eric Clearinghouse on Disabilities and Gifted Education.

Evans, J. H., Bird, K. M., Ford, L. A., Green, J. L., and Bischoff, R. A. (1992). Strategies for overcoming resistance to the integration of students with disabilities in neighborhood schools: A case study. *CASE in Point, 7*(1), 1–15.

Gaddy, B., McNulty, B., and Waters, T. (2002). The reauthorization of the individuals with disabilities education act: Moving toward a more unified system. Aurora, CO: Mid-continent Research for Education and Learning. *Studies in Education, 11,* 13–29.

Goor, M. B., and Schwenn, J. O. (1995). *Leadership for special education administration: A case based approach.* Fort Worth, TX: Harcourt Brace.

Goor, M., Schwenn, J., and Boyer, L. (1997). Preparing principals for leadership in special education. *Intervention in School and Clinic, 32*(3), 133–141.

Greyerbiehl, D. (1993). Educational policies and practices that support the inclusion of students with disabilities in the general education classroom. Charleston, WV: West Virginia Developmental Disabilities Planning Council.

Hegler, K. L. (1995, April). The "what, why, who and if" of inclusion processes in rural schools: Supporting teachers during attitude and teaching behavior change. Paper presented at the seventy-third Annual International Convention of the Council of Exceptional Children, Indianapolis, IN.

Hyatt, N. E. (1987). Perceived competencies and attitudes of a select group of elementary school administrators relative to preparation and experience in administering special education programs. Dissertation Abstracts International, 48(02A), 361.

Katsiyannis, A. (1994, November). Individuals with disabilities: The school principal and 504. *NASSP, 78*(565), 6–10.

Kirner, M., Vautour, J. A., and Vautour, M. B. (1993, March). Enhancing instructional programs within the schools: Training school principals in special education administration. Paper presented at the International Conference of the Learning Disabilities Association, San Francisco.

Morton, C. (2000). Characteristics of principals as a leader as perceived by teachers of special education. The University of Toledo.

Murray, L. B. (1993). Putting it all together at the school level: A principal's perspective. Integrating General and Special Education, J. I. Goodlad and T. C. Lovitt, eds., New York: Merrill.

Nardone, A. J. (1999). The campus administrator as instructional leader in acquisition of knowledge of special education legal issues. (Doctoral dissertation, University of New Mexico, 1999). Dissertation Abstracts International, 60, 04A.

National Association of Secondary Principals (NASSP). (2003). House approves special education legislation. Reston, VA: NASSP.

National Association of Secondary Principals (NASSP). (2001). NASSP gearing up for IDEA reauthorization. Reston, VA: NASSP.

National Association of State Board of Education (NASDE). (1991, October). Section 504 of the rehabilitation act of 1973: Old problems and emerging issues for public schools. Liaison Bulletin. Alexandria, VA: NASBE.

Patterson, J., Bowling, D., and Marshall, C. (2000). Are principals prepared to manage special education dilemmas? *National Association of Secondary School Principals Bulletin, 84*(613), 9–20.

Praisner, C. (2003). Attitudes of elementary school principals toward inclusion of students with disabilities. *Exceptional Children, 69*(2), 135–145.

Praisner, C. L. (2000). Attitudes of elementary school principals toward the inclusion of students with disabilities in general education classes. (Doctoral dissertation, Lehigh University, 2000). Dissertation Abstracts International, 61(07), 2661.

Rhys, H. J. (1996). The principal's role in special education: building-level administrators' knowledge of special education issues as these apply to their administrative role. (Doctoral dissertation, University of Kansas, 1996). Dissertation Abstracts International, 57, 07A.

Salisbury, C., and Smith, B. J. (1991). The least restrictive environment: Understanding the options. *Principal, 7*(1), 24–25, 27.

Sirotnik, K. A. and Kimball, K. (1994). The unspecial place of special place of special education in programs that prepare school administrators. *Journal of School Leadership, 4*(6), 598–630.

Smith, J. O., and Colon, R. J. (1998). Legal responsibilities toward students with disabilities: What every administrator should know. *NAASP Bulletin, 81,* 40–53.

Stoler, R. D. (1992). Perceptions of regular education teachers toward inclusion of all handicapped students in their classrooms. *Clearing House, 65*(1), 60–62.

Tucker, N. (2002, November 15). Judge orders D.C. contract schools paid. *The Washington Post,* p. B03.

United States Department of Education (2002). *Twenty-fourth annual report to congress on the implementation of individuals with disabilities act.* Washington, DC: Education Publication Center, U.S. Department of Education.

Van Horn, G. P., Burrello, L. C., and DeCue, L. (1992). An instructional leadership framework: The principal's leadership role in special education. *The Special Education Leadership Review, 1,* 41–54.

Part IV

CREATING THE FUTURE

Ed.D. and Ph.D. Program Designs in Educational Leadership and Administration: The Challenging Present and Changing Future

KAETLYN LAD, EDWARD GRAHAM, AND JAMES CENGIZ GULEK

IN 2002, A PRELIMINARY STUDY OF ED.D. AND PH.D. PROgrams in Educational Leadership and Administration (Lad and Graham, 2003) was undertaken to investigate the design of programs including factors such as faculty load, size of programs, program delivery and semester hours, use of cohort models, and number of seminar and research courses. In 2003, a follow-up study of Ed.D. and Ph.D. programs was undertaken to investigate the design of courses offerings, course delivery using the Internet, comprehensive examinations, dissertation committee composition, and dissertation chairing compensation. Results of the studies indicate few significant differences in the designs of Ed.D. and Ph.D. Programs in Educational Leadership in the samples of these studies.

OVERVIEW OF STUDIES

This article presents and discusses selected findings of two studies investigating the design of Ed.D. and Ph.D. programs in Educational Leadership and Administration. The first study, conducted in 2002, was intended to be a preliminary investigation of Ed.D. and Ph.D. programs in educational leadership and educational administration in the United States. Information was gathered regarding various components of both Ed.D. and Ph.D. programs, including such things as the design of programs in terms of size, private vs. public, course focus, size and time of classes, use of cohort models, and doctoral faculty assignments and expectations in terms of workload. Preliminary information was also gathered regarding the use of the Internet for delivery of instruction in these programs. The second study was implemented in 2003. The purpose of the second study was to investigate the design of courses offerings, course delivery, comprehensive examinations, dissertation committee composition, and dissertation chairing compensation in order to describe a model of the typical Ed.D. program and the typical Ph.D. program in educational leader-

ship and administration. It was the intent of the research to gather information to formulate the basis for a more advanced study of doctoral programs focusing on accountability issues in educational leadership and administration.

As K–12 public school districts across the country are being held accountable for the learning of their students, programs in the higher education arena are feeling pressure to demonstrate the success of these programs. As the notion of accountability continues to move into higher education, faculty in doctoral programs who prepare school leaders for influential positions in public school systems will be required to measure the success of their programs.

Higher education programs credentialing school administrators are already being required to demonstrate student success (Korostoff and Paull, 2001; Gilbert, 1996). Several states, most notably Texas, have included in the State Rules and Regulations, a mandate that graduates of credential programs successfully pass state tests designed to demonstrate mastery of a particular knowledge base. Texas monitors passing rates of graduates of administrative credentialing programs (i.e., percentage of students passing with a 90 percent rate necessary for continued accreditation from the state.)

In light of the movement toward greater accountability, colleges and universities across the nation may soon be expected to demonstrate the success of their doctoral programs and their graduates. These studies were a preliminary step to a future, more advanced study that will focus on accountability issues in doctoral programs.

BACKGROUND

From 1986 to 1998, according to Gerald and Hussar (2002), the number of doctoral degrees in the United States increased from 34,041 to 46,010, with a slight decrease to 44,077 in 1998–1999. Further, the number of doctoral degrees granted in the United States is expected to increase to 46,800 by 2012. Gerald and Hussar noted that by 2010, the doctoral degree may be the new benchmark for promotion to district-level positions, as it already is for the superintendency in most states across the nation. Ed.D. and Ph.D. programs in educational leadership and administration vary in regard to many program characteristics, including, for example, semester hour requirements, course content, student/professor contact hours, use of full-time and part-time instructors, and cohort versus traditional program models (Levin and O'Donnell, 1999; Miller and Irby, 1999). With such a variety of models, it is difficult even to begin the process of studying accountability issues and investigating which programs appear to be successful models in preparing education administrators.

How will success of doctoral programs in educational leadership and administration be defined and measured? The success of doctoral programs may be defined in terms of the grade point average or the number of the students applying to and completing particular programs, or program success may be defined in terms of the professional careers of program graduates. However *successful* is defined, it can only become more important to program enrollment as competition for students increases due to the development and implementation of new programs (Foster, 2001; Levin, 1998; Miller and Irby, 1999; Slater and Martinez, 2000; Smallwood, 2001).

The movement toward measuring student success in K–12 education has brought about the resurfacing of the quantitative/qualitative debate in regard to educational research (Barone, 2001; Levin and O'Donnell, 1999; Mayer, 2000). As a result of the quantitative definitions of student success in K–12, the number and type of required research courses for doctoral students in educational leadership and administration has emerged as an area of controversy (Mayer, 2001; Page, 2001; Riehl, Larson, Short, and Reitzug, 2000; Young, 2001). Finding a way to design graduate programs in educational research with adequate depth and breadth while maintaining a balanced and reasonable program for practitioners has emerged as one problem for faculty in doctoral programs (Mertz, 2001; Paul and Marfo, 2001). Mertz (2001) suggested designing a doctoral seminar focused on diverse research traditions as one possible solution to this dilemma. Because doctoral programs will be expected (as they should be) to prepare education leaders to use research to improve the *practice* of education as well as

to prepare education leaders for the needs of the *future* (Pallas, 2001), the issue of research courses in doctoral programs needs to be addressed.

The introduction of the Internet has made alternate ways of transmission of knowledge available to doctoral programs. Institutions have incorporated the use of the Internet into doctoral programs in educational leadership and administration in a variety of ways and to varying degrees (Davies and Quick, 2001; Foster, 2001). Some programs have experimented with on-line course delivery while most programs have expected students to access research on-line (Hartley and Bendixen, 2001). A study by Linder, Dooley, and Murphy (2001) reported that use of the Internet for delivery of courses in doctoral students has influenced student competencies and has changed the role of the doctoral faculty in significant ways (Davies and Quick, 2001).

The use of the cohort model, particularly in Ed.D. programs, has become the popular mode of program delivery in educational administration (Miller and Irby, 1999), and has undoubtedly influenced the design of educational leadership and administration of doctoral programs (Scribner and Donaldson, 2001). An increase in the practice of using the cohort model (Teitel, 1997; Muth and Barnet, 2001) in doctoral programs in the last five years (Scribner and Donaldson, 2001), the use of the Internet for research, and the use of the Internet for course delivery (Card and Horton, 2000), have all had an impact on the workload and workday of faculty participating in these doctoral programs. Detailed knowledge regarding the design and requirements of current doctoral programs in leadership and administration may assist educators with the task of defining and designing measures for determining the success of doctoral programs.

METHODOLOGY OF THE FIRST STUDY

A survey for the first study was designed and reviewed by a panel of full-time doctoral professors of educational leadership and administration in the graduate school of education from a nationally ranked university. Questions regarding size, whether public or private, semester hours spent in particular types of coursework, enrollment issues, professor workload, and Internet use were included in the survey. Slight modifications were made for clarification as a result of the panel's review.

In the first mailing, 256 copies of the survey were mailed to institutions of higher education in the United States classified in the 2001 Higher Education

Directory as Carnegie Doctoral/Research institutions. The survey was modified slightly after the first mailing to improve the clarity of responses, though the content of the survey was not substantively altered. The revised survey was mailed to the 183 colleges and universities listed as having doctoral programs in educational leadership or administration in *US News and World Report, 2001* that were not sent questionnaires in the first mailing. This sample was from a consensus-like activity as everyone on the two lists was contacted and the sample consisted of those who responded. The intent was to reach all colleges and universities in the country having a doctoral program in educational leadership or administration through either the first or second mailing.

The survey contained two segments; one segment dealt with Ed.D. programs and the other segment dealt with Ph.D. programs. Since questions regarding faculty workload were identical on both surveys, the responses were combined into one data set for analysis. In order to have consistency in the data, the term *semester hours* was consistently used in reporting findings and results rather than using the terms *credits* or *units*. In addition, quarter hours were converted into semester hours (conversion formula: quarter hours/1.5 = semester hours).

Descriptive statistics were used as part of the analysis. The demographic responses (size of the institution, public/private, and program type) were cross-tabulated to the responses regarding the questionnaire segments. A second analysis of the data included a two-step process. First, the demographic responses (size of the institution, public/private, and program type) were cross-tabulated to the responses regarding programmatic aspects of the respective programs. This information was used to collapse variables responses to cell sizes appropriate for analytical purposes. For example, with the variable describing the institution size, the responses huge (over 40,000) and large (15,001–40,000) were collapsed into one response, as were the responses for medium (6,001–15,000) and small (under 6,000). This strategy then allowed for the cross-tabulate size cells to remain within the parameters required for generalized chi-square procedures, which were used to assess the association between the demographic responses, which characterize the institution, and the programmatic responses, which characterize the program. The focus of this study was a comparison between Ed.D. and Ph.D. programs in institutions having only one type program.

Based on the chi-square procedures, candidate independent variables were picked for Analysis of Variance (ANOVA) in an attempt to understand these data at a higher level. No statistical significant relationships, however, were found using the ANOVA procedure. As a result, means were evaluated using *t*-tests and categorical variables were evaluated using generalized chi-square procedures.

RESULTS OF THE FIRST STUDY

Descriptive statistics were used to summarize information gathered from the first survey (Data Set 1). In Data Set 1, the sample size was 41 (Ed.D. programs, N = 33; and Ph.D. programs, N = 8). Data Set 2 combined responses from both surveys (N = 75). The data from Set 1 indicated that most institutions with programs in educational leadership or administration are between 6,000 and 40,000 in total institutional enrollment. Results indicated that the total semesters hours needed to complete each program varied little in this sample. The Ed.D. programs in the sample had a larger mean of total hours than did the Ph.D. programs. Both Ed.D. and Ph.D. programs have 63–65 hours of course requirements for program completion. Cohorts were clearly the model of choice in both types of programs though the mean for cohort size and class size was greater for Ed.D. programs that for the Ph.D. programs in the sample. The Ph.D. programs averaged about seven months longer to complete and averaged about 10 percent greater adherence to Carnegie hour requirements than did the average Ed.D. programs in the sample. Both Ed.D. and Ph.D. programs in this sample, whether at public or private institutions, used the cohort model as the preferred model of program delivery. This finding supports the notion from the literature that cohort models are favored by doctoral programs (Scribner and Donaldson, 2001).

The Ph.D. and Ed.D. programs in this sample differed little in the number of semester hours of research courses included as part of the programs. Ed.D. programs averaged 14 semester hours of research coursework while Ph.D. programs averaged 12 semester hours. Traditional thinking is that the research requirements of the Ph.D. surpass the research requirements for the Ed.D., which was not supported by this study. The findings of the study support the idea of the controversy over research requirements doctoral programs indicated by Mertz (2001) and Paul and Marfo (2001). Fifteen percent more of the Ed.D. full-time faculty were expected to chair dissertations (with no added release time) than were Ph.D. full-time faculty.

Ph.D. faculty in this sample averaged one more course taught per semester than did Ed.D. faculty.

Data set 2 included 19 private institutions and 56 public institutions. In Data Set 2, the statistical findings of this study focused on differences and similarities between institutional size (huge/large and medium/small), program type (Ed.D. and Ph.D.), program with respect to faculty course load, and other related information. Many findings of this study were intriguing, but because there were no statistically significant relationships found among variables more study is necessary.

The statistical differences in Data Set 2 derived from this sample indicated the following: the average number of dissertations chaired by Ed.D. full-time faculty members was greater than that chaired by Ph.D. full-time faculty members; a higher percentage of classes were taught by adjunct faculty at medium/small institutions than at huge/large institutions; a higher percentage of dissertations were chaired by adjunct faculty at medium/small institutions than at huge/large institutions; a higher percentage of dissertations were chaired by adjunct faculty at private institutions than at public institutions; adjunct faculty at medium/small institutions chaired a higher percent of total dissertations completed than did adjunct faculty at huge/large institutions; and, the majority of courses were taught on weeknights at huge/large institutions while the majority of courses were taught on weekends at small/medium institutions.

METHODOLOGY OF THE SECOND STUDY

The survey used to collect the data for the second study was designed using the information collected in the first study and added areas of data collection that would define, in more depth, the design of Ph.D. and Ed.D. programs in educational leadership and administration. The second survey was designed to collect information relating to such items as Carnegie units (credits) taught in content areas such as leadership, management, ethics, change, policy, quantitative and qualitative research preparation, the composition of doctoral committees, instructor release time for dissertation chairing, completion of written and oral comprehensive examinations, and the extent to which the Internet is used for course delivery in Ph.D. and Ed.D. programs in educational leadership and administration. Data collected in the targeted areas for Ed.D. programs were compared with the same data collected for Ph.D. programs.

The source of the sample for the study was the 21st Edition, *Educational Administration Directory, 2002–2003* (Lane, 2003) that provides a service to the profession of educational administration and leadership by providing information that will help improve communication between the faculties of the Educational Administration departments throughout the United States and Canada. The survey was mailed to the department members of 50 Ph.D. and 50 Ed.D. programs in educational leadership and administration in the United States who were, in this study, randomly selected from the Directory. Follow-up calls were made to increase response rate. Twenty-nine Ph.D. (58 percent) and 27 (54 percent) of Ed.D. surveys were completed and returned. Total survey return was 56 for an overall return rate of 56 percent.

RESULTS OF THE SECOND STUDY

Descriptive statistics were conducted to understand the overall design of doctoral programs in the areas surveyed and describe the similarities and differences between the Ed.D. and Ph.D. programs. The *t*-test and chi-square statistical analyses were used to test if there is a significant difference between the Ed.D. and Ph.D. programs in terms of the number of units offered in core content areas, content and delivery of comprehensive exams, composition of dissertation committee, position of the dissertation chair, faculty compensation, and delivery of doctoral courses.

Ed.D. and Ph.D. programs showed similarity in many ways and did not show any statistically significant differences in a number of measures. Several of the statistical analyses that showed significant differences were that Ph.D. programs offer significantly more units in finance ($F = 4.90$, $p<.05$); whereas Ed.D. programs offer significantly more units in dissertation proposal writing ($F = 13.17$, $p<.005$) and seminar discussion of readings ($F = 4.45$, $p<.05$). Significantly more Ph.D. programs include part-time faculty ($F = 5.73$, $p<.05$) and practitioners ($F = 5.04$, $p<.05$) in the dissertation committee. Ed.D. programs offer significantly more courses entirely on-line ($F = 4.58$, $p<.05$). Significantly more Ph.D. programs have written (Chi-Square $= 6.98$, $p<.05$), on-site no books/notes (Chi-Square $= 6.76$, $p<.05$) comprehensive exams. Significantly more Ed.D. programs include a full-time dissertation chair outside of the department (Chi-Square $= 8.32$, $p<.005$).

Results indicate that a typical doctoral program in educational administration and leadership is semester-based; offers 3 units in management, curriculum, change process, finance, educational law, qualitative research, and dissertation proposal writing; and 3–6 units in leadership, organization, supervision/evaluation, educational policy/politics, and quantitative research. Among the least emphasized areas that were surveyed were ethics/values, adult learning, and seminar discussion of readings. A typical doctoral program included written and on-site no books/notes exam; but majority of programs had no oral or take-home exams. Written comprehensive exams typically had 4–6 questions. Most dissertation committees included full-time faculty along with a research professor and were composed of 4–5 members. Part-time faculty and practitioners were not common on dissertation committees. A typical dissertation chair was a full-time professor of leadership, chosen by student, and compensated with reduced teaching load. A part-time chair appointed from within or outside of the department within outside the program faculty was not typical. A typical doctoral program did not offer on-line courses; however, chat rooms, discussion boards, and website use for courses are becoming more popular. The majority of doctoral programs made course syllabi available on-line and are currently developing/planning future on-line courses.

IMPLICATIONS FOR CHANGE

The data presented in this study may assist institutions of higher education in understanding the present design of Ed.D. and Ph.D. doctoral programs in educational leadership and administration and comparing Ed.D. and Ph.D. programs as they are currently being implemented in the United States. Institutions will be able to compare the studied components of today's programs noting differences that may represent program innovations. This information from these two studies of present Ed.D. and Ph.D. program design might be used in comparing and evaluating present program structure and in presenting models for consideration when changing future program design to meet the challenges of today's world. The data may provide information that is helpful in determining and defining the course requirements, content area requirements, research requirements, comprehensive examination content and procedures, use of the cohort model and cohort size, dissertation committee composition, faculty workload and chairing compensation, and use of the Internet in course delivery in Ed.D. and Ph.D. programs in educational leadership and administration.

IMPLICATIONS FOR FUTURE STUDY

The results of these two studies offer numerous avenues for future large-scale research projects. A future study comparing the "successfulness" of students who have completed doctoral programs of different demographic design and different program delivery modes would seem relevant. In order to undertake a study of doctoral program "successfulness," one must be able to compare student success in programs of similar and varying design.

Results may assist in creating and implementing a more detailed study of such programs regarding accountability for program success. The information presented here may assist members of present programs in making decisions about their own doctoral programs and for investigating what measures of accountability are appropriate given program designs. As the emphasis on accountability continues to move into the realm of higher education, an increase in the number of studies regarding accountability and the success of doctoral programs will likely emerge. Such data would assist institutions of higher education in making decisions regarding program improvement.

REFERENCES

Barone, T. (2001). Science, art, and the predispositions of educational researchers. *Educational Researchers, 30*(7), 24–28.

Card, K. A., and Horton, L. (2000). Providing access to graduate education using computer-mediated communication. *International Journal of Instructional Media, 27*(3), 235–245.

Davies, T., and Quick, D. (2001). Reducing distance through distance learning: The community college leadership doctoral program at Colorado State University. *Community College Journal of Research and Practice, 25*(8), 607–620.

Foster, A. L. (2001). Texas fines distance-learning institution as diploma mill. *The Chronicle of Higher Education, 48*(13), A29.

Gerald, D. E., and Hussar, W. J. (2002). *Projections of Educational Statistics to 2012*. National Center for Educational Statistics, NCES 2002–030.

Gilbert, S. W. (1996). Making the most of a slow revolution. *Change, 28*(2), 10–23.

Hartley, K., and Bendixen, L. D. (2001). Educational research in the Internet age: Examining the role of individual characteristics. *Educational Researcher, 30*(9), 22–26.

Korostoff, M., and Paull, R. C. (2001). Identifying the moving target: The principal shortage, California's administrative services credential program and the Steinberg bill. *Educational Leadership and Administration: Teaching and Program Development, 13*, 123–137.

Lad, K., and Graham, E. (2003). A preliminary study of the structure of Ed.D. and Ph.D. programs in educational leadership and administration. *Educational Leadership and Administration: Teaching and Program Development, 15*, 125–137.

Lane, K. E. (2003). Educational Administration Directory 2002–2003. Proactive Publications: Lancaster, PA.

Levin, J. R., and O'Donnell, A. (1999). What to do about educational research's credibility gaps? *Issues in education, 5*, 177–229.

Levin, R. A. (1998). Engaging doctoral candidates in action research. *Teaching Education, 9*(2), 125–133.

Linder, J. R., Dooley, K. E., and Murphy, T. H. (2001). Differences in competencies between doctoral student on-campus and at a distance. *American Journal of Distance Education, 15*(2), 25–40.

Mayer, R. E. (2000). What is the place of science in educational research? *Educational Researcher, 29*(6), 38–39.

Mayer, R. E. (2001). Resisting the assault on science: The case for evidence-based reasoning in educational research. *Educational Researcher, 30*(7), 29–30.

Metz, M. H. (2001). Intellectual border crossing in graduate education: A report from the field. *Educational Researcher, 30*(5), 12–18.

Miller, W., and Irby, R. (1999). An inquiry into the exigency of a beginning doctoral cohort in educational leadership. *College Student Journal, 33*(3), 358–363.

Muth, R., and Barnett, B. (2001). Making the case for cohorts: Identifying research gaps, improving professional preparation, and gaining political support. *Educational Leadership and Administration: Teaching and Program Development, 13*, 111–122.

Page, R. N. (2001). Reshaping graduate preparation in educational research methods: One school's experience. *Educational Researcher, 30*(5), 19–25.

Pallas, A. M. (2001). Preparing education doctoral students for epistemological diversity. *Educational Researcher 30*(5), 6–11.

Paul, J. L., and Marfo, K. (2001). Preparation of educational researchers in philosophical foundation of inquiry. *Review of Educational Research, 71*(4), 525–547.

Riehl, C., Larson, C. L., Short, P. M., and Reitzug, U. C. (2000). Reconceptualizing research and scholarship in educational administration: Learning to know, knowing to do, and doing to learn. *Educational Administration Quarterly 36*(3), 391–427.

Scribner, J., and Donaldson, J. F. (2001). The dynamics of group learning in a cohort: From non-Learning to transformative learning. *Educational Administration Quarterly, 37*(5), 605–636.

Slater, C., and Martinez, B. (2000). Transformational leadership in the planning of a doctoral program. *The Educational Forum, 64*(4), 308–316.

Smallwood, S. (2001). Graduates students give their programs mixed reviews in new questionnaire. *The Chronicle of Higher Education, 48*(10), A18.

Teitel, L. (1997). Understanding and harnessing the power of the cohort model in preparing educational leaders. *Peabody Journal of Education, 72*(2), 66–85.

Young, L. J. (2001). Border crossings and other journeys: Revisioning the doctoral preparation of education researchers. *Educational Researcher, 30*(5), 3–5.

Academic Reading Assignments and the Graduate Student

JULIE COMBS

IN A RECENT SURVEY, 82 PERCENT OF THE COLLEGE STUDENTS sampled admitted that they read their college textbooks little or not at all (Sikorski, Rich, Saville, Buskist, Drogan, and Davis, 2002). During informal discussions, some students revealed that they do not complete assigned readings and are frustrated by the selections. Proficient reading is a prerequisite for the expected scholarship for students engaged in graduate level studies. Reading assignments offer background information that can be used to facilitate active classroom activities to extend and deepen understanding of content. When students do not complete reading assignments, learning at higher levels is limited. The purpose of this study is to identify reading practices of graduate level students. By understanding student preferences and practices related to academic reading, professors should be able to select appropriate texts and facilitate effective reading strategies that can improve student learning.

PROCEDURES

This study utilized an exploratory qualitative design and was guided by these two research questions: (a) What motivates graduate-level students to read academic assignments, and (b) How do the principles of adult learning theories apply to assignment of class reading? Specifically the investigation involved defining the problem, locating relevant sources, summarizing and evaluating information from the retrieved sources, and interpreting the information to understand trends and issues related to graduate students' reading practices.

After the research questions were defined, research reports were found using a variety of indexes in education, social sciences, and business. The search for reports was systematic and documented to include as many relevant studies as possible within the past 20 years. All research reports were evaluated for empirical strengths and weaknesses.

Findings were categorized and three themes were formulated to answer the first research question. Next, these themes were compared to theories regarding adult learning to validate the themes and to provide a theoretical explanation of the findings. From this analysis, specific conclusions were identified and will direct future investigations of graduate level reading practices. This study provides initial findings to guide an on-going action research project for the purpose of improving graduate-level instruction.

FINDINGS

Bischoping (2003) noted that few studies had evaluated the reading practices of students at the university level. The search confirmed this finding. No studies were found with graduate students as subjects, rather all studies involved students at the undergraduate level. Also, no studies were found that included students enrolled in educational leadership programs. Because of these limitations, the first research question was modified to explore the reading practices of undergraduate level students.

Three studies reported on textbook usage and comprehension of textbook content by undergraduate students enrolled in psychology classes (Sikorski et al., 2002; Taraban, 2000; Weiten, Guadagno, and Beck, 1996). Williams (1997) studied the effects of instructional approaches to motivate reading in undergraduate geography students. Bischoping (2003) surveyed undergraduate students from business, humanities, and social sciences along with their instructors to examine the overall perceptions of selected readings. After an analysis of the findings, three general reasons were identified to explain student completion of assigned reading. These three categories were relevance, financial impact, and overall workload issues.

Relevance

Students were more likely to complete reading assignments when they had a personal reason to do so such as having an interest in the material or in earning a desired grade. In a study surveying entry level psychology students approximately 80 percent reported reading the text very little or not at all (Sikorski et al., 2002). Moreover, students rated the study practices that best prepared them for exams. Approximately 60 percent of the students believed that taking notes and studying them, without reading the text resulted in acceptable outcomes. Bischoping (2003) found that students preferred reading selections that were contemporary, easy to read, and related to their personal backgrounds. Students reported they were more likely to read selections when they perceived the materials to be personally meaningful, supportive of course objectives, or aligned with assessments.

Williams (1997) observed the effect of different strategies used to motivate student completion of reading assignments in undergraduate geography classes. After explaining to the class the relevance of the reading assignment and its importance to the course's content, Williams observed little change in student behavior and concluded that encouragement from the instructor as an isolated strategy for reading assignment completion was ineffective. Williams hypothesized that the influence and leadership of peers would lead to higher completion rates and assigned students the task of preparing and leading discussion questions on the assigned reading. Based on student survey data, Williams concluded that peer influence alone was an ineffective motivator. Next, unannounced quizzes were administered to assess knowledge of the reading. Although students were unhappy with this approach, they indicated in a survey that they were more motivated by quizzes and assignments as opposed to internal factors of a desire to learn or self-motivation. When asked what types of strategies would motivate the students to complete reading assignments, approximately 70 percent of the students responded that graded written assignments such as reading notes, quizzes, summaries, or comprehension questions were most effective.

Test preparation and course grades were found to be of major importance to students (Liow and Betts, 1993). Students often assessed the relevance of the reading assignment based on its connection to course exams (Bischoping, 2003). Sikorski et al. (2002) reported that approximately 16 percent of the students believed that reading the text was not necessary to receive an acceptable grade in the course. Instead, students believed that attending class, taking notes, and studying the notes were of greater value than reading the textbook in relation to their final course grade. Sikorski et al. concluded that instructors should utilize methods that will increase student accountability for reading by utilizing quizzes and non-volunteer class discussions.

Although students valued materials that helped them earn acceptable grades, instructors were found to place much less emphasis on student grades when selecting reading materials (Bischoping, 2003; Liow and Betts, 1993). Instructors listed different criteria when choosing effective reading material and supplied pedagogical reasons for material selection including connection to the course themes, level of reading difficulty, and diversity of perspectives. Furthermore, instructors were less likely to consider factors deemed important to students such as ease of reading, test preparation or review activities, and material costs (Bischoping, 2003).

Regarding text selection, Bischoping (2003) found that instructors reported having great autonomy in their choices of course materials. Moreover, text decisions were most often made in isolation in that instructors rarely discussed selections with colleagues or professional librarians. Bischoping concluded that professional discussions with colleagues and students could lead to better selections. An analysis of the available studies found that undergraduate students were more likely to complete reading assignments when content from the reading was assessed and included in their course grade.

Financial Impact

Students were more likely to complete reading assignments when they perceived the costs of the materials to be affordable and of good value. Approximately 70 percent of the students surveyed did not purchase a required course textbook (Sikorski et al., 2002). One factor listed by students when deciding to buy the textbook focused on the bookstore's willingness to buy the book back at the end of the semester. In this university's case, the selected textbook could not be returned. Three-fourths of the students that did not purchase the textbook borrowed a copy from a friend. Many of the students listed financial reasons or explained that the text was of little value. At a second university studied, 18 percent of the students did not buy the required course textbook even though the bookstore would buy back the text.

Of this 18 percent of students that did not purchase the book, 54 percent believed the book was unnecessary and 21 percent indicated the book was too expensive. When instructors were asked about criteria used in reading selections for the course, financial concerns were not listed (Bischoping, 2003). In the studies reviewed, undergraduate students believed that costs impacted their decisions to complete course reading assignments.

Workload

Students were more likely to complete reading assignments when they perceived the assignment to be of reasonable length and when they had time to do so. Sikorski et al. (2002) reported that of the undergraduate students that purchased a course text, 82 percent read the textbook very little or not at all. For the students that did read the course materials, they estimated that they spent less than three hours per week on reading assignments. Focusing on the perceived workloads of adult part-time students, Chambers (1992) concluded that instructors who overload students with excessive work harm the learning of students, as overload results in surface level learning as opposed to deeper levels of understanding. Specifically, she argued that

> if students are to learn well, to engage in deep learning, then teachers must ensure that the curriculum allows them to do so: they must ensure that time is allowed for students actively to engage in academic discourses in the ways outlined earlier [calculating workload hours based on reading rates], rather than being constantly driven by the need to complete a multitude of tasks as best they can. (p. 153)

Chambers suggested a formula to calculate a course's workload based on the work of Whalley (1982). The formula calculated estimated time to complete the reading by categorizing text according to its difficulty level. For example, material that is easy to read received an estimation of 100 words per minute while more difficult texts received a rate of 40 words per minute. Chambers explained that these rates were more than reading fluency speeds as they incorporated study and reflection time. Chambers concluded that students were more likely to complete assignments when they perceived the workload to be of reasonable amount. Moreover, in a related study, workload was shown to be a factor in a student's decision to drop out of the university (Woodly and Parlett, 1983).

Students were asked about their reading assignment preferences and reported that they wanted less reading material for their courses (Bischoping, 2003). In the studies reviewed, undergraduate students attributed relevance, costs, time, and workload concerns as reasons for completing or not completing course reading assignment. The next question was proposed to compare the results of the literature review with existing theories about how adults learn. How do the students' reasons for completing reading assignments synthesized from these studies align with theories regarding the learning preferences of adults?

Adult Learning Theories

Knowles (1968) differentiated adult learning and was the first to term adult learning "andragogy" as compared to pedagogy which is used to define learning principles for children. Since then, andragogy, self-directed learning, and transformational learning have become a few of the theories explaining the needs of adult learners (Merriam, 2001). These theories suggest that adults have different learning needs than children, need less direction, desire more choice, and want immediate application. Knowles (1980) defined five characteristics of the adult learner: (a) can direct his own learning, (b) has extensive background experiences and knowledge, (c) has learning needs related to his social roles, (d) is most interested in immediate application of knowledge, and (e) is motivated to learn more by internal factors than external factors.

Although adult learning theory has been the topic of many studies and applied in several disciplines, Zemke (2002) stated that andragogy is no longer a cogent explanation of adult learning. Merriam and Caffarella (1991) stated that andragogy is a widely known theory of adult learning that has produced more "controversy, philosophical debate, and critical analysis than any other concept/theory/model proposed thus far" (pp. 249–250). The assumptions of andragogy have been tested and challenged with adult students. Bale and Dudney (2000) studied the learning preferences of Generation X college students (born between 1961 to 1981) and found that they preferred both pedagogical and andragogical elements in the undergraduate classroom. For example, students reported a preference for direction from an authority as opposed to self-directed learning experiences. At the same time, Generation X students indicated a desire for relevant connections, applications, and use of active participation teaching strategies. Bale and Dudney concluded that instructors should provide a comprehensive syllabus and detailed grading rubrics for assignments and utilize guest speakers, current journals articles, case studies, and group work teaching strategies.

In the studies reviewed, some of the students' reasons for completing reading assignments aligned with principles of adult learning. One characteristic stated by Knowles (1980) was that adult learners were most interested in immediate application of knowledge. This issue of relevance was dominant in the studies reviewed. Students were more likely to read assignments when they believed the reading selections were contemporary and related to their personal backgrounds (Bischoping, 2003).

Another characteristic of adult learners was that they were motivated to learn more by internal factors than external factors (Knowles, 1980). The results of the studies reviewed provided mixed results relating to this characteristic of adult learners. Many of the university students believed that course grades were a motivating factor when deciding to complete reading assignments (Bischoping, 2003; Liow and Betts, 1993). Are course grades an external factor or an internal factor related to achievement and success? Perhaps course grades represent both external and internal factors, depending on the specific student. Some students may be motivated primarily by the learning represented by earning a specific grade. Others may be motivated to earn a specific grade in order to complete the requirements for a degree or to obtain financial reward. The studies did not provide enough information to determine the levels of internal or external motivation of students related to earning course grades. On the other hand, one specific external factor, costs of reading materials, was found to be a motivating factor for students. Similar to the findings regarding the need for external motivation by Generation X college students (Bale and Dudney, 2000), this review suggests that adult learners are more focused on external factors such as costs, time, and grades as opposed to internal factors related to learning and personal improvement. The remaining three principles of adult learning including self-directed learning, use of background experience, and connecting learning to adult's social roles could not be analyzed based on the data given in the studies.

DISCUSSION

If reading is an essential skill needed for students to obtain knowledge necessary in pursuit of higher education, then more attention and study should be devoted to the reading practices of adult learners. One finding of this study was that students valued relevance as a factor in their decisions to read assignments. Instructors did consider relevant content when selecting reading (Bischoping, 2003) but should extend consideration toward materials that will relate to the students' background experiences, career goals, and current life applications. Furthermore, if the completion of reading is a necessary learning activity of the course, then knowledge gained from the reading should be included in course assessments. By connecting the reading to evaluation, instructors communicate that the reading is relevant for the course and is necessary for achieving the course objectives. Students stated that they were more motivated to read when they knew that assessment was tied to the reading (Bischoping, 2003; Liow and Betts, 1993; Sikorski et al., 2002; Williams, 1997). Connecting the reading to the course grade appears to be one of the most effective ways to motivate students to read.

In addition to the criteria of relevance, instructors should consider costs of materials and workload issues of their students when selecting assignments. Both of these concerns emerged as motivating factors for students but were not reported by instructors as considerations (Bischoping, 2003; Sikorski et al., 2002). In addition, instructors reported rarely discussing selections with colleagues (Bischoping, 2003). Such dialogue with their peers could result in the consideration of additional criteria related to the specific needs of their students regarding workload or financial issues.

Some of the principles of adult learning theory were supported by college students' reasons to complete reading assignments, while other principles did not match. Of greatest congruence was the principle of relevance and life application. By focusing on relevance when selecting reading materials, instructors will increase the probability that students will participate in the desired learning activities. Of least congruence was the principle of self-directed learning. Although more data were needed, the general findings did not show that the adult students in the studies were motivated by self-directed, intrinsic reasons. Additional inquiry is needed to determine the relevance of adult learning theories for the various age groups served in higher education.

Because of the lack of studies about college students' reading practices and the limited disciplines represented by the studies reviewed, more research is needed to understand this essential learning skill. Additionally, more research is needed to test adult learning theories with graduate-level students.

CONCLUSIONS

This study was designed to investigate the reading practices of graduate level students. Because no studies with graduate students could be located, undergraduate students' practices were analyzed. Students considered factors of relevance, financial impact, and workload when deciding to complete assigned reading. Instructors selected different criteria than did their students when choosing reading assignments. Instructors considered the assignment's connection to course content and text difficulty levels. Furthermore, instructors were less likely to consider test preparation or student financial concerns when selecting texts. Therefore, the implications of this study are that instructors should consider applying adult learning theory principles of relevance when selecting assignments and should review workload and financial concerns of students in their learning communities. The selection of more relevant and meaningful reading assignments should result in higher student participation. By knowing the factors involved in a student's decision to complete course reading assignments, instructors can increase their effectiveness in monitoring and evaluating deeper levels of learning.

REFERENCES

Bale, J. M., and Dudney, D. (2000). Teaching Generation X: Do andragogical learning principles apply to undergraduate finance education? *Financial Practice and Education, 10*, 216–227.

Bischoping, K. (2003). Selecting and using course readings: A study of instructors' and students' practices. *Canadian Journal of Higher Education, 33*(1), 25–58.

Chambers, E. (1992). Work-load and the quality of student learning. *Studies in Higher Education, 17*(2), 141–153.

Knowles, M. S. (1968). Andragogy, not pedagogy. *Adult Leadership, 16*(10), 350–353, 386.

Knowles, M. S. (1980). *The modern practice of adult education: from pedagogy to andragogy* (2nd ed). New York: Cambridge Books.

Liow, S. R., and Betts, M. (1993). Course design in higher education: A study of teaching methods and educational objectives. *Studies in Higher Education, 18*(1), 65–79.

Merriam, S. B. (2001, Spring). Andragogy and self-directed learning: Pillars of adult learning theory. *New Directions for Adult and Continuing Education, 89*, 3–13.

Merriam, S. B., and Caffarella, R. S. (1991). *Learning in adulthood*. San Francisco: Jossey-Bass.

Sikorski, J. F., Rich, K., Saville, B. K., Buskist, W., Drogan, O., and Davis, S. F. (2002). Student use of introductory tests: Comparative survey findings from two universities. *Teaching of Psychology, 29*(4), 312–313.

Taraban, R., Rynearson, K., and Kerr, J. (2000). College students' academic performance and self-reports of comprehension strategy use. *Reading Psychology, 21*(4), 283–308.

Weiten, W., Guadagno, R. E., and Beck, C. A. (1996). Students' perceptions of textbook pedagogical aids. *Teaching of Psychology, 23*(2), 105–107.

Whalley, P. (1982). Argument in text and the reading process. In A. Flammer and W. Kintsch (Eds.), *Discourse Processing*. Amsterdam: North Holland.

Williams, A. M. (1997). Making the most of assigned readings: Some alternative strategies. *Journal of Geography in Higher Education, 21*(3), 363–372.

Woodley, A., and Partlett, M. (1983, Autumn). Student drop-out. *Teaching at a Distance, 24*, 2–23.

Zemke, R. A. (2002, Sept.). Pocket guide to useful learning theories. *Training, 39*(9), 90–91.

Changing the Future: How Doctoral Students' Changing Perceptions of Social Justice Transforms Practice

SANDRA HARRIS AND BETTY ALFORD

NEARLY 100 YEARS AGO, DEWEY (1916) SUGGESTED THE importance of educator opportunities to change the future when he wrote that as educators influence what and how society learns, the world is continually constructed and reconstructed. Yet, attitudes of leadership today often are embedded with a "privileged perspective which largely ignores issues of status, gender, and race" (Gosetti and Rusch, 1995, p. 12.) Too often, this fosters leadership attitudes that are closed-minded and intolerant, and results in continually sustaining inequity through stratifying groups of people (Rusch, 2002).

Even though a goal of social justice is that all individuals have access to resources in order to meet essential needs that lead to equitable school environments, there remains a disparity in the academic achievement levels of historically oppressed groups and their Anglo counterparts (Barton, 2004). This is evidenced in the dropout rates of students coming from minority and/or low socioeconomic backgrounds which are considerably higher than those who come from Anglo families and/or more privileged economic environments (Texas Education Agency, 2002). Consistent with this, Spring (2004) reported a 1999 study by Gary Orfield that suggested that segregation with all of its inequities is still "an educational pattern" in the United States (p. 123).

At the same time, national and state standards challenge school leaders to "capitalize on diversity to create a school culture that promotes respect and success for all students" (National Policy Board for Educational Administration, 2001, Standard 2 narrative explanation). However, in order for issues of power and privilege to lead to a more just and equitable understanding of educational leadership, today's administrators must create a vision for their schools founded upon moral and spiritual attitudes, language, and practices that understand and include words, such as "compassion," "forgiveness," "wisdom," and "humil-

ity" (Beck and Foster, 1999; Tillman, 2002). Therefore, this paper explores the perceptions of social justice issues and resultant changes in practice of educators enrolled in an educational leadership doctoral program.

CONCEPTUAL FRAMEWORK

Dantley (2001) argued that it is time to offer an alternative to the "positivist, empiricist methods of reform" traditionally embedded in our understandings (p. 3) and challenged educational leaders to consider three principles posited by Cornell West (1988). These spiritual principles, deep-seated moralism, inescapable opportunism, and aggressive pessimism have the capacity to change the embedded assumptions and behaviors of all involved. Dantley (2001) referred to deep-seated moralism as *principled leadership* which manifests itself in a careful and critical reflection of one's position on issues of justice, democracy, and fairness. This happens when leaders reflect critically about the democratic efficacy of administrative decisions and procedures being implemented.

Dantley's second principle, inescapable opportunism, is the notion of *pragmatic leadership* which challenges leaders to consciously consider the contradictions of spoken philosophies of democratic schools and the realities facing our schools. This is evidenced when school leaders commit to a willingness to change their beliefs when they recognize the conflict inherent in what they say they believe and what they observe happing in schools. The third principle, profound pessimism, leads to Dantley's idea of *purposive leadership*, which is focused on conscious actions that transform schools. In other words, education leaders must reflect on where they stand regarding social justice, they must question this disconnect between what they say and what they do, and, finally, leaders must consider how schools can be transformed into schools where social justice abounds.

Making Our Schools More Just

Apple (1999) noted that throughout the United States many contradictory proposals have been offered to make our schools more just. Some of these "fixes" have suggested greater forms of governmental control, especially considering equity and the oppressed. For example, Hirsch (1999) suggested that the school should use a common curriculum in order to eliminate the extremes of wealth and poverty. Anderson (1996) argued that administrative practices that continue to track students are responsible for ineffective schools. Mahar (2001) challenged teachers to incorporate visual thinking and the graphic process into the classroom in order to create a climate where there is little failure. Crow and Matthews (1998) argued that a rigorous curriculum is a defining characteristic of a successful school. Lin (2001) emphasized the fundamental characteristic of caring because when people sincerely care they find ways to be just, fair and equitable. However, regardless of strategy used, Slavin (1998) emphasized that the only way to decrease the equity gap in academic performance of children is to increase the achievement of disadvantaged and minority students. After all, as Scheurich and Skrla argue it is "our spiritual duty as educators to create schools that are equitable; schools that serve literally all children really well" (2003, p. 7).

Dantley's (2001) suggestion that principled leadership, pragmatic leadership and purposive leadership, lead to the transformation of schools is consistent with Foster (1986) who challenged leaders to engage in discourse about the direction of leadership within our society "concerned with how lives should be lived" (p. 57). Additionally, Lambert (2002) challenged leaders to "explore current practices, beliefs, and assumptions that serve as a basis for posing inquiry questions" (p. 89). Likewise, Sarason (2002) challenged school leaders to speak and not remain silent about needed changes so that the "imaginativeness of which its members are capable" may be heard (p. 141). Thus, an essential component of learning that leads to knowing is the principle that "deeper transformation is fostered by understanding of oneself and by becoming conscious of and examining the social construction of one's identity (Ettling, 2003, p. 8). In agreement with this, Tatum (1997) and Howard (1999) asserted that a fundamental process in this challenge to achieve common goals lies in educators becoming comfortable with their own identity. This process of critical reflection, grounded in identification and evaluation of personal identity and its related biases, has profound implications for schools to be transformed into equitable learning communities.

METHODOLOGY

Sample

We surveyed 64 students who had either completed or were nearing completion of a new doctoral program which had graduated five cohorts. Fifty-one responded, and 25 were female and 26 were male. Forty-three students were white, while six were African American and two were Hispanic. We combined the African American and Hispanic students into one category due to the small number. Twenty-two students were less than 40 years old and 29 were over 40 years of age. The majority of the respondents were principals or superintendents (36), 10 worked in the central office, and five were classroom teachers. Thirty-three students were employed in rural areas of Texas, while 18 worked in suburban or urban areas.

Data Collection

Sixty-four students who had completed the doctoral program or were nearing completion were mailed a 26-question survey in the summer of 2004. The questions asked students to critically reflect using Dantley's three principles as a guiding framework:

- principled leadership (what do you believe about social justice issues?)
- pragmatic leadership (considering the reality of social justice, what changes have occurred in your beliefs?)
- purposive leadership (considering reality and your own changing beliefs regarding social justice, what changes have occurred in your practice?).

Fifty-one students responded. The stated goal of the doctoral program was to prepare educators to transform educational settings into ones that were socially just. The first questions queried students if this goal had been met. Then, participants rated the importance of social justice issues as they related to their leadership role using a 5-point Likert-type scale of 1 (least important) to 5 (most important). They also rated how well their course work heightened understandings and critical analysis about these issues using the same scale. In open-ended questions, students described how their perceptions of social justice issues had changed. Additionally, students were asked to describe a situation with which they had dealt in the past year and explain how their understandings about social justice concepts influenced this event.

Data Analysis

SPSS was used to generate frequencies and cross-tabs disaggregated the data by ethnicity (combining Hispanic and African American into one category), location, age, and gender. Means were generated and independent samples, *t* tests and *Oneway ANOVA*, were calculated to analyze for statistical significance at *p*<.05. The survey had a reliability coefficient of .9379 which is high.

FINDINGS

Principled Leadership—What Do You Believe?

We began by asking respondents to reflect on their beliefs about social justice issues and rate how well the doctoral program had met the goal of preparing educators to bring about educational settings that are socially just through the course work. Overall responses indicated that participants felt the doctoral program gave social justice high importance. They responded that "the goal was evident in course content" (*M* = 4.63, *SD* = .53) and "evident in learning experiences" (*M* = 4.65, *SD* = .48). They reported that "the goal resulted in a focus on multicultural settings" with a mean of 4.45 (*SD* = .64).

How Important Is It To Know About Social Justice Issues?

The next question asked participants to critically reflect on the importance of gaining knowledge about all of the social justice issues that were listed. Responses rated all items important with means that ranged from 4.57 to 3.90. (See Table 1). They considered gaining knowledge about providing equitable school environments for all and meeting needs of students of low socio-economic status as most important.

The issue of least concern was the item "overcoming discrimination due to sexual orientation." This raised a concern because the issue of sexual orientation has recently become a major concern to schools where students have attempted to set up clubs for "gay" students within this area. Additionally, student sexual orientation is often reported as an issue leading to students being bullied which can negatively affect the climate of the entire school (Harris and Petrie, 2003).

When responses were further analyzed with independent sample *t*-tests for location, age and ethnicity no statistically significant differences were found. No significant findings were reported when Oneway ANOVA analyzed for differences in job status. However, when analyzed by gender, two categories: promoting an appreciation for ethnic differences and increasing opportunities for marginalized groups were identified as significantly more important to females than to males. An interesting finding is that in every category rating importance of gaining knowledge about social justice issues, females reported a higher mean than males. (See Table 1 for over-all means.)

How Has Course Work Heightened Understanding?

The next question asked participants to rate how the course work and activities had heightened their understanding and critical analysis of social justice areas relating to leadership. The mean response range for these questions was 4.588 to 3.784. Once again, the lowest mean dealt with overcoming discrimination due to sexual orientation, which suggested the need for future course work to include this topic in more depth. (See Table 2.)

When social justice issues were disaggregated and further analyzed with independent sample *t* tests and

Table 1. Importance of Gaining Knowledge About Social Justice Issues as They Relate to Leadership

Social Justice Issue	Mean	Std. Dev.
Providing school environments equitable for all	4.57	610
Meeting needs of students of low SES	4.51	.731
Closing achievement gap between ethnic/economic	4.45	.673
*Promoting appreciation for ethnic differences	4.45	.673
**Increasing opportunities for marginalized groups	4.45	.855
Overcoming gender bias	4.35	.770
Responding to needs of students w/disabilities	4.39	.665
Promoting multiculturalism	4.33	.771
Overcoming sexual orientation discrimination	3.9	1.063

Notes:
n = 51
*p<.05 by gender (females *M* = 4.64; males *M* = 4.192)
**p<.05 by gender (females *M* = 4.56; males *M* = 4.076)
Scale: 1(least important) – 5 (most important)

**Table 2. Rate the Degree that Doctoral Course Work and Activities Heightened
Your Understanding and Critical Analysis of Social Justice Areas Related To Leadership**

Social Justice Issue	Mean	Std. Dev.
Providing school environments equitable for all	4.588	.638
Meeting needs of students of low SES	4.451	.756
*Promoting appreciation for ethnic differences	4.411	.697
***Promoting multiculturalism	4.411	.779
**Increasing opportunities for marginalized groups	4.313	.860
Closing achievement gap between ethnic/economic	4.294	.831
Overcoming gender bias	4.254	.820
Responding to needs of students w/disabilities	4.137	.775
Overcoming sexual orientation discrimination	3.783	1.136

Notes:
n = 51
*$p < .05$ by gender (females M =4.640; males 4.192)
**$p < .05$ by gender (females M = 4.560; males 4.076)
***$p < .05$ by age (less than 40 M = 4.136; over 40 years of age M = 4.6207)

Oneway ANOVA, there were no significant findings by ethnicity, location or by job description. However, those respondents older than 40 years of age indicated that doctoral course work and activities heightened understandings and critical analysis significantly more for promoting multiculturalism than for those who were less than 40 years of age. This is a reasonable expectation considering that it was likely older students had been away from university coursework longer and had not been exposed to multiculturalism education.

When data were analyzed by gender, two categories were statistically significant at the $p < .05$ level. Females reported that course work and activities heightened understanding and critical analysis of the social justice issue of promoting an appreciation for ethnic differences and increasing opportunities for marginalized groups. Once again, it was interesting to note that in every category, females reported a higher mean than males regarding heightened understandings of social justice issues.

What Was the Most/Least Important Area To Be Addressed?

In open-ended questions, participants were asked to identify the area of social justice which was most important and least important for educators to address. Half (50 percent) indicated that providing school environments that are equitable for all was the most important area for educators to address. The item "increasing opportunities for marginalized groups" was selected by 25 percent of the students and 15 percent selected "promoting an appreciation for ethnic differences." Another 10 percent selected "meeting the needs of students of low socio-economic status" as most important to be addressed.

One individual commented that the issue of providing an environment that was equitable for all was most important because "educators must make sure that all children are given the opportunity to succeed so they can become informed citizens in a caring society." Another pointed out that "in this time of standards and accountability, it is easy to get caught up in the politics of education, instead of the needs of the students."

Determining the area of least importance for educators to address was difficult and over half of the participants suggested that all were important and chose not to specify one as least important noting that "none can be identified as unimportant." However, the 25 who identified a least-important issue specified that it was the issue of overcoming sexual discrimination. One respondent added that it was also "time for the pendulum to swing back to reasonableness" regarding special education needs. Another commented that "closing the achievement gap has already been address with standardized testing."

Pragmatic Leadership—What Changes Have Occurred in Your Beliefs?

Next, participants were asked to critically reflect on their socially just beliefs and the realities that exist within their schools. All of the participants indicated that their perceptions of social justice had changed as a result of the doctoral program. One major theme—increased awareness of social justice issues—emerged as a result of the program components which emphasized readings, synthesis writing, diverse guest speakers, panels, class discourse, and reflection.

While all respondents reported that they had become more aware of social justice issues, they also noted that they were now "more aware of injustices on my campus." Over 75 percent indicated that this had caused them to identify their own prejudices and biases and become "more aware of my hidden self." This was an important step to leading them to become more pro-active in dealing with social justice issues in their personal and professional lives.

Participants also expressed a renewed awareness of the meaning of social justice and how it can impact other people. For example, one respondent stated that initially "he had not given credence to Friere's notion that 'You can't fully understand oppression unless you have been oppressed.'" He indicated that this was a "landmark moment" for him. Another admitted that she had never realized all of the various issues that were involved, such as oppression, language, power, and the need for discourse. Still, another acknowledged his "naiveté kept [him] from seeing what [his] studies were presenting."

The increased awareness of lack of equity led several participants to comment that their perceptions "have been challenged" regarding social justice. One pointed out that her perceptions had not changed, but her "viewpoints had definitely increased." She wrote that this would make her a better educator, because she had "always had a heart for the under-served . . . my knowledge was just limited." Others noted that their weaknesses in the area of social justice were due to "lack of exposure" to people with diverse backgrounds. Because the program enabled students to read about and work closely with people of other races, they felt that they "have been able to grow as a result."

Purposive Leadership—What Changes Have Occurred in Your Practice?

When considering reality and doctoral student changing beliefs, all participants reported that they are transforming their practice in many ways to better understand and include marginalized groups. As experiences were shared, it was obvious that graduates as well as current doctoral students were responding to the challenge with purposeful action to better address social justice issues on their campuses.

Students are implementing changes in their practice. Each of the 51 participants indicated that they are implementing changes in their practice to be more socially just. One student shared the following experience:

We received a Palestinian student—rather than treating him indifferently, I purposefully made an attempt to provide congenial respect.

Another wrote:

I have become aware of how bilingual programs are "schools within schools" which are in actuality segregation devices. I came to this realization after reading about subtractive schooling.

Still another student shared this:

I dealt with a young African American male in the area of sexual misbehaviors. I delved into his cultural background and was able to redirect his behaviors. Discussions in class allowed me to understand the need as well as to promote social justice.

Other selected student comments included the following:

A teacher made a comment she thought was funny, however I could tell that the student did not. In private, I visited with the teacher about her racial comment and its effect on the student.

We have a high population of economically disadvantaged students. I no longer believe that people are economically disadvantaged because they are lazy. Now, I work harder to motivate these kids.

I am amazed how low the issues of social justice are considered from different lenses. I have encouraged teacher friends to read articles about social justice.

I became aware of a community conflict where an oppressed group was taking sides with their oppressors and they were not even aware this was happening. . . . I was able to encourage them to understand why this was not a good move for them.

I changed my dissertation topic, so that I could learn more about social justice issues and how to help my campus in this regard.

I am working with my teachers to increase their expectations for low SES students. We need to have high expectations for all students!

I don't laugh at certain kinds of jokes anymore.

Our low SES kids were not participating in extra-curricular activities. I began a program that targeted these students for involvement.

There are challenges to transforming practice. Transforming practice is not always easy. For example, one respondent wrote that becoming more aware of the importance and need for socially just schools had caused her to "become more vocal about helping all students to achieve success." This need to become more vocal was expressed by others also. However, at the same time, several students pointed out that becoming "vocal is not easy and might change some relationships on my campus . . . but they need to become aware of this also."

Participants also reported much frustration in transforming practice with regard to standardized accountability measures, indicating that "my hands are tied." One student wrote that "It is difficult, though not impossible, to focus on the rights and needs of each student, and their differences, when the state system wants educators to focus on everyone achieving the same material at the same time." Another argued that a "cookie cutter curriculum is anti-social justice!" One student agreed with an article by a well-known education leader that stated that "standardized accountability locks us into a minimum standard and does not allow for expansion." Several expressed the belief that most school decisions "are only made to improve test scores . . . not to improve opportunities for a good education."

At the same time, other students believed that "even though it is difficult," purposive leadership had a positive effect on standardized accountability systems because it provided motivation "for giving instruction to students who have been ignored in the past." Unfortunately, these same students felt that under-served students "still do not receive the same enrichment opportunities." While all of the students wrote at some point about the need for a care ethic, one student stated this especially well, when he wrote that "we are all family" and indicated that it was every educator's responsibility to be a leader who "mirrored care and understanding to ensure social justice."

CONCLUSION

Within the framework of principled leadership (critically reflect on beliefs), doctoral graduates and students who participated in this survey indicated that they considered social justice issues important, especially providing equitable school environments for all students, meeting the needs of students of low socioeconomic status, closing the achievement gap between ethnic and economic groups, and promoting an appreciation for ethnic differences. The one area where critical reflection occurred least was that of sexual orientation discrimination.

Regarding pragmatic leadership (recognize belief changes needed), overwhelmingly students reported that increasing awareness and having their perceptions challenged led them to consciously consider the contradictions of spoken philosophies of democratic schools and the realities that exist in our schools which led to changing beliefs. Purposive leadership (changes in practice) comments reinforced that changed beliefs identified a need for purposefully changing actions and these transforming actions are occurring on school campuses due to their enhanced understanding of social justice issues.

This study has significance for educational leaders and leadership programs in considering the importance of reflecting on social justice issues, evaluating belief issues within students of all ages, and then implementing changes that can occur to transform the schooling experience for all students. Findings suggest the need to encourage the necessary dialogue of social justice theory as it relates to best practice in the schools. People think about themselves and others in terms of social identities (Gollwitzer and Kirchof, 1998) and they create narratives to help them understand themselves and their identities (McAdams, 1999). This reflective, discursive practice is an essential component to transforming schools (Rusch, 2002). Framed within Dantley's principled leadership, pragmatic leadership, and purposive leadership, doctoral students in this study, engaged in critical, reflective analysis, recognized the need for social justice, developed an awareness that led to changing behaviors, and transformed their own practices to lead their schools to become more socially just. This study suggests that when improving social justice in schools is a program goal, and students are encouraged to critically reflect on what they believe, paradigms of social justice leadership are changed and practice is transformed. This is critical to changing the future of schools and ultimately changing the future. "Never doubt that a small group of thoughtful committed citizens can change the world. Indeed, it is the only thing that ever has" (Margaret Mead, in Blaydes, 2003, p. 75).

REFERENCES

Anderson, G. L. (1996). What does practitioner research look like? *Teaching and Change, 3*(2), 173–206.

Apple, M. (1999). Teacher assessment ignores social injustice. *Education Digest, 65*(2), 24–28.

Barton, P. (2004). Why does the gap persist? *Educational Leadership, 62*(3), 8–13.

Beck, L., and Foster, W. (1999). Administration and community: Considering challenges, exploring possibilities.

In J. Murphy and K. Louis (Eds.), *Handbook of research on educational administration* (2nd ed., pp. 337–358). San Francisco: Jossey-Bass.

Blaydes, J. (2003). *The educator's book of quotes.* Thousand Oaks, CA: Corwin Press.

Crow, G. M., and Matthews, L. J. (1998). *Finding one's way: How mentoring can lead to dynamic leadership.* Thousand Oaks, CA: Corwin Press.

Dantley, M. (2001). *Transforming school leadership through Cornel West's notions of African American Prophetic spirituality.* Paper presented at The University Council for Educational Administration, November 2001.

Dewey, T. (1916). *Democracy and education.* New York: Macmillan.

Ettling, D. (2003). The praxis of sustaining transformative change. *TCRecord On-line.* Retrieved on February 20, 2004, from http://www.tcrecord.org/.

Foster, W. (1986). *Paradigms and promises.* Buffalo: Prometheus Books.

Gollwitzer, P. M., and Kirchof, O. (1998). The willful pursuit of identity. In J. Heckhausen and C. S. Dweck (Eds.), *Motivation and self-regulation across the life span* (pp. 389–423). New York: Cambridge University Press.

Gosetti, P., and Rusch, E. (1995). Re-examining educational leadership: Challenging assumptions. In D. Dunlap and P. Schmuck (Eds.), *Women leading in education* (pp. 11–35). New York: State University of New York Press.

Harris, S., and Petrie, G. (2002). *Bullying: The Bullies, the bullied, the victims.* Lanham, MD: Scarecrow Education.

Hirsch, E. D. (1999). Americanization and the schools. *Clearing House, 72*(3), 136–139.

Howard, G. (1999). *We can't teach what we don't know.* New York: The New Press.

Lambert, L. (2002). Leadership as a form of learning: Implications for theory and practice. In G. Perreault and F. Lunenburg (Eds.), *The changing world of school administration* (pp. 80–90). Lanham, MD: Scarecrow Education.

Lin, Q. (2001). Toward a caring-center multicultural education within the social justice context. *Education, 1,* 107–114.

Mahar, D. (2001). Social justice and the class community: Opening the door to possibilities. *Educational Journal, 90,* 107–114.

McAdams, D. P. (1999). Personal narratives and the life story. In L. A. Pervin and O. P. John (Eds.), *Handbook of personality: Theory and research* (2nd ed., pp. 478–500). New York: Guilford Press.

National Policy Board for Educational Administration. (2001). *ELCC/NCATE standards for advanced programs in educational leadership.* Retrieved on January 15, 2002, from www.npbea.org/ELCC.

Rusch, E. (2002). The (un)changing world of school leadership: A journey from discourse to practice. In G. Perreault and F. Lunenburg (Eds.), *The changing world of school administration* (pp. 60–79). Lanham, MD: Scarecrow Education.

Sarason, S. (2002). A call for professional-organizational self-scrutiny. In G. Perreault and F. Lunenburg (Eds.), *The changing world of school administration* (pp. 131–143). Lanham, MD: Scarecrow Education.

Scheurich, J. J., and Skrla, L. (2003). *Leadership for equity and excellence.* Thousand Oaks, CA: Corwin Press.

Slavin, R. (1998). Can education reduce social inequality? *Educational Leadership, 55*(4), 6–11.

Spring, J. (2004). *Deculturalization and the struggle for equality* (4th ed.). New York: McGraw-Hill.

Tatum, B. (1997). *Why are all the black kids sitting together in the cafeteria?* New York: Basic Books.

Texas Education Agency. (2001). *Division of Performance Reporting. Academic Excellence Indicator System. 2000–2001—State performance report.* Retrieved October 6, 2002, from www.tea.state.tx.us/perfreport/aeis/2001/state.html.

Tillman, L. (2002). The impact of diversity in educational administration. In G. Perreault and F. Lunenburg (Eds.), *The changing world of school administration* (pp. 144–156). Lanham, MD: Scarecrow Education.

West, C. 1988. *Prophetic fragments.* Grand Rapids, MI: African World Press.

Online vs. Face-to-Face Instruction: Similarities, Differences, and Efficacy

DAVID BARNETT AND LOLA AAGAARD

ADVANCES IN TECHNOLOGY HAVE LED TO AN EXPLOSION OF online university programs. Online programs compete for students that were once served primarily in traditional, face-to-face university programs. Given the additional options students have when choosing degree programs, faculty members are often encouraged by the university administration to change courses that heretofore had been face-to-face to an online setting. This change in instructional delivery has led to the need to examine instructional practices, evaluate their applicability and effectiveness, and determine their impact on student learning. This study analyzed four courses that were taught in both formats to varying extents: Research for the Instructional Leader, School Finance, Superintendent Practicum and School Law. The factors compared across delivery formats included instructional strategies, actual student achievement, and student perceptions of the efficacy of each format.

BACKGROUND AND LITERATURE REVIEW

Educational reform has been front and center since the release of *A Nation at Risk* in 1983. Every facet of the schooling process has been examined to stem the "rising tide of mediocrity" that threatened the very existence of the American educational system (National Commission on Excellence in Education, 1983, p. 5). This examination has included the expectations placed on students, the ways schools are structured, instructional process and procedures, and the practices of educators who lead the schools. This careful analysis of American education has led, in part, to a review of the ways in which teachers and school leaders are trained.

A number of studies have examined the leadership component of the schooling process (National Commission on Excellence in Educational Administration, 1987; Council of Chief State School Officers, 1996; Thomas B. Fordham Institute, 2003). Each of these studies had an impact not only on what effective school leaders do on a daily basis, but more notably on how aspiring school leaders are trained to perform these tasks. University programs designed to prepare school leaders are often accredited based on the program's adherence to standards identified by these reform initiatives (e.g., Interstate School Leaders Licensure Consortium: Standards for School Leaders) and their graduates are expected to have the skills necessary to implement the identified standards.

The adoption of these standards by several states has facilitated reform efforts among university school leadership programs promoting program review, curriculum alignment, and course content analysis. Generally speaking, national leadership standards focus on developing future leaders' interpersonal skills, promoting ethical behavior and facilitating their ability to formulate and share a vision for their schools with students, parents and other stakeholders. Effective leaders attend to the culture both within the school and the larger political/social culture that often impacts the school. They collaborate with families and communities and effectively use the schools' resources (e.g., human, time, financial, etc.) for the benefit of improved student achievement. There is general agreement on "what" the focus of school leadership programs should be, but "how" that focus might best be achieved is still under review.

Comparisons of Face-to-Face and Online Instruction

Many studies (Kassop, 2003; O'Malley, 1999; Smith, Ferguson, and Caris, 2001; Taylor and Maor, 2000) have compared aspects of face-to-face and online teaching, exploring the advantages/disadvantages of both delivery methods. These studies suggest advantages may be found in either approach depending on the course objectives and the methods used to accomplish those objectives. A recent meta-analysis of such studies concluded that the skill of the instructor and the types of activities in which students are involved are more of a predictor of student success than is the medium that is used to deliver the instruction (Bernard, Abrami, Lou, Borokhovski, Wade, and Wozney, 2004).

Face-to-face educational administration preparation programs have commonly used a particular set of instructional strategies to develop school leaders, including role playing, investigations of case studies, simulation activities, and completion of authentic tasks designed to match the expectations of effective school leaders. These traditional instructional strategies may need to be modified as leadership preparation courses go online. For example, class discussions involving twenty or more students in a face-to-face setting can become thought provoking and insightful. When those same twenty students are involved in an online synchronous discussion, however, it may become unwieldy and confusing. Communication cues such as body language and tone of voice that are often obvious in a face-to-face setting are all but nonexistent in online, synchronous discussions. Additionally, in face-to-face settings normally only one person speaks at a time. In an online setting, unless managed correctly, many students often try to "talk" at the same time leaving participants somewhat bewildered about the direction the discussion is taking. Asynchronous discussion board postings can alleviate this concern, but the immediate give and take of a live discussion is lost.

Providing students who are pursuing certification as school leaders opportunity to gather information from a variety of sources, to hear opinions that may differ from their own, and to develop consensus-building skills are key components in educational leadership training. One of the ways in which this is accomplished is through case studies that present a variety of challenges that students are to solve. It is recognized that in a real world setting there would be considerably more information available not found in the case study, however enough information is provided around which decisions and recommendations may be made. In-class discussions can be lively with students' deep-seated beliefs and philosophies guiding their responses and sometimes being questioned. Do online course-based discussions influence student opinions in the same way as those conducted face-to-face?

Methodology and Results

Students in four graduate classes—Research for the Instructional Leader, School Finance, Superintendent Practicum and School Law—were given the opportunity to examine and discuss case studies dealing with various issues faced by today's school leaders. Regardless of delivery format, the instructor acted solely as the facilitator, allowing students to take the lead in the discussions, pose questions of one another, challenge one another's opinions and solutions of the cases and provide explanation for their own thoughts. Additionally, some assignments and course resources were available only online while other assignments and resources were provided in the more traditional manner through hard copy and texts.

After participating in a variety of instructional strategies involving online and face-to-face activities students were asked to respond to a number of questions in which they evaluated the effectiveness of the instructional techniques. Seventy-three students responded to a survey with items using a Likert-type scale (1 = strongly disagree to 5 = strongly agree). The students also participated in focus groups in which they were encouraged to discuss the two instructional environments. Participating students were divided into groups based on the certification they were pursuing. The subgroups and the number in each subgroup (shown in parentheses following each group) are as follows: supervisor of instruction (11), counselor (4), superintendent (21), and principal (37). Because of the small number in the counselor group its responses may have limited applicability to the larger population of students pursuing certification as a counselor.

RESULTS

Discussions

SYNCHRONOUS. The first two statements of the survey asked students to rate their reflectivity while participating in face-to-face and synchronous discussions (see Table 1).

In both environments (i.e., online and face-to-face) the overall average response of 4.32 indicates students were in general agreement that either format for discussion allowed for reflection. Three of the four subgroups (supervisor, counseling and principal certification) rated the impact of online discussions as having equal or greater impact on their reflectivity. The effect size of this difference for supervisor candidates was very large (0.95, based on a joint standard deviation of 0.58), while the difference for the principal candidates was very small (0.19, std = 0.94). In contrast, the fourth subgroup (superintendent) rated

Table 1. Response Reflectivity—Synchronous Discussions

	Online			Face-to-Face		
Subgroup	N	Mean	(St. dev)	N	Mean	(St. dev)
Supervisor	11	4.91	(0.30)	11	4.36	(0.67)
Counselor	4	4.75	(0.50)	4	4.75	(0.50)
Superintendent	21	4.05	(1.02)	19	4.68	(0.49)
Principal	37	4.24	(0.30)	35	4.06	(0.67)
Total Sample	73	4.32	(1.01)	69	4.32	(0.76)

Online item: "Online discussions allow me to be reflective in responding to my peers' ideas." Face-to-face item: "Face-to-face discussions allow me to be reflective in responding to my peers' ideas."

face-to-face discussions as having a greater impact than synchronous virtual discussions (medium large effect size = 0.66, std = 0.95). It may be noted that students pursuing superintendent certification already have certification as a principal and/or supervisor and most of them are practicing school leaders. Moreover, follow-up focus groups revealed that most of the students in this subgroup had limited or no experience in an online setting while pursuing their principal/supervisor certification.

ASYNCHRONOUS. Questions three and four sought to compare the impact of face-to-face discussions with asynchronous virtual discussions (see Table 2). Students were asked whether class discussions (some lasting several days or weeks) influenced their ideas about the topic.

As a group, students rated online discussions as more likely to make them rethink their positions than face-to-face discussions, but the effect size was extremely small (0.13, std = 0.91). Subgroups were split in their opinions with supervisors (large effect = 0.82, std = 0.78) and principals (small effect = 0.23, std = 0.92) indicating that asynchronous discussions had a greater impact on their ideas than did discussion in a face-to-face class. On the other hand counselors (moderately small effect = 0.39, std = 0.64) and superintendents (small effect = 0.26, std = 0.98) rated face-

to-face class discussions as more influential in causing them to rethink their ideas.

Comments from focus groups illustrated both positions.

- Discussion board [asynchronous] discussions cause me to reflect on my own thinking even before I enter into the discussion. It's not a spur of the moment kind of discussion, but rather, a discussion that requires me to examine my own ideas, beliefs, and opinions. And, when I do post ideas on the Discussion Board, they're more in-depth than those that I'll post when involved in real-time [synchronous] discussions.
- When I read the ideas of my classmates on the Discussion Board, I see that some of them are deep thinkers, much more than I am. And, I examine their thoughts, opinions and ideas; sometimes challenging, sometimes asking for clarification, and sometimes finding my own deep-seated beliefs being challenged. I also note that EVERYONE is involved in Discussion Board discussions. With the computer keeping track of who says what (and knowing that class participation is a part of my grade) I want to make sure that my ideas are presented.
- While I see the place for Discussion Board discussions, I like the give and take that's found in a REAL classroom. I need to see someone's reaction, hear

Table 2. Response Reflectivity—Asynchronous Discussions

	Online			Face-to-Face		
Subgroup	N	Mean	(St. dev)	N	Mean	(St. dev)
Supervisor	11	4.64	(0.50)	11	4.00	(0.89)
Counselor	4	4.00	(0.00)	4	4.25	(0.96)
Superintendent	20	3.75	(0.94)	19	4.00	(0.78)
Principal	37	4.24	(0.93)	35	4.03	(0.92)
Total Sample	72	4.15	(0.93)	69	4.03	(0.89)

Online item: "The ideas and responses of my colleagues to my ideas posted on Discussion Board prompted me to rethink some of my ideas."
Face-to-face item: "The ideas and responses of my colleagues to my ideas presented in class prompted me to rethink some of my ideas."

Table 3. Effectiveness of Environments

	Online			Face-to-Face		
Subgroup	N	Mean	(St. dev)	N	Mean	(St. dev)
Supervisor	11	3.36	(0.81)			
Counselor	4	3.00	(0.00)			
Superintendent	20	2.65	(0.88)	21	3.76	(0.77)
Principal	36	2.92	(1.16)	35	3.43	(1.04)
Total Sample	71	2.91	(1.02)	56	3.55	(0.99)

Online item: "Online classes are more effective than face-to-face classes."
Face-to-face item: "Face-to-face classes are more effective than online classes."

their tone of voice, and look them in the eye when I confront them. Sometimes when my ideas are challenged on the Discussion Board I'm not sure if the challenge is confrontational or intellectual. I have reflected on my own ideas when I've been challenged on the Discussion Board, but I've done the same thing in a face-to-face setting as well.

Overall Effectiveness

Another question in the survey asked students to rate the overall effectiveness of online vs. face-to-face classes (see Table 3). When asked if online classes were more effective than face-to-face classes, students in the supervisor and counseling group were undecided, with average ratings around 3.0. The survey was modified later to gather student opinion from the remaining two sub-groups about whether face-to-face classes were more effective than online classes.

Generally speaking, students perceived face-to-face classes as somewhat more effective than online classes (medium effect size = 0.59, std = 1.09), although superintendent candidates felt more strongly about it (very large effect = 1.05, std = 1.06) than principal candidates (medium effect = 0.46, std = 1.12). Comments from the focus groups seemed to indicate that students' opinion on the issue of relative effectiveness varied depending on the quality of their prior online experiences of the students.

- I've had three online classes. Two of them were great with the professors giving feedback on individual assignments. Yet, in the other class, all we did was answer questions on the quizzes following each section with the computer scoring the quiz. When I e-mailed the professor he rarely would respond to me as a person. Sometimes I felt like I was in the way of whatever else he was doing. I'm glad that I didn't have him for my first online class or I wouldn't have taken another one. Professors need to put themselves in our place and let us know when we're doing things right and when we're not.

- The only experience I've had with online instruction is this class. I like being able to go on Blackboard and have all the material I need for the class right there for me. Also, I know that when I have a question I can send the question by e-mail and get a response usually within a day or so.

- Call me old-fashioned, but I guess I'll always prefer coming to class and interacting with the teacher and my classmates. It's the kind of teaching I know about and it's the kind of teaching I'm most comfortable with. Don't get me wrong, I suppose there's a place for the computer in instruction, but I like flesh and blood.

In addition to comparing the two environments, students were asked to rate the effectiveness of online classes (see Table 4). Without exception, all students indicated that online classes were effective with supervisor candidates being the most positive in their ratings.

Student Achievement

In addition to student opinion, class averages of students who were in strictly face-to-face School Finance classes were compared with School Finance students who were involved approximately 50 percent of the time in an online setting. The content of the classes was the same and the same instructor taught all classes. The average student course grade (based on a 4 point scale) in the classes that were solely face-to-face was 3.65 while the average in the blended classes was 3.63, indicating almost no difference in students' mastery of the expected content.

Table 4. Effectiveness of Online Classes

Subgroup	N	Mean	(St. dev)
Supervisor	11	4.82	(0.60)
Counselor	4	4.00	(0.00)
Superintendent	19	4.05	(0.78)
Principal	33	4.18	(0.88)
Total Sample	67	4.24	(0.85)

Item: "Online classes are an effective way to learn."

The instructor kept a record of issues regarding teaching in the two delivery formats. Two of these were related to student achievement.

- Some of the technical aspects of the course took longer online than it did face-to-face. For example, I work through the state funding formula to show students how much student attendance impacts the amount of money schools receive. When meeting face-to-face, I can work through at least two examples in one class setting. In an online setting, I'm only able to get through one example. To account for this time difference, I work through at least one example with the students online and then post the key for the other examples online. Students are then asked to work through the other examples and check their work. A comparison of students' grades indicates that both groups of students do equally well when completing assignments based on this concept.
- When I assign students to groups I often require them to meet virtually. I assign myself to each group so that I might receive group e-mails and participate in their discussions. In a class that's strictly face-to-face, I'm not able to monitor group discussion. Being able to monitor group discussions has allowed me to more effectively guide students' understanding of some of the concepts we discuss.

Blended Classes

With some students preferring online classes and some students preferring face-to-face classes perhaps a compromise is the best solution. When asked if they preferred classes that are partially face-to-face and partially online, 85 percent of the students tended to agree or strongly agree resulting in an average response of 4.28. (See Table 5.) (Note: The survey was revised after supervisor and counseling students responded to the survey. Therefore they did not respond to this item.)

Responses from students in focus groups also seemed to support this class structure.

- There are times when I come to class and, at the end of class I think, "Why wasn't this information simply presented online?" My time is important and after driving for two hours, I want discussion that's pertinent and compelling. There are times when I do need to hear and see my classmates and the instructor. But, there are lots of times when what's presented in class could just as easily have been posted on Blackboard.
- After teaching all day, I'm glad that I sometimes have the option to complete an assignment on my own time. Scheduling around night responsibilities makes it nearly impossible to come to campus on the same night every week. I don't particularly like never seeing others in my class, but I do like instructors who realize that effective instruction can happen in a virtual world. I wish ALL instructors would at least experiment with technology. We have it in all of our classrooms—university professors who don't use technology are sending a message they may not intend.

Given the interest in online classes, students were asked how many (none, more or all) classes they would prefer to take online (see Table 6).

Two-thirds of the students indicated they would like to take more classes online while the remaining third was almost equally split between wanting no classes online and wanting all of them online. The distribution in the sub-groups was similar except that one quarter of supervisor candidates were more inclined toward all online classes, while an equal portion of superintendent candidates wanted no online classes at all.

Academic Dishonesty

The final survey item asked students to respond to their perception of student dishonesty in an online environment compared to a face-to-face environment. Despite technology that would seem to make student dishonesty easier (e.g., plagiarism by copying and pasting from one document to another) and online instructors who may never actually see their students,

Table 5. Blended Class Interest

Subgroup	N	Mean	(St. dev)
Supervisor			
Counselor			
Superintendent	19	4.47	(0.76)
Principal	33	4.18	(0.83)
Total Sample	52	4.28	(0.86)

Item: "I prefer classes that are partially face-to-face and partially online."

Table 6. Interest in Online Classes

Subgroup	None Percent	More Percent	All Percent
Supervisor	9	64	27
Counselor	0	100	0
Superintendent	26	63	11
Principal	18	68	15
Total sample	18	68	15

Item: "How many of your classes would you prefer to take online?"

Table 7. Student Dishonesty

Subgroup	Mean	St. Dev.	N
Supervisor	1.55	(0.93)	11
Counselor	2.50	(0.58)	4
Superintendent	2.68	(0.76)	19
Principal	2.64	(0.99)	33
Total Sample	2.63	(0.95)	67

Item: "There are more instances of student dishonesty (e.g., cheating on exams, plagiarism, etc.) in online classes than face-to-face courses."

respondents tended to disagree slightly that an online environment results in more student dishonesty than occurs in a face-to-face classroom (see Table 7).

Student Participation in Class Discussion

Because students reported that their ideas were influenced by the comments and opinions of their classmates, the percent of students participating in discussions online was compared with the percent of students participating in discussions in face-to-face classes. In every instance, the percent of students participating in online discussions surpassed the percent of students participating in face-to-face classes by at least 15 percent (see Table 8).

Involvement of all students in class is a goal of most instructors and it is often a requirement in online classes. Therefore, in this particular instructional strategy, online classes seem to be more effective in including a larger percentage of students in discussions than are face-to-face classes. Furthermore, focus group comments from students tended to support the notion that their online discussions, while frequently requiring more of their time, also provided them opportunity to be more reflective and thoughtful in their responses. During focus group discussions students acknowledged that the computer keeps track of how often they speak and what they say, while in face-to-face discussions there typically is not a record of their comments. While online comments are often less spontaneous than those made in a face-to-face setting, students more frequently make an effort to participate in the discussion.

Table 8. Percent of Students Involved in Discussions

Course	Delivery Mode	
	Online	Face-to-Face
School Finance	98	81
Practicum	100	85
Research	100	84

Implications and Suggestions for Additional Research

The results of this study are another contribution to the growing literature comparing online and face-to-face courses. The conclusions provided here may be somewhat limited in scope because all students were a part of a leadership training program at one university. Students pursuing other degrees (e.g., accounting, engineering, etc.) may respond differently based on the content of their coursework. Despite these caveats, the results aligned with many other studies that indicate essentially no difference in academic outcome between the two delivery formats. Student opinion and preferences varied, however.

Because some students prefer verbal instruction, while other students learn best through written instruction, and still others prefer a more active, kinesthetic approach, the challenge of incorporating various learning styles into an online setting needs additional attention. University faculty members should examine the objectives of the course and, whenever possible, seek to provide instruction in a manner using a combination of instructional delivery methods.

As the influence and use of technology continues to increase, on-going examination of this resource and how it might be used most effectively in the preparation of educational administrators is essential. School leaders must be able to work effectively with people. Therefore, as educational leadership courses move more and more to an online setting, requiring aspiring leaders to interact with people in a positive, helpful way, judging the effectiveness of these interactions, and offering suggestions for growth will be critical. Models for how school leadership preparation may be enhanced in a virtual world will be critical to the survival and growth of educational leadership programs.

REFERENCES

Bernard, R., Abrami, P., Lou, Y., Borokhovski, E., Wade, A., and Wozney, L. (2004). How does distance education compare with classroom instruction? A meta-analysis of empirical literature. *Review of Educational Research, 74*(3), 379–439.

Chenoweth, T., Carr, C., and Ruhl, T. (2002, August). *Best practice in educational leadership programs.* Paper presented at the Administrator Licensure Planning Forum, Eugene, OR.

Council of Chief State School Officers. (1996). *Standards for school leaders.* Washington, DC: Interstate School Leaders Licensure Consortium.

Kassop, M. (2003, June). Ten ways online education matches, or surpasses, face-to-face learning. *The Technol-*

ogy Source. Retrieved July 28, 2004, from http://ts.mivu
.org default.asp?show=article&id=1059.

National Commission on Excellence in Education. (1983).
A nation at risk: The imperative for educational reform.
Washington, DC: U.S. Department of Education.

National Commission on Excellence in Educational Administration Report. (1987). *Leaders for America's schools.*
Tempe, AZ: University Council for Educational Administration.

O'Malley, J. (1999). Students' perceptions of distance learning, online learning and the traditional classroom. *Online
Journal of Distance Learning Administration, 2*(4). Retrieved September 1, 2004, from http://www.westga.edu/
~distance/omalley24.html.

Smith, G., Ferguson, D., and Caris, M. (2001). Online vs.
face-to-face. *Technological Horizons in Education, 28*(9),
18–22.

Taylor, P., and Maor, D. (2000). Assessing the efficacy of
online teaching with the Constructivist Online Learning
Environment Survey. *Teaching and Learning Forum 2000.*
Retrieved August 2, 2004, from http://lsn.curtin.edu.au/
tlf/tlf2000/taylor.html.

Thomas B. Fordham Institute. (2003). *Better leaders for
America's schools: A manifesto.* Washington, DC.

School Leadership and the Role of Policy, Politics, and Advocacy: Implications for Leadership Training

GENNIVER BELL

For the fact is that today . . . millions of my fellow citizens are needlessly exposed to hazard because they have neither the inclination nor the knowledge to advance their own interest and to protect themselves from the political decisions brought about by powerful others.

—Halperin, *A Guide for the Powerless and Those Who Don't Know Their Own Power*

IN THIS DAY AND AGE, FEW WILL DISAGREE THAT THE ROLE of the school administrator has changed. The increasing political nature of education and the increasing encroachment of the federal government in the business of education have placed new demand on school leaders. Cooper, Fusarelli and Randell (2004) contend that we live in an age when educational leaders need to be well informed and familiar with education policy and the politics surrounding the creation and implementation of those policies. Yet, little attention is paid to the macro-level forces and actors who often create school policies preferring to focus on the day-to-day operations of individual schools or districts. Nevertheless, more and more school leaders perceive their major problems as statewide and national in both scope and origin (Cooper, Furaselli and Randell, 2004; Kowalski, 1995).

School administrators are now faced with contemporary policy demands that exceed their traditional capacity for action (Honig, 2004). The context of schooling is changing day-by-day. School leaders must now joggle these demands and mandates imposed by an increasingly complex society. Issues of accountability abound, while limited resources continue to persist. Imposed shared governance or the reallocation of authority without regard for the integration of complex ideologies, and demands for high teacher quality while teacher shortages are on the rise are just a few policy issues administrators must tackle. Too often these mandates are imposed by "powerful others"

without input from those responsible for implementing the legislative reform measures (Bell and Johnson, 2003). These demands have ushered in a need for more knowledge and sophisticated skills in the areas of public policy, politics and advocacy. Despite the importance of policies affecting education, limited attention has been given to the need for more comprehensive training of leaders to address the political challenges of the future. Berg and Hall (1999) concluded: "It is evident that few preparation programs forthrightly acknowledge the political process or foster the involvement of prospective administrators in the political process." (p. 10). Traditionally, the focus on policy training is reserved at the doctorate level, leaving perspective and young administrators without the proper tools to address the issues of the job. Moreover, even at the advanced level, most programs focus on analyses of current policy issues rather than the process and skills for shaping policy action.

PURPOSE AND BACKGROUND

This paper seeks to evoke an awareness of the critical need for developing political educational leaders. A brief historical perspective and a theoretical approach for developing political leaders through a public policy and advocacy development approach are provided. Secondly, the paper will outline some critical areas in the development of political leaders. Finally, the discussion will offer practical and proven strategies for enhancing the political knowledge, confidence and skills of future leaders within the five critical areas.

The new era of reform and accountability, as well as budget constraints dominate the policy discussions. Nevertheless, school administrators are generally missing from the policy agenda development and legislation crafting stages. The results are needless exposure of American children to educational hazards that serve to impede progress and place many students at risk (Bell and Johnson, 2003). School administrators are in a unique position to influence policy and legislation at all levels (Kennedy, 2000). Yet, education leaders traditionally have viewed themselves as having limited power to influence policy at state and federal levels. Moreover, few possess the skills needed to significantly influence the political process. Their voices are largely ignored. Elaine Hopson (2004), a state legislator and former superintendent, states: "After being drafted into the political arena, I realized how naïve I was in substance and in procedure, and how simplistic were the short courses on 'How an idea becomes a law'" (¶ 2). Frances Fowler (2003) purported:

> Educational leaders need to be literate about policy and the policy process. The time is long past (if indeed there ever were such time), when administrators could tell themselves that politics and education don't mix and then sit complacently on the sideline while others made important policy decisions for schools. In today's rapidly changing policy environment, those who lead our schools must have a basic understanding of educational policy and how it is made. Otherwise they are likely to make serious blunders. (p. viii)

School leaders have a professional responsibility to advocate for children; but advocacy cannot exist without political involvement. Advocacy and powerlessness cannot function together (Bell and Johnson, 2003). Suzanne Bassi (2004), a state legislator and former superintendent, contends: "Being an effective lobbyist for education issues is truly one of the most important jobs anyone involved with education, from administrator to parent volunteers, can do" (¶ 1). Effective advocacy requires action and voice. Too often administrators are naïve of the substance, content, complexities and procedures of the political arena and, therefore, lack the skills and confidence to manipulate school reform issues in a positive direction. Advocacy is the first line of defense in the public policy process and the political arena. According to Corbell (2000), advocacy is "standing up or speaking up" (p. 1). Dettmer (1995) defines advocacy as "giving active support to a cause, putting out a call to take a position on an issue, and acting to see that it is resolved" (p. 389). Johnson and Johnson (1991) elaborated:

> Advocacy is the presenting of a position, and providing reasons why others should adopt it. You present, teach and advocate your position and its rationale. Decisions and conclusions are reached through a process of argument and counterargument aimed at persuading others to adopt, modify or drop positions.

Advocating a positions and defending it against refutation require engaging in considerable cognitive rehearsal and elaboration, which in turn results in increase understanding of the position and the more frequent use of higher level reasoning. (p. 278)

The nature of advocacy would suggest that school leaders need to develop the disposition, knowledge and the skills to influence policy agendas, craft or recraft reform legislation and build support among various groups. This would require, among other things, knowledge of various advocacy models such as the one proposed by Gallagher (1993). In this model Gallagher describes the essential components of advocacy: *goal, target, knowledge, message, delivery mode, and evaluation*. The model provides a framework for approaching concrete and sustainable advocacy efforts. This model would suggest then that school leaders need knowledge and skills not only in the political and public policy processes but also in areas of marketing, communication strategies, lobbying techniques, and evaluation methods to chart progress as well as to disseminate sound data. Kenneth Wong (2004) suggested that teachers too have a role in advocating change. If this is accurate, then principals have the added burden of guiding, encouraging and fostering the political skills and knowledge of their teachers.

Advocacy is the foundation through which educational leaders chart their course through the public policy and political process. It is the foundation on which administrators function as effective instructional leaders. Without the desire, knowledge and zeal to advocate for children, forging a path through policy and politics will be fruitless.

Traditionally, when we speak of policy in educational settings, the immediate assumption is the review of current policy or the analysis of the implementation impact on schools. Little attention is given to the advocacy component of influencing policy at its various stages.

Public policy as a discipline is a relatively new adventure. In 1951 Harold Lasswell advanced the notion of *policy science* as an emerging field of study (Cooper et. al, 2004). Lasswell suggested that a rigorous and scientific approach to policy studies would offer a framework for crafting good policy. Anderson (1984) and others would soon follow with what is now a public policy framework. The policy process defined by public policy theorist included six stages: (a) issues definition, (b) agenda setting, (c) policy formation, (d) policy adoption, (e) implementation, and (f) policy evaluation.

In this model, the *issues definition* stage identifies a problem and elevates the problem from an individual to a social problem which becomes a political issue. The problem can only become an issue if the advocates are successful in garnering public support. Thus, the *issues definition* stage is the foundation for all policies, advocacy and the political process. As issues gain public support, they become formalized in the political process as policy agendas.

The *policy agenda* stage introduces the formal political process. It is at this stage that political networks among policy makers must be formulated. Policy formation is the initiation of the formal political/governmental process. It is the actual drafting of legislation, administrative rule or a court decision.

As Hopson (2004) reminded us, "How a bill becomes law is not a simplistic matter." The *policy adoption* stage therefore, is a critical stage of involvement for school leaders and encompasses all of the skill of the previous stages. During this stage bills are drafted and moved through the legislative process by formal and informal procedures. Bills are drafted, analyzed, re-drafted, and assigned appropriation based on the commitment of the supporters and the strength of advocates. It is at this stage that the visibility and voice of leaders is most critical.

The *implementation stage* is the transforming of a statute or law into practice. This stage is reliant upon *intermediaries*—those charged with the responsibility of implementation. Educators historically have been delegated as the intermediaries to implement education policies, often without adequate funding, even though we had no significant input in the drafting of the legislation and our experiences tell us that the policies proposed are not good for children. School leaders are often faced with the task of motivating organizations to carry out the (often unpopular) mandates of legislation that could serve to be detrimental to children.

Evaluation then is a critical stage of the policy process. The *evaluation stage* should provide sound assessments to determine the effectiveness of the policy. It should provide accurate research data for refining the policy through a feedback mechanism that flows through all previous stages of the policy process. Knowledge of evaluation procedures and cost effective analysis methods can provide essential information for feedback purposes.

The author adapted the model to include a final step: The *continuation/modification/termination stage.* It is this stage where only school leaders and educa-

tors, in general, can provide the most accurate information. The voices of leaders are needed in challenging policy makers to adhere to recommendations regarding the viability of current policies. If policies are found to not meet the needs of education, termination should be swift.

Thus, to successfully maneuver through the policy process stages, school leaders most have adequate training and practical experiences to expose them to the complexities of the process. To advance the issues of education for the benefit of all children, leaders need a voice and must be present at the table, crafting policy and influencing legislation for the improvement of education. Unfortunately, most educators view their roles as discussants or at best *implementers* of policy, rather than active *engagers* in the various policy development stages (Bell and Johnson, 2003). It is critical that school leaders have a thorough understanding of the stages, the skills and strategies to positively influence each stage. Leaders must be visible and vocal with the defining of issues as with the more traditional role of implementation.

University Responsibilities

The development of political leadership skills requires a sound foundation in the theory, supported by diverse practical experiences (Bell and Johnson, 2003). As Educational Administration programs seek to restructure their programs to meet ISLLC, NCATE and/or state standards, we must be reminded that true education goes beyond mere standards. To address only the standards means to meet minimum requirements. As we address issues of instructional leadership, curriculum, school law and finance, we must be cognizant of the fact that we have not properly prepared our students if we have not exposed them to the realities of the ever encompassing political process and the theories for making sound political decisions. Effective instructional leadership cannot occur without a strong voice (advocate) for children (Bell and Johnson, 2003). We must instill a responsibility of advocacy in prospective school leaders through development of strong political awareness. No amount of instructional leadership can circumvent the destruction of ill conceived yet mandated policies.

University programs should help students to understand that policy is not made in a vacuum. Training programs should introduce students to theories and models that provide insight into how policy decisions are made and how administrators can utilize these concepts to influence reform efforts. Moreover, students should be equipped with practical experiences that will expose them to the real political environment. Bell and Johnson (2003) outlined some basis concepts for developing sound training and development programs. The model includes:

- Theoretical and practical applications of the public policy and political process;
- Knowledge and understanding of various policy instruments;
- Development of public relations and marketing skills;
- Knowledge and understanding of economic, social and political systems and their impact on the policy/political process; and
- Development of advocacy and lobbying skills (p. 7).

These concepts provide an umbrella for addressing the complexities within the discipline. It takes into account the knowledge, skills and disposition needed not only to address policy concerns, but also skills needed for effective leaders.

Given the enormous task of training school leaders, the question becomes . . . how can universities infuse the policy component into their programs? Although the author advocates for a policy course, many of the components can be incorporated into existing courses or field experiences. Technology also serves as a wonderful tool for addressing these concepts and many others. Given school administrators' limited time, no longer is it necessary to travel to the State Legislative Buildings to address issues and to be involved in the policy/political process. Even though personal appearances during the legislative sessions and at committee hearings are always encouraged, the use of technology is more practical for practicing administrators. There are many on-line activities that can be used effectively to enhance the student's understanding and personal comfort level.

The following are four practical web-based exercises that can be used in the development of political leaders. These activities can be used as component of a policy/politics class or can be utilized in other leadership courses.

Exercise # 1: Introduction to the Legislative Process

All states legislatures have web sites that provide a wealth of information. Usually there is educational information regarding the legislative process and information on each of the state legislators. The instructor can develop a worksheet with questions that would require students to maneuver the web site in order to obtain information and confidence. The worksheet can include such items as: (a) identification of local legislators; (b) identification of standing committees for both Houses and education related committee memberships; (c) identification of current legislative actions; (d) provide status and history of (xxx) bills related to education; and (e) trace the legislative steps for a bill becoming law.

Exercise # 2: Policy Position Paper

Have students identify current education agenda issues in your state. They should select an issue and write a concise position paper addressing the issue, providing sound documentation and data to support their position. The student should identify a state legislator with an interest in the issue. The position paper should be emailed to the legislator. To ensure that the paper is forwarded, require that the email document be copied to you.

Exercise # 3: Bill Analyses and Tracking

Provide students with a list of current House or Senate Bills (i.e., SB1234, HB564) related to education. Require the students to locate the bills via the web site and conduct an analysis of each bill. The analysis should include (a) bill sponsor(s); (b) summary of the bill; (c) appropriation requirements; (d) bill history/current status; and (e) a personal analysis of the bill's impact on education.

Exercise # 4: Think Tank Analyses

Provide web sites to various policy/political organizations (Think Tanks) addressing educational issues. Require the students to select one organization provided and conduct a search and identify at least three other organizations. The student should identify the organization; provide a brief history; identify the current issues addressed by the organization; provide an ideological assessment of the organizational views; and provide a personal assessment of the organization's impact on education.

CONCLUSION

University programs must provide future leaders with the opportunities to master political skills that produce results. The recent No Child Left Behind legislation is a poignant reminder of the need for political leadership skills. In this day of increasing federal and state involvement in education, truly effective leadership cannot occur without sufficient mastery of skills in policy, politics and advocacy (Bell and Johnson,

2003). Educational leadership programs must show the way towards education advocacy and political savvy.

REFERENCES

Anderson, J. (1984). *Public policymaking* (3rd ed.). New York: Holt, Rinehart and Winston.

Bassi, S. (2004). Relationships matters [Electronic Version]. *The School Administrator, 3*(61), 6–7.

Bell, G., and Johnson, J. (2003). School leadership development revisited: Infusing policy, politics and advocacy. *The AASA Professor, 26*(2), 6–10.

Berg, J., and Hall, G. (1999). Intersection of political leadership and educational excellence: A neglected leadership domain. *AASA Professor, 23*(3), 7–12.

Cooper, B. S., Fusarelli, L. D., and Randell, E. V. (2004). *Better policies, better schools: Theories and applications.* Boston: Pearson.

Corbell, L. D. (2000). Parental involvement in three local school districts: Methods maintaining support. Unpublished master's thesis, University of Arkansas, Little Rock.

Dettmer, P. (1995). Building advocacy and public support for gifted education. In J. L. Genschaft, M. Bireley and C. L. Hollinger (Eds.), *Serving gifted and talented students: A resource foe school personnel* (pp. 389–403). Austin, TX: PRO-ED.

Fowler, F. (2004). *Policy studies for educational leaders: An introduction* (2nd ed.). Upper Saddle River, NJ: Pearson Merrill Prentice Hall.

Halperin, S. (1981). *A guide for the powerless and those who don't know their own power: A mini-manual on the American political process.* Washington, DC: The Institute for Educational Leadership.

Honig, M. (2004). The new middle management: Intermediary organizations in education policy implementation. *Educational Evaluation and Policy Analysis, 36*(1), 65–87.

Hopson, E. (2004). Truth and politics. *The School Administrator, 3*(61), 12.

Johnson, D., and Johnson, F. (1991). *Joining together: Group theory and group skills* Engelwood Cliffs, NJ: Prentice Hall.

Kawalski, T. (1995). *Keepers of the flame: Contemporary urban superintendents.* Thousand Oaks, CA: Corwin Press.

Lasswell, H. (1951). The policy orientation. In D. Lerner and H. Lasswell (Eds.), *The policy sciences* (pp. 3–15). Stanford, CA: Stanford University Press.

Wong, K. (2004). A discussion on the politics of education. *The Southern Journal of Teaching and Education.* Retrieved June 29, 2004, from http://www.sjteonline.com/winter2004kwong.htm.

Preparing School District Administrators to be Recruiters and Interviewers

JOE NICHOLS

EACH YEAR THOUSANDS OF PROSPECTIVE TEACHERS AND educational leaders are recruited and interviewed for positions in the nation's schools. When a school district employs a person for one these positions, it is making a potential million-dollar investment in salaries, benefits and professional development over a teacher's career. In order to invest the school district's resources wisely, educational leaders must know how to recruit and interview personnel in order to discern the best possible applicants for positions available. This study describes how a course taught at the postgraduate level prepares candidates to be recruiters and interviewers. It discusses course strategies and provides a protocol, developed by course participants, who may be used to interview prospective principals.

INTRODUCTION

Each year thousands of school districts across the nation employ instructional and leadership staff. In the process of employing personnel for positions, school district administrators are usually charged with the tasks of recruiting and interviewing potential staff members.

Why should university preparation programs devote significant efforts toward teaching prospective educational leaders to be effective recruiters? According to Smith (2005), "the question isn't whether you can fill a . . . position or how to fill it, but rather can you do it well. Good instructional programs rely on having high quality staff members" (p. 50). All school districts, urban and rural, those with increasing enrollments and those with declining enrollments, need to be prepared to conduct recruiting activities. "Recruitment . . . should be common to all school districts. Talent and skills are scarce commodities. School districts are ethically bound to find the most talented and skilled people available to achieve their mandate of educating children" (Rebore, 2004, p. 93).

Why should university preparation programs teach their prospective educational leaders to be effective interviewers? Smith states that "the single most important decision you make for students is to hire a teacher. If you don't think the teachers in your school are more important than the curriculum, think of this: What would you rather have: the ten best basketball plays or the ten best basketball players?" (p. 73). Rebore (2004) discussed the importance of interviewing in not only selecting the best person for a position, but also fostering a positive image of the school district.

> The interviewer has extremely important responsibilities. Not only does he or she direct the interview by asking questions, but also he or she must record the respondent's answers and present the respondent with a favorable image of the school district. Through the interview process, the interviewer must evaluate and come to a conclusion about the suitability of each candidate. (p. 124)

Arkansas State University's format for teaching future educational leaders to be effective recruiters and interviewers is a major component in the course entitled School Personnel Administration. The course is presented in a fashion that provides participants opportunities to engage in authentic experiences in developing protocols for recruiting and interviewing prospective staff. The protocols culminate with course participants actually conducting interviews and making recommendations for employment.

ESTABLISHING THE NEED—CLARIFYING TASKS

It was estimated in the early 1990's that the United States would have a need for 87,000 teachers by decade's end. This dilemma was caused by several factors including class size reduction mandates, growth in enrollment, and attrition of the teaching profession due to retirement. Making matters worse is the fact that new teachers were leaving the profession at an alarming rate (Ingersol and Smith, 2003).

School districts may wish to consider the practices of those in the business world in the process of recruiting and interviewing personnel. According to Caggiano (1998), many in the business world have recruiting and interviewing protocols that are unique to their needs. Interview questions are framed that are specific to a certain industry or position within an industry. As in industry, school districts are also unique from one to another especially when one considers the many different job titles and job descriptions involved in educating children.

During the brief time allocated to interviewing personnel, many are discussing details that could have been provided during a recruiting phase of employment. If the business world were applied to education, issues such as district goals, employee expectations, salary, benefits, and community offerings could have been provided to an applicant in a portfolio prior to the interview and would have assisted in expediting the entire process. When the recruiting and interviewing are not approached as separate functions, applicants are provided with little opportunity to verbalize and reveal the skills they bring to the profession. The interviewer often dominates discussions during the interview by articulating the district's strengths, philosophies of teaching, and discipline. Sirbasku (2002) describes the pitfalls to this approach to interviewing:

> In most job searches, those responsible for doing the hiring sell the job before they select a candidate. This approach is backwards. Why sell the job to someone who isn't a candidate? After all, a savvy applicant may be a good "interview"—well-groomed, friendly, professional, enthusiastic, interested, a good listener, etc. What happens in this case is the recruiter starts doing the talking, telling about the job requirements before the interview starts. It's the candidate who's doing the listening, learning how to appeal to the recruiter. The result is that, since most individuals can mask their true tendencies for at least 45 minutes, the interviewer rarely gets an accurate picture of the job candidate. Alternatively, why not learn profiles of interviewees before taking the time to sell the job? (p. 32)

A study conducted by Nichols (2004) indicated that interviewing protocols in rural school districts rarely existed. In a study of eighty-three rural school districts with student populations of less than one thousand, less than 1 percent had protocols in place to interview prospective staff. The study indicated that personnel conducting the interviews did most of the talking and used interview time to provide information about their school districts. Rarely were applicants afforded opportunities that provided interviewers insight into the skills the applicant would bring to the district. Lines of questioning appeared, for the most part, to be spontaneous.

When teaching future educational leaders to interview, the legal parameters of the process cannot be overlooked. Whether questions are simply asked or they are asked and recorded, interviewers should use extra caution in following legal guidelines throughout the process. According to Montoya (HR Focus, 1997), an attorney for the Equal Employment Opportunity Council (EEOC), "The strength in hiring cases has come primarily from extraneous comments that are made on interview sheets. It's amazing what some people will write in the margin" (p. 60). Rebore (2004) describes the interviewing process as one that is "essentially a conversation between two or more individuals to generate information about the candidate; it also has profound legal implications" (p. 131).

1. *Name*: It is lawful to inquire if an applicant has worked under a different name or nickname in order to verify work or educational records; it is unlawful to ask questions in an attempt to discover the applicant's ancestry, lineage, or national origin.
2. *Age*: For a minor, requiring proof of age in the form of a work permit or certificate of age is lawful; it is unlawful to require adults to present a birth certificate or baptismal record to a district.
3. *Race*: To request information about distinguishing physical characteristics is legal; to ask the color of the applicant's skin, eyes, etc., is illegal if this indicates directly or indirectly race or skin color.
4. *Religion*: All inquiries are illegal.
5. *Sex*: Inquiries regarding sex are permissible only when a bona fide occupational qualification exists.
6. *Ethnic Background*: It is illegal to ask which languages the applicant reads, writes, or speaks fluently; inquiries about the applicant's national origin are illegal.
7. *Marital and Family Status*: Questions to determine if a man or woman can meet specific work schedules are lawful; inquiries about being married, single, divorced, etc., are unlawful.
8. *Credit Rating*: All questions about charge accounts or credit rating are unlawful.
9. *Work Experience*: It is lawful to ask why an applicant wants to work for a particular company or in-

stitution; asking what kind of supervisor the applicant prefers is unlawful.

10. *Life Style*: Asking about future career plans is lawful; asking an applicant if he/she drinks alcoholic beverages or takes drugs is unlawful. (p. 128)

When teaching future school leaders to be effective recruiters and interviewers Messmer (1995) suggests the following format be considered:

Write out a list of questions before the interview. Prioritize them by category by budgeting a reasonable amount of time for the entire interview. While you may not have time to ask every question, this approach will keep you focused. Give candidates ample time to respond. Thoughtful silence does not mean indecision. Don't rush in with another question to fill that silent period. Remember, the interview is a time for you to listen, not talk. (p. 35)

UTILIZING AUTHENTIC PROBLEM-BASED TEACHING STRATEGIES

Most, if not all, textbooks written on the topic of school personnel administration contain at least one chapter that discusses recruiting and interviewing potential staff. Lengthy passages are contained that discuss the importance of recruiting and interviewing personnel that will enable a school district to do the best possible job in educating students and reaching the goals outlined by the district.

Though textbooks provide vast varieties of good information regarding this process, the actual process of recruiting and interviewing is often not experienced by educational leaders until they are in positions of employment in school districts. For many, their only experiences with recruiting and interviewing have been those encountered when they were recruited and interviewed by a school district.

Learning by experience has long been documented an effective teaching methodology by many in the field of education. The central focus in a pragmatic teaching philosophy places emphasis on students' learning by utilizing a hands-on approach. The root of the word *Pragmatism* is a Greek word meaning work.

"Pragmatism is a philosophy that encourages us to seek out the processes and do the things that work best" (Ozman and Craver, 2003, p. 127).

Probably the best-known pragmatist in the twentieth century was John Dewey. With his experimental methodologies, Dewey emphasized that learning by experience is the best form of learning from as early as kindergarten through the most sophisticated levels of education (Gutek, 2004). Gutek further observes that Pragmatists believe that education "needs to be concerned with real flesh and blood issues that make a concrete difference in human life" (p. 72).

For teachers who are emphasizing experiential learning, Ozman and Craver suggest the following:

A properly prepared and motivated teacher will make suggestions and arouse student interests to help launch new learning projects. Indeed the role of the teacher is to help students grow, and this means leading them into new areas of knowledge to help make their understandings, skills, and abilities become deeper, more complex, and more sophisticated. (p. 149)

Eggen and Kauchak (1996) cite the inquiry method of teaching and learning as "one of the most effective ways to help them develop their higher-order and critical-thinking skills" (p. 236). The teacher's role in this process is to be "a facilitator of the process rather than merely lecturing and presenting information to the students" (p. 240). "The inquiry method, while seemingly remote and academic, is very much a part of our every day lives" (p. 271). Candidates preparing for careers in school administration have a great need to recruit and select personnel as part of the cadre of tasks they must perform in their positions.

THE COURSE: SCHOOL PERSONNEL ADMINISTRATION

School Personnel Administration is a course taught in the Specialist in Education Degree (Ed. S.) program at Arkansas State University. The course is designed to prepare district-level school educational leaders to effectively manage the personnel functions necessary to maintain a school district. Included in this course are preparations for leadership and management in the following areas:

1. Recruiting and interviewing potential staff;
2. Staff development and evaluation;
3. Reduction in force;
4. Employee termination; and
5. Collective negotiations.

THE COURSE PROJECT: RECRUITING AND INTERVIEWING PERSONNEL FOR SCHOOL DISTRICTS

An in-depth exploration of the leadership and management functions of recruiting and interviewing potential staff is experienced in this course by the participants. In this exploration, course participants work in collaborative groups to create a protocol to recruit and interview staff. Participants engage in the following activities to develop their protocol:

1. Review literature that identifies the legal constraints of recruiting and interviewing staff and distinguishes the tasks of recruiting and interviewing.
2. Develop a job description for the staff position for which they are developing the protocols.
3. Develop a protocol for recruiting a staff member.
4. Develop a protocol for interviewing a staff member.
5. Conduct an actual interview using the protocol.
6. Select an applicant and make an oral and written recommendation for employment to the board of education.
7. Construct a professional development plan for the applicant recommended for employment.

Each semester, a different position is identified as the one the course participants will recruit and interview. In the past three semesters, course participants have developed protocols for recruiting and interviewing a classroom teacher, a special education teacher, and a mid-level principal.

USING PROFESSIONAL LITERATURE TO SET THE STAGE

The text used to guide the course participants in discerning the tasks of recruiting and interviewing, as well as functioning within a legal framework, is *Human Resources Administration in Education: A Management Approach* (Rebore, 2004). At least one three-hour class session is dedicated to discussing the confusion that often exists among educational leaders in distinguishing between the tasks involved in recruiting and interviewing prospective staff. Also in this class session, the legal parameters of recruiting and interviewing are discussed with the expectation that protocols developed by the course participants will be compliant with EEOC standards and regulations.

Course participants also review appropriate professional literature to discern the necessary tasks required to function in the position for which they are developing the protocols. These tasks are identified from professional journals, web sites, and textbooks that specifically detail the performance standards for the positions.

DEVELOPING A JOB DESCRIPTION

After a particular position is determined in which course participants will engage in recruiting and interviewing activities, a job description is written for the position. Course participants, working in collaborative groups of five or less, review professional literature and then discuss the competencies and capacities they desire to be included in the job description. Discussions are moderated by the professor and guidance is provided to course participants to ensure that the descriptions are not so long as to be cumbersome, yet not so brief as to not include necessary detail and expectations.

The job description is utilized as one of the references for constructing the protocols for recruiting and interviewing.

DEVELOPING COMPONENTS OF A RECRUITING PROTOCOL FOR A MID-LEVEL PRINCIPAL

Course participants were given the task of developing a protocol of recruiting a mid-level principal for a school district. Related research was discussed explaining the importance of distinguishing between the tasks of recruiting and interviewing. Twelve course participants were asked to collaboratively develop a packet of information that would be available for recruiting purposes and were asked to develop a plan to disseminate the packet to job applicants.

The dissemination plan that course participants designed was as follows:

1. Send applications to all who requested one.
2. Review each application and acknowledge the receipt of the application with a letter.
3. Establish a pool of candidates from applications received.
4. Send each candidate a letter with time for their interview and provide each with a packet of information regarding the school district and community (recruiting packet), and identify the personnel who would be conducting the interview.
5. Send a letter to applicants who would not be interviewed with a letter stating that they were not in the applicant pool.

The recruitment packet contained the following information about the school district:

1. The school district's web site and information that could be found thereon.
2. A job description for the position as it appears in the district's policy manual.
3. The district's organizational chart.
4. A salary schedule and descriptions of benefits.

5. A packet of information that may be provided by the area chamber of commerce that included information about the community that would be important to persons moving into the district.

AN INTERVIEWING PROTOCOL: THE BASIS FOR WHAT IS ASKED OF APPLICANTS FOR THE MID-LEVEL PRINCIPALSHIP

In order to develop interview questions for the mid-level principalship, course participants were guided to establish interview questions that had a theoretical basis and that were legally compliant. After discussing lines of questioning that would be considered illegal, course participants formatted questions that complied with the Americans with Disabilities Act and questions that were compliant with ethical and legal parameters set forth by the Equal Employment Opportunities Commission (EEOC).

In order to develop interview questions with an articulated research base, course participants selected competencies of school leaders that were described by the Interstate School Leadership Licensure Consortium (ISLLC, 1996). They were familiar with these components as they had been the basis for most of the courses they had encountered in their programs of study. The ISLLC Standards are as follows:

Standard 1. A school administrator is an educational leader who promotes the success of all students by facilitating the development, articulation, implementation, and stewardship of a vision of learning that is shared and supported by the school community.
Standard 2. A school administrator is an educational leader who promotes the success of all students by advocating, nurturing, and sustaining a school culture and instructional program conducive to student learning and staff professional growth.
Standard 3. A school administrator is an educational leader who promotes the success of all students by ensuring management of the organization, operations, and resources for a safe, efficient, and effective learning environment.
Standard 4. A school administrator is an educational leader who promotes the success of all students by collaborating with families and community members, responding to diverse community interests and needs, and mobilizing community resources.
Standard 5. A school administrator is an educational leader who promotes the success of all students by acting with integrity, fairness, and in an ethical manner.

Standard 6. A school administrator is an educational leader who promotes the success of all students by understanding, responding to, and influencing the larger political, social, economic, legal, and cultural context. (p. 10–21)

Course participants discussed each of the six standards and developed a key word or phrase that described each. The following key words were developed:

1. Standard One: Vision
2. Standard Two: Instruction
3. Standard Three: Management
4. Standard Four: Collaboration
5. Standard Five: Ethics
6. Standard Six: Politics

After the six key words were identified, course participants were guided to develop a set of questions that addressed each of the six standards. They were instructed to develop a line of questions and be prepared to script respondents' answers by recording key words or phrases. Course participants developed thirty-two questions to be included in the protocol and also developed a rubric for scoring the responses. The maximum score for each response had a value of two points and a minimum score had a value of zero points. A score of zero points indicated, in the interviewer's observation, that the applicant had little or no understanding of a meaningful response to the question. A score of one point indicated that the applicant had a response, in the interviewer's observation, which demonstrated a satisfactory understanding of the question. A score of two points indicated that the applicant's response, in the interviewer's observation, demonstrated significant insight into the question and was able to articulate that insight in a response. A maximum score of 64 was attainable. To determine the interview team's score of an applicant's interview, each team member's score was added and an average score was calculated. To determine the protocol's content validity, course participants interviewed the course professor and scripted and scored the professor's responses.

CONDUCTING INTERVIEWS

The twelve course participants were organized into three interview teams with each team having four members. Three candidates in the university's Masters Degree Program in Educational Leadership consented to participate in mock interviews. While one interview team conducted an interview, the remaining two teams observed and scripted. Each member of the interview team was assigned specific interview questions and was responsible for asking those questions and clarifying their content when clarification was sought by the applicant. Although applicants were given the latitude to ask for clarification of any question they did not understand, interviewers were instructed not to respond in a fashion that would prompt a specific answer. Each applicant was asked the same questions from the interview protocol.

APPLICANTS IN MOCK INTERVIEWS

The three applicants participating in the mock interviews came from very diverse backgrounds in their respective teaching fields. Applicant 1 was a special education teacher at the middle school level with eighteen years of teaching experience and had concentrated her program of study on Special Education Administration and the mid-level principalship. Applicant 2 was a mid-level assistant principal with one year of administrative experience and twenty-seven years of teaching experience at the fifth grade level. She had concentrated her course of study on the mid-level principalship. Applicant 2 also revealed in the process that she had Parkinson's Disease. Applicant 3 was a middle school music instructor with five years teaching experience and was concentrating her program of study on the mid-level principalship.

SCORING THE INTERVIEWS

After the three interviews were conducted, the course participants met in their respective interview teams and shared individual rubric scores. Each team engaged in discussions regarding the rationale for assigning scores to specific questions. From the scripting, course participants defended the scores they assigned to an applicant's responses. After the discussions concluded, the teams calculated a combined score and determined which applicant would be recommended for employment. Scores of the three applicants are reflected in Table 1.

CONCLUSIONS

The scores from Table 1 indicate that Applicant 2 had the highest score in the interview. In dialogue among course participants after the conclusion of the interviews, other factors not measured in the protocol were discussed that could have possibly impacted decisions of the interviewers in making an employment recommendation to the board of education. Factors such as

Table 1. Applicants' Scores on Interview Questions

Applicant	Team 1 Score	Team 2 Score	Team 3 Score
Applicant 1	49	52	49.5
Applicant 2	52	56.3	52
Applicant 3	41	51	51

poise, enthusiasm, and appearance were discussed. Course participants determined that Applicant 2 approached the interview with "more poise and polish" than the other two applicants. When asked a question, Applicant 2 repeated it in a statement and then proceeded to respond. Years of experience in teaching and a year of administrative experience appeared to provide Applicant 2 an advantage in the process.

With the exception of Team 1's score of Applicant 3, the remaining two applicants had scores that were similar. From discussions among course participants, Applicant 2's years of teaching experience and year of administration appeared to provide her with more insight into the educational process than had been encountered by Applicants 1 or 3. Several of the questions that were asked referred to the education of children with disabilities which provided an advantage to Applicant 1 since her primary focus of study was Special Education Administration.

All three teams indicated that Applicant 2 would be their recommendation to the board of education for the principal's position, although one interview team indicated that they might recommend Applicant 3 for the position if the attendance center for which they were interviewing was not experiencing personnel or student achievement problems. They cited her enthusiasm toward the educational process and toward children in general.

LEARNING BY DOING:
PERCEPTIONS OF COURSE PARTICIPANTS

Near the conclusion of the semester, the university conducted a student evaluation of the course and its instructor. This evaluation is conducted without the physical presence of the instructor. This "hands-on" approach has been extremely popular among course participants. Some of their unsolicited comments were as follows:

1. The hands-on experiences for this course have been really great.
2. The group working as a team helps to understand how working in a school will be.
3. The hands-on work makes theories more real and gives you an idea of how to apply it.

4. The course has provided me with a wonderful hands-on leaning experience. The setting was cooperative learning and everyone was involved in communicative learning and interaction. It allowed me to think as a leader.

This approach, I feel, better prepared us for the job field. I thought I knew it all. The course has really opened my eyes to dealing with personnel issues . . . especially recruiting and interviewing personnel.

TARGETS AND CHALLENGES

As educational leadership programs prepare district-level leaders, little will be more important than ensuring that these future leaders have the skills necessary to identify and employ a competent staff. Common complaints among practitioners and the consistent observations of critics have been that knowledge and skills required on the job are not taught in administrator preparation programs (Pepper, 1988). Providing activities of authenticity in courses ensures that a school leader's encounter with the interview process has been on the side of the interviewer and not only the interviewee.

As educational leadership programs focus on "learning by doing," many opportunities exist for professors to authenticate activities for their students. Few activities could be more meaningful than having program candidates experience the process of staff recruitment and selection. When certified staff members are employed, they truly represent a million dollar investment over the course of their careers. The million dollar investment consists of the cost of salaries, benefits, and professional development. The impact that staff members will have in the lives of students, school districts, and communities cannot be calculated in financial terms alone. Their impact truly reaches to the very core of educating the nation's children and their selection to positions of such great importance should be encountered in a fashion that recognizes that importance.

REFERENCES

Caggiano, C. (1998). What were you in for? *Inc., 20,* 117.

Council of Chief State School Officers. (1996). Interstate school leadership licensure consortium: Standards for school leaders. Washington, DC: Council of Chief State School Officers.

Eggen, P., and Kauchak, D. (1996). *Strategies for teachers: Teaching content and thinking skills* (3rd ed.). Boston, MA: Allyn and Bacon.

Gutek, G. (2004). *Philosophical and ideological voices in education.* Boston, MA: Allyn and Bacon.

Ingersoll, R. M., and Smith, T. M. (2003). The wrong solution to the teacher shortage. *Educational Leadership, 60,* 30–33.

Messmer, M. (1995). The art and science of conducting a job interview. *Business Credit, 97,* 35–36.

Nichols, J. (2004). Recruiting and interviewing in rural school districts: protocol or potluck? *Rural Educator 26*(1), 40–46

Ozman, H., and Craver, S. (2003). *Philosophical foundations of education* (7th ed.). Columbus, OH: Merrrill-Prentice Hall.

Pepper, J. B. (1988). Clinical education for school superintendents and principals: The missing link. In D. E. Griffiths, R. T. Stout, and P. R. Forsyth (Eds.), *Leaders for America's Schools* (pp. 360–366). Berkeley, CA: McCutchan.

Rebore, R. (2004). *Human resources administration: A management perspective* (7th ed.). Boston, MA: Allyn and Bacon.

Sirbasku, J. (2002). Secrets of finding and keeping good employees. *USA Today, 130,* 32–34.

Smith, R. (2005). *Human resources administration: A school based prospective* (7th ed.). Larchmont, NY: Eye on Education.

APPENDIX: INTERVIEW QUESTIONS AND SCORING RUBRIC

Directions to Interviewer: Ask each question and clarify any misunderstanding that the person being interviewed may have. After the question is addressed by the applicant, provide a score in the indicated area. Use your scripted notes to support the following score: 0 = applicant's response indicated little or no understanding of a meaningful resolution to the question; 1 = applicant's response indicated a satisfactory resolution of the question; 2 = applicant's response indicated significant insight into the resolution of the question and articulated that insight in the response.

Vision
1. How would you ensure that students and staff have high expectations?
2. Discuss the importance of student and staff morale.
3. What is your definition of equitable and equal access to all your school has to offer?
4. How would you ensure open communication to all stakeholders in your attendance center?
5. What are your ideas of effective classroom management?
6. Describe a safe school environment.
7. How will you make yourself accessible to the stakeholders in your attendance center?
8. What can a student expect from you as their principal?

9. Describe your openness to innovations in education.
10. Describe loyalty.
11. Describe your perception of fairness.
12. Describe your work ethic.

Instruction

13. How would you ensure students with disabilities are receiving an appropriate education?
14. Describe your instructional leadership style.
15. What do you perceive as an effective classroom learning environment?

Management

What do you consider to be the management functions of the following?

16. Daily Routine
17. Discipline Policy
18. Physical Plant
19. Classified Personnel
20. Certified Personnel
21. Scheduling

Collaboration

How would you receive input from and provide feedback to the following?

22. Students
23. Parents
24. Staff
25. Community

Ethical Leadership

From a leadership standpoint, what do the following terms mean to you?

26. Honesty
27. Trust
28. Legal

Politics

Describe your understanding of the importance of the following as they relate to the political structure of the principalship:

29. Teacher Factions
30. Informal Power
31. Board of Education
32. Media

ADA/EEOC Compliance

You have been provided with the job description of this position. Is there any reason as to why you could not perform the duties of this position?

Preparing Superintendents for Bond Campaigns

Steve Neill

IN THE LATE NINETIES, A SCHOOL BOARD IN A SMALL Kansas community examined their facility needs and decided that a bond election was necessary. In the recent past, district facility needs had been addressed using capital outlay money but that was no longer feasible. District leadership developed a five million dollar plan to include major upgrades at all buildings with what they viewed as positive implications for all subjects and programs. The board decided to seek a bond election and conducted a modest informational campaign designed to apprise the community of the board's concerns and goals for the future as reflected in the building project.

When Election Day came, over 60 percent of the voters rejected the bond issue. The result came as a complete shock to advocates on the board of education and they decided it was important to understand what went wrong. The board commissioned a study team from an area university to examine the causes for such an overwhelming rejection of the bond issue.

The study team conducted interviews with a variety of community leaders and stakeholders. As the team began to determine patterns from the resulting data, one overriding fact became clear. The board had overestimated the communities' willingness to accept the board's view of district needs and had assumed that people would simply go along without a vigorous bond campaign. When one board member was asked, "Why didn't you mount a more strenuous campaign?" he replied, "The community has always supported bond elections." When asked the date of the last successful campaign, he paused, thought a moment and said, "Well, I guess it was 1967."

As states and their various levels of government continue to feel the effects of economic uncertainty, financing public education continues to be a central issue. Superintendents find themselves having to meet ever-increasing expectations with decreasing resources. One specific area, where this trend is especially felt, is the maintenance and construction of educational facilities. Superintendents must decide whether to use scarce resources to solve current problems or to invest in the district's future by maintaining or upgrading facilities.

In various ways, state governments allow their school districts to raise additional funds through the issuance of bonds. The process requires a bond election where the community is asked to approve a certain level of indebtedness for an expressed purpose.

Clearly, school boards and superintendents cannot assume that community support exists for a bond issue simply because district leadership sees the need. In order that the bond issue may have the best possible chance of passage, a vigorous, well-planned, and effective campaign is essential. The strategies for such a campaign must be the result of intelligent and extensive planning using the best available information. As the financial health of school districts continues to decline, the need for an effective campaign is all the more important.

The bond campaign is unique for a school district because this process is not a common practice for dealing with other district business, and superintendents often have little training or experience in dealing with the issues and strategies involved. The resulting difficulties facing superintendents when they endeavor to promote a bond issue motivated the development of this study.

BACKGROUND: THE SUPERINTENDENT AND BOND CAMPAIGNS

Based on their role as the district's educational leader, school superintendents have the primary responsibility of leading bond issue efforts (Lunenburg and Ornstein, 1991). Since superintendents rarely receive formal training in the political and managerial strategies associated with bond issues, passage often proves problematic. Although university training programs for district administration provide instruction in leadership, finance, plant and facilities, consensus building, and budgetary management, little instruction is specifically committed to the unique issues associated with the development and passage of bond issues. Specific course content varies based on the instructor. University texts designed specifically to deal with facility issues speak briefly about bond issues and seldom, if ever, about effective strategies (Castaldi, 1994; Davidson, 1987; Heim, Lyman, and Wilson, 1990; Konnert, 1995). Because of inconsistent university curriculum related to bond issues, superintendents are forced to learn on the job.

RESEARCH DESIGN AND METHODOLOGY

Superintendents, who had been successful in previous bond campaigns, were asked to identify critical strategies that they believe were the most salient in contributing to a successful bond issue. The same question was put to superintendents who had not been successful in a recent bond campaign. Finally, an examination was made regarding the affect on a bond issue referendum of the political and cultural context present in the community.

The study used a quantitative approach through the development and administration of a survey. A survey was developed based on bond issue campaign strategies identified in a review of literature and piloted with Kansas superintendents. The process of survey development yielded twelve different strategies that are most often used in bond campaigns. The twelve identified strategies were:

1. District designed informational brochures.
2. Information community meetings.
3. Door-to-door campaigns to promote the bond issue.
4. Get out the vote campaigns.
5. Involving students and teachers in promoting the bond issue.
6. Letters-to-the-editor campaigns in the local paper.
7. Developing media support.
8. Relating the bond issue to educational goals.
9. Speakers bureau of proponents to speak to community groups.
10. Targeting certain community groups during the campaign.
11. Telephone campaigns to promote the bond issue.
12. Displaying pro-bond issue yard signs.

The survey was sent to Kansas superintendents who led a bond campaign during a two-year period (1999–2001). The superintendents were asked to complete the survey which was designed to establish a ranking of the twelve strategies both as they were practiced in a prior campaign and how they would be used in a future election.

LESSONS LEARNED

The study resulted in several significant lessons for superintendents and boards of education.

Emphasize Communication with the Community

Bond campaigns should always place communication as a high priority through informational meetings and brochures. Stakeholders need a source of information that is accurate and does not require a major commitment of time and energy. They want to know the facts but they do not want to expend the effort required to investigate issues on their own.

Informational meetings and brochures consistently received strong support from all superintendents. Informing the public is clearly an important strategy to bond success. It would have been reasonable to expect wide variations in the highest priority strategies between those who managed successful campaigns and those who experienced electoral defeat. Instead, the variations chronicled in the study came in those strategies ranked third through twelfth.

The informational meetings and brochures should portray to interested stakeholders that the board of education is proposing a well-planned design that is aimed at improving the education of district students. Stressing the educational impact appears to have a positive influence on stakeholders. Voters appear to be willing to vote for projects that address an existing educational need.

Target Stakeholders with a Vested Interest

Successful superintendents placed more emphasis on strategies that informed or involved stakeholders who had an existing interest in the bond issue. In contrast, unsuccessful superintendents tended to use strategies designed to communicate with stakeholders regardless of their level of interest. Unsuccessful superintendents, for example, emphasized door-to-door and telephone campaign strategies. Strategies were designed to involve every stakeholder. It appears that targeting those stakeholders with an existing interest will translate into a willingness to vote. Focusing district resources on communicating with stakeholders who will not vote may be an inappropriate use of limited resources.

Examine the Opinions and Concerns of Stakeholders

Every community is clearly different with germane issues varying dramatically from one district to another. Assumptions made regarding the potential support or opposition from any particular group such as senior citizens, farmers, and the business sector position the passage of the bond issue at risk. Far too often, superintendents assume that groups like senior citizens will be opposed to the campaign because they live on fixed incomes and they no longer have children in school. The study found that, when approached properly, senior citizens could be active supporters of the bond issue. This applies to all the various interest groups that superintendents might find in their school districts.

Relate the Bond Issue to Educational Goals

The study found that efforts that related building needs to educational goals were effective strategies. Voters were more likely to vote for building improvements if the district could relate the improvement specifically to quality education. Superintendents should keep in mind that a majority of district patrons are in support of quality education. Different definitions of "quality" may exist but voters recognize the impact that effective PK–12 education has on the community.

Consider the Impact of Unique Community Circumstances

Superintendents indicated that certain circumstances unique to their communities had a major impact on the eventual results of the bond campaign.

Taxes

Superintendents indicated that the specific tax situation in their communities had impact on the passage of their bond elections. The promise of no tax increase was an important factor in the passage of several bond issues. One superintendent reported that the bond included "no mill increase and still had 27 percent no vote."

Another tax related issue involved the tax rate levied by other entities in the community. One community struggled with their bond issue because, "Our property tax is extremely high with a community college assessing 40 mil." The only positive impact from the tax situation involved the prevalence of low interest rates during the time of the bond campaign. Lower interest rates allowed the district to ask for a larger project with more of the money going to the actual building itself. Patrons were also impacted by the argument that waiting for improvements would make the eventual bill considerably higher if interest rates rose to prior levels.

Past Elections

Superintendents indicated that the community's experience with prior bond issues influenced their campaigns. In some communities, the influence of prior bond elections went back 20 years. A superintendent reported that his district faced a communication problem with the community in overcoming the errors of a prior election:

> The facilities committee had worked for over a year in determining the needs of the community and school district. The facilities committee had made a recommendation to the BOE for a $5.2 million project that provided about 42,000 square feet of construction. When I examined the documents collected from the community meetings, it looked like the recommendation by the facilities committee did not follow the perceived needs of the community. Needless to say, that bond election failed by a vote of 2 to 1. The facilities committee was reorganized and the BOE hired a consultant (retired superintendent) that led them through the process of discovering the need. After almost a year the facilities committee recommended to the BOE a project that would construct about 41,000 square feet at a cost of $3.6 million. This proposal did include the perceived needs of the community. This bond election passed by a vote of 2 to 1.

One superintendent reported failure in five previous bond issue campaigns before passage was achieved. Seeking community input and following it were crucial in final passage for some campaigns. One superintendent pointed out:

> A yearlong community task force process was used to define the scope and design of the proposal. The task force was at least 70 percent community members. We kept BOE and district staff in low profile in creating the plan. The plan was from the community and not the "school establishment."

Unique Local Issues

Superintendents frequently mentioned the importance of what could reasonably be called unique local issues. One such issue involved the condition of specific facilities. One district passed a bond issue only after the fire marshal required half a million dollars in repairs. Another district faced the loss of a building without necessary roof repairs. The superintendent reported, "We had to repair the roof of our high school. We either repaired the building or we would close it very soon."

Several superintendents believed that making use of current facilities was crucial as an alternative to building new ones. One campaign gained the support of elderly stakeholders through the improvement of a 1919 building that many of them had attended. Another district suffered a defeat in their bond election in part because of the proposal to change the location of the high school. Still another district gained support from middle school parents by nixing a plan to move ninth graders to the high school. The superintendent felt that "Maintaining a separate attendance center for [grades] 6–8 instead of moving them to the [high school] won votes of middle school parents."

Consider the Impact of Community Make-up

Concerning the impact of social, economic, and ethnic background of their community, superintendents indicated two important themes: One, the role of the economy; and two, community demographic factors that influenced bond passage.

Economy

Some superintendents indicated that the economy was stronger at the time of their campaigns. One postulated that the issue would have failed during the more difficult economic times when this study was conducted. Specific negative economic issues mentioned included aircraft lay-offs and the price of wheat.

Positive economic issues also existed. One superintendent reported that his community saw educational improvement as crucial to economic development. Another superintendent felt that the state's financial problems actually helped. He reported that "[We had a] concern about state's financial position [and the] possible loss or reduction in state aid for capital improvements."

Demographics

A wide range of demographic issues surfaced in superintendent responses. The most often mentioned demographic was the variance in age in a community. Superintendents mentioned a large elderly population as being a campaign factor. No consistent positive or negative factor was reported resulting from a large elderly population. One superintendent reported, "I think our community has an aging population with many having no children in school. This became an issue." Another superintendent said, "We have an older population that favors education. This support helped. We kept this population informed."

The percentage of stakeholders with children in school was also identified as a factor. One superintendent reported that it was an advantage to their bond campaign to have 40 percent to 50 percent of the families with children in school. Another superintendent reported a decided disadvantage when 85 percent of their stakeholders had no family members in the public schools. Some superintendents reported a growing school aged population as a benefit while other districts with an increasingly older population saw it as a challenge.

The superintendent of a large, urban district reported variance in ethnicity as an issue. The district was poor and ethnically diverse. The superintendent reported that opponents predicted bond failure because the community was too diverse to get behind an issue. The bond issue passed. The superintendent felt, "We are one of the poorest communities in the state. Also, heavily minority. Many said the community would not vote for a tax increase. But the community rallied behind an issue of pride and equity."

Other factors that influenced individual campaigns positively included the community's desire for the best possible schools, rapid community growth, and the community's growing need for an educated workforce. Additional negative factors involved general conservatism of the community, the impact of specific religious groups that opposed taxes, and opposition from the agricultural community.

Consider the Impact of Anti-Bond Issue Interest Groups

Responses regarding political issues centered on interest groups. A small number of campaigns reported the existence of interest groups that opposed the issue and those already in existence that also opposed the proposed projects. The number of responses did not indicate that this was a widespread problem for bond campaigns.

A small number of superintendents reported the development of groups that were specifically organized to oppose the bond campaign. One superintendent gave this account:

> The first election attempt did have a special interest group that came out at the final hour with a strong argument to vote "no" on the proposed bond election.

They took out a large ad in the weekly paper that did not allow time for a rebuttal. They also did a bulk mailing to all registered voters depicting their interpretation of how much taxes an individual would have to pay that owned a $50,000 home.

One community lost their campaign due to lack of support from the community's business organizations while another campaign was impacted by opposition from city government.

One superintendent reported that his district's campaign used the existence of an opposing interest group in a positive way during the next election: "The current group supporting the bond issue was a coalition of groups supporting and opposing previously defeated bond issues. That gave this group tremendous credibility. Perception: If this group can get together and support this issue, it must be good."

CONCLUSION

Superintendents developing and leading bond campaigns faced a combination of variables that were unique from one district to another. Although many factors existed in multiple districts, no specific factor or factors consistently occurred in a majority of the districts. Superintendents reported that each district had a unique combination of factors. The combination of multiple factors caused each district to face a unique voting climate. One community had opposition from elderly voters but support from the local businesses while another had business support but opposition from city government. Although both districts enjoyed business support, the voting climate was very different because of the combination of other factors. Clearly, a successful campaign must examine the factors that are unique to their communities and develop specific strategies to target those issues.

Based on the results of this study, superintendents must examine their future bond issue campaigns in the light of strategies that will be most effective. They must clearly communicate the purpose of the bond issue and its role in the education of students. They must target communication efforts to those stakeholders whose interest in the campaign will translate into voting. They must identify the role that special interest groups are playing in community and avoid making assumptions about special interest group's views on the bond issue. Moreover, the superintendent must set clear priorities in terms of strategies to be used based on their potential impact and the resources available in the campaign. A clearly defined strategy that makes the greatest use of available resources will provide the superintendent with the best chance of obtaining the kind of physical resources that can aid district teachers in the education of our students.

REFERENCES

Castaldi, B. (1994). Educational facilities: Planning, modernization, and management. Needham Heights, MA: Allyn and Bacon.

Davidson, J. (1987). The superintendency—Leadership for effective schools. Jackson, MS: The Kelwynn Press.

Heim, M. O., Lyman, L. R., Wilson, A. P., Winn, W. O, and Dykes, A. R. (1990). The superintendency and the school board: The call for excellence. Manhattan, KS: The Master Teacher, Inc.

Konnert, M. W. (1995). The school superintendency: Leading education into the 21st century. Lancaster, PA: Technomic.

Lunenburg, F. C., and Ornstein A. C. (1991). Educational administration: Concepts and practices. Belmont, CA: Wadsworth.

Finishing the Preparation of School Leaders: Can Preparation Programs and School Districts Partner to Produce the Leaders Schools Need?

CHERYL MCFADDEN AND KERMIT BUCKNER

THE PAST TWO DECADES HAVE BEEN CHALLENGING TIMES for schools and for the principals who lead them. As Bottoms and O'Neill (2001) have observed, "Increasingly, state accountability systems are placing the burden of school success—and individual student achievement—squarely on the principal's shoulders" (p. 4). Federal legislation in the form of the *No Child Left Behind (NCLB) Act of 2001* has increased that pressure. Concurrently, principal preparation programs have been criticized for failing to adequately prepare their candidates for the increasingly difficult task of school leadership (Brent, 1998). In an era when principals were under intense pressure to improve their schools, generally measured by student achievement, principal preparation programs have been called upon to prepare candidates who know how to close achievement gaps, to increase student learning, to improve teaching and learning, and to effectively manage their schools. This challenge has caused principal preparation faculties to examine everything they do and to seek new ways to prepare their candidates for school leadership. This article suggests that the reform of preparation programs alone has not been and may never be enough to ensure that school leaders have been fully prepared to meet the challenges they will face in their schools. We contend that a key ingredient in the preparation of school leaders has been missed. The key element that has been missed has been the linkage of preparation and induction. We also presented the result of a three-year pilot study in which a school district and principal preparation program partnered to continue preparation and to induct school leaders.

BACKGROUND

Traditional principal preparation programs have been under attack for the past two decades as the emphasis of school leadership shifted from management of the school operations to instructional leadership. The Southern Regional Education Board (SREB) with the

support of the Wallace Foundation has been a leader in calling for the restructuring of school leader preparation. In *Preparing a New Breed of School Principals: It's Time for Action*, Bottoms and O'Neill (2001) called for "universities to create school leadership preparation programs that will make a difference in improving schools and student achievement" (p. 25). To accomplish that task the SREB set the following goals for themselves:

1. Create a leadership preparation prototype outside of the traditional university-based program, demonstrate it and market it.
2. Create a network of higher education institutions that have an interest in working together to reshaping the traditional leadership preparation program by giving greater emphasis to the knowledge and skills needed by school leaders to improve curriculum, instruction, and student achievement.
3. Work with one or more state leadership academies to design, pilot, and refine a leadership academy program that prepares existing and emerging leaders to plan and carry out comprehensive middle grades and high school reform.
4. Establish a regional goal for improving leadership around a single priority—raising student achievement in middle grades and high schools—and develop indicators for tracking progress in achieving the goal over the next decade.

The SREB suggested that the redesign of public schools was contingent on the redesign of the programs that prepared their leaders. This intense focus on raising student achievement was indicative of the increased attention being directed toward the instructional leadership role of the principal.

The role of instructional leader was assigned to the principal in part because of school effectiveness research that found principal behavior to be a factor in school effectiveness (Levine and Lezotte, 1990;

Sammons, Hillman and Mortimore, 1995). More recent research, however, has concluded that educational leadership has been, at best, an indirect influence on student achievement. A recent meta-analysis of the research on educational leadership's direct impact on student achievement reported that not more that 1 percent of the variance in student achievement was associated with differences in educational leadership. This meta-analysis further revealed that there was no evidence for a direct effect of educational leadership on student achievement in secondary schools (Witziers, Bosker and Kruger, 2003). One of the major problems researchers encountered when they studied the impact of leader behavior on student achievement was controlling the many variables with which they were confronted when they examined student achievement. The debate over the impact of leader behavior on student achievement has made it difficult for those who are redesigning preparation programs to define the key knowledge and skills essential to effective instructional leadership. Whether leader behavior has been a significant factor in student and school success has been and will, likely, continue to be debated. There has been much less debate, however, over the need for the reform of preparation programs and the need for program candidates to be more focused on instructional issues.

In 1996 the alliance of associations representing education administrators, the National Policy Board for Educational Administration (NPBEA), created a set of national standards for school leaders. These standards, the Interstate School Leaders Licensure Consortium (ISLLC) Standards, were the first national standards for school leaders. They were developed under the direct supervision of the Council of Chief State School Officers (CCSSO) by a team of individuals that included representatives from each of the NPBEA member associations as well as representatives from 24 states. The ISLLC Standards were created to call attention to the need for school leaders to focus on student learning, to influence their evaluation, and to be prepared differently. The Standards called on educational leaders to steward a vision of learning, promote schools that were conducive to learning, collaborate with families and their communities, promote fair and ethical behavior, advocate for students in the larger social and political context, and effectively manage the learning environment (CCSSO, 1996). The Standards sent a clear message to those who prepare school leaders. That message was embodied in an ISLLC based licensure exam that many candidates would be required to take and in the accreditation standards for preparation programs that would mirror the Standards.

The ISLLC Standards were used as the basis for the School Leaders Licensure Assessment (SLLA), created by the Education Testing Service, and for the National Council for the Accreditation of Teacher Education (NCATE) Special Program Area (SPA) for school administration. The SLLA was adopted by a significant number of states as a requirement of an administrator license. This requirement increased the pressure on preparation programs to address the Standards in states that require candidates to take the SLLA. The school administration SPA, the Education Leadership Constituent Council (ELCC), has served as the accrediting body for all K–12 administrator preparation programs. Preparation programs wishing to receive recognition through ELCC and NCATE were required to address the ISLLC Standards as a part of their application process.

The ELCC modified the ISLLC Standards to fit the context of preparation in 2002. The resulting ELCC standards reflected the initial ISLLC Standards with one significant addition. The ELCC Standards included a seventh standard that defined a "structured, sustained, standards-based experience(s) in authentic settings" (National Policy Board for Educational Administration [NPBEA], 2002).

Preparation programs have made progress in shifting from an "educate the school manager" focus to an "educate the instructional leader" focus during the past two decades. This fact has been documented by the increased percentage of institutions that have been accredited by the ELCC since it began its work in the mid-1990s (NPBEA, 2002). This improvement, reflected in accreditation success, has not quieted critics such as the SREB who continue to call for major restructuring and alternative routes to school leader preparation. School systems continue to report that they cannot find qualified candidates to fill their vacancies and school leaders struggle to solve the numerous problems they encounter in their schools.

In 2003 a study was conducted in North Carolina to determine if induction services were being provided for the state's novice principals (Spencer, 2003). The data collected in that study from approximately half of the state's school districts revealed that only two of the school districts (3.7 percent) had formal induction programs for their new school leaders. This study also included a review of induction across a number of professions outside of education. When comparing induction services available to professionals in medicine, law, business, the military, and other professions with induction services available to school leaders, it was clear that school leaders were not being supported during the critical beginning years of their careers on the same level as are other professionals. Induction services have been provided to individuals to help them use the knowledge and skills taught during their preparation into effective action within the real world context. In this paper, we have suggested that the missing element in the preparation has been induction. In addition, we have suggested that preparation programs and school districts they serve should and can partner to provide induction services. Finally, we have suggested that a three-year pilot study of how a preparation program and school district partnered to induct school leaders can illuminate some of the issues, questions, and benefits that might arise in other such partnerships.

In summary, during the past two decades expectations placed on school leaders have shifted from a school manager orientation to an instructional leader orientation. School leaders have been held accountable for the achievement of students and have been expected to focus their attention on teaching and learning. Preparation programs that prepare school leaders have been criticized for not preparing their candidates to be instructional leaders. Standards have been created that require preparation programs to prepare their candidates to be instructional leaders. Research has been mixed regarding the influence of leader behavior on student achievement. Even though expectations for school leaders increased, few school districts have provided induction services for their new administrators. We have suggested partnerships provide opportunities for school districts and preparation programs to solve their mutual problems. Such partnerships have provided opportunities for school districts to induct their new leaders and opportunities for preparation programs to connect with the realities of school leadership and finish the preparation begun during class meetings and internships.

THE PROBLEM

School districts have struggled to improve student achievement, to make schools safer, to find and retain qualified teachers and principals, and to close achievement gaps. Districts have also struggled to find the time and the resources to train and develop high potential individuals who have shown *leadership qualities.* Principal preparation programs have been criticized for inadequately preparing their candidates for the rigors of school leadership, but they too have found it difficult to identify the knowledge and skills that the research has supported to teach instructional leaders. The ISLLC Standards include behavior, knowledge, and disposition outcomes for each Standard, but these Standards have provided little guidance regarding the kinds of preparation that will equip candidates to achieve those outcomes. As a matter of fact, the knowledge base for education administration has been a topic of hot debate for over a decade. In a review of principal preparation programs, Anderson (1991) reported that principals have been dissatisfied with preparation programs for many years. Principal preparation programs have struggled to provide students with the skills needed to translate knowledge into practical application. Preparation programs have been accused of being disconnected from the daily realities of public schools (Institute of Educational Leadership, 2000). As a result, some graduates have felt inadequately prepared for school leadership following graduation. Physicians, attorneys, and business leaders generally have participated in induction program before they have been expected to handle the most difficult problems in their professions. In contrast, principals and teachers have generally been assigned the most challenging tasks in their profession during their first year on the job with little or no induction. It is only through a structured induction process that the goals of principal preparation programs and the goals school districts establish for their new school leaders may be ensured. Academicians and practitioners working together have an opportunity to meet the challenge of fully preparing future educational leaders for the complex and ever-changing environments in which they work.

THE PROGRAM

One university based principal preparation program and a local school district in eastern North Carolina formed a partnership to finish the preparation of district leaders and to induct the district's newly hired school leaders. This partnership began as the result of discussions between the district superintendent and a professor at the local university. The district was interested in involving the university in the design of a program to help its assistant principals get ready to become principals. As the discussions progressed, individuals working in the university preparation program saw an opportunity to become more involved with current school leadership issues and with the realities of school leadership in its service area. University personnel agreed to become involved with the project. In order to facilitate the process, a committee comprised of principals, assistant principals, central office personnel, and university faculty were assembled to develop and implement the program. One of the first tasks to be accomplished was to address the following questions:

1. What were the benefits to the LEA and the university?
2. How would the university and the LEA work together (authority and responsibility)?
3. Who would provide the resources (money, facilities, and materials)?
4. How would we attract the right candidates?
5. What would be the requirements for the program?
6. What would the program content be?
7. How would the program be evaluated?
8. How would the program be sustained?

The committee attempted to answer all of these questions prior to implementing the program. However, over the past three years, many answers were revised as the program modifications were made to accommodate the needs of the school district and the university. The remainder of this article addressed each of these questions as it described the program that was developed. The program, referred to as the *Principal Leadership Academy*, has just completed its third year.

Benefits of the Program

The public school members of the planning committee agreed that the program would best serve the district by developing individuals who had shown leadership qualities and were viable candidates for vacant principal positions and by providing induction services for new principals who had participated in the program as assistant principals. The goal of the *Principal Leadership Academy* was to help participants develop the knowledge, dispositions, and skills needed to effectively lead a district school and to provide support for new principal during an induction period. As a consequence of developing strong instructional leaders, it was hoped that there would also be an improvement in student achievement and a reduction in the attrition rate among teachers and administrators in the district.

The university faculty members saw in this partnership the opportunity to make sure their preparation program reflected the realities of school leadership.

University faculty working in the program would have first hand experience in working with principals who were engaged in solving authentic districts problems and dealing with the realities of instructional leadership in an accountability driven state.

Working Together

Initially, the planning committee decided that all decisions regarding the program would be made collaboratively by the school district's director of professional development and the university's co-directors of the program. This subcommittee of the planning committee met regularly to develop the components of the program. It was decided that the Leadership Academy participants should contact the director of professional development regarding issues such as seminar attendance. Due to the importance of maintaining confidentiality among the participants and the co-directors, it was agreed that the co-directors would not discuss any issues that arose during school visits or seminars with district administrators. The superintendent and other district administrators were to be informed on a regular basis as to the progress of the program (seminar topics, activities, program evaluation, and other relevant information), but not about the discussions and reflections that took place during activities and visits.

Resources for the Program

The co-directors developed a budget for the first year of the program. The budget included books, materials, fees for guest speakers, salaries for faculty from the College of Health and Human Performance, and other costs associated with the participants receiving a complete medical examination and evaluation. The budget did not include salaries for the co-directors. The university's contribution was the co-directors involvement in the program. The district agreed to fund the budget ($5,000) with professional development funds. The first Leadership Academy program consisted of six monthly half-day seminars (three in both the fall and spring), three to four site leadership/wellness visits to each participant, and a one-week summer institute.

The budget for the second year was increased to $10,000. This increase was needed so that participants could attend professional development conferences and to fund a second cohort of participants who entered the program at the beginning of the second year. Again, the co-directors did not receive a salary. At the conclusion of the second year, the co-directors met with the director of professional development and the superintendent and presented three different plans for year three. The first plan was for the continuation of the existing program. The second plan added more site visits for the assistant principals in the program and included one year of induction services for individuals who had completed the program and been promoted to principal positions. The second plan included funds to release one of the university co-directors for one course. The third plan, nicknamed the "Cadillac" plan included all of the components of the second plan, but added training on coaching and mentoring for principals with assistant principals in the program and for mentoring and coaching new principals for two years. The superintendent without any hesitation selected the "Cadillac" plan. The cost for this plan was $25,000.

Attracting the Right Candidates

The school district has 33 schools (six high schools, six middle schools, six K–8 schools, 14 elementary schools, and one Pre-K center). The district employed 33 principals and 36 assistant principals. Twenty-seven percent of the district's principals are eligible to retire in 2004 and by 2009 that number will increases to 48 percent. The director of professional development, with the approval of the planning committee, developed an application and an evaluation rubric to evaluate applicants. The first section of the application consisted of school employment information. The second section asked the applicants to list activities that had influenced their professional growth. The last section asked the applicants to reflect on several questions. For example, during the interview candidates were asked, "Under what conditions and on what specific topics should schools seek 'consensus' as a method for making decisions?" Interview questions and an evaluation rubric were also developed.

In October 2001, the director of professional development conducted a session for all its assistant principals in which the Leadership Academy was described. The assistant principals were given an opportunity to ask questions. In addition to asking questions about the level of commitment and seminar topics, many questions arose as to the necessity for the program and the consequence of not participating. The co-director and the director of professional development described the benefits of the program and assured interested individuals that acceptance into the Leadership Academy did not guarantee participants would be employed as principals. Prospective participants were told the program offered them an opportunity to continue their preparation. The director of professional development then sent each assistant principal an application and invited them to apply. During the next month, the applicants were interviewed and notified of their status. Eight applicants were accepted into the program in year one, six were accepted in year two, and seven were accepted in year three. Cohorts 1 and 2 have completed the program and the members of cohort 3 are in their second year.

Program Requirements

Applicants were required to have a minimum of three years of experience as an assistant principal. Participants were required to attend monthly half-day seminars during the academic year and a one-week summer institute in summer between year one and year two. Attendance and participation was mandatory. Since the Leadership Academy was a two-year program, successful completion of year one was a prerequisite for advancing to year two.

Program Content

The goal of the Leadership Academy was to develop individuals with the knowledge, dispositions, and skills needed to provide effective school leadership. The specific objectives of the program were:

1. Participants would use daily experiences to record observations about leader's effectiveness in self and others, report select observations to colleagues, and engage in discussions about the effectiveness of leadership behaviors.
2. Participants would create a professional development plan based upon personal and school needs, record experiences in a journal, and share learning with their reflection teams.
3. Participants would participate in activities that would enable them to better understand their own and other's action.
4. Participants would demonstrate the ability to make better decisions based on new knowledge and skills.
5. Participants would demonstrate the ability to use research and professional literature to enhance their leadership knowledge and skills.
6. Participants would be able to explain the relationship between health parameters and effective school leadership.

The ISLLC Standards and the ISLCC Collaborative Professional Development Process provided the framework for the Leadership Academy. The research conducted by Waters, Marzano, and McNulty (2003) that identified 21 leadership characteristics linked to changes in students' test scores was also incorporated into the content.

A major component of the Leadership Academy was the monthly seminars during the academic year. Table 1 lists some of the topics for these seminars. Participants were also provided with research articles and books to read that were pertinent to the seminar topics.

Another component of the Leadership Academy was the Summer Institute. The Summer Institute was conducted over a one-week period and included two components: an instructional leadership seminar and a health/wellness component. Leader 123, an Instructional leadership program developed by the National Association of Secondary School Principals (NASSP), has been used as the instructional leadership program during two summers. The goal of Leader 123 was to develop instructional leaders who have skills in planning, developing, measuring, and implementing the school changes needed to improve the learning process. Participants in this program also learn key behaviors for sensitivity, delegating, post-performance and real-time coaching, self-development and seeking feedback on performance.

The health/wellness component included a complete medical examination, physical fitness examination, and seminars in nutrition and stress management. The health/wellness component was delivered by faculty from the College of Health and Human Performance at the university. The purpose of this component of the Leadership Academy was to make participants aware of important health parameters that affect their quality of life and their professional performance. Faculty from the College of Health and Human Performance provided a complete "Cardiovascular Disease Risk Factor Identification/Reduction Program" for each participant. Tests and evaluations

included in this program were: complete blood and urinalysis, medical and exercise inventories, resting and exercise electrocardiogram, cardiopulmonary examination by a physician, lung function testing, body composition assessment (hydrostatic and skinfolds), strength and flexibility assessment, and symptom limited maximal treadmill stress test with physician interpretation. At the conclusion of the testing, each participant received a follow-up report and a personalized exercise prescription. In consultation with an exercise physiologist and health educator, each participant was required to develop a plan for implementing and monitoring their personal exercise prescription.

In the stress management component of the program, participants learned to anticipate stressful events, to manage day-to-day stress and to prevent stress overload. Participants took a variety of computerized assessments including "Life Experiences Test," "Type-A Personality Profile" and "Stress Vulnerability Test" to discover their current level of stress. Faculty shared current information about the health effects of stress and the importance of an effective comprehensive stress management program. Specific stress management techniques were also discussed. Faculty assisted each participant in developing an effective personalized stress management plan.

Program Evaluation

There were three assessments identified to measure the effectiveness of the program. The first assessment was the number of participants receiving appointments as principals or receiving recognition by the district for outstanding performance. The second and third assessments consisted of surveys of participant satisfaction.

In cohort 1, five participants (63 percent) have been appointed principals and one has been appointed to a central office position. The one who was appointed to

Table 1. Leadership Academy Seminar Topics

Topic
Personal and Professional Needs Assessment Using the FIRO-B and the 360 Instruments
Conflict Management Styles Using the Thomas-Kilmann Conflict Mode Instrument
Evaluating Learning and Conferencing Skills
Legal Issues and Ethics
Mentoring and Coaching
Making University Partnerships Work
Purpose Driven Leadership: Define, Communicating, and Maintaining the Vision
Teaching Recruitment and Retention
Leading Schools in an Era of Accountability
Internal and External Publics
Inclusive Schools for Children with Significant Developmental Disabilities

a central office position was also the district's assistant principal of the year. One member of this cohort accepted a director's position at the university. Two of the six members (33 percent) of cohort 2 and two of the seven members (29 percent) of cohort 3 have been appointed principals. One member of cohort 2 was the recipient of the district's assistant principal of the year award during the second year of her Leadership Academy experience. One member of cohort 3 has been eliminated from the program for unprofessional conduct and behavior. This decision was made by the superintendent.

The evaluators developed two formal assessment instruments. The first assessment instrument was designed to be completed at the end of the program and the second instrument to be completed at the conclusion of both year one and two. In the first assessment, participants were asked to complete a survey designed to: (a) to ascertain the perceptions of participants to the Leadership Academy Program and (b) to ascertain the perceptions of participants of the importance of the Program to job requirements. Specifically, the survey was designed to address the following five questions:

1. To what extent did participants believe that the Leadership Academy Program provided adequate preparation for school administration?
2. To what extent did participants believe that the Leadership Academy provided adequate preparation in areas important to job requirements?
3. To what extent were perceptions of program and importance to job requirements for ISLLC Standards related?
4. To what extent did participants believe that the ISLLC indicators were important to job effectiveness?
5. To what extent did participants believe that the ISLLC standards were important to job effectiveness?

The first section of the survey contained selected demographic information. The second section attempted to obtain their perceptions of the adequacy of the Leadership Academy Program and the importance of the Program to job requirements. This section included information regarding the knowledge, dispositions, and performance indicators of the ISLLC Standards for School Leaders to measure the Leadership Academy participants perceived adequacy of training as described in the ISLLC indicators and the relevance of these indicators to job requirements. The

six ISLLC Standards were limited to 40 indicators—7 knowledge indicators, 9 dispositions indicators, and 24 performance indicators. A Likert Scale, with numerical value, was used to quantify responses related to participants' perceptions of the adequacy of the Leadership Academy Program, the relationship of the Program to actual job requirements, the extent to which the adequacy of the Program and the importance of the job requirements relate to the 40 ISLLC indicators, and the extent to which the adequacy of preparation and the importance to job requirements relate to the ISLLC Standards. The third section of the survey contained three open-ended questions asking participants to identify the most important and least important concepts and to identify other important concepts not addressed in the current program.

Cohort 1 and 2 had six participants to complete the program. Cohort 3 is in the second year of program and has six members remaining in the program. As a result, only six participants each year (total of 12) have completed this survey. Since the evaluators were dealing with such a small number, descriptive statistics (frequency distributions, means, and percentages) were calculated for the following: (a) The participants' perceptions of the adequacy of the program, (b) the relationship of the program to actual job requirements, (c) the extent to which the adequacy of program and the importance to job requirements relate to the ISLLC indicators, and (d) the extent to which the adequacy of program and importance to job requirements related to the ISLLC Standards.

Since many of the participants have been appointed principals and/or have been transferred to different schools or the central office during the past three years, the evaluators chose to examine the data from this instrument upon conclusion of the program for cohort 1 and 2. Table 2 provides current demographic information for members of all three cohorts.

Twenty-eight percent were age 30–39 (n = 5), 50 percent were 40–49 (n = 9), and 22 percent (n = 4) were 50–59. Twenty-two percent were males (n = 4) and 78 percent were females (n = 14). Their current school assignments ranged from 39 percent serving in elementary schools (n = 7), 28 percent in K–8 schools, 22 percent in middle schools (n = 4), and 11 percent in high schools (n = 2). They ranged in teaching experience: 56 percent in elementary (n = 10), 17 percent in middle school (n = 3), and 28 percent in high school (n = 5). All the participants had three years or more of experience as assistant principals as this was a requirement for applying to the Leadership Academy.

Table 2. Demographic Information for Leadership Academy Participants

	Cohort 1	Cohort 2	Cohort 3
Age			
0–39	1	2	2
40–49	5	4	4
50–59	0	0	0
Gender			
Male	2	0	2
Female	4	6	4
School Assignment			
Elementary	2	3	1
K–8	1	2	2
Middle School	2	1	1
High School	0	0	2
Central Office	1	0	0
Teaching Experience			
Elementary	3	4	3
K-8	0	0	0
Middle School	1	2	0
High School	2	0	3

Note. 18 participants.

All of the participants in cohort 1 and 2 (12 participants) either strongly agreed or agreed to the adequacy of the program, the relationship of the program to actual job requirements, the extent to which the adequacy of preparation and the importance to job requirements relate to the ISLLC indicators, and the extent to which the adequacy of preparation and importance to job requirements related to the ISLLC Standards. The participants indicated that all six of the ISLLC Standards are important to the job. The participants identified Standard 3's knowledge and performance indicators, particularly legal issues impacting school operations, effective problem framing and problem solving skills, effective conflict resolution skills, effective group-process and consensus building-skills, and effective communication skills.

The second assessment instrument was a survey of open-ended questions administered to cohort 2 at the completion of the program and cohort 3 (12 participants) at the end of the second year. In response to the importance of the planning, journaling, and on-the-job reflections, one participant wrote, "I have been able to use my professional development successfully going into my principalship. . . . " Another commented, "It helped me look at my weaknesses and strengths. This process also helped me understand where I spend the majority of my time and how I might better use my time." Another participant responded, "Only by reflecting on the job that we are doing can we improve. The journaling was difficult to keep going on a regular basis."

When asked about the importance of the monthly seminars, one participant wrote, "I particularly liked this portion of the program. Developing trust in a learning organization was a helpful presentation for reflection." Another one wrote, "I have found the sharing with my colleagues especially valuable. The cohort has provided a positive networking opportunity." Several participants share this comment: "It helped me get a feel for what other administrators were going through and the problems I had were pretty universal."

Overwhelmingly, the participants identified the site visits as one of the most important component of the program. One comment about the site visits included "Cheryl and Kermit (co-directors) have come to know me better on a professional level and have had a chance to see my work environment and give advice and guidance that is specific to my circumstances." Another participant wrote, "The visits have given me an insight that I probably would've not had. I enjoyed the 'straight' talk. Having someone taking an interest in me has caused me to take an interest in myself."

When asked about the most valuable part of the Leadership Academy, one participant wrote "The opportunity to examine and glean best practice from a group of motivated leaders, in a setting that is focused on progressive educational leadership." Another responded that "the summer session has been the most valuable part of the Academy for me, especially the health component."

Finally, the participants were asked to identify elements that were absent from the program. One participant commented, "More time for activities . . . to share experiences . . . share best practice . . . books/journal articles to read . . . " Several participants expressed this sentiment: "More opportunities to come together."

The evaluators made several conclusions based on the results of the second survey. Participants wanted to share their professional experiences with other school leaders. They appreciated the dialogues with members of their cohorts and the co-directors. The participants enjoyed learning about their self and others in a safe environment. They were allowed to make mistakes and be forgiven. One participant referred to the Leadership Academy as a "period of grace." Finally, the participants wanted to improve their leadership skills and increase their knowledge base through research and professional literature. Their ultimate goal was to be able to integrate this knowledge into best practice and improve student achievement.

Sustaining the Program

The Leadership Academy has completed its third year. To date, the school district has provided $40,000 to support the Academy. The university has provided support for the Academy in terms of in-kind contributions (only one of the co-directors has received a one course reduction per semester for one year). As other school districts are learning about the program, the university has had many requests to implement the program throughout eastern North Carolina. The co-directors have submitted several grant proposals to private industry but have been unsuccessful in securing funds. The dean of the College of Education at the university and the co-directors have met with six superintendents in the region (including the one involved in the current program) and have expanded the Leadership Academy Program to include all of these districts. During the past four years, a steel mill has built a mill in this region and employs 300 people. The steel mill has reported profitable earnings this year. In addition, the steel mill has received tax abatements for four years from the state and will continue to do so for several more years. The dean and the co-directors are in the process of submitting a proposal to the executives of this steel mill for funding. If successful, the Leadership Academy Program would involve school leaders in six school districts in eastern North Carolina.

The superintendent involved in this Leadership Academy has been very impressed with the success of the program. He has already committed more funds for the 2004–2005 school year. The co-directors and the director of professional development will continue to seek both private and public funds to support this endeavor.

SUMMARY AND CONCLUSION

This article has called attention to the need to change the way principals were prepared to lead schools in an era of accountability. In the light of general agreement regarding this need, the only question that remained was how to do it. One answer that was presented was to adopt and adapt the induction models used by other professions to complement preparation with induction. Such an approach was presented in which a preparation program and school district partnered to conduct post preparation program work and to induct new administrators.

One three-year pilot study has not provided data that would support the implementation of post preparation and induction program partnerships on a wide scale. It did, however, provide enough evidence to warrant further study and experimentation. This partnership demonstrated that services provided by individuals whose primary duty was to prepare school leaders can make a difference in the continued preparation and induction of new school leaders. The partnership has also served to provide professors with authentic situations for their classes and with a much better understanding of the realities of school leadership.

The participants in this pilot study have concluded that the effort was successful and that program goals were accomplished for all parties involved. As this preparation program considers how best to expand this program to include other school districts, a number of questions will have to be answered. These questions are also valid for other preparation programs interested in creating similar partnerships. The basic questions to be answered are the following:

1. What are the specific needs (school district and preparation program) to be addressed?
2. What are the program costs? What will each partner contribute to the cost?
3. How will the program be managed and by whom?
4. How will participants be selected?
5. How will program director(s) be held accountable?
6. How will the program be evaluated?

Any partnership is a work in progress. This was certainly the case with the pilot study reported here. A trusting relationship between the preparation program and school district will be an essential ingredient. This kind of partnership can also serve to strengthen the trust between school districts and the school districts they serve.

REFERENCES

Anderson, M. E. (1991). *Principals: How to train, recruit, select, induct, and evaluate leaders for America's schools.* Eugene, OR: ERIC Clearinghouse on Educational Management, University of Oregon. (ERIC Document Reproduction Service No. ED337843.)

Bottoms, G., and O'Neill, K. (2001). *Preparing a new breed of school principals: It's time for action.* Retrieved August 2004 from http://www.sreb.org.

Brent, B. O. (1998). Teaching in educational administration. *Newsletter of the American Educational Research Association, 5*(2).

Council of Chief State School Officers [CCSSO]. (1996). *Standards for School Leaders.* Retrieved August 2004 from http://www.ccsso.org.

Institute for Educational Leadership, Inc. (2000). *Leadership for student learning: Reinventing the principalship.* Washington, DC: Author.

Levine, D., and Lezotte, L. (1990). *Unusually effective schools: A review and analysis of research and practice.* Madison, WI: National Center for Effective Schools Research and Development.

National Policy Board for Educational Administration [NPBEA]. (2002). *Standards for Advanced Programs in Educational Leadership.* Retrieved August 2004 from http://www.npbea.org.

Sammons, P., Hillman, J., and Mortimore, P. (1995). *Key characteristics of effective schools: A review of school effectiveness research.* London: OFSTED.

Spencer, K. (2003). *A study of formal induction programs in North Caroline for public school principals: Identifying key components of the North Carolina principal induction programs.* Unpublished doctoral dissertation, East Carolina University, Greenville, NC.

Waters, J. T., Marzano, R. J., and McNulty, B. A. (2003). *Balanced leadership: What 30 years of research tells us about the effect of leadership on student achievement.* Aurora, CO: Mid-continent Research for Education and Learning. Retrieved August 2004 from http://www.mcrel.org.

Witziers, B., Bosker, R., and Kruger, M. (2003). Educational leadership and student achievement: The elusive search for an association. *Educational Administration Quarterly, 39*(3), 389–425.

University-Authorized Charter Schools: A Unique Component of the School Choice Movement

DOUGLAS THOMAS, JAMES MACHELL, AND JIM BOWMAN

THROUGHOUT HISTORY AMERICAN PUBLIC SCHOOLS HAVE been viewed as a vehicle for improving the lives of young people and for responding to a wide array of social conditions. Competing forces place varying demands on public schools and confusion persists concerning several critical questions: What is the purpose of public school education? To whom do the public schools belong? To whom are the public schools accountable? These questions and others related to ownership and control of public schools have been the source of fierce debate and continue to be key issues that must be addressed as we develop a vision for public schooling for the twenty-first century.

Our nation's public schools have experienced numerous trends in the twentieth century. An overarching issue through which many developments can be viewed focuses on the questions of who controls the public schools and to whom the schools should be accountable. At times thoughtful educators have taken the responsibility for developing a vision for the education of young people and created learning environments and educational programs where that vision came alive. Conversely, educational practitioners often find themselves in a more reactive mode where their actions are taken in response to criticism from those outside the educational community.

A factor closely related to the control of public schools is public perception of the quality of those schools. In 1983 "A Nation at Risk" (National Commission on Excellence in Education) reported to the American public that our nation's public schools were failing miserably. One might argue that, over the course of the last seventeen years of the twentieth century, the public perception of the quality of America's public schools has never been more negative.

The high level of dissatisfaction for public schools has increased pressure on public schools and policy makers. Such pressure has manifested itself in several forms. Control mechanisms imposed by state govern-ment through the development of statewide curriculum frameworks, assessment programs, and centralized control over instructional materials have stripped educators at the building and district level from much authority. State legislation geared toward encouraging alternatives to public schools represents another level of pressure to which educators are now reacting.

This paper examines charter schools, specifically university-authorized charter schools, and the issues related to ownership and control of public schools. Understanding these issues will provide insights into some of the challenges and opportunities that face public schools, the educational community, and the larger society in the twenty-first century. The remainder of the paper is organized into three sections. The section that follows directly provides a general overview of charter schools as a school choice option and charter school legislation. The recent phenomenon of university-authorized charter schools including specific examples of what is occurring at one state university that is now in the process of sponsoring charter schools is examined in section two. In section three the authors attempt to forecast the impact of university-authorized charter schools on the future of the larger educational community, including K–12 public schools, universities, and other related entities.

CHARTER SCHOOLS

As a result of the growing public dissatisfaction with the public schools, several school choice options have been explored as a means for parents and others to exercise greater control and ownership. Hlebowitsh (1995) observed that the debate over school choice "revolves around a dualism that frames the main purpose of the school to be either in the best interests of the individual and the family or the best interests of society . . . most advocates of choice have contended that schools should be devoted to the individual and that the family is, therefore, the most effective agent in

303

shaping the school experience" (p. 6). Others (Boyer, 1992; Jones and Ambrosie, 1995; Manno, Finn, Bierlein and Vanourek, 1998) have noted the social, educational, legislative, political, and organizational trends that support school choice as a viable option to traditional public schools. It remains to be seen exactly how tuition tax credits and school voucher systems as school choice options will ultimately affect public education. However, charter schools as options for school choice have already made a considerable impact.

Charter schools are public schools that operate under a "contract" or charter with a school, district, or state. The charter includes the terms under which the school must operate (including provisions for fiscal management and accountability for student achievement) and the charter may be revoked if the school violates these conditions. The concept behind charter schools maintains that those responsible for operating a charter school trade ". . . rules and regulations for freedom and results" (Manno et al., 1998, p. 490). Typically, charter schools are freed from bureaucratic control mechanisms from the local district and state department levels yet are held accountable for measuring and reporting student performance. Conceptually, charter schools afford those who operate them and the clients they serve (students and parents) much greater levels of control and ownership over the school through the limitation or suspension of bureaucratic controls imposed by district-level boards and state government.

The charter school movement has gained momentum. Minnesota passed the nation's first charter law in 1991. In 1998, the National Study for Charter Schools reported that "by fall 1997 there were approximately 700 charter schools operating in 29 states and the District of Columbia" (U.S. Department of Education, 1998, p. 4). The same report indicated that 279 new charter schools were opened during the 1997–1998 school year and that during the 1997 legislative session four states (Mississippi, Nevada, Ohio, and Pennsylvania) passed charter school legislation. In 1998, Missouri and Virginia passed charter school laws, bringing the total number of states with charter school legislation to 34. By 2003 that number increased to 40 states, Puerto Rico, and the District of Columbia, (U.S. Department of Education, 2004).

According to the U.S. Department of Education website for charter schools, charter schools are one of the fastest growing innovations in education policy, enjoying broad bipartisan support from governors, state legislators, and past and present secretaries of education. In 1997, President Clinton called for the creation of 3,000 charter schools by the year 2002. In 2002, President Bush called for $200 million to support charter schools. Since 1994, the U.S. Department of Education has provided grants to support the development of charter schools (U.S. Dept. of Education, 2004).

The U.S. Department of Education (2004) reported that 41 states and the District of Columbia have passed legislation authorizing charter schools. Currently, 37 of these states have charter schools in operation, with 2,971 schools providing services to approximately 703,000 students. This is a 15 percent increase from the previous year and a 40 percent increase since 1999 (U. S. Department of Education, 2004).

While the growth in the number of states with charters legislation, schools opening, and the number of students served by these schools is impressive, studies on the impact of these schools are just starting to emerge. In 1995, Bierlein noted that, at that time, no formal studies or data existed on the impact of charter schools. However, informal reports revealed several noteworthy findings about charter schools at that time including the following: (a) numerous "at-risk" students were being served by charter schools; (b) unique learning environments were being created in response to teacher and parental desires; (c) unique community and business partnerships were being formed; (d) unique opportunities for teachers had surfaced; (e) larger percentages of existing funds were being focused on instructional activities; and (f) effects across the broader system were becoming visible. Bierlein concluded that "conceptually, charter schools are intended to not only serve the students within their walls, but to help initiate other changes" (p. 19).

There have been studies identifying the challenges faced by charter schools. The National Study of Charter Schools found that the following challenges related to implementing charter schools: (a) resource limitations: (b) political resistance and regulations imposed by state or local boards; (c) internal conflicts; and (d) difficulties with teacher unions (U.S. Department of Education, 1998, p. 14).

Nathan (1998) noted challenges that are internal and external. Internal challenges include: (a) how to assess student achievement; (b) how to meet needs of disabled students; (c) how to most effectively organize governance structures; (d) how to best organize teaching and learning activities; and (e) how to attract a broad range of students. External challenges include:

(a) the impact of allowing more than one potential sponsor; (b) insufficient and weak charter school laws; (c) the involvement of for-profit corporations; (d) questionable research findings; (e) facilities; and (f) skepticism of educators and board members.

The National Study for Charter Schools also identified characteristics of charter schools and of students who attend charter schools. Most charter schools are small, many utilize non-traditional grade configurations, and most are newly created (as opposed to being converted from an existing public school) (U.S. Department of Education, 1988, p. 9). Charter school students are similar to those in public schools in terms of distribution of racial and income characteristics and those in several states have a higher proportion of schools that predominately serve students of color (U.S. Department of Education, 1998, p. 10–11).

Bierlein (1995) found several elements that make charter schools an appealing reform concept. Charter schools: (a) focus on results; (b) remain public schools; (c) enhance educational choice options; (d) permit true decentralization; (e) enable local school boards to become policy boards; and (f) provide a more market-driven educational system (p. 13). Bierlein observed "overall, these elements—all within a public school setting—have made charter schools a very attractive reform initiative for policymakers, educators, and parents alike" (p. 15).

The National Study of Charter Schools also reported several factors that make charter schools attractive to parents. These included: (a) there is a perceived need for alternatives to public schools and charter schools are in high demand; (b) many parents are dissatisfied with the public schools; and (c) charter schools offer an alternative vision for education that focuses on academics plus other attractions including a more positive learning environment and high standards (U.S. Department of Education, 1998, p. 12–13).

Among the findings of the Charter Schools in Action study was that the charter schools studied were "genuine centers of innovation" (Manno et al., 1998, p. 490). The authors of the study suggest that those "committed to revitalizing public education should welcome charter schools as a giant step toward the reinvention of public education in America" (Manno et al., 1998, p. 490). The study's findings suggest traits of charter schools that can serve as examples for other public schools. Charter schools are: (a) consumer-oriented focusing on responding to student needs; (b) created to serve the diverse needs and priorities of clients; (c) accountable, results-oriented and focused on student learning; (d) professional and free from bureaucratic control and micro-management; and (e) emphasize intimacy and mission.

Charter school laws vary from state to state. The nature or "strength" of charter school legislation is a critical factor that affects the proliferation and operation of charter schools. Four key areas in the political debate involved with charter school legislation include: (a) organizer options—Many want to exclude private schools from obtaining charters; (b) sponsorship options—Many want only the local board to sponsor them, not state boards or universities; (c) legal and fiscal autonomy—Many want charter schools to remain part of the district and not become autonomous entities; and (d) employee requirements and protection—Many want to require certification and maintain district-level bargaining and tenure provisions (Bierlein, 1995, p. 15–16).

Bierlein (1995) described the characteristics of "stronger" charter school laws. In states with stronger laws, "charter schools can be sponsored by entities other than local boards (or have strong appeal process), are granted a great deal of financial and legal autonomy, and are granted automatic freedom from most state and local rules" (p. 16). As a result, more charter school activity is occurring in those states. Bierlein (1995) described states with "weaker" laws as "often no more than enhanced site-based decision-making experiments. They remain part of the school district, have limited control over budget and personnel matters, and often must seek waiver on a case-by-case basis . . . limited chartering activity is occurring in states with weaker laws" (p. 16).

A key component of "strong" charter school legislation is the availability of a non-local board sponsorship or an appeal process. "Five years of experience show that the details of state charter laws matter enormously. The five states with the 'strongest' laws allow some entity other than local school boards, such as a state board of education or public university, to sponsor charters. As of December 1995, the five states with the strongest laws had 222 charter schools, compared to only 14 schools in the five states with the weakest laws" (Nathan, 1996, p. 20). The eight states providing for the authorization of charter schools by universities are all ranked as states with moderate to strong charter legislation (Center for Educational Reform, 2004).

Missouri's charter school legislation is contained in Missouri Senate Bill 781 relating to school desegregation, school funding and urban schools and was passed by the Missouri General Assembly in May of

1998. The law provides for charter schools to be established only in Kansas City and St. Louis. As such, the statute is perceived to be a political response to dissatisfaction with the two urban school districts of the state. There are several key features of the Missouri legislation that make it a "strong" charter school law. The law

1. contains no cap on the number of schools that can be developed with some restrictions on the number of locations and limited to the St. Louis and Kansas City School Districts;
2. allows local school boards, four-year public colleges or universities or public community colleges in the same or adjoining county to be charter school sponsors;
3. allows for an unlimited number of new charter schools but limits conversions of existing public schools;
4. exempts charter schools from all laws and rules pertaining to schools except those pertaining to health, safety, minimum educational standards and federal anti-discrimination policies;
5. allows charter schools to operate as nonprofit corporations;
6. allows charter schools to be eligible to receive and use transportation funding and to provide or contract for student transportation services;
7. requires the school district where the charter school pupil resides to pay the state and local share of the per-pupil operating revenues, plus any other federal or state aid received on behalf of the child;
8. allows charter school personnel to participate in the applicable school retirement system of the district in which the charter school is located;
9. requires one third of a sponsor's charters should give enrollment preference to dropouts or at-risk students;
10. requires that admissions cannot be limited to or based on an individual's race or ability; and
11. permits charter schools to affiliate with a four-year college, university or community college for specified purposes.

The Missouri charter school legislation was passed during a time period in which both the Kansas City and St. Louis school districts, and the state of Missouri, were anticipating the end of long and expensive desegregation programs. The desegregation plans ordered by the federal courts, beginning in 1972 for St. Louis and 1975 for Kansas City, are considered by most experts to be America's most costly—over $3 billion since 1980. The state of Missouri became liable for a portion of the costs associated with the cases. These districts receive about $47 million per year from the state for desegregation (Boyer and Ghan, 1998, p. 9). With the end of the state and locally funded desegregation program in sight, urban education issues were perceived to be a high priority in the state legislature and led to the passage of the charter school legislation.

The identification and promotion of "stronger" charter school laws has become a top priority for charter school advocates (Nathan, 1996; Premack, 1996; Wood and Smith, 1996). According to Premack (1996), the presence of alternative charter granting agencies is a key factor in forcing "local districts to be more responsive and solicitous if they want to play an active role" (p. 13). Wood and Smith (1996) outline several critical components needed for "successful legislation," listing the need to allow numerous "public" organizations to sponsor charter schools as the number one component for effective charter school laws. As the political support for charter schools continues to grow, and new and revised legislation is adopted, the role of sponsoring agencies, other than local school boards will be increasingly prominent in the charter school movement.

UNIVERSITY-AUTHORIZED CHARTER SCHOOLS

University-authorized charter schools are a recent phenomenon. Of the 41 states with charter school legislation, only eight have provisions for accreditation or sponsorship by institutions of higher education. All eight of these states are ranked as states with "strong charter school legislation" (Center of Educational Reform, 2004). The states include Florida, Indiana, Michigan, Minnesota, Missouri, New York, North Carolina, and Wisconsin.

Although the role of universities as sponsoring agencies is limited, it has generated some impressive activity in the charter school movement. For example, Michigan's law allows four different entities to authorize charter schools: state public universities, community colleges, intermediate school districts, and local school districts. Of the 43 charters operating in Michigan during the 1995–1996 school year, 33 were chartered by state universities, while only two were chartered by local school districts (Goenner, 1996). Especially active in this charter activity, Central Michigan University has established a Charter School Office and Resource Center, has developed a rigorous chartering process, and has granted 31 charters to date (Goenner, 1996; Premack, 1996).

Missouri provides another example of one state university that is responding quickly to recent legislation permitting charter school sponsorship. Since the passage of charter legislation in 1998, 28 charters have been authorized in Missouri. In 2003–2004, 27 schools were operating, serving approximately 12,130 students (U.S. Department of Education, 2004). Universities sponsored 26 of these 28 schools, with the other two schools being sponsored by the Kansas City and St. Louis school districts.

NEW RELATIONSHIPS, NEW ROLES

As a potential charter school sponsor under the new legislation, Central Missouri State University immediately found itself involved in new and unique relationships and dialogues. The first wave of new relationships facilitated by the charter school initiative involved discussions and interactions with members of the educational and political establishments. In response to the passage of charter school legislation, a private corporation that provides professional development training to educators in the Kansas City metropolitan area established the Kansas City Charter School Sponsor Consortium. This consortium facilitated communication among the different parties, highlighted the charter school movement, and established a forum for dialogue. In addition to the "local" players, university personnel were introduced to "outsiders" (i.e., educational consultants and non-profit organizations, interested in the charter movement).

Another wave of dialogue facilitated by the university's involvement with the charter school process was generated internally among university personnel. A college task force was created and committees established. This activity generated a great deal of dialogue among university colleagues concerning the charter school movement, the legislative mandates of the new law, and what the role of the university should be. Much of these internal discussions converged upon the "anti-public school" perception that both higher education and public school personnel had concerning charter schools. Would sponsoring a charter school adversely affect relationships between universities and public school leaders?

The immediate and future allocation of time and personnel was another topic of concern discussed intensely within the ranks of the university. It soon became very clear that being involved in the charter school movement was going to be a time consuming venture. The statutes did not provide for any financial support for sponsors. Could universities just decide not to be involved? Who was going to establish the guidelines? Who was going to review the applications? Who would be responsible for monitoring the schools in the future? What is the capacity for sponsorship?

A third wave of relationships that developed as a consequence of the university's role in sponsoring charter schools involved the actual charter school applicants. They were now players in a new game, sanctioned by law, ripe with past disappointment and frustrations, but consumed with hope and enthusiasm. It was the first time for many of the university faculty members to witness first hand how disillusioned and disenfranchised many of these applicants were with the existing school system. They did not talk of school systems and educational philosophy. Instead, they talked of neighbor after neighbor who moved to the suburbs when their kids turned five, of wanting a school that did not change principals six out of eight years or whose teachers were not transferred without cause or purpose, and they talked of wanting to help students learn to read and to finish high school. These applicants included parents with children in public schools and private schools, principals from both private and public schools, retired teachers who ran a day care facility for economically disadvantaged families, directors of community outreach centers, and representatives from Hispanic and Italian cultural centers.

As the university ventured down the early paths of the charter school movement, the new and unique relationships, interactions, and dialogues that occurred helped set the stage for a commitment to facilitation and active partnership. These relationships, especially with the actual charter school applicants, assisted in personalizing the need for charter schools to those involved.

Issues related to control and ownership of schools has been raised several times throughout the paper. As Central Missouri State University continues to consider the role of the university in sponsoring charter schools, issues that speak to control and ownership must be considered. It appears that the university's involvement in charter schools in Kansas City serves to assist the parents and educators who are establishing these schools in gaining a greater measure of control and ownership of the schools. Simultaneously, such efforts serve to limit the level of control and ownership traditionally held by the local district board and the state department of education. Surely, Central Missouri State University's decision to sponsor charter schools will be viewed by some as empowering and by others as a threat.

EXAMINING THE UNIVERSITY'S ROLE

Several factors appear to be important in understanding the proactive response by Central Missouri State University to requests for charter school sponsorship. University decision-making on sponsoring charter schools was influenced by a number of key issues, including: (a) compatibility with university and college mission; (b) legislative intent; (c) perceived liabilities to the university; and (d) the projected impact upon the students of Kansas City.

Mission Congruency

SERVICE. A primary component in the mission of Central Missouri State University and in the College of Education and Human Services is service. Early in the process of considering the feasibility and desirability of sponsoring charter schools it became clear that key decision makers at Central Missouri State University believed that to do so was consistent with their vision of service.

IMPROVING TEACHER PREPARATION. Another priority for the College of Education and Human Services focuses on preparing teachers to work in schools in a wide variety of communities, including urban settings. Sponsoring charter schools in the Kansas City metropolitan area and developing positive working relationships with those who manage and operate such schools would provide a variety of K–12 educational settings appropriate for student field-based experiences. This urban experience complements existing student field experiences in small and mid-size suburban and rural schools.

TEACHER RECRUITMENT. By partnering with schools and community organizations within Kansas City, CMSU hopes to recruit and attract additional students to the University, especially those who might be interested in the field of education. The ethnic diversity that exists in Kansas City and in Missouri is not represented in the teacher preparation programs across the state, including CMSU. Less than 10 percent of the candidates enrolled in the teacher certification program at Central Missouri State University are minority students. Central hopes to improve this situation and recruit more minority students, especially those of African American and Hispanic heritage, to its programs in education.

Another key concern is the acute teacher shortage impacting the urban areas. With its involvement within the city, Central Missouri State University faculty will be able to develop relationships with key representatives of educational and community organizations that would foster the identification and recruitment of additional candidates interested in becoming public school teachers and administrators. This would include non-traditional and second-career candidates who might quality for alternative certification, as well as those entering a traditional teacher preparation program. By recruiting and preparing individuals from the urban area, it is more likely these beginning educators will be inclined to go back to their home neighborhoods and communities to teach.

Legislative Intent

The statute clearly designated four-year universities with teacher preparation programs as potential sponsors. Not only does the statute designate universities as sponsors, it also creates the potential for other higher education institutions to become "affiliate" universities with the goal of developing educational partnerships with the urban charter schools. It is clear that the intent of the law was that Central Missouri State University and other state universities would get involved with charter schools as a method of improving urban education in Kansas City and St. Louis.

Potential Liabilities

Perceived liabilities were also important factors that had to be considered regarding charter school sponsorship decisions. Several important questions emerged in the deliberations on the college campus during the months following the passage of the charter school law. Many of these questions were related to perceived liability of sponsoring charter schools, including: Are there any financial liabilities for CMSU if it agrees to sponsor a charter school? Does the university have the time and personnel to sponsor urban charter schools? What if a school fails to meet its fiscal management plan? What happens if CMSU sponsors a charter school and it fails? How will our role as a charter school sponsor be perceived by traditional public school advocates? How will the university's role be perceived by educators and other stakeholders in Kansas City?

PUBLIC RELATIONS. The University had to weigh the effect of the "anti-public school" perception that some higher education and public school personnel had concerning charter schools against the perceived benefits. Will charter school sponsorship be interpreted by other constituents (including public school teachers and administrators who are current students and/or alumni) as "selling out" public schools? There have been anti-charter school positions taken by leading administrator and school board organizations within the state (Ritter, 1998; Ward, 1998). The position of practitioners and existing policy makers is not likely to change in the immediate future. What consequences will this have upon the university and its long history of working with public (in a traditional sense) educators? There was concern that sponsoring charter schools could adversely affect our relationships with area public school leaders.

Media coverage of charter school developments accentuated this concern. In a March 1999 *Kansas City Star* article titled "Charter plans linked to KC school clashes," highlighted confrontations involving students, community patrons, and school leaders (White, 1999). Later that same month another article contained the following quote from a Kansas City school board member regarding the university's role in the charter school movement, "You have a bunch of well-meaning white males in the middle of nowhere imposing policies on the city." In that same article the president of the board described the university as "renegade" (Shelly, 1999).

TIME AND PERSONNEL. The allocation of time and personnel was another topic of concern discussed intensely within the ranks of the university. As the university navigated through the roles and responsibilities of sponsorship, it soon became clear that involvement in the charter school movement was going to be a time-consuming venture. The statutes did not provide for any financial support for sponsors, and thus existing personnel would have to assume the extra responsibilities stemming from the requirements of sponsorship. During the hectic months of this first year of charter school legislation, university personnel provided hundreds, if not thousands, of hours of service toward the charter school initiative.

Improving Urban Education

Another benefit for the university would include the opportunity to work with urban educators in the city. By being involved in the development and implementation of urban educational centers from the beginning, faculty members at CMSU would have the opportunity to impact a variety of educational settings in the city. Faculty would have opportunities to provide guidance and professional development to the schools. Faculty would also be involved in the evaluation and analysis of the schools, with opportunities to provide feedback and participate in the development of school improvement models. By creating centers of innovation and competition within the urban dis-

tricts, and by having the higher education institutions taking a leading role in these ventures, charter schools provide a direct path to urban reform and renewal at both the K–12 and higher education settings.

FUTURE ROLES

What does the future hold for university-authorized charter schools? What will be the effect of such university involvement into this school choice option on K–12 public schools? How will it affect the relationship and roles of these universities with local school districts, state departments of education, and other affected agencies and organizations? By tracking what has occurred with charter schools since 1991 and beginning to understand and use information from lessons being learned at universities that are involved in this activity one can begin to get a sense for what may occur in the future.

It seems clear that charter schools and other options for school choice are increasing. One can expect to continue to see an increase in the number of charter schools, especially in those states where strong laws exist that encourage their development and permit groups other than local school boards to provide sponsorship. As the number and variety of charter schools grow and as research detailing the effects of these programs on student learning becomes available, one can expect to see a cross-fertilization of ideas and strategies. As different approaches to meeting the needs of various communities of learners are found to be effective, surely we will see public schools borrowing and using some of these ideas. One of the major concepts behind the encouragement of school choice is to provide motivation for educators to examine new ways of meeting students' needs. In time, charter schools will encourage such innovations to occur.

The partnerships forged between the various charter school groups and the university will provide a bridge across institutional boundaries that currently cause collaboration to be awkward. Colleges of education involved in these efforts will expand the number and variety of sites available for students to use as laboratory settings and venues for field experiences. In institutions such as Central Missouri State University, where there tends to be a lack of diverse settings for student field experiences, this benefit should be particularly helpful and striking. Ultimately pre-service teachers who are being prepared in these colleges and universities will benefit from these expanded opportunities.

The relationships and roles of universities, school districts, state departments of education and other affected agencies and organizations will change over time. Initially, relationships between these groups will become more strained and competition for resources will add to the initial difficulty in this area. Ultimately one of two outcomes will be realized. The path taken will be determined by responses to the questions outlined in the beginning of this paper: What is the purpose of public school education? To whom do the public schools belong? To whom are the public schools accountable? One future path may be a continuing reinforcement of institutional barriers and a perception of others from outside one's own organization as "interfering" with our children's education.

The other path, the one the authors predict will be followed, will find universities, local school districts, state departments of education, and other agencies and organizations removing institutional barriers and collaborating more closely to find the best ways to meet all of the learning needs of all of the students in the public schools. As this process takes place, we will see that the important answers to the overarching questions are: The purpose of public school education is to serve the needs of students and society. Public schools belong to and should be accountable to all of us. Likewise, we should all be accountable for helping the public schools continually improve in meeting the needs of our young people.

REFERENCES

Bierlein, L. A. (1995). Charter schools: A new approach to public education. *NASSP Bulletin, 79*(572), 12–20.

Boyer, E. L. (1992). *A special report on school choice.* Princeton, NJ: Carnegie Foundations for the Advancement of Teaching.

Boyer, P., and Ghan, B. (1998, Winter). Dissecting desegregation: A look at the differences and similarities between the desegregation cases in St. Louis and Kansas City. *Show Me Education,* 8–11.

Center for Educational Reform (2004). Retrieved December 31, 2004, from www.edreform.com.

Goenner, J. N. (1996). Charter schools: The revitalization of public education. *Phi Delta Kappan, 78,* 32–36.

Hlebowitsh, P. S. (1995). Can we find the traditional American school in the idea of choice? *NASSP Bulletin, 79*(572), 1–11.

Jones, W. A., and Ambrosie, F. (1995). What are the challenges inherent in schools for choice? *NASSP Bulletin, 79*(572), 21–32.

Manno, B. V., Finn, C. E., Bierlein, L. A., and Vanourek, G. (1998). How charter schools are different: Lessons and implications from a national study. *Phi Delta Kappan, 79,* 488–498.

Nathan, J. (1996). Early lessons of the charter school movement. *Educational Leadership, 54*(2), 16–20.

Nathan, J. (1998). Heat and light in the charter school movement. *Phi Delta Kappan, 79,* 499–505.

National Commission on Excellence in Education. (1983). *A nation at risk.* Washington, DC: U.S. Government Printing Office.

Premack, E. (1996). Charter schools: A status report. *School Business Affairs, 62*(12), 10–15.

Ritter, J. (1998, Spring). The charter school dilemma. *Show Me Education,* 18–19.

Shelly, B. (1999, March 31). Glitches in charter school plans. *The Kansas City Star,* p. B1.

U.S. Department of Education (1998). *A national study of charter schools.* Office of Educational Research and Improvement, Washington, D.C.

U.S. Department. of Education (2004). Retrieved December 31, 2004, from www.uscharterschools.org/pub/uscs_docs/o/history.htm.

Ward, C. D. (1998, Winter). Charter schools are no answer. *Show Me Education,* 7.

White, T. (1999, March 17). Charter plans linked to KC school clashes. *The Kansas City Star,* p. B1.

Wood, C. R., and Smith, S. (1996). Critical components of charter schools: An analysis by state. *School Business Affairs, 62*(12), 28-33.

The Learning Curve of Principal Work

SHOBHANA RISHI AND FRED MUSKAL

PRINCIPALS FACE MYRIAD CHALLENGES IN THEIR WORK IN the age of accountability reform (Lashway, 2002; Wanzare and LaCosta, 2001). How best to train and support principals to meet these demands has gained increasing attention (Brown and Flanary, 2004) while the pool of qualified candidates continues to dwindle (Young, Peterson, and Short, 2002). New perspectives that add to our knowledgebase on the work of principals and how it is learned are needed. The present study uses grounded theory to examine the work experiences of novice and veteran principals to define concerns at the beginning of their careers and after ten or more years on the job; recommendations based on the perspective of principals as learners are presented.

BACKGROUND OF THE STUDY

The nature of principal work has been investigated from a variety of angles. Earlier observational studies revealed the daily activities of principals to be characterized by long hours, high volume of varied tasks in rapid pace, and fragmentation due to frequent interruptions (Martin and Willower, 1981; Kmetz and Willower, 1982; Bredeson, 1985). Blumberg (1987) characterized principal work as a "craft" that could, unlike art, be demystified and communicated. He also recommended talking to principals about their work in order to understand the intentions behind the appearance of disparate actions and events that characterize principal work upon observation (p. 43).

Assumptions about how principal work is learned are reflected in methods of preparation of principals. Traditional approaches to administrative training consist of coursework in school management, leadership, and supervision with an introduction to school law, union negotiations, and politics (Cooper and Boyd, 1987). Yet, new principals and scholars have continued to confirm the significance of experiential learning (Akerlund, 1988; Gill, 1992; Mannon, 1991;

Oliver, 1992; Peterson, 1987) and that situations exert a greater force than theory in determining action in administrative work (Murphy and Hallinger, 1987). University preparation programs for administration usually provide some field-based experiences in order to address the gap between declarative knowledge and procedural knowledge (Daresh and Playko, 1992; Ohde and Murphy, 1993). Induction, formation, and mentoring have been used to facilitate the transition from coursework to practice (Daresh, 1990; Daresh, 1995; Daresh and Playko, 1992).

The gap between theory and practice continues to be an issue (Hart and Bredeson, 1996; Daresh and Playko, 1992). Peterson (1985) applied the Kolb model of experiential learning to reveal the problems of on-the-job learning due to the characteristics of the work, properties of the organization, and norms of the occupation which tend to make learning slow, counterproductive, and biased (p. 189). Although the effective implementation of mentoring still poses a challenge, it includes the possibility of guarding against some of the obstacles to learning from experience (Daresh, 2004). New perspectives on the work of principals are needed to understand the concerns of practice from a learner's perspective.

METHODOLOGY

This study used grounded theory to analyze interview data from fifteen elementary school principals. Creswell (1998) recommends qualitative methodology if the inquiry seeks to find out *how* or *why* to describe what is going on, the topic needs to be explored, and a detailed view of the topic needs to be presented (p. 17). The purpose of this study was to explore the nature of principals' work from the point of view of principals in the field and to describe categories based on how principals view their work. Categories for principal work were defined and analyzed using the Dreyfus and Greenfield models.

311

Sampling and Data Collection

The sample of fifteen elementary school principals was from two similar-sized large school districts in central California. Eight of the fifteen principals were novices beginning their second or third year of practice. The criterion of one to three years of experience for novice principals was based on a phone consultation with Dr. Patricia Benner who has done extensive work with the Dreyfus model (theoretical model used to analyze data in this study) in the areas of clinical nursing practice (Benner, 1984) as well as on the basis of an informal survey conducted with veteran principals on "How long it took for them to get the hang of the job." The seven veteran principals were all from the same district and all with the exception of one had fifteen or more years of experience. One veteran principal was in his tenth year.

The standardized open-ended interview was used to collect data because it allows the respondents to present their experiences in their own terms while yielding data that is systematic and thorough as a result of the use of guiding questions to standardize the interviews. This method also retains flexibility for follow-up investigations as needed (Patton, 1990, p. 281).

The interview questions were developed by the researchers and based upon the Dreyfus model. All interviews were conducted on principals' school site except for one. Interviews were taped and assigned name and number codes to protect participants before being transcribed. The following questions guided the interviews:

1. What were the most salient or challenging parts of the job at the beginning or early part of your career? When do you think you mastered them? Which ones remain?
2. Describe a mistake you made during your first two years that you have corrected. What was the most difficult part of the job when you started and how has it changed?
3. What new issues have emerged this year?
4. What would you like to see happen this year and how do you intend to implement your plans?
5. How do you define success as a principal? Has your definition changed over the course of your career? How?
6. How do you know you have learned something new on the job?

Data Analysis

Open coding in this study began with a close reading of the novice interviews for any "events" that stood out to the researcher. Strauss and Corbin (1998) explain the process of generating categories as a sequence of the activities of closely examining data, breaking them down into discrete parts, and comparing them for similarities and differences which allows for the differentiation and discrimination among categories (p. 102). The mistakes, challenges, difficulties, surprises and successes reported by respondents were labeled as events that were significant to novices in their new work. The veteran group's responses regarding their challenges during their first two years were added to the novice list. All events that are listed were found to recur in the data.

Labeled events were classified for the general phenomenon they revealed, and categories were defined. For example, data revealed that novice principals experienced the various demands on their time and began to cope with these demands in different ways; thus the category of "time management" emerged to reflect this dominant concern of novice principals. Memos about the issues related to time management revealed dimensions of this category. The structure of codes includes *topics*, *dimensions*, and *categories*. The topics are the labels for events recognized as significant by respondents. *Dimensions* are groups of topics that share a common property, and dimensions belong to a *category* (See Tables 1 and 2).

Finally, the categories for novice and veteran groups were analyzed using the Dreyfus model to see which ones were significant for different levels of experience, and classified according to the domains of administrator work as described by Greenfield (1995).

THEORETICAL MODELS

The Dreyfus Model

The Dreyfus model of learning specifies a process in which people begin a task by learning rules, then, after incorporating experience, move beyond the rules to functioning in experiential and intuitive based ways (Dreyfus and Dreyfus, 1986). The learning process incorporates learning and adapting to tasks by incorporating experiential lessons into one's intuition as one becomes increasingly proficient. Learners all begin as Novices and may proceed to Advanced Beginner, Competent Performer, Proficient Performer, and, finally, to Expert level. Learners may also choose to quit, settle at a level, or be unable to progress further because of personal limitations or lack of interest. Although principals begin their careers at different stages of development, develop within their careers at

Table 1. Novice Codes

Category	Dimensions	Topics
A. Time Management		a. Surprise at amount of work b. Surprise at the extent of responsibilities c. Mistakes of omission d. Missed deadlines e. Time away from site f. Lengthy discipline investigations g. Need to check procedures h. Work hours i. Sort, prioritize, delegate
B. Teachers	B1. Credibility	a. Supervising peers b. Being younger than teachers c. Self-confidence d. Thinking of yourself as the "boss" e. Elementary instruction and curriculum f. Handling younger children
	B2. Rapport	a. Building relationships b. Teacher attacks c. Fear of principal d. Support for teachers e. Not being too friendly
	B3. Managing adults	a. Shock at teacher behavior b. Inflexibility of teachers c. Listen more d. Give only appropriate information
	B4. Making decisions	a. Consult teachers before making a decision b. Communicate decisions clearly c. Stand your ground
C. District Office		a. Knowing who is who b. Procedures c. Meeting their director's expectations d. Support from their director e. Higher salaries f. Feedback g. Accountability

Table 2. Veteran Codes

Category	Dimensions	Topics
D. Adaptation	D1. Change in demographics	a. English language learners b. Increased drug use c. Increase in single parent homes d. New school site
	D2. Change in district demands	a. Management styles b. Accountability c. Meeting AYP and API d. New programs e. Formalized monitoring f. Teacher contract constraints g. Budget constraints
	D3. Professional engagement	a. Sense of fulfillment b. Projects c. Retirement

different rates, and may operate on more than one stage simultaneously, as learners they can be placed within one of the Dreyfus levels of learning. Distinctive features of the five levels may be summed up as follows:

Novice. New to the field or context, the Novice relies on external rules/procedures/formulas to complete a task. At this stage the learner does not know what there is to know in the field.

Advanced Beginner. Having had a chance to try out rules, the Advanced Beginner understands the jargon and his theoretical knowledge interacts with his experiences as he is becoming familiar with the context. However, he may not understand the implications of actions and their interrelation. He still checks procedures to reflect and check his understanding.

Competent Performer. Having internalized routine rules and procedures, the Competent Performer is more aware of the factors involved in the field and their significance. He selects focus and devises own plan, which includes inaction. At this level, the learner knows what he needs to know and do to be effective in his job though he may not necessarily know how to do it or do it perfectly.

Proficient Performer. No longer performing in an analytical mode, the mass of experience of the Proficient Performer allows holistic processing of new situations. Whereas problem-solving and decision-making at the earlier stages is more deliberate, now it is more fluid and comes from an established perspective and stance. The learner develops his or her "own style" based on selected overall priorities and stance.

Expert. Giving the virtuoso performance, the Expert, does not have to think about what to do or how to do it. His plethora of experience allows him to understand each new situation in its uniqueness, and he understands deeply that there are no guarantees and therefore outcomes do not baffle him or her. Massive practice is required for this level of performance.

Greenfield Cross Sectional Model

The Greenfield (1995) model describes the work of educational administration as encompassed in the following five dimensions: (a) Moral, (b) Social/Interpersonal, (c) Managerial, (d) Instructional, and (e) Political. These dimensions of work are based on the interactions between the administrator's perspectives, abilities, skills, values, and motives and the demand environment of principals' work. Greenfield's (1995) model takes into account the following three unique features of schools as organizations: (a) the moral character of schools, (b) a highly educated, autonomous, and permanent workforce, and (c) regular and unpredictable threats to organizational stability. Greenfield adds, "The magnitude of these role demands and the nature of relations among them will change depending on other variables including group, organizational, and community factors" (p. 69).

The Greenfield model is especially appropriate for this study as it accounts for the contextual factors of principals' work that are significant to the problems of practice and that influence individual principals' experience and perceptions. The novice and veteran codes were examined with the Greenfield model in order to describe how the different aspects of the principal work changed in significance with growing experience.

FINDINGS AND DISCUSSION

The findings of this study indicated that first and second year principals must first focus on managerial and social-interpersonal skills. Leadership may develop later, but these skills are the base of the principal's job. Once these skills have been mastered, principals are prepared for mentoring by other principals.

The First and Second Year Concerns

Results of this study (Table 1) confirmed the findings of earlier research about the difficulties faced by principals in their first and second years:

1. Time management and role definition
2. Developing rapport, establishing credibility, and managing teachers, parents, and other adults
3. Responding to feedback and demands from district office
4. Training and support with district procedures.

All topics in the novice data that indicated a discovery or element of surprise by principals regarding their work on the new job relate in some manner to the concepts of role clarity and role expectations. Role clarity had been identified as an area of difficulty for new principals in a number of studies (Barton, 1998; Daresh, 1986; Gorious, 1999; Gussner, 1974; Hurley, 1989; Mannon, 1991; Mascaro, 1973; O'Brien, 1988; Oliver, 1992). Role expectation was cited by Greenfield (1977) as a determinant of positive socialization outcomes for principals; principals' role expectation indicated lack of preparation for the realities of the job encountered by them (Duke et al., 1984).

Other concerns of novices as identified in the Novice data also confirm previous studies. Time as a unifying concept was identified by Mascaro (1973); principals' preoccupation with sorting and prioritizing were identified as key activities in the first two stages of the Parkay and Hall (1992) model of principal socialization; and the critical role that social interpersonal skills play in principals' work has been noted (Daresh and Playko, 1992; Wolcott, 1984; Greenfield, 1987; Greenfield, 1995).

The added hurdle of being new to the district reflects the urgency of organizational socialization over professional socialization (Hart, 1993). The importance of and lack of feedback were concerns voiced by novice principals (Barton, 1998; Gorious, 1999; Gussner, 1974; Hurley, 1989; Mannon, 1991; Mascaro, 1973; O'Brien, 1988; Oliver, 1992).

Early Career Challenges

The performance and behavior of principals in their first two years indicated that they function as learners at Novice and Advanced Beginner Levels of the Dreyfus model (Table 3). Veteran principals have mastered the routine tasks that confront Novices. The Dreyfus model generates an understanding of principal behaviors and performance in the first three years with attention to their needs as learners.

As learners at the Novice Level, principals must rely on external rules and procedures. Doing routine tasks takes more time when you are in the process of learning how things work. At the same time, sorting and prioritizing are also difficult to do in the early years on the job, precisely because one does not know what is more important, which compounds the time issue.

Some principals were at the Advanced Beginner Level towards the end of their first year and by the start of the second year. This level is defined by the learner's initial incorporation of experiences on the job. The issues with teachers covered a broad range of topics related to developing rapport, establishing credibility, and managing adults. These related concerns showed how novice principals quickly began to learn from mistakes they made and from their observations of teacher behaviors. As noted in previous research, social-interpersonal skills and abilities in the processes of communicating and listening played an important role in managing people and developing rapport and credibility (Greenfield, 1987, 1995; Duke, 1986).

In summary, novice issues reflect many concerns and experiences of principals identified in previous research and using the Dreyfus model conceptual-izes these issues as learning skills, which makes them more amenable to training, i.e., to administrative preparation.

Veteran Principals

Veteran principals with ten or more years perform at the Competent Performer and Proficient levels. At these levels, the routine operation of a site has been mastered and does not require additional energy and time from the principal. Principals have shown they can manage the routine operations of the site to a level deemed satisfactory by the three main stakeholders: district office, teachers, and parents.

RECOMMENDATIONS

Principal Needs by Years on the Job

FIRST YEAR ON THE JOB. Studies continue to demonstrate that the most powerful learning for principal work occurs through on-the-job experiences (Peterson, 1987; Mannon, 1991; Oliver, 1992; Daresh, 1990, 1995). Daresh and Playko (1992) stressed the need for an intermediate step, such as formation, to help new administrators get ready for the challenges of the principalship. Learning through experience in the absence of proper feedback and reflection, however, can also be "mis-educative" (Daresh and Playko, p. 44). Data suggested that the first year is markedly different and principals begin at the Novice Level, though they may progress to the Advance Beginner Level. Principals at the Novice Level will benefit from "rules of thumb" as well as clear directives to consolidate or chunk tasks and prioritize their work. In addition to the personal wisdom that each individual brings to the job, rules of thumb that take into account district culture and priorities can be given to novices by their supervisors or peers for common situations encountered in administrative work.

RECOMMENDATION. New principals will benefit from printed guides and calendars that outline requirements and upcoming events in the district, to enable them to plan, organize, and prioritize their tasks in order to better manage their time. Individual districts or school sites can keep a list of specific responsibilities and tasks in relation to the day-to-day *operations* of the site. These can then guide the new principal in establishing credibility with both the staff and district office.

RECOMMENDATION. Visiting model sites or being shown model systems for organization of tasks will help novices in finding a system that works for them and that is satisfactory for district office.

Table 3. Principals as Learners: Novice and Veteran Codes Interpreted with the Dreyfus Model of Learning

Novice (N): First stage/level in the Dreyfus model of skill acquisition. Novice is in process of identifying the different factors and terms of the new work context. This stage is characterized by the novice's complete reliance on externally supplied rules and procedures. When presented with a task or situation, the novice must follow explicit instruction or direction that does not require prior knowledge of the context. The instructions at this stage could be followed by almost anyone.

- Relies on book knowledge, manuals, personal experience and guidance from others (Codes: Ag, B4-a, Ca, Cb, Cc, Cf, D1-d, D2-d)
- In process of recognizing factors involved in principal work (Codes: Aa, Ab, Ac, Ah, B1-d, B3-a, Ca)

N101, N102, N103, N104, N105, N106, N107, V107, V111, V112

Advanced Beginner (AB): Second stage/level in the Dreyfus model of skill acquisition. The advanced beginner has had a chance to try out the rules learned on the job and is getting to know the context of work. At this stage, the learner's book knowledge interacts with work experiences. The Advanced Beginner learns by trial and error and learning depends on the learner's unique way of understanding work experiences as they occur. At this stage the learner still relies on external prompts and may refer to rules and procedures, but continues to reflect, check and predict new experiences to broaden his understanding

- Beginning to learn from mistakes
- Supplies more of own sense-making for learning from experience (Codes: B2-a, B2-e, B3-b, B3-c, B3-d, B4, D1-a)

N102, N104, N106, N107, V107, V109, V112

Competent Performer (CP): Third stage/level in the Dreyfus model of skill acquisition. The CF has had enough experience to internalize routine rules and procedures. The CF is familiar with the context and may be overwhelmed by the amount of data or information that presents itself since it is now visible. The CP still needs a plan to operate, but now it is a plan made by the learner. The CP must interpret and decide what is important; failure or success depends on choices made by the CP. At this stage to not take action is also an action selected by the CP.

- Routine rules and procedures have been internalized
- Makes own plan and chooses focus
- Takes responsibility for what he/she does and does not do
- Conveys sense of knowing what is at stake (Codes: D1, D2)

V107, V108, V109, V110, V111, V112, V113

Proficient Performer (PP): Fourth stage/level in the Dreyfus model of skill acquisition. The PP is performing in a mode beyond analytical rationality. The mass of experience allows the PP to process new situations more holistically and to consider actions to address them in a more intuitive manner. The learner's perspective that is the result of varied experiences allows them to have their own stance.

Mass of experience allows holistic and intuitive processing of problems and solutions (D)
Conveys a stance (D)

V107, V109, V110, V111, V113

Expert (E): Fifth of the five stages of the Dreyfus model of skill acquisition. The E does not have to think about what to do, how to do it, or when to do it but simply does what works. Even if it fails in a given circumstance, the E is not baffled due to abundant experience. The E understands that there are no guarantees, even though there are calculated probabilities that have been incorporated unconsciously into their intuitive decisions (Dreyfus, 1986).

Insufficient data

RECOMMENDATION. Workshops on required district paperwork and the management of routine operations should help them to become more efficient managers. Workshops that focus on specific tasks that must be accomplished such as the process of making a categorical budget or conducting textbook inventory will serve new principals well since time spent in the in-service will not be construed as time away from their work.

RECOMMENDATION. A major concern for new principals is the management of teachers. Skills that are encompassed in principals' work with teachers are listening and communication skills, an understanding of interpersonal styles, and some general insights about motivations and personality styles. Workshops and in-services on social interpersonal styles and strategies will add to a principal's repertoire at any stage and level of practice.

RECOMMENDATION. It is also advisable that principals gather information about expectations that a particular site staff and parents have for their principal through informal and formal surveys and socials.

Years Two and Three on the Job

How long principals will remain at the Advanced Beginner Level is dependent on individual abilities, skills, motivations, and values as well as learning outcomes at the Advanced Beginner Level. Principals at the Advanced Beginner Levels, usually in their second and third years, will benefit greatly from feedback and guided reflection on their job experiences.

RECOMMENDATION. It is critical for principals in their second and third years to receive feedback and have opportunities to dialogue with other experienced principals and mentor principals who can facilitate reflection on their work experiences.

RECOMMENDATION. Workshops for specific tasks such as budgets, textbook inventory, and other tasks can be organized and provided as needed and requested by novices.

Although the ideas of mentoring are hardly new, their adequate and consistent application remains a challenge. Theorists such as Schön (1991), Hart and Bredeson (1996), and Daresh and Playko (1992) offer models to supply the critical components of reflection and feedback. Thinking about the cause and effect relationships of events in administrative work may seem at times to be diametrically and diabolically opposed to efficiency and practicality. It is our contention that thoughtful reflection can expedite subsequent decision making.

Four or More Years on the Job

By the fourth year on the job, principals have mastered routine tasks of management, and may benefit greatly by working with novices as mentors.

RECOMMENDATION. Assign experienced principals as mentors to Advanced Beginner principals, i.e., to those who have mastered the basics of school management specified in the foregoing.

The mentor-novice relationship can be a mutually instructive one. It can help veterans by giving them a chance to consolidate their own learning. Novices will benefit greatly from a mentor who engages with them in dialogue and can facilitate reflection on their job experience.

Observations of administrators' career patterns show a prevalence of irregularities in the paths leading up to the principalship (Magel, 1992; Morford, 2001; Small, 1994). Administrators who aspire to be principals must recognize the arduous and encompassing nature of the enterprise. Since prior socialization experiences as students and teachers may not give adequate role expectations, pre-service programs and school districts should provide information about the actual responsibilities of the principal role. Experience in various leadership positions prior to assuming the principalship will also help reduce the learning curve on the job during the first couple of years. List of specific job duties at each school site, since these vary slightly according to school traditions and cultures, will help eliminate some of the mistakes of omission.

CONCLUSIONS

This study has examined the complexity of the beginning work lives of new principals. Applying the Dreyfus model to the interviews of 15 principals and the literature, it is apparent that districts, schools, and veteran principals can develop learning tools to make the transition from Novice to Advanced Beginner and Competent Performer an easier task by developing systematic ways to prepare Novices for what we all know will happen in the early years on the school site. This will prepare new principals for benefiting from mentoring by veterans. Easing the managerial and interpersonal burdens that all principals must go through should enable better and stronger development of principals at a time when good principals are increasingly needed and demanded by the school's stakeholders.

REFERENCES

Akerlund, P. M. (1988). The socialization of first-year principals and vice principals (Doctoral dissertation, Seattle University, 1988). *Dissertation Abstracts International, 49, 08A,* 2029.

Barton, D. H. (1998). The role of principal socialization as it relates to school restructuring (Doctoral dissertation, University of Oregon, 1998). *Dissertation Abstracts International, 59, 09A,* 3294.

Benner, P. E. (1984). *From Novice to Expert: Excellence in clinical nursing practice.* Menlo Park: Addison-Wesley Publishing Co.

Blumberg, A. (1987). The Work of principals: A touch of craft. In W. Greenfield (Ed.), *Instructional Leadership Concepts, Issues and controversies* (pp. 38–55). Newton, MA: Allyn and Bacon, Inc.

Blumberg, A., and Greenfield, W. (1980). *The Effective Principal: Perspectives on school leadership.* Boston: Allyn & Bacon, Inc.

Bredeson, P. V. (1985). An analysis of the metaphorical perspectives of school principals. *Educational Administration Quarterly, 21*(1), 29–50.

Brown, F., and Flanary, D. (2004). How many principal preparation groups does it take to screw in "the" light bulb? *NCPEA Leadership Review, 5*(2), 2–3.

Cooper, B. S., and Boyd, W. L. (1987). The evolution of training for school administrators. In J. Murphy and P. Hallinger (Eds.), *Approaches to Administrative Training in Education* (pp. 3–27). Albany: SUNY Press.

Creswell, J. W. (1998). *Qualitative Inquiry and Research Design.* New Delhi: Sage Publications.

Daresh, J. C. (1986). Support for beginning principals: First Hurdles are highest. *Theory into Practice, 23,* 168–173.

Daresh, J. C. (1990, May 1990). Formation: the missing ingredient in administrator preparation. *NASSP Bulletin,* 1–5.

Daresh, J. C. (1995). Research base on mentoring for educational leaders: what do we know? *Journal of Educational Administration, 33*(5), 7–16.

Daresh, J. C. (2004). Mentoring school leaders: Professional promise or predictable problems? *Educational Administration Quarterly, 40,* 495–517.

Daresh, J. C., and Playko, M. A. (1992). *The Professional Development of School Administrators: Preservice, Induction and Inservice Applications.* Boston: Allyn and Bacon.

Dreyfus, H. L., and Dreyfus, S. E. (1986). *Mind over machine: The power of human intuition and expertise in the era of the computer.* New York: The Free Press.

Duke, D. L. (1986). The Aesthetics of leadership. *Educational Administration Quarterly, 22*(1), 7–27.

Duke, D. L., Isaacson, N. S., Sagor, R., and Schmuck, P. A. (1984). Transition to leadership: An investigation of the first year of the principalship: Paper sponsored by Lewis and Clark College.

Gill, N. (1992). Socialization tactics, self-efficacy, and role innovation of public school principals. (Doctoral dissertation, University of Colorado, 1992). *Dissertation Abstracts International, 54,* 03A, 0752.

Gorius, P. A. (1999). Sensemaking during the induction phase of socialization of a neophyte principal: A researcher's reflections. (Doctoral dissertation, University of Saskatchewan, 1999). *Dissertation Abstracts International, 60,* 12A, 4262.

Greenfield, W. D. J. (1977). Administrative candidacy: a process of new role learning, part 2. *Journal of Educational Administration, 15*(2), 171–193.

Greenfield, W. D. J. (1987). Moral Imagination and interpersonal competence: antecedents to instructional leadership. In W. D. J. Greenfield (Ed.), *Instructional Leadership: Concepts, issues and controversies* (pp. 56–73). Newton: Allyn and Bacon, Inc.

Greenfield, W. D. J. (1995). Toward a theory of school administration: the centrality of leadership. *Educational Administration Quarterly, 31*(1), 61–85.

Gussner, W. P. (1974). The socialization of a school administrator. Unpublished doctoral dissertation, Washington University, St. Louis, Missouri.

Hart, A. W. (1993). Principal Succession: Establishing Leadership in Schools. Albany: SUNY Press.

Hart, A. W., and Bredeson, P. V. (1996). *The Principalship: A Theory of Professional Learning and Practice.* New York: McGraw-Hill, Inc.

Hurley, J. (1989). The organizational socialization of high school principals: A description and analysis. (Doctoral dissertation, University of Wisconsin, 1989). *Dissertation Abstracts International, 50,* 12A, 3808.

Kmetz, J. T., and Willower, D. J. (1982). Elementary principals' work behavior. *Educational Administration Quarterly, 18*(4), 62–78.

Lashway, L. (2003). Role of the school leader. Eugene, OR: ERIC Clearinghouse on Educational Management (ERIC Digest No. 141).

Magel, S. (1992). Modes of development for school principals: Pathways to success. (Doctoral dissertation, Pepperdine University, 1992). *Dissertation Abstracts International, 53,* 03A, 0677.

Mannon, G. (1991). The Socialization of the Principalship. *Dissertation Abstracts International, 52,* 11A, 3787.

Martin, W. J., and Willower, D. J. (1981). The managerial behavior of high school principals. *Educational Administration Quarterly, 17,* 69–90.

Mascaro, F. G. (1973). *The Early on-the-job socialization of first-year elementary principals.* Unpublished doctoral dissertation, University of California, Riverside, California.

Morford, L. M. (2001). Learning the ropes or being hung: The socialization of new principals in rural high schools. (Doctoral dissertation, State University of New York at Albany, 2001). *Dissertation Abstracts International, 62,* 2A, 4015.

Murphy, J., and Hallinger, P. (1987). New directions in the professional development of school administrators: A synthesis and suggestions for improvement. In J. Murphy and P. Hallinger (Eds.), *Approaches to Administrative Training in Education.* Albany: SUNY Press.

O'Brien, D. E. (1988). Taking the role of principal: A qualitative investigation of socialization during the first year (Doctoral dissertation, Kent State University, 1988). *Dissertation Abstracts International, 50,* 06A, 1513.

Ohde, K. L., and Murphy, J. (1993). The development of expertise: Implications for school administrators. In Hallinger, P., Leithwood, K., and Murphy, J. (Eds.), *Cognitive Perspectives on Educational Leadership* (pp. 75–87). New York: Teachers College Press.

Oliver, J. B. (1992). A comparative case study of the moral and technical socialization of five first year elementary school. (Doctoral dissertation, University of Utah, 1992). *Dissertation Abstracts International, 53,* 08A, 2632.

Patton, M. Q. (1990). *Qualitative evaluation and research methods (2nd ed.).* Newbury Park, CA: Sage Publications.

Peterson, K. D. (1985). Obstacles to learning from experience and principal training. *The Urban Review, 17*(3), 189–200.

Peterson, K. D. (1987). Administrative control and instructional leadership. In W. Greenfield (Ed.), *Instructional leadership: Concepts, issues, and controversies.* Newton, MA: Allyn & Bacon.

Schön, D. (1991) *The reflective practitioner: how professionals think in action.* Great Britain: Arena Ashgate Publishing Limited.

Small, S. R. (1994). If I knew then what I know now: Principals reflect on their first year of practice. (Doctoral dissertation, Syracuse University, 1994). *Dissertation Abstracts International, 55,* 08A, 2241.

Strauss, A., and Corbin, J. (1998). *Basics of qualitative research: Techniques and procedures for developing grounded theory (2nd ed.).* Thousand Oaks, CA: Sage Publications.

Wanzare, Z., and De La Costa, J. L. (2001). Rethinking the instructional leadership role of the school principal: Challenges and prospects. *Journal of Educational Thought, 35*(3), 269–295.

Wolcott, H. F. (1984). *The man in the principal's office: An ethnography.* Prospect Heights, IL: Waveland Press, Inc.

Young, M. D., Petersen, G. T., and Short, P. M. (2002). The complexity of substantive reform: A call for interdependence among key stakeholders. *Educational Administration Quarterly, 38(2),* 137–175.

Competencies for Educational Technology Directors: Perceptions of Public School Technology Directors

NIDELIA MONTOYA AND GARY IVORY

SINCE THE 1983 PUBLICATION OF *A NATION AT RISK* (National Commission on Excellence in Education, 1983) and culminating most recently in *No Child Left Behind* (*NCLB*) (Department of Education, 2001a), educators and the rest of the public have sought to improve education. Simultaneously, there has been increasing competition for the resources to improve education and moves by elected officials to seize the initiative for educational decision making away from traditional education leaders (Reyes, Wagstaff, and Fusarelli, 1999). These pressures have moved some to propose that technology can help improve education (Department of Education, 2001b). Writers urge that technology can advance both leadership and instruction. It may increase leader effectiveness by automating "back office" functions that consume administrators' time, for example, accounting for funds, supplies, pupils, and their grades; helping them plan and manage time better; enabling them to update their knowledge of research and best practices; facilitating the analysis of management information; and improving communication among educators and learners (Ivory, 2001; President's Committee of Advisors on Science and Technology, 1997). Some of those administrative functions will be carried out centrally in the district; others are better handled at the campus level. On the instruction side, some expect technology to (a) give students access to a greater wealth of learning materials and opportunities for productive interactions with others, (b) foster more engaging and challenging forms of pedagogy, (c) enable longer and more flexible work periods and more cross-disciplinary learning, and (d) facilitate students' demonstrating their learning in a greater variety of ways (Gonzales, 2001; National Council for Accreditation of Teacher Education (NCATE), 1997; Technology Counts, 2002; Wiburg, 2001). This faith has been demonstrated by investment in technology (Digest of Education Statistics, 2001; Technology Counts, 2002; NCATE, 1997).

STANDARDIZATION OF TECHNOLOGY APPLICATIONS IN EDUCATION

Though administrative and instructional applications of technology may be discussed in the same venues, they will differ with respect to the amount of standardization that characterizes them. Instructional applications are unlikely to be standardized because of the range, decentralization of, and controversy over instructional methodology (Picciano, 2002). As for administrative applications, some will be centralized and others may not. Centralized applications have included processing transactions, compiling and analyzing information, and supporting decision making. In this respect, the school district's Information Systems (IS) Department may have been similar to the IS department in any organization. It may have tended to centralize control; to have performed independently from the rest of the organization; and to have treated tasks primarily as requiring technical skill, rather than management, organizational or human relations skills. All three of these characteristics seem to be changing. In the early 1990s, three articles reported on a survey of Information System (IS) professionals in business and professors of business administration to elicit their ratings of the importance of knowledge and skill requirements both for the present and future, and to determine how university professors' perceptions matched those of IS professionals (Farwell, Kuramoto, Lee, Trauth, and Winslow, 1992; Lee, Trauth, and Farwell, 1995; Trauth, Farwell, and Lee, 1993). Because of the survey's sponsorship by the Boston Chapter of the Society for Information Management, we refer to it hereinafter as the "Boston SIMS study." Researchers surveyed IS professionals and professors in New England on their ratings of the importance of three categories of items: (a) task activities, (b) interpersonal/ management skills, and (c) technical skills. From their findings they identified knowledge and skill requirements likely to increase in importance and those likely to decrease.

Task Activities

Findings from the Boston SIMS study suggested that providing support and service to meet user's needs would increase in importance as IS development and use were distributed throughout the organization. Other important task activities would be integrating networks, and integrating new business applications with existing applications. These last two, prompted Farwell et al. to describe a new role for the IS professional as "the integrator," integrating departments and functions as corporations merged, downsized, and globalized (1992, p. 299).

Interpersonal and Management Skills

The Boston SIMS findings suggested that interpersonal and management skills and knowledge of the organization's business would increase dramatically in importance. As off-the-shelf software became cheaper and easier to use, departments within organizations would develop their own applications and IS staffs. Then they would demand support from the organization's central IS department in using and maintaining those applications. This would require IS workers to work closely with others outside the IS department and therefore to have far more interpersonal and management skills and to know more about all aspects of the organization.

Technical Skills

The Boston SIMS study suggested there would be more need in the future for technical skills in the following: Networks, communications, relational databases, fourth generation languages, systems integration, information access and security, data access and management, and firm-specific technologies.

LEADERSHIP SKILLS FOR TECHNOLOGY IN PREK–12 SCHOOL DISTRICTS

Delfin (1995) replicated the Boston SIMS study nationally with public school technology directors. She found a similar need for technology directors to be able to integrate technology issues with organizational ones. Delfin's public school technology directors rated interpersonal and management skills high; they also rated high those task activities related to public school problems and dealing with others; and they gave the lowest ratings to technical skills. Delfin's findings suggested the new paradigm identified by Farwell et al. (1992) for business and industry was also applicable to the public schools. But Delfin did not survey professors who prepared public school technology directors.

Since then, the Information Technology Association of America (1997) has raised a concern that universities were not sufficiently preparing students for the IS world of practice. But there has been little attention to the competency and skill requirements for education technology directors, and to whether university faculties are contributing to the development of them (Bromley and Jacobson, 1997). The Technology Standards for School Administrators Collaborative (TSSA Collaborative, n.d.), created a list of standards later adopted by the International Society for Technology in Education as its National Educational Technology Standards for Administrators (NETS-A). But these standards do not address technology directors specifically. We offer here a study of current perceptions of school district technology directors, specifically addressing three questions:

1. What is the correlation between technology directors' and professors ratings of the importance of knowledge and skills in the three areas of (a) task activities, (b) technical skill, and (c) interpersonal and management skills?
2. How do public school technology directors and professors teaching technology courses in units of education rate the importance of each of the three areas?
3. Within each of the three areas, what knowledge and skill requirements are more important?

METHOD

Instrument

We updated the Boston SIMS survey based on the advice of IS experts and findings from a pilot test. The updated survey asked respondents to rate the importance of 55 knowledge and skill requirements for public school technology directors on a five-point Likert-type scale with 1 indicating "Not important" and 5 indicating "Important." We asked respondents to rate each item for the present (2002) and the future (2005). Finally, we posted the survey on the World Wide Web and identified and recruited public school technology directors and professors to take it.

Participants

In all, 175 public school technology directors responded to the survey from 16 states. Delfin (1995) reported the greatest number of public school technology directors in her study to have specialized in education. Therefore, we identified professors who taught graduate educational technology courses in

Table 1. Correlations Among Ratings of Knowledge and Skill Requirements for Public School Technology Directors: Present (2002) and Future (2005)

Respondents	Directors: Present	Professors: Present	Directors: Future	Professors: Future
Technology Directors' Ratings for the Present	—	.97	.99	.97
Professors' Ratings for the Present	—	—	.96	.99
Technology Directors' Ratings for the Future	—	—	—	.96
Professors' Ratings for the Future	—	—	—	—

units of education. We invited these professors to participate and received usable surveys from 50 professors in 19 states.

RESULTS

Table 1 shows the correlations among ratings of the importance of knowledge and skills requirements for public school technology directors by technology directors and professors for the present and future. There was near perfect correlation among all ratings.

Table 2 shows the average ratings given to task activities, interpersonal and management skills, and technical skills by technology directors and professors for the present and the future. In all cases, the highest mean ratings went to interpersonal and management skills followed by task activities. Technology skills consistently came in last. Because of the strong agreement between technology directors and professors, for the remainder of this article, we will focus on the responses of technology directors.

Importance of Task Activities

Table 3 shows the ratings (decreasing according to their ratings for the present) of task activities by technology directors. The first thing to notice is that rankings for the present and the future are almost identical, suggesting that public school technology directors in 2002 did not see upcoming changes in their roles.

We note also that Farwell et al.'s (1992) findings about the future importance of task activities were generally confirmed by our survey, with some notable variations. Our technology directors' top two ratings, both for the present and the future went to "Manage/Plan district IT strategies, strategic applications,

technology architecture," and "Support information access and security," which were lower in Farwell et al.'s study. And integration activities, which ranked in the top three in the Boston SIMS studies, ranked much lower with public school technology directors. Farwell et al.'s prediction about the enhanced role of "the integrator" appears not to have come true for the public school technology directors in this study. Another surprising finding was the low rankings of two items about supporting users: "Support end-use computing (e.g., information center, hotline)" and "Support user-developed systems." Our public school technology directors did not rank highly those items related to users' demands. We will propose reasons for this below.

Importance of Interpersonal and Management Skills

Table 4 shows close agreement between the present and future ratings for interpersonal and management skills. As we noted above, in general, interpersonal and management skills rated higher than the other two categories (Table 2).

The Boston SIMS studies suggested interpersonal and management skills would become more important as IS professionals would have to resist the temptation to make any task "the end in itself" and instead keep in sight the "larger goal that the system is trying to accomplish" (Lee, Trauth, and Farwell, 1995, p. 316). This prediction was accurate for public school technology directors as the items in third- through fifth-place were "Focus on technology as a means, not an end"; "Work cooperatively in a one-on-one and project team environment"; and "Plan and execute work in a collaborative environment." Tied for sev-

Table 2. Means (Standard Deviations) Across Knowledge and Skill Requirements of Ratings by Public School Technology Directors and Education Professors

	Technology Directors		Education Professors	
	Present	Future	Present	Future
Task Activities	4.1 (0.59)	4.25 (0.58)	4.0 (0.52)	4.1 (0.50)
Interpersonal and Management Skills	4.6 (0.16)	4.7 (0.16)	4.6 (0.18)	4.6 (0.18)
Technical Skills	3.5 (0.88)	3.6 (0.96)	3.4 (0.66)	3.6 (0.70)

Table 3. Task Activities: Present (2002) and Future (2005) Ratings by Public School Technology Directors

Ratings for the Present		*Ratings for the Future*	
1. Manage/Plan district IT strategies, strategic applications, technology architecture	4.75	Manage/Plan district IT strategies, strategic applications, technology architecture	4.83
2. Support information access and security	4.70	Support information access and security	4.77
3.5. Manage/Plan feasibility/approval process for new systems and technology	4.67	Manage/Plan feasibility/approval process for new systems and technology	4.77
3.5. Analyze public school problems and IS solutions	4.67	Analyze public school problems and IS solutions	4.75
5. Manage/Plan system development/project implementation	4.64	Manage/Plan system development/project implementation	4.73
6. Train and educate users	4.63	Train and educate users	4.67
7. Implement system evaluation processes	4.47	Implement system evaluation processes	4.58
8. Integrate existing and new applications	4.40	Implement new or changed computer supported processes	4.55
9. Implement new or changed computer supported processes	4.38	Integrate existing and new applications	4.50
10. Integrate networks	4.31	Integrate networks	4.48
11. Implement data management procedures	4.25	Implement data management procedures	4.41
12. Analyze software packages; evaluation and selections	4.23	Integrate data types (e.g., video, voice)	4.38
13. Support hardware	4.22	Support existing portfolio of applications	4.28
14. Support existing portfolio of applications	4.21	Support hardware	4.23
15. Support end-user computing (e.g., information center, hotline)	4.13	Support end-user computing (e.g., information center, hotline)	4.22
16. Train and educate IT professionals	4.05	Train and educate IT professionals	4.20
17. Integrate data types (e.g., video, voice)	3.98	Analyze software packages; evaluation and selections	4.18
18. Develop databases	3.58	Develop databases	3.75
19. Support user-developed systems	2.97	Support user-developed systems	3.12
20. Develop applications software; purchase and tailor	2.94	Develop applications software; purchase and tailor	3.03
21. Develop in-house applications	2.84	Develop in-house applications	2.91

Table 4. Interpersonal and Management Skills: Present (2002) and Future (2005) Ratings by Public School Technology Directors

Ratings for the Present		*Ratings for the Future*	
1. Be self-directed and proactive	4.86	Be self-directed and proactive	4.85
2. Accomplish assignments	4.84	Accomplish assignments	4.85
3. Focus on technology as a means, not an end	4.82	Work cooperatively in a one-on-one and project team environment	4.84
4. Work cooperatively in a one-on-one and project team environment	4.79	Plan and execute work in a collaborative environment	4.84
5. Plan and execute work in a collaborative environment	4.78	Focus on technology as a means, not an end	4.83
7. Learn new technologies	4.72	Understand technological trends	4.80
7. Plan, organize, and lead projects	4.72	Plan, organize, and lead projects	4.76
7. Understand technological trends	4.72	Learn new technologies	4.75
9. Plan, organize and write clear, concise, effective memos, reports and documentation	4.69	Plan, organize and write clear, concise, effective memos, reports and documentation	4.72
10. Understand the public school environment	4.64	Interpret public school problems and develop appropriate technical solutions	4.71
11. Interpret public school problems and develop appropriate technical solutions	4.62	Understand the public school environment	4.68
12. Develop and deliver effective, informative, and persuasive presentations	4.53	Develop and deliver effective, informative, and persuasive presentations	4.5
13. Deal with ambiguity	4.52	Deal with ambiguity	4.53
14. Teach others	4.51	Teach others	4.52
15. Learn public school functions	4.47	Learn public school functions	4.51
16. Be sensitive to organizational culture/politics	4.41	Be sensitive to organizational culture/politics	4.46
17. Be close to customers and maintain productive user or client relationships	4.32	Be close to customers and maintain productive user or client relationships	4.36

enth place were three items, one of which seems to emphasis general management skills, "Plan, organize, and lead projects," and two which focus on keeping up with developments in technology, "Learn new technologies" and "Understand technological trends."

Importance of Technical Skills

Table 5 shows the ratings of technical skills by technology directors.

Farwell et al.'s 1992 respondents had rated networks the most important technical skill for the future. Participants in our pilot study had suggested we modify the item on networks to cover "Networks, Internet, Extranet, Wireless Networking Technologies," and our respondents rated this item the highest technical skill both for present and future. Based on the pilot study, we had added two other items to the survey, "Web based applications and/or web page publishing/development" and "Operating systems: Network (Windows NT/2000 or Novell Netware)," which came in second and third in our rankings. "Systems integration" ranked high both with the Boston SIMS respondents and with ours. "Decision support systems" came in fifth in our study, much higher than in the Boston SIMS study. Finally, public school technology directors gave much lower priority to "Fourth-generation languages" than had the Boston SIMS study.

The technical skills portion of our survey was missing more responses than were the other two portions.

For example, out of the 175 technology directors who participated in rating knowledge and skill requirements for the present, on average 170 (97 percent) rated the task activities and 172 (98 percent) rated the interpersonal and management skills, but only 146 (83 percent) rated the technical skills. Professors responded similarly. Thus, we have five items receiving lower than 80 percent response rates for the present from both technology directors (N<140) and professors (N<40): (a) assembly language; (b) COBOL, or other third generation languages (structured programming); (c) fourth generation languages; (d) distributed processing; and (e) systems analysis/structured analysis. Strangely, two of the items (distributed processing and systems analysis/structured analysis) were ranked in the top ten by those who rated them, though they were not even responded to by 20 percent of our participants. A third item which the Boston SIMS data suggested would decrease in importance, systems life cycle management, ranked sixth in our study, but with only 82 percent of technology directors and 78 percent of professors responding to it.

DISCUSSION

Comparing These Findings to Those of the Boston SIMS Study

In the Boston SIMS study, the professors reported different perceptions from those of practitioners. In

Table 5. Technical Skills: Present (2002) and Future (2005) Ratings by Public School Technology Directors

Ratings for the Present		Ratings for the Future	
1. Networks, Internet, Extranet, Wireless Networking Technologies	4.48	Networks, Internet, Extranet, Wireless Networking Technologies	4.69
2. Web based applications and/or web page publishing/development	4.27	Web based applications and/or web page publishing/development	4.53
3. Operating systems: Network (Windows NT/2000 or Novell Netware)	4.24	Systems Integration	4.36
4. Systems Integration	4.20	Operating systems: Network (Windows NT/2000 or Novell Netware)	4.29
5. Decision support systems	4.07	Decision support systems	4.25
6. Systems life cycle management	4.04	Systems life cycle management	4.23
7. Operating systems: Micros	3.92	Telecommunications and Voice/Data integration	4.20
8. Telecommunications and Voice/Data integration	3.79	Systems analysis/structured analysis	3.99
9. Systems analysis/structured analysis	3.79	Operating systems: Micros	3.84
10. Distributed processing	3.65	Distributed processing	3.80
11. Relational databases	3.62	Relational databases	3.80
12. Data management (e.g., data modeling, data warehousing)	3.51	Data management (e.g., data modeling, data warehousing)	3.74
13. Operating systems: Mainframe	2.87	Operating systems: Mainframe	2.78
14. Application programming languages	2.54	Application programming languages	2.61
15. Fourth generation languages	2.12	Fourth generation languages	2.20
16. Assembly language	1.95	Assembly language	1.91
17. COBOL, or other third generation languages (structured programming)	1.75	COBOL, or other third generation languages (structured programming)	1.66

this survey the education professors' perceptions correlated highly with those of public school technology directors. It may be that the education professors tended to have had more practical experience than those in the Boston SIMS study, not having gone straight through school to become professors, so that their perceptions are more aligned to the education workplace. Furthermore, in the ten years since the Boston SIMS study, technology has become more available and user friendly so that neither technology directors nor professors can escape the realization that high levels of technical skills may no longer be as necessary, and both place more emphasis on interpersonal and management skills and task activities. But we caution not to over interpret this finding. Though *perceptions* of professors and technology directors are similar, we lack evidence of what the directors actually *do* and the professors actually *teach.*

Our survey confirmed the findings of both the Boston SIMS study and Delfin (1995) that interpersonal and management skills were perceived as more important than traditional IS activities and technical skills. But we do not argue for de-emphasizing all task activities and technical proficiencies in preparing public school technology directors. In fact, if we use as a rule of thumb that we should consider important any skill to which technology directors gave a mean "future" score above four, then seven of the 17 technical skills are still important, as are 17 of the 22 task activities. Furthermore, as Farwell et al. (1992) explained, the shift in emphasis from traditional technical skills to interpersonal and management skills may indicate not that we should de-emphasize technical proficiency, but only that there will be more than one career path for IS professionals. Most organizations, including public schools will still need some highly skilled technical specialists. But, now technical expertise will not be the sole path to leadership in IS roles. Those who want to lead public schools in technology use will have to acquire many other competencies and may not, in fact, need to maintain high levels of technical expertise because they can hire experts.

The other important insight from the Boston SIMS study is that the central IS department may not be the only place to employ IS professionals, because IS functions will be displaced throughout the organization, with each department doing more of its own IS work and thus needing to employ IS specialists. Different departments, then, will call on the central IS department for support as well as products, and IS departments will have to respond.

Given that prediction, it is surprising that the public school technology directors in our study gave comparatively low rankings to items about supporting users' needs. They rated the item "Support end-user computing (e.g., information center, hotline)" 4.13 for the present and 4.22 for the future, but this score placed it only fifteenth of all task activities for both the present and future. The item "Support user-developed systems" came in even lower, with a 2.17 for the present and 3.12 for the future, ranking among the bottom three task activities.

This may be related to the work of public schools. The work is instruction, distributed throughout buildings away from the technology department; teachers think of technology in terms of software to accomplish specific instructional tasks; therefore, they do not consider the centralized IS department a source of help; and they do not demand its support.

Simultaneously, unlike in business and industry, where the IS function is being distributed throughout the organization, pressures for accountability data impel the centralization of IS functions in public schools. Thus public school technology directors must respond to forces different from those the Boston SIMS study projected for business and industry.

Implications for Preparation of Public School Technology Directors

Our survey results have implications for preparing public school technology directors. Most important, and noted in recent literature on preparation of school leaders (Cambron-McCabe and Cunningham, 2002; Glasman, Cibulka, and Ashby, 2002; Young, Peterson, and Short, 2002), is that academe and practice must cooperate to make preparation programs in school leadership relevant to the practice of school leadership. We do not believe universities should simply look to practitioners for the design of all aspects of preparation, but they should balance their perceptions against practitioners'. We further urge that preparation programs for technology directors involve field-based practice to involve the cooperative work in public schools that our findings show will constitute their futures.

This study asked only for practitioners' and professors' perceptions of importance of knowledge and skill requirements, not for their behavior with regard to them. Investigating professors' actual teaching behavior would be a study beyond our means. But NCATE (2002) already urges that academic departments and colleges of education examine their own practices for their effects. In the same spirit, we urge professors to reflect on the relative importance of the three areas studied here: task activities, interpersonal and management skills, and technical skills; and on the rankings of the items which compose them. We urge them to examine their curricula for the match between the perceptions of importance revealed in this study and the content of their courses. Higher education leaders should consider these findings also in the design of preparation programs for public school technology leaders. With the disparate competencies required of technology leaders, no single department or college can provide all the preparation needed. Collaboration among departments may be as important, then, as collaboration between universities and public school systems.

Future Research

Finally, we recommend this study be replicated every few years to monitor the work requirements of public school technology directors, so data will be available to guide decisions regarding preparing and employing them, and developing their skills. But locating and recruiting public school technology directors and professors of technology for this survey was labor-intensive and its representativeness is questionable. Future research could produce better representation and information if it were sponsored by professional educational technology organizations. Finally, we recommend the survey be revised regularly, in particular with regard to items on which we had low scores or low response-rates, to determine whether they should be replaced. The current study and future similar efforts offer the hope of more effective preparation, selection, and professional development of public school technology directors; better educational technology leadership; and thus better education.

REFERENCES

Bromley, H., and Jacobson, S. (1997). Technology and change in school administrator preparation. In K. C. Westbrook (Ed.), *Technology and the educational workplace: Understanding fiscal impacts* (pp. 127–149). Thousand Oaks, CA: Corwin Press.

Cambron-McCabe, N., and Cunningham, L. (2002). National commission for the advancement of educational leadership: Opportunity for transformation. *Educational Administration Quarterly, 38*(2), 289–299.

Delfin, A. P. (1995). Perceptions of technology directors as to the importance of specific knowledge and skill require-

ments. (Doctoral dissertation, New Mexico State University, 1995). *Dissertation Abstracts International, 56* (09A), 3384.

Department of Education (2001a). *No Child Left Behind.* Retrieved July 6, 2003, from http://www.ed.gov/offices/OESE/esea/.

Department of Education (2001b). *Enhancing Education through Technology Act of 2001.* Retrieved July 6, 2003, from http://www.ed.gov/legislation/ESEA02/pg34.html.

Digest of Education Statistics (2001). *Public schools and school classrooms with access to the Internet, by school characteristics: 1994 to 2000.* Retrieved July 26, 2003, from http://nces.ed.gov/pubs2002/digest2001/tables/dt421.as.

Farwell, D. W., Kuramoto, L., Lee, D., Trauth, E. M., and Winslow, C. (1992). A new paradigm for IS: The educational implications. *Information Systems Management, 9*(2) 7–14.

Glasman, N., Cibulka, J., and Ashby, D. (2002). Program self-evaluation for continuous improvement. *Educational Administration Quarterly, 38*(2), 257–288.

Gonzales, C. L. (2001). How administrators become technology leaders. In G. Ivory (Ed.), *What works in computing for school administrators* (pp. 211–224). Lanham, MD: Scarecrow.

Information Technology Association of America. (1997). *Help wanted: The IT workforce gap at the dawn of a new century.* (ERIC Document Reproduction Service No. ED 407491.)

Ivory, G. (Ed.). (2001). *What works in computing for school administrators.* Lanham, MD: Scarecrow.

Lee, D. M. S., Trauth, E. M., and Farwell, D. (1995). Critical skills and knowledge requirements of IS professionals: A joint academic/industry investigation. *MIS Quarterly, 19*(3), 313–340.

National Commission on Excellence in Education (1983). *A nation at risk: The imperative for educational reform.* Retrieved July 8, 2003, from http://www.ed.gov/pubs/NatRisk/.

NCATE (1997). *Technology and the new professional teacher, preparing for the 21st century.* (ERIC Document Reproduction Service No. ED412201.)

NCATE (2002). *Professional standards for the accreditation of schools, colleges, and departments of education.* Retrieved July 30, 2003, from http://ncate.org/2000/unit_stnds_2002.pdf.

Picciano, A. G. (2002). *Educational leadership and planning for technology* (3rd ed.). Upper Saddle River, NJ: Merrill Prentice Hall.

President's Committee of Advisors on Science and Technology (1997). *Report to the President on the Use of Technology to Strengthen K–12 Education in the United States.* Retrieved July 25, 2003, from http://www.ostp.gov/PCAST/k-12ed.html.

Reyes, P., Wagstaff, L. H., and Fusarelli, L. (1999). Delta forces: The changing fabric of American society and education. In J. Murphy and K. S. Louis (Eds.), *Handbook of research on educational administration* (2nd. ed., pp. 183–201). San Francisco, CA: Jossey-Bass.

Technology Counts (2002). [Special issue]. *Education Week, 21*(55).

Trauth, E. M., Farwell, D. W., and Lee, D. (1993). The IS expectation gap: Industry expectations versus academic preparation. *MIS Quarterly, 17*(3), 293–303.

TSSA Collaborative (n.d.). *Technology standards for school administrators.* Retrieved July 27, 2003, from http://cnets .iste.org/tssa/pdf/tssa.pdf.

Wiburg, K. M. (2001). Effective planning for technology. In G. Ivory (Ed.), *What works in computing for school administrators* (pp. 225–245). Lanham, MD: Scarecrow.

Young, M. D., Peterson, G. J., and Short, P. M. (2002). The complexity of substantive reform: A call for interdependence among key stakeholders. *Educational Administration Quarterly, 38*(2), 137–175.

Collaborating to Groom Effective School Leaders

WILLIAM RUFF AND ELEANOR PERRY

RECENTLY IN A MEETING WITH THE PUBLIC SCHOOL SUPER-intendents of the region, principal preparation was discussed and all agreed that three qualities were most prized in a principal: (a) instructional leadership, (b) the ability to connect with people (teachers and parents) and (c) entrepreneurial acumen. This conversation mirrored the traits identified by Cuban (1988), as well as others (Katz, 1955; Yukl, 1981), as needed by all educators—instructional, political, and managerial. With the plethora of accountability programs, the instructional and political strands have gained prominence in discussions of school leadership and leadership preparation (Ruff and Shoho, 2002). However, the managerial skills are no less important. All three of Cuban's strands must be integrated for effective leadership. Yet, the need to increase capacity within our schools to meet the demands made by public policy (such as No Child Left Behind, 2001), forces the nature of this management strand to be proactive in nature—to be entrepreneurial.

Charter school visionaries are a unique blend of educators and entrepreneurs who need special training to develop both educational and business leadership skills, especially in areas supporting fiduciary responsibilities and financial planning. Although the need for such understanding is not seen as critical for a public school principal, it does impact how schools are run. For example, currently the economy in many states is contracting. School funding and educational programs are being cut at an alarming rate to balance the districts' budgets. Would as many programs or the same programs be cut if the capacity for fiduciary matters extended beyond the district's business manager? Many educational leaders study school finance, school personnel and other management courses when pursuing a Master's degree and administrative certification, but in almost all programs, these courses are taught within the College of Education. Is there a better way to prepare our public school leaders for demands currently unseen?

This article describes a unique leadership preparation program developed to prepare effective charter school leaders and explores its methods as an inquiry into assumptions governing traditional principal preparation.

PROFESSIONAL PREPARATION FOR AN EMERGING ROLE

In the bureaucratic model of educational leadership, roles and responsibilities were meticulously defined and elaborated, but as schooling becomes less hierarchical, what should the school leader do? The relevancy of this question is made more urgent by the fact that as school leaders are being asked to share power, they are simultaneously being held to higher standards of accountability (Deasy, 2000; No Child Left Behind Act, 2001; Silva, Gimbert and Nolan, 2000). Meyer and Macmillan (2001) postulated two criteria for an emerging conceptualization of educational leadership.

First, leadership must be reconceptualized to describe the act or process of creating and sustaining an environment in which teachers can carry on their highly complex socially textured task of instruction. Second, the definition must also recognize and encompass the continuously expanding role that principals are assuming (p. 14).

Such criteria place institutional outcomes as more important than individual efforts. Yet, if a new generation of educational leaders is to be adequately trained for the practice of leadership in continuously changing contexts, our instruction must provide students with the ability to apply general principles of practice to specific contexts. Such instruction necessitates learning in multiple contexts from multiple perspectives. From a variety of experiences, tacit understandings will be called into question allowing reflection and learning. "The outcomes of our [educational leadership] programs require the same confronting of our own tacit assumptions, theories-in-use, or mental models that we prescribe for our students" (Kottkamp, 2002, p. 3).

Jackson and Kelley (2002) note five successful practices seen in exceptional leadership preparation programs—problem-based learning, cohorts, collaborative partnerships, field experiences, and use of technology. In many preparation programs, the internship is used to provide field experience to aspiring school leaders. "The internship is both a capstone of educational endeavor and a beginning experience in meeting the demands of a new position in educational leadership" (Martin, Wright and Danzig, 2003, p. xix). Traditionally, the internship is among the last courses taken in the preparation program. Yet, sequencing a preparation program so that students are indoctrinated with theory before offering opportunities to acquire experience in the practice from which the theory is derived serves to separate theory from practice rather than integrate the two. The integration of theory and practice is essential to developing expertise for practice in an array of changing contexts. Furthermore, national standards (i.e., Educational Leadership Consortium Council [ELCC]) and many state standards focus on knowledge application. Competency in applying knowledge presupposes active learning opportunities. Spiraling the curriculum such that field experiences are distributed among classroom activities seems to be a more efficient way of preparing leaders to appropriately apply knowledge to changing contexts. In fact, Kelley and Peterson (2000) suggested that the experiential component be viewed as the core of preparation supported by classroom content to augment reflection of practice. A distributed internship provides an approach intertwining practice with theory and facilitating student ability to apply knowledge appropriately to a given context.

Browne-Ferrigo (2003) noted, "The making of a principal is an intricate process of learning and reflection that requires socialization into a community of practice and assumption of a new identity" (p. 471). The distributed internship directly provides the means of facilitating learning and reflection. The field experience provides a basis for learning and the classroom promotes an opportunity for reflection. Additionally, the distributed internship situates the student in a leadership context. As a result, the socialization, inculcation of shared assumptions about leadership, and formation of identity begins as the student enters a preparation program and develops as the student matriculates. In the traditional internship, the socialization process is delayed until the end of the preparation program. By extending the socialization process through a distributed internship, shared assumptions of leadership and leadership identity are more likely to be ingrained. Additionally, the context of the socialization process is more likely to be varied with a distributed internship. Furthermore, the distributed internship can be structured to promote socialization across a variety of contexts; whereas, such opportunities are limited in a traditional internship due its relatively short duration.

LEADERSHIP FOR EDUCATIONAL ENTREPRENEURS (LEE)

LEE is a masters program that bridges a Masters of Education program with a Masters of Business Administration program. Perry (1999) identified major gaps in how training was delivered to charter owner/operators who must function in both business and educational environments. Some organizations addressed these needs by offering one-shot workshops or year-long internships; yet, charter leaders wanted more substantial training leading to supervisory certification or a Masters degree based on their specialized needs. Traditional educational leadership programs did not provide both the instructional and business skills needed by charter leaders.

The LEE program was created to provide the necessary coursework for this new breed of educational leader and facilitate the professional development partnerships necessary to establish a networked community. It addressed the gap noted by Perry (2001) in three ways. First, the LEE program provided a unique individualized curriculum. Students gain a solid foundation integrating theory and practice, experience relevant coursework, and develop long-term networking opportunities for collegial and university support. Second, the LEE program provided a flexible delivery of courses. Courses are delivered on-line in 7-week blocks complimented with face-to-face regional meetings. Third, the LEE program required a distributed internship providing students a field placement each semester of the program. Each of five field placements immersed students into a different type of organizational culture to garner a variety of perspectives on schooling—a professional organization, a government organization, a non-profit organization, a for-profit organization and finally a performance-challenged public school. Overall, the LEE program created powerful university/charter school partnership bringing together charter school leaders from across the country with regional education laboratories, charter school associations, policy institutes, regional resource centers and other universities.

The significance of the LEE program in terms of leadership preparation is two-fold. First, this model represents a significant rethinking in how a major university delivers a graduate program to meet the needs of a specialized population of school leaders. It is a giant step in commitment to meeting the needs of this new breed of university student. Accordingly, its successes and failures allow other universities to reassess how they deliver their leadership programs and technical assistance. Second, the Office of Educational Research and Improvement's (OERI's) (2001) report showed that charter schools seem to be producing a ripple effect—perhaps inducing broader, long lasting systemic change nationwide. Such long lasting systemic change is not necessarily limited to the charter schools, but must necessarily include the quality of leadership within the schools and the preparation and connectedness of those leaders to the broader educational system.

The LEE program was a collaborative effort among multiple constituencies. It provided a replicable model showing how key stakeholders in school systems, higher education, government, regional educational laboratories, businesses and foundations can work together to produce strong educational leaders. Information collected from students, faculty, as well as key stakeholders from the U.S. Department of Education, regional laboratories, businesses and foundations, combined with data gathered from program artifacts, were analyzed to determine existing patterns and the points considered to be relevant for program replication as well as transferable elements with the potential to enhance traditional leadership preparation programs.

The distributed internship presented a significant challenge, but rewarding experience for students. Each student was assigned a mentor at the beginning of the program. In addition to facilitating site placements and monitoring fieldwork, the mentors provided significant affective and academic support. Initially, the field placements were conceived by the students to be a traditional internship, resulting in students becoming overwhelmed at the prospect of trying to complete five internships and completing coursework. Improving the connection between field placements and coursework decreased student stress levels and facilitated the ability to apply principles to practice. Emphasis was placed on the connection between the site placement and schooling. Moving the locus of the site activities from the site to the connection between schools and the site helped student to envision the proper role of the placement. For many of the students the different site placements have played a direct role in broadening professional networks. This was expected in planning the distributed internship. An unanticipated consequence was a noticeable increase in self-efficacy. Several students assumed community leadership roles. This seems to suggest that field placements outside of schools as well as inside schools encourage increased leadership activities and recognition of leadership at the community level. A more systematic study of this phenomenon is necessary before any conclusions can be reached. Additionally, research needs to extend to post-graduation activities.

Although the issue of charter schools remains contentious among educators, the preparation of charter school leaders provided a means of benchmarking traditional leadership preparation. By examining the LEE program, tacit assumptions long ago embedded in the preparation programs of common school principals can be questioned, discussed and changed. Arygris (1999) writes about barriers to organizational learning and that an inability to discuss common assumptions limits the organization's ability to learn, improve, or build increased capacity. With the No Child Left Behind Act at the national level and a plethora of accountability systems being implemented by an increasing number of states, the demands made by the public upon our schools has never been greater. To meet these demands, schools must increase current levels of capacity. School leaders must be skilled to accomplish this increase in organizational capacity and, in turn, leadership preparation programs must provide potential leaders with these skills. This requires the questioning of tacit yet foundational assumptions embedded within the programs. Seeing educational leadership preparation from a different view, the view of the LEE program, can potentially promote the capacity of traditional leadership preparation programs.

REFERENCES

Argyris, C. (1999). *On organizational learning (2nd ed.)*. Malden, MA: Blackwell Publishers Inc.

Cuban, L. (1988). *The managerial imperative and practice of leadership in schools*. Albany, NY: State University of New York Press.

Deasy, J. E. (2000). Moving from oversight to insight: One community's journey with its superintendent. *Phi Delta Kappan, 82*(1), 13–15.

Ferrigno-Browne, T. (2003). Becoming a principal: Role conception, initial socialization, role-identity transformation, purposeful engagement. *Educational Administration Quarterly, 39*(4), 468–503.

Jackson, B. L., and Kelley, C. (2002). Exceptional and innovative programs in educational leadership. *Educational Administration Quarterly, 38*(2), 192–212.

Katz, R. L. (1955). Skills of an effective administrator. *Harvard Business Review.*

Kelley, C., and Peterson, K. (2000, November). The work of principals and their preparation: Addressing critical needs for the 21st century. Paper presented at the annual conference of the University Council for Educational Administration in Albuquerque, NM.

Martin, G. E., Wright, W. F., and Danzig, A. B. (2003). *School leader internship: Developing, monitoring and evaluating your leadership experience.* Larchmont, NY: Eye on Education.

Meyer, M. J., and McMillian, R. B. (2001). The principal's role in transition: Instructional leadership ain't what it used to be. *International Electronic Journal for Leadership in Learning, 5(13).* Retrieved online Jun 18, 2004, from http://www.ucalgary.ca/~iejll/.

No Child Left Behind Act of 2001, Public Law 107–110 (2001).

Office of Educational Research and Improvement. (2001). *The challenge and opportunity: Impact of charter schools on districts.* Washington, DC: U.S. Government Press.

Perry, E. (2001). Charter school and university leaders: Partners transforming higher education. *Charter School Journal, 1,* 2–3.

Perry, E. (1999). Redefining management education: Charter school leaders carve their own niche. Pour un renouvellement de l'enseignement de las Gestion. Actes du Symposium organize a l'occasion du 30eme anniversaire de l'lSG. Tunis.

Ruff, W. G., and Shoho, A. R. (2002). Toward Understanding Leadership in Learning Communities: Mental Models of Instructional Leadership. Paper Presented at the University Council for Educational Administration Annual Conference, Pittsburgh, PA. Nov. 2002.

Silva, D. Y., Gimbert, B., and Nolan, J. F. (2000). Sliding the door: Locking and unlocking possibilities for teacher leadership. *Teachers College Record, 102*(4), 779–804.

Yukl, G. (1981). *Leadership in organizations.* Camden, NJ: Prentice-Hall.

About the Editors

Connie L. Fulmer earned her Ph.D. in Educational Administration at the Pennsylvania State University. Currently, she serves as coordinator of the Administrative Leadership and Policy Studies Division [ALPS] in the School of Education at the University of Colorado at Denver. Dr. Fulmer coordinates the work of the ALPS faculty and their principal partners in delivering six metro-area leadership academies and one statewide distance-learning program. Her most recent 2005 publication is included in A. Tattnal, J. Osorio and A. Visscher (Eds.), *Information Technology and Educational Management in the Knowledge Society* (pp. 37–46) New York: Springer, and is titled "Managing accountability innovations in distance-learning programs."

Frederick L. Dembowski earned the Ed.D. degree from the University of Rochester, New York. He is currently the Hibernian Endowed Professor of Educational Leadership and Head of the Department of Educational Leadership and Technology at Southeastern Louisiana University. His most recent major publication is *Effective School District Management*, published by AASA in 1999. He is currently serving as the editor of the *AASA Journal of Scholarship and Practice*, and is a member of Executive Board of the National Council of Professors of Educational Administration (NCPEA).